A-Z SHE

D1076596

CONT...

Key to Map Pages	2-3
Large Scale City Centre	4-5
Map Pages	6-143

Index to Streets, Towns, Villages & selected Places of Interest	144-221
Index to Hospitals & Hospices	222-223
Index to Stations	224

REFERENCE

Motorway	**M1**
A Road	**A61**
Under Construction	
Proposed	
B Road	**B6150**
Dual Carriageway	
One-way Street	→
Traffic flow on A Roads is also indicated by a heavy line on the driver's left.	→
Restricted Access	
Pedestrianized Road	
Track / Footpath	
Residential Walkway	
Railway Level Crossing Station Heritage Sta. Tunnel	
Supertram The boarding of Supertrams at stops may be limited to a single direction, indicated by the arrow. Stop	
Built-up Area BURGESS ST.	
Local Authority Boundary	– · – · – ·
National Park Boundary	
Posttown Boundary	
Postcode Boundary Within Posttowns	

Map Continuation **86** Large Scale City Centre **4**	
Car Park (selected)	ℙ
Park & Ride	P+
Church or Chapel	†
Fire Station	■
Hospital	Ⓗ
House Numbers A & B Roads only 5 13	
Information Centre	🄳
National Grid Reference	435
Police Station	▲
Post Office	★
Toilet	▽
with facilities for the Disabled	♿
Viewpoint	⁜ ☀
Educational Establishment	⌐
Hospital or Hospice	⌐
Industrial Building	⌐
Leisure or Recreational Facility	⌐
Place of Interest	⌐
Public Building	⌐
Shopping Centre or Market	⌐
Other Selected Buildings	⌐

SCALE

Map Pages 6-143 1:18,103	Map Pages 4-5 1:9051
0 — ¼ — ½ Mile	0 — ⅛ — ¼ Mile
0 — 250 — 500 — 750 Metres	0 — 100 — 200 — 300 Metres
3½ inches (8.89 cm) to 1 mile 5.52 cm to 1 km	7 inches (17.78 cm) to 1 mile 11.05 cm to 1 km

Copyright of Geographers' A-Z Map Company Ltd.

Head Office:
Fairfield Road, Borough Green, Sevenoaks, Kent, TN15 8PP
Telephone: 01732 781000 (Enquiries & Trade Sales)
01732 783422 (Retail Sales)

www.a-zmaps.co.uk

Copyright © Geographers' A-Z Map Co. Ltd.

Ordnance Survey® This product includes mapping data licensed from Ordnance Survey® with the permission of the Controller of Her Majesty's Stationery Office.

© Crown Copyright 2002
All rights reserved Licence number 100017302

Edition 3 2002   Edition 3b 2005

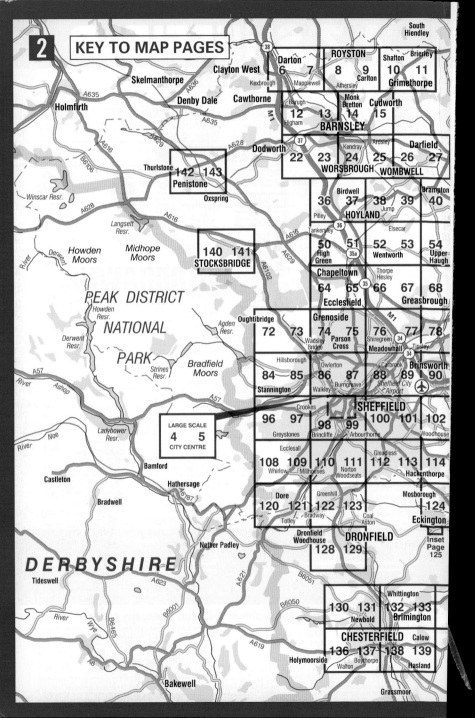

2 KEY TO MAP PAGES

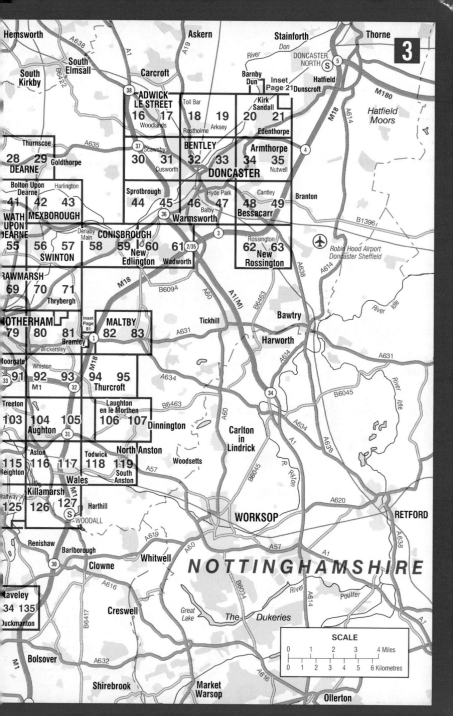

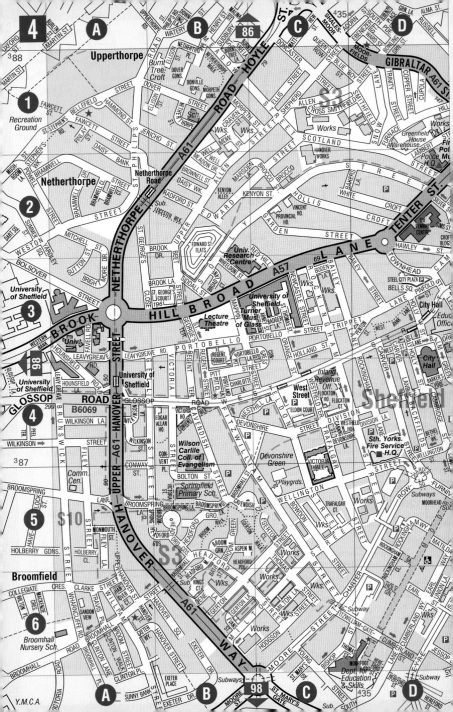

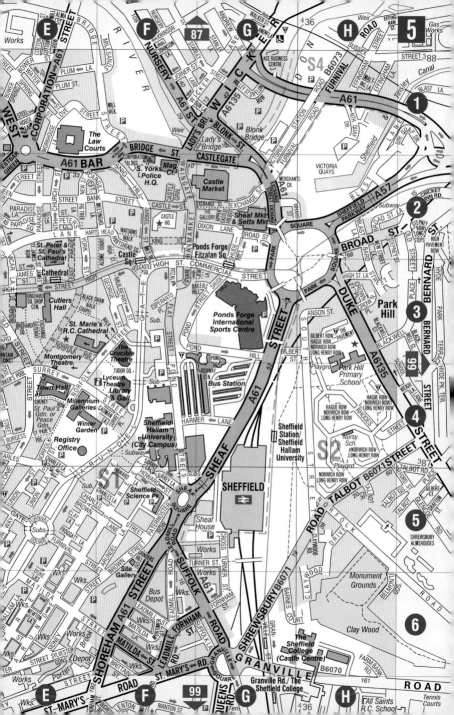

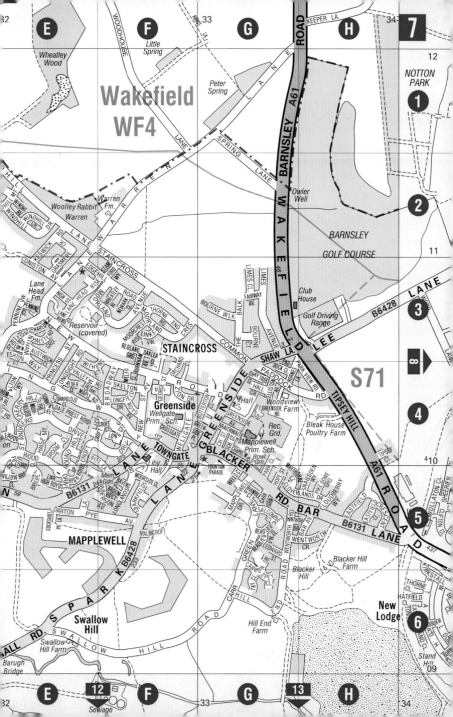

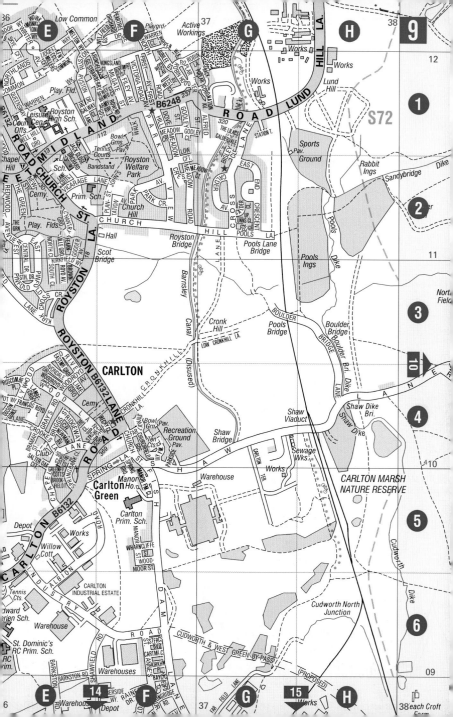

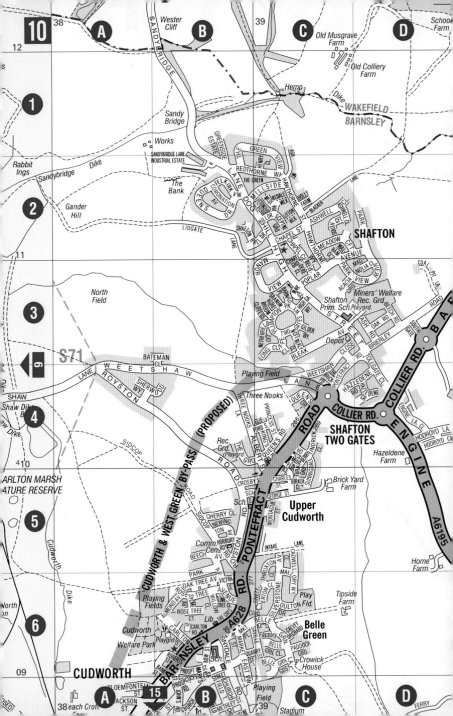

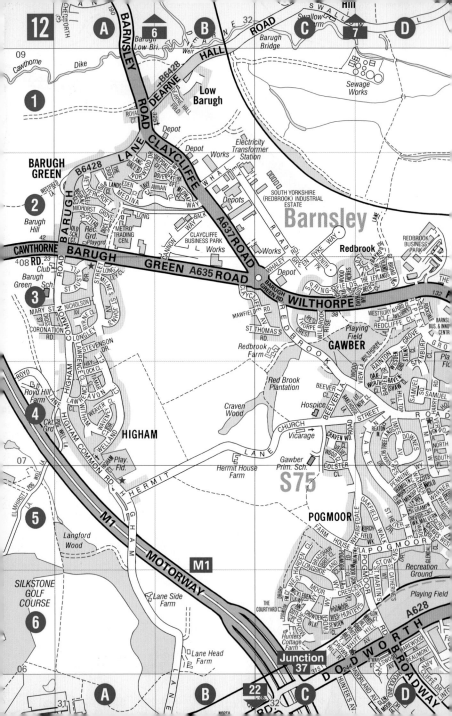

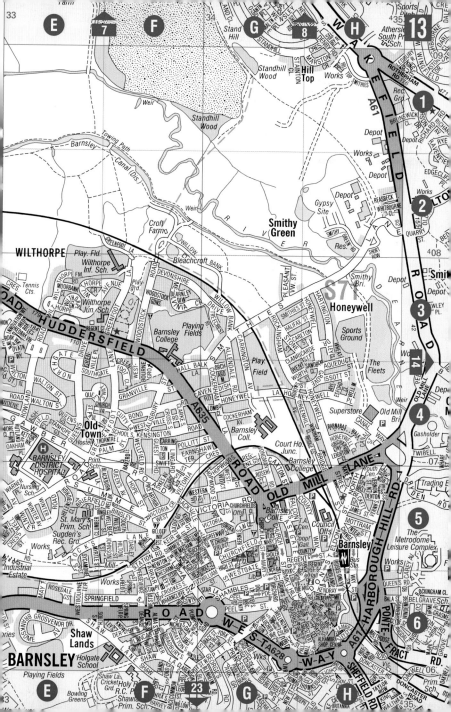

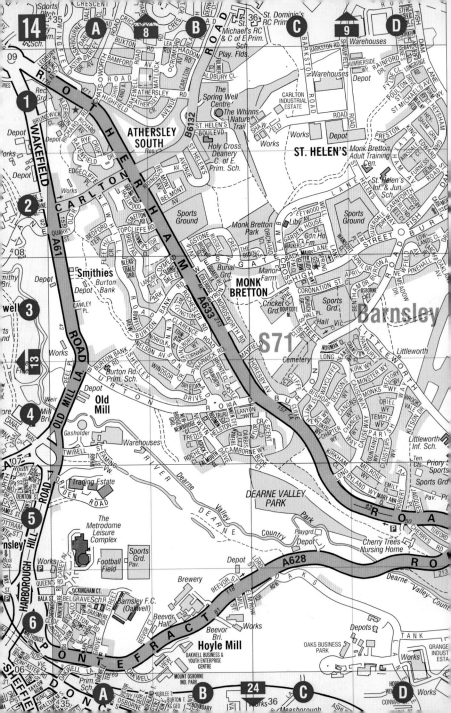

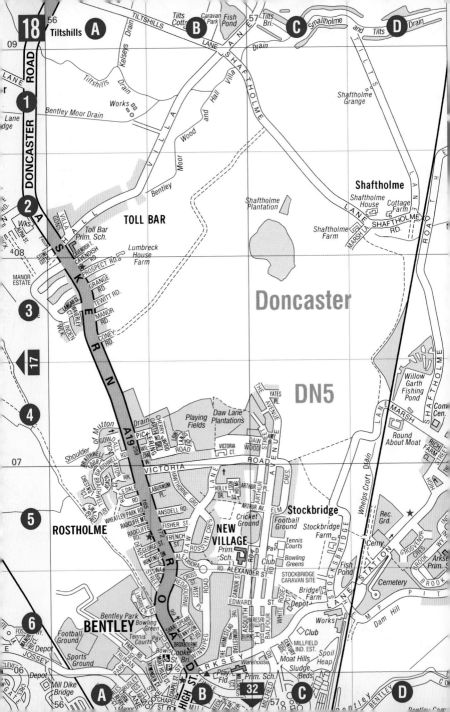

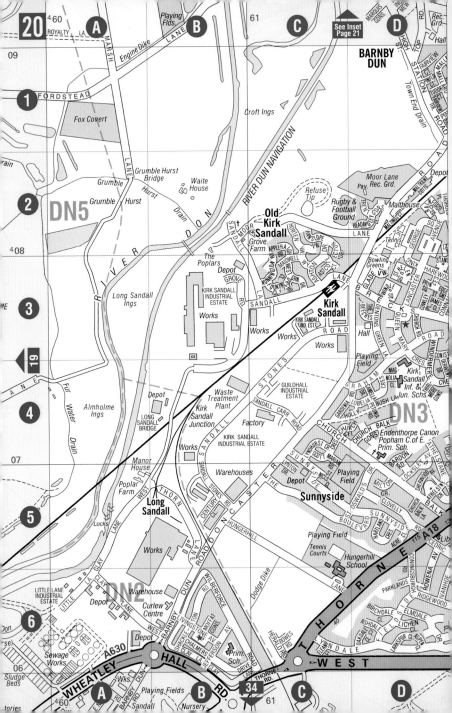

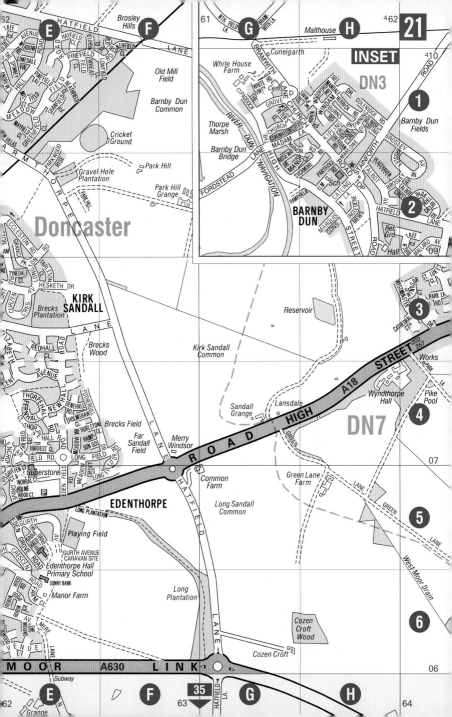

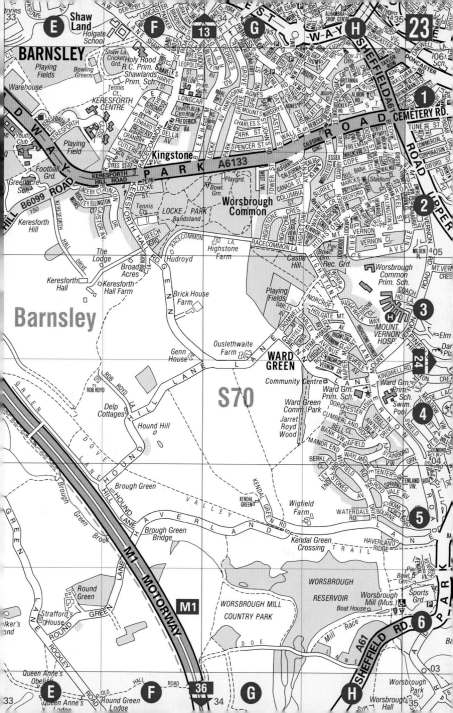

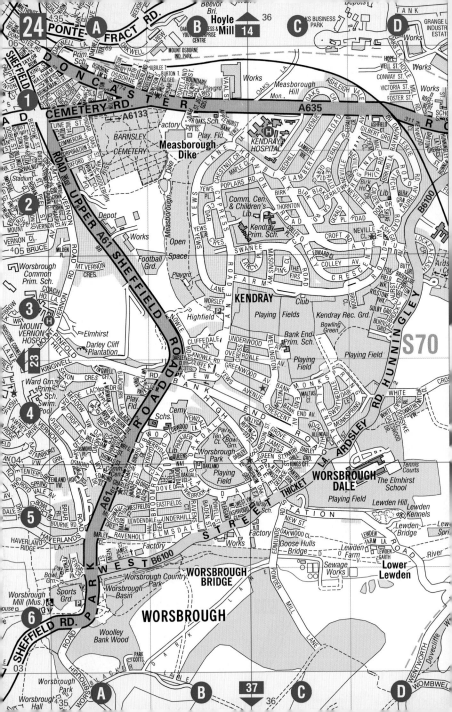

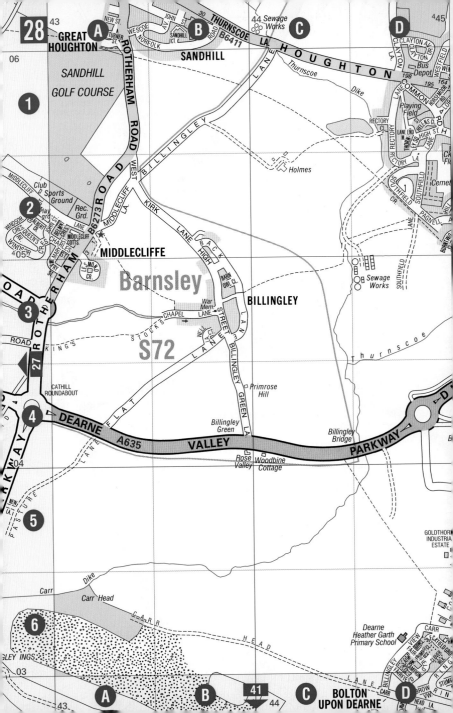

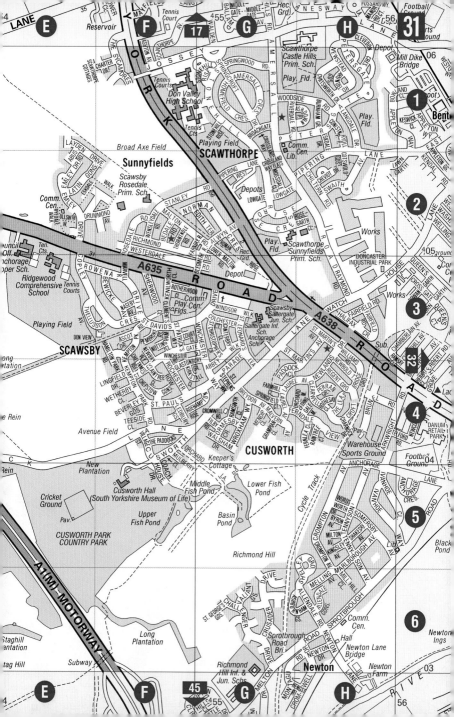

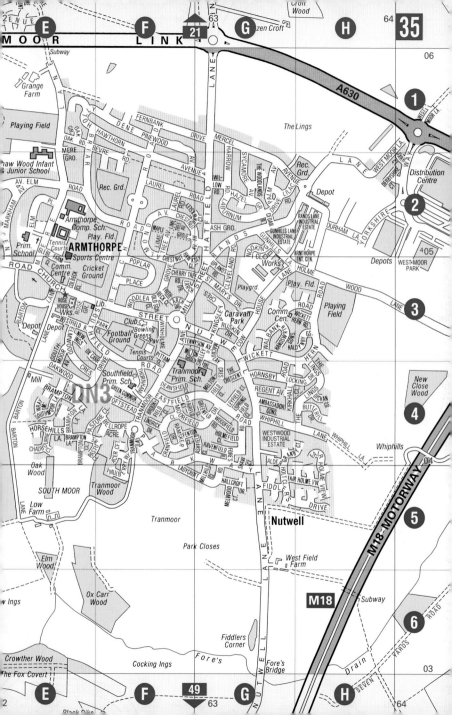

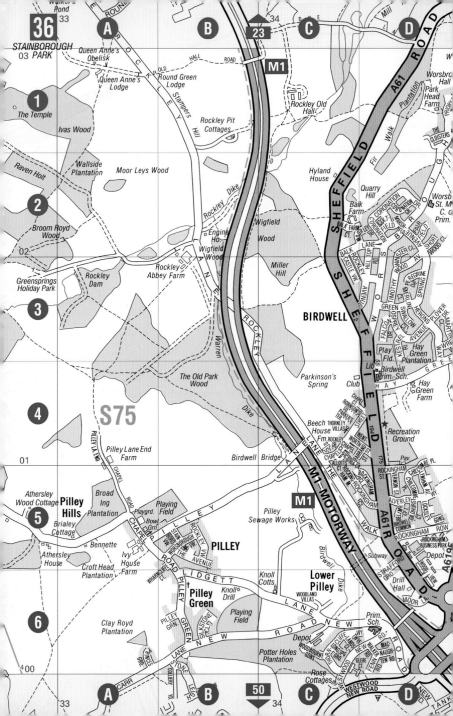

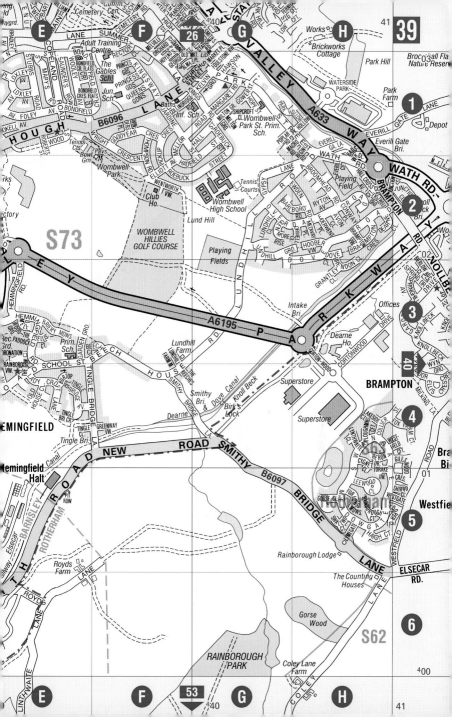

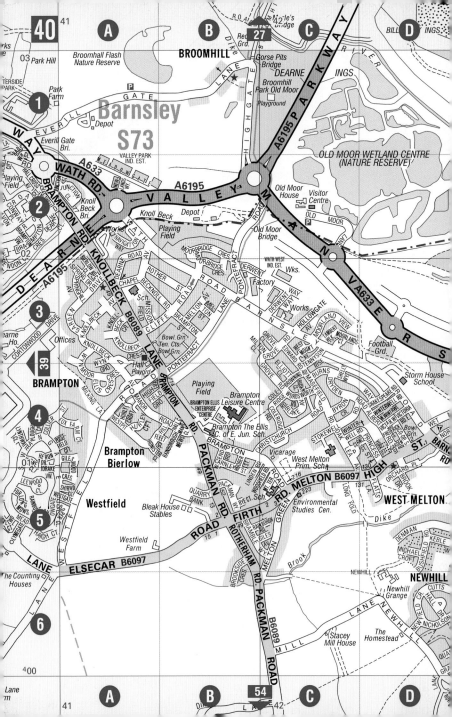

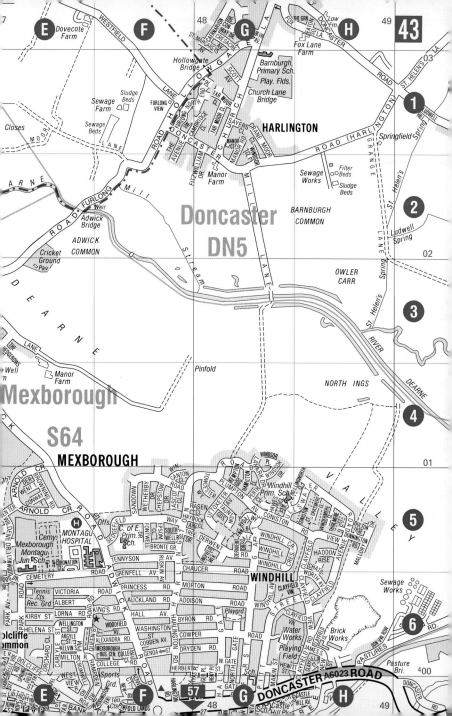

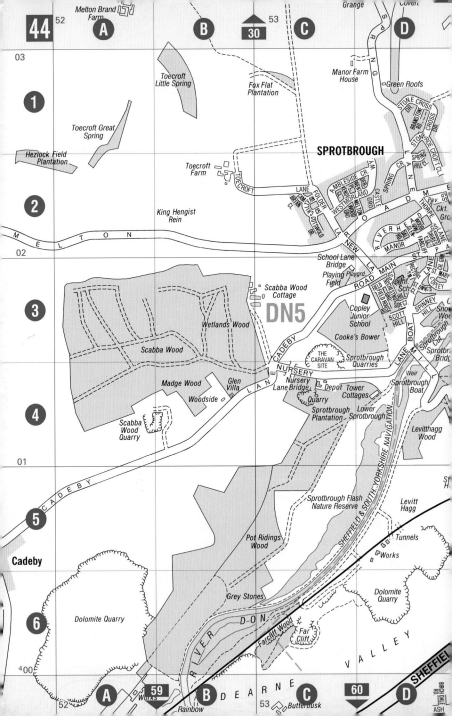

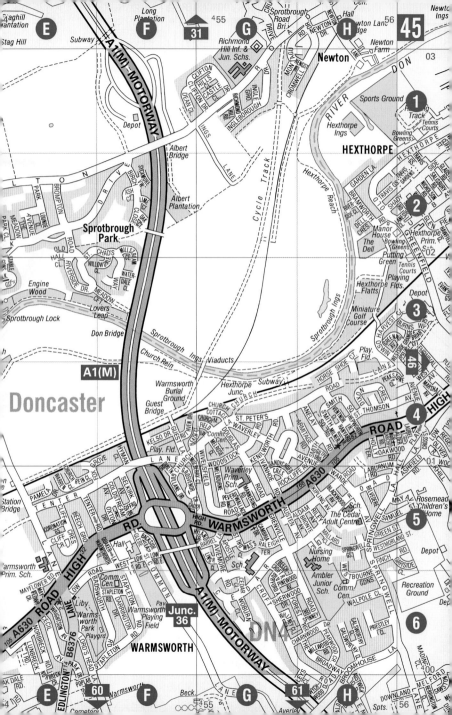

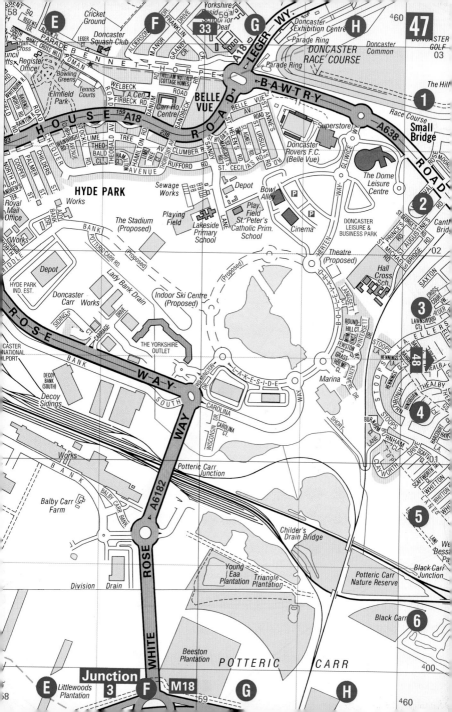

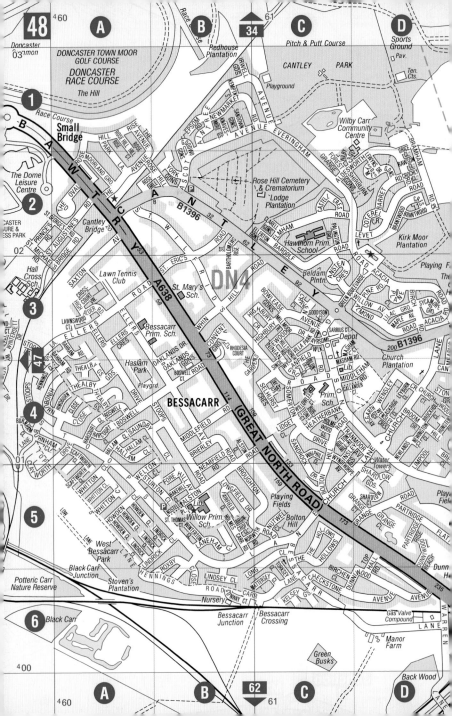

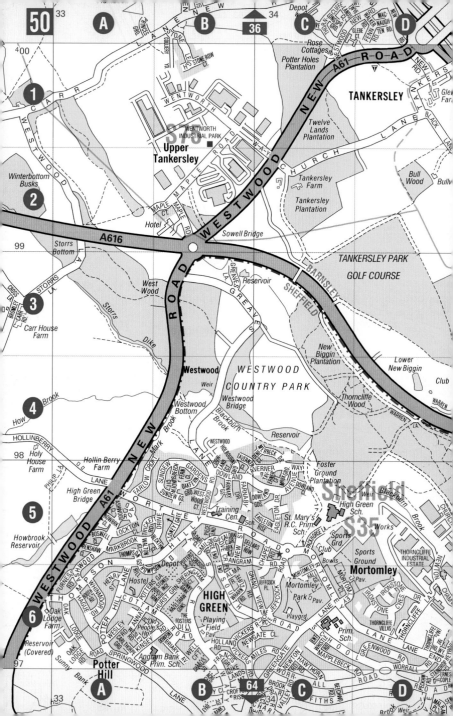

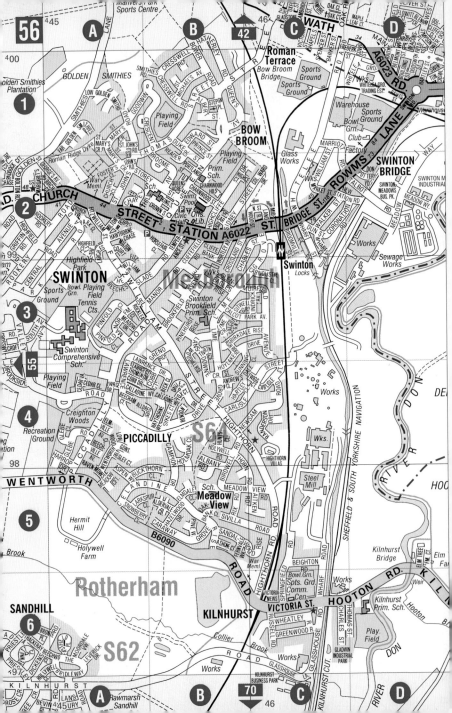

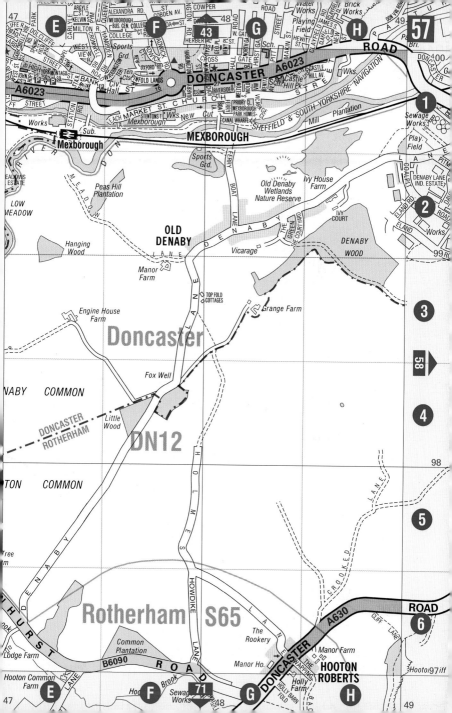

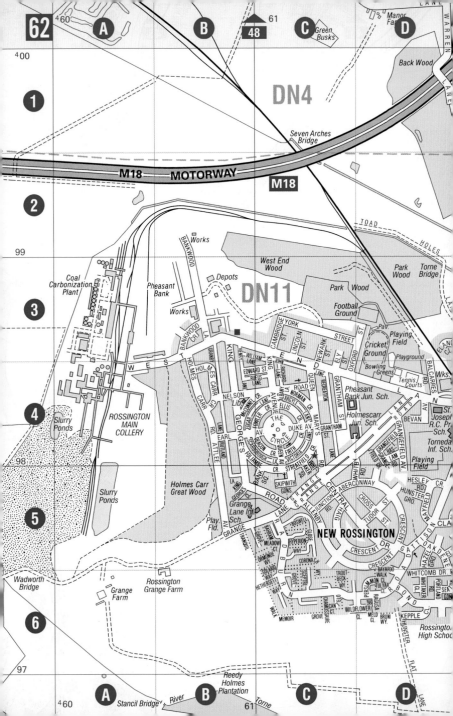

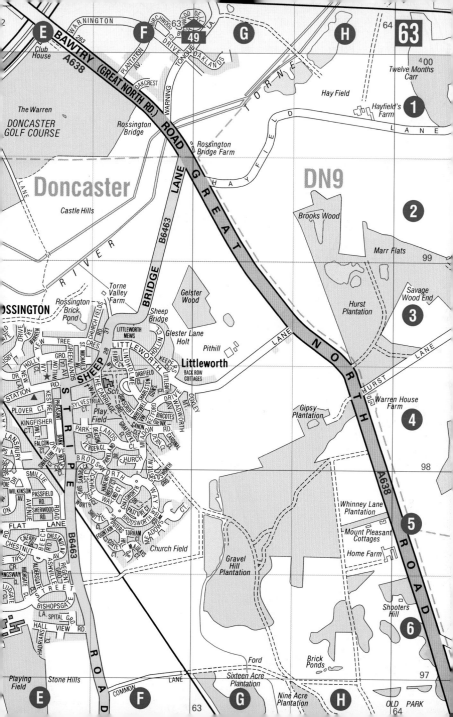

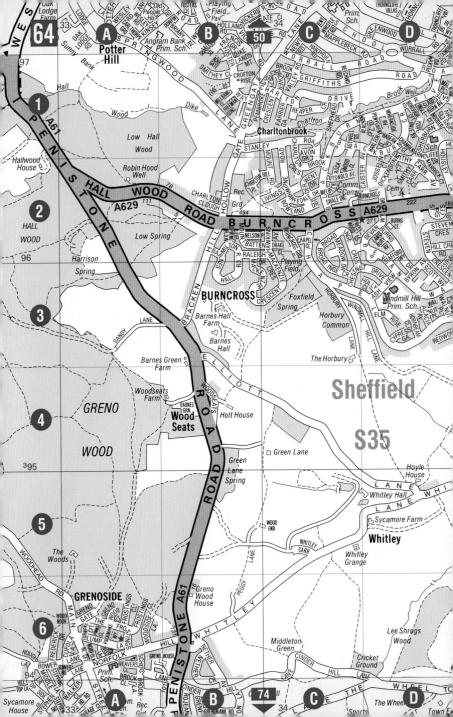

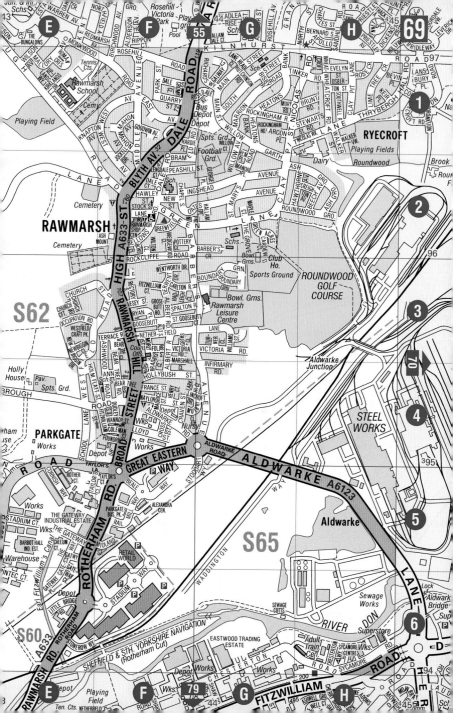

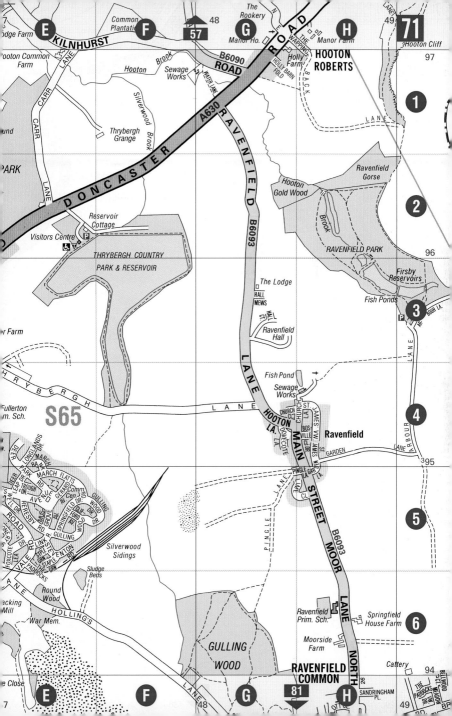

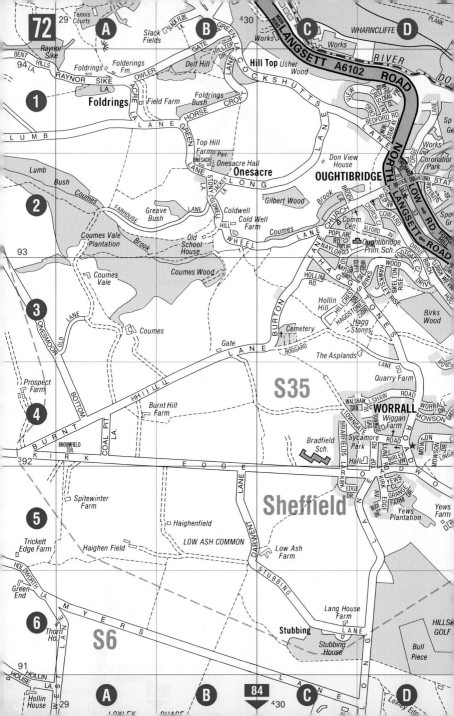

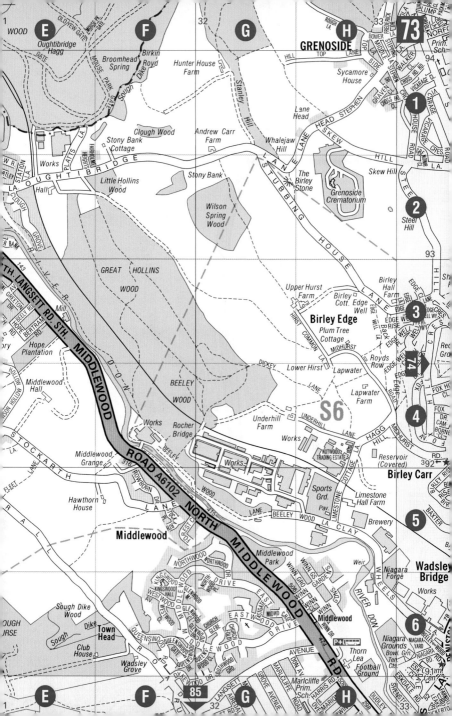

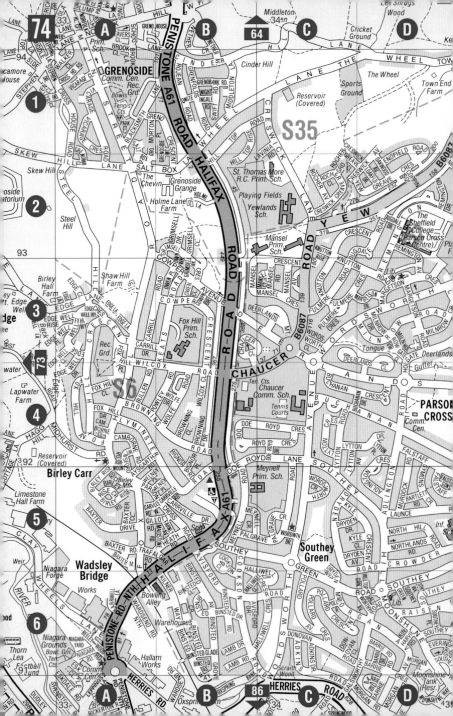

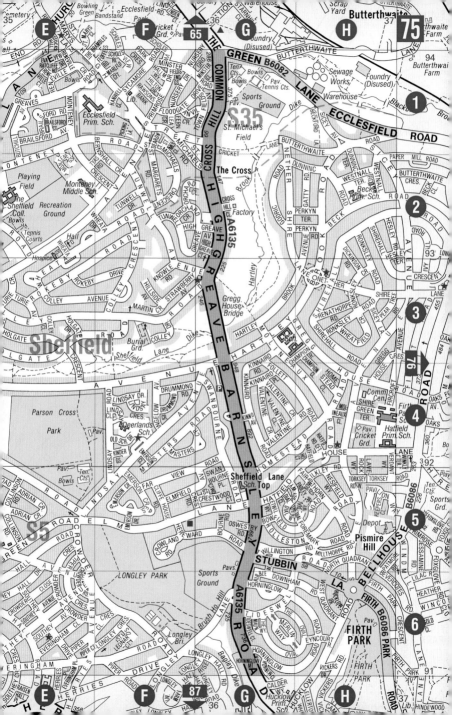

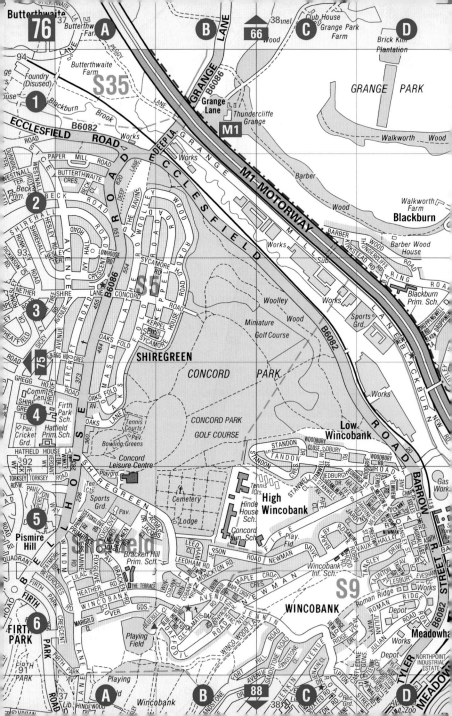

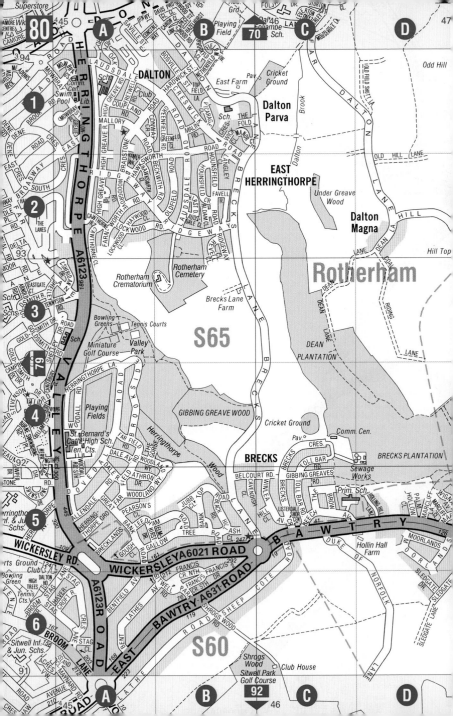

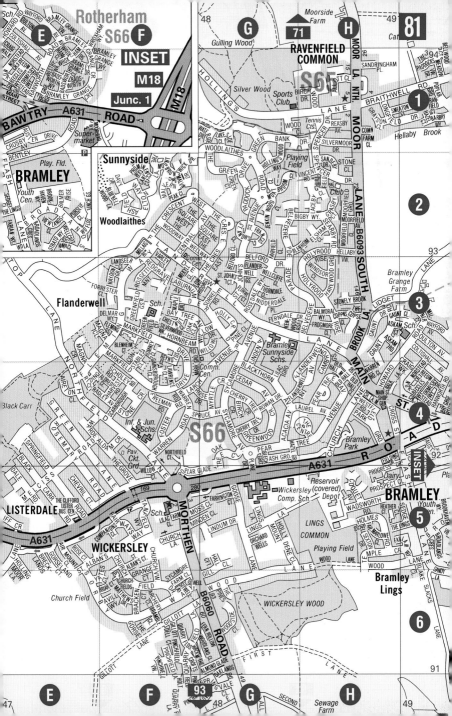

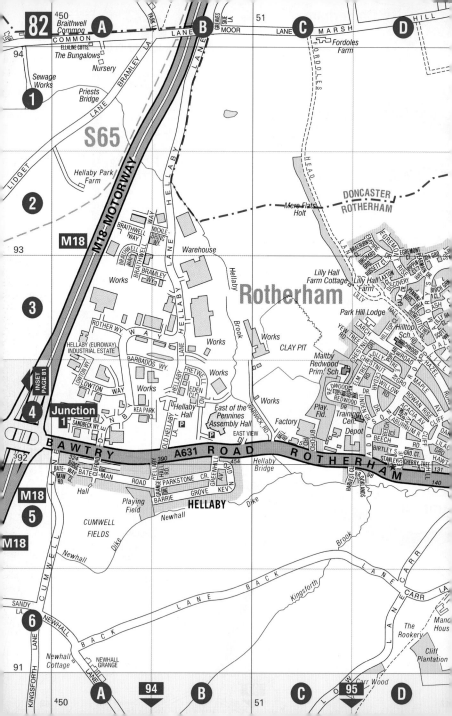

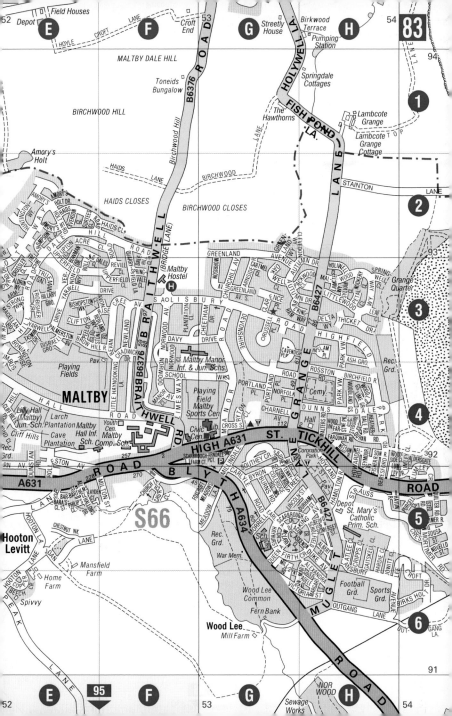

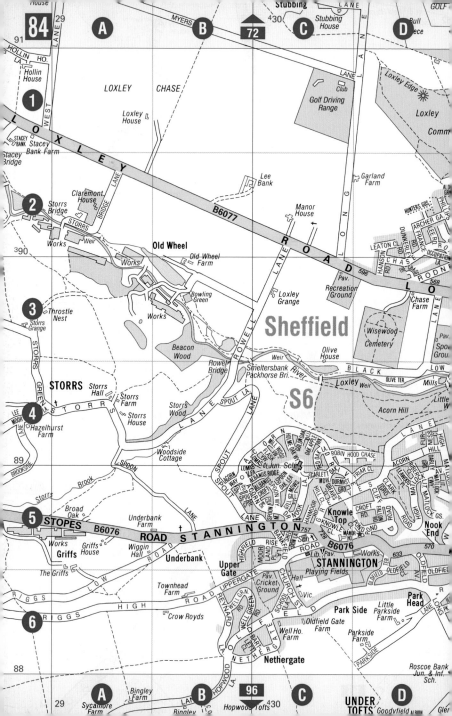

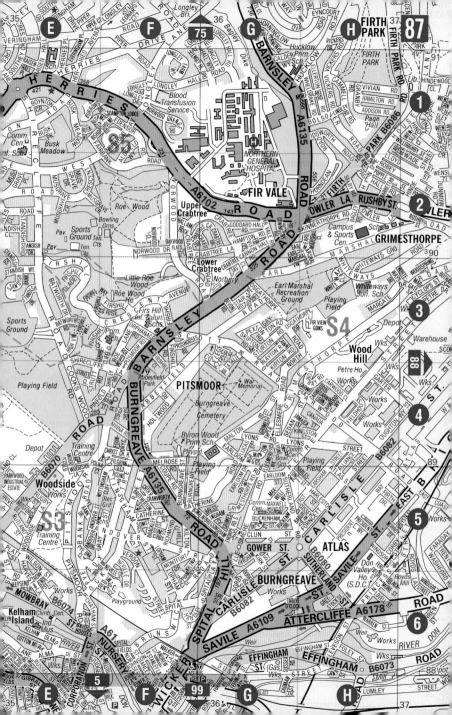

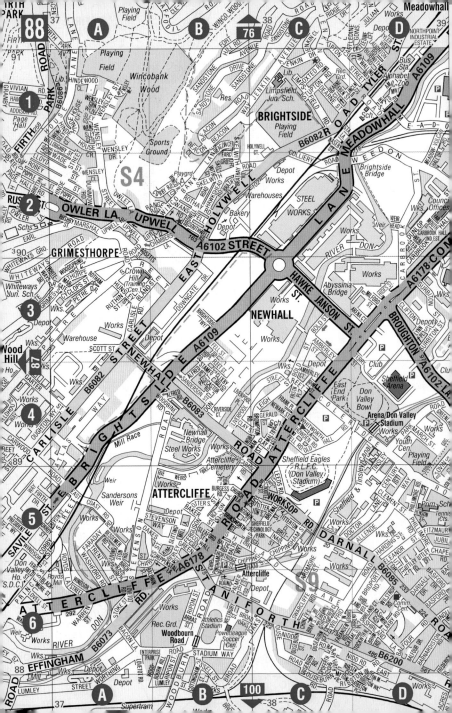

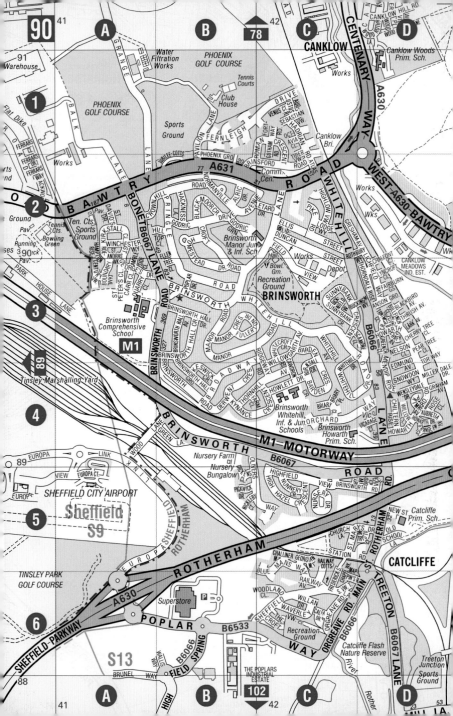

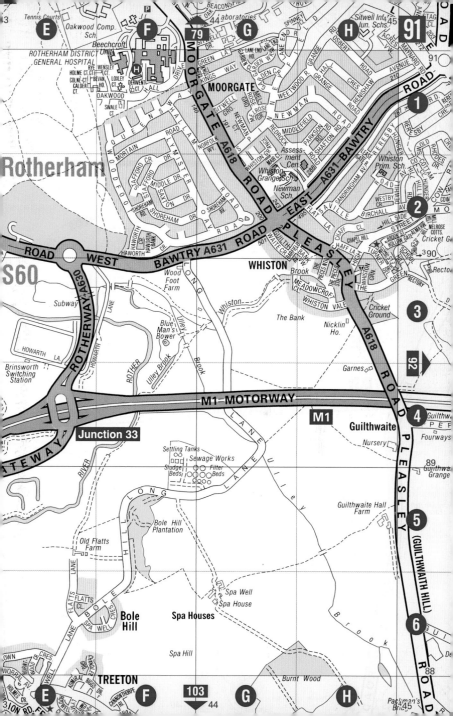

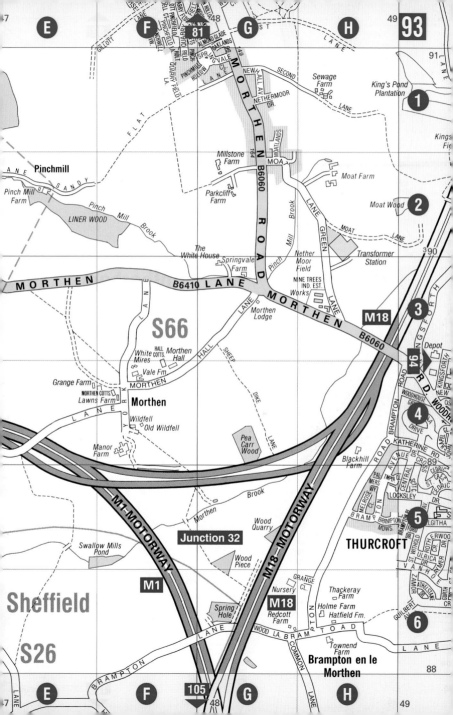

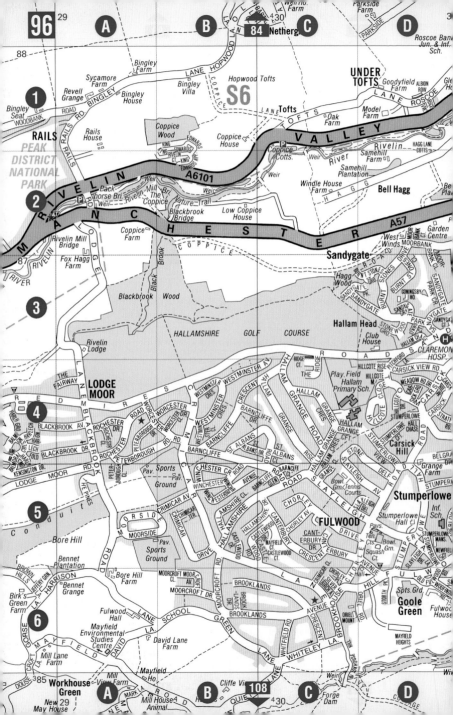

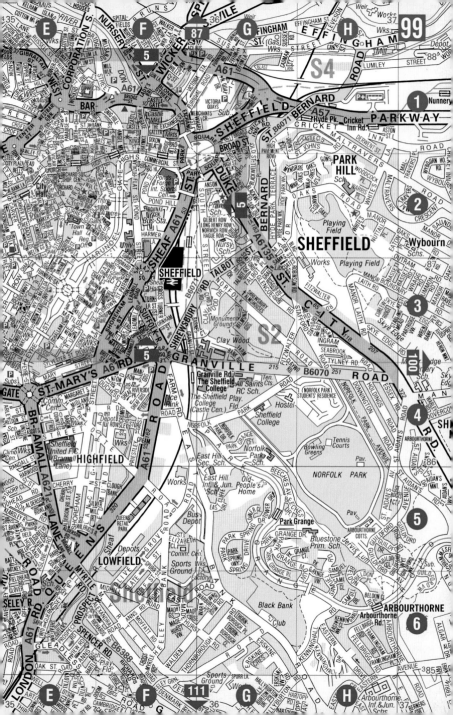

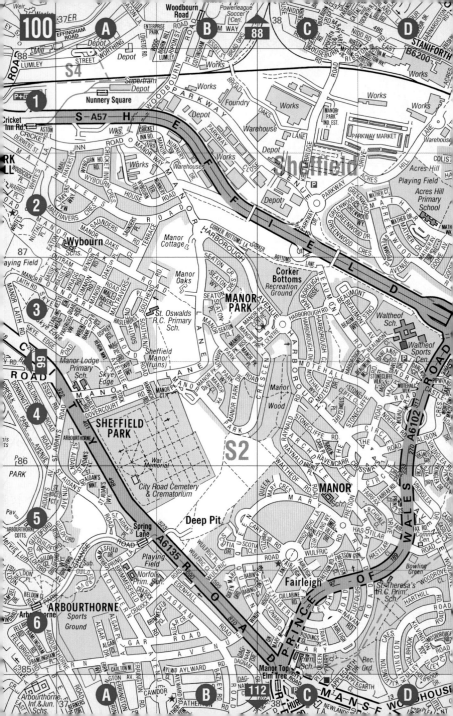

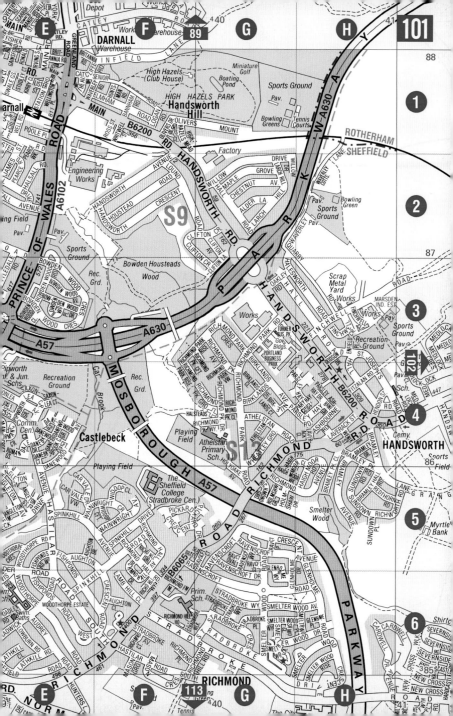

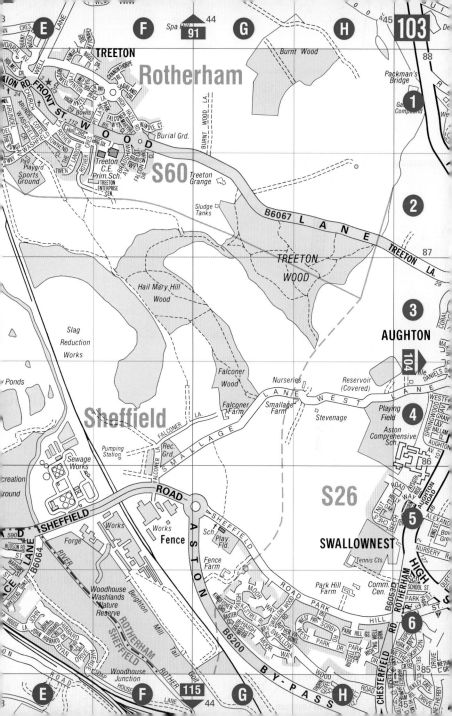

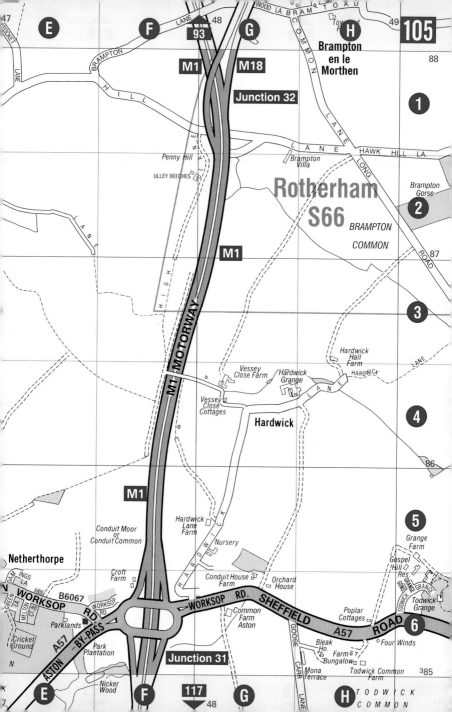

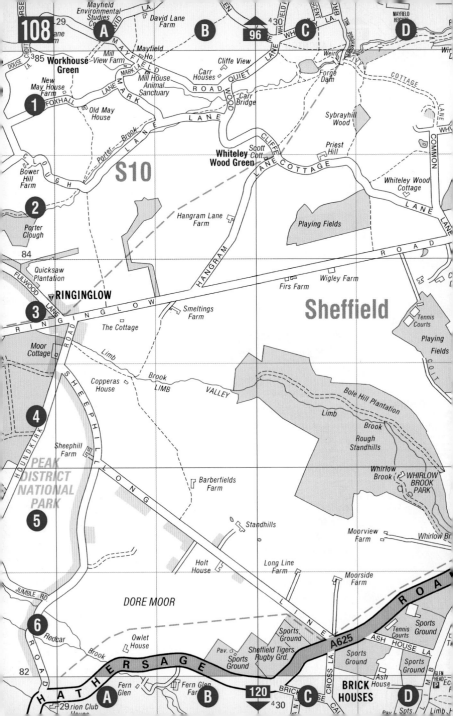

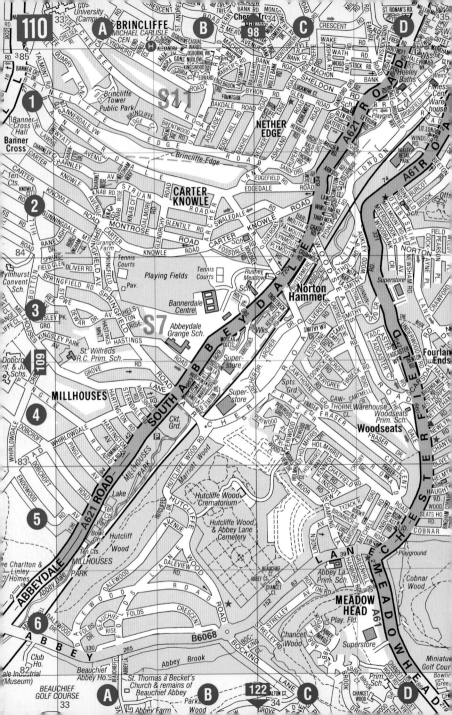

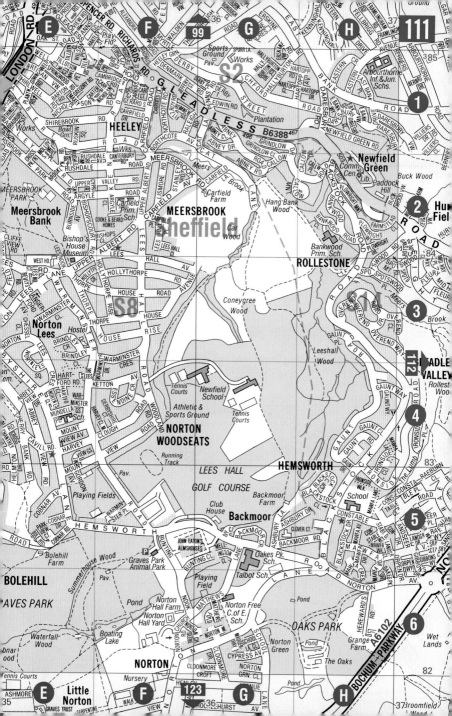

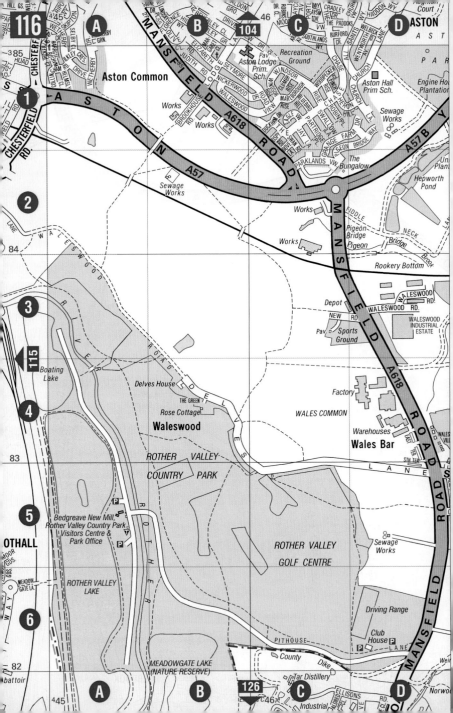

Sheffield
S26

WALES

KIVETON PARK

Kiveton
Bridge

M1 MOTORWAY

TODWICK
COMMON

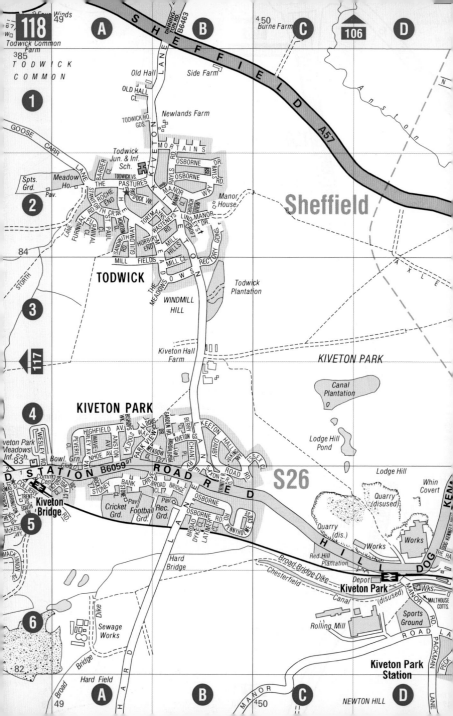

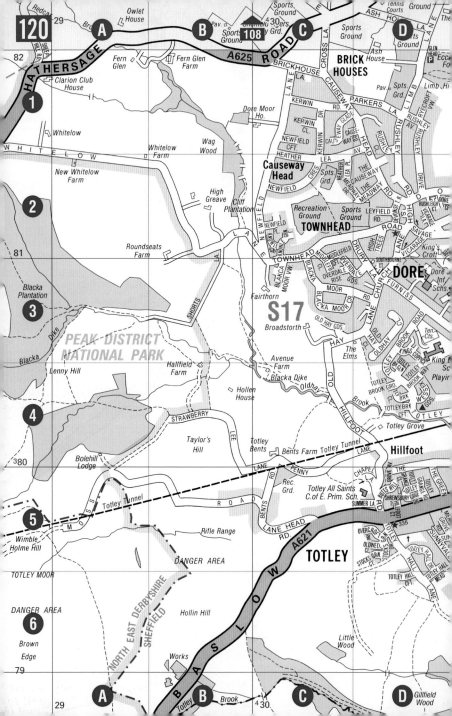

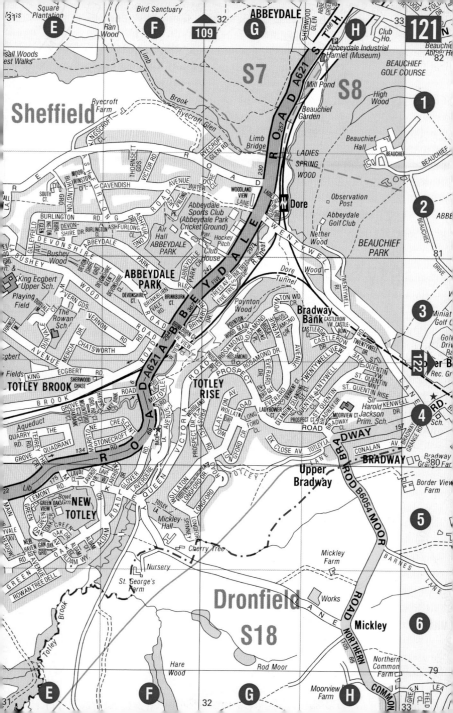

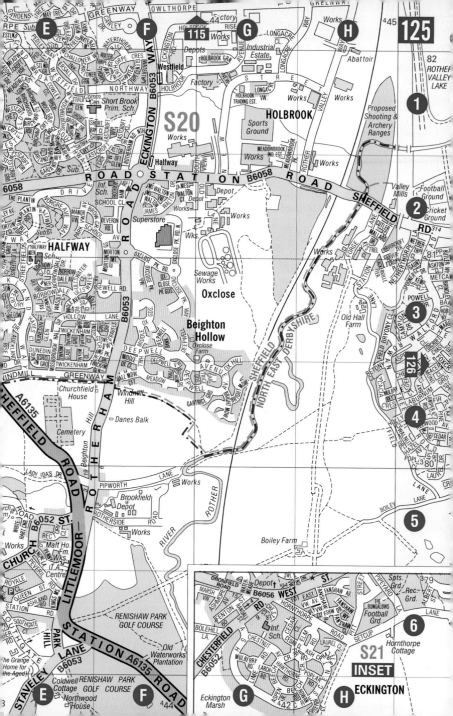

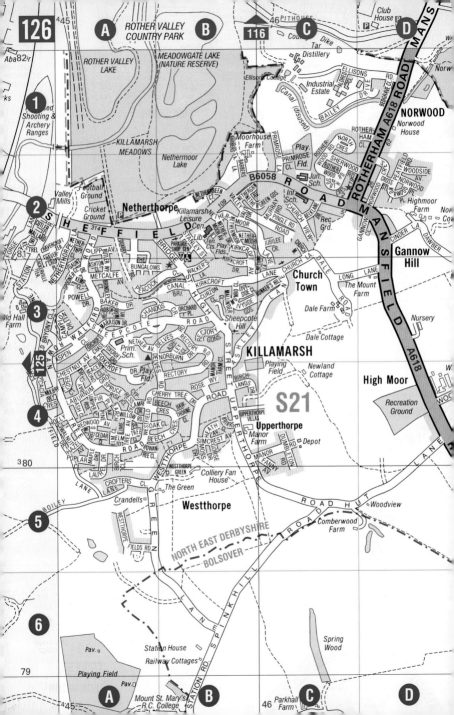

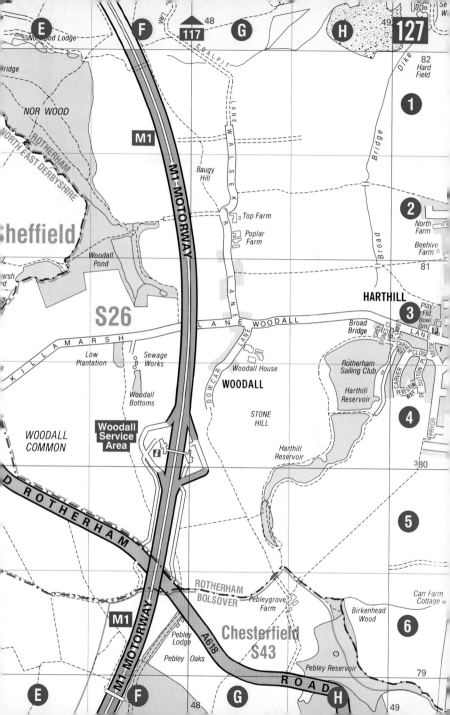

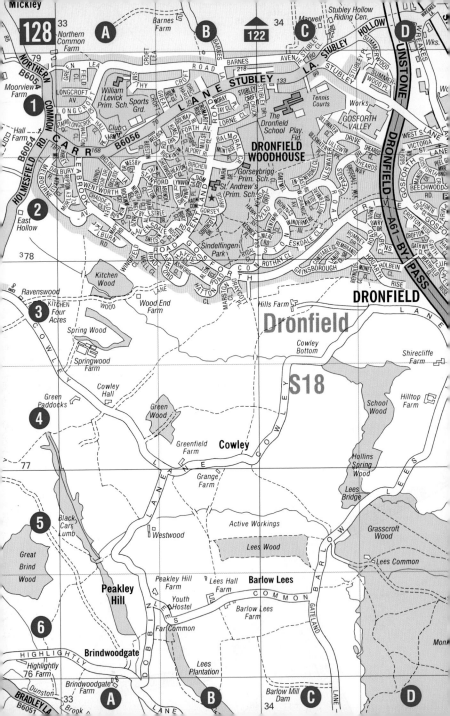

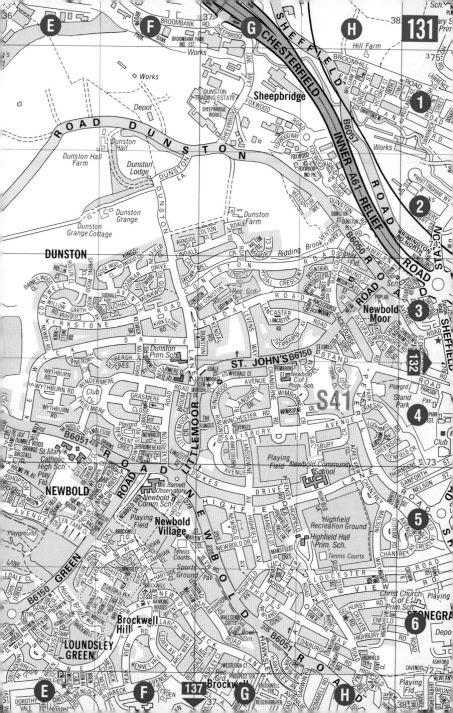

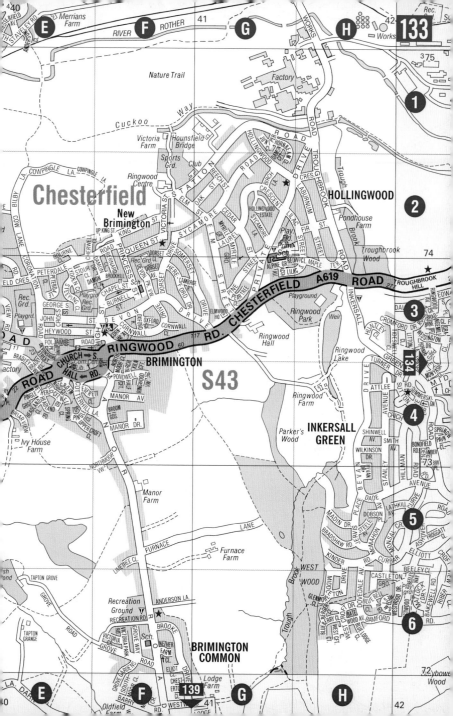

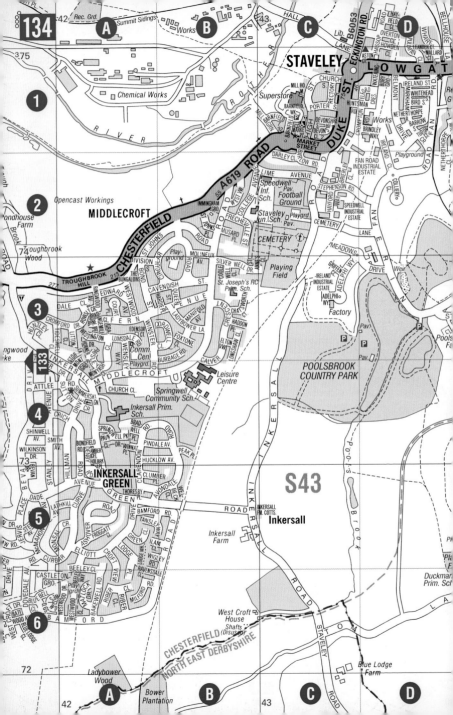

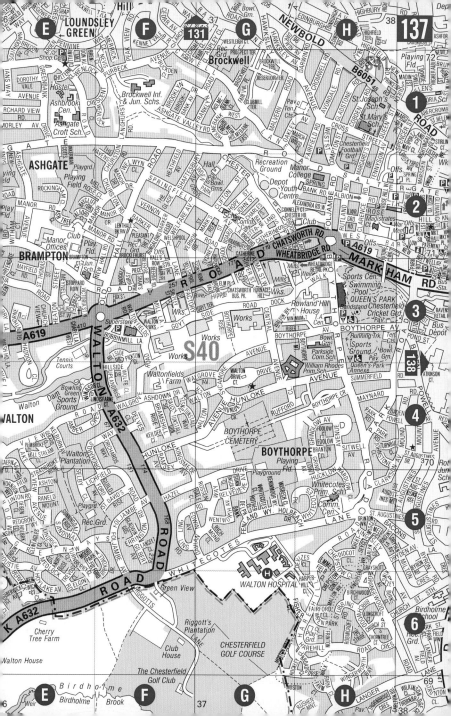

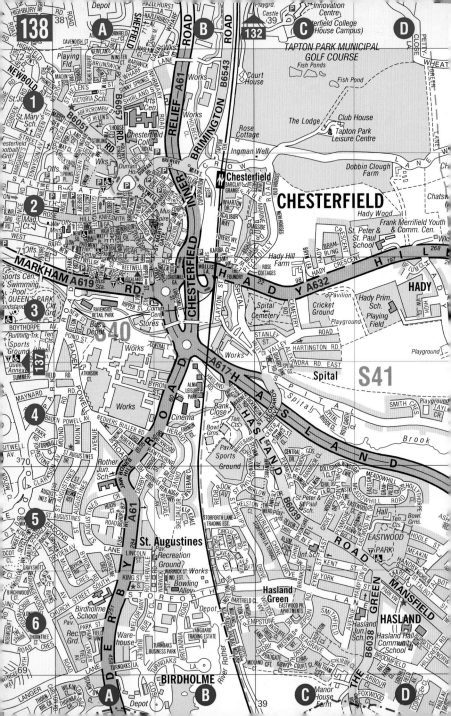

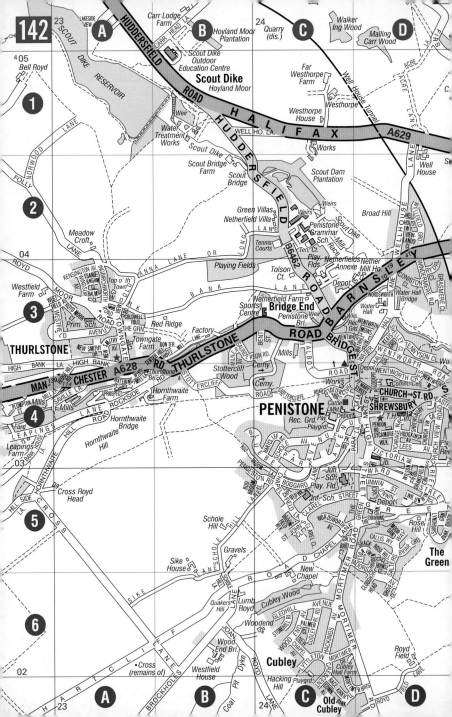

INDEX

Including Streets, Places & Areas, Industrial Estates,
Selected Subsidiary Addresses and Selected Places of Interest.

HOW TO USE THIS INDEX

1. Each street name is followed by its Posttown or Postal Locality and then by its map reference; e.g. Abbey Brook Clo. *S8* . . . .6C **110** is in the Sheffield 8 Postal District and is to be found in square 6C on page **110**. The page number being shown in bold type.
A strict alphabetical order is followed in which Av., Rd., St., etc. (though abbreviated) are read in full and as part of the street name; e.g. Abbeyfield Rd. appears after Abbey Farm Vw. but before Abbey Glen.

2. Streets and a selection of Subsidiary names not shown on the Maps, appear in the index in *Italics* with the thoroughfare to which it is connected shown in brackets; e.g. *Abbeydale Ct. S17* . . . .2G *121 (off Ladies Spring Dri.)*

3. Places and areas are shown in the index in **bold type**, the map reference to the actual map square in which the town or area is located and not to the place name; e.g. **Abbeydale**. . . .6H 109

4. An example of a selected place of interest is **Abbeydale Golf Course**. . . .2H 121

5. Map references shown in brackets; e.g. Abney St. *S1* . . . .2D **98** (3C **4**) refer to entries that also appear on the large scale pages **4-5**.

GENERAL ABBREVIATIONS

All : Alley	Est : Estate	Pde : Parade
App : Approach	Fld : Field	Pk : Park
Arc : Arcade	Gdns : Gardens	Pas : Passage
Av : Avenue	Gth : Garth	Pl : Place
Bk : Back	Ga : Gate	Quad : Quadrant
Boulevd : Boulevard	Gt : Great	Res : Residential
Bri : Bridge	Grn : Green	Ri : Rise
B'way : Broadway	Gro : Grove	Rd : Road
Bldgs : Buildings	Ho : House	Shop : Shopping
Bus : Business	Ind : Industrial	S : South
Cvn : Caravan	Info : Information	Sq : Square
Cen : Centre	Junct : Junction	Sta : Station
Chu : Church	La : Lane	St : Street
Chyd : Churchyard	Lit : Little	Ter : Terrace
Circ : Circle	Lwr : Lower	Trad : Trading
Cir : Circus	Mc : Mac	Up : Upper
Clo : Close	Mnr : Manor	Va : Vale
Comn : Common	Mans : Mansions	Vw : View
Cotts : Cottages	Mkt : Market	Vs : Villas
Ct : Court	Mdw : Meadow	Vis : Visitors
Cres : Crescent	M : Mews	Wlk : Walk
Cft : Croft	Mt : Mount	W : West
Dri : Drive	Mus : Museum	Yd : Yard
E : East	N : North	
Embkmt : Embankment	Pal : Palace	

POSTTOWN AND POSTAL LOCALITY ABBREVIATIONS

Adw S : Adwick-le-Street	*Brim* : Brimington	*Edl'tn* : Edlington
Adw D : Adwick-upon-Dearne	*B'wth* : Brinsworth	*Else* : Elsecar
A'ley : Alverley	*Brod* : Brodsworth	*Flan* : Flanderwell
Ans : Anston	*Burn* : Burncross	*Gawber* : Gawber
App : Apperknowle	*Cad* : Cadeby	*Gold* : Goldthorpe
Ard : Ardsley	*Cal* : Calow	*Greasb* : Greasbrough
Ark : Arksey	*Cant* : Cantley	*Gt Hou* : Great Houghton
Ark T : Arkwright Town	*Car* : Carlton	*Gren* : Grenoside
Arm : Armthorpe	*Cat* : Catcliffe	*Grim* : Grimethorpe
Ash : Ashgate	*C'town* : Chapeltown	*Grin* : Grindleford
Ast : Aston	*Ches* : Chesterfield	*Haigh* : Haigh
Auc : Auckley	*Clif* : Clifton	*Half* : Halfway
Aug : Aughton	*Coal A* : Coal Aston	*Harl* : Harley
Bal : Balby	*Con* : Conisbrough	*H'ton* : Harlington
Blbgh : Barlborough	*Cry P* : Crystal Peaks	*H'hill* : Harthill
Barl : Barlow	*Cud* : Cudworth	*Harw* : Harworth
Barn : Barnburgh	*Cusw* : Cusworth	*Has* : Hasland
Barn D : Barnby Dun	*Cut* : Cutthorpe	*H'by* : Hellaby
B'ley : Barnsley	*Dalt* : Dalton	*H'fld* : Hemingfield
Bar G : Barugh Green	*D'fld* : Darfield	*Hems* : Hemsworth
Baw : Bawtry	*Dart* : Darton	*Hick* : Hickleton
Beig : Beighton	*Deep* : Deepcar	*Hghm* : Higham
Ben : Bentley	*Den M* : Denaby Main	*High* : Highfields
Bes : Bessacarr	*Dinn* : Dinnington	*High G* : High Green
Birdw : Birdwell	*Dod* : Dodworth	*H Hoy* : High Hoyland
Bla H : Blacker Hill	*Donc* : Doncaster	*H'brk* : Holbrook
Bsvr : Bolsover	*Donc F* : Doncaster Finningley Airport	*Holl* : Hollingwood
Bols : Bolsterstone	*Dron* : Dronfield	*Holm* : Holmesfield
Bol D : Bolton-upon-Dearne	*Dron W* : Dronfield Woodhouse	*Holy* : Holymoorside
B'well : Braithwell	*Duck* : Duckmanton	*Hood G* : Hood Green
Braml : Bramley	*D'ville* : Dunsville	*Hoot L* : Hooton Levitt
Bram : Brampton	*E'mr* : Eastmoor	*Hoot R* : Hooton Roberts
Bram B : Brampton Bierlow	*E'wd T* : Eastwood Trad. Est.	*Hoy* : Hoyland
Bram M : Brampton-en-le-Morthen	*E'fld* : Ecclesfield	*H'swne* : Hoylandswaine
Bran : Branton	*Eck* : Eckington	*Ink* : Inkersall
Brie : Brierley	*E'thpe* : Edenthorpe	*Intake* : Intake

Jump : Jump
Kil : Killamarsh
Kiln : Kilnhurst
K'wth : Kimberworth
King : Kingston
Kirk S : Kirk Sandall
K Ind : Kirk Sandall Ind. Est.
Kiv P : Kiveton Park
Kiv S : Kiveton Park Station
Lghtn : Laughton
L Hou : Little Houghton
Lund : Lundwood
Maltby : Maltby
Manv : Manvers
M'well : Mapplewell
Marr : Marr
Mar L : Marsh Lane
Mas M : Mastin Moor
Mexb : Mexborough
M'brng : Micklebring
Mill G : Millhouse Green
Monk B : Monk Bretton
Morth : Morthen
Mosb : Mosborough
New C : New Crofton
New R : New Rossington
New W : New Whittington
N Ans : North Anston
Notton : Notton
Old Br : Old Brampton
Old De : Old Denaby
Old E : Old Edlington
Old W : Old Whittington
O'bri : Oughtibridge
Owl : Owlthorpe
Oxs : Oxspring
P'gte : Parkgate

P'stne : Penistone
Pick : Pickburn
Pool : Poolsbrook
Rav : Ravenfield
Rawm : Rawmarsh
Ridg : Ridgeway
Ross : Rossington
Roth : Rotherham
Roy : Royston
Scaw : Scawsby
Scawt : Scawthorpe
Scho : Scholes
Shaf : Shafton
Shut : Shuttlewood
Silk : Silkstone
Silk C : Silkstone Common
Soth : Sothall
S Elm : South Elmsall
S Hien : South Hiendley
S Kirk : South Kirkby
Spin : Spinkhill
Spro : Sprotbrough
S'bgh : Stainborough
S'ton : Stainton
Stann : Stannington
Stav : Staveley
S'bri : Stocksbridge
S'side : Sunnyside
Swait : Swaithe
Swal : Swallownest
Swint : Swinton
Tank : Tankersley
Temp N : Temple Normanton
Thpe H : Thorpe Hesley
Thor S : Thorpe Salvin
Thry : Thrybergh

Thur : Thurcroft
T'land : Thurgoland
Thurls : Thurlstone
Thurn : Thurnscoe
Tins I : Tinsley Ind. Est.
Tod : Todwick
Toll B : Toll Bar
Tree : Treeton
Ulley : Ulley
Uns : Unstone
Upt : Upton
Wadw : Wadworth
Wal : Wales
Wal B : Wales Bar
Walt : Walton
Warm : Warmsworth
Wat : Waterthorpe
Wath D : Wath-upon-Dearne
W'wth : Wentworth
W'fld : Westfield
Whar S : Wharncliffe Side
Whis : Whiston
Whit M : Whittington Moor
Wick : Wickersley
Wing : Wingerworth
Womb : Wombwell
Wood : Woodhouse
W'land : Woodlands
W'sett : Woodsetts
Wool : Woolley
Worr : Worrall
Wors : Worsbrough
Wors B : Worsbrough Bridge
Wors D : Worsbrough Dale
Wort : Wortley

A

Abbey Brook Clo. S8 . . . . .6C 110
Abbey Brook Ct. S8 . . . . .6C 110
Abbey Brook Dri. S8 . . . . .6C 110
Abbey Brook Gdns. S8 . . . . .6C 110
Abbey Clo. Lghtn 6F 95
Abbey Ct. S8 . . . . .6B 110
Abbey Cres. S7 . . . . .6H 109
Abbey Cft. S7 . . . . .6H 109
Abbey Cft. Ches 4C 130
Abbeydale. 6H 109
Abbeydale Ct. S17 . . . . .2G 121
   (off Ladies Spring Dri.)
Abbeydale Dri. S7 . . . . .3B 110
Abbeydale Golf Course. 2H 121
Abbeydale Ind. Hamlet. 6H 109
                 (Museum)
Abbeydale Park. 3F 121
Abbeydale Pk. Cres. S17 . . . . .3F 121
Abbeydale Pk. Ri. S17 . . . . .2E 121
Abbeydale Rd. S7 . . . . .4B 110
Abbeydale Rd. S. S17 & S7 . . . . . . .3F 121
Abbey Farm Vw. Cud 2H 15
Abbeyfield Rd. S4 . . . . .4F 87
Abbey Glen. Maltby 2D 94
Abbey Grange. S7 . . . . .6H 109
Abbey Grn. Dod 3C 22
Abbey Gro. Lund 4E 15
Abbeyhill Clo. Ash 1B 136
Abbey La. S7 & S8 . . . . .5G 109
Abbey La. S11 . . . . .4G 109
Abbey La. B'ley 5E 15
Abbey La. Lghtn 4G 95
Abbey La. Dell. S8 . . . . .6H 109
Abbey Sq. B'ley 3E 15
Abbey Vw. Dri. S8 . . . . .4E 111
Abbey Vw. Rd. S8 . . . . .4E 111
Abbey Wlk. Donc 4G 31
Abbey Way. N Ans 4B 106
Abbot La. Wool 1F 7
Abbots Clo. Cud 2H 15
Abbotsford Dri. Thur 5A 94
Abbots Mdw. Soth 6G 115
Abbots Rd. B'ley 4F 15
Abbott St. Donc 1B 46
Abdy. 3D 54
Abdy Rd. Rawm & Swint 4C 54
Abdy Rd. Roth 5F 67

Abell St. Thry 5C 70
Aberconway Cres. New R 5C 62
Abercorn Rd. Donc 5A 34
Abercrombie St. Ches 1A 138
Aberford Gro. Else 5D 38
Abingdon Gdns. Roth 4B 68
Abingdon Rd. Donc 4H 33
Abney Clo. S14 . . . . .1G 111
Abney Clo. Ches 5E 131
Abney Dri. S14 . . . . .1G 111
Abney Rd. S14 . . . . .1G 111
Abney St. S1 . . . . .2D 98 (3C 4)
Abrafact Ind. Ct. S6 . . . . .2B 86
Abus Rd. Donc 2E 31
Acacia Av. Braml 4G 81
Acacia Av. C'town 3D 64
Acacia Av. Holl 3G 133
Acacia Av. Maltby 4D 82
Acacia Ct. Ben 5A 18
Acacia Cres. Kil 4H 125
Acacia Gro. Con 5C 58
Acacia Gro. Shaf 3C 10
Acacia Rd. S5 . . . . .5A 76
Acacia Rd. Donc 3D 48
Ace Bus. Cen. S3 . . . . . . .6F 87 (1G 5)
Ace Clo. Maltby 4F 119
Acer Av. S9 . . . . .4F 89
Acer Cft. Arm 4F 35
Ackworth Dri. S9 . . . . .2H 89
Acorn Cft. Roth 5B 68
Acorn Dri. S6 . . . . .5C 84
Acorn Hill. S6 . . . . .4D 84
         (in two parts)
Acorn Ridge. Walt 1D 125
Acorn St. S3 . . . . .6E 87 (1D 4)
Acorn Way. S6 . . . . .5B 84
Acorn Way. Grim 6F 11
Acre Clo. E'thpe 5D 20
Acre Clo. Maltby 4B 94
      (Sycamore Dri.)
Acre Clo. Maltby 2E 83
      (Upperfield Rd.)
Acre Ga. High G 1B 64
Acre La. H'swne 1D 142
Acre La. Whar S 1A 72
Acres Hill La. S9 . . . . .2D 100
Acres Hill Rd. S9 . . . . .1D 100
Acres Vw. Roth 6H 79
Acres Vw. Clo. Ches 4H 131
Adastral Av. S12 . . . . .5C 112
Addison Rd. S5 . . . . .1H 87

Addison Rd. Maltby 4D 82
Addison Rd. Mexb 6F 43
Addison Sq. Dinn 4F 107
Addy Clo. S6 . . . . .6C 86
Addy Clo. Bal 6C 46
Addy St. S6 . . . . .6C 86
Adelaide Rd. S7 . . . . .1B 110
Adelaide St. Maltby 6H 83
Adelphi St. S6 . . . . .6C 86
Adelphi Way. Stav 3C 134
Adkins Dri. S5 . . . . .6C 74
Adkins Rd. S5 . . . . .6C 74
Adlard Rd. Donc 3H 33
Adlington Cres. S5 . . . . .5D 74
Adlington Rd. S5 . . . . .5D 74
Admiral Biggs Dri. Tree 1E 103
Admirals Crest. Scho 5D 66
Adrian Cres. S5 . . . . .5E 75
Adsetts St. S4 . . . . .2A 88
Adwick Av. Toll B 2H 17
Adwick Ct. Mexb 1F 57
Adwick La. Adw S 1E 17
Adwick le Street. 1E 17
Adwick Pk. Manv 5B 42
Adwick Rd. Mexb 4D 42
Adwick Sports Cen. & Swimming Pool.
. . . . .3D 16
Adwick-upon-Dearne. 3D 42
Agden Rd. S7 . . . . .5C 98
Agnes Rd. B'ley 1G 23
Agnes Rd. Dart 5C 6
Agnes Ter. B'ley 1G 23
Ainsdale Av. Gold 5F 29
Ainsdale Clo. Roy 1D 8
Ainsdale Ct. B'ley 2D 14
Ainsdale Rd. Roy 1D 8
Ainsley Rd. S10 . . . . .1A 98
Ainsty Rd. S7 . . . . .6D 98
Ainthorpe Rd. Toll B 2H 17
Aintree Av. Donc 1B 48
Aintree Clo. Donc 4F 31
Aintree Dri. Mexb 5F 43
Aintree Rd. S6 . . . . .1G 85
Airdale Rd. Dart 5A 6
Aireton Clo. Flan 4E 81
Aireton Rd. B'ley 5G 13
Aireton Rd. Roth 5E 81
Air Mt. Clo. Wick 5E 81
Aisby Dri. Ross 3E 63

Aisthorpe Rd. *S8* 4D **110**
Aitken Rd. *Kiln* 5C **56**
Aizlewood Rd. *S8* 6D **98**
    (in two parts)
Akley Bank Clo. *S17* 4F **121**
Alan Rd. *Dart* 5B **6**
Alba Clo. *D'fld* 3C **26**
Albanus Cft. *S6* 5C **84**
Albanus Ridge. *S6* 5C **84**
Albany Av. *C'town* 3F **65**
Albany Clo. *Womb* 3G **25**
Albany La. *New R* 4C **62**
Albany Rd. *S7* 6D **98**
Albany Rd. *Donc* 3A **46**
Albany Rd. *Kiln* 4B **56**
Albany Rd. *S'bri* 3D **140**
Albany St. *Roth* 3E **79**
Albert Av. *New W* 1D **132**
Albert Cres. *L Hou* 2H **27**
Albert Rd. *S8* 1E **111**
Albert Rd. *S12* 4C **114**
Albert Rd. *Gold* 4G **29**
Albert Rd. *Mexb* 6E **43**
Albert Rd. *P'gte* 3F **69**
Albert Rd. *Wath D* 4D **40**
Albert St. *B'ley* 6H **13**
Albert St. *Cud* 4C **10**
Albert St. *Eck* 6D **124**
Albert St. *Maltby* 5H **83**
Albert St. *Roth* 3C **78**
Albert St. *Swint* 1B **56**
Albert St. *Thurn* 1E **29**
Albert St. E. *B'ley* 6H **13**
Albert St. N. *Ches* 2H **131**
Albert Ter. Rd. *S6* 6C **86**
Albion Dri. *Thurn* 1H **29**
Albion Ho. *B'ley* 1H **23**
Albion Pl. *Donc* 6E **33**
Albion Rd. *Car* 6E **9**
Albion Rd. *Ches* 2H **137**
Albion Rd. *Roth* 3E **79**
Albion Row. *S6* 1D **96**
Albion St. *S6* 1C **98**
Albion Ter. *B'ley* 1A **24**
Albion Ter. *Donc* 2B **46**
Alcester Rd. *S7* 6D **98**
Aldam Clo. *S17* 5E **121**
Aldam Clo. *Roth* 2B **80**
Aldam Cft. *S17* 5E **121**
Aldam Rd. *S17* 5E **121**
Aldam Rd. *Donc* 5H **45**
Aldam Way. *S17* 5E **121**
Aldbeck Cft. *Dart* 6C **6**
Aldbury Clo. *B'ley* 1B **14**
Aldcliffe Cres. *Donc* 1F **61**
Aldene Av. *S6* 2F **85**
Aldene Glade. *S6* 2F **85**
Aldene Rd. *S6* 1F **85**
Alder Chase. *Scho* 5E **67**
Alder Clo. *M'well* 4E **7**
Aderford Dri. *Bal* 1H **61**
Alder Gro. *D'fld* 5D **26**
Alder Gro. *Donc* 4A **46**
Alder Holt Clo. *Arm* 4G **35**
Alder La. *S9* 2G **101**
Alder M. *Hoy* 6A **38**
Alderney Rd. *S2* 6E **99**
Aldersgate Clo. *New R* 5E **63**
Aldersgate Ct. *Maltby* 4H **83**
Alders Grn. *S6* 2D **84**
Alderson Av. *Rawm* 6F **55**
Alderson Clo. *Swal* 4B **104**
Alderson Dri. *B'ley* 1A **14**
Alderson Dri. *Donc* 1F **47**
Alderson Pl. *S2* 5E **99**
Alderson Rd. *S2* 5D **98**
Alderson Rd. N. *S2* 5E **99**
    (in two parts)
Alders, The. *Holy* 6A **136**
Aldervale Clo. *Swint* 5B **56**
Aldesworth Rd. *Donc* 2C **48**
Aldfield Way. *S5* 2F **87**
Aldham Cotts. *Womb* 4A **26**
Aldham Cres. *Womb* 3G **25**
Aldham Ho. La. *Womb* 5H **25**
Aldham Ind. Est. *Womb* 4A **26**
Aldine Ct. *S1* 3F **5**
Aldous Clo. *Kiv P* 4A **118**
Aldous Way. *Kiv P* 4A **118**
Aldred Clo. *Kil* 1C **126**
Aldred Clo. *Wick* 4F **81**
Aldred Ct. *Roth* 4E **79**
Aldred Rd. *S10* 6A **86**

Aldred St. *Roth* 4E **79**
Aldrin Way. *Maltby* 3E **83**
Aldwarke. **5H 69**
Aldwarke La. *Roth* 4G **69**
Aldwarke Rd. *P'gte* 4F **69**
Alexander St. *Ben* 6B **18**
Alexandra St. *S11* 1B **110**
Alexandra Cen. *P'gte* 5F **69**
Alexandra Ridge. *S6* 1G **77**
Alexandra Gdns. *S11* 1B **110**
Alexandra Rd. *S2* 6F **99**
Alexandra Rd. *Adw S* 1F **17**
Alexandra Rd. *Ben* 5B **18**
Alexandra Rd. *Donc* 3B **46**
Alexandra Rd. *Dron* 1F **129**
Alexandra Rd. *Mexb* 6F **43**
Alexandra Rd. *Swal* 5A **104**
Alexandra Ter. *B'ley* 1F **25**
Alford Av. *O'bri* 2D **72**
Alford Clo. *B'ley* 3D **12**
Alford Clo. *Ches* 2E **137**
Alfred Rd. *S9* 4B **88**
    (in two parts)
Alfred St. *Roy* 1G **9**
Algar Clo. *S2* 6A **100**
Algar Cres. *S2* 6B **100**
Algar Dri. *S2* 6A **100**
Algar Pl. *S2* 6A **100**
Algar Rd. *S2* 6A **100**
Alhambra Shop. Cen. *B'ley* 6H **13**
Alice Rd. *Roth* 2B **78**
Alice Way. *Uns* 5H **129**
Alison Clo. *Swal* 6B **104**
Alison Cres. *S2* 4D **100**
Alison Dri. *Swal* 6B **104**
Allatt St. *Roth* 3E **79**
Allatt Clo. *B'ley* 1H **23**
Alldred Cres. *Swint* 4A **56**
Allenby Clo. *S8* 2C **122**
Allenby Cres. *New R* 5C **62**
Allenby Dri. *S8* 2C **122**
Allendale. *Wors* 4C **24**
Allendale Cr. *Wors* 4C **24**
Allendale Dri. *Hoy* 6A **38**
Allendale Gdns. *Donc* 6H **31**
Allendale Rd. *B'ley* 3G **13**
Allendale Rd. *Dart* 5B **6**
Allendale Rd. *Donc* 6H **31**
Allendale Rd. *Hoy* 6H **37**
Allendale Rd. *Roth* 5A **80**
Allende Way. *S9* 5D **88**
Allen Rd. *Beig* 5F **115**
Allen St. *S3* 1D **98** (1C **4**)
Allerton St. *Donc* 5D **32**
Allestree Dri. *Dron W* 2A **128**
All Hallows Dri. *Maltby* 5E **83**
Alliance St. *S4* 4H **87**
Alliss Rd. *Bran* 3H **49**
Allott Clo. *Rav* 1H **81**
Allott Cres. *Jump* 4C **38**
Allotts Ct. *Birdw* 4C **36**
Allott St. *Else* 6C **38**
Allott St. *Hoy* 6F **37**
Allpits Rd. *Cal* 2F **139**
All Saints Clo. *Wath D* 5E **41**
All Saints Sq. *Den M* 1C **58**
All Saints Sq. *Roth* 3D **78**
All Saints Way. *Ast* 1C **116**
Allsopps Yd. *Bla H* 2H **37**
Allt St. *P'gte* 3F **69**
Alma Cres. *Dron* 6E **123**
Alma Leisure Pk. *Ches* 4B **138**
Alma Rd. *High G* 6B **50**
Alma Rd. *Roth* 4D **78**
Alma Row. *Whis* 2A **92**
Alma St. *S3* 6E **87** (1D **4**)
Alma St. *B'ley* 6F **13**
Alma St. *Womb* 1F **39**
Alma St. W. *Ches* 3G **137**
Almholme. **2G 19**
Almholme La. *Ark* 4E **19**
    (in two parts)
Almond Av. *Arm* 2F **35**
Almond Av. *Cud* 6B **10**
Almond Clo. *Cal* 2G **139**
Almond Clo. *Maltby* 4E **83**
Almond Dri. *Kil* 4A **126**
Almond Glade. *Wick* 6G **81**
Almond Pl. *Brim* 4E **133**

Almond Pl. *Wath D* 6F **41**
Almond Rd. *Donc* 3D **48**
Almond Tree Rd. *Wal* 5E **117**
Alms Hill Cres. *S11* 4F **109**
Alms Hill Dri. *S11* 4F **109**
Alms Hill Glade. *S11* 4F **109**
Alms Hill Rd. *S11* 4F **109**
Almshouses. *W'wth* 3C **52**
Alney Pl. *S6* 5B **74**
Alphabet Zoo. **1D 88**
Alpha Rd. *Roth* 2H **79**
Alpha St. *Toll B* 2H **17**
Alpine Clo. *S'bri* 3C **140**
Alpine Cft. *S'bri* 3C **140**
Alpine Gro. *Holl* 3G **133**
Alpine Rd. *S6* 6B **86**
Alpine Rd. *S'bri* 3C **140**
Alport Av. *S12* 2G **113**
Alport Clo. *S12* 2G **113**
Alport Gro. *S12* 2G **113**
Alport Pl. *S12* 3G **113**
Alport Ri. *Dron W* 1B **128**
Alport Rd. *S12* 2G **113**
Alric Dri. *B'ley* 6E **15**
Alric Dri. *B'wth* 2B **90**
Alrich M. *S'bri* 2B **140**
Alsing Rd. *S9* 6E **77**
Alston Clo. *Donc* 4B **48**
Alston Rd. *Donc* 5B **48**
Alton Clo. *S11* 5G **109**
Alton Clo. *Dron W* 3B **128**
Alton Clo. *Walt* 5D **136**
Alton Way. *M'well* 4E **7**
Alum Chine Clo. *Has* 5C **138**
Alvaston Wlk. *Den M* 2C **58**
Alverley. **2F 61**
Alverley La. *Donc* 1G **61**
Alverley Vw. *A'ley* 2G **61**
Alverley Way. *Birdw* 5D **36**
Alwyn Av. *Donc* 2G **31**
Amalfi Clo. *D'fld* 4D **26**
Ambassador Gdns. *Arm* 4G **35**
Amber Cres. *Ches* 4E **137**
Amber Cft. *Ink* 4A **134**
Amberley Ct. *S9* 4C **88**
Amberley St. *S9* 3C **88**
Ambler Ri. *Aug* 4A **104**
Ambleside Clo. *B'wth* 3A **90**
Ambleside Clo. *Ches* 4E **131**
Ambleside Clo. *Half* 3E **125**
Ambleside Cres. *Spro* 2C **44**
Ambleside Gro. *B'ley* 1G **25**
Ambleside Wlk. *Ans* 1H **119**
Amen Corner. *Roth* 2C **78**
    (in two parts)
America La. *Rawm & Wath D* 4B **54**
Amersall Cres. *Donc* 1G **31**
Amersall Rd. *Donc* 1G **31**
Amesbury Clo. *Ches* 4G **131**
Amory's Holt Clo. *Maltby* 2E **83**
Amory's Holt Dri. *Maltby* 2E **83**
Amory's Holt Rd. *Maltby* 2E **83**
Amory's Holt Way. *Maltby* 3D **82**
Amos Rd. *S9* 1D **88**
Amy Rd. *Ben* 4C **18**
Anchorage Cres. *Donc* 5A **32**
Anchorage La. *Donc* 4H **31**
Ancona Ri. *D'fld* 3D **26**
Ancote Clo. *B'ley* 6C **12**
Anderson Clo. *New W* 1E **133**
Anderson La. *Brim* 6F **133**
Andover Dri. *S3* 5E **87**
Andover St. *S3* 5E **87**
Andrew La. *S3* 6F **87** (1G **5**)
    (off Walker St.)
Andrews Pl. *Roth* 1A **78**
Andrew St. *S3* 6F **87** (1G **5**)
Anelay Rd. *Donc* 1H **45**
Anfield Rd. *Donc* 4C **48**
Angel La. *W'wth* 5H **53**
Angel St. *S3* 1F **99** (2F **5**)
Angel St. *Bol D* 2A **138**
Angel Yd. *Ches* 2A **138**
Angerford Av. *S8* 3E **111**
Anglesey Rd. *Dron* 3D **128**
Angleton Av. *S2* 5E **101**
Angleton Clo. *S2* 5E **101**
Angleton Gdns. *S2* 5E **101**
Angleton Grn. *S2* 5E **101**
Angleton M. *S2* 5E **101**

Angram Rd. *High G* 5B **50**
Annan Clo. *Bar G* 2B **12**
Annat Pl. *High G* 6A **50**
Annesley Clo. *S8* 2D **122**
Annesley Clo. *Has* 5C **138**
Annesley Rd. *S8* 1D **122**
Anne St. *Dinn* 2F **107**
Anns Rd. *S2* 6E **99**
Ann St. *P'gte* .4F **69**
Ansdell Rd. *Ben* 5B **18**
Ansell Rd. *S11* 1G **109**
Anson Gro. *B'wth* 3D **90**
Anson St. *S2* 2G **99** (3H **5**)
Ansten Cres. *Donc* 3C **48**
Anston Av. *Kiv P* 4A **118**
Anston Clo. *Ans* 1F **119**
Antrim Av. *S10* 3B **98**
Anvil Clo. *S6* 5E **85**
Anvil Cres. *E'fld* 1F **75**
Apley Rd. *Donc* 1D **46**
Apollo St. *Rawm* 6H **55**
Apostle Clo. *Donc* 5G **45**
Appleby Clo. *Dart* 4D **6**
Appleby Rd. *Donc* 5A **34**
Appleby Wlk. *Ans* 6F **107**
Applegarth Clo. *S12* 1C **112**
Applegarth Dri. *S12* 1C **112**
Applehaigh Dri. *Kirk S* 2C **20**
Applehaigh Gro. *Roy* 1C **8**
Applehaigh Vw. *Roy* 2C **8**
Applehurst Bank. *B'ley* 1B **24**
Appleton Clo. *Dalt* 6B **70**
Appleton Gdns. *Ben* 2A **32**
Appleton Way. *Donc* 1H **31**
Appleton Way. *Wors* 4A **24**
Appletree Dri. *Dron* 2E **129**
Appletree Wlk. *Dron* 2F **129**
(off Appletree Dri.)
April Clo. *B'ley* 3D **14**
April Dri. *B'ley* 3D **14**
Aqueduct St. *B'ley* 4H **13**
Arbour Clo. *Ches* 6D **138**
Arbour Cres. *Thur* 5B **94**
Arbour Dri. *Thur* 5B **94**
Arbour La. *Rav* 4H **71**
Arbourthorne. 6A **100**
Arbourthorne. *S2* 4A **100**
Arbourthorne Cotts. *S2* 5H **99**
Arbourthorne Est. *S2* 1A **112**
Arbourthorne Rd. *S2* 6H **99**
Arcade, The. *S9* 6E **77**
Arcade, The. *B'ley* 6H **13**
Archdale Clo. *S2* 5D **100**
Archdale Pl. *S2* 5C **100**
Archdale Rd. *S2* 4C **100**
Archer Dri. *S8* 4B **110**
(in two parts)
Archer Ga. *S6* 2D **84**
Archer Ho. *Roth* 2E **79**
(off Wharncliffe Hill)
Archer La. *S7* 2B **110**
Archer Rd. *S8* 4B **110**
Archery Clo. *Wick* 6F **81**
Archibald St. *S7* 1C **110**
Archway Cen. *S1* 2F **99** (4G **5**)
Arcon Pl. *Rawm* 1G **69**
Arcubus Av. *Swal* 5B **104**
Ardeen Rd. *Donc* 5G **33**
Arden Clo. *Ches* 6E **131**
Arden Ga. *Donc* 1F **61**
Ardmore St. *S9* 6C **88**
Ardsley. 1G **25**
Ardsley Av. *Ast* 6C **104**
Ardsley Gro. *Owl* 5H **113**
Ardsley Dri. *Owl* 5H **113**
Ardsley Gro. *Owl* 5H **113**
Ardsley M. *B'ley* 1G **25**
Ardsley Rd. *Ches* 2D **136**
Ardsley Rd. *Wors* 4C **24**
Arena Ct. *S9* 3D **88**
Argyle Clo. *S8* 2F **111**
Argyle La. *New R* 4C **62**
Argyle Rd. *S8* 2E **111**
Argyle St. *Mexb* 6E **43**
Argyll Av. *Donc* 4H **33**
Arklow Clo. *Has* 5B **138**
Arklow Rd. *Donc* 5G **33**
Arksey. 5D **18**
Arksey Comn. La. *Ark* 5E **19**
Arksey La. *Ben* 6B **18**
Arkwright Rd. *Donc* 4H **31**
Arley St. *S2* .4E **99**

Arlington Av. *Ast* 5D **104**
Arlott Way. *Edl'tn* 2C **60**
Armer St. *Roth* 3C **78**
Armitage Rd. *Deep* 4F **141**
Armitage Rd. *Donc* 4H **45**
Armroyd La. *Hoy* 1A **52**
Arms Pk. Dri. *Half* 3F **125**
Armstead Rd. *Beig* 4G **115**
Armstrong Wlk. *Maltby* 3E **83**
Armthorpe. 3E **35**
Armthorpe Enterprise Cen. *Arm* 2H **35**
Armthorpe La. *Barn D* 2E **21**
Armthorpe La. *Donc* 4G **33**
Armthorpe Rd. *S11* 5F **97**
Armthorpe Rd. *Donc* 4G **33**
Armthorpe Sports Cen. 3E **35**
Armyne Gro. *B'ley* 6E **15**
Army Row. *Roy* 1F **9**
Armytage Ind. Est. *Whit M* 3B **132**
(Brimington Rd. N.)
Armytage Ind. Est. *Whit M* 2A **132**
(Station Rd.)
Arncliffe Dri. *B'ley* 6D **12**
Arncliffe Dri. *C'town* 1D **64**
Arndale Precinct. *Maltby* 4G **83**
Arnold Av. *S12* 5D **112**
Arnold Av. *B'ley* 6B **8**
Arnold Cres. *Mexb* 5E **43**
Arnold Rd. *Roth* 3H **79**
Arnold St. *S6* 4A **86**
Arnside Clo. *Ches* 2F **131**
Arnside Rd. *S8* 2C **110**
Arnside Rd. *Maltby* 3G **83**
Arnside Ter. *S8* 2C **110**
Arran Hill. *Thry* 4D **70**
Arran Rd. *S10* 2H **97**
Arras St. *S9* 6B **88**
Arren Clo. *Barn D* 1H **21**
Arrowsmith Ho. *Roth* 2E **79**
(off Wharncliffe Hill)
Arthington St. *S8* 1E **111**
Arthur Av. *Ben* 5B **18**
Arthur Pl. *Ben* 5B **18**
Arthur Rd. *S'bri* 3C **140**
Arthur St. *Ben* 5C **18**
Arthur St. *Rawm* 6G **55**
Arthur St. *Roth* 2C **78**
Arthur St. *Swal* 6B **104**
Arthur St. *Wors* 4A **24**
Artisan Vw. *S8* 1E **111**
Arundel Av. *Dalt* 6B **70**
Arundel Av. *Tree* 1E **103**
Arundel Clo. *Ches* 3H **131**
Arundel Clo. *Dron W* 2B **128**
Arundel Cotts. *Tree* 1E **103**
Arundel Ct. *S11* 3F **109**
Arundel Ct. *Stav* 1C **134**
(off Devonshire St.)
Arundel Cres. *Tree* 1E **103**
Arundel Gdns. *Donc* 1H **31**
Arundel Gdns. *Roy* 1E **9**
Arundel Ga. *S1* 2F **99** (4F **5**)
Arundel La. *S1* 3F **99** (5F **5**)
Arundell Dri. *B'ley* 2F **15**
Arundel Rd. *C'town* 1E **65**
Arundel Rd. *Roth* 4F **79**
Arundel Rd. *Tree* 1E **103**
Arundel St. *S1* 3E **99** (6E **5**)
Arundel St. *Tree* 1E **103**
Arundel Vw. *Jump* 4C **38**
Ascension Clo. *Maltby* 5H **83**
Ascot Av. *Donc* 2B **48**
Ascot Clo. *Mexb* 5F **43**
Ascot Dri. *Donc* 3F **31**
Ascot St. *S2* 4E **99**
Ashberry Clo. *Thurn* 1F **29**
Ashberry Gdns. *S6* 6B **86**
Ashberry Rd. *S6* 6B **86**
Ashbourne Clo. *Ches* 6C **130**
Ashbourne Gro. *S13* 4H **101**
Ashbourne Gro. *O'bri* 3E **73**
Ashbourne Rd. *S13* 4H **101**
Ashbourne Rd. *B'ley* 6C **8**
Ashburnham Gdns.
Donc 6G **31**
Ashburton Clo. *Adw S* 1C **16**
Ashbury Dri. *S8* 5G **111**
Ashbury La. *S8* 5G **111**
Ashby Ct. *B'ley* 1F **23**
Ash Clo. *Kil* 4A **126**
Ash Clo. *Roth* 5B **80**
Ash Cotts. *Womb* 3H **25**
Ash Ct. *Maltby* 3D **82**

Ash Ct. *Spro* .2F **45**
Ashcourt Dri. *Bal* 1H **61**
Ash Cres. *Deep* 3F **141**
Ash Cres. *Eck* 6G **125**
Ash Cres. *Mexb* 5D **42**
Ashcroft. 5B **52**
Ashcroft Clo. *Edl'tn* 4A **60**
Ashcroft Dri. *Old W* 1B **132**
Ashdale Clo. *E'thpe* 6D **20**
Ash Dale Rd. *Warm* 1B **60**
Ashdell. *S10* 3A **98**
Ashdell La. *S10* 3A **98**
Ashdell Rd. *S10* 3A **98**
Ashdene Ct. *Swint* 5B **56**
Ashdown Dri. *Ches* 4F **137**
Ashdown Gdns. *Soth* 4G **115**
Ashdown Pl. *Donc* 1H **31**
Ash Dyke Clo. *Dart* 6D **6**
Asher Rd. *S7* 5D **98**
Ashes La. *W'wth* 5B **52**
Ashfield Clo. *S12* 3B **112**
Ashfield Clo. *Arm* 4G **35**
Ashfield Clo. *B'ley* 4E **13**
Ashfield Ct. *S'foot* 1D **24**
Ashfield Dri. *S12* 3B **112**
Ashfield Rd. *Deep* 3F **141**
Ashfield Rd. *Donc* 5A **46**
Ashfield Rd. *Has* 5D **138**
Ashfield Way. *S'side* 2F **81**
Ashford Clo. *Dron W* 3B **128**
Ashford Ct. *Ches* 6A **132**
Ashford Rd. *S11* 5B **98**
Ashford Rd. *Dron W* 3B **128**
Ashfurlong Clo. *S17* 2F **121**
Ashfurlong Dri. *S17* 2F **121**
Ashfurlong Pk. *S17* 2F **121**
Ashfurlong Rd. *S17* 2E **121**
Ashgate. 2E **137**
Ashgate Av. *Ches* 2E **137**
Ashgate Clo. *S10* 3A **98**
Ashgate La. *S10* 3A **98**
Ashgate Rd. *S10* 3A **98**
Ashgate Rd. *Ash* 1A **136**
Ashgate Rd. *Ches* 1D **136**
Ashgate Valley Rd. *Ches* 1F **137**
Ash Gro. *S10* 3B **98**
Ash Gro. *Arm* 2G **35**
Ash Gro. *B'ley* 2D **24**
Ash Gro. *Con* 4C **58**
Ash Gro. *Maltby* 3H **83**
Ash Gro. *Rawm* 2H **69**
Ash Gro. *Wick* 4G **81**
Ash Ho. La. *S17* 6D **108**
Ashland Ct. *S7* 1C **110**
Ashland Rd. *S7* 1C **110**
Ashland Rd. *Eck* 6E **125**
Ash La. *Deep* 3G **141**
Ashleigh. *Brie* 2G **11**
Ashleigh Av. *S12* 2B **112**
Ashleigh Clo. *Old W* 1B **132**
Ashleigh Ct. *Eck* 6H **125**
Ashleigh Cft. *S12* 2B **112**
Ashleigh Dri. *S12* 2B **112**
Ashleigh Gdns. *Roth* 5B **68**
Ashleigh Pl. *S12* 2B **112**
Ashleigh Va. *B'ley* 1C **24**
Ashley Clo. *Kil* 3B **126**
Ashley Cft. *Roy* 1D **8**
Ashley Gro. *Ast* 6B **104**
Ashley Ind. Est. *Roth* 2D **78**
Ashley La. *Kil* 3B **126**
Ashmore Av. *Eck* 6G **125**
Ashmount. *S6* 4A **74**
Ash Mt. *Rawm* 2F **69**
Ash Mt. Roth 3F **79**
(off Doncaster Rd.)
Ash Mt. *Shaf* 1C **10**
Ashopton Rd. *Ches* 5E **131**
Ashover Clo. *Wors* 5A **24**
Ashover Rd. *Ink* 5A **134**
Ashpool Clo. *S13* 1A **114**
Ashpool Fold. *S13* 1A **114**
Ash Ridge. *Swint* 3B **56**
Ash Rd. *Shaf* 3D **10**
Ash Rd. *Wath D* 6G **41**
Ash Row. *B'ley* 6C **14**
Ash St. *S6* 5C **86**
Ash St. *Mosb* 1C **124**
Ash St. *Womb* 3G **25**
Ashton Av. *Donc* 6F **17**
Ashton Clo. *Ches* 5E **130**
Ashton Clo. *Kil* 3A **126**

Ashton Dri.—Balcarres Rd.

Ashton Dri. Kirk S 3C 20
Ash Tree Clo. Ches 2E 137
Ash Tree Ct. S9 5D 76
(off Eccles St.)
Ashurst Clo. S6 5E 85
Ashurst Clo. Ches 6B 130
Ashurst Dri. S6 4E 85
Ashurst Pl. S6 5E 85
Ashurst Rd. S6 4E 85
Ash Va. Ches 2D 136
Ash Vw. C'town 3D 64
Ash Vw. Roth 4B 68
Ashville. New R 5E 63
Ashwell Clo. Shaf 2C 10
Ashwell Gro. Roth 1H 79
Ashwell Rd. S13 1A 114
Ashwood Clo. Bran 3G 49
Ashwood Clo. High G 5A 50
Ashwood Clo. Wors 5B 24
Ashwood Ho. Adw S 2E 17
Ashwood Rd. High G 6A 50
Ashwood Rd. P'gte 3F 69
Ashworth Dri. Roth 5F 67
Askam Ct. Braml 3H 81
Askam Rd. Braml 3H 81
Askern Ho. Donc 1C 46
(off St James St.)
Askern Rd. Toll B 2H 17
Askew Ct. S'bri 4E 141
Askrigg Clo. Donc 4D 48
Asline Rd. S2 5E 99
Aspen Clo. E'thpe 6D 20
Aspen Clo. Kil 3A 126
Aspen Gro. D'fld 5E 27
Aspen Rd. Eck 6G 125
Aspen Wlk. Maltby 4C 82
Aspen Way. Roth 4B 78
Aspen Way. Swint 5A 56
Aspley Clo. Ches 6G 131
Asquith Rd. S9 5D 76
Asquith Rd. Ben 6B 18
Astcote Ct. Kirk S 3C 20
Aster Clo. Ans 3F 119
Aster Clo. Beig 4F 115
Aston. 6D 104
Aston By-Pass. S13 5G 103
Aston Clo. Dron 6G 123
Aston Clo. Swal 4B 104
Aston Common. 1B 116
Aston Ct. Stav 1D 134
Aston Dri. B'ley 1A 14
Aston Forge Ct. Ast 6D 104
Aston La. Aug 3B 104
Aston St. S2 1H 99
Aston Towers. Dron 6G 123
Astwell Gdns. C'town 1C 64
Atebanks Ct. Bal 1H 61
Athelstan Clo. S13 4G 101
Athelstane Cres. E'thpe 4D 20
Athelstane Dri. Thur 6A 94
Athelstane Rd. Con 3D 58
Athelstan Rd. S13 4G 101
Athersley Cres. B'ley 1A 14
Athersley Gdns. Owl 5A 114
Athersley North. 5B 8
Athersley Rd. B'ley 1A 14
Athersley South. 1A 14
Atherton Clo. S2 1B 112
Atherton Rd. S2 1B 112
Atholl Clo. Walt 5D 136
Atholl Cres. Donc 4A 34
Athol Rd. S8 3C 110
Athorpe Gro. Dinn 4E 107
Athorpe Rd. Dinn 4E 107
Athron Dri. Roth 5A 80
Athron Ind. Est. Donc 5E 33
(off Athron St.)
Athron St. Donc 5E 33
Atkin Pl. S2 5E 99
Atkinson Ct. Ches 4A 138
Atlantic Cres. S8 3C 122
Atlantic Dri. S8 3C 122
Atlantic Rd. S8 3B 122
Atlantic Wlk. S8 3C 122
Atlantic Way. S8 3C 122
Atlas. 5H 87
Atlas St. S4 5H 87
Atlas St. B'wth 2C 90
Atlas Way. S4 4A 88
Atlee Clo. Maltby 5H 83
Atlow Clo. Ches 6D 130
Atrium. Cry P 5E 115
Atterby Dri. Ross 3E 63
Attercliffe. 5B 88
Attercliffe Comn. S9 4C 88
Attercliffe Rd. S4 & S9 6H 87
Attlee Av. New R 4B 62
Attlee Cres. D'fld 4G 27
Attlee Rd. Ink 4H 133
Aubretia Av. B'wth 4D 90
Auburn Rd. Edl'tn 3B 60
Auckland Av. S6 3E 85
Auckland Dri. Half 3D 124
Auckland Ri. Half 3E 125
Auckland Rd. Donc 4E 33
Auckland Rd. Mexb 6F 43
Auckland's Pl. Ches 3A 138
Auckland Way. Half 3E 125
Audrey Rd. S13 6E 101
Aughton. 4A 104
Aughton Av. Aug 4A 104
Aughton Clo. S13 6F 101
Aughton Cres. S13 5E 101
Aughton Dri. S13 5E 101
Aughton La. Ast 5C 104
Aughton Rd. Aug 5A 104
Augustus Rd. B'wth 1C 90
Aukley Rd. S8 2D 110
Aunby Dri. Swal 5B 104
Austen Av. Donc 5G 45
Austen Dri. Braml 1E 81
Austerfield Av. Donc 2A 32
Austin Clo. S6 3E 85
Austin Ct. S6 2E 85
Austwick Clo. Donc 1F 61
Austwick Clo. M'well 3E 7
Austwick Wlk. B'ley 5F 13
Autumn Clo. Thur 5C 94
Autumn Dri. Maltby 3G 83
Avenue 1. Has 5B 138
Avenue 2. Has 5B 138
Avenue 3. Has 5B 138
Avenue 4. Has 5B 138
Avenue 5. Has 5B 138
Avenue 6. Has 5B 138
Avenue 7. Has 5B 138
Avenue 8. Has 5B 138
Avenue Ct. S10 5G 97
Avenue Rd. S7 1D 110
Avenue Rd. Ches 3A 132
Avenue Rd. Donc 4E 33
Avenue Rd. Wath D 6G 41
Avenue, The. S9 1E 101
Avenue, The. Beig 3F 115
Avenue, The. Ben 6C 18
Avenue, The. Donc 1A 48
Avenue, The. Dron 1F 129
Avenue, The. H'ton 1F 43
Avenue, The. Maltby 2E 95
Avenue, The. Roy 1G 9
Avenue, The. Tank 5B 36
Aviemore Rd. Donc 5G 45
Avill Way. Wick 6F 81
Avisford Dri. S5 6B 74
Avisford Rd. S5 5B 74
Avoca Av. Donc 5G 33
Avocet Way. Thpe H 1B 66
Avon Clo. Dron 6F 123
Avon Clo. Hghm 4A 12
Avon Clo. Maltby 3F 83
Avon Clo. Womb 2H 39
Avondale Dri. B'ley 4E 9
Avondale Rd. S6 3H 85
Avondale Rd. Ches 1H 137
Avondale Rd. Donc 6G 33
Avondale Rd. Ink 5B 134
Avondale Rd. Roth 2A 78
Avon Gro. C'town 1C 64
Avon Mt. Roth 2A 78
Avon St. B'ley 6A 14
Axholme Ct. Donc 4F 33
Axholme Rd. Donc 4E 33
Axle La. Ans 3D 118
Aylesbury Ct. S9 5D 76
Aylesbury Cres. S9 6D 76
Aylesbury Rd. Donc 5H 33
Aylesford Clo. B'ley 4H 13
Aylsham Dri. Ast 6C 104
Aylward Clo. S2 6B 100
Aylward Rd. S2 6B 100
Aymer Dri. Thur 5A 94
Ayrsome Wlk. Donc 3C 48
Aysgarth Av. B'ley 1H 25
Aysgarth Clo. Donc 4D 48
Aysgarth Ri. Swal 5A 104
Aysgarth Rd. S6 5A 74
Ayton Wlk. Ben 5A 18
Azalea Clo. Ans 4F 119

B

Babington Clo. S2 6B 100
Babington Ct. S2 6B 100
Babur Rd. S4 5H 87
Backfield Ri. C'town 1E 65
Backfields. S1 2E 99 (4D 4)
Back La. S10 1F 97
Back La. S17 4F 121
Back La. Ans 1G 119
Back La. B'ley 3C 14
Back La. Cal 4H 139
Back La. Cusw 4D 30
Back La. Eck 6A 124
Back La. Hoot R 1H 71
Back La. L Hou 2B 28
Back La. Maltby & Hoot L 6A 82
Back La. Old E 6A 60
Back La. Oxs 6G 143
Back La. P'stne 4D 142
Back La. Rawm 1C 68
Back La. S'bri 2A 140
Back La. Thry 3D 70
Back La. Woodh 1C 114
Back La. W. Roy 1C 8
Backmoor. 5G 111
Backmoor Cres. S8 5G 111
Backmoor Rd. S8 5G 111
Bk. Poplar Ter. Roy 1G 9
Back Row. Cant 2F 49
Bk. Row Cotts. Ross 4F 63
Backside La. Warm 5F 45
Bacon La. S9 6A 88
Bacons La. Ches 5H 137
Baden Powell Av. Ches 4H 137
Baden Powell Rd. Ches 3A 138
Baden St. Roth 2C 78
Baden St. Wors 5B 24
Badger Clo. S13 6C 102
Badger Clo. Walt 5D 136
Badger Dri. S13 6C 102
Badger La. S1 3C 4
Badger Pl. S13 6C 102
Badger Ri. S13 6C 102
Badger Rd. S13 6C 102
Badgers Holt. Bran 3H 49
Badsley Ct. Roth 3G 79
Badsley Moor La. Roth 4F 79
Badsley St. Roth 3F 79
Badsley St. S. Roth 4F 79
Badsworth Clo. Braml 1E 81
Badsworth Clo. Womb 1H 39
Badsworth Pl. Braml 1E 81
Badsworth Rd. Warm 6E 45
Badsworth Way. Braml 1E 81
Bage Hill. Walt 6A 136
Bagger Wood Hill. Hood G 6A 22
Bagger Wood Rd. T'land & Hood G 6A 22
Bagley Rd. S4 2H 87
Bagshaw's Rd. S12 1D 112
Bagshot St. S11 5B 98
Bahram Gro. New R 5C 62
Bahram Rd. Donc 3A 48
Bailey Dri. Kil 1C 126
Bailey La. S1 2D 98 (3C 4)
Bailey M. Scawt 6G 17
Bailey St. S1 2E 99 (3D 4)
Bainbridge Rd. Donc 2B 46
Baines Av. Edl'tn 4A 60
Baines Wood Clo. Ches 3E 131
Bainton Dri. B'ley 2F 23
Bakehouse La. B'ley 4C 12
Bakehouse La. Eck 6D 124
Baker Dri. Kil 3A 126
Bakers Hill. S1 2F 99 (3G 5)
Bakers La. S1 1E 99 (2C 4)
Baker St. S9 5B 88
Baker St. Dinn 3C 106
Bakewell Rd. B'ley 1A 14
Bakewell Rd. Ink 6A 134
Balaclava La. S6 5C 86
Balaclava Rd. S6 5C 86
Bala St. B'ley 6H 13
Balby. 3B 46
Balby Carr Bank. Donc 3C 46
(in two parts)
Balby Rd. Donc 3B 46
Balby St. Den M 2D 58
Balcarres Rd. New R 4D 62

Baldwin Av. *Donc* 4A **32**
Baldwin St. *S9* 6A **88**
Balfour Dri. *S9* 6D **88**
Balfour Rd. *S9* 6D **88**
Balfour Rd. *Ben* 6C **18**
Balk Farm Ct. *Birdw* 2C **36**
Balk La. *Birdw* 2C **36**
Balk La. *Braml* 4H **81**
Balk La. *B'wth* 1A **90**
Balkley La. *D'fld* 4G **27**
Balk, The. *Ark* 2D **18**
Balk, The. *M'well* 3G **7**
Balk, The. *Roth* 3B **68**
Ballam Av. *Donc* 6G **17**
Ballfield Av. *Dart* 5A **6**
Ballfield La. *Dart* 5A **6**
Ballidon Clo. *Ches* 5E **131**
Ballifield Av. *S13* 4A **102**
Ballifield Clo. *S13* 4A **102**
Ballifield Cres. *S13* 4B **102**
Ballifield Dri. *S13* 4B **102**
Ballifield Pl. *S13* 4A **102**
Ballifield Ri. *S13* 4B **102**
Ballifield Rd. *S13* 4A **102**
Ballifield Way. *S13* 4A **102**
Ball Rd. *S6* .3H **85**
Ball St. *S3* .6D **86**
Balmain Dri. *S6* 2H **85**
Balmain Rd. *S6* 2H **85**
Balmer Ri. *Braml* 2E **81**
Balm Grn. *S1* 2E **99** (3D **4**)
Balmoak La. *Ches* 5C **132**
Balmoral Clo. *Thurls* 3A **142**
Balmoral Ct. *S11* 3F **109**
Balmoral Cres. *S10* 4A **96**
Balmoral Cres. *Dron W* 1B **128**
Balmoral Glen. *S10* 4A **96**
Balmoral M. *S10* 4A **96**
Balmoral Rd. *S13* 1C **114**
Balmoral Rd. *Donc* 5F **33**
Balmoral Way. *Braml* 3H **81**
Baltic La. S9 . . . . .5B **88**
(off Baltic Rd.)
Baltic Rd. *S9* 5B **88**
Baltic Way. *S9* 5B **88**
Bamford Av. *B'ley* 1A **14**
Bamford Clo. *Dod* 2A **22**
Bamford Rd. *Ink* 6H **133**
Bamforth St. *S6* 4B **86**
Banbury Clo. Den M 2D **58**
(off Thrybergh Ct.)
Bank Clo. *S7* 1C **110**
Bank Clo. *Roth* 6H **67**
Bank Ct. *Brim* 3D **132**
Bank End Av. *Wors* 4C **24**
Bank End Clo. *Bol D* 1A **42**
Bank End Rd. *Wors* 4B **24**
Bankfield La. *S6* 5C **84**
Bankfield Rd. *S6* 3G **85**
Bank Ho. La. *Thurls* 4A **142**
Bank Ho. Rd. *S6* 6A **86**
Bank La. *Bols* 6G **141**
Bank Rd. *Ches* 5A **132**
Bank Sq. *New R* 5C **62**
Bank St. *S1* 1F **99** (2E **5**)
Bank St. *Ans* 2F **119**
Bank St. *B'ley* 2H **23**
Bank St. *Brim* 3D **132**
Bank St. *Ches* 2G **137**
Bank St. *Cud* 6B **10**
Bank St. *Donc* 2C **46**
Bank St. *Hoy* 6H **37**
Bank St. *Mexb* 1E **57**
Bank St. *S'foot* 1E **25**
Bank Ter. S10 . . . . .2A **98**
(off Parker's La.)
Bank Top Rd. *Roth* 5B **80**
Bank Vw. *S12* 4C **114**
Bank Vw. *Whis* 2H **91**
Bankwood Clo. *S14* 2H **111**
Bank Wood Clo. *Ches* 4D **130**
Bankwood Cres. *New R* 3B **62**
Bankwood La. *New R* 2B **62**
Bankwood Rd. *S14* 2H **111**
Banner Ct. *S11* 1H **109**
Banner Cross. **1H 109**
Banner Cross Dri. *S11* 1H **109**
Banner Cross Rd. *S11* 2H **109**
Bannerdale Clo. *S11* 1A **110**
Bannerdale Rd. *S11 & S7* 1A **110**
Bannerdale Vw. *S11* 1A **110**
Bannham Rd. *S9* 1F **101**
Bannister Ho. *Donc* 3G **33**

Bar Av. *M'well* 5H **7**
Barbados Way. *H'by* 3A **82**
Barber Balk Clo. *Roth* 6H **67**
Barber Balk Rd. *Roth* 1H **77**
Barber Clo. *Tod* 2A **118**
Barber Cres. *S10* 1B **98**
Barber Pl. *S10* 1B **98**
Barber Rd. *S10* 1B **98**
Barberry Way. *Rav* 1H **81**
Barber's Av. *Rawm & P'gte* 2F **69**
Barber's Cres. *Rawm* 2G **69**
Barbers La. *Kil* 1B **126**
(in two parts)
Barber's Path. *Mexb* 6D **42**
Barber St. *Hoy* 5A **38**
Barber Wood Rd. *Roth* 2C **76**
Barbon Clo. *Ches* 6G **131**
Barbot Hall Ind. Est. *P'gte* 5E **69**
Barbot Hill Dri. *Greasb* 5C **68**
Barbot Hill Rd. *Roth* 5C **68**
Bar Cft. *Ches* 5F **131**
Barclay Grange. *Ches* 2B **138**
Barcroft Flatt. *B'ley* 3C **12**
Barden Cres. *B'wth* 3C **90**
Barden Dri. *B'ley* 4D **12**
Bardolf Rd. *Donc* 2C **48**
Bardon Rd. *E'thpe* 4D **20**
Bard St. *S2* 2G **99** (2H **5**)
Bardwell Rd. *S3* 5D **86**
Barewell Hill. *Brie* 1G **11**
(in two parts)
Barfield Av. *Whis* 2G **91**
Barfield Rd. *Hoy* 5A **38**
Barholme Clo. *Ches* 4D **130**
Barholm Rd. *S10* 3F **97**
Bari Clo. *D'fld* 3C **26**
Baring Rd. *Roth* 3D **76**
Barkby Rd. *S9* 5C **76**
Barker Fold. *Ches* 2F **137**
Barker La. *Ches* 2F **137**
Barkers Cft. *Roth* 4H **67**
Barkers La. *Con* 4H **59**
Barker's Pl. *S6* 4A **86**
Barker's Pool. *S1* 2E **99** (4D **4**)
Barker's Rd. *S7* 1B **110**
Barker St. *Mexb* 1C **56**
Bark Meadows. *Dod* 2C **22**
Barkston Rd. *B'ley* 6E **9**
Bar La. *M'well* 5H **7**
Barlborough Rd. *Womb* 2G **39**
Barlby Gro. *S12* 4C **114**
Barley Clo. *Wors* 5A **24**
Barley Cft. La. *Dinn* 5F **107**
Barley La. *Ash* 6C **130**
Barley M. *Dron W* 1A **128**
Barley Vw. *Thurn* 2F **29**
Barleywood Rd. *S9* 5E **89**
Barlow. **1A 130**
Barlow Dri. *S6* 5G **85**
Barlow Lees. **6B 128**
Barlow Lees La. *Dron* 6C **128**
Barlow Rd. *S6* 5G **85**
Barlow Rd. *Ches* 2B **130**
Barlow Rd. *Stav* 2C **134**
Barlow Vw. *Dron* 4F **129**
Barmouth Rd. *S7* 2C **110**
Barnabas Wlk. *B'ley* 4H **13**
Barnard Av. *Coal A* 6H **123**
Barnardiston Rd. *S9* 6D **88**
Barnburgh Ho. *Edl'tn* 2C **60**
Barnburgh La. *Gold & Barn* 5G **29**
Barnby Dun. **2H 21**
Barnby Dun Rd. *Donc* 2H **33**
Barncliffe Clo. *S10* 5C **96**
Barncliffe Cres. *S10* 4B **96**
Barncliffe Dri. *S10* 4B **96**
Barncliffe Glen. *S10* 5C **96**
Barncliffe Rd. *S10* 4B **96**
Barn Clo. *Ches* 5F **131**
Barnes Av. *Dron W* 1B **128**
Barnes Ct. *S2* 3F **99** (6G **5**)
Barnes Ct. Swint 4A **56**
(off Lawrence Dri.)
Barnes Grn. *Gren* 4B **64**
Barnes Hall Rd. *Burn* 2B **64**
Barnes La. *Dron W* 5H **121**
Barnes Rd. *Ches* 4E **139**
Barnet Av. *S11* 2E **109**
Barnet Rd. *S11* 2E **109**
Barnfield Av. *S10* 2E **97**
Barnfield Clo. *S10* 2E **97**
Barnfield Clo. *Stav* 1C **134**
Barnfield Dri. *S10* 3E **97**

Barnfield Rd. *S10* 2E **97**
Barnfield Ter. *Stav* 1C **134**
Barnfield Wlk. *Stav* 1C **134**
Barnfold Pl. *Shaf* 3C **10**
Barnham Clo. *Ches* 5D **136**
Barn Owl Clo. *L Hou* 3B **28**
Barnsdale Av. *Owl* 5A **114**
Barnside Clo. *P'stne* 5D **142**
Barnsley. **6H 13**
Barnsley Av. *Con* 3C **58**
Barnsley Bus. & Innovation Cen.
    B'ley 3D **12**
Barnsley Crematorium. *B'ley* 2G **25**
Barnsley F.C. **6A 14**
Barnsley Golf Course. **2H 7**
Barnsley Rd. *S5 & S4* 4G **75**
Barnsley Rd. *Brie* 3E **11**
Barnsley Rd. *Cud* 1G **15**
Barnsley Rd. *D'fld* 2D **26**
Barnsley Rd. *Dart & Bar G* 5C **6**
Barnsley Rd. *Dod* 2A **22**
Barnsley Rd. *Gold* 4E **29**
Barnsley Rd. *Hick & Marr* 2A **30**
Barnsley Rd. *Hoy* 3H **37**
Barnsley Rd. *Marr & Donc* 2B **30**
Barnsley Rd. *Notton* 2G **7**
Barnsley Rd. *P'stne & H'swne* 3C **142**
Barnsley Rd. *Thpe H* 6A **52**
Barnsley Rd. *Wath D* 3B **40**
Barnsley Rd. *Womb* 4H **25**
(in three parts)
Barnstone St. *Donc* 2A **46**
Barnwell Cres. *Womb* 4H **25**
Baron St. *S1* .4E **99**
Barrack La. *S6* 5C **86**
Barracks Fld. Ter. *Else* 6C **38**
Barratt Rd. *Eck* 6D **124**
Barrel La. *Donc* 5G **45**
Barret Rd. *Donc* 2D **48**
Barretta St. *S4* 2H **87**
Barrick M. *Roth* 2H **77**
Barrie Cres. *S5* 6D **74**
Barrie Dri. *S5* 6D **74**
Barrie Gro. *H'by* 5B **82**
Barrie Rd. *S5* 6D **74**
Barrie Rd. *Donc* 5B **46**
Barrow. **4C 52**
Barrowby Rd. *Roth* 6G **79**
Barrowfield Gate. **3C 52**
Barrow Fld. La. *W'wth* 3C **52**
Barrowfield Rd. *Thurn* 2F **29**
Barrow Hill. *W'wth* 4A **52**
Barrow Rd. *S9* 5D **76**
Barrow St. *Stav* 1D **134**
Barrow, The. *W'wth* 4B **52**
Barry Rd. *Brim* 1F **139**
Bartholomew Clo. *Whis* 1B **92**
Bartholomew St. *Womb* 6A **26**
Bartin Clo. *S11* 2H **109**
Bartle Av. *S12* 3B **112**
Bartle Dri. *S12* 3B **112**
Bartle Rd. *S12* 3B **112**
Bartlett Clo. *S6* 6C **84**
Bartlett Rd. *S5* 5D **74**
Bartle Way. *S12* 3B **112**
Barton Cres. *Ches* 5C **130**
Barton La. *Arm* 3E **35**
(in two parts)
Barton Pl. *Con* 4D **58**
Barton Rd. *S8* 1E **111**
Barugh Green. **3A 12**
Barugh Grn. Rd. *Bar G & B'ley* 2A **12**
Barugh La. *Bar G* 2A **12**
Base Green. **4D 112**
Basegreen Av. *S12* 4D **112**
Basegreen Clo. *S12* 4E **113**
Basegreen Cres. *S12* 4D **112**
Basegreen Dri. *S12* 4D **112**
Basegreen Pl. *S12* 4D **112**
Basegreen Rd. *S12* 4D **112**
Basegreen Way. *S12* 4E **113**
Basford Clo. *S9* 6D **88**
Basford Dri. *S9* 6D **88**
Basford M. *S9* 6E **89**
Basford Pl. *S9* 6D **88**
Basford St. *S9* 6D **88**
Basil Av. *Arm* 2C **34**
Basil Clo. *Ches* 2A **138**
Basildon Rd. *Thurn* 1E **29**
Basil Griffith Ct. S3 . . . . .3F **87**
(off Orphanage Rd)
Baslow Cres. *Dod* 2A **22**

Baslow Rd. *S17* 6B **120**
Baslow Rd. *B'ley* 6D **8**
Baslow Rd. *E'mr* 4A **136**
Bassett Pl. *S2* 3H **99**
Bassett Rd. *S2* 3A **100**
Bassey Rd. *Bran* 3H **49**
Bassingthorpe La. *Roth* 5B **68**
Bass Ter. *Donc* 6E **33**
Bastock Rd. *S6* 2B **86**
Bateman Clo. *Cud* 3A **10**
Bateman Rd. *H'by* 5A **82**
(in two parts)
Bateman Sq. *Thurn* 1E **29**
Batemoor. **3E 123**
Batemoor Clo. *S8* 3E **123**
Batemoor Dri. *S8* 3E **123**
Batemoor Pl. *S8* 3E **123**
Batemoor Rd. *S8* 3E **123**
Batemoor Wlk. S8 . . . .*3E 123*
(off Batemoor Clo.)
Batesquire. *Soth* 5F **115**
Bates St. *S10* 6A **86**
Batewood Av. *Ink* 6H **133**
Bath St. *S1* 3D **98** (6B **4**)
Battison La. *Wath D* 1D **54**
Batt St. *S8* .5E **99**
Batty Av. *Cud* 1G **15**
Batworth Dri. *S5* 3E **87**
Batworth Rd. *S5* 3E **87**
Baulk Farm Clo. *Roth* 3B **68**
Bawtry Ga. *S9* 1G **89**
Bawtry Rd. *S9 & B'wth* 1G **89**
Bawtry Rd. *Donc* 1H **47**
Bawtry Rd. *H'by* 4A **82**
Bawtry Rd. *Rk & Wick* 5C **80**
Baxter Av. *Donc* 5E **33**
Baxter Clo. *S6* 5A **74**
Baxter Clo. *Swal* 6G **103**
Baxter Ct. *Donc* 5E **33**
Baxter Dri. *S6* 5A **74**
Baxter Ga. *Donc* 6C **32**
Baxter M. *S6* 5A **74**
Baxter Rd. *S6* 5A **74**
Bayardo Wlk. *New R* 6D **62**
Baycliff Clo. *B'ley* 1D **14**
Baycliff Dri. *Ches* 2E **137**
Bay Ct. *Kil* 4A **126**
Bayford Way. *Womb* 6D **26**
Baysdale Cft. *Mexb* 2D **124**
Bay Tree Av. *Flan* 3F **81**
Bazley Rd. *S2* 1B **112**
Beacon Clo. *S9* 1B **88**
Beacon Cft. *S9* 1B **88**
Beacon Rd. *S9* 1B **88**
Beaconsfield Rd. *Donc* 2A **46**
Beaconsfield Rd. *Roth* 6G **79**
Beaconsfield St. *B'ley* 1G **23**
Beaconsfield St. *Mexb* 6D **42**
Beacon Vw. *Else* 6C **38**
Beacon Way. *S9* 1B **88**
Beale Way. *P'gte* 5F **69**
Beancroft Clo. *Wadw* 6H **61**
Bear Tree Clo. *P'gte* 3F **69**
Bear Tree Rd. *P'gte* 3F **69**
Bear Tree St. *P'gte* 4F **69**
Beauchamp Rd. *Roth* 6H **67**
Beauchief. **1B 122**
Beauchief. *S8* 1H **121**
Beauchief Abbey. **1A 122**
Beauchief Abbey La. *S8* 6A **110**
Beauchief Clo. *Deep* 4H **141**
Beauchief Ct. *S8* 5C **110**
Beauchief Dri. *S8* 2A **122**
Beauchief Golf Course. **1H 121**
Beauchief Ri. *S8* 6A **110**
Beaufort Rd. *S10* 2B **98**
Beaufort Rd. *Donc* 5H **33**
Beaulieu Clo. *M'well* 5G **7**
Beaulieu Vw. *M'well* 5G **7**
Beaumont Av. *S2* 3C **100**
Beaumont Av. *B'ley* 6D **12**
Beaumont Av. *W'land* 1B **16**
Beaumont Clo. *S2* 3D **100**
Beaumont Cres. *S2* 3C **100**
Beaumont Dri. *Roth* 4H **79**
Beaumont M. *S2* 4D **100**
Beaumont Rd. *Dart* 6A **6**
Beaumont Rd. N. *S2* 3C **100**
Beaumont St. *Hoy* 6F **37**
Beaumont Way. *S2* 3C **100**
Beaver Av. *S13* 5B **102**
Beaver Clo. *S13* 5B **102**
Beaver Dri. *S13* 5B **102**

Beaver Hill. **5B 102**
Beaver Hill Rd. *S13* 5B **102**
Beccles Way. *Braml* 1E **81**
Beck Clo. *S5* 2A **76**
Beck Clo. *Swint* 4B **56**
Beck Cft. *Hoy* 1G **51**
Becket Av. *S8* 3B **122**
Becket Cres. *S8* 3C **122**
Becket Cres. *Roth* 5F **67**
Becket Rd. *S8* 3C **122**
Beckett Hospital Ter. *B'ley* 1H **23**
Beckett Rd. *Donc* 4E **33**
Becket St. *B'ley* 5H **13**
Becket Wlk. *S8* 3B **122**
Beckfield Gro. *Bol D* 6D **28**
Beckford La. *S5* 1H **75**
Becknoll Rd. *Bram* 3A **40**
Beck Rd. *S5* 2H **75**
Beckton Av. *Wat* 5E **115**
Beckton Gro. *Wat* 5E **115**
Beckwith Rd. *Dinn* 3C **106**
Beckwith Rd. *Roth* 2B **80**
Bedale Ct. *Roth* 5F **79**
Bedale Rd. *S7* 1D **100**
Bedale Rd. *Donc* 2F **31**
Bedale Wlk. *Shaf* 2C **10**
Bedford Clo. *Ans* 6D **106**
Bedford Rd. *O'bri* 1D **72**
Bedford St. *S6* 6D **86**
Bedford St. *B'ley* 2H **23**
Bedford St. *Maltby* 5H **83**
Bedford Ter. *B'ley* 2A **14**
Bedgebury Clo. *Soth* 6H **115**
Bedgrave Clo. *Kil* 1D **126**
Bedgreave New Mill. **5A 116**
Beecham Ct. *Swint* 4A **56**
Beech Av. *Cud* 5B **10**
Beech Av. *Rawm* 2H **69**
Beech Av. *Roth* 5C **80**
Beech Clo. *Brie* 2G **11**
Beech Clo. *Maltby* 4D **82**
Beech Ct. *D'fld* 4E **27**
Beech Cres. *Eck* 6G **125**
Beech Cres. *Kil* 4A **126**
Beech Cres. *Mexb* 6C **42**
Beechcroft Rd. *Donc* 5G **45**
Beechdale Clo. *Ches* 1F **137**
Beech Dri. *Bran* 2H **49**
Beech en Hurst. S8 . . . .*5E 79*
(off Reneville Rd.)
Beeches Av. *S2* 5G **99**
Beeches Dri. *S2* 5G **99**
Beeches Gro. *Beig* 4G **115**
Beeches Rd. *Wal* 4F **117**
Beeches, The. *H'fld* 4F **39**
Beeches, The. *Kirk S* 3D **20**
Beeches, The. *Swal* 6B **104**
Beeches, The. *Swint* 3A **56**
Beechfern Clo. *High G* 5B **50**
Beechfield Clo. *Bol D* 1A **42**
Beechfield Rd. *Donc* 1D **46**
Beech Gro. *B'ley* 2F **23**
Beech Gro. *Ben* 1B **32**
Beech Gro. *Con* 4D **58**
Beech Gro. *Dinn* 6F **107**
Beech Gro. *Warm* 5E **45**
Beech Gro. *Wick* 4G **81**
Beech Hill. *Con* 3E **59**
Beech Hill Rd. *S10* 3A **98**
Beech Ho. Rd. *H'fld* 3F **39**
Beechlea. *Thurn* 1E **29**
Beech Rd. *Arm* 3F **35**
Beech Rd. *Maltby* 4D **82**
Beech Rd. *New R* 5E **63**
Beech Rd. *Shaf* 3D **10**
Beech Rd. *Wath D* 5G **41**
Beech St. *B'ley* 1H **23**
Beech St. *Holl* 2G **133**
Beech Tree Clo. *Cant* 2F **49**
Beech Vs. *Roth* 1G **79**
Beechville Av. *Swint* 4A **56**
Beech Way. *Dron* 6E **123**
Beechs Way. *Warm* 5H **103**
Beechwood Clo. *E'thpe* 6E **21**
Beechwood Clo. *Rawm* 6H **55**
Beechwood Clo. *Wath D* 2F **55**
Beechwood Lodge Flats. *Roth* 2F **79**
Beechwood Rd. *S6* 3H **85**
Beechwood Rd. *Donc* 2D **128**
Beechwood Rd. *High G* 1C **64**
Beechwood Rd. *Roth* 5G **79**

Beechwood Rd. *S'bri* 4D **140**
Beechwood Wlk. Edl'tn *4A 60*
(off Broomvale Wlk.)
Beeden Clo. *Thry* 4D **70**
Beehive Rd. *S10* 1B **98**
Beehive Rd. *Ches* 3F **137**
Beehive Yd. *Ches* 3F **137**
Beeley Clo. *Ink* 5A **134**
Beeley St. *S2* 4D **98**
Beeley Vw. *Walt* 6E **137**
Beeley Way. *Ink* 6A **134**
Beeley Wood La. *S6* 4F **73**
Beeley Wood Rd. *S6* 6A **74**
Beely Rd. *O'bri* 3E **73**
Beeston Clo. *Dron W* 1A **128**
Beeston Sq. *B'ley* 5B **8**
Beeton Rd. *S8* 2D **100**
Beet St. *S3* 2D **98** (2B **4**)
Beetwell St. *Ches* 3A **138**
Beever Clo. *B'ley* 4C **12**
Beever La. *B'ley* 4C **12**
Beeversleigh. Roth *3E 79*
(off Clifton La.)
Beevers Rd. *Roth* 5F **67**
Beever St. *Gold* 4H **29**
Beever Ct. *B'ley* 6A **14**
Beever St. *B'ley* 6B **14**
Begonia Clo. *Ans* 3E **119**
Beighton. **3G 115**
Beighton Hollow. 3F **125**
Beighton Rd. *S12* 4B **114**
Beighton Rd. *S13* 1C **114**
Beighton Rd. *Kiln* 5C **56**
Beighton Rd. E. *Wat* 4D **114**
Belcourt Rd. *Roth* 5B **80**
Beldon Clo. *S2* 6H **99**
Beldon Pl. *S2* 6H **99**
Beldon Rd. *S2* 6H **99**
Belford Clo. *Braml* 3G **81**
Belford Dri. *Braml* 3G **81**
Belfry Gdns. *Brie* 4E **49**
Belfry Way. *Dinn* 6G **107**
Belgrave Dri. *S10* 4D **96**
Belgrave Pl. *Swal* 6A **104**
Belgrave Rd. *S10* 4E **97**
Belgrave Rd. *B'ley* 6A **14**
Belgrave Sq. *S2* 5E **99**
Belklane Dri. *Kil* 2C **126**
Bellamy Clo. *Roth* 4H **79**
Bell Bank Vw. *Wors* 4H **23**
Bellbank Way. *B'ley* 5B **8**
Bellbrooke Av. *D'fld* 2D **26**
Bellbrooke Pl. *D'fld* 2D **26**
Bellefield St. *S3* 1C **98** (1A **4**)
Belle Green. **6C 10**
Belle Grn. Clo. *Cud* 6C **10**
Belle Grn. Gdns. *Cud* 6C **10**
Belle Grn. La. *Cud* 6C **10**
Belle Vue. **1G 47**
Belle Vue Av. *Donc* 1G **47**
Belle Vue Clo. *Brim* 3D **132**
Belle Vue Rd. *Mexb* 6E **43**
Bellfields, The. *Thpe H* 2A **66**
Bell Hagg. **2D 96**
Bellhagg Rd. *S6* 5H **85**
Bellhouse La. *Stav* 1D **134**
Bellhouse Rd. *S5* 5H **75**
Bellhouse Vw. *Stav* 1D **134**
Bellis Av. *Donc* 3A **46**
Bellmer Clo. *B'ley* 2A **14**
Bellmer Cft. *Birdw* 5D **36**
Bellows Clo. *Rawm* 2F **69**
Bellows Rd. *Rawm* 2F **69**
Bellrope Acre. *Arm* 4F **35**
Bellscroft Av. *Thry* 5C **70**
Bells Sq. *S1* 2E **99** (3D **4**)
Bell St. *Ast* 6D **104**
Bellwood Cres. *Hoy* 6G **37**
Belmont. *Cud* 3H **15**
Belmont Av. *B'ley* 2B **14**
Belmont Av. *C'town* 2E **65**
Belmont Av. *Donc* 2C **46**
Belmont Cres. L *Hou* 2A **28**
Belmont Dri. *Stav* 1D **134**
Belmont Dri. *S'bri* 3E **141**
Belmonte Gdns. *S2* 3G **99** (6H **5**)
Belmont St. *Ches* 3A **132**
Belmont St. *Mexb* 1D **56**
Belmont St. *Roth* 3A **78**
Belper Rd. *S7* 1D **110**
Belridge Clo. *B'ley* 3D **12**
Belsize Rd. *S10* 5E **97**
Beltoft Way. *Con* 2G **59**

Belton Clo. *Dron W* 2A **128**
Belvedere. *Donc* 5H **45**
Belvedere Av. *Ches* 5G **137**
Belvedere Clo. *Ans* 2H **119**
Belvedere Clo. *Ches* 5C **136**
Belvedere Clo. *Shaf* 3C **10**
Belvedere Dri. *D'fld* 2D **26**
Belvedere Pde. *Braml* 2G **81**
Belvoir Av. *Barn* 1G **43**
Ben Bank Rd. *Silk C & Dod* 3A **22**
Bence Clo. *Dart* 6C **6**
Bence Farm Ct. *Dart* 6C **6**
Bence La. *Dart* 5A **6**
Ben Clo. *S6* .2F **85**
Benita Av. *Mexb* 1G **57**
Ben La. *S6* 2F **85**
Benmore Dri. *Soth* 6H **115**
Bennett Clo. *Rawm* 6H **55**
Bennetthorpe. *Donc* 1E **47**
Bennett St. *S2* 5D **98**
Bennett St. *Roth* 3G **77**
Bennimoor Way. *Ches* 5G **137**
Benson Rd. *S2* 3A **100**
Bentfield Av. *Roth* 6A **80**
Bentham Dri. *B'ley* 3D **14**
Bentham Rd. *Ches* 6G **131**
Bentham Way. *M'well* 3E **7**
Bent Hills La. *Whar S* 1A **72**
Bentinck Clo. *Donc* 1D **46**
Bentinck St. *Con* 3F **59**
Bent La. *Stav* 1E **135**
Bent Lathes Av. *Roth* 6A **80**
Bentley. **1B 32**
Bentley Av. *Donc* 1A **46**
Bentley Clo. *B'ley* 2E **15**
Bentley Comn. La. *Ben* 1C **32**
Bentley Moor. **1H 17**
Bentley Moor La. *Adw S* 1G **17**
Bentley Rise. **3B 32**
Bentley Rd. *S6* 6G **85**
Bentley Rd. *Braml* 2E **81**
Bentley Rd. *C'town* 4F **65**
Bentley Rd. *Donc* 2A **32**
Bentley St. *Roth* 6D **78**
Benton Ct. *Roth* 2H **77**
Benton Ter. *Swint* 4B **56**
Benton Way. *Roth* 2H **77**
Bents Clo. *S11* 2E **109**
Bents Clo. *C'town* 2E **65**
Bents Cres. *S11* 3F **109**
Bents Cres. *Dron* 6G **123**
Bents Dri. *S11* 2E **109**
Bents Green. **2F 109**
Bents Grn. Av. *S11* 1E **109**
Bents Grn. Pl. *S11* 2E **109**
Bents Grn. Rd. *S11* 1F **109**
Bents La. *Dron* 6G **123**
(in two parts)
Bents Rd. *S11* 2F **109**
Bents Rd. *S17* 5C **120**
Bents Rd. *Roth* 1H **77**
Bent St. *P'stne* 3C **142**
Bents Vw. *S11* 2E **109**
Benty La. *S10* 2F **97**
Beresford Rd. *Maltby* 5H **83**
Beresford St. *Ben* 6C **18**
Berkeley Cft. *Roy* 1D **8**
Berkeley Precinct. *S11* 5B **98**
Berkley Clo. *Wors* 4H **23**
Bernard Clo. *Brim* 3F **133**
Bernard Gdns. S2 . . . .*2G* **99**
(off Bernard St.)
Bernard Rd. *S2 & S4* 1H **99**
Bernard Rd. *Edl'tn* 4B **60**
Bernard St. *S2* 2G **99** (3H 5)
Bernard St. *Rawm* 6H **55**
Bernard St. *Roth* 4E **79**
Berners Clo. *S2* 2A **112**
Berners Dri. *S2* 1A **112**
Berners Pl. *S2* 1A **112**
Berners Rd. *S2* 1A **112**
Berneslai Clo. *B'ley* 5G **13**
Bernshall Cres. *S5* 1F **75**
Berresford Rd. *S11* 5B **98**
Berrington Clo. *Donc* 1G **61**
Berry Av. *Eck* 6C **124**
Berrydale. *Wors* 4B **24**
Berry Dri. *Kiv P* 4B **118**
Berry Edge Clo. *Con* 4G **59**
Berry Holme Clo. *C'town* 2E **65**
Berry Holme Ct. *C'town* 2E **65**
Berry Holme Dri. *C'town* 2E **65**
Berrywell Av. *P'stne* 5E **143**

Bertram Rd. *O'bri* 3E **73**
Berwick Av. *Ches* 6E **137**
Berwick Clo. *Ches* 6E **137**
Berwick Ct. *Ches* 6E **137**
Berwick Way. *Donc* 4A **34**
Berwyn Clo. *Ches* 6E **131**
Bessacarr. **5B 48**
Bessacarr La. *Donc* 5C **48**
Bessemer Pk. *Roth* 5B **78**
Bessemer Pl. *S9* 6A **88**
Bessemer Rd. *S9* 5A **88**
Bessemer Ter. *S'bri* 2D **140**
Bessemer Way. *Roth* 4A **78**
Bessingby Rd. *S6* 4A **86**
Bethel Rd. *Roth* 1F **79**
Bethel St. *Hoy* 5B **38**
Bethel Wlk. *S1* 4D **4**
Betjeman Gdns. *S10* 4A **98**
Betony Clo. *Kil* 4H **125**
Beulah Rd. *S6* 2B **86**
Bevan Av. *New R* 4D **62**
Bevan Clo. *Else* 5C **38**
Bevan Cres. *Maltby* 3F **83**
Bevan Dri. *Ink* 5H **133**
Bevan Ho. *Roth* 1F **91**
Bevan Way. *C'town* 2D **64**
Bevercotes Rd. *S5* 6H **75**
Beverley Av. *Wors* 3H **23**
Beverley Clo. *B'ley* 6A **8**
Beverley Clo. *Swal* 6B **104**
Beverley Gdns. *Donc* 4F **31**
Beverley Rd. *Donc* 3G **33**
Beverleys Rd. *S8* 3E **111**
Beverley St. *S9* 5C **88**
Bevin Pl. *Rawm* 1H **69**
Bevre Rd. *Arm* 1F **35**
Bewdley Ct. *Roy* 1F **9**
Bewicke Av. *Donc* 3F **31**
Bhatia Clo. *Mexb* 6E **43**
Bib La. *Lghtn* 4E **95**
Bickerton Rd. *S6* 1A **86**
Bierlow Clo. *Bram* 3A **40**
Bigby Way. *Braml* 2H **81**
Bignor Pl. *S6* 4B **74**
Bignor Rd. *S6* 4B **74**
Big Six. *Tree* 1F **103**
Bilby La. *Brim* 2E **133**
Billam Pl. *Roth* 6G **67**
Billam St. *Eck* 6B **124**
Billingley. **3B 28**
Billingley Dri. *Thurn* 2E **29**
Billingley Grn. La. *L Hou* 3B **28**
Billingley La. *Thurn* 2B **28**
Billingley Vw. *Bol D* 1H **41**
Bilston St. *S6* 4B **86**
Binders Rd. *Roth* 6G **67**
Binfield Rd. *S8* 2D **110**
Bingham Ct. *S10* 5G **97**
Bingham Pk. Cres. *S11* 6G **97**
Bingham Pk. Rd. *S11* 6G **97**
Bingham Rd. *S8* 5D **110**
Bingley Dri. *Thurn* 5F **13**
Bingley La. *S6* 1A **96**
Bingley St. *B'ley* 5F **13**
Binsted Av. *S5* 6B **74**
Binsted Clo. *S5* 6B **74**
Binsted Cres. *S5* 6B **74**
Binsted Cft. *S5* 6B **74**
Binsted Dri. *S5* 6B **74**
Binsted Gdns. *S5* 6B **74**
Binsted Glade. *S5* 6B **74**
Binsted Gro. *S5* 6B **74**
Binsted Rd. *S5* 6B **74**
Binsted Way. *S5* 6B **74**
Biram Wlk. *Else* 1D **52**
(off Forge La.)
Birchall Av. *Whis* 2H **91**
Birch Av. *C'town* 3E **65**
Birch Clo. *Kil* 5A **126**
Birch Clo. *Spro* 2F **45**
Birch Ct. *Swint* 2A **56**
Birch Cres. *Wick* 4G **81**
Birchdale Clo. *E'thpe* 6D **20**
Birchen Clo. *Donc* 6F **131**
Birchen Clo. *Donc* 6C **48**
Birchen Clo. *Dron W* 2B **128**
Birches Fold. *Coal A* 5G **123**
Birches La. *Coal A* 5G **123**
Birch Farm Av. *S8* 1E **123**
Birchfield Cres. *Dod* 1C **22**
Birchfield Rd. *Maltby* 4H **83**
Birchfield Wlk. *B'ley* 5D **12**
Birch Grn. Clo. *Maltby* 3D **82**

Birch Gro. *Con* 3F **59**
Birch Gro. *O'bri* 3E **73**
Birch Hall Golf Course. **6H 129**
Birch Ho. Av. *O'bri* 3D **72**
Birchitt Clo. *S17* 4A **122**
Birchitt Pl. *S17* 4A **122**
Birchitt Rd. *S17* 4A **122**
Birchitt Vw. *Dron* 6E **123**
Birch Kiln Cft. *Brim* 4F **133**
Birchlands Dri. *Kil* 4B **126**
Birch La. *Holl* 2G **133**
Birch Pk. Ct. *Roth* 3A **78**
Birch Rd. *S9* 5A **88**
Birch Rd. *B'ley* 2D **24**
Birch Rd. *Donc* 3D **48**
Birch Tree Clo. *Barn D* 1E **21**
Birch Tree Rd. *S'bri* 4D **140**
Birchtree Rd. *Thpe H* 4B **66**
Birchvale Rd. *S12* 4F **113**
Birchwood Av. *Rawm* 1F **69**
Birchwood Clo. *Maltby* 3D **82**
Birchwood Clo. *W'fld* 1E **125**
Birchwood Ct. *Ches* 6H **137**
Birchwood Ct. *Donc* 6F **49**
Birchwood Cres. *Ches* 6H **137**
Birchwood Cft. *W'fld* 1E **125**
Birchwood Dell. *Donc* 6F **49**
Birchwood Dri. *Rav* 1H **81**
Birchwood Gdns. *W'fld* 1E **125**
Birchwood Gro. *W'fld* 1E **125**
Birchwood La. *B'well* 2G **83**
Birchwood Ri. *W'fld* 1E **125**
Birchwood Vw. *W'fld* 1E **125**
Birchwood Way. *W'fld* 1E **125**
Bircotes Wlk. *Ross* 4F **63**
Bird Av. *Womb* 1E **39**
Birdholme. **6A 138**
Birdholme Cres. *Ches* 5A **138**
Bird St. *Stav* 1D **134**
Birdwell. **4D 36**
Birdwell Comn. *Birdw* 5D **36**
Birdwell Rd. *S4* 2B **88**
Birdwell Rd. *Dod* 3D **22**
Birdwell Rd. *Kiln* 5B **56**
Birk Av. *B'ley* 2C **24**
Birkbeck Ct. *High G* 5B **50**
Birk Cres. *B'ley* 2C **24**
Birk Grn. *B'ley* 2D **24**
Birk Ho. La. *B'ley* 2D **24**
Birklands Av. *S13* 4G **101**
Birklands Clo. *S13* 4G **101**
Birklands Dri. *S13* 4G **101**
Birk Rd. *B'ley* 2C **24**
Birks Av. *S13* 1B **114**
Birks Holt Dri. *Maltby* 6H **83**
Birks Rd. *Roth* 6G **67**
Birks Wood Dri. *O'bri* 3D **72**
Birk Ter. *B'ley* 2C **24**
Birkwood Av. *Cud* 3H **15**
Birley Brook Dri. *Ches* 4D **130**
Birley Carr. **4A 74**
Birley Cft. *Ches* 4D **130**
Birley Edge. **3H 73**
Birley Estate. **4F 113**
Birley La. *S12* 5E **113**
Birley Moor Av. *S12* 4G **113**
Birley Moor Clo. *S12* 4G **113**
Birley Moor Cres. *S12* 4G **113**
Birley Moor Dri. *S12* 5G **113**
Birley Moor Pl. *S12* 5G **113**
Birley Moor Rd. *S12* 2F **113**
Birley Moor Way. *S12* 5G **113**
Birley Ri. Cres. *S6* 5A **74**
Birley Ri. Rd. *S6* 5A **74**
Birley Spa. **3H 113**
Birley Spa Clo. *S12* 3B **114**
Birley Spa Dri. *S12* 3B **114**
Birley Spa La. *S12* 4H **113**
Birley Spa Wlk. S12 . . . .*3B* **114**
(off Carter Lodge Dri.)
Birley Stone, The. **2H 73**
Birley Va. Av. *S12* 3E **113**
Birley Va. Clo. *S12* 3E **113**

Birley Vw. *Worr* 4D **72**
Birley Wood Golf Course. **5G 113**
Birstall Clo. *Ches* 4E **131**
Birthwaite Rd. *Dart* 4A **6**
Birtley St. *Maltby* 4D **82**
Bisby Rd. *Rawm* 1G **69**
Biscay La. *Wath D* 4E **41**
Biscay Way. *Wath D* 5F **41**
Bishopdale Ct. *Mosb* 6A **114**
Bishopdale Dri. *Mosb* 1A **124**
Bishopdale Ri. *Mosb* 6A **114**
Bishop Gdns. *S13* 1A **114**
Bishopgarth Clo. *Donc* 3B **32**
Bishop Hill. *S13* 1A **114**
Bishops Clo. *S8* 2F **111**
Bishopscourt Rd. *S8* 2E **111**
Bishopsgate La. *New R* 6E **63**
Bishopsholme Clo. *S5* 1E **87**
Bishopsholme Rd. *S5* 1E **87**
Bishop's House Mus. **2E 111**
Bishopstoke Ct. Roth 2G *79*
        (off Doncaster Rd.)
Bishopston Wlk. *Maltby* 3E **83**
Bishop St. *S3* 3D **98** (6C **4**)
Bishops Wlk. *Ches* 5A **138**
Bishops Way. *B'ley* 4C **14**
Bishops Way. *Kiv P* 4A **118**
Bisley Clo. *Roy* 2G **9**
Bismarck St. *B'ley* 2H **23**
Bitholmes La. *Deep* 5H **141**
Bittern Vw. *Thpe H* 1C **66**
Blacka Moor Cres. *S17* 3C **120**
Blacka Moor Rd. *S17* 3C **120**
Blackamoor Rd. *Swint* 4E **55**
Blacka Moor Vw. *S17* 3C **120**
Blackberry Flats. Half 2E *125*
        (off Halfway Dri.)
Blackbird Av. *B'wth* 3D **90**
Blackbrook Av. *S10* 4A **96**
Blackbrook Dri. *S10* 4A **96**
Blackbrook Rd. *S10* 4A **96**
Blackburn. **3D 76**
Blackburn Cres. *C'town* 1C **64**
Blackburn Cft. *C'town* 1D **64**
Blackburn Dri. *C'town* 2C **64**
Blackburne St. *S6* 4B **86**
Blackburn La. *B'ley* 5F **13**
Blackburn La. *Roth* 3D **76**
Blackburn La. *Wors* 4A **24**
Blackburn Meadows Nature Reserve.
. . . .**4H 77**
Blackburn Rd. *Roth* 4D **76**
Blackburn St. *Wors* 4A **24**
Black Carr Rd. *Wick* 4E **81**
Blackdown Av. *Ches* 6D **130**
Blackdown Av. *Wat* 5D **114**
Blackdown Clo. *Wat* 5D **114**
Blacker Grange. *Bla H* 3H **37**
Blacker Hill. **2H 37**
Blacker La. *Shaf* 2C **10**
Blacker La. *Wors* 1E **37**
Blacker Rd. *M'well* 4G **7**
Blackheath Clo. *B'ley* 6D **8**
Blackheath Rd. *B'ley* 6D **8**
Blackheath Wlk. *B'ley* 6D **8**
Black Hill Rd. *Roth* 5B **80**
Black La. *S6* 4D **84**
Black La. *Hoy* 1D **50**
        (in two parts)
Blackmoor Cres. *B'wth* 2B **90**
Blackmore St. *S4* 6H **87**
Blacksmith La. *Cal* 1G **139**
Blacksmith La. *Gren* 1A **74**
Blacksmith Sq. Else 1D *52*
        (off Wath Rd.)
Blackstock Clo. *S14* 5H **111**
Blackstock Cres. *S14* 5H **111**
Blackstock Dri. *S14* 5H **111**
Blackstock Rd. *S14* 2H **111**
Black Swan Wlk. *S1* 3E **5**
Blackthorn Av. *Braml* 4G **81**
Blackthorn Clo. *Has* 5D **138**
Blackthorn Clo. *High G* 5B **50**
Blackthorne Clo. *Edl'tn* 4A **60**
Blackwell Clo. *S2* 2G **99** (3H **5**)
Blackwell Ct. *S2* 2G **99** (3H **5**)
Blackwell Pl. *S2* 2G **99** (3H **5**)
Blackwood Av. *Donc* 5H **45**
Blagden St. *S2* 2G **99**
Blair Athol Rd. *S11* 1H **109**
Blake Av. *Donc* 3F **33**
Blake Av. *Wath D* 4C **40**
Blake Clo. *Braml* 6H **81**

Blake Gro. Rd. *S6* 6C **86**
Blakeley Clo. *B'ley* 3A **8**
Blakeney Rd. *S10* 2A **98**
Blake St. *S6* 6B **86**
Blandford Dri. *Ches* 4G **131**
Bland La. *S6* 2F **85**
        (in two parts)
Bland St. *S4* 3A **88**
Blast La. *S4* 1G **99** (1H **5**)
        (in two parts)
Blaxton Clo. *Owl* 5A **114**
Blayton Rd. *S4* 3G **87**
Bleachcroft Way. *B'ley* 2E **25**
Bleak Av. *Shaf* 3C **10**
Bleakley Clo. *Shaf* 3C **10**
Bleasdale Gro. *B'ley* 3A **14**
Blenheim Av. *B'ley* 1G **23**
Blenheim Clo. *Braml* 2G **81**
Blenheim Clo. *Dinn* 5E **107**
Blenheim Ct. *Dart* 3F **81**
Blenheim Cres. *Mexb* 6D **42**
Blenheim Gdns. *S11* 2G **109**
Blenheim Gro. *B'ley* 1F **23**
Blenheim M. *S11* 2G **109**
Blenheim Rd. *B'ley* 1F **23**
Blocks, The. *Cud* 3B **130**
Bloemfontein St. *Cud* 1G **15**
Blonk St. *S1* 1F **99** (1G **5**)
Bloomfield Ri. *Dart* 4E **7**
Bloomfield Rd. *Dart* 4D **6**
Bloomhouse. **4D 6**
Bloomhouse La. *Dart* 3C **6**
Blossom Cres. *S12* 4D **112**
Blow Hall Cres. *Edl'tn* 3C **60**
Blow Hall Riding. *Edl'tn* 4D **60**
Blucher St. *B'ley* 6G **13**
Bluebell Av. *P'stne* 4C **142**
Bluebell Clo. *S5* 6A **76**
Bluebell Clo. *Hoy* 1G **51**
Bluebell Clo. *Ink* 6H **133**
Bluebell Rd. *S5* 5B **76**
Bluebell Rd. *Dart* 2C **6**
Bluebell Wood La. *S'side* 2F **81**
Blueberry Clo. *Ink* 6H **133**
Bluebird Hill. *Ast* 1C **116**
Blue Boy St. *S3* 1D **98** (1C **4**)
Bluelodge Clo. *Ink* 6H **133**
Blue Mans Way. *Cat* 5C **90**
Bluestone Clo. *Donc* 4C **48**
Blundell St. *B'ley* 2D **14**
Blyde Rd. *S5* 2G **87**
Bly Rd. *D'fld* 3D **26**
Blyth Av. *Rawm* 2F **69**
Blyth Clo. *Ches* 5D **136**
Blyth Clo. *Whis* 2B **92**
Blythe St. *Womb* 6A **26**
Blyth Rd. *Maltby* 5F **83**
Boardman Av. *Rawm* 5C **54**
Boat La. *Spro* 3D **44**
Bobbinmill La. *Ches* 3F **137**
Bochum Parkway. *S8* 2E **123**
Bocking Clo. *S8* 6B **110**
Bocking Hill. *Deep* 3F **141**
Bocking La. *S8* 6B **110**
Bocking Ri. *S8* 1C **122**
Boden La. *S1* 2D **98** (3C **4**)
Boden Pl. *S9* 6E **89**
Bodmin Ct. *B'ley* 4B **14**
Bodmin St. *S9* 5B **88**
Bodmin Way. *Ches* 6E **131**
Boggard La. *O'bri* 3C **72**
Boggard La. *P'stne* 5C **142**
Boiley La. *Kil* 5H **125**
Boland Rd. *S8* 4B **122**
Bold St. *S9* .4C **88**
Bole Clo. *Womb* 5D **26**
Bolehill. **4H 139**
        (Calow)
Bolehill. **5E 111**
        (Greenhill)
Bole Hill. **6F 91**
        (Treeton)
Bole Hill. *S8* 5E **111**
Bole Hill. *Cal* 4G **139**
Bole Hill. *Tree* 6F **91**
Bole Hill Clo. *S6* 5H **85**
Bole Hill La. *S10* 1G **97**
Bolehill La. *Eck* 6G **125**
Bole Hill Rd. *S6* 1F **97**
Bolehill Vw. *S10* 6H **85**
Bolsover Rd. *S5* 1H **87**
Bolsover Rd. *Mas M* 1H **135**
Bolsover Rd. E. *S5* 2H **87**

Bolsover St. *S3* 2C **98** (3A **4**)
Bolsterstone. **6E 141**
Bolton Hill Rd. *Donc* 5C **48**
        (in two parts)
Bolton Rd. *Swint* 2H **55**
Bolton Rd. *Wath D* 5A **42**
Bolton Rd. Workshops. *Wath D* 4B **42**
Bolton St. *S3* 3D **98** (3B **4**)
Bolton St. *Den M* 1B **58**
Bolton-upon-Dearne. **1A 42**
Bond Clo. *Donc* 1C **46**
Bondfield Av. *New R* 5E **63**
Bondfield Cres. *Womb* 1E **39**
Bondfield Cres. Flats. *Womb* 1E **39**
        (in two parts)
Bondfield Rd. *Ink* 4A **134**
Bond Rd. *B'ley* 4F **13**
Bond St. *New R* 6D **62**
Bond St. *Stav* 3A **134**
Bond St. *Womb* 6B **26**
Bonet La. *B'wth* 2A **90**
Bonington Ri. *Maltby* 3E **83**
Bonsall Ct. Ches 4F *131*
        (off Bowness Rd.)
Bonville Gdns. *S3* 1B **4**
Booker Rd. *S8* 5C **110**
Bookers La. *Dinn* 3B **106**
        (in two parts)
Bookers Way. *Dinn* 4B **106**
Booth Clo. *Thur* 5C **94**
Booth Clo. *Wat* 5D **114**
Booth Cft. *Wat* 5D **114**
Booth Pl. *Rawm* 6E **55**
Booth Rd. *High G* 6A **50**
Booth St. *Hoy* 5A **38**
Booth St. *Roth* 3B **68**
Bootle St. *S9* 5C **88**
Borough Rd. *S6* 3A **86**
Borrowdale Av. *Half* 3E **125**
Borrowdale Clo. *B'ley* 1G **25**
Borrowdale Clo. *Half* 3E **125**
Borrowdale Cres. *Ans* 6F **107**
Borrowdale Dri. *Half* 3E **125**
Borrowdale Rd. *Half* 3E **125**
Boston Castle. **5E 79**
Boston Castle Gro. *Roth* 5E **79**
Boston Castle Ter. *Roth* 5E **79**
Boston St. *S2* 4D **98**
Bosville Clo. *Rav* 4H **71**
Bosville Rd. *S10* 2H **97**
Bosville St. *P'stne* 5E **143**
Bosville St. *Roth* 1B **80**
Boswell Clo. *High G* 5A **50**
Boswell Clo. *New R* 5C **62**
Boswell Clo. *Roy* 1D **8**
Boswell Ct. *Donc* 4B **48**
Boswell Rd. *Donc* 4A **48**
Boswell St. *Wath D* 1F **55**
Boswell St. *Roth* 4F **79**
Bosworth Rd. *Adw S* 1C **16**
Bosworth St. *S10* 1H **97**
Botanical Rd. *S11* 4A **98**
Botham St. *S4* 3H **87**
Botsford St. *S3* 5E **87**
Boulder Bri. La. *Car* 3G **9**
Boulder Hill. **3H 85**
Boulevard, The. *E'thpe* 5C **20**
Boulton Clo. *Ches* 6C **130**
Boundary Av. *Donc* 2A **34**
Boundary Clo. *Edl'tn* 2C **60**
Boundary Clo. *Stav* 1E **135**
Boundary Dri. *Brie* 2G **11**
Boundary Grn. *Rawm* 3G **69**
Boundary Rd. *S2* 3H **99**
Boundary St. *B'ley* 1B **24**
Boundary Wlk. *B'wth* 3A **90**
Bourne Clo. *Brim* 2E **133**
Bourne Ct. *M'well* 3G **7**
Bourne Rd. *S5* 5G **75**
Bourne Rd. *Wors* 5H **23**
Bourne Wlk. *M'well* 3G **7**
Bow Bri. La. *Roth* 5C **78**
Bow Broom. **1B 56**
Bowden Gro. *Dod* 2B **22**
Bowden Wood Av. *S9* 3E **101**
Bowden Wood Clo. *S9* 3E **101**
Bowden Wood Cres. *S9* 3E **101**
Bowden Wood Dri. *S9* 3E **101**
Bowden Wood Pl. *S9* 3E **101**
Bowden Wood Rd. *S9* 3E **101**
Bowdon St. *S1* 3D **98** (5C **4**)
Bowen Dri. *Thry* 5D **70**

Bowen Rd. *Roth* 1F **79**
Bower Clo. *Roth* 6G **67**
Bower Farm Rd. *Old W* 1B **132**
Bower Hill. *Oxs* 6H **143**
Bower Ho. *Gren* 6A **64**
Bower La. *Gren* 6A **64**
Bower Rd. *S10* 1B **98**
Bower Rd. *Swint* 6B **42**
Bowers Fold. *Donc* 6D **32**
Bower Spring. *S3* 1E **99** (1E **5**)
Bower St. *S3* 1E **99** (1E **5**)
Bower Va. *Edl'tn* 4A **60**
Bowes Rd. *E'thpe* 6C **20**
Bowfell Vw. *B'ley* 3A **14**
Bowfield Clo. *S5* 5H **75**
Bowfield Ct. *S5* 5G **75**
(off Etwall Way)
Bowfield Rd. *S5* 5G **75**
Bowland Clo. *Donc* 1H **31**
Bowland Cres. *Wors* 5H **23**
Bowland Dri. *C'town* 2C **64**
Bowland Dri. *Walt* 6D **136**
Bowlease Gdns. *Donc* 3C **48**
Bowling Grn. St. *S3* 6E **87** (1D **4**)
Bowman Clo. *S12* 5B **112**
Bowman Dri. *S12* 5B **112**
Bowman Dri. *Maltby* 2E **83**
Bowness Clo. *Ches* 4F **131**
Bowness Clo. *Dron W* 2C **128**
Bowness Dri. *Bol D* 2A **42**
Bowness Rd. *S6* 4A **86**
Bowness Rd. *Ches* 4F **131**
Bowood Rd. *S11* 5B **98**
Bowshaw. 5D **122**
Bowshaw. *Dron* 6D **122**
Bowshaw Av. *S8* 4E **123**
Bowshaw Clo. *S8* 4E **123**
Bowshaw Vw. *S8* 4E **123**
Bow St. *Cud* 6B **10**
Boyce St. *S6* 6B **86**
Boyd Rd. *Wath D* 2F **55**
Boyland St. *S3* 5D **86**
Boynton Cres. *S5* 1E **87**
Boynton Rd. *S5* 2D **86**
Boythorpe. 4G **137**
Boythorpe Av. *Ches* 3G **137**
Boythorpe Cres. *Ches* 4H **137**
Boythorpe Mt. *Ches* 3H **137**
Boythorpe Ri. *Ches* 3G **137**
Boythorpe Rd. *Ches* 3H **137**
Bracken Clo. *Bran* 2H **49**
Bracken Ct. *Wick* 6F **81**
Brackendale Clo. *Brim* 4D **132**
Brackenfield Gro. *S12* 3F **113**
Bracken Hill. *Burn* 3B **64**
Bracken Moor. 4E **141**
Bracken Moor La. *S'bri* 4E **141**
Bracken Rd. *S5* 5A **76**
(in two parts)
Brackley St. *S3* 5F **87**
Bradberry Balk La. *Womb* 5A **26**
Bradbourne Clo. *Stav* 3A **134**
Bradbury Clo. *Ches* 2G **137**
Bradbury's Clo. *P'gte* 4F **69**
Bradbury St. *S8* 1E **111**
Bradbury St. *B'ley* 6F **13**
Bradfield Rd. *S6* 3A **86**
Bradford Rd. *Donc* 1A **34**
Bradford Row. *Donc* 6D **32**
Bradgate. 2A **78**
Bradgate Clo. *Roth* 2A **78**
Bradgate Ct. *Roth* 2H **77**
Bradgate Cft. *Ches* 6C **138**
Bradgate Ho. Clo. *Roth* 2A **78**
Bradgate La. *Roth* 2H **77**
Bradgate Pl. *Roth* 1A **78**
Bradgate Rd. *Roth* 1A **78**
Bradlea Ri. *Rawm* 6G **55**
Bradley Av. *Womb* 6A **26**
Bradley Clo. *Brim* 4E **133**
Bradley La. *Barl* 6A **128**
Bradley St. *S10* 6H **85**
Bradley Way. *Brim* 3E **133**
Bradmarsh Way. *Roth* 5C **78**
Bradshaw Av. *Tree* 2F **103**
Bradshaw Clo. *B'ley* 5C **12**
Bradshaw Rd. *Ink* 5H **133**
Bradshaw Way. *Tree* 2F **103**
Bradstone Rd. *Roth* 2A **80**
Bradway. 4A **122**
Bradway Bank. 3H **121**
Bradway Clo. *S17* 4H **121**
Bradway Dri. *S17* 4H **121**

Bradway Grange Rd. *S17* 4A **122**
Bradway Rd. *S17* 4H **121**
(in two parts)
Bradwell Av. *Dod* 3C **22**
Bradwell Clo. *Dron W* 2A **128**
Bradwell Pl. *Ink* 4A **134**
Bradwell St. *S2* 1F **111**
Braeburn Clo. *Maltby* 2D **82**
Braemar Rd. *Donc* 6G **33**
Braemore Rd. *S6* 2G **85**
Brailsford Av. *S5* 1E **75**
Brailsford Ct. *S5* 1E **75**
Brailsford Rd. *S5* 1E **75**
Braithwaite M. *M'well* 4G **7**
(off Braithwaite St.)
Braithwaite St. *M'well* 4G **7**
Braithwell Ct. *Ben* 4A **18**
Braithwell Rd. *Ben* 5A **18**
Braithwell Rd. *Maltby* 4F **83**
Braithwell Rd. *Rav* 1H **81**
Braithwell Wlk. *Den M* 1B **58**
Braithwell Way. *H'by* 2A **82**
Bramah St. *B'ley* 4E **9**
Bramall La. *S2* 4E **99**
Bramall La. *S'bri* 1B **140**
Bramble Clo. *Wick* 6F **81**
Brambles, The. *E'fld* 1E **75**
Brambles, The. *Roy* 1C **8**
Bramble Way. *Wath D* 5B **40**
Brambling Ct. *Ches* 2C **138**
Bramblings, The. *Donc* 5E **49**
Bramcote Av. *B'ley* 5A **8**
Brameld Rd. *Rawm* 2F **69**
Brameld Rd. *Swint* 2H **55**
Bramham Ct. S9 . . . . .6D **88**
(off Bramham Rd.)
Bramham Rd. *S9* 6D **88**
Bramham Rd. *Donc* 1D **48**
Bramley. 4H **81**
Bramley Av. *S13* 5H **101**
Bramley Av. *Ast* 5C **104**
Bramley Carr. *B'ley* 2D **22**
Bramley Clo. *Mosb* 2C **124**
Bramley Ct. *S10* 2H **97**
Bramley Ct. *Den M* 2B **58**
Bramley Dri. *S13* 4H **101**
Bramley Grange Cres. *Braml* 1E **81**
Bramley Grange Dri. *Braml* 1E **81**
Bramley Grange Ri. *Braml* 1E **81**
Bramley Grange Vw. *Braml* 1E **81**
Bramley Grange Way. *Braml* 1F **81**
Bramley Hall Rd. *S13* 5H **101**
Bramley La. *S13* 4H **101**
Bramley La. *Rav* 1A **82**
Bramley Lings. 5H **81**
Bramley M. *Eck* 6D **124**
Bramley Pk. Cvn. Site. *Mar L* 6A **124**
Bramley Pk. Clo. *S13* 5H **101**
Bramley Pk. Rd. *S13* 4H **101**
Bramley Way. *H'by* 3A **82**
Brampton. 2F **137**
(Chesterfield)
Brampton. 3A **40**
(Rotherham)
Brampton Av. *Thur* 5H **93**
Brampton Bierlow. 4A **40**
Brampton Clo. *Arm* 4E **35**
Brampton Clo. *Ches* 2E **137**
Brampton Ct. *Owl* 5A **114**
Brampton Cres. *Womb* 2H **39**
Brampton Ellis Enterprise Cen.
Bram B 4B **40**
Brampton en le Morthen. 6H **93**
Brampton La. *Arm* 4E **35**
Brampton La. *Ulley* 1F **105**
Brampton Meadows. *Thur* 5H **93**
Brampton Rd. *Thur* 6H **93**
Brampton Rd. *Wath D* 4B **40**
Brampton Rd. *Womb* 2H **39**
Brampton St. *Bram* 3B **40**
Brampton Vw. *Womb* 2H **39**
Bramshill Clo. *Soth* 6G **115**
Bramshill Ct. *Soth* 6G **115**
Bramshill Ri. *Ches* 4F **137**
Bramwell Clo. *S3* 1C **98** (2A **4**)
Bramwell Ct. *S3* 1C **98** (2A **4**)
Bramwell Dri. *S3* 1C **98** (2A **4**)
Bramwell St. *S3* 1C **98** (2A **4**)
Bramwell St. *Roth* 2E **79**
Bramwith La. *Barn D* 1G **21**
(in two parts)
Bramwith Rd. *S11* 5F **97**
Bramworth Rd. *Donc* 2H **45**

Branchcroft Dri. *Bal* 1H **61**
Brandene Clo. *Cal* 2G **139**
Brander Clo. *Bal* 6C **46**
Brand La. *Spro* 5B **30**
Brandon St. *S3* 4F **87**
Brandreth Clo. *S6* 6C **86**
Brandreth Rd. *S6* 6C **86**
Brand's La. *Dinn & W'sett* 6H **107**
Branksome Av. *B'ley* 6E **13**
Branksome Chine Av. *Has* 6C **138**
Bransby St. *S6* 6B **86**
Branstone Rd. *Spro* 1D **44**
Branton. 3H **49**
Branton Clo. *Ches* 4H **137**
Branton Ga. Rd. *Bran* 1H **49**
Branton Ter. *Bran* 3H **49**
Brantwood Cres. *Donc* 2D **48**
Brathay Clo. *S4* 2B **88**
Brathay Rd. *S4* 2B **88**
Brayford Rd. *Bal* 1H **61**
Bray St. *S9* 6C **88**
Bray Wlk. *Roth* 5E **67**
Brearley Av. *Deep* 4F **141**
Brearley Av. *New W* 1D **132**
Brearley Cen., The. *S9* 4F **89**
Breckland Rd. *Ches* 5D **136**
Brecklands. *Roth* 5A **80**
Brecklands. *Wick* 5E **81**
Breck La. *Dinn* 3F **107**
Brecks. 5C **80**
Brecks Cres. *Roth* 4C **80**
Brecks La. *Kirk S* 3D **20**
Brecks La. *Roth* 2B **80**
Brecon Clo. *Ches* 5C **136**
Brecon Clo. *Soth* 5G **115**
Brendon Av. *Ches* 1E **137**
Brendon Clo. *Womb* 3H **39**
Brent Clo. *Ches* 6F **131**
Brentwood Av. *S11* 1B **110**
Brentwood Clo. *Hoy* 1G **51**
Brentwood Rd. *S11* 1B **110**
Brentwood Vs. *Roth* 2E **79**
Bressingham Clo. *S4* 5G **87**
Bressingham Rd. *S4* 5G **87**
Bressingham Rd. N. *S4* 5F **87**
Bretby Clo. *Donc* 4D **48**
Bretby Rd. *Ches* 5C **130**
Brettas Pk. *B'ley* 2A **14**
Brett Clo. *Rawm* 5C **54**
Bretton Clo. *Brie* 3G **11**
Bretton Clo. *Ches* 6C **130**
Bretton Clo. *Dart* 5A **6**
Bretton Gro. *S12* 4F **113**
Bretton Ho. Donc 1C **46**
(off St James St.)
Bretton Rd. *Dart* 5A **6**
Bretton Vw. *Cud* 2G **15**
Brewery Rd. *Wath D* 4F **41**
Brewery St. *Ches* 2B **138**
Breydon Av. *Donc* 4G **31**
Briar Clo. *Ches* 6G **131**
Briar Ct. *Wick* 6F **81**
Briar Cft. *Bal* 3A **46**
Briardene Clo. *Ches* 6B **130**
Briarfield Av. *S12* 4C **112**
Briarfield Cres. *S12* 4C **112**
Briarfield Rd. *S12* 4C **112**
Briarfields La. *Worr* 4C **72**
Briar Gro. *Brie* 2G **11**
Briar Gro. *P'stne* 5D **142**
Briar Ri. *Wors* 5A **24**
Briar Rd. *S7* 1C **110**
Briar Rd. *Arm* 1E **35**
Briars Clo. *Kil* 4B **126**
Briar Vw. *Brim* 4E **133**
Briary Av. *High G* 6B **50**
Briary Clo. *B'wth* 4C **90**
Brickhouse La. *S17* 1C **120**
Brick Houses. 1C **120**
Brickhouse Yd. *Ches* 2G **137**
Brick St. *S10* 1H **97**
Brickyard, The. *Shaf* 4C **10**
Brickyard Wlk. *Ches* 2A **138**
Bridby St. *S13* 1D **114**
Bri. Bank Clo. *Ches* 5F **131**
Bridge End. 3C **142**
Bridge Gdns. *B'ley* 4H **13**
Bridgegate. *Roth* 2D **78**
Bridge Gro. *Donc* 4H **31**
Bridge Hill. *O'bri* 2D **72**
Bridgehouses. *S3* 6E **87**
Bridge Inn Rd. *C'town* 1E **65**

Bridgelake Dri. *Bal* 1H **61**
Bridge La. *Thurn* 2F **29**
Bridge Rd. *Donc* 3A **48**
Bridge St. *S3* 6E **87** (1E **5**)
(in two parts)
Bridge St. *B'ley* 4H **13**
Bridge St. *Bol D* 6F **29**
Bridge St. *Ches* 4A **138**
Bridge St. *Dart* 4C **6**
Bridge St. *Donc* 1B **46**
Bridge St. *Kil* 2B **126**
Bridge St. *P'stne* 3C **142**
Bridge St. *Roth* 2D **78**
Bridge St. *Swint* 2C **56**
Bridle Clo. *C'town* 1E **65**
Bridle Cres. *C'town* 1E **65**
Bridle Rd. *Mas M* 2F **135**
Bridle Stile. *Mosb* 2C **124**
Bridle Stile Clo. *Mosb* 2C **124**
Bridle Stile Gdns. *Mosb* 2B **124**
Bridleway, The. *Rawm* 6A **56**
Bridport Rd *S9* 6D **88**
Brier Clo. *Wat* 6D **114**
Brierfield Clo. *B'ley* 5E **13**
Brierley. 2F **11**
Brierley Clo. *Dart* 5E **7**
Brierley Clo. *Stav* 2C **134**
Brierley Rd. *Dalt* 6C **70**
Brierley Rd. *Donc* 4B **48**
Brierley Rd. *Grim & Brie* 4F **11**
Brierley Rd. *Shaf* 3D **10**
Brierley Rd. *S Hien* 1E **11**
Brier St. *S6* 3A **86**
Briery Meadows. *H'fld* 3E **39**
Briery Wlk. *Roth* 4B **68**
Brigadier Hargreaves Ct. *S13* . . .1A **114**
Briggs St. *B'ley* 4E **9**
Bright Mdw. *Half* 4G **125**
Brightmore Dri. *S3* 2C **98** (3A **4**)
Brighton St. *Grim* 6G **11**
Brighton Ter. Rd. *S10* 1A **98**
Brightside. 1C **88**
Brightside La. *S9* 4A **88**
Brightside Way. *S9* 3B **88**
Brimington. 3F **133**
Brimington Common. 6F **133**
Brimington Rd. *Ches* 1B **138**
Brimington Rd. N. *Ches* 2A **132**
(in two parts)
Brimmesfield Clo. *S2* 6A **100**
Brimmesfield Dri. *S2* 5A **100**
Brimmesfield Rd. *S2* 6A **100**
Brinckman St. *B'ley* 1H **23**
Brincliffe. 6A **98**
Brincliffe Clo. *Ches* 4D **136**
Brincliffe Ct. *S7* 1C **110**
Brincliffe Cres. *S11* 6A **98**
Brincliffe Edge Clo. *S11* 1A **110**
Brincliffe Edge Rd. *S11* 1H **109**
Brincliffe Gdns. *S11* 6A **98**
Brincliffe Hill. *S11* 6H **97**
Brindley Clo. *S8* 3E **111**
Brindley Ct. *Kil* 3A **126**
Brindley Cres. *S8* 3E **111**
Brindley Rd. *Ches* 5A **132**
Brindley Way. *Stav* 1D **134**
Brindwoodgate. 6A **128**
Brinkburn Clo. *S17* 3F **121**
Brinkburn Ct. *S17* 3F **121**
Brinkburn Dri. *S17* 3F **121**
Brinkburn Va. Rd. *S17* 3F **121**
Brinsford Rd. *B'wth* 2B **90**
Brinsworth. 3B **90**
Brinsworth Hall Av. *B'wth* 3B **90**
Brinsworth Hall Cres. *B'wth* 3B **90**
Brinsworth Hall Dri. *B'wth* 3B **90**
Brinsworth Hall Gro. *B'wth* 4B **90**
Brinsworth La. *B'wth* 3B **90**
Brinsworth Rd. *B'wth* 4A **90**
(in two parts)
Brinsworth St. *S9* 5B **88**
Brinsworth St. *Roth* 3C **78**
Bristol Gro. *Donc* 3G **33**
Bristol Rd. *S11* 4A **98**
Britain St. *Mexb* 1D **56**
Britannia Clo. *B'ley* 1H **23**
Britannia Ho. *B'ley* 1H **23**
Britannia Rd. *S9* 1E **101**
(in two parts)
Britannia Rd. *Ches* 6B **138**
Britland Clo. *B'ley* 5C **12**
Britnall St. *S9* 5C **88**
(in two parts)

Briton Sq. *Thurn* 1G **29**
Briton St. *Thurn* 1G **29**
Brittain St. *S1* 3F **99** (6F **5**)
Britten Ho. *Donc* 3G **33**
Broachgate. *Donc* 1G **31**
Broad Bri. Clo. *Kiv P* 5B **118**
Broadcarr Rd. *Hoy* 3H **51**
Broadcroft Clo. *Beig* 3H **115**
Broad Dyke Clo. *Kiv P* 5B **118**
Broad Elms Clo. *S11* 3F **109**
Broad Elms La. *S11* 4E **109**
Broadfield Ct. *S8* 1D **110**
Broadfield Rd. *S8* 1D **110**
Broadfield Way. *S8* 1D **110**
Broadgorse Clo. *Ches* 6H **137**
Broadhead Rd. *Deep* 4F **141**
Broad Inge Cres. *C'town* 2C **64**
Broadlands. *Braml* 2E **81**
Broadlands Av. *Owl* 5A **114**
Broadlands Clo. *Owl* 5B **114**
Broadlands Cres. *Braml* 2E **81**
Broadlands Cft. *Owl* 5B **114**
Broadlands Ri. *Owl* 5B **114**
Broad La. *S1* 2D **98** (3B **4**)
Broad La. Ct. *S1* 2D **98** (3B **4**)
Broadley Rd. *S13* 6E **101**
Broad Oaks. *S9* 6B **88**
Broadoaks Clo. *Ches* 2B **138**
Broadoaks Clo. *Dinn* 5E **107**
Broad Oaks La. *S9* 1B **100**
Broadoaks Rd. *Dinn* 4E **107**
Broad Pavement. *Ches* 2A **138**
Broad Riding. *Edl'tn* 4D **60**
Broad St. *S2* 1F **99** (2G **5**)
(in two parts)
Broad St. *Hoy* 5H **37**
Broad St. *P'gte* 4F **69**
Broad St. La. *S2* 1G **99** (2H **5**)
Broadwater. *Bol D* 1G **41**
Broadway. *B'ley* 6D **12**
Broadway. *B'wth* 4B **90**
Broadway. *M'well* 4F **7**
Broadway. *Roth* 2H **79**
Broadway. *Swint* 3H **55**
Broadway Av. *C'town* 3F **65**
Broadway Clo. *Swint* 3H **55**
Broadway Ct. *B'ley* 6D **12**
Broadway E. *Roth* 2H **79**
Broadway, The. *Donc* 6H **45**
Brocco Bank. *S11* 5A **98**
Brocco La. *S3* 1D **98** (2C **4**)
Brocco St. *S3* 1D **98** (2C **4**)
Brockfield Clo. *Wors* 4A **24**
Brockhill Ct. *Brim* 3F **133**
Brockhole Clo. *Donc* 4D **48**
Brockholes Farm. 4H **49**
Brockholes La. *Bran* 4H **49**
Brockholes La. *P'stne* 6A **142**
Brockhurst Way. *Thry* 5D **70**
Brocklehurst Av. *S8* 1G **123**
Brocklehurst Av. *B'ley* 3D **24**
Brocklehurst Ct. *Ches* 2F **137**
Brocklehurst Piece. *Ches* 3F **137**
Brockwell. 1G **137**
Brockwell Ct. *Ches* 5F **131**
Brockwell Hill. 6F **131**
Brockwell La. *Ches* 5F **131**
Brockwell La. *Cut* 4B **130**
Brockwell Pl. *Ches* 1G **137**
Brockwell Ter. *Ches* 1G **137**
Brockwell Wlk. *Ches* 6F **131**
Brockwood Clo. *S13* 6C **102**
Brodsworth Bus. Pk. *Brod* 3B **16**
Brodsworth Ho. *Donc* 1C **46**
(off St James St.)
Brodsworth Way. *Ross* 4E **63**
Bromcliffe Pk. *B'ley* 2E **15**
Bromehead Way. *Ches* 4F **131**
Bromfield Ct. *Roy* 1F **9**
Bromley Carr Rd. *Wort* 3A **50**
Brompton Rd. *S9* 4C **88**
Brompton Rd. *Spro* 2E **45**
Bromwich Rd. *S8* 5C **110**
Bronte Av. *Donc* 5H **45**
Bronte Clo. *B'ley* 4B **14**
Bronte Gro. *Mexb* 5F **43**
Bronte Pl. *Rawm* 6H **55**
Brookbank Rd. *Ches* 1F **137**
Brook Clo. *Ast* 6C **104**
Brook Clo. *Gren* 6A **64**
Brook Cft. *Ans* 2F **119**
Brook Cft. *S'bri* 3E **141**
Brookdale Rd. *C'town* 4E **51**

Brook Dri. *S3* 1D **98** (2B **4**)
Brook Dri. *Wath D* 5D **40**
Brooke Dri. *Brim* 6F **133**
Brooke St. *Donc* 4D **32**
Brooke St. *Hoy* 5H **37**
Brook Farm M. *Wath D* 4E **41**
Brookfield Av. *Ches* 3C **136**
Brookfield Av. *Swint* 3B **56**
Brookfield Clo. *Arm* 4F **35**
Brookfield Clo. *Dalt* 6B **70**
Brookfield M. *Ark* 5E **19**
Brookfield Rd. *S7* 6D **98**
Brookfields Pk. *Manv* 3H **41**
Brookfield Ter. *B'ley* 5E **9**
Brookfield Yd. *S7* 6D **98**
Brook Grn. *S12* 4B **114**
Brookhaven Way. *Braml* 2E **81**
Brook Hill. *S3* 2C **98** (3A **4**)
Brook Hill. *Thpe H* 2B **66**
Brookhill Rd. *Dart* 5A **6**
Brookhouse. 4E **95**
Brookhouse Clo. *S12* 4B **114**
Brookhouse Ct. *S12* 4B **114**
(off Brookhouse Dri.)
Brookhouse Dell. *Thur* 4C **94**
Brookhouse Dri. *S12* 4B **114**
Brookhouse Hill. *S10* 6C **96**
Brookhouse La. *Lghtn* 5E **95**
Brookhouse La. *Ast* 1B **116**
Brooklands. *Maltby* 5D **82**
Brooklands Av. *S10* 6B **96**
Brooklands Cres. *S10* 6B **96**
Brooklands Dri. *S10* 6B **96**
Brooklands Pk. *Dinn* 4C **106**
Brooklands Way. *Dinn* 4D **106**
Brook La. *S3* 2D **98** (3B **4**)
Brook La. *S12* 4B **114**
Brook La. *Braml* 3H **81**
Brook La. *Gren* 1A **74**
Brook La. *O'bri* 2C **72**
Brooklyn Dri. *Ches* 1F **137**
Brooklyn Pl. *S8* 2E **111**
Brooklyn Rd. *S8* 2E **111**
Brooklyn Works. *S3* 6E **87**
Brook M. *Ans* 2F **119**
Brook Rd. *S8* 2D **110**
Brook Rd. *Con* 3F **59**
Brook Rd. *High G* 1C **64**
Brook Rd. *Roth* 1H **79**
Brook Row. *S'bri* 4E **141**
Brookside. 3D **136**
Brookside. *Con* 4E **59**
Brookside. *Roth* 4A **80**
Brookside. *Swint* 4H **55**
Brookside Bar. *Ches* 3B **136**
Brookside Clo. *S12* 4B **114**
Brookside Ct. *P'gte* 5D **68**
Brookside Cres. *Wath D* 6B **40**
Brookside Dri. *B'ley* 3D **24**
Brookside Glen. *Ches* 3B **136**
Brookside La. *S6* 5A **84**
Brook Sq. *Con* 4E **59**
Brook St. *Whis* 2H **91**
Brookvale. *B'ley* 4D **14**
Brook Va. *Ches* 3G **137**
Brookview Ct. *Dron* 6E **123**
Brook Way. *Ark* 5D **18**
Brook Yd. *Ches* 2G **137**
Broom. 5F **79**
Broom Av. *Roth* 5H **79**
Broombank Pk. *Ches* 1F **131**
Broombank Pk. Ind. Est. *Ches* 1F **131**
Broombank Rd. *Ches* 1F **131**
Broom Chase. *Roth* 5F **79**
Broomcliffe Gdns. *Shaf* 3C **10**
Broom Clo. *S2* 4D **98**
Broom Clo. *B'ley* 3D **24**
Broom Clo. *Bol D* 6D **28**
Broom Clo. *Ches* 4F **131**
Broom Clo. *Dart* 4E **7**
Broom Clo. *S'side* 2G **81**
Broom Clo. *Wath D* 1G **55**
Broom Cft. *Roth* 5G **79**
Broom Cres. *Roth* 5F **79**
Broomcroft. *Dod* 3D **22**
Broomcroft Pk. *S11* 4F **109**
Broom Dri. *Roth* 6H **79**
Broome Av. *Swint* 3B **56**
Broomfield. 3B **98**
Broomfield Av. *Has* 6D **138**
Broomfield Clo. *B'ley* 1D **22**
Broomfield Ct. *S'bri* 3F **141**
Broomfield Gro. *Roth* 5F **79**

Broomfield Gro. *S'bri* 4F **141**
Broomfield La. *S'bri* 4E **141**
Broomfield Rd. *S10* 3B **98**
Broomfield Rd. *S'bri* 3F **141**
Broomfield Ter. *O'bri* 4A **72**
Broom Fld. Wlk. *P'stne* 5C **142**
Broom Gdns. *Brim* 4F **133**
Broom Grange. *Roth* 5G **79**
Broom Grn. *S3* 3D **98** (5B **4**)
Broom Gro. *Ans* 4F **119**
Broom Gro. *Roth* 4F **79**
Broomgrove Cres. *S10* 3B **98**
Broomgrove Hall. *S10* 3B **98**
Broomgrove La. *S10* 3B **98**
Broomgrove Rd. *S10* 3B **98**
Broomhall Pl. *S10* 3C **98** (6A **4**)
Broomhall Rd. *S10* 4C **98** (6A **4**)
Broomhall St. *S3* 3C **98** (6A **4**)
(in three parts)
Broomhead Ct. *M'well* 5F **7**
Broomhead La. *Womb* 2H **39**
Broomhill. **1B 40**
(Darfield)
Broomhill. **3A 98**
(Sheffield)
Broomhill. *Den M* 1A **58**
Broomhill Clo. *Eck* 6B **124**
Broom Hill Dri. *Donc* 4D **48**
Broomhill La. *Bol D* 6G **27**
Broomhill Rd. *Old W* 1H **131**
Broomhill Vw. *Bol D* 2H **41**
Broomhouse La. *Edl'tn & Donc* 4B **60**
(in two parts)
Broomhouse La. Ind. Est. *Edl'tn* 2C **60**
Broom La. *Roth* 5G **79**
Broom Riddings. *Roth* 5B **68**
Broom Rd. *Roth* 4F **79**
Broomroyd. *Wors* 5B **24**
Broomspring Clo. *S3* 3C **98** (5B **4**)
Broomspring La. *S10* 3C **98** (5A **4**)
(in four parts)
Broom St. *S10* 3C **98** (6A **4**)
Broom Ter. *Roth* 4F **79**
Broomvale Wlk. *Edl'tn* 4A **60**
Broom Valley Rd. *Roth* 4E **79**
Broomville St. *Swint* 2C **56**
Broom Wlk. *S3* 5B **4**
Broomwood Clo. *Beig* 4G **115**
Broomwood Gdns. *Beig* 4G **115**
Brosley Av. *Barn D* 1H **21**
Brotherton St. *S3* 5F **87**
Brough Grn. *Dod* 4C **22**
Broughton Av. *Donc* 2A **32**
Broughton La. *S9* 3D **88**
Broughton Rd. *S6* 2A **86**
Broughton Rd. *Ches* 4F **131**
Broughton Rd. *Donc* 5B **48**
Brow Clo. *Wors* 3H **23**
Brow Cres. *Half* 2E **125**
Brow Hill Rd. *Maltby* 3E **83**
Brownell St. *S3* 1D **98** (2B **4**)
Brown Hills La. *S10* 6A **96**
Browning Av. *Donc* 5B **46**
(in two parts)
Browning Clo. *S6* 4B **74**
Browning Clo. *B'ley* 2B **14**
Browning Ct. *Ches* 2D **136**
Browning Ct. *Roth* 4H **79**
Browning Dri. *S6* 4B **74**
Browning Dri. *Roth* 3H **79**
Browning Rd. *S6* 4A **74**
Browning Rd. *Barn D* 1H **21**
Browning Rd. *Mexb* 5E **43**
Browning Rd. *Roth* 3H **79**
Browning Rd. *Wath D* 4C **40**
Brown La. *S1* 3E **99** (5E **5**)
Brown La. *Coal A* 6G **123**
Brownroyd Av. *Roy* 3E **9**
Browns Sq. *H'fld* 4D **38**
Brown St. *S1* 3F **99** (5F **5**)
Brown St. *Roth* 2B **78**
Brow, The. *Roth* 5C **80**
Brow Vw. *Bol D* 1H **41**
Broxbourne Gdns. *Ben* 6B **18**
Broxholme La. *Donc* 5D **32**
Broxholme Rd. *S8* 4D **110**
Bruce Av. *B'ley* 2H **23**
Bruce Cres. *Donc* 4H **33**
Bruce Rd. *S11* 5B **98**
Bruncroft Clo. *Donc* 5B **48**
Brunel Rd. *Donc* 4H **31**
Brunel Way. *Cat* 6A **90**
Bruni Way. *New R* 6D **62**

Brunswick Clo. *B'ley* 1H **13**
Brunswick Dri. *S'side* 2F **81**
Brunswick Rd. *S3* 6F **87**
Brunswick Rd. *Roth* 5F **79**
Brunswick St. *S10* 2C **98** (4A **4**)
Brunswick St. *Ches* 1A **138**
Brunswick St. *Thurn* 1H **29**
Brunt Rd. *Rawm* 1H **69**
Brushfield Rd. *S12* 3F **113**
Brushfield Rd. *Ches* 6B **130**
Bryn Lea. *Ches* 2C **138**
Bryony Clo. *Kil* 3H **125**
Bubwith Rd. *S9* 1D **88**
Buchanan Clo. *S5* 4C **74**
Buchanan Dri. *S5* 4C **74**
Buchanan Rd. *S5* 4C **74**
Buckden Clo. *Ches* 1F **137**
Buckden Rd. *B'ley* 5F **13**
Buckenham Clo. *S4* 5G **87**
Buckenham St. *S4* 5G **87**
Buckingham Clo. *Dron W* 1B **128**
Buckingham Ct. *Roy* 1D **8**
Buckingham Rd. *Con* 2D **58**
Buckingham Rd. *Donc* 5F **33**
Buckingham Way. *B'wth* 3C **90**
Buckingham Way. *Maltby* 3G **83**
Buckingham Way. *Roy* 1D **8**
Buckleigh Rd. *Wath D* 1E **55**
Buckley Ct. *B'ley* 1H **23**
Buckley Ho. *B'ley* 1H **23**
Buckthorn Clo. *Swint* 5A **56**
Buckwood Vw. *S14* 2H **111**
Bude Ct. *B'ley* 4C **14**
Bude Rd. *Donc* 3B **46**
Bullen Rd. *S6* 4A **74**
Bullfinch Clo. *B'wth* 3D **90**
Bungalow Rd. *Edl'tn* 3B **60**
Bungalows, The. *Ches* 2F **137**
(Barker La.)
Bungalows, The. *Ches* 2A **132**
(Brimington Rd. N.)
Bungalows, The. *Ches* 4G **131**
(Littlemoor)
Bungalows, The. *Ches* 3B **138**
(off Piccadilly Rd.)
Bungalows, The. *Eck* 6C **124**
(off West St.)
Bungalows, The. *Eck* 6H **125**
(Pitt St.)
Bungalows, The. *Kil* 3A **126**
Bungalows, The. *Rawm* 6E **55**
(Jackson Cres.)
Bungalows, The. *Rawm* 1F **69**
(off Middle Av.)
Bungalows, The. *Stav* 3A **134**
Bungalows, The. *Tree* 1E **103**
Bunker's Hill. *Kil* 3C **126**
Bunting Clo. *S8* 5F **111**
Bunting Clo. *Walt* 4D **136**
Bunting Ho. *Old W* 1B **132**
Bunting Nook. *S8* 5F **111**
Burbage Clo. *Dron W* 1B **128**
Burbage Gro. *S12* 2F **113**
Burbage Rd. *Stav* 4B **134**
Burcot Rd. *S8* 2D **110**
Burcroft. **3F 59**
Burcroft Clo. *Hoy* 6F **37**
Burcroft Hill. *Con* 2F **59**
Burden Clo. *Donc* 1C **46**
Burford Av. *Donc* 6G **45**
Burford Cres. *Ast* 6C **104**
Burgen Rd. *Roth* 6G **67**
Burgess Clo. *Has* 6D **138**
Burgess Rd. *S9* 5B **88**
Burgess St. *S1* 2E **99** (4E **5**)
Burghley Clo. *Dinn* 5E **107**
Burgoyne Clo. *S6* 5B **86**
Burgoyne Rd. *S6* 5B **86**
Burkinshaw Av. *Rawm* 5F **55**
Burkitt Dri. *Mas M* 1F **135**
Burleigh Ct. *B'ley* 6H **13**
Burleigh St. *B'ley* 1H **23**
Burley Clo. *Ches* 6A **138**
Burlington Arc. *B'ley* 6H **13**
(off Eldon St.)
Burlington Clo. *S17* 2E **121**
Burlington Ct. *S6* 6C **86**
Burlington Glen. *S17* 2E **121**
Burlington Gro. *S17* 2E **121**
Burlington Ho. *Ches* 2A **138**
(off Burlington St.)
Burlington Rd. *S17* 2E **121**
Burlington St. *S6* 6C **86** (1A **4**)

Burlington St. *Ches* 2A **138**
Burman Rd. *Wath D* 6F **41**
Burnaby Ct. *S6* 4B **86**
Burnaby Cres. *S6* 5B **86**
Burnaby Grn. *S6* 4B **86**
Burnaby Rd. *S6* 4B **86**
Burnaby St. *Donc* 1C **46**
Burnaby Wlk. *S6* 5B **86**
Burnaston Clo. *Dron W* 2A **128**
Burnaston Wlk. *Den M* 2C **58**
Burnbridge Rd. *Old W* 1B **132**
Burncross. **2C 64**
Burncross Dri. *C'town* 2D **64**
Burncross Gro. *C'town* 2C **64**
Burncross Rd. *Burn & C'town* 2C **64**
Burnell Rd. *S6* 2A **86**
Burnell St. *Brim* 3F **133**
Burnett Clo. *P'stne* 5E **143**
Burns Clo. *Ches* 6H **137**
Burns Ct. *C'town* 2D **64**
Burngreave. **5G 87**
Burngreave Bank. *S4* 5F **87**
Burngreave Rd. *S3* 4F **87**
Burngreave St. *S3* 5F **87**
Burn Gro. *C'town* 3G **65**
Burngrove Pl. *S3* 4F **87**
Burnham Av. *M'well* 4F **7**
Burnham Clo. *Donc* 4H **47**
Burnham Gro. *Donc* 1H **31**
Burnham Way. *D'fld* 4D **26**
Burn Pl. *B'ley* 6A **8**
Burnsall Cres. *B'wth* 4C **90**
Burnsall Gro. *B'ley* 3D **24**
Burns Clo. *Ches* 6H **137**
Burns Ct. *C'town* 2D **64**
Burns Dri. *C'town* 2D **64**
Burns Dri. *Dron* 3G **129**
Burns Dri. *Roth* 3H **79**
Burnside Av. *S8* 2E **111**
Burns Rd. *S6* 1B **98**
Burns Rd. *Barn D* 1H **21**
Burns Rd. *Dinn* 5G **107**
Burns Rd. *Donc* 5B **46**
Burns Rd. *Maltby* 5G **83**
Burns Rd. *Roth* 3G **79**
Burns St. *Ben* 6B **18**
Burns Way. *Bal* 3A **46**
Burns Way. *Wath D* 4C **40**
Burnt Hill La. *O'bri* 4A **72**
Burnt Stones Clo. *S10* 3D **96**
Burnt Stones Dri. *S10* 3D **96**
Burnt Stones Gro. *S10* 3D **96**
Burnt Tree La. *S3* 6D **98** (1B **4**)
(in two parts)
Burntwood Clo. *Thurn* 2D **28**
Burntwood Cres. *Tree* 6E **91**
Burnt Wood La. *Tree* 1G **103**
Burntwood Rd. *Grim* 6H **11**
Burrell St. *Roth* 3D **78**
Burrowfield Av. *S6* 2A **86**
Burrows Dri. *S5* 1E **87**
Burrows Gro. *Womb* 6H **25**
Burrs Wood Cft. *Ches* 4D **130**
Bursden Clo. *Old W* 2A **132**
Burton Av. *B'ley* 3D **14**
Burton Av. *Donc* 3B **46**
Burton Bank Rd. *B'ley* 4A **14**
(in two parts)
Burton Cres. *B'ley* 2E **15**
Burton La. *O'bri* 3C **72**
Burtonlees Ct. *Donc* 4C **48**
Burton Rd. *S3* 5D **86**
Burton Rd. *B'ley* 4A **14**
Burton Rd. Bus. Pk. *B'ley* 2E **15**
Burton St. *S6* 4B **86**
Burton St. *B'ley* 4G **13**
Burton Ter. *B'ley* 1B **24**
Burton Ter. *Donc* 3B **46**
Burtop Cft. *H'fld* 4E **39**
Burying La. *W'wth* 2A **52**
Bushey Wood Gro. *S17* 2D **120**
Bushey Wood Rd. *S17* 3E **121**
Bushfield Rd. *Wath D* 5D **40**
Busk Knoll. *S5* 1E **87**
Busk Mdw. *S5* 1E **87**
Busk Pk. *S5* 1E **87**
Busley Gdns. *Ben* 1A **32**
(in two parts)
Butcher St. *Thurn* 1E **29**
Butchill Av. *S5* 1E **75**
Bute St. *S10* 2H **97**
Butler Rd. *S6* 4G **85**
Butler Way. *Kil* 2A **126**
Butterbusk. *Con* 3G **59**
Butterbusk Green. **1A 60**

Buttercross Dri. *L Hou* 1G **27**
Butterfield Ct. *Bram* 3A **40**
Butterill Dri. *Arm* 4H **35**
Butterley Dri. *B'ley* 3D **24**
Butterleys. *Dod* 2C **22**
Buttermere Clo. *Ans* 6E **107**
Buttermere Clo. *Bol D* 2A **42**
Buttermere Clo. *Ches* 4F **131**
Buttermere Clo. *Mexb* 5G **43**
Buttermere Dri. *Dron W* 2C **128**
Buttermere Rd. *S7* 3C **110**
Buttermere Way. *B'ley* 1H **25**
Buttermilk La. *Bsvr* 6H **135**
Butterthwaite. . . . . **.6H 65**
Butterthwaite Cres. *S5* 2A **76**
Butterthwaite La. *E'fld* 1G **75**
Butterthwaite Rd. *S5* 1G **75**
Butterton Clo. *M'well* 4G **7**
Butterton Dri. *Ches* 6C **130**
Butt Hole Rd. *Con* 3G **59**
Button Hill. *S11* 3H **109**
Button Row. *S'bri* 3D **140**
Butts Hill. *S17* 5D **120**
Buxton Rd. *B'ley* 6C **8**
Byath La. *Cud* 1H **15**
Byford Rd. *Maltby* 4C **82**
Byland Way. *B'ley* 5D **14**
Byram Ct. *Bal* 6C **46**
Byrley Rd. *Roth* 6G **67**
Byrne Clo. *Bar G* 3A **12**
Byron Av. *Bal* 5A **46**
(in two parts)
Byron Av. *C'town* 3D **64**
Byron Av. *Donc* 5H **31**
Byron Clo. *Dron* 4G **129**
Byron Cres. *Wath D* 4C **40**
Byron Dri. *B'ley* 3B **14**
Byron Dri. *Roth* 3G **79**
Byron Rd. *S7* 1B **110**
Byron Rd. *Beig* 5G **115**
Byron Rd. *Ches* 5A **138**
Byron Rd. *Dinn* 5G **107**
(in two parts)
Byron Rd. *Maltby* 5G **83**
Byron Rd. *Mexb* 6F **43**
Byron St. *Ches* 4B **138**

C

Cadeby. . . . . **.5A 44**
Cadeby Av. *Con* 3C **58**
Cadeby Ho. Donc 1C **46**
(off St James St.)
Cadeby La. *Spro* 5A **44**
Cadeby Rd. *Spro* 3C **44**
Cadman Ct. *Mosb* 3D **124**
Cadman Ct. *S1* 2E **99** (4F 5)
Cadman Rd. *S12* 2E **113**
Cadman St. *S4* 1G **99**
Cadman St. *Mosb* 3C **124**
Cadman St. *Wath D* 5G **41**
Cadwell Clo. *Cud* 5C **10**
Caernarvon Clo. *Ches* 5E **137**
Caernarvon Cres. *Bol D* 1H **41**
Caernarvon Dri. *Barn* 1G **43**
Caernarvon Rd. *Dron* 3F **129**
Caine Gdns. *Roth* 3G **77**
Cairns Rd. *S10* 3F **97**
Cairns Rd. *Beig* 3F **115**
Caister Av. *C'town* 2D **64**
Caistor Av. *B'ley* 2E **23**
Calcot Grn. *Swint* 3B **56**
Calcot Pk. Av. *Swint* 3B **56**
Caldbeck Gro. *High G* 5B **50**
Caldbeck Pl. *Ans* 6F **107**
Calder Av. *Roy* 2G **9**
Calder Clo. *Roy* 2G **9**
Calder Ct. *Roth* 1E **91**
Calder Cres. *B'ley* 2D **24**
Calder Rd. *Bol D* 2B **42**
Calder Rd. *Roth* 5H **67**
Calder Ter. *Con* 2E **59**
Caldervale. *Roy* 1G **9**
Calder Way. *S5* 1G **87**
Caldey Rd. *Dron* 3E **129**
California Cres. *B'ley* 2H **23**
California Dri. *Cat* 6C **90**
California Dri. *C'town* 3E **65**
California Gdns. *B'ley* 1H **23**
California St. *B'ley* 2G **23**
California Ter. *B'ley* 2G **23**
Calladine Way. *Swint* 4A **56**

Callander Ct. *Donc* 4C **48**
Callis La. *P'stne* 6E **143**
Callis Way. *P'stne* 5D **142**
Callow Dri. *S14* 2H **111**
Callow Mt. *S14* 2G **111**
Callow Pl. *S14* 2H **111**
Callow Rd. *S14* 2G **111**
Callum Ct. *P'gte* 5E **69**
Callywhite La. *Dron* 2F **129**
Calner Cft. *Soth* 5H **115**
Calow. . . . . **.2F 139**
Calow Brook Dri. *Has* 5E **139**
Calow Green. . . . . **.5H 139**
Calow La. *Has & Cal* 5D **138**
Calow La. Ind. Est. *Has* 5E **139**
Calstock Clo. *Ches* 1C **136**
Calver Clo. *Dod* 3C **22**
Calver Cres. *Stav* 4B **134**
Calverley Gdns. *Womb* 6C **26**
Calvert Rd. *S9* 5E **89**
Calvert St. *Hoy* 6F **37**
Calvey Orchard. *Cud* 6C **10**
Camborne Clo. *S6* 4A **74**
Camborne Rd. *S6* 4A **74**
Camborne Way. *B'ley* 4B **14**
Cambourne Clo. *Adw S* 1D **16**
Cambria Dri. *Donc* 5G **45**
Cambrian Clo. *Ches* 5F **131**
Cambrian Clo. *Spro* 2C **44**
Cambridge Clo. *H'ton* 1F **43**
Cambridge Ct. S1 . . . . .2E **99** (4D 4)
(off Carver St.)
Cambridge Cres. *Roth* 2G **79**
Cambridge Pl. *Roth* 2G **79**
Cambridge Rd. *S8* 1F **111**
Cambridge Rd. *Brim* 3F **133**
Cambridge Rd. *Deep* 4H **141**
Cambridge St. *S1* 2E **99** (4D 4)
Cambridge St. *Mexb* 6C **42**
Cambridge St. *New R* 3C **62**
Cambridge St. *Roth* 3G **79**
Camdem Gdns. *Braml* 4H **81**
Camdale Ri. *S12* 6H **113**
Camdale Vw. *S12* 6H **113**
Camden Pl. *Donc* 1C **46**
Camellia Clo. *Con* 4F **59**
Camellia Dri. *Kirk S* 4D **20**
Camlough Wlk. *Ches* 2B **138**
Cammell Rd. *S5* 1H **87**
Camms Clo. *Eck* 5D **124**
Camm St. *S6* 5A **86**
Campbell Dri. *Roth* 4H **79**
Campbell St. *Roth* 3C **68**
Camping La. *S8* 5C **110**
Campion Clo. *Bol D* 6D **28**
Campion Dri. *Kil* 3A **126**
Campion Dri. *Swint* 4B **56**
Campo La. *S1* 2E **99** (3D 4)
Campsall Dri. *S10* 2G **97**
Campsall Fld. Clo. *Wath D* 1E **55**
Campsall Fld. Rd. *Wath D* 6E **41**
Canada St. *S4* 4H **87**
Canada St. *B'ley* 2G **23**
Canal Bri. *Kil* 3B **126**
Canal St. *S4* 6H **87**
Canal St. *B'ley* 4H **13**
Canal Way. *B'ley* 4H **13**
Canal Wharf. *Ches* 1B **138**
Canal Wharfe. *Mexb* 1G **57**
Canary Ct. *S'side* 2F **81**
Canberra Ri. *Bol D* 1H **41**
Canklow. . . . . **.6D 78**
Canklow Hill Rd. *Roth* 6D **78**
Canklow Meadows Ind. Est. *B'wth* 3D **90**
Canklow Rd. *Roth* 6D **78**
Canning St. *S1* 2D **98** (4C 4)
Cannock St. *S6* 3A **86**
Cannon Hall Rd. *S5* 2G **87**
Cannonthorpe Ri. *Tree* 1F **103**
Cannon Way. *B'ley* 2B **12**
Canon Clo. *Ross* 4F **63**
Canons Way. *B'ley* 4C **14**
Cantelo Ct. *New R* 6C **62**
Canterbury Av. *S10* 5C **96**
Canterbury Clo. *Donc* 3G **31**
Canterbury Clo. *Roth* 4H **79**
Canterbury Cres. *S10* 5C **96**
Canterbury Dri. *S10* 5C **96**
Canterbury Rd. *S8* 2F **111**
Canterbury Rd. *Donc* 3F **33**
Cantilupe Cres. *Ast* 5B **104**
Cantley. . . . . **.2F 49**

Cantley La. *Donc* 2B **48**
Cantley Mnr. Av. *Donc* 5E **33**
Cantrell Clo. *Brim* 3D **132**
Capel Ri. *Brim* 3D **132**
Capel St. *S6* .4B **86**
(in two parts)
Caperns Rd. *Ans* 2H **119**
Capri Ct. *D'fld* 3C **26**
Capthorne Clo. *Ches* 6B **130**
Cvn. Site, The. *Spro* 3C **44**
Caraway Gro. *Swint* 5B **56**
Carbis Clo. *B'ley* 4B **14**
Carbrook. . . . . **.3D 88**
Carbrook Hall Ind. Est. *S9* 2D **88**
Carbrook Hall Rd. *S9* 2D **88**
Carbrook St. *S9* 3D **88**
Cardew Clo. *Rawm* 2G **69**
Cardigan Rd. *Donc* 4A **34**
Cardinal Clo. *Ross* 4F **63**
Cardoness Dri. *S10* 3E **97**
Cardoness Rd. *S10* 3F **97**
Cardwell Av. *S13* 6H **101**
Cardwell Dri. *S13* 6H **101**
Carey Av. *B'ley* 5A **14**
Carfield Av. *S8* 2F **111**
Carfield La. *S8* 2G **111**
Carfield Pl. *S8* 2F **111**
Carisbrooke Rd. *Donc* 5G **33**
Carlby Rd. *S6* 4G **85**
Carley Dri. *W'fld* 6F **115**
Carlingford Rd. *Roth* 6G **79**
Carlin St. *S13* 1G **113**
Carlisle Clo. Ches 1G **131**
Carlisle Pl. Roth 2E **79**
(off Nottingham St.)
Carlisle Rd. *S4* 3A **88**
Carlisle Rd. *Donc* 2H **33**
Carlisle St. *S4* 6G **87**
Carlisle St. *Kiln* 4B **56**
(in two parts)
Carlisle St. *Roth* 2E **79**
Carlisle St. E. *S4* 5H **87**
Carlisle Ter. *Dinn* 4F **107**
Carlthorpe Gro. *High G* 6A **50**
Carlton. . . . . **.4F 9**
Carlton Av. *Roth* 3F **79**
Carlton Clo. *Mosb* 3C **124**
Carlton Green. . . . . **.5F 9**
Carlton Ho. Cud 6B **10**
Carlton Ho. Donc 1C **46**
(off Bond Clo.)
Carlton Ho. Donc 5E **33**
(off Highfield Rd.)
Carlton Ind. Est. *B'ley* 1C **14**
(in two parts)
Carlton Ind. Est. *Car* 6E **9**
Carlton Marsh Nature Reserve. . . . . . . **.5H 9**
Carlton M. *S2* 6A **100**
Carlton Rd. *S6* 1H **85**
Carlton Rd. *B'ley* 2A **14**
Carlton Rd. *Ches* 6H **137**
Carlton Rd. *Donc* 4E **33**
Carlton Rd. *Rawm* 3F **69**
Carlton St. *B'ley* 3G **13**
Carlton St. *Cud* 6B **10**
Carlton St. *Grim* 6G **11**
Carlton Ter. *Car* 4G **9**
Carlyle Rd. *Maltby* 5G **83**
Carlyle St. *Mexb* 6E **43**
Carlyon Gdns. *Ches* 5H **137**
Carnaby Rd. *S6* 4A **86**
Carnarvon St. *S6* 6C **86**
Carnforth Rd. *B'ley* 2D **14**
Carnley St. *Wath D* 4B **40**
Carnoustie Av. *Ches* 5E **137**
Carnoustie Clo. *Swint* 3C **56**
Carolina Ct. *Donc* 4G **47**
Carolina Way. *Donc* 4G **47**
Carpenter Cft. *S12* 1E **113**
Carpenter Gdns. *S12* 1E **113**
Carpenter M. *S12* 1E **113**
Carr. . . . . **.2E 95**
Carr Bank Clo. *S11* 5F **97**
Carr Bank Dri. *S11* 5E **97**
Carr Bank La. *S11* 5E **97**
Carr Clo. *B'wth* 3A **90**
Carr Clo. *Deep* 4G **141**
Carrcroft Ct. *Deep* 4H **141**
Carrfield Clo. *Dart* 5B **6**
Carrfield Ct. *S8* 1F **111**
Carrfield Dri. *S8* 1F **111**
Carrfield La. *S2* 1F **111**
Carr Fld. La. *Bol D* 6D **28**

Carrfield Rd. *S8* 1F 111
Carrfield St. *S8* 1F 111
Carr Fold. *Deep* 4H 141
Carr Forge Clo. *S12* 3A 114
Carr Forge La. *S12* 3A 114
Carr Forge Mt. *S12* 3A 114
Carr Forge Pl. *S12* 3B 114
Carr Forge Rd. *S12* 3A 114
Carr Forge Ter. *S12* 3A 114
Carr Forge Vw. *S12* 3B 114
Carr Forge Wlk. S12 ....*3B 114*
　　　　　(off Carter Lodge Dri.)
Carr Furlong. *B'ley* 4B 8
Carr Grange Light Ind. Est. *Donc* 2D 46
Carr Grn. *Bol D* 6E 29
Carr Grn. *M'well* 5G 7
Carr Grn. La. *M'well* 6G 7
Carr Gro. *Deep* 4G 141
Carr Head. **4H 141**
Carr Head La. *Bol D* 6A 28
Carr Head La. *P'stne* 1B 142
Carr Hill. *Donc* 3B 46
Carr Ho. Rd. *Donc* 2D 46
Carriage Dri. *Donc* 3E 47
Carriage Way, The. *Ross* 4F 63
Carrill Dri. *S6* 3A 74
Carrill Rd. *S6* 3A 74
Carrington Av. *B'ley* 3G 13
Carrington Rd. *S11* 5H 97
Carrington St. *B'ley* 4F 13
Carrington St. *Roth* 4F 79
Carrington Ter. *Kiv P* 5H 117
Carr La. *Bes* 6B 48
Carr La. *Con* 5F 59
Carr La. *Donc* 2D 46
Carr La. *Dron W* 1A 128
Carr La. *Hoot L & Maltby* 5D 82
Carr La. *Maltby & Lghtn* 2E 95
Carr La. *P'stne* 6F 141
Carr La. *Thry* 1E 71
Carr La. *Ulley* 2D 104
Carr La. *Wadw* 6H 61
Carr La. *Wort & Tank* 1A 50
Carron Dri. *M'well* 5G 7
Carr Rd. *S6* 5A 86
Carr Rd. *Deep* 5F 141
Carr Rd. *Edl'tn* 4A 60
Carr Rd. *Wath D* 5G 41
Carrs La. *Cud* 2H 15
Carr St. *B'ley* 2D 14
Carr Vw. Av. *Donc* 3B 46
Carr Vw. Rd. *Roth* 1F 77
Carrville Dri. *S6* 5B 74
Carrville Rd. *S6* 5B 74
Carrville Rd. W. *S6* 5A 74
Carrwell La. *S6* 6A 74
Carrwood Rd. *B'ley* 6E 15
Carsick. **4E 97**
Carsick Gro. *S10* 4D 96
Carsick Hill. **4D 96**
Carsick Hill Cres. *S10* 4D 96
Carsick Hill Dri. *S10* 4E 97
Carsick Hill Rd. *S10* 4D 96
Carsick Hill Way. *S10* 4D 96
Carsick Vw. Rd. *S10* 4D 96
Carsington Clo. *Ches* 6D 130
Carson Mt. *S12* 4D 112
Carson Rd. *S10* 2H 97
Carterhall La. *S12* 5E 113
Carterhall Rd. *S12* 5D 112
Carter Knowle. **2B 110**
Carter Knowle Av. *S11* 2H 109
Carter Knowle Rd. *S11 & S7* 2H 109
Carter Lodge Av. *S12* 3A 114
Carter Lodge Dri. *S12* 3B 114
Carter Lodge Pl. *S12* 3B 114
Carter Lodge Ri. *S12* 3B 114
Carter Lodge Wlk. S12 ....*3B 114*
　　　　　(off Carter Lodge Dri.)
Carter Pl. *S8* 1F 111
Carter Rd. *S8* 1E 111
Cartmel Clo. *Dron W* 2C 128
Cartmel Clo. *Maltby* 3G 83
Cartmel Ct. *B'ley* 6F 9
Cartmel Cres. *Ches* 3F 131
Cartmell Ct. *S8* 3C 110
Cartmell Cres. *S8* 4D 110
Cartmell Hill. *S8* 3C 110
Cartmell Rd. *S8* 3C 110
Cartmel Wlk. *Dinn* 6F 107
Cart Rd. *C'town* 6E 51
Car Va. Dri. *S13* 5E 101
Car Va. Vw. *S13* 5E 101

Carver Clo. *H'hill* 4H 127
Carver Dri. *Dinn* 5E 107
Carver La. *S1* 2E **99** (3D **4**)
Carver St. *S1* 2E **99** (3D **4**)
Carver Way. *H'hill* 3H 127
Carwood Clo. *S4* 4H 87
Carwood Grn. *S4* 4H 87
Carwood Gro. *S4* 4H 87
Carwood La. *S4* 4H 87
Carwood Rd. *S4* 4H 87
Carwood Way. *S4* 4H 87
Cary Rd. *S2* 5B 100
Cary Rd. *Eck* 6B 124
Castell Cres. *Donc* 2C 48
Castle Av. *Con* 3E 59
Castle Av. *Ross* 5F 63
Castle Av. *Roth* 6D 78
Castlebeck. **4E 101**
Castlebeck Av. *S2* 4D 100
Castlebeck Ct. S2 ....*4E 101*
　　　　　(off Castlebeck Av.)
Castlebeck Cft. *S2* 4E 101
Castlebeck Dri. *S2* 5D 100
Castlebeck Gro. *S2* 5E 101
Castle Clo. *Dod* 3C 22
Castle Clo. *Monk B* 4B 14
Castle Clo. *P'stne* 5E 143
Castle Clo. *Spro* 1G 45
Castle Ct. *S2* 1H 99
Castle Cres. *Con* 2E 59
Castledale Cft. *S2* 5D 100
Castledale Gro. *S2* 5E 101
Castledale Pl. *S2* 5D 100
Castledine Ct. *Bal* 1H 61
Castledine Cft. *S9* 1D 88
Castledine Gdns. *S9* 1C 88
Castle Din. *Hood G* 1A 68
Castlegate. *S3* 1F **99** (2G **5**)
Castle Green. **5E 143**
Castle Grn. *S3* 1F **99** (2F **5**)
Castle Grn. *Lghtn* 1D 106
Castle Gro. *Spro* 2D 44
Castle Gro. Ter. *Con* 2F 59
Castle Hill. *Con* 3E 59
Castle Hill. *Eck* 5D 124
Castle Hill Av. *Mexb* 1H 57
Castle Hill Clo. *Eck* 5D 124
Castle Hills Rd. *Donc* 6G 17
Castle Ho. *S3* 3H 99
Castle La. *P'stne* 5E 143
Castle M. *Scawt* 6H 17
Castlereagh St. *B'ley* 6G 13
Castlerigg Way. *Dron W* 2C 128
Castle Row. *S17* 3H 121
Castlerow Clo. *S17* 3H 121
Castlerow Dri. *S17* 3H 121
Castlerow Vw. *S17* 3H 121
Castle Sq. S1 ....2F **99**
　　　　　(off High St.)
Castle St. *S3* 1F **99** (2F **5**)
Castle St. *B'ley* 1G 23
Castle St. *Con* 3E 59
Castle St. *P'stne* 5E 143
Castle Ter. *Con* 3E 59
Castleton Gro. *Ink* 6H 133
Castle Vw. *Birdw* 3C 36
Castle Vw. *Dod* 1B 22
Castle Vw. *Eck* 6D 124
Castle Vw. *Edl'tn* 4B 60
Castle Vw. *Hood G* 6A 22
Castle Wlk. S2 ....1H **99**
　　　　　(off St John's Rd.)
Castlewood Clo. *S10* 5C 96
Castlewood Cres. *S10* 5B 96
Castlewood Dri. *S10* 5C 96
Castlewood Rd. *S10* 5C 96
Castle Yd. *Ches* 3A 138
Castor Rd. *S9* 4B 88
Casual Wards. *S11* 6B 98
Catania Ri. *D'fld* 3C 26
Catch Bar La. *S6* 1A 86
Catchford Vw. *Ches* 4D 130
Catcliffe. **5D 90**
Catcliffe Rd. *S9* 1E 101
Cathedral Cft. *D'ville* 3H 21
Catherine Av. *Swal* 6B 104
Catherine Ct. *Ches* 2G 137
Catherine Rd. *S4* 5F 87
Catherine St. *S3* 5F 87
Catherine St. *Ches* 2G 137
Catherine St. *Donc* 1D 46
Catherine St. *Mexb* 6D 42
Catherine St. *Roth* 3E 79
Cathill Rd. *Bol D* 5G 27

Cathill Roundabout. *D'fld* 4A 28
Cat La. *S2 & S8* 1G 111
Catley Rd. *S9* 6E 89
Catling La. *Barn D* 2H 21
Cattal St. *S9* 6C 88
Catterick Clo. *Den M* 3A 58
Catterick Ho. *Roth* 2F 79
Cauldon Dri. *Ches* 6C 130
Caulk La. *Swait* 4E 25
　　　　　(in three parts)
Causeway Gdns. *S17* 1C 120
Causeway Glade. *S17* 1C 120
Causeway Head. **1C 120**
Causeway Head Rd. *S17* 1C 120
Causeway, The. *S17* 2D 120
Cavendish Av. *S6* 2E 85
Cavendish Av. *S17* 2F 121
Cavendish Clo. *Roth* 5B 80
Cavendish Ct. *S3* 3D **98** (5B **4**)
Cavendish Ct. *Ches* 6A 132
Cavendish Pl. *Maltby* 3G 83
Cavendish Ri. *Dron* 3D 128
Cavendish Rd. *S11* 6A 98
Cavendish Rd. *B'ley* 4G 13
Cavendish Rd. *Roth* 3A 78
Cavendish Rd. *Toll B* 3A 18
Cavendish St. *S3* 2D **98** (4B **4**)
Cavendish St. *Ches* 2A 138
Cavendish St. *Stav* 3A 134
Cavendish St. N. *Old W* 1A 132
Cavendish Ter. *Toll B* 2A 18
Cavill Rd. *S8* 4E 111
Cawdor Rd. *S2* 1A 112
Cawdor St. *Ben* 6B 18
Cawdron Clo. *Dalt* 6B 70
Cawdron Ri. *B'wth* 4C 90
Cawley Pl. *B'ley* 3A 14
Cawston Rd. *S4* 3G 87
Cawthorne Clo. *S8* 4C 110
Cawthorne Clo. *Dod* 3C 22
Cawthorne Clo. *Roth* 2A 80
Cawthorne Gro. *S8* 4C 110
Cawthorne La. *Dart* 6A 6
Cawthorne Rd. *Bar G* 2A 12
Cawthorne Rd. *Roth* 2A 80
Cawthorne Vw. *H'swne* 1F 143
Caxton Clo. *New W* 1D 132
Caxton La. *S10* 3H 97
Caxton Rd. *S10* 3A 98
Caxton Rd. *W'land* 2D 16
Caxton St. *B'ley* 5G 13
Caythorpe Clo. *Lund* 2G 15
Cayton Clo. *B'ley* 6A 8
Cecil Av. *Dron* 1E 129
Cecil Av. *Warm* 6E 45
Cecil Rd. *Dron* 6E 123
Cecil Sq. *S2* 5D 98
Cedar Av. *Ches* 6F 131
Cedar Av. *Mexb* 5D 42
Cedar Av. *Wick* 4G 81
Cedar Clo. *Donc* 6G 45
Cedar Clo. *Eck* 6G 125
Cedar Clo. *Kil* 4A 126
Cedar Clo. *Roy* 1C 8
Cedar Clo. *S'bri* 4D 140
Cedar Clo. *Swint* 4A 56
Cedar Cres. *B'ley* 2B 24
Cedar Dri. *Maltby* 4D 82
Cedar Gro. *Con* 5C 58
Cedar Nook. *Kiv P* 5G 117
Cedar Rd. *Arm* 2G 35
Cedar Rd. *Donc* 6G 45
Cedar Rd. *S'bri* 4D 140
Cedars, The. *S10* 3H 97
Cedar St. *Holl* 2G 133
Cedar Va. *Swint* 4A 56
Cedar Way. *C'town* 3D 64
Cedric Av. *Con* 4C 58
Cedric Ct. *Thur* 5A 94
Cedric Cres. *Thur* 5A 94
Cedric Rd. *E'thpe* 5D 20
Celandine Ct. *S17* 4G 121
Celandine Gdns. *S17* 4G 121
Celandine Gro. *D'fld* 5E 27
Celandine Ri. *Swint* 5A 56
Celtic Ct. *Roth* 5H 67
Cemetery Av. *S11* 4B 98
Cemetery La. *Stav* 2C 134
Cemetery Rd. *S11* 5C 98
Cemetery Rd. *B'ley* 1A 24
Cemetery Rd. *Bol D* 2A 42
Cemetery Rd. *Ches* 3C 138
Cemetery Rd. *Dron* 3F 129

Cemetery Rd. *Grim* 6G **11**
Cemetery Rd. *Jump* 4C **38**
Cemetery Rd. *Mexb* 6E **43**
Cemetery Rd. *Wath D* 1E **55**
Cemetery Rd. *Womb* 6B **26**
Cemetery Rd. *W'land* 3C **16**
Cemetery Ter. *Brim* 4E **133**
Centenary Way. *Roth* 4C **78**
Centenary Works. Roth *3C 78*
           (off Centenary Way)
Central Av. *Ben* .1B **32**
Central Av. *Dinn* 3G **137**
Central Av. *Grim* 5G **11**
Central Av. *Roth* 2H **79**
Central Av. *S'side* 2F **81**
Central Av. *Swint* 3H **55**
Central Av. *W'land* 3C **16**
Central Boulevd. *Donc* 3H **33**
Central Bus. Pk. *Roth* 3C **78**
Central Dri. *Cal* 2F **139**
Central Dri. *Has* 4C **138**
Central Dri. *New R* 5C **62**
Central Dri. *Rawm* 5C **54**
Central Dri. *Roy* .2E **9**
Central Dri. *Thur* 5A **94**
Central M. *Dinn* 5G **107**
Central Pde. *Roth* 3H **79**
Central Pavement. Ches *2A 138*
           (off Market Pl.)
Central Rd. *Roth* 3D **78**
Central St. *Ches* 4C **138**
Central St. *Gold* 3G **29**
Central St. *Hoy* .6F **37**
Central Ter. *Ches* 3B **138**
Central Ter. *Edl'tn* 3B **60**
Central Wlk. *Brim* 4D **132**
Centre Riding. *Wadw* 6F **61**
Centre, The. *Braml* 4H **81**
Centurion Bus. Pk. *Roth* 4A **78**
Centurion Retail Pk. *Donc* 4B **32**
Centurion St. *Roth* 4A **78**
Centurion Way. *Donc* 4B **32**
Century Clo. *K Ind* 5B **20**
Century Ct. *Edl'tn* 2C **60**
Century Gdns. *Ben* 6C **18**
Century St. *S9* 5D **88**
Century Vw. *B'wth* 3A **90**
Chadbourne Clo. *Arm* 4E **35**
Chaddesden Clo. *Dron W* 2A **128**
Chaddesdon Wlk. *Den M* 1D **58**
Chadwick Dri. *Maltby* 3F **83**
Chadwick Gdns. *Ark* 5E **19**
Chadwick Rd. *S13* 6E **101**
Chadwick Rd. *Donc* 4B **32**
Chadwick Rd. *W'land* 3C **16**
Chaff Clo. *Whis* .2H **91**
Chaffinch Av. *B'wth* 3D **90**
Chaff La. *Whis* 2H **91**
Chalfont Ct. *B'wth* 3D **90**
Challands Clo. *Has* 5C **138**
Challands Way. *Has* 5C **138**
Challenger Dri. *Spro* 6G **31**
Challiner M. *Cat* .5C **90**
Challoner Grn. *W'fld* 1E **125**
Challoner Way. *W'fld* 1E **125**
Chalmers Dri. *Donc* 6B **20**
Chaloner Heights. *Bla H* 2H **37**
Chamberlain Av. *Donc* 3A **32**
Chamberlain Ct. *C'town* 1D **64**
Chambers Av. *Con* 3C **58**
Chambers Dri. *C'town* 6E **51**
Chambers Gro. *C'town* 6E **51**
Chambers La. *S4* 2B **88**
Chambers Rd. *Hoy* 4H **37**
Chambers Rd. *Roth* 6H **67**
Chambers Valley Rd. *C'town* 6E **51**
Chambers Vw. *C'town* 6E **51**
Chamossaire. *New R* 6C **62**
Champion Clo. *S5* 3H **75**
Champion Rd. *S5* 3H **75**
Chancel Way. *B'ley* 4C **14**
Chancery Pl. *Donc* 6C **32**
Chancet Ct. *S8* 6C **110**
Chancet Wood. *S8* 1D **122**
Chancet Wood Clo. *S8* 1D **122**
Chancet Wood Dri. *S8* 1D **122**
Chancet Wood Ri. *S8* 1D **122**
Chancet Wood Rd. *S8* 6D **110**
Chancet Wood Vw. *S8* 1D **122**
Chandler Gro. *Tree* 6E **91**
Chandos Cres. *Kil* 3A **126**
Chandos St. *S10* 3A **98**

Chaneyfield Way. *Ches* 4D **130**
Channing Gdns. *S6* 4B **86**
Channing St. *S6* .4B **86**
Chantrey Av. *Ches* 5H **131**
Chantrey Rd. *S8* 4D **110**
Chantry Bri. *Roth* 2D **78**
Chantry Clo. *Donc* 4E **49**
Chantry Gro. *Roy* .2E **9**
Chantry Pl. *Kiv P* 4B **118**
Chantry Vw. *Mexb* 6G **43**
Chantry Vw. *Roth* 3C **78**
Chapel Av. *Bram* 3A **40**
Chapel Clo. *S10* .4F **97**
Chapel Clo. *Birdw* 4C **36**
Chapel Clo. *Burn* 2C **64**
Chapel Clo. *Roth* 3A **68**
Chapel Clo. *Shaf* 2C **10**
Chapel Clo. *Thur* 4A **94**
Chapel Ct. *Birdw* 4C **36**
Chapel Ct. *Wath D* 6E **41**
Chapelfield Cres. *Thpe H* 2B **66**
Chapelfield Dri. *Thpe H* 2B **66**
Chapel Fld. La. *P'stne* 5C **142**
Chapelfield La. *Thpe H* 2B **66**
Chapelfield Mt. *Thpe H* 2B **66**
Chapelfield Pl. *Thpe H* 2B **66**
Chapelfield Rd. *Thpe H* 1B **66**
Chapel Fld. Wlk. *P'stne* 5C **142**
Chapelfield Way. *Thpe H* 2B **66**
Chapel Hill. *Bla H* 2H **37**
        (off Wentworth Rd.)
Chapel Hill. *Swint* 2A **56**
Chapel Hill. *Whis* 2H **91**
Chapel La. *S9* 5C **88**
Chapel La. *S17* 5D **120**
Chapel La. *B'ley* .5E **9**
Chapel La. *Bran* 3H **49**
Chapel La. *Con* .4E **59**
Chapel La. *Gt Hou* 1G **27**
Chapel La. *L Hou* 3B **28**
Chapel La. *P'stne* 5C **142**
Chapel La. *Roth* 4D **78**
Chapel La. *Thurn* 1H **29**
Chapel La. *Wort* 1G **141**
Chapel La. *E. Has* 6D **138**
Chapel La. *W. Ches* 3E **137**
Chapel M. *M'well* .4G **7**
Chapel M. *Swint* 2A **56**
Chapel Pl. *B'ley* .1F **25**
Chapel Ri. *Ans* .2F **119**
Chapel Rd. *Burn & C'town* 3C **64**
Chapel Rd. *High G* 5C **50**
Chapel Rd. *Tank* 5A **36**
Chapel St. *B'ley* .1F **25**
Chapel St. *Ben* .1B **32**
Chapel St. *Birdw* 4C **36**
Chapel St. *Bol D* .1A **42**
Chapel St. *Brim* 3F **133**
Chapel St. *Ches* 3A **132**
        (Brimington Rd.)
Chapel St. *Ches* *3A 132*
        (off Station Rd.)
Chapel St. *Greasb* 3B **68**
Chapel St. *Grim* .6G **11**
Chapel St. *Hoy* .6F **37**
Chapel St. *Mexb* 6C **42**
Chapel St. *Mosb* 3C **124**
Chapel St. *Rawm* 2F **69**
Chapel St. *Shaf* .2C **10**
Chapel St. *Thurn* 1E **29**
Chapel St. *Woodh* 1B **114**
Chapel Ter. *S10* .4F **97**
Chapeltown. 2F **65**
Chapeltown Baths. 2E **65**
Chapeltown Rd. *E'fld* 5F **65**
Chapel Vw. *Arm* 2D **34**
Chapel Vw. *Thurls* 3A **142**
        (off View Rd.)
Chapel Wlk. *S1* 2E **99** (3E **5**)
Chapel Wlk. *Ans* 3F **119**
Chapel Wlk. *Cat* .6C **90**
Chapel Wlk. *Mexb* 1E **57**
Chapel Wlk. *Rawm* 6D **54**
Chapel Wlk. *Roth* 3C **78**
        (in two parts)
Chapel Way. *Kiv P* 5H **117**
Chapel Way. *Rawm* 6D **54**
Chapelwood Rd. *S9* 5D **88**
Chapel Yd. *Dron* 1E **129**
Chapman St. *S9* .5D **76**
Chappell Clo. *H'swne* 1F **143**
Chappell Dri. *Donc* 4C **32**
Chappell Rd. *H'swne* 1F **143**

Chapter Way. *B'ley* 4C **14**
Charity St. *B'ley* .1F **15**
Charles Ashmore Rd. *S8* 1D **122**
Charles Cres. *Arm* 2D **34**
Charles Cres. Flats. *Arm* 2D **34**
Charles La. *S1* 2E **99** (4E **5**)
        (in two parts)
Charles Rd. *Wath D* 6G **41**
Charles Sq. *High G* 6B **50**
Charles St. *S1* 2E **99** (4E **5**)
        (in two parts)
Charles St. *B'ley* .1G **23**
Charles St. *Ches* 2G **137**
Charles St. *Cud* .5C **10**
Charles St. *Dinn* 3F **107**
Charles St. *Donc* 4E **33**
Charles St. *Gold* .4F **29**
Charles St. *Kiln* .6C **56**
Charles St. *L Hou* 2A **28**
Charles St. *Rawm* 6H **55**
Charles St. *Swint* 3B **56**
Charles St. *Thur* .4A **94**
Charles St. *Wors* 5A **24**
Charlotte La. *S1* .4B **4**
Charlotte Rd. *S1 & S2* 4E **99**
Charltonbrook. .1C **64**
Charlton Brook Cres. *C'town* 1C **64**
Charlton Clough. *C'town* 2B **64**
Charlton Dri. *High G* 1C **64**
Charlton Hill Ri. *C'town* 2B **64**
Charnell Av. *Maltby* 4G **83**
Charnley Av. *S11* 2A **110**
Charnley Clo. *S11* 1H **109**
Charnley Dri. *S11* 2A **110**
Charnley Ri. *S11* 2A **110**
Charnock Av. *S12* 5D **112**
Charnock Cres. *S12* 4C **112**
Charnock Dale Rd. *S12* 5C **112**
Charnock Dri. *S12* 4D **112**
Charnock Dri. *Cusw* 4H **31**
Charnock Gro. *S12* 5D **112**
Charnock Hall. .5D **112**
Charnock Hall Rd. *S12* 5C **112**
Charnock Vw. Rd. *S12* 5C **112**
Charnock Wood Rd. *S12* 5D **112**
Charnwood Ct. *Soth* 5G **115**
Charnwood Dri. *Donc* 6H **45**
Charnwood Gro. *Roth* 2H **77**
Charnwood Ho. *Swint* 2B **56**
Charnwood St. *Swint* 2B **56**
Charter Arc. *B'ley* 6H **13**
Charter Dri. *Scawt* 1F **31**
Charter Row. *S1* 3E **99** (6C **4**)
Charter Sq. *S1* 3E **99** (5D **4**)
Chasecliff Clo. *Ches* 6F **131**
Chase Rd. *S6* 3D **84**
Chase, The. *S6* .3D **84**
Chase, The. *S10* .4B **98**
        (off Clarkegrove Rd.)
Chase, The. *Ast* .1C **116**
Chatfield Rd. *S8* 5C **110**
Chatham Ho. *Roth* 3E **79**
        (off Doncaster Ga.)
Chatham St. *S3* .6E **87**
Chatham St. *Roth* 3E **79**
Chatsworth Av. *Ches* 3D **136**
Chatsworth Av. *Mexb* 5H **43**
Chatsworth Bus. Pk. *Ches* 3G **137**
Chatsworth Clo. *Ast* 6D **104**
Chatsworth Ct. *S11* 3F **109**
Chatsworth Ct. *Stav* 3B **134**
Chatsworth Cres. *Donc* 1H **31**
Chatsworth Dri. *Ross* 5F **63**
Chatsworth Pk. Av. *S12* 2C **112**
Chatsworth Pk. Dri. *S12* 2C **112**
Chatsworth Pk. Gro. *S12* 2C **112**
Chatsworth Pk. Ri. *S12* 2C **112**
Chatsworth Pk. Rd. *S12* 2C **112**
Chatsworth Pl. *Dron W* 1B **128**
Chatsworth Ri. *B'wth* 3D **90**
Chatsworth Ri. *Dod* 2A **22**
Chatsworth Rd. *S17* 3E **121**
Chatsworth Rd. *B'ley* 1A **14**
Chatsworth Rd. *Ches* 3B **136**
Chatsworth Rd. *Roth* 3B **78**
Chatterton Dri. *Roth* 5H **79**
Chaucer Clo. *S5* .3B **74**
Chaucer Dri. *Dron* 4G **129**
Chaucer Ho. Roth *4H 79*
        (off Browning Rd.)
Chaucer Rd. *S5* .4B **74**
Chaucer Rd. *Ches* 3H **131**
Chaucer Rd. *Mexb* 5F **43**

Chaucer Rd. *Roth* 5H **79**
Cheadle St. *S6* 3A **86**
Cheapside. *B'ley* 6H **13**
Checkstone Av. *Donc* 6C **48**
Chedworth Clo. *Dart* 6C **6**
Cheedale Av. *Ches* 6E **131**
Cheedale Clo. *Ches* 5F **131**
Cheedale Wlk. *Ches* 6F **131**
Cheetham Dri. *Maltby* 3G **83**
Chelmsford Av. *Ast* 5C **104**
Chelmsford Dri. *Donc* 3F **33**
Chelsea Ct. *S11* 6A **98**
Chelsea Ri. *S11* 6A **98**
Chelsea Rd. *S11* 6A **98**
Cheltenham Ri. *Donc* 4F **31**
Cheltenham Rd. *Donc* 4A **34**
Chelwood Ct. *Bal* 6C **46**
Chemist La. *Roth* 2C **78**
Cheney Row. *S1* 4E **5**
Chepstow Clo. *Ches* 5H **137**
Chepstow Dri. *Mexb* 5F **43**
Chepstow Gdns. *Ches* 6H **137**
Chepstow Gdns. *Donc* 4F **31**
Chequer Av. *Donc* 1E **47**
Chequer Rd. *Donc* 6D **32**
Cheriton Av. *Adw S* 1C **16**
Cherry Bank Rd. *S8* 4E **111**
Cherry Brook. *Roth* 1H **79**
Cherry Clo. *Cud* 5B **10**
Cherry Clo. *Roy* 1C **8**
Cherry Gth. *Ben* 4B **18**
Cherry Gro. *Con* 5B **58**
Cherry Gro. *Gold* 4E **29**
Cherry Gro. *New R* 5E **63**
Cherry Hills. *Dart* 4E **7**
Cherry La. *Donc* 5B **32**
Cherrys Rd. *B'ley* 5D **14**
Cherry St. *S2* 5E **99**
Cherry St. S. *S2* 5E **99**
Cherry Tree Clo. *S11* 6B **98**
Cherry Tree Clo. *B'wth* 3D **90**
Cherry Tree Clo. *M'well* 4G **7**
Cherry Tree Ct. *S11* 6B **98**
Cherry Tree Cres. *Wick* 4G **81**
Cherry Tree Dell. *S11* 6B **98**
Cherry Tree Dri. *S11* 6B **98**
Cherry Tree Dri. *Kil* 4B **126**
Cherry Tree Hill. **6B 98**
Cherry Tree Pl. *Wath D* 6F **41**
Cherry Tree Rd. *S11* 6B **98**
Cherry Tree Rd. *Arm* 3F **35**
Cherry Tree Rd. *Donc* 1B **46**
Cherry Tree Rd. *Maltby* 4D **82**
Cherry Tree Rd. *Wal* 5E **117**
Cherry Tree St. *Hoy & Else* 5B **38**
Cherry Wlk. *C'town* 2E **65**
Chertsey Clo. *Ches* 5H **137**
Cherwell Clo. *Brim* 2E **133**
Chesham Rd. *B'ley* 6F **13**
Cheshire Rd. *Donc* 4E **33**
Chessel Clo. *S8* 3E **111**
Chesterfield. **2A 138**
Chesterfield Av. *New W* 1E **133**
Chesterfield Crematorium. *Brim* 5D **132**
Chesterfield Golf Course. **6G 137**
Chesterfield Inner Relief Rd.
   Ches 1G **131**
Chesterfield Mus. & Art Gallery. **2B 138**
Chesterfield Rd. *S8* 5D **110**
Chesterfield Rd. *Bsvr* 6H **135**
Chesterfield Rd. *Brim* 4D **132**
Chesterfield Rd. *Cal* 3E **139**
              (Hady Hill)
Chesterfield Rd. *Cal & Duck* 3H **139**
            (Top Rd.)
Chesterfield Rd. *Dron* 2E **129**
Chesterfield Rd. *Eck* 6G **125**
Chesterfield Rd. *Holl & Stav* 3G **133**
Chesterfield Rd. *Swal* 1H **115**
          (in two parts)
Chesterfield Rd. S. *S8* 4E **123**
Chesterfield Small Bus. Cen. Ches 4A **132**
       (off Pottery La. W.)
Chesterhill Av. *Dalt* 6C **70**
Chester Ho. *Ches* 2G **137**
Chester Rd. *Donc* 3F **33**
Chester St. *Ches* 2G **137**
Chesterton Clo. *Brim* 1F **139**
Chesterton Rd. *Donc* 5C **46**
Chesterton Rd. *E'wd T* 1G **79**
Chesterton Way. *E'wd T* 6H **69**
Chesterwood Dri. *S10* 3H **97**
Chestnut Av. *S9* 2G **101**

Chestnut Av. *Arm* 2F **35**
Chestnut Av. *Beig* 2F **115**
Chestnut Av. *Brie* 3F **11**
Chestnut Av. *Donc* 2H **33**
Chestnut Av. *Eck* 6G **125**
Chestnut Av. *Kil* 4A **126**
Chestnut Av. *Kiv P* 4G **117**
Chestnut Av. *New R* 5E **63**
Chestnut Av. *Roth* 2H **79**
Chestnut Av. *S'bri* 4D **140**
Chestnut Av. *Wath D* 1F **55**
Chestnut Clo. *Dron* 3G **129**
Chestnut Clo. *Flan* 3F **81**
Chestnut Ct. *B'ley* 2H **23**
Chestnut Ct. *Ben* 5A **18**
Chestnut Cres. *B'ley* 2B **24**
Chestnut Dri. *C'town* 3C **64**
Chestnut Gro. *Con* 4C **58**
Chestnut Gro. *Dinn* 3F **107**
Chestnut Gro. *Maltby* 4D **82**
Chestnut Gro. *Mexb* 5D **42**
        (in two parts)
Chestnut Gro. *Spro* 3D **44**
Chestnut Gro. *Thurn* 2F **29**
Chestnut Rd. *Swal* 5H **103**
Chestnut Wlk. *Hoot L* 5E **83**
Chevet Ho. Donc 1C **46**
      (off St James St.)
Chevet Ri. *Roy* 1D **8**
Chevet Vw. *Roy* 1C **8**
Cheviot Dri. *Donc* 2H **31**
Cheviot Wlk. *B'ley* 5D **12**
Cheviot Way. *Ches* 6E **131**
Chevril Ct. *Wick* 5E **81**
Chichester Rd. *S10* 1H **97**
Chilcombe Pl. *Birdw* 5D **36**
Childers St. *Donc* 2E **47**
Chiltern Clo. *Ches* 1E **137**
Chiltern Ct. Ches 1E **137**
      (off Brendon Av.)
Chiltern Cres. *Spro* 2C **44**
Chiltern Ri. *B'wth* 4D **90**
Chiltern Rd. *Donc* 2H **31**
Chiltern Wlk. *B'ley* 5D **12**
Chilton St. *B'ley* 1A **24**
Chilwell Clo. *B'ley* 4B **8**
Chilwell Gdns. *B'ley* 4B **8**
Chilwell M. *B'ley* 4B **8**
Chindit Ct. *Dinn* 4F **107**
Chinley St. *S9* 6C **88**
Chippingham Pl. *S9* 5B **88**
Chippingham St. *S9* 5B **88**
Chippinghouse Rd. *S7 & S8* 6D **98**
Chiverton Clo. *Dron* 1E **129**
Chorley Av. *S10* 5C **96**
Chorley Dri. *S10* 5C **96**
Chorley Pl. *S10* 6C **96**
Chorley Rd. *S10* 6C **96**
Christchurch Av. *Ast* 5C **104**
Christchurch Flats. Wath D 4C **40**
      (off Masefield Rd.)
Christ Chu. Rd. *S3* 4F **87**
Christ Chu. Rd. *Donc* 5D **32**
Christchurch Rd. *Wath D* 4C **40**
Christ Chu. Ter. *Donc* 6E **33**
Church Av. *Rawm* 3E **69**
Church Balk. *E'thpe* 4C **20**
Church Balk Gdns. *E'thpe* 4D **20**
Church Balk La. *E'thpe* 5D **20**
Church Clo. *Dart* 5C **6**
Church Clo. *Ink* 4A **134**
Church Clo. *Kiv P* 5F **117**
Church Clo. *Maltby* 5F **83**
Church Clo. *O'bri* 2D **72**
Church Clo. *Rav* 4G **71**
Church Clo. *Swint* 2A **56**
Church Corner. *Lghtn* 6F **95**
Church Cottage M. Donc 4G **45**
Church Ct. *Ans* 3G **119**
Church Ct. *Donc* 4D **48**
Church Cft. *E'thpe* 4C **20**
Church Cft. *Rawm* 3E **69**
Churchdale Rd. *S12* 3F **113**
Church Dri. *Brie* 3F **11**
Church Dri. *W'wth* 4C **52**
Churchfield. *B'ley* 5G **13**
Churchfield Av. *Cud* 1H **15**
Churchfield Clo. *Ben* 1A **32**
Churchfield Clo. *Dart* 5A **6**
Churchfield Ct. *B'ley* 5G **13**
Churchfield Ct. *Dart* 5B **6**

Churchfield Cres. *Cud* 1H **15**
Church Fld. Dri. *Wick* 5F **81**
Churchfield Gdns. *Car* 4F **9**
Churchfield La. *Dart* 5A **6**
Church Fld. La. *W'wth* 5B **52**
Church Fields. *Roth* 2G **77**
Churchfields. *Wick* 6F **81**
Churchfields Cvn. Site. Ben 1A **32**
      (off Church St.)
Churchfields Clo. *B'ley* 5G **13**
Church Fields Rd. *Ross* 3F **63**
Churchfield Ter. *Cud* 1H **15**
Church Fld. Vw. *Bal* 4G **45**
Church Fold. *S6* 6G **73**
Church Fold. *B'ley* 5G **13**
Church Glebe. *S6* 6G **73**
Church Grn. *Spro* 3D **44**
Church Grn. *Wath D* 5E **41**
Church Grn. *B'ley* 3C **14**
Church Heights. *H'swne* 1F **143**
Church Hill. *Roy* 2F **9**
Church Hill. *Whis* 2A **92**
Churchill Av. *Donc* 3A **32**
Churchill Av. *Maltby* 3G **83**
Churchill Rd. *S10* 2A **98**
Churchill Rd. *Donc* 3E **33**
Churchill Way. *C'town* 5D **50**
Church La. *S9* 5B **88**
Church La. *S12* 4C **114**
Church La. *S17* 3D **120**
Church La. *Adw S* 1E **17**
Church La. *Ast* 1D **116**
      (in two parts)
Church La. *Barn D* 1G **21**
Church La. *Beig* 4G **115**
Church La. *Bes* 5C **48**
Church La. *Braml* 4H **81**
Church La. *Cal* 2F **139**
Church La. *Cat* 5C **90**
Church La. *Ches* 2A **138**
Church La. *Dinn* 4D **106**
Church La. *H'ton* 1G **43**
Church La. *Kil* 3C **126**
Church La. *Maltby* 5F **83**
Church La. *Rav* 4H **71**
Church La. *Tank* 2C **50**
Church La. *Tree* 1E **103**
Church La. *Wadw* 6H **61**
      (in two parts)
Church La. *Warm* 4F **45**
      (in two parts)
Church La. *Wath D* 5E **41**
Church La. *Wick* 5F **81**
Church La. *Woodh* 1B **114**
Church La. *Wors* 5G **13**
      (Churchfield)
Church La. *Wors* 1D **36**
      (Worsbrough Rd.)
Church La. M. *Braml* 4H **81**
Church Lea. *Hoy* 1A **52**
Church Mdw. Rd. *Ross* 4F **63**
Church Meadows. *Cal* 2F **139**
Church Meadows. *Dinn* 5E **107**
Church M. *Ben* 1A **32**
Church M. *Bol D* 2A **42**
Church M. *Kil* 2C **126**
Church M. *Mexb* 1G **57**
Church M. *Mosb* 2D **124**
Church Rein Clo. *Warm* 5E **45**
Church Rd. *Barn D* 1G **21**
Church Rd. *Den M* 1C **58**
Church Rd. *Edl'tn* 2B **60**
Church Rd. *Kirk S* 3D **20**
Church Rd. *Wadw* 6H **61**
Churchside. *Cal* 2F **139**
Churchside. *Has* 6D **138**
Church St. *S1* 2E **99** (3E **5**)
Church St. *S6* 6C **84**
Church St. *Arm* 3E **35**
Church St. *B'ley* 5G **13**
Church St. *Ben* 1A **32**
Church St. *Bol D* 1A **42**
Church St. *Brie* 2F **11**
Church St. *Brim* 4E **133**
Church St. *Cal* 2F **139**
Church St. *Car* 4F **9**
Church St. *Con* 3E **59**
Church St. *Cud* 1H **15**
Church St. *D'fld* 4F **27**
Church St. *Dart* 5C **6**
Church St. *Donc* 5C **32**
Church St. *Dron* 2E **129**

Church St. E'fld 6E 65
Church St. Eck 5E 125
Church St. Else 6C 38
Church St. Gawber 4C 12
Church St. Greasb 2G 77
Church St. Jump 4B 38
Church St. M'well 4G 7
Church St. Mexb 1F 57
Church St. O'bri 2C 72
Church St. P'stne 4D 142
Church St. Rawm 3E 69
Church St. Roth (S60) 3D 78
Church St. Roth (S61) 3A 68
Church St. Roy 2E 9
Church St. Stav 1C 134
Church St. Swint 2H 55
Church St. Thur 5B 94
Church St. Thurn 1E 29
Church St. Wal 5F 117
Church St. Wath D 5E 41
Church St. Womb 1F 39
Church St. Clo. Thurn 1E 29
Church St. N. Old W 1A 132
Church St. S. Ches 6H 137
(in two parts)
Church St. W. Ches 3E 137
Church Ter. Dod 2A 22
Church Town. 3C 12
Church Vw. Ast 6D 104
Church Vw. Barn 1G 43
Church Vw. B'ley 4F 13
Church Vw. Ches 3E 137
Church Vw. Cud 1H 15
Church Vw. D'fld 4G 27
Church Vw. Donc 5C 32
Church Vw. Edl'tn 4A 60
Church Vw. Hoy 6F 37
Church Vw. Kil 2C 126
Church Vw. Swint 2A 56
Church Vw. Thry 4D 70
Church Vw. Tod 2B 118
Church Vw. Wadw 6H 61
Church Vw. Wick 5F 81
Church Vw. Woodh 1C 114
Church Vw. Cres. P'stne 4D 142
Church Vw. Rd. P'stne 4D 142
Church Wlk. Ches 2A 138
(off Stephenson Pl.)
Church Wlk. Den M 1C 58
Church Wlk. Thurn 1E 29
(off Church St.)
Church Way. Adw S 1D 16
Church Way. Ches 2A 138
Church Way. Donc 5C 32
Churcroft. B'ley 3C 12
Churston Rd. Ches 2F 137
Cinder Bri. Rd. Roth 3C 68
Cinderhill La. S8 ....1F 123
Cinder Hill La. Gren & E'fld 1B 74
Cinderhill Rd. Roth 5G 67
Cinder Hills Way. Dod 2C 22
Cinder La. Kil 2D 126
Circle Clo. S2 ....5D 100
Circle, The. S2 ....4C 100
Circle, The. High G 6C 50
Circle, The. New R 4C 62
Circuit, The. W'land 1B 16
Circular Rd. Has 5B 138
Circular Rd. Stav 3B 134
City Rd. S2 & S12 ....3H 99
City Road Cemetery & Crematorium.
S2 ....5A 100
Clanricarde St. B'ley 3G 13
Clara Pl. K'wth 3H 77
Clare Ct. Roth 2D 78
Clarehurst Rd. D'fld 3E 27
Clarel Clo. P'stne 5C 142
Clarel Gdns. Donc 2C 48
Clarel St. P'stne 5C 142
Claremont Cres. S10 ....2B 98
Claremont Pl. S10 ....2B 98
Claremont St. Roth 3H 77
Clarence Av. Donc 3B 46
Clarence La. S3 ....4D 98
Clarence Pl. Maltby 3G 83
Clarence Rd. S6 ....3H 85
Clarence Rd. B'ley 3B 14
Clarence Rd. Ches 2H 137
Clarence Sq. Dinn 4G 107
Clarence St. Ches 2H 137
Clarence St. Dinn 4G 107
Clarence St. Wath D 4C 40
Clarendon Ct. S11 ....5E 97

Clarendon Dri. S10 ....5E 97
Clarendon Rd. S10 ....5E 97
Clarendon Rd. Ink 5A 134
Clarendon Rd. Roth 2F 79
Clarendon St. B'ley 6F 13
Clark Av. Donc 1E 47
Clark Av. Edl'tn 5B 60
Clarke Av. Dinn 2C 106
Clarke Av. Thur 5C 94
Clarke Ct. Dinn 3F 107
Clarke Dell. S10 ....4B 98
Clarke Dri. S10 ....4B 98
Clarkegrove Rd. S10 ....4B 98
Clarkehouse Rd. S10 ....4A 98
Clarkes Cft. Womb 6B 26
Clarke Sq. S2 ....5D 98
Clarke St. S10 ....3C 98 (6A 4)
Clarke St. B'ley 4F 13
Clarke St. Thurn 1G 29
Clark Gro. S6 ....5D 84
Clarks Cft. Adw S 1D 16
Clarkson Av. Ches 5H 137
Clarkson St. S10 ....2C 98
Clarkson St. Wors 4C 24
Clark St. Hoy 4H 37
Clarney Av. D'fld 3D 26
Clarney Pl. D'fld 3E 27
Claycliffe Av. B'ley 3B 12
Claycliffe Bus. Pk. B'ley 2B 12
Claycliffe Rd. Bar G & B'ley 1B 12
Claycliffe Ter. B'ley 1F 23
Claycliffe Ter. Gold 4G 29
Clayfield Av. Mexb 6H 43
Clayfield Clo. Mexb 6H 43
Clayfield Ct. Mexb 6H 43
Clayfield La. W'wth 4D 52
Clayfield Rd. Hoy 3H 37
Clayfield Rd. Mexb 6H 43
Clayfields. Donc 6A 46
Clayfield Vw. Mexb 5H 43
(in three parts)
Clay Flat La. New R 5D 62
Clay La. S1 ....5E 5
Clay La. Donc 6B 20
Clay La. W. Donc 5A 20
(in two parts)
Clay Pit La. Rawm 2G 69
Clay Pits La. S'bri 2A 140
Clayroyd. Wors 5B 24
Clay St. S9 ....4B 88
(in two parts)
Clayton Av. Thurn 1D 28
Clayton Cres. Wat 5E 115
Clayton Dri. Thurn 1D 28
Clayton Hollow. Wat 5E 115
Clayton La. Thurn 1D 28
Clayton St. Ches 3B 138
Clay Wheels La. S6 ....5H 73
Claywood Dri. S2 ....3G 99 (6H 5)
Claywood Rd. S2 ....3G 99 (5H 5)
(Claywood Dri.)
Claywood Rd. S2 ....4G 99
(Granville Rd.)
Clayworth Dri. Donc 5H 47
Clear Vw. Grim 5G 11
Clearwell Cft. Cusw 4H 31
Cleeve Hill Gdns. Wat 5D 114
Clematis Rd. S5 ....6B 76
Clement M. Roth 3G 77
Clementson Rd. S10 ....1A 98
Clement St. S9 ....5D 88
Clement St. Roth 3G 77
Clevedon Cres. Donc 6H 17
Clevedon Way. Maltby 2H 83
Clevedon Way. Roy 1D 8
Cleveland Rd. Arm 3G 35
Cleveland St. S6 ....6C 86
Cleveland St. Donc 1C 46
Cleveland Way. Ches 1D 136
Cliff Ct. Den M 2B 58
Cliff Cres. Warm 5E 45
Cliff Dri. D'fld 4G 27
Cliffe Av. Wors 4B 24
Cliffe Bank. Swint 2B 56
Cliffe Clo. Brie 2F 11
Cliffe Ct. B'ley 4C 14
Cliffe Cres. Dod 2A 22
Cliffedale Cres. Wors 3B 24
Cliffe Farm Dri. S11 ....6G 97
Cliffe Fld. Rd. S8 ....2D 110
Cliffefield Rd. Swint 2B 56
Cliffe Ho. Rd. S5 ....5F 75

Cliffe La. B'ley 4C 14
Cliffe Rd. S6 ....5G 85
Cliffe Rd. Bram 3A 40
Cliffe Vw. Rd. S8 ....2E 111
Cliff Hill. Maltby 4D 82
Cliff Hills Clo. Maltby 4E 83
Cliff La. Brie 3E 11
Cliff La. Con 6H 57
Clifford Av. Thry 5E 71
Clifford Clo. Ches 3D 136
Clifford Lister Bus. Cen., The.
Wick 5E 81
Clifford Rd. S11 ....6B 98
Clifford Rd. H'by 5A 82
Clifford Rd. Roth 6G 67
Clifford St. Cud 4C 10
Clifford Wlk. Den M 2A 58
Cliff Rd. S6 ....5D 84
Cliff Rd. D'fld 4G 27
Cliff St. S11 ....4D 98
Cliff St. Mexb 1E 57
Cliff Ter. B'ley 6A 14
Cliff Vw. Den M 1B 58
Clifton. 2F 79
Clifton Av. S9 ....2G 101
Clifton Av. B'ley 5A 8
Clifton Av. Roth 3G 79
Clifton Bank. Roth 3E 79
Clifton Clo. B'ley 5A 8
Clifton Cres. S9 ....2F 101
Clifton Cres. Donc 3H 33
Clifton Cres. N. Roth 3F 79
Clifton Cres. S. Roth 3F 79
Clifton Dri. Spro 1F 45
Clifton Gdns. Brie 2E 11
Clifton Gro. Roth 3F 79
Clifton Hill. Con 4E 59
Clifton La. S9 ....3G 101
Clifton La. Con 5F 59
Clifton La. Roth 3E 79
Clifton Mt. Roth 3E 79
Clifton Pk. Mus. 3F 79
Clifton Ri. Maltby 3E 83
Clifton Rd. Grim 6G 11
Clifton St. S9 ....3D 88
Clifton St. B'ley 1A 24
Clifton St. Ches 2G 137
Clifton Ter. Con 3F 59
Clifton Ter. Roth 3E 79
Clinton La. S10 ....3C 98 (6A 4)
Clinton Pl. S10 ....4C 98 (6A 4)
Clinton Wlk. S10 ....3C 98 (6A 4)
Clipstone Av. B'ley 5B 8
Clipstone Gdns. S9 ....5E 89
Clipstone Rd. S9 ....5E 89
Clixby Rd. S9 ....4B 88
Cloisters, The. Donc 4E 49
Cloisters, The. Wors 1D 36
Cloisters Way. B'ley 4B 14
Cloonmore Cft. S8 ....6G 111
Cloonmore Dri. S8 ....6G 111
Close, The. B'ley 4E 15
Close, The. Bran 3H 49
Close, The. Car 4E 15
Close, The. Dinn 5F 107
Cloudberry Way. M'well 5H 7
Clough Bank. S2 ....5F 99
Clough Bank. Roth 2B 78
(in two parts)
Clough Fields. 1F 97
Clough Fields. S10 ....1F 97
Clough Fields Rd. Hoy 6G 37
Clough Grn. Roth 2C 78
Clough Gro. O'bri 2E 73
Clough Head. P'stne 6D 142
Clough La. S10 ....2A 108
Clough Rd. S1 & S2 ....4E 99
Clough Rd. Hoy 6H 37
Clough Rd. Roth 3B 78
(in two parts)
Clough St. Roth 2B 78
Clough, The. Ches 4E 139
Clough Wood Vw. O'bri 3D 73
Clovelly Rd. E'thpe 5D 20
Clover Ct. S8 ....5H 111
Clover Gdns. S5 ....6A 76
Clover Grn. Roth 5G 67
Cloverlands Dri. M'well 5G 7
Clover Wlk. Bol D 6D 28
Club Garden Rd. S11 ....5D 98
(in two parts)
Club Garden Wlk. S11 ....4D 98
(off London Rd.)

Club Mill Rd. *S6* 2C **86**
Clubmill Ter. *Ches* 1G **137**
Club St. *S11* 5D **98**
Club St. *B'ley* 3C **14**
Club St. *Hoy* 6F **37**
Clumber Pl. *Ink* 5A **134**
Clumber Ri. *Ast* 1C **116**
Clumber Rd. *S10* 4E **97**
Clumber Rd. *Donc* 2F **47**
Clumber St. *B'ley* 5E **13**
Clun Rd. *S4* 5G **87**
Clun St. *S4* 5G **87**
Clyde Rd. *S8* 1D **110**
Clyde St. *B'ley* 6H **13**
Coach Ho. Dri. *Donc* 5F **31**
Coach Ho. La. *B'ley* 3H **23**
Coach Houses, The. S10 . . . . .1B **98**
(off Moorgate Av.)
Coach Rd. *Roth* 3B **68**
Coach Rd. *W'wth* 4H **51**
Coal Aston. 5G **123**
Coalbrook Av. *S13* 5D **102**
Coalbrook Gro. *S13* 5D **102**
Coalbrook Rd. *S13* 5D **102**
Coalby Wlk. B'ley 5G **13**
(off Prospect St.)
Coal Pit La. *Brie* 3D **10**
Coal Pit La. *O'bri* 4A **72**
Coal Pit La. *S'bri* 5D **140**
Coalpit La. *Wal* 6F **117**
Coalpit Rd. *Den M* 2A **58**
Coal Riding La. *Roth* 3D **80**
Coates St. *S2* 3G **99**
Cobb Ct. *Swint* 4B **56**
Cobb Dri. *Swint* 4A **56**
Cobcar Av. *Else* 6D **38**
Cobcar Clo. *Else* 5C **38**
Cobcar La. *Else* 5C **38**
Cobcar St. *Else* 6C **38**
Cock Alley. .4G **139**
Cockayne Pl. *S8* 2D **110**
Cockerham Av. *B'ley* 4G **13**
Cockerham La. *B'ley* 4G **13**
Cockhill La. *S'ton* 6A **60**
(in two parts)
Cockpit La. *P'stne* 4D **142**
Cockshot La. *Deep* 5E **141**
Cockshot Pit La. *M'well* 5E **7**
Cockshutt Av. *S8* 1B **122**
Cockshutt Dri. *S8* 1B **122**
Cockshutt St. *S8* 1B **122**
Cockshutts La. *O'bri* 1B **72**
Coggin Mill Way. *Roth* 4A **78**
Coisley Hill. 2H **113**
Coisley Hill. *S13* 1H **113**
Coisley Rd. *S13* 2A **114**
Coit La. *S11* 4D **108**
Coke Hill. *Roth* 4D **78**
Coke La. *Roth* 4D **78**
Colbeck Clo. *Arm* 3E **35**
Colby Pl. *S6* 6F **85**
Colchester Ct. *Donc* 3G **31**
Colchester Rd. *S10* 1H **97**
Coldstream Av. *Warm* 5F **45**
Coldwell Hill. *O'bri* 2B **72**
Coldwell La. *S10* 2E **97**
Coldwell's Fold. *Thurls* 3A **142**
Coleford Rd. *S9* 5E **89**
Coleman St. *P'gte* 4F **69**
Coleridge Av. *B'ley* 3B **14**
Coleridge Gdns. *S9* 5D **88**
Coleridge Rd. *S9* 4C **88**
Coleridge Rd. *Barn D* 1H **21**
Coleridge Rd. *Maltby* 5G **83**
Coleridge Rd. *Roth* 2F **79**
Coleridge Rd. *Wath D* 4C **40**
Coley La. *Bram B & W'wth* 6H **39**
Colister Dri. *S9* 1E **101**
Colister Gdns. *S9* 2D **100**
College Av. *Stav* 2B **134**
College Clo. *S4* 3G **87**
College Ct. *S4* 3G **87**
College Ct. *Mexb* 6F **43**

College La. *Roth* 3D **78**
(off College St.)
College Pk. Clo. *Roth* 6E **79**
College Rd. *Donc* 1C **46**
(in two parts)
College Rd. *Mexb* 6F **43**
College Rd. *Roth* 3B **78**
(in two parts)
College Rd. Roundabout.
Roth 2C **78**
College St. *S10* 3B **98**
College St. *Roth* 3D **78**
College Ter. *D'fld* 4E **27**
College Wlk. Roth 2D **78**
(off Frederick St.)
College Wlk. Shop. Cen.
Roth 2D **78**
(off Frederick St.)
Collegiate Cres. *S10* 4B **98** (6A **4**)
Colley Av. *B'ley* 3E **75**
Colley Av. *B'ley* 3C **24**
Colley Clo. *S5* 3E **75**
Colley Cres. *S5* 3F **75**
Colley Cres. *B'ley* 2C **24**
Colley Dri. *S5* 3F **75**
Colley Pl. *B'ley* 2C **24**
Colley Rd. *S5* 3E **75**
Collier Rd. *Shaf* 4C **10**
Colliers Clo. *S13* 1B **114**
Collier St. *Bram* 4H **39**
Colliery Clo. *Dinn* 3E **107**
Colliery Clo. *Stav* 2D **134**
Colliery La. *Thurn* 3F **29**
Colliery Rd. *S4* 2C **88**
Colliery Rd. *Kiv P* 5H **117**
Colliery Vs. *Thur* 3B **94**
Colliery Yd. *Tank* 1B **50**
Collin Av. *S6* 2G **85**
Collindridge Rd. *Womb* 1F **39**
Collingbourne Av. *Soth* 6G **115**
Collingbourne Dri. *Soth* 6G **115**
Collingham Rd. *Swal* 1A **116**
Collins Clo. *Dod* 2A **22**
Collinson Rd. *S5* 5E **75**
Collins Yd. Dron 2F **129**
(off Mill La.)
Collishaw Clo. *Has* 5C **138**
Colne Ct. *Roth* 1E **91**
Colonel Ward Dri. *Swint* 2C **56**
Colonnades Shop. Cen. Donc 6C **32**
(off Duke St.)
Colster Clo. *B'ley* 5C **12**
Coltfield. *Birdw* 2D **36**
Coltishall Av. *Braml* 3H **81**
Colton Clo. *Ches* 2G **131**
Columbia St. *B'ley* 2G **23**
Columbus Way. *Maltby* 3E **83**
Colver Rd. *S2* 5E **99**
(in two parts)
Colvin Clo. *Ark* 6E **19**
Colwall St. *S9* 5B **88**
Commerce St. *C'town* 1F **65**
Commercial Rd. *Gold* 5E **29**
Commercial St. *S1* 2F **99** (3G **5**)
Commercial St. *B'ley* 1A **24**
Common Farm Clo. *Rav* 1H **81**
Common La. *S11* 1D **108**
Common La. *Ark* 2G **19**
Common La. *Bram M* 6G **93**
Common La. *Con & Clif* 6F **59**
Common La. *Cut* 3A **130**
Common La. *Deep* 5G **141**
Common La. *Harw* 6F **63**
Common La. *Rav* 1A **82**
Common La. *Roy* 1E **9**
(in two parts)
Common La. *Thur* 6D **94**
Common La. *Warm* 5F **45**
Common La. *Wath D* 5H **41**
(Doncaster Rd.)
Common La. *Wath D* 3B **42**
(Mexborough Rd., in two parts)
Common Rd. *Ans* 3D **106**
(Monk's Bri. Rd.)
Common Rd. *Ans* 4A **106**
(Pocket Handkerchief La.)
Common Rd. *Brie* 3G **11**
Common Rd. *Con* 4G **59**
Common Rd. *Thurn* 1D **28**
Common Side. 2B **112**
Commonside. *S10* 1A **98**
Common, The. *E'fld* 6F **65**
Commonwealth Vw. *Bol D* 1H **41**

Companions Clo. *Wick* 5F **81**
Compton St. *S6* 5H **85**
Compton St. *Ches* 2H **137**
Conalan Av. *S17* 4H **121**
Conanby. 3C **58**
Conan Rd. *Con* 3D **58**
Concorde M. *Donc* 5D **32**
Concord Leisure Cen. 4A **76**
Concord Rd. *S5* 3A **76**
Concord Vw. Rd. *Roth* 4E **77**
Conduit La. *S10* 1A **98**
Conduit Rd. *S10* 1A **98**
Conery Clo. *Thry* 5E **71**
Coney Rd. *Toll B* 3A **18**
Congress St. *S1* 2D **98** (3C **4**)
Coningsburgh Rd. *E'thpe* 5D **20**
Coningsby Ho. *S10* 3D **96**
Coningsby Rd. *S5* 2G **87**
Conisborough Castle. 3E **59**
Conisborough Castle Vis. Cen. 3E **59**
Conisbrough. 3E **59**
Coniston Av. *Dart* 3E **7**
Coniston Clo. *Ans* 1H **119**
Coniston Clo. *P'stne* 3D **142**
Coniston Ct. *Mexb* 5H **43**
Coniston Dri. *Bol D* 2A **42**
Coniston Dri. *Donc* 1F **61**
Coniston Pl. *Donc* 1H **31**
Coniston Rd. *S8* 2C **110**
Coniston Rd. *B'ley* 6A **14**
Coniston Rd. *Ches* 3F **131**
Coniston Rd. *Donc* 5A **34**
Coniston Rd. *Dron W* 3B **128**
Coniston Rd. *Kirk S* 3D **20**
Coniston Rd. *Mexb* 5G **43**
Coniston Ter. *S8* 2C **110**
Coniston Way. *Ches* 3F **131**
Connaught Dri. *Kirk S* 3D **20**
Connelly Ct. *Ches* 2G **137**
Conrad Dri. *Maltby* 3E **83**
Constable Clo. *S14* 5H **111**
Constable Clo. *Dron* 2C **128**
Constable Clo. *Flan* 3F **81**
Constable Dri. *S14* 5H **111**
Constable La. *Dinn* 4F **107**
Constable Pl. *S14* 5A **112**
Constable Rd. *Wath D* 5E **41**
Constable Rd. *S14* 5H **111**
Constable Way. *Dalt* 6A **70**
Constitution Hill. *Cad* 1F **59**
(in two parts)
Convent Gro. *Donc* 3B **48**
Convent Pl. *S3* 2D **98** (4B **4**)
Convent Wlk. *S3* 2D **98** (4B **4**)
Conway Ct. *Bes* 6B **48**
Conway Cres. *Roth* 1A **80**
Conway Dri. *Barn* 1G **43**
Conway Dri. *Bran* 3H **49**
Conway Pl. *Womb* 2H **39**
Conway St. *S3* 2C **98** (1A **4**)
Conway St. *B'ley* 1D **24**
Conway Ter. *Mexb* 5E **43**
Conyers Dri. *Ast* 5B **104**
Conyers Rd. *Donc* 4B **32**
Coo Hill. *S13* 1C **114**
Cook Av. *Maltby* 3E **83**
Cooke & Beard Homes. *S8* 2F **111**
Cooke St. *Ben* 1A **32**
Cookson Clo. *S5* 5B **74**
Cookson Rd. *S5* 6B **74**
Cookson St. *Donc* 3B **46**
Cooks Rd. *Beig* 5G **115**
Cooks Wood Rd. *S3* 4E **87**
Coole Well Clo. *Stav* 3B **134**
Coombe Pl. *S10* 2A **98**
Coombe Rd. *S10* 2A **98**
Co-operative Cotts. *Brie* 2F **11**
Co-operative Cotts. *Pool* 4E **135**
Co-operative St. *Cud* 1G **15**
Co-operative St. *Gold* 4G **29**
Co-operative St. *Wath D* 4D **40**
Cooper Clo. *Bram* 5A **40**
Cooper Gallery. 5H **13**
Cooper Rd. *Dart* 5A **6**
Coopers Ter. *Donc* 6D **32**
Cooper St. *Donc* 2E **47**
Copeland Rd. *Womb* 1E **39**
Cope St. *B'ley* 2H **23**
Copley Av. *Con* 3C **58**
Copley Cres. *Donc* 3E **31**
Copley Gdns. *Spro* 3D **44**

Copley Pl. *Roth* 1A **78**
Copley Rd. *Donc* 5D **32**
Copley St. *S8* 1E **111**
Copper Beech Clo. *Beig* 4G **115**
Copper Beech Cres. *Hoot L* 6E **83**
Copper Clo. *B'ley* 1H **23**
Copper St. *S3* 1E **99** (1D **4**)
Coppice Av. *B'ley* 3D **12**
Coppice Clo. *Has* 6D **138**
Coppice Clo. *S'bri* 2B **140**
Coppice Gdns. *Roth* 5B **68**
Coppice La. *S6* 1B **96**
Coppice La. *Harl* 4H **51**
Coppice Rd. *S10* 2B **96**
Coppice Rd. *High* 5D **16**
Coppice, The. *Roth* 5E **67**
Coppice Vw. *S10* 2F **97**
Coppicewood Ct. *Bal* 1H **61**
Coppins Clo. *Braml* 3H **81**
Coppin Sq. *S5* 2D **74**
Copse, The. *Braml* 3H **81**
Coquet Av. *Braml* 5H **81**
Coral Clo. *Aug* 3A **104**
Coral Dri. *Aug* 3A **104**
Coral Pl. *Aug* 3A **104**
Coral Way. *Aug* 3A **104**
Corby Rd. *S4* 2B **88**
Corby St. *S4* 5H **87**
Cordwell Av. *Ches* 3E **131**
Cordwell Clo. *Stav* 3B **134**
Corker Bottoms. **3C 100**
Corker Bottoms La. *S2* 2B **100**
Corker Rd. *S12* 1C **112**
Cornfield Clo. *Ash* 6C **130**
Corn Hill. *Con* 4F **59**
Cornish St. *S6* 6D **86**
(in two parts)
Cornish Way. *P'gte* 5E **69**
Cornwall Av. *Brim* 3F **133**
Cornwall Clo. *B'ley* 3B **14**
Cornwall Clo. *Brim* 3F **133**
Cornwall Dri. *Brim* 3F **133**
Cornwall Rd. *Donc* 4H **33**
Cornwell Clo. *Rawm* 5C **54**
Coronach Way. *New R* 5C **62**
Coronation Av. *Dinn* 3F **107**
Coronation Av. *Kiv P* 5G **117**
Coronation Av. *Roy* 1G **9**
Coronation Av. *Shaf* 2B **10**
Coronation Bri. *Roth* 3B **78**
Coronation Cotts. *Barn D* 1G **21**
Coronation Ct. *Mexb* 5E **43**
Coronation Cres. *Birdw* 2D **36**
Coronation Dri. *Birdw* 2D **36**
Coronation Dri. *Bol D* 1H **41**
Coronation Gdns. *Warm* 5E **45**
Coronation Rd. *Bar G* 3A **12**
Coronation Rd. *Brim* 3E **133**
Coronation Rd. *Donc* 4B **46**
Coronation Rd. *Hoy* 5H **37**
Coronation Rd. *Rawm* 1A **70**
Coronation Rd. *S'bri* 3D **140**
Coronation Rd. *Swint* 2C **56**
Coronation Rd. *Wath D* 5G **41**
Coronation St. *B'ley* 3C **14**
Coronation St. *D'fld* 3F **27**
Coronation St. *Thurn* 1G **29**
Coronation Ter. *B'ley* 1F **25**
Coronation Ter. *H'fld* 3E **39**
Corporation Bldgs. *S3* 2F **5**
Corporation St. *S3* 1E **99** (1E **5**)
Corporation St. *B'ley* 2A **24**
Corporation St. *Ches* 2B **138**
(in two parts)
Corporation St. *Roth* 3D **78**
Cortina Ri. *D'fld* 3C **26**
Corton Wood Dri. *Bram* 3H **39**
Cortonwood Ho. Donc 1C **46**
(off Bond Clo.)
Cortworth. 4F **53**
Cortworth La. *W'wth* 4F **53**
Cortworth Pl. *Else* 5D **38**
Cortworth Rd. *S11* 3G **109**
Corve Way. *Ches* 6B **130**
Corwen Pl. *S13* 1A **114**
Cosgrove Ct. *E'thpe* 5E **21**
Cossey Rd. *S4* 5H **87**
Coterel Cres. *Donc* 2D **48**
Cotleigh Av. *S12* 4A **114**
Cotleigh Clo. *S12* 4A **114**
Cotleigh Cres. *S12* 4A **114**
Cotleigh Dri. *S12* 4A **114**
Cotleigh Gdns. *S12* 4A **114**

Cotleigh Pl. *S12* 4A **114**
Cotleigh Rd. *S12* 4A **114**
Cotleigh Way. *S12* 4A **114**
Cotswold Av. *C'town* 2C **64**
Cotswold Clo. *B'ley* 5D **12**
Cotswold Clo. *Ches* 6E **131**
Cotswold Cres. *Whis* 2A **92**
Cotswold Dri. *Ast* 6C **104**
Cotswold Dri. *Spro* 2C **44**
Cotswold Gdns. *Donc* 2H **31**
Cotswold Rd. *S6* 3H **85**
Cottage Clo. *Pool* 3E **135**
Cottage La. *S11* 2C **108**
Cottam Clo. *Whis* 2A **92**
Cottam Rd. *High G* 6A **50**
Cottenham Rd. *Roth* 2F **79**
Cotterdale Gdns. *Womb* 6D **26**
Cotterhill La. *Brim* 4E **133**
Cottesmore Clo. *B'ley* 4E **13**
Cotton Mill Hill. *Holy* 6A **136**
Cotton Mill Row. *S3* 6E **87** (1E **5**)
Cotton Mill Wlk. *S3* 6E **87**
Cotton St. *S3* 6E **87** (1E **5**)
Coultas Av. *Deep* 5F **141**
Countess Rd. *S1* 4E **99**
County Ct. *B'ley* 5H **13**
County Way. *B'ley* 5H **13**
(in two parts)
Coupe Rd. *S3* 5F **87**
Coupland Rd. *Roth* 1A **80**
Court Clo. *Donc* 3F **31**
Court Pl. *Stav* 3A **134**
Courtyard, The. *B'ley* 6C **12**
Courtyard, The. *Old De* 2G **57**
Coventry Gro. *Donc* 2H **33**
Coventry Rd. *S9* 6E **89**
Cover Clo. *Harl* 4H **51**
Coverdale Rd. *S7* 2C **110**
Cover Dri. *D'fld* 3F **27**
Coverleigh Rd. *Wath D* 1F **55**
Cow Clo. *O'bri* 2D **72**
Cow Ho. La. *Arm* 3G **35**
Cow La. *S11* 4G **109**
(Abbey La.)
Cow La. *S11* 2E **133**
(Greystones)
Cow La. *Brim* 2E **133**
Cowley. **4B 128**
Cowley Clo. *Ches* 2B **138**
Cowley Dri. *C'town* 3G **65**
Cowley Gdns. *W'fld* 1E **125**
Cowley Grn. *Womb* 1D **38**
Cowley Hill.
C'town & Thpe H 3G **65**
Cowley La. *C'town* 2F **65**
Cowley La. *Holm* 3A **128**
Cowley Pl. *Kirk S* 3D **20**
Cowley Rd. *O'bri* 3D **72**
Cowley Vw. Clo. *C'town* 3E **65**
Cowley Vw. Rd. *C'town* 3F **65**
Cowlishaw Rd. *S11* 5A **98**
Cowood St. *Mexb* 1D **56**
Cowper Av. *S6* 3B **74**
Cowper Cres. *S6* 3B **74**
Cowper Dri. *S6* 3B **74**
Cowper Dri. *Roth* 5H **79**
Cowper Rd. *Mexb* 6F **43**
Cowpingle La. *Brim* 2E **133**
(in two parts)
Cowrakes Clo. *Whis* 2A **92**
Cow Rakes La. *Whis* 2A **92**
Coxley Clo. *Ross* 5F **63**
Coxley Mt. *Ross* 4G **63**
Cox Pl. *S6* 2F **85**
Cox Rd. *S6* 2F **85**
Crabtree Av. *S5* 3G **87**
Crabtree Clo. *S5* 2G **87**
Crabtree Ct. *B'ley* 1F **25**
Crabtree Cres. *S5* 2G **87**
Crabtree Dri. *S5* 2G **87**
Crab Tree Hill La.
H'swne 1E **143**
Crabtree La. *S5* 2G **87**
Crabtree Pl. *S5* 2G **87**
Crabtree Rd. *S5* 2F **87**
Cradley Dri. *Ast* 6C **104**
Cradock M. *S2* 6A **100**
Cradock Rd. *S2* 6A **100**
Craganour Pl. Den M 2B **58**
(off Bolton St.)
Cragdale Gro. *Mosb* 2D **124**
Craglands Gro. *Ches* 6C **130**

Cragside Clo. *Ches* 2C **138**
Crags Rd. *Den M* 2D **58**
Crag Vw. Clo. *O'bri* 1D **72**
Crag Vw. Cres. *O'bri* 1D **72**
Craigholme Cres. *Donc* 2A **34**
Craig Wlk. *Braml* 1E **81**
Craithie Rd. *Donc* 5F **33**
Crakehall Rd. *E'fld* 4D **64**
Cramfit Clo. *Ans* 1F **119**
Cramfit Cres. *Dinn* 4D **106**
Cramfit Rd. *Ans* 6C **106**
Cramlands. *Dod* 2C **22**
Cranborne Dri. *Dart* 4D **6**
Cranborne Rd. *Ches* 4G **131**
Cranbrook Rd. *Donc* 4E **33**
Cranbrook St. *B'ley* 1F **23**
Crane Dri. *Roth* 2G **77**
Crane Moor Clo. *H'ton* 1G **43**
Crane Rd. *Roth* 5G **67**
Crane Well La. *Bol D* 1C **42**
Cranfield Clo. *Arm* 4F **35**
Cranford Ct. *Owl* 5A **114**
Cranford Dri. *Owl* 4A **114**
Cranford Gdns. *Roy* 1D **8**
Cranleigh Gdns. *Adw S* 2C **16**
Cranleigh Rd. *Mas M* 1F **135**
Cranston Clo. *B'ley* 3D **14**
Cranswick Way. Con 3G **59**
(off Milner Ga. Ct.)
Cranwell Ct. *Gold* 5E **29**
Cranwell Rd. *Cant* 4F **49**
Cranworth Clo. *Roth* 2G **79**
Cranworth Pl. *S3* 5F **87**
Cranworth Rd. *S3* 5F **87**
Cranworth Rd. *Roth* 1F **79**
Craven Clo. *S9* 6E **89**
Craven Clo. *Donc* 3C **48**
Craven Clo. *Roy* 1D **8**
Craven Rd. *Ches* 6H **131**
Craven St. *S3* 1D **98** (1B **4**)
Craven St. *P'gte* 4F **69**
Craven Wood Clo. *B'ley* 4C **12**
Crawford Rd. *S8* 3D **110**
Crawshaw Av. *S8* 1B **122**
Crawshaw Gro. *S8* 1B **122**
Crawshaw Rd. *Donc* 1A **46**
Cream St. *S2* 4F **99**
Crecy Av. *Donc* 5A **34**
Creighton Av. *Rawm* 2H **69**
Cresacre Av. *Barn* 1G **43**
Crescent E., The. *S'side* 2G **8**
Crescent End, The. *Thur* 5B **94**
Crescent Rd. *S7* 6C **98**
Crescent Rd. *Holy* 6A **136**
Crescent, The. *S17* 4E **121**
Crescent, The. *Arm* 4G **35**
Crescent, The. *B'ley* 3D **12**
Crescent, The. *Bol D* 6F **29**
Crescent, The. *Brim* 4C **132**
Crescent, The. *Con* 3C **58**
Crescent, The. *Cud* 6B **10**
Crescent, The. *Dinn* 4G **107**
Crescent, The. *E'thpe* 5E **21**
Crescent, The. *Edl'tn* 2B **60**
Crescent, The. *Holy* 6A **136**
Crescent, The. *Hood G* 6A **22**
Crescent, The. *Roth* 2E **79**
Crescent, The. *Swint* 3H **55**
Crescent, The. *Thur* 5B **94**
Crescent, The. *W'land* 3B **16**
Crescent W., The. *S'side* 2F **81**
Cresswell Rd. *S9* 1E **101**
Cresswell Rd. *Swint* 3B **56**
Cresswell St. *B'ley* 5E **13**
Crest Rd. *S5* 5F **75**
Crestwood Ct. *S5* 5G **75**
Crestwood Gdns. *S5* 5G **75**
Creswell St. *Mexb* 1D **56**
Creswick Av. *S5* 2C **74**
Creswick Clo. *Ches* 5D **136**
Creswick Clo. *Roth* 1B **80**
Creswick Greave. *Gren* 2C **74**
Creswick Greave Clo. *S5* 2C **74**
Creswick La. *Gren* 1C **74**
Creswick Rd. *Roth* 1B **80**
Creswick St. *S6* 5B **86**
(in two parts)
Creswick Way. *S6* 5B **86**
Crewe Hall. *S10* 4A **98**
Crich Av. *B'ley* 6C **8**
Crich Rd. *Ink* 4A **134**
Cricketers Wlk. S2 . . . . .1H **99**
(off St John's Rd.)

Cricket Inn Cres. S2 . . . . .2A 100
Cricket Inn Rd. S2 . . . . .1G 99 (2H 5)
                (in two parts)
Cricket La. E'fld 1G 75
Cricket Vw. Rd. Harl 4H 51
Crimicar Av. S10 . . . . .5B 96
Crimicar Clo. S10 . . . . .6C 96
Crimicar Dri. S10 . . . . .5B 96
Crimicar La. S10 . . . . .4B 96
Crimpsall. 6A 32
Crimpsall Rd. Donc 1B 46
Cripps Av. New R 4E 63
Cripps Clo. Maltby 5H 83
Crispin Clo. S12 . . . . .3C 112
Crispin Dri. S12 . . . . .3C 112
Crispin Gdns. S12 . . . . .3C 112
Crispin Rd. S12 . . . . .3C 112
Crochley Clo. Donc 2D 48
Croft Av. Roy 2D 8
Croft Bldgs. S1 . . . . .2D 4
Croft Clo. S11 . . . . .4F 109
Croft Clo. Lghtn 6F 95
Croft Clo. Womb 2H 39
Croft Ct. E'thpe 4D 20
Croft Dri. M'well 4E 7
Crofters Clo. Kil 5A 126
Crofters Ct. Bal 6C 46
Croft La. S11 . . . . .4F 109
Croft Lea. Dron W 1A 128
Crofton Av. S6 . . . . .1H 85
Crofton Clo. Dron 2D 128
Crofton Dri. Bol D 6E 29
Crofton Ri. High G 1B 64
Crofton Ri. Dron 2D 128
Croft Rd. S6 .5D 84
Croft Rd. S12 . . . . .2D 112
Croft Rd. B'ley 2C 24
Croft Rd. B'wth 2B 90
Croft Rd. Donc 6G 45
Croft Rd. Hoy 4H 37
Crofts Dri. Thry 5C 70
Crofts, The. Roth 3D 78
Crofts, The. Wick 6F 81
Croft St. Roth 4B 68
Croft St. Wors 4A 24
Croft, The. Ard 5D 18
Croft, The. B'ley 2A 12
Croft, The. Cat 6C 90
Croft, The. Con 4E 59
Croft, The. Else 1C 52
Croft, The. H'swne 1F 143
Croft, The. Swint 3H 55
Croft Vw. Ink 5A 134
Cromarty Ri. Dron W 1B 128
Cromer Clo. Rawm 1F 69
Cromer Rd. Donc 5A 34
Cromford Av. B'ley 1B 14
Cromford Clo. Donc 5E 49
Cromford Ct. Ches 4F 131
          (off Bowness Rd.)
Cromford Dri. Stav 3H 133
Cromford St. S2 . . . . .4F 99
Crompton Av. B'ley 1F 23
Crompton Av. Donc 5H 31
Crompton Rd. Donc 1H 33
Crompton Rd. Stav 1D 134
Cromwell Dri. Donc 1G 45
Cromwell Ho. Donc 4G 31
Cromwell Mt. Wors 3G 23
Cromwell Rd. Ches 1H 137
Cromwell Rd. Donc 4B 32
Cromwell Rd. Mexb 6E 43
Cromwell St. S6 . . . . .6A 86
Cronkhill La. B'ley 4F 9
                (in two parts)
Crooked La. Con 6H 57
Crooke Ho. La. B'ley 1D 26
Crookes. 2H 97
Crookes. S10 .1H 97
Crookes La. B'ley 4D 8
                (in two parts)
Crookesmoor. 1B 98
Crookesmoor Dri. S6 . . . . .1B 98
Crookesmoor Rd. S6 & S10 . . . . .2A 98
Crookes Rd. S10 . . . . .2A 98
Crookes Rd. Donc 5A 46
Crookes St. B'ley 6F 13
Crookes Valley Rd. S10 . . . . .1B 98
Crookhill Clo. Edl'tn 4A 60
Crookhill Pk. Golf Course. 6G 59
Crookhill Rd. Con 3F 59
Cropston Clo. Ches 6C 138
Cropton Rd. Roy 2D 8

Crosby Av. Braml 1E 81
Crosby Ct. B'ley 2D 14
Crosby Rd. S8 . . . . .4D 110
Crosby St. Cud 5B 10
Cross Allen Rd. Beig 5F 115
Cross Bank. Donc 4B 46
Cross Bedford St. S6 . . . . .6C 86
Cross Burgess St. S1 . . . . . . .2E 99 (4E 5)
Cross Butcher St. Thurn 1E 29
Cross Chantrey Rd. S8 . . . . .4E 111
Crosscourt Vw. Bes 3A 48
Cross Dri. S13 . . . . .1B 114
Crossfield Dri. Wath D 6E 41
Crossfield Gdns. High G 5B 50
Cross Ga. Donc 3A 32
Crossgate. M'well 4F 7
Cross Ga. Mexb 1G 57
Crossgate. Thurn 2F 29
Crossgates. Wadw 6H 61
Cross Gilpin St. S6 . . . . .5C 86
Cross Hill. Brie 2F 11
Cross Hill. E'fld 2G 75
Cross Hill Clo. S5 . . . . .2G 75
Cross Ho. Clo. Gren 1H 73
Cross Ho. Rd. Gren 1A 74
Cross Keys La. Hoy 5E 37
Crossland Dri. S12 . . . . .4C 112
Crossland Pl. S12 . . . . .3C 112
Crossland St. Swint 3B 56
Crossland Way. Donc 1G 31
Crossland Way Flats.
     Donc 2G 31
Cross La. S10 .1H 97
Cross La. S17 . . . . .1C 120
Cross La. Coal A 4G 123
                (Dyche La.)
Cross La. Coal A 6G 123
              (Green La.)
Cross La. Dron 2E 129
Cross La. Roy 2E 9
Cross La. S'bri 5A 142
         (Hornthwaite Hill Rd.)
Cross La. S'bri 2A 140
          (Smithy Moor La.)
Cross La. Wort .3A 50
Crossley Clo. Maltby 3E 83
Cross Myrtle Rd. S2 . . . . .6F 99
Cross Pk. Rd. S8 . . . . .2E 111
Crosspool. 3F 97
Cross Rd. Thur 4A 94
Cross Smithfield. S3 . . . . . . .1D 98 (1C 4)
Cross St. St. Roth 4C 68
Cross St. S13 . . . . .1B 114
Cross St. B'ley 3C 14
Cross St. B'ley 4F 13
Cross St. Bar G 3A 12
Cross St. Ben .6B 18
Cross St. Braml 4H 81
Cross St. Brim 3E 133
Cross St. Ches 1H 137
Cross St. Donc 4A 46
Cross St. Edl'tn 3B 60
Cross St. Gold 4H 29
Cross St. Greasb 4C 68
Cross St. Hoy .6F 37
Cross St. Kil .2D 126
Cross St. K'wth 3A 78
Cross St. Maltby 4G 83
Cross St. New R 5D 62
Cross St. P'gte 4F 69
Cross St. Thry .5C 70
Cross St. Wath D 5E 41
Cross St. Wors 3B 24
Cross, The. 2G 75
Cross Turner St. S2 . . . . . . .3F 99 (5G 5)
Cross Wlk. S11 . . . . .4D 98
          (off London Rd.)
Crossway. Swint 3H 55
Crossways. Bol D 1A 42
Crossways. Donc 2H 33
Crossways N. Donc 2H 33
Crossways S. Donc 3H 33
Crossways, The. S2 . . . . .4D 100
Crowden Wlk. B'ley 6C 12
Crowder Av. S5 . . . . .5D 74
Crowder Clo. S5 . . . . .6E 75
Crowder Cres. S5 . . . . .6E 75
Crowder Rd. S5 . . . . .5E 75
Crowgate. Ans 4E 119
Crowland Rd. S5 . . . . .5F 75
Crow La. Ches 2B 138
Crowley Dri. Wath D 1E 55
Crown Av. B'ley 2A 24

Crown Clo. B'ley 2A 24
Crown Co. Roth 1G 77
Crown Hill Rd. B'ley 6C 12
Crownhill Rd. B'wth 2A 90
Crown Pl. S2 . . . . .2G 99 (3H 5)
Crown Rd. Ches 6A 132
Crown St. B'ley 2A 24
Crown St. Hoy .5H 37
Crown St. Swint 2B 56
Crown Well Ct. B'ley 1F 25
        (off Coronation Ter.)
Crown Well Hill. Ard 1F 25
Crowther Pl. S7 . . . . .5D 98
Crow Tree La. Adw D 3D 42
                (in two parts)
Croydon St. S11 . . . . .5D 98
Cruck Clo. Dron W 1B 128
Cruise Rd. S11 . . . . .5F 97
Crummock Rd. S7 . . . . .2C 110
Crummock Way. B'ley 1H 25
Crumpsall Dri. S5 . . . . .2D 86
Crumpsall Rd. S5 . . . . .1D 86
Crumwell Rd. Roth 5F 67
Crusader Dri. Spro 6G 31
Crystal Peaks Shop. Cen.
     Cry P 5E 115
Cubley. 6C 142
Cubley Brook Ct. P'stne 5C 142
Cudley Ri. Rd. P'stne 6C 142
Cudworth. 6B 10
Cudworth Vw. Grim 6G 11
Cullabine Rd. S2 . . . . .6C 100
Cull Row. Deep 4H 141
Cumberland Av. Donc 5H 33
Cumberland Clo. Hoy 4A 38
Cumberland Clo. Wors 4H 23
Cumberland Cres. C'town 3F 65
Cumberland Dri. B'ley 1F 25
Cumberland Pl. Den M 2B 58
Cumberland Rd. Hoy 4A 38
Cumberland St. S1 . . . . .3E 99 (6D 4)
Cumberland Way. S1 . . . . . .3E 99 (6D 4)
Cumberland Way. Bol D 2A 42
Cumbrian Wlk. B'ley 5D 12
Cumwell La. H'by 6A 82
Cundy Cross. 5E 15
Cundy St. S6 . . . . .6A 86
Cunliffe St. Coal A 5G 123
Cunningham Rd. Donc 1D 46
Cupola. S3 . . . . .1E 99 (1D 4)
Cupola La. Gren 6A 64
Cupola Yd. Roth 3C 78
Curbar Curve. Ink 5H 133
Curlew Av. Eck 6B 124
Curlew Ct. Ross 4E 63
Curlew Ridge. S2 . . . . .3H 99
Curlew Ri. Thpe H 1C 66
Curzen Cres. Kirk S 3E 21
Curzon Av. Dron 3D 128
Curzon Co. Kil 3B 126
Cusworth. 4F 31
Cusworth Gro. Ross 5F 63
Cusworth Hall. .5F 31
      (S. Yorkshire Mus. of Life)
Cusworth Ho. Donc 1C 46
           (off St James St.)
Cusworth La. Donc 4F 31
Cusworth Pk. Country Pk. 5E 31
Cusworth Rd. Donc 2A 32
Cuthbert Bank Rd. S6 . . . . .4B 86
Cuthbert Rd. S6 . . . . .4B 86
Cutler Clo. Kil .2H 125
Cutlers Av. B'ley 1F 23
Cutlers Wlk. S2 . . . . .6E 99
Cuttholme Clo. Ches 1D 136
Cuttholme Rd. Ches 1D 136
Cuttholme Way. Ches 1E 137
Cutthorpe. 4B 130
Cutthorpe Common End. 4C 130
Cutthorpe Grange. Ches 4C 130
Cutthorpe Rd. Ches 4B 130
Cutts Av. Wath D 6D 40
Cutts Fld. Vw. Roy 1D 8
Cutts Ter. S8 . . . . .6D 98
Cutty La. B'ley .4F 13
Cyclops St. S4 .3A 88
Cygnet Clo. Bram 4H 39
Cypress Av. S8 . . . . .6G 111
Cypress Clo. Kil 4A 126
Cypress Ga. C'town 3D 64
Cypress Gro. Con 5B 58
Cypress Rd. B'ley 2B 24
Cyprus Rd. S8 . . . . .2E 111

Cyprus Ter. *S6* 5B **86**
(off Burgoyne Rd.)

D

Dade Av. *Ink* 5H **133**
Daffodil Rd. *S5* 6B **76**
Dagnam Clo. *S2* 1B **112**
Dagnam Cres. *S2* 6B **100**
Dagnam Dri. *S2* 6B **100**
Dagnam Pl. *S2* 1C **112**
Dagnam Rd. *S2* 6B **100**
Daisy Bank. *S3* 1C **98** (1A **4**)
Daisy Wlk. *S3* 1D **98** (2B **4**)
Daisy Wlk. *Beig* 4F **115**
Dalbury Rd. *Dron W* 2A **128**
Dalby Gdns. *Soth* 6G **115**
Dalby Gro. *Soth* 5H **115**
Dale Av. *Roth* 4A **80**
Dalebrook Ct. *S10* 4E **97**
Dalebrook M. *S10* 4E **97**
Dale Clo. *B'ley* 6C **8**
Dale Clo. *Stav* 3A **134**
Dale Ct. *Rawm* 2F **69**
Dale Grn. Rd. *Wors* 5H **23**
Dale Gro. *Bol D* 2H **41**
Dale Hill Clo. *Maltby* 3F **83**
Dale Hill Rd. *Maltby* 3D **82**
Dale Rd. *Con* 3E **59**
Dale Rd. *Dron* 3F **129**
Dale Rd. *Kil* 3C **126**
Dale Rd. *Rawm* 2F **69**
Dale Rd. *Roth* 5A **80**
Dale Rd. *Wick* 5E **81**
Dale Side. *S10* 4H **97**
Dale St. *Rawm* 1F **69**
Daleswood Av. *B'ley* 6D **12**
Daleswood Dri. *Wors* 4D **24**
Dale, The. *S8* 4D **110**
Daleview Rd. *S8* 5B **110**
Dalewood Av. *S8* 6A **110**
Dalewood Clo. *Ches* 4E **139**
Dalewood Dri. *S8* 6H **109**
Dalewood Rd. *S8* 6A **110**
Dalmore Rd. *S7* 2A **110**
Dalton. **1A 80**
Dalton Ct. *S8* 6D **98**
Dalton Ct. *Den M* 2B **58**
Dalton Ho. *Roth* 6H **79**
Dalton La. *Roth* 6B **70**
Dalton Magna. **2D 80**
Dalton Parva. **1B 80**
Dalton Ter. *B'ley* 1A **24**
Damer St. *S10* 2B **98**
Dam Head. *Roth* 2B **68**
Dam Ings La. *Ast* 6E **105**
Damon Dri. *Brim* 3F **133**
Damson Cft. *Holl* 1G **133**
Damsteads. *Donc* 2C **22**
Danby Av. *Old W* 1B **132**
Danby Rd. *Kiv P* 4B **118**
Danebrook Clo. *S2* 4E **101**
Danebrook Ct. *S2* 4E **101**
Danebrook Dri. *S2* 4E **101**
Danesthorpe Clo. *Donc* 3A **34**
Dane St. *Thurn* 1G **29**
Dane St. N. *Thurn* 1G **29**
Dane St. S. *Thurn* 1G **29**
Danesway. *Donc* 6H **17**
Danethorpe Way. *Con* 5C **58**
Danewood Av. *S2* 4E **101**
Danewood Cft. *S2* 4E **101**
Danewood Gdns. *S2* 4E **101**
Danewood Gro. *S2* 4E **101**
Daniel Hill. *S6* 6C **86**
Daniel Hill Ct. *S6* 6B **86**
Daniel Hill M. *S6* 6C **86**
Daniel Hill St. *S6* 6B **86**
Daniel Hill Ter. *S6* 6C **86**
Daniel Hill Wlk. *S6* 6C **86**
Daniel La. *Rawm* 1B **68**
Daniels Dri. *Aug* 4A **104**
Dannemora Clo. *S9* 4E **89**
Dannemora Dri. *S9* 4E **89**
Danum Ct. *Den M* 2B **58**
Danum Dri. *Roth* 2F **79**
Danum Retail Pk. *Donc* 4A **32**
Danum Rd. *Donc* 1F **47**
Dara St. S9 . . . . .5D **76**
(off Fife St.)
Darcy Clo. *Swal* 5B **104**
Darcy Rd. *Eck* 6C **124**

Daresbury Clo. *S2* 1H **111**
Daresbury Pl. *S2* 1H **111**
Daresbury Pl. *S2* 1H **111**
Daresbury Rd. *S2* 1H **111**
Daresbury Vw. *S2* 1H **111**
Darfield. **4F 27**
Darfield Av. *Owl* 5H **113**
Darfield Clo. *Owl* 5H **113**
Darfield Clo. *Ross* 4F **63**
Darfield Ho. Donc 1C **46**
(off St James St.)
Darfield Rd. *Cud* 2H **15**
Dargle Av. *Donc* 4G **33**
Darhaven. *D'fld* 3E **27**
Dark La. *B'ley* 2D **22**
Dark La. *Brim* 1E **139**
Dark La. *Cal* 3F **139**
Dark La. *Wors* 6B **24**
Darley Av. *B'ley* 1A **14**
Darley Av. *Wors* 3G **23**
Darley Cliff Cotts. *Wors* 3B **24**
Darley Clo. *B'ley* 6C **8**
Darley Clo. *H'hill* 3H **127**
Darley Clo. *Stav* 2C **134**
Darley Gro. *S6* 4D **84**
Darley Gro. *Wors* 4C **24**
Darley Pk. *Roth* 4H **77**
Darley Ter. *B'ley* 5F **13**
Darley Yd. *Wors* 4B **24**
Darnall. **1E 101**
Darnall Dri. *S9* 6D **88**
Darnall Rd. *S9* 5C **88**
Darnley Dri. *S2* 5C **100**
Darrington Dri. *Warm* 6F **45**
Darrington Pl. *B'ley* 4E **15**
Dartmouth Rd. *Donc* 5F **49**
Darton. **4C 6**
Darton Hall Clo. *Dart* 4D **6**
Darton Hall Dri. *Dart* 4D **6**
Darton La. *Dart & M'well* 5D **6**
Dartree Clo. *D'fld* 1D **24**
Dartree Clo. *D'fld* 3D **26**
Dartree Wlk. *D'fld* 3D **26**
Dart Sq. *S3* 1C **98** (2A **4**)
Darwall Clo. *High G* 5B **50**
Darwent La. *Worr* 5B **72**
Darwent Rd. *Ches* 5C **132**
Darwin Av. *Ches* 6G **131**
Darwin Clo. *S10* 3F **97**
Darwin La. *S10* 3F **97**
Darwin Rd. *S6* 1H **85**
Darwin Rd. *Ches* 1H **137**
Darwin Yd. Else 1D **52**
(off Distillery Side)
Darwynn Av. *Swint* 2G **55**
Davey La. *Thurn* 3F **29**
Davian Way. *Ches* 5G **137**
David Clo. *S13* 6D **102**
David La. *S10* 6A **96**
Davies Dri. *Swint* 4B **56**
Davis Clo. *Dalt* 6B **70**
Davis St. *Roth* 2G **79**
Davy Dri. *Maltby* 3F **83**
Davy Dri. *S'side* 2F **81**
Davy Rd. *Den M* 2A **58**
Dawber La. *Kil* 2D **126**
Daw Cft. Av. *Wors* 4A **24**
Dawlands Clo. *S2* 3D **100**
(in two parts)
Dawlands Dri. *S2* 4D **100**
Daw La. *Ben* 5B **18**
Dawson Av. *Rawm* 5C **54**
Dawson Cft. *Roth* 3A **68**
Dawson La. *Wath D* 1E **55**
Dawson La. *Kiv P* 5H **117**
Daw Wood. *Ben* 4C **18**
Dayhouse La. *B'ley* 2D **12**
Dayhouse Way. *B'ley* 3D **12**
Daykin Clo. *Dart* 5B **6**
Daylands Av. *Con* 4C **58**
Day St. *B'ley* 1G **23**
Deacon Clo. *Ross* 4F **63**
Deacon Cres. *Maltby* 5G **83**
Deacon Cres. *New R* 4C **62**
Deacons Way. *B'ley* 4C **14**
Deadman's Hole La. *S9* 5G **77**
Deadman's Hole La. *Roth* 4A **78**
Deakins Wlk. *S10* 4F **97**
Dean Clo. *Ross* 4F **63**
Dean Clo. *Spro* 1F **45**
Deane Fld. Vw. *Wat* 5D **114**
Deanhead Ct. *Owl* 5A **114**

Deanhead Dri. *Owl* 5H **113**
Dean La. *Roth* 3C **80**
Deansfield Clo. *Arm* 4F **35**
Dean St. *B'ley* 6F **13**
Deans Way. *B'ley* 3C **14**
Dearden Ct. *E'fld* 1F **75**
Dearne. **4G 29**
Dearne Clo. *Womb* 2H **39**
Dearne Ct. *S9* 1C **88**
Dearne Hall Fold. *Bar G* 1B **12**
Dearne Hall Rd. *Bar G* 1B **12**
Dearne Mills - Darton Bus. Pk.
Dart 5C **6**
Dearne Rd. *Bram* 3A **40**
Dearne Rd. *Wath D & Bol D* . . .3G **41**
Dearne Rd. Flatlets. Bol D . . . .
(off Dearne Rd.)
Dearneside Leisure Cen. 5G **29**
Dearne St. *S9* 1C **88**
Dearne St. *Con* 2F **59**
Dearne St. *Dart* 4D **6**
Dearne Valley Parkway. *Hoy* . . .5E **37**
Dearne Valley Parkway. *L Hou* . .4A **28**
Dearne Valley Parkway. *Womb* . .2A **40**
Dearne Vw. *Gold* 4F **29**
Dearneway. *Wath D* 5F **41**
Dearnley Vw. *B'ley* 3F **13**
Deben Clo. *Ches* 5E **137**
Decoy Bank. *Donc* 3D **46**
Decoy Bank N. *Donc* 2D **46**
Decoy Bank S. *Donc* 3D **46**
Deepcar. **3H 141**
Deepdale Cft. *Bar G* 2B **12**
Deepdale Rd. *Roth* 3G **77**
Deep La. *S5* 2A **76**
Deep Pit. **5B 100**
Deepwell Av. *Half* 3F **125**
Deepwell Bank. *Half* 3F **125**
Deepwell Ct. *Half* 3F **125**
Deepwell Vw. *Half* 3F **125**
Deerlands Av. *S5* 3C **74**
Deerlands Clo. *S5* 3C **74**
Deerlands Mt. *S5* 3B **74**
Deerlands Rd. *Ches* 2D **136**
Deer Leap Dri. *Thry* 5E **71**
Deer Pk. Clo. *S6* 5E **85**
Deer Pk. Pl. *S6* 5E **85**
Deer Pk. Rd. *S6* 5E **85**
Deer Pk. Rd. *Thry* 4E **71**
Deer Pk. Vw. *S6* 5E **85**
Deer Pk. Way. *S6* 5F **85**
De Houton Clo. *Tod* 2A **118**
Deightonby St. *Thurn* 1G **29**
De Lacy Dri. *Wors* 4A **24**
Delamere Clo. *Soth* 5G **115**
De La Salle Dri. *S4* 4G **87**
Delf St. *S2* 6F **99**
Della Av. *B'ley* 1F **23**
Dell Av. *Grim* 5G **11**
Dell Cres. *Donc* 2H **45**
Dell, The. *Ches* 2D **136**
Delmar Way. *Flan* 3F **81**
Delph Bank. *Ches* 5G **137**
Delph Edge. *Wort* 1G **141**
Delph Ho. Rd. *S10* 2F **97**
Delta Pl. *Roth* 2H **79**
Delta Way. *Maltby* 3H **83**
Delves Av. *S12* 3C **114**
Delves Clo. *S12* 3C **114**
Delves Clo. *Ches* 4F **137**
Delves Dri. *S12* 4C **114**
Delves La. *Ben* 5B **18**
Delves Pl. *S12* 4B **114**
Delves Rd. *S12* 4B **114**
Delves Rd. *Kil* 3B **126**
Delves Ter. *S12* 4B **114**
Denaby Av. *Con* 4B **58**
Denaby La. *Old De & Den M* . . .6E **57**
Denaby La. Ind. Est. *Den M* . . .2A **58**
(Coal Pit Rd.)
Denaby La. Ind. Est. *Den M* . . .2A **58**
(Pitman Rd.)
Denaby Main. **1C 58**
Den Bank. **2E 97**
Den Bank Av. *S10* 2E **97**
Den Bank Clo. *S10* 2F **97**
Den Bank Cres. *S10* 2E **97**
Den Bank Dri. *S10* 2E **97**
Denbrook La. *Con* 5F **59**
Denby Rd. *B'ley* 6B **8**
Denby Rd. *Ink* 4A **134**
Denby St. *S2* 4D **98**
Denby St. *Ben* 5A **18**

Denby Way. *H'by* 4A **82**
Dene Clo. *Wick* 5G **81**
Dene Cres. *Roth* 1H **79**
Denehall Rd. *Kirk S* 4E **21**
Dene La. *S3* 3D **98** (6B **4**)
Dene Rd. *Roth* 1H **79**
Denham Rd. *S11* 4C **98**
Denholme Clo. *S3* 6F **87**
Denison Rd. *Donc* 1B **46**
Denman Rd. *Wath D* 5D **40**
Denman St. *Roth* 1E **79**
Denmark Rd. *S2* 1F **111**
Denson Clo. *S2* 1F **111**
Dent La. *S12* 5H **113**
Dentons Grn. La. *Kirk S* 3D **20**
Denton St. *B'ley* 5H **13**
Derby Pl. *S2* 1G **111**
Derby Rd. *Ches & Wing* 6A **138**
Derby Rd. *Donc* 1A **34**
Derbyshire Ct. *S8* 4F **111**
Derbyshire Ct. *Arm* 2H **35**
Derbyshire La. *S8* 2D **110**
Derby St. *S2* 1F **111**
Derby St. *B'ley* 6F **13**
Derby Ter. *S2* 1G **111**
Derriman Av. *S11* 3H **109**
Derriman Clo. *S11* 3H **109**
Derriman Dri. *S11* 3H **109**
Derriman Glen. *S11* 3H **109**
Derriman Gro. *S11* 3H **109**
Derry Gro. *Thurn* 2E **29**
Derwent Clo. *Ans* 6F **107**
Derwent Clo. *B'ley* 6D **8**
Derwent Clo. *Dron* 6F **123**
Derwent Ct. *S17* 4G **121**
Derwent Ct. *Roth* 1F **91**
Derwent Cres. *B'ley* 6D **8**
Derwent Cres. *B'wth* 4B **90**
Derwent Cres. *Ches* 4F **131**
Derwent Dri. *C'town* 2C **64**
Derwent Dri. *Kirk S* 4D **20**
Derwent Dri. *Mexb* 5G **43**
Derwent Dri. *Rawm* 3F **69**
Derwent Gdns. *Gold* 5G **29**
Derwent Ho. Ches 4F **131**
(off Ullverston Rd.)
Derwent Pl. *Spro* 2D **44**
Derwent Pl. *Womb* 2H **39**
Derwent Rd. *B'ley* 6C **8**
Derwent Rd. *Dron* 6F **123**
Derwent Rd. *Mexb* 5G **43**
Derwent Rd. *Roth* 4A **68**
Derwent St. *S2* 1H **99**
Derwent Ter. *Mexb* 5E **43**
Derwent Way. *Wath D* 3B **40**
De Sutton Pl. *H'hill* 4H **127**
Deveron Rd. *Half* 2F **125**
Devizes Clo. *Ches* 5H **137**
Devon Ct. *Den M* 3B **58**
Devon Dri. *Brim* 3F **133**
Devon Pk. Vw. *Brim* 3F **133**
Devon Rd. *S4* 3G **87**
Devonshire Av. E. *Has* 5C **138**
Devonshire Clo. *S17* 3F **121**
Devonshire Clo. *Ches* 3H **131**
Devonshire Clo. *Dron* 3D **128**
Devonshire Clo. *Stav* 1C **134**
Devonshire Ct. *S17* 3F **121**
Devonshire Ct. *Brim* 4D **132**
Devonshire Dri. *S17* 2E **121**
Devonshire Dri. *Ans* 5E **107**
Devonshire Dri. *B'ley* 3F **13**
Devonshire Glen. *S17* 3F **121**
Devonshire Gro. *S17* 3E **121**
Devonshire La. *S1* 2D **98** (4C **4**)
Devonshire Pk. *Brim* 3E **133**
Devonshire Rd. *S17* 2E **121**
Devonshire Rd. *Donc* 4H **33**
Devonshire Rd. *Maltby* 3G **83**
Devonshire Rd. E. *Has* 5C **138**
Devonshire St. *S3* 2D **98** (4B **4**)
Devonshire St. *Brim* 3E **133**
Devonshire St. Ches 2A **138**
(off Holywell St.)
Devonshire St. *Roth* 3B **78**
Devonshire St. *Stav* 1C **134**
Devonshire Ter. Rd. *S17* 2D **120**
Devonshire Vs. Ches 3H **131**
(off Occupation Rd.)
Dewar Dri. *S7* 3A **110**
Dewhill Av. *Whis* 2H **91**
Dial Clo. *S5* 5G **75**
Dial Ho. Rd. *S6* 3G **85**

Dial, The. *S5* 5H **75**
Dial Way. *S5* 5G **75**
Diamond St. *Womb* 6B **26**
Dickan Gdns. *Arm* 4H **35**
Dickens Clo. *Cat* 5B **90**
Dickenson Ct. *C'town* 2D **64**
Dickenson Rd. *Ches* 4B **138**
Dickens Rd. *Rawm* 6H **55**
Dickey La. *S6* 4G **73**
Dickinson Pl. *B'ley* 2H **23**
Dickinson Rd. *S5* 2H **75**
Dickinson Rd. *B'ley* 2H **23**
Didcot Clo. *Ches* 5H **137**
Digby Clo. *Roth* 1G **77**
Dike Hill. *Harl* 4A **52**
Dikelands Mt. *High G* 1B **64**
Dillington Rd. *B'ley* 2H **23**
Dillington Sq. *B'ley* 2H **23**
Dillington Ter. B'ley 2H **23**
(off Hornby St.)
Dingle Bank. *Cal* 4E **139**
Dingle La. *Cal* 4E **139**
(in two parts)
Dinmore Clo. *Donc* 1G **61**
Dinnington. 4F **107**
Dinnington Bus. Cen.
Dinn 3E **107**
Dinnington Rd. *S8* 3D **110**
Dinnington Rd. *Tod* . . . . . .1B **118** & 6A **106**
(in two parts)
Dirleton Dri. *Warm* 5F **45**
Discovery Way. *Maltby* 3D **82**
Discovery Way. *Whit M* 2A **132**
Disraeli Gro. *Maltby* 3E **83**
Distillery M. *Else* 1D **52**
Distillery Side. *Else* 1D **52**
Ditchingham St. *S4* 5G **87**
Division La. *S1* 2E **99** (4D **4**)
Division St. *S1* 2D **98** (4C **4**)
Division St. *Stav* 3A **134**
Dixon La. *S1* 1F **99** (2G **5**)
Dixon Rd. *S6* 2H **85**
Dixon Rd. *Ches* 3B **138**
Dixon Rd. *Edl'tn* 3A **60**
Dixon St. *S6* 6D **86**
Dixon St. *Roth* 2E **79**
Dobbin St. *S11* 6G **97**
Dobbin Hill. *S11* 1G **109**
Dobbin La. *Barl* 6A **128**
Dobcroft Av. *S7* 5H **109**
Dobcroft Clo. *S11* 3G **109**
Dobcroft Rd. *S11 & S7* 3G **109**
Dobie St. *B'ley* 1H **23**
Dobroyd Ter. *Jump* 4B **38**
Dobson Pl. *Ink* 5H **133**
Dobsyke Clo. *Wors* 4D **24**
Dockin Hill Rd. *Donc* 5D **32**
Dock Wlk. *Ches* 3G **137**
Doctor La. *S9* 5C **88**
Dodds Clo. *Roth* 5C **78**
Dodd St. *S6* 4A **86**
Dodson Dri. *S13* 3H **101**
Dodworth St. *Mexb* 1D **56**
Dodworth. 2B **22**
Dodworth Bottom. 3B **22**
Dodworth Bus. Pk. *Dod* 1A **22**
Dodworth Grn. Rd. *Dod* 3A **22**
Dodworth Rd. *B'ley* 1C **22**
Doe La. *Wors* 6G **23**
Doe Quarry La. *Dinn* 3F **107**
Doe Quarry Pl. *Dinn* 4G **107**
Doe Quarry Ter. *Dinn* 4F **107**
Doe Royd Cres. *S5* 4B **74**
Doe Royd Dri. *S5* 4C **74**
Doe Royd La. *S5* 4B **74**
Dog Cft. La. *Ark* 6G **19**
Dog Hill. *Shaf* 2B **10**
Dog Hill Dri. *Shaf* 2C **10**
Dog Kennels Hill. *Kiv S* 5D **118**
Dog Kennels La. *Kiv S & Ans* 5D **118**
Dog La. *B'ley* 6G **13**
Dolcliffe Clo. *Mexb* 6D **42**
Dolcliffe Common. 6F **43**
Dolcliffe Rd. *Mexb* 6E **43**
Doles Av. *Roy* 2D **8**
Doles Cres. *Roy* 2D **8**
Doles La. *Whis* 3A **92**
Doleswood Dri. *Lghtn* 1E **107**
Dome Leisure Cen., The. 2H **47**
Domine La. *Roth* 3D **78**
Dominoe Gro. *S12* 2F **113**
Don Av. *S6* 6G **73**

Doncaster. 6C **32**
Doncaster Ga. *Roth* 3E **79**
Doncaster Golf Course. 1E **63**
Doncaster Ind. Pk. *Donc* 3H **31**
Doncaster International Railport.
Donc 3D **46**
Doncaster La. *W'land* 2E **17**
(in two parts)
Doncaster Leisure & Bus. Pk. 2H **47**
Doncaster Mus. & Art Gallery. 6D **32**
Doncaster Pl. *Roth* 2G **79**
Doncaster Race Course. 1H **47**
Doncaster Rd. *Arm & Bran* 3D **34**
Doncaster Rd. *Barn* 1H **43**
(in two parts)
Doncaster Rd. *B'ley & S'foot* 6H **13**
Doncaster Rd. *Bran* 3H **49**
Doncaster Rd. *Cant & Bran* 3F **49**
Doncaster Rd. *Con* 3F **59**
Doncaster Rd. *Dalt & Thry* 6A **70**
Doncaster Rd. *D'tld* 3F **27**
Doncaster Rd. *E'thpe & Kirk S* 5B **20**
Doncaster Rd. *Gold & Hick* 4G **29**
Doncaster Rd. *H'ton* 1F **43**
Doncaster Rd. *Mexb* 1F **57**
Doncaster Rd. *Pick* 3A **16**
Doncaster Rd. *Roth* 3E **79**
Doncaster Rd. *Thry & Con* 2E **71**
Doncaster Rd. *Toll B* 2H **17**
Doncaster Rd. *Wath D* 5G **41**
Doncaster Rovers F.C. 1G **47**
Doncaster Squash Club. 6E **33**
Doncaster St. *S3* 1D **98** (1C **4**)
Doncaster Town Moor Golf Course.
. . . . .6A **34**
Don Dri. *B'ley* 2D **24**
Donetsk Way. *S12* 5B **114**
Don Hill Height. *Wort & Deep* 1E **141**
Donnington Rd. *S2* 4H **99**
Donnington Rd. *Mexb* 5H **43**
Donovan Clo. *S5* 6C **74**
Donovan Rd. *S5* 6C **74**
Don Pottery Yd. *Swint* 2D **56**
Don Rd. *S9* .4B **88**
Donstone Vw. *Dinn* 5D **106**
Don St. *Con* 2F **59**
Don St. *Donc* 4D **32**
Don St. *P'stne* 5F **143**
Don St. *Roth* 4D **78**
Don Ter. *Thurls* 3B **142**
Don Valley Stadium. 5C **88**
Don Vw. *Donc* 3E **31**
Don Vw. Row. *Mexb* 6H **43**
Dorchester Pl. *Mexb* 4H **23**
Dorcliffe Lodge. *S10* 5G **97**
Dore. 2D **120**
Dore & Totley Golf Course. 4B **122**
Dore Clo. *S17* 2G **121**
Dore Ct. S17 . . . . .2G **121**
(off Ladies Spring Ct.)
Dore Ho. Ind. Est. *S13* 5C **102**
Dore Rd. *S17* 2D **120**
Dorking St. *S4* 6G **87**
Dorothy Hyman Sports Cen. 1H **15**
Dorothy Rd. *S6* 2H **85**
Dorothy Va. *Ches* 1E **137**
Dorset Av. *Brim* 3F **133**
Dorset Clo. *Brim* 3F **133**
Dorset Cres. *Donc* 4A **34**
Dorset Dri. *Brim* 3F **133**
Dorset St. *S10* 3C **98**
Douglas Rd. *S3* 5D **86**
Douglas Rd. *Ches* 5C **132**
Douglas Rd. *Donc* 4G **45**
Douglas St. *Roth* 3E **79**
Douse Cft. La. *S10* 1A **108**
Dovebush Way. *Bar G* 2B **12**
Dovecliffe Rd. *Womb* 6E **25**
Dove Clo. *Bol D* 1B **42**
Dove Clo. *Womb* 2H **39**
Dovecote La. *Rav* 4G **71**
Dovecote M. *Monk B* 3C **14**
Dovecott Lea. *Soth* 4H **115**
Dovedale. *Wors* 5B **24**
Dovedale Av. *Ink* 6H **133**
Dovedale Ct. *Ches* 4G **131**
Dovedale Pl. *Wors* 5B **24**
Dovedale Rd. *S7* 2B **110**
Dovedale Rd. *Roth* 5A **80**
Dove Hill. *Roy* 1F **9**
Dove La. *Ast* 1C **116**
Dovercourt Rd. *S2* 4A **100**

Dovercourt Rd.—East Mall

Dovercourt Rd. *Roth* 2A **78**
Dover Gdns. *S3* 1D **98** (1B **4**)
Doveridge Clo. *Old W* 1A **132**
Dove Rd. *Womb* 2H **39**
Dover Rd. *S11* 4A **98**
Dover St. *S3* 1D **98** (1B **4**)
Doveside Dri. *D'fld* 5D **26**
Dove Valley Trail. *Silk C* 4A **22**
Dove Valley Trail. *Wors* 5C **24**
Dowcar La. *H'hill* 4G **127**
Dowdeswell St. *Ches* 1A **138**
Dowfin. *High G* 6B **50**
Dowland Av. *High G* 5B **50**
Dowland Clo. *High G* 5C **50**
Dowland Ct. *High G* 5B **50**
Dowland Gdns. *High G* 5C **50**
Downes Cres. *B'ley* 4D **12**
Downgate Dri. *S4* 3B **88**
Downham Rd. *S5* 6G **75**
Downing La. *S3* 6D **86** (1B **4**)
Downing Rd. *S8* 1C **122**
Downing Sq. *P'stne* 5D **142**
Downland Clo. *Donc* 1F **61**
Downlands. *Brim* 4D **132**
Down's Row. *Roth* 3D **78**
Dragoon Ct. *S6* 4B **86**
Drake Clo. *Burn* 2C **64**
Drake Head La. *Con* 3G **59**
(in two parts)
Drakehouse. **4D 114**
Drake Ho. Cres. *Wat* 4D **114**
Drakehouse La. *Beig* 4F **115**
Drake Ho. La. W. *Beig* 4F **115**
Drake Ho. Retail Pk. *Beig* 4D **114**
Drake Ho. Way. *Wat* 4E **115**
Drake Rd. *Donc* 3E **33**
Drake Rd. Maltby 5H 83
(off Tickhill Rd.)
Drake Ter. *Brim* 3C **132**
Drake Vw. *Bram* 5H **39**
Dransfield Av. *P'stne* 5D **142**
Dransfield Clo. *S10* 3F **97**
Dransfield Rd. *S10* 3E **97**
Draycott Pl. *Dron W* 3B **128**
Driver St. *S13* 5D **102**
Drive, The. *S6* 1H **85**
Drive, The. *E'thpe* 5E **21**
Dronfield. **2E 129**
Dronfield Ind. Est. *Dron* 2G **129**
Dronfield Rd. *Eck* 6A **124**
Dronfield Woodhouse. **2B 128**
Dropping Well. **1G 77**
Droppingwell Farm Clo. *Roth* 6F **67**
Droppingwell Rd. *Roth* 3D **76**
Drover Clo. *High G* 1C **64**
Drummond Av. *Donc* 2E **31**
Drummond Cres. *S5* 4F **75**
Drummond Rd. *S5* 4F **75**
Drummond St. *Roth* 2D **78**
(in two parts)
Drury Farm Ct. *B'ley* 6C **12**
Drury La. *S17* 2D **120**
Drury La. *Coal A* 6G **123**
Dryden Av. *S5* 5C **74**
Dryden Av. *Ches* 5A **138**
Dryden Dri. *S5* 5C **74**
Dryden Rd. *S5* 5C **74**
Dryden Rd. *B'ley* 5A **14**
Dryden Rd. *Donc* 5C **46**
Dryden Rd. *Mexb* 6F **43**
Dryden Rd. *Roth* 5H **79**
Dryden Rd. *Wath D* 4C **40**
Dryden Way. *S5* 6C **74**
Dublin Rd. *Donc* 4G **33**
Duchess Rd. *S2* 4F **99** (6F **5**)
Duckham Dri. *Ast* 1C **116**
Duckmanton. **3H 139**
(Calow)
Duckmanton. **6E 135**
(Inkersall Green)
Duckmanton Rd. *Duck* 6E **135**
Ducksett La. *Eck* 6D **124**
Dudley Rd. *S6* 1H **85**
Dudley Rd. *Donc* 6H **33**
Dudley St. *P'gte* 4F **69**
Duftons Clo. *Con* 2F **59**
Dugdale Dri. *S5* 2D **74**
Dugdale Rd. *S5* 2C **74**
Duke Av. *Maltby* 5H **83**
Duke Av. *New R* 4C **62**
Duke Cres. *B'ley* 1H **23**
Duke Cres. *Roth* 6G **67**
Duke La. *S1* 3E **99** (6E **5**)
Duke of Norfolk La. *Wick* 5C **80**
Dukeries Dri. *Ans* 6E **107**
Duke's Cres. *Edl'tn* 2B **60**
Dukes Dri. *Ches* 5G **131**
Dukes La. *Roth* 1F **77**
(in two parts)
Dukes Pl. *Roth* 5H **79**
Duke St. *S2* 2G **99** (3H **5**)
Duke St. *B'ley* 1H **23**
Duke St. *Ches* 3A **132**
Duke St. *Dinn* 3F **107**
Duke St. *Donc* 6C **32**
Duke St. *Hoy* 5A **38**
Duke St. *Mosb* 3D **124**
Duke St. *Stav* 1C **134**
Duke St. *Swint* 1B **56**
Dumbleton Rd. *Kil* 4C **126**
Dumble Wood Grange. *Ches* 4E **131**
Dumfries Row. *B'ley* 2A **24**
Duncan Rd. *S10* 1H **97**
Duncan St. *B'wth* 2C **90**
Duncombe St. *S6* 6A **86**
Dundas Rd. *S9* 6G **77**
Dundas Rd. *Donc* 3E **33**
Dundonald Rd. *Ches* 4A **138**
Dunedin Glen. *Half* 3E **125**
Dunedin Gro. *Half* 3E **125**
Dunella Dri. *S6* 2H **85**
Dunella Pl. *S6* 2G **85**
Dunella Rd. *S6* 2H **85**
Dun Fields. *S3* 6D **86**
Dunford Ct. *Wath D* 5G **41**
Dunkeld Rd. *S11* 2H **109**
Dunkerley Rd. *S6* 2D **84**
Dun La. *S3* 6D **86**
Dunleary Rd. *Donc* 5G **33**
Dunlin Clo. *Thpe H* 1B **66**
Dunlop St. *S9* 2D **88**
Dunmere Clo. *B'ley* 2A **14**
Dunmow Rd. *S4* 2A **88**
Dunninc Rd. *S5* 2H **75**
Dunninc Ter. *S5* 2H **75**
Dunniwood Av. *Donc* 6C **48**
Dunniwood Reach. *Bes* 5D **48**
Dunns Dale. *Maltby* 4H **83**
Dunscroft Gro. *Ross* 4F **63**
Dunstan Rd. *Maltby* 5E **83**
Dunston. **3F 131**
Dunston Ct. *Ches* 2H **131**
Dunston La. *Ches* 2F **131**
Dunston Pl. *Ches* 2H **131**
Dunston Rd. *Ches* 3C **130**
Dunston Trad. Est. *Ches* 1G **131**
Dun St. *S3* 6D **86**
Dun St. *Swint* 2C **56**
Durham Av. *New W* 1C **132**
Durham Clo. *New W* 1D **132**
Durham La. *S10* 2B **98**
Durham La. *Arm* 2H **35**
Durham Pl. *Roth* 5H **79**
Durham Rd. *S10* 2C **98**
Durham Rd. *Donc* 2F **33**
Durham St. *Maltby* 5H **83**
Durley Chine Dri. *Has* 5C **138**
Durlstone Clo. *S12* 2C **112**
Durlstone Cres. *S12* 2C **112**
Durlstone Dri. *S12* 2C **112**
Durlstone Gro. *S12* 2C **112**
Durmast Gro. *S6* 5C **84**
Durnan Gro. *Rawm* 5C **54**
Durnford Rd. *Donc* 4E **33**
Durrant Rd. *Ches* 2A **138**
Durvale Ct. *S17* 3E **121**
Dutton Rd. *S6* 2B **86**
Duxford Ct. *Donc* 5E **49**
Dyche Clo. *S8* 3F **123**
Dyche Dri. *S8* 3F **123**
Dyche La. *S8 & Coal A* 2E **123**
Dyche Pl. *S8* 3F **123**
Dyche Rd. *S8* 3F **123**
Dycott Rd. *Roth* 2H **77**
Dyer Rd. *Jump* 4C **38**
Dye Works Yd. *Holy* 6A **136**
Dykes Hall Gdns. *S6* 3H **85**
Dykes Hall Pl. *S6* 2H **85**
Dykes Hall Rd. *S6* 2G **85**
Dykes La. *S6* 3G **85**
Dyke Va. Av. *S12* 3A **114**
Dyke Va. Clo. *S12* 3A **114**
Dyke Va. Pl. *S12* 3A **114**
Dyke Va. Rd. *S12* 2H **113**
Dyke Va. Way. *S12* 3A **114**
Dykewood Dri. *S6* 1F **85**
Dyson Pl. *S11* 5B **98**
Dyson St. *B'ley* 2F **23**

E

Eaden Cres. *Hoy* 5B **38**
Eagleton Dri. *High G* 5C **50**
Eagleton Ri. *High G* 5C **50**
Eagle Vw. *Ast* 1C **116**
Ealand Way. *Con* 2G **59**
Eaming Vw. *B'ley* 4A **14**
Earl Av. *Maltby* 5G **83**
Earl Av. *New R* 4B **62**
Earldom Clo. *S4* 5G **87**
Earldom Dri. *S4* 5G **87**
Earldom Rd. *S4* 4G **87**
Earldom St. *S4* 5G **87**
Earlesmere Av. *Donc* 3A **46**
Earl Marshal Clo. *S4* 2H **87**
Earl Marshal Dri. *S4* 2G **87**
Earl Marshall Sports Cen. **2H 87**
Earl Marshal Rd. *S4* 3G **87**
Earl Marshal Vw. *S4* 2G **87**
Earlsmere Dri. *B'ley* 1G **25**
Earlston Dri. *Donc* 3B **32**
Earl St. *S1* 3E **99** (6D **4**)
(in two parts)
Earl Way. *S1* 3E **99** (6D **4**)
Earnshaw Hall. *S10* 4H **97**
Earnshaw Ter. *B'ley* 4F **13**
Earsham St. *S4* 5G **87**
Earth Cen., The. **1D 58**
Easedale Clo. *Ches* 6B **130**
East Av. *Rawm* 1F **69**
East Av. *Swint* 3H **55**
East Av. *Womb* 6H **25**
East Av. *W'land* 3C **16**
E. Bank Clo. *S2* 1H **111**
E. Bank Pl. *S2* 1H **111**
E. Bank Rd. *S2* 4F **99**
E. Bank Vw. *S2* 1H **111**
E. Bank Way. *S2* 1H **111**
E. Bawtry Rd. *Roth* 2H **91**
E. Cliffe Dri. *S2* 5G **99**
E. Coast Rd. *S9* 5A **88**
East Cres. *Duck* 5E **135**
East Cres. *Roth* 2H **79**
East Cres. *S'bri* 3C **140**
East Cft. *Bol D* 1A **42**
Eastcroft Clo. *W'fld* 1F **125**
Eastcroft Dri. *W'fld* 2E **125**
Eastcroft Glen. *W'fld* 1F **125**
Eastcroft Vw. *W'fld* 2F **125**
Eastcroft Way. *W'fld* 1F **125**
East Dene. **2G 79**
E. Earsham St. *S4* 5H **87**
E. End Cres. *Roy* 2G **9**
Eastern Av. *S2* 1H **111**
Eastern Av. *Dinn* 5G **107**
Eastern Clo. *Dinn* 4G **107**
Eastern Cres. *S2* 1H **111**
Eastern Dri. *S2* 6H **99**
Eastern Wlk. *S2* 6H **99**
Eastfield Av. *P'stne* 4D **142**
Eastfield Clo. *M'well* 5H **7**
Eastfield Cres. *Lghtn* 6G **95**
Eastfield Cres. *M'well* 5H **7**
E. Field La. *Lghtn* 6H **95**
Eastfield Pl. *Rawm* 6A **56**
Eastfield Rd. *S10* 6H **85**
(in two parts)
Eastfield Rd. *Arm* 4F **35**
Eastfield Rd. *Dron* 3G **129**
Eastfields. *Wors* 5B **24**
Eastgate. *S6* 6G **73**
Eastgate. *B'ley* 5G **13**
Eastgate Ct. *Roth* 3H **79**
E. Glade Av. *S12* 4G **113**
E. Glade Clo. *S12* 4G **113**
E. Glade Cres. *S12* 4G **113**
E. Glade Dell. *S12* 3G **113**
E. Glade Pl. *S12* 4G **113**
E. Glade Rd. *S12* 3G **113**
E. Glade Sq. *S12* 4G **113**
E. Glade Way. *S12* 3G **113**
Eastgrove Rd. *S10* 4B **98**
East Herringthorpe. **2B 80**
E. Laith Ga. *Donc* 6D **32**
Eastleigh. *Roth* 1G **79**
Eastleigh Ct. *Has* 5D **138**
E. Lodge La. *Roth* 3C **68**
East Mall. *Cry P* 4E **115**

Eastmoor Gro. *B'ley* 3E **9**
Eastmoor Rd. *Brim* 1F **139**
East Pde. *S1* 2E **99** (3E **5**)
East Pinfold. *Roy* 2E **9**
East Rd. *S2* 6F **99**
East Rd. *Oxs* 6G **143**
East Rd. *Roth* 2H **79**
E. Side Clo. *Ches* 3B **132**
E. Side Rd. *Ches* 3B **132**
East St. *D'fld* 3E **27**
East St. *Dinn* 4F **107**
East St. *Donc* 2C **46**
East St. *Gold* 3H **29**
East Ter. *Kiv P* 4D **116**
E. Vale Dri. *Thry* 5D **70**
East Vw. *Ches* 3A **138**
East Vw. *Cud* 6B **10**
East Vw. *H'by* 4B **82**
East Vw. *Jump* 4B **38**
E. View Av. *Eck* 6H **125**
E. View Ter. *S6* 2H **85**
Eastwell Gro. *Womb* 2H **39**
East Whitwell. 4D **140**
Eastwood. 1G **79**
Eastwood. *S6* 6G **73**
Eastwood Av. *Ans* 2G **119**
Eastwood Clo. *Has* 5D **138**
Eastwood Ct. *Roth* 1G **79**
Eastwood Dri. *Cal* 3H **139**
Eastwood Ho. Roth 2F **79**
           (off Doncaster Rd.)
Eastwood La. *Roth* 2E **79**
Eastwood Mt. *Roth* 3G **79**
Eastwood Pk. Apartments.
    Ches .6C **138**
Eastwood Pk. Dri. *Has* 5D **138**
Eastwood Rd. *S11* 5B **98**
Eastwood Trad. Est. *Roth* 6G **69**
Eastwood Va. *Roth* 1G **79**
Eastwood Vw. *Roth* 1H **79**
Eaton Pl. *S2* 2H **99**
Eaton Sq. *Barn* 1H **43**
Ebenezer Pl. *S3* 6E **87** (1D **4**)
Ebenezer Pl. *Else* 6C **38**
Ebenezer St. *S3* 6E **87** (1D **4**)
Eben St. *S9* 1C **88**
Ecclesall. 2G **109**
Ecclesall Rd. *S11* 3G **109**
Ecclesall Rd. S. *S11* 5E **109**
Ecclesall Woods Forest Walks. 1D **120**
Eccles Dri. *Edl'tn* 5B **60**
Ecclesfield. 6E **65**
Ecclesfield Common. 6G **65**
Ecclesfield Rd. *S5 & S9* 1H **75**
Ecclesfield Rd. *C'town* 2F **65**
Eccles St. *S9* 5D **76**
Eccleston Rd. *Kirk S* 2E **21**
Eckington. 6E **125**
Eckington Hall. *Mosb* 4D **124**
Eckington Rd. *Beig* 1F **125**
           (in two parts)
Eckington Rd. *Coal A* 5G **123**
Eckington Rd. *Stav* 1C **134**
Eckington Way. *Cry P* 3D **114**
Ecton Dri. *Kirk S* 2C **20**
Edale Ct. *Ches* 4G **131**
Edale Ri. *Dod* 2A **22**
Edale Rd. *S11* 6G **97**
Edale Rd. *Roth* 3H **77**
Edderthorpe. 1E **27**
Edderthorpe La. *D'fld* 1E **27**
Eddyfield Rd. *Oxs* 5G **143**
Eden Clo. *Bar G* 2A **12**
Eden Clo. *H'by* 4B **82**
Edencroft Dri. *E'thpe* 4E **21**
Eden Dri. *S6* 3E **85**
Edenfield Clo. *B'ley* 1D **14**
Eden Fld. Rd. *E'thpe* 5E **21**
Eden Glade. *Swal* 5B **104**
Eden Gro. *Donc* 1A **46**
Eden Gro. *Swal* 5B **104**
Eden Gro. Rd. *E'thpe* 5E **21**
Edenhall Rd. *S2* 6B **100**
Edensor Ct. *Stav* 3A **134**
Edensor Rd. *S5* 1F **87**
Eden Ter. *Mexb* 5E **43**
Edenthorpe. 5E **21**
Edenthorpe Dell. *Owl* 5B **114**
Edenthorpe Gro. *Owl* 5C **114**
Edgar Allan Ho. *S3* 4B **4**
Edgar La. *New R* 4B **62**
Edgbaston Way. *Edl'tn* 2C **60**
Edge Bank. *S7* 1C **110**

Edgebrook Rd. *S7* 1B **110**
Edgecliffe Pl. *B'ley* 2A **14**
Edge Climbing Cen., The. 4E **99**
Edge Clo. *S6* 3A **74**
Edgedale Rd. *S7* 2B **110**
Edgefield Rd. *S7* 2C **110**
Edge Grn. *Kirk S* 3D **20**
Edge Hill Rd. *S7* 1B **110**
Edgehill Rd. *Donc* 2A **34**
Edgehill Rd. *M'well* 3E **7**
Edgelands Ri. *Cud* 2H **15**
Edge La. *S6* 3A **74**
           (in three parts)
Edgemount Rd. *S7* 2C **110**
Edge Well Clo. *S6* 3A **74**
Edge Well Cres. *S6* 3A **74**
Edge Well Dri. *S6* 4A **74**
Edge Well La. *S6* 3H **73**
Edge Well Pl. *S6* 3H **73**
Edge Well Ri. *S6* 3A **74**
Edge Well Way. *S6* 3A **74**
Edinburgh Av. *Bol D* 1H **41**
Edinburgh Clo. *B'ley* 3B **14**
Edinburgh Ct. Ches 1H **137**
          (off Highfield Rd.)
Edinburgh Dri. *Ans* 6D **106**
Edinburgh Rd. *Ches* 6H **131**
Edinburgh Rd. *Hoy* 4A **38**
Edith Ter. *Donc* 2G **31**
Edlington La. *Edl'tn & Warm* 2C **60**
Edlington La. *Old E & Edl'tn* 6A **60**
Edlington Riding. Edl'tn 4C **60**
Edlington Sports Cen. & Swimming Pool.
  . . . . .5B **60**
Edmonton Clo. *B'ley* 5C **12**
Edmund Av. *S17* 3A **122**
Edmund Av. *B'wth* 4D **90**
Edmund Clo. *S17* 3B **122**
Edmund Dri. *S17* 3B **122**
Edmund Rd. *S2* 5F **99** (6F **5**)
Edmunds Rd. *Wors* 5C **24**
Edmund St. *Ches* 3H **131**
Edmund St. *Wors* 5A **24**
Edna St. *Bol D* 1A **42**
Edward Clo. *B'ley* 2C **24**
Edward Pl. *S11* 1B **110**
Edward Rd. *Adw S* 1F **17**
Edward Rd. *Gold* 5E **29**
Edward Rd. *Wath D* 3C **40**
Edward St. *S3* 1D **98** (2B **4**)
Edward St. *Arm* 2D **34**
Edward St. *Ben* 6B **18**
Edward St. *D'fld* 4E **27**
Edward St. *Dinn* 4F **107**
Edward St. *Eck* 6D **124**
Edward St. *Hoy* 5H **37**
Edward St. *M'well* 5G **7**
Edward St. *New R* 4B **62**
Edward St. *Stav* 3A **134**
Edward St. *S'bri* 3D **140**
Edward St. *Swint* 1B **56**
Edward St. *Thurn* 1E **29**
Edward St. *Womb* 6C **26**
Edward St. Flats. *S3* 1D **98** (2B **4**)
Edwin Av. *Ches* 5F **137**
Edwin Rd. *S2* 1G **111**
Edwin Rd. *W'land* 3C **16**
Edwins Clo. *B'ley* 6B **8**
Effingham La. *S4* 1G **99** (1H **5**)
Effingham Rd. *S4 & S9* 6H **87**
Effingham Sq. Roth 2D **78**
        (off Effingham St.)
Effingham St. *S4* 1G **99** (1H **5**)
Effingham St. *Roth* 3D **78**
           (in two parts)
Egerton Clo. *S3* 3D **98** (5C **4**)
Egerton La. *S1* 3D **98** (6B **4**)
Egerton Rd. *Dron* 1F **129**
Egerton Rd. *Swal* 6B **104**
Egerton St. *S1* 3D **98** (6B **4**)
Egerton Wlk. *S3* 5B **4**
Eggington Clo. *Donc* 4F **49**
Egmanton Rd. *B'ley* 4B **8**
Egremont Clo. *Maltby* 2D **82**
Egremont Ri. *Maltby* 2D **82**
Eilam Clo. *Roth* 1G **77**
Eilam Rd. *Roth* 1G **77**
Eland Clo. *Ross* 3D **62**
Eland Rd. *Den M* 2A **58**
Elcroft Gdns. *Beig* 5F **115**
Elder Av. *Ans* 2H **119**
Elder Ct. *Kil* 4A **126**
Elder Dri. *Roth & S'side* 3F **81**

Elder Gro. *Con* 4C **58**
Eldertree Rd. *Thpe H* 3B **66**
Elder Way. *Ches* 2A **138**
Eldon Arc. B'ley 6H **13**
             (off Eldon St.)
Eldon Ct. *S1* 2D **98** (4C **4**)
Eldon Rd. *Roth* 1F **79**
Eldon St. *S1* 2D **98** (4C **4**)
Eldon St. *B'ley* 6H **13**
Eldon St. N. *B'ley* 5H **13**
Eleanor Ct. *E'thpe* 6C **20**
Eleanor St. *S9* 5D **88**
Elgin Clo. *Ches* 6E **137**
Elgin St. *S10* 2H **97**
Elgitha Dri. *Thur* 5A **94**
Eliot Clo. *Brim* 6F **133**
Elizabeth Av. *Kirk S* 3E **21**
Elizabeth Rd. *Ast* 1B **116**
Elizabeth St. *Gold* 4G **29**
Elizabeth St. *Grim* 6G **11**
Elizabeth Way. Roth 3C **78**
             (off Vine Clo.)
Elkstone Rd. *Ches* 6C **130**
Ellaline Cotts. *Rav* 1A **82**
Elland Clo. *B'ley* 6A **8**
Ella Rd. *S4* 4G **87**
Ellavale. *Else* 5C **38**
Ellenborough Rd. *S6* 3H **85**
Ellen Tree Clo. *B'wth* 2B **90**
Ellerker Av. *Donc* 1B **46**
Ellers Av. *Donc* 3A **48**
Ellers Cres. *Donc* 3A **48**
Ellers Dri. *Donc* 3A **48**
Ellershaw La. *Con* 4C **58**
Ellershaw Rd. *Con* 4D **58**
           (in two parts)
Ellers Rd. *Donc* 3A **48**
Ellerton Gdns. *Donc* 2C **48**
Ellerton Rd. *S5* 1H **87**
Ellesmere Rd. *S4* 5G **87**
           (in two parts)
Ellesmere Rd. N. *S4* 4G **87**
Ellesmere Ter. *Donc* 3F **79**
Ellesmere Wlk. *S4* 5G **87**
Ellington Ct. *B'ley* 2E **23**
Elliot Rd. *S6* 1B **98**
Elliott Av. *Womb* 2F **39**
Elliott Clo. *Wath D* 4C **40**
Elliott Ct. *Roth* 2E **79**
Elliott Dri. *Ink* 5A **134**
Elliott Dri. *Roth* 5H **67**
Elliott La. *Gren* 4B **64**
Elliott M. Roth 2H **77**
           (off Benton Way)
Elliottville St. *S6* 5A **86**
Ellis Av. *Wath D* 1D **54**
Ellis Ct. *H'fld* 3E **39**
Ellis Cres. *Bram* 4A **40**
Ellis Cres. *New R* 4C **62**
Ellisons Rd. *Kil* 1C **126**
Ellison St. *S3* 1D **98** (1B **4**)
           (in two parts)
Ellis St. *S3* 1D **98** (1C **4**)
Ellis St. *B'wth* 2C **90**
Elliston Av. *M'well* 4G **7**
Ellorslie Dri. *S'bri* 3E **141**
Ellwood. *B'ley* 3E **15**
Elmbridge Clo. *Roy* 2G **9**
Elm Clo. *Barn D* 2H **21**
Elm Clo. *Ches* 4H **131**
Elm Clo. *Kil* 4A **126**
Elm Clo. *Ross* 5F **63**
Elm Ct. *Wors* 5B **24**
Elm Cres. *Ben* 5C **18**
Elm Cres. *Mosb* 1C **124**
Elmdale Clo. *Swint* 5B **56**
Elmdale Dri. *E'thpe* 6D **20**
Elm Dri. *Kil* 4A **126**
Elmfield Av. *S5* 5F **75**
Elmfield Rd. *Donc* 1D **46**
Elmfield Rd. *New R* 5D **62**
Elm Grn. La. *Con* 3E **59**
Elm Gro. *Roth* 4B **68**
Elmham Rd. *S9* 1F **101**
Elmham Rd. *Donc* 2C **48**
Elmhirst Dri. *Roth* 5A **80**
Elmhirst La. *Silk* 5A **12**
Elm La. *S5* 5F **75**
Elm Lodge Farm Clo.
    Ches .4H **131**
Elmore Rd. *S10* 2A **98**
Elm Pl. *Arm* 2E **35**
Elm Pl. *B'ley* 2D **14**

Elm Pl. *Ches* 3G **137**
Elm Pl. *Rawm* 2G **69**
Elm Ri. *C'town* 3D **64**
Elm Rd. *Arm* 2E **35**
Elm Rd. *Beig* 3G **115**
Elm Rd. *Eck* 6H **125**
Elm Rd. *Mexb* 5C **42**
Elm Row. *B'ley* 6B **14**
Elmsdale. *Wors* 5B **24**
Elm St. *Holl* 2F **133**
Elm St. *Hoy* 6F **37**
Elm Tree Clo. *Ans* 2H **119**
Elm Tree Cres. *Dron* 6E **123**
Elm Tree Farm Ct. *Hoot R* 5D **56**
Elm Tree Hill. 1D **112**
Elm Tree Rd. *Maltby* 4D **82**
Elmtree Rd. *Thpe H* 4B **66**
Elmview Rd. *S9* 5D **76**
Elmville Av. *Swint* 4A **56**
Elm Wlk. *Thurn* 1F **29**
Elm Way. *Wath D* 1G **55**
Elmwood Av. *W'land* 1B **16**
Elmwood Cres. *Arm* 3E **35**
Elmwood Dri. *Mosb* 3D **124**
Elmwood Ho. *Holl* 3G **133**
Elsecar. 6C **38**
Elsecar Heritage Centre,
  Newcomen Beam Engine. 1D **52**
Elsecar Ho. Donc 1C **46**
  (off Bond Clo.)
Elsecar Rd. *Bram B* 5A **40**
Elsecar Steam Railway. 1D **52**
Elsham Clo. *Braml* 2H **81**
Elstead Clo. *Bar G* 2A **12**
Elstree Dri. *S12* 3D **112**
Elstree Rd. *S12* 3D **112**
Elsworth Clo. *Donc* 2C **46**
Elton La. *S'side* 2F **81**
Elton St. *Ches* 3A **138**
Elton Vw. *Stav* 3B **134**
Elvaston Clo. *Dron W* 2A **128**
Elwin Ct. *Bal* 1H **61**
Elwis St. *Donc* 5B **32**
Elwood Rd. *S17* 3A **122**
Ely Rd. *Donc* 2F **33**
Ely St. *New R* 3C **62**
Embankment Rd. *S10* 2A **98**
Emerson Clo. *S5* 4F **75**
Emerson Cres. *S5* 5F **75**
Emerson Dri. *S5* 5F **75**
Emily Clo. *B'ley* 5D **14**
Emily Rd. *S7* 1C **110**
Emley Dri. *Donc* 2E **31**
Emley Ho. Donc 1C **46**
  (off St James St.)
Emmetfield Clo. *Ches* 5H **137**
Empire Dri. *Maltby* 2D **82**
Empire Rd. *S7* 6D **98**
Empire Ter. *Roy* 1F **9**
Emsley Av. *Cud* 3H **15**
Endcliffe Av. *S10* 4A **98**
Endcliffe Crescent. 4H **97**
Endcliffe Cres. *S10* 3H **97**
Endcliffe Edge. 4G **97**
Endcliffe Edge. *S10* 4H **97**
Endcliffe Glen Rd. *S11* 4A **98**
Endcliffe Gro. Av. *S10* 4G **97**
Endcliffe Hall Av. *S10* 4G **97**
Endcliffe Ri. Rd. *S11* 4A **98**
Endcliffe Ter. Rd. *S10* 4A **98**
Endcliffe Va. Av. *S11* 5A **98**
Endcliffe Va. Rd. *S10* 4H **97**
Endcliffe Way. *Donc* 2A **34**
Endfield Rd. *S5* 2D **74**
Endowood Rd. *S7* 5H **109**
Endowood Rd. *Ches* 5C **136**
Enfield Pl. *S13* 3H **101**
Enfield Rd. *Ches* 6H **131**
Engine La. *Gold* 5H **29**
Engine La. *Shaf* 4D **10**
Engline La. Clo. *Shaf* 4D **10**
Ennerdale Av. *Half* 3E **125**
Ennerdale Clo. *Ans* 6E **107**
Ennerdale Clo. *Dron W* 2C **128**
Ennerdale Clo. *Mexb* 5G **43**
Ennerdale Cres. *Ches* 4E **131**
Ennerdale Dri. *Half* 3E **125**
Ennerdale Rd. *B'ley* 1H **25**
Ennerdale Rd. *Donc* 3A **34**
Ennis Cres. *Donc* 4G **33**
Enterprise Cen. *Gold* 5G **29**
Enterprise Pk. *S9* 6A **88**
Entwistle Rd. *High G* 6C **50**

Epping Gdns. *Soth* 5G **115**
Epping Gro. *Soth* 5G **115**
Epsom Clo. *Mexb* 5F **43**
Epsom Rd. *Donc* 1B **48**
Epworth Ct. *Ben* 1B **32**
  (off Chapel St.)
Erin Rd. *Pool & Duck* 3D **134**
Ernest Copley Ho. *High G* 1D **64**
  (off Peckham Rd.)
Errington Av. *S2* 1A **112**
Errington Clo. *S2* 1A **112**
Errington Cres. *S2* 1A **112**
Errington Rd. *S2* 1A **112**
Errington Rd. *Ches* 5F **137**
Errington Way. *S2* 6A **100**
Erskine Cres. *S2* 6G **99**
Erskine Rd. *S2* 6G **99**
Erskine Rd. *Roth* 1E **79**
Erskine Vw. *S2* 1G **111**
Eshton Ct. *M'well* 3E **7**
Eshton Wlk. *B'ley* 6F **13**
Eskdale Clo. *S6* 1A **86**
Eskdale Clo. *Dron W* 2C **128**
Eskdale Dri. *Donc* 1H **31**
Eskdale Rd. *S6* 1A **86**
Eskdale Rd. *B'ley* 1G **25**
Eskdale Rd. *Roth* 4H **67**
Eskdale Wlk. *Donc* 2E **31**
Eslaforde Ter. *Roth* 1H **79**
  (off Doncaster Rd.)
Esperanto Pl. *S1* 3F **5**
Essendine Cres. *S8* 4F **111**
Essex Av. *Donc* 6H **33**
Essex Clo. *Kiv P* 4B **118**
Essex Rd. *S2* 4H **99**
Essex Rd. *B'ley* 2H **23**
Essoldo Chambers. Roth 3D **78**
  (off High St.)
Estate Rd. *Rawm* 6E **55**
Estone Dri. *Swal* 5B **104**
Ettrick Clo. *Ches* 6E **131**
Etwall Clo. *Ches* 5C **130**
Etwall Way. *S5* 5G **75**
Europa Clo. *S9* 5A **90**
Europa Dri. *S9* 3F **89**
Europa Link. *S9* 4F **89**
Europa Vw. *S9* 5H **89**
Euston Way. *Dinn* 3C **106**
Evans St. *S1* 6B **4**
Evanston Gdns. *Donc* 3A **46**
Eva Ratcliffe Ho. *S5* 1E **75**
Eveline St. *Cud* 1H **15**
Evelyn Av. *Donc* 5H **33**
Evelyn Clo. *Donc* 5H **33**
Evelyn Rd. *S10* 2H **97**
Evelyn St. *Rawm* 1H **69**
Evelyn Ter. *B'ley* 1A **24**
Everard Av. *S17* 4G **121**
Everard Dri. *S17* 4G **121**
Everard Glade. *S17* 4G **121**
Everett Clo. *Brim* 4E **133**
Everill Clo. *Womb* 2H **39**
Everill Ga. La. *Womb* 1H **39**
  (in two parts)
Everingham Clo. *S5* 6E **75**
Everingham Cres. *S5* 6D **74**
Everingham Pl. *S5* 1E **87**
Everingham Rd. *S5* 6E **75**
Everingham Rd. *Donc* 1C **48**
Everson Clo. *Maltby* 2E **83**
Everton Rd. *S11* 5A **98**
Evesham Clo. *S9* 6D **76**
Ewden Rd. *Womb* 2H **39**
Ewden Village. 6E **141**
Ewden Way. *B'ley* 6C **12**
Ewers Rd. *Roth* 3H **77**
Ewood Dri. *Donc* 3C **48**
Excalibur Way. *Ches* 2B **138**
Excelsior Ct. *Con* 3E **59**
Exchange Gateway. *S1* 3E **5**
Exchange Pl. *S2* 2G **5**
Exchange St. *S2* 1F **99** (2G **5**)
Exchange St. *Donc* 2C **46**
Exeter Dri. *S3* 4D **98** (6B **4**)
Exeter Pl. *S3* 4D **98** (6B **4**)
Exeter Rd. *Donc* 3G **33**
Exeter Way. *S3* 3C **98** (6A **4**)
Exley Av. *S6* 6G **85**
Eyam Clo. *Dod* 2A **22**
Eyam Rd. *S10* 2H **97**
Eyncourt Rd. *S5* 6H **75**
Eyre Gdns. *Ches* 1H **137**
Eyre Gdns. *High G* 1B **64**

Eyre La. *S1* 3E **99** (6E **5**)
Eyre St. *S1* 4E **99** (6D **4**)
Eyre St. E. *Ches* 6C **138**

F

Fabian Way. *Braml* 2E **81**
Factory La. *Donc* 6C **32**
Factory St. *Ches* 3F **137**
Fairbank Rd. *S5* 1E **87**
Fairbank Vw. *Whis* 2A **92**
Fairburn Clo. *S6* 6E **85**
Fairbarn Dri. *S6* 6E **85**
Fairbarn Pl. *S6* 6E **85**
Fairbarn Rd. *S6* 6E **85**
Fairbarn Way. *S6* 6E **85**
Fairburn Gdns. *B'wth* 3D **90**
Fairburn Gro. *Else* 5D **38**
Fair Clo. *Ches* 1G **137**
Fairfax Dri. *S2* 5D **100**
Fairfax Rd. *S2* 5D **100**
  (in two parts)
Fairfax Rd. *Donc* 5H **33**
Fairfield. *Birdw* 2D **36**
Fairfield. *Bol D* 6D **28**
Fairfield Clo. *Braml* 2G **81**
Fairfield Clo. *Brim* 3D **132**
Fairfield Clo. *Donc* 5B **48**
Fairfield Ct. *Arm* 4F **35**
Fairfield Ct. *Ash* 1B **136**
Fairfield Ct. *Womb* 5D **26**
Fairfield Dri. *Ash* 1B **136**
Fairfield Heights. *S10* 3H **97**
Fairfield Rd. *Ches* 1H **137**
Fairfield Rd. *Donc* 3H **31**
Fairford Clo. *Ches* 6H **137**
Fairford Clo. *Donc* 5E **49**
Fairholme Heights. *O'bri* 2E **73**
Fair Holme Vw. *Arm* 5G **35**
Fairleigh. .5C **100**
Fairleigh. *S2* 6C **100**
Fairleigh Dri. *Roth* 5E **79**
Fairmount Gdns. *S12* 4A **114**
Fairthorn Rd. *S5* 5H **75**
Fair Vw. *Ches* 1G **137**
Fair Vw. Av. *W'land* 2B **16**
Fairview Clo. *Bran* 4H **49**
Fairview Clo. *Hoy* 6G **37**
Fairview Ct. *Barn D* 1D **20**
Fair Vw. Dri. *Ast* 6C **104**
Fairview Rd. *Dron* 6E **123**
Fairview Ter. *Barn D* 1D **20**
Fairview Vs. *Barn D* 1E **21**
Fairway. *Dod* 3C **22**
Fairway Av. *M'well* 3G **7**
Fairways. *Wick* 5F **81**
Fairway, The. *S10* 4A **96**
Fair Winds Clo. *Dron* 2E **129**
Faith St. *B'ley* 1F **15**
Falcon Clo. *Adw S* 1D **16**
Falcon Ct. *Ross* 4E **63**
Falcon Dri. *Birdw* 3D **36**
Falcon Dri. *Tree* 2F **103**
Falconer Clo. *Dart* 4B **6**
Falconer La. *S13* 5F **103**
Falconer Way. *Tree* 1F **103**
Falcon Knowle Ing. *Dart* 4A **6**
Falcon Ri. *Dron* 6H **123**
Falcon Rd. *Dron* 6G **123**
Falcon St. *B'ley* 5G **13**
Falcon Way. *Dinn* 6E **107**
Falcon Yd. Ches 2A **138**
  (off Low Pavement)
Falding St. *C'town* 2F **65**
Falding St. *Roth* 3C **78**
Falkland Ri. *Dron* 3E **129**
Falkland Rd. *S11* 1G **109**
Fall Bank Cres. *Dod* 2A **22**
Fall Bank Ind. Est. *Dod* 2A **22**
Fallon Rd. *S6* 5D **84**
Falmouth Clo. *B'ley* 4B **14**
Falmouth Rd. *S7* 2C **110**
Falstaff Cres. *S5* 5D **74**
Falstaff Rd. *S5* 5D **74**
Fane Cres. *Swal* 5B **104**
Fanny Av. *Kil* 4C **126**
Fan Rd. *Stav* 2D **134**
Fan Rd. Ind. Est. *Stav* 2C **134**
Fanshaw Av. *Eck* 6H **125**
Fanshaw Bank. *Dron* 2E **129**
Fanshaw Clo. *Eck* 6H **125**

Fanshaw Dri. *Eck* 6H **125**
Fanshaw Rd. *Dron* 1F **129**
Fanshaw Rd. *Eck* 6H **125**
Fanshaw Way. *Eck* 6H **125**
Faraday Rd. *S9* 5A **88**
Faranden Rd. *S9* 6C **88**
Farcliff. *Spro* .2D **44**
Far Cres. *Roth* 2H **79**
Far Cft. *Bol D* 1A **42**
Farcroft Gro. *S4* 2B **88**
Far Dalton La. *Roth* 6C **70**
Fardell Gdns. *Braml* 5H **81**
Far Fld. Clo. *E'thpe* 4E **21**
Far Fld. La. *B'ley* 1E **15**
Far Fld. La. *Wath D* 5H **41**
Farfield Pk. *Manv* 4H **41**
Farfield Rd. *S3* 5C **86**
Far Fld. Rd. *E'thpe* 4E **21**
Far Fld. Rd. *Roth* 4A **80**
Fargate. *S1* 2E **99** (3E **5**)
Far Golden Smithies. *Swint* 1A **56**
Farhouse La. *O'bri* 2A **72**
Farish Pl. *S2* 1F **111**
Far La. *S6* 2H **85**
Far La. *Roth* .1H **79**
Far Lawns. *Car* 4F **9**
Farlawns Ct. *Bal* 1H **61**
Farlow Cft. *High G* 5A **50**
Farm Bank Rd. *S2* 3G **99** (6H **5**)
Farm Clo. *S12* 5D **112**
Farm Clo. *B'ley* 3C **14**
Farm Clo. *B'wth* 4B **90**
Farm Clo. *Ches* 6H **137**
Farm Clo. *Coal A* 5F **123**
Farm Clo. *E'thpe* 6E **21**
Farm Ct. *Adw S* 1E **17**
Farm Cres. *Mosb* 3C **124**
Farm Fields Clo. *Wat* 6D **114**
Farm Grange. *Donc* 1G **61**
Farmhill Clo. *Donc* 4G **31**
Far Moor La. *B'ley* 5C **12**
Far Moor Clo. *H'ton* 1G **43**
Farmoor Gdns. *Soth* 5H **115**
Farm Rd. *S2* 4F **99** (6G **5**)
Farm Rd. *B'ley* 3B **24**
Farmstead Clo. *S14* 2H **111**
Farm Vw. Clo. *S12* 4B **114**
Farm Vw. Clo. *Roth* 1F **77**
Farm Vw. Dri. *S12* 4B **114**
Farm Vw. Gdns. *S12* 4B **114**
Farm Vw. Rd. *Roth* 1F **77**
Farm Wlk. *Mosb* 2C **124**
Farm Way. *D'fld* 3E **27**
Farnaby Dri. *High G* 5B **50**
Farnaby Gdns. *High G* 5B **50**
Farnborough Dri. *Donc* 5E **49**
Farndale Av. *Walt* 5D **136**
Farndale Rd. *S6* 1A **86**
Farndale Rd. *Donc* 2F **31**
Farnley Av. *S6* 5B **74**
Farnon Clo. *Ches* 4B **138**
Farnsworth Ct. *Has* 5D **138**
Farnsworth St. *Has* 5C **138**
Farnworth Rd. *Roth* 2A **80**
Far Pl. *Roth* .2H **79**
Farquhar Rd. *Maltby* 4H **83**
Farrand St. *Birdw* 4C **36**
Farrar Rd. *S7* 6D **98**
Farrar St. *B'ley* 6F **13**
Farrier Ga. *High G* 1C **64**
Farriers Way. *Bal* 6C **46**
Farringdon Dri. *New R* 6E **63**
Farrington Ct. *Wick* 5G **81**
Farrow Clo. *Dod* 2C **22**
Farthing Gale M. *Donc* 4H **31**
Far Townend. *Dod* 2B **22**
Far Vw. Rd. *S5* 5F **75**
Far Vw. Ter. *B'ley* 2G **23**
Farwater Clo. *Dron* 3E **129**
Farwater La. *Dron* 2D **128**
Fathers Gdns. *Kiv P* 5H **117**
Favell Rd. *S3* 2C **98** (3A **4**)
Favell Rd. *Roth* 2B **80**
Fawcett St. *S3* 1C **98** (1A **4**)
(in two parts)
Fearn Ho. Cres. *Hoy* 6G **37**
Fearnley Rd. *Hoy* 6G **37**
Fearn's Bldgs. P'stne 4C **142**
(off Stottercliffe Rd.)
Fearnville Gro. *Roy* 2E **9**
Felkin St. *Ches* 2B **138**
Felkirk Vw. *Shaf* 2B **10**
Fellbrigg Rd. *S2* 6H **99**

Fellowsfield Way. *Roth* 2G **77**
Fellows Wlk. *Womb* 5H **25**
Fell Rd. *S9* 4C **88**
Fell St. *S9* 3B **88**
Fence. **5F 103**
Fen Ct. *E'thpe* 5E **21**
Fenland Way. *Ches* 5G **137**
Fenney La. *S11* 5E **109**
Fenn Rd. *Tank* 6D **36**
Fensome Way. *D'fld* 3E **27**
Fenton Clo. *Arm* 4F **35**
Fenton Cft. *Roth* 1A **78**
Fenton Fields. *Roth* 1A **78**
Fenton Rd. *S Elm* 5A **68**
Fenton St. *Eck* 6G **125**
Fenton St. *Roth* 2H **77**
Fentonville St. *S11* 5B **98**
Fenton Way. *Roth* 5B **68**
Feoffees Rd. *E'fld* 1F **75**
Ferguson St. *S9* 5B **88**
Ferham Clo. *Roth* 3A **78**
Ferham Pk. Av. *Roth* 3A **78**
Ferham Rd. *Roth* 3A **78**
Fern Av. *Beig* 3F **115**
Fern Av. *Donc* 2A **32**
Fern Av. *Stav* 3A **134**
Fern Bank. *Adw S* 1D **16**
Fern Bank. *K'wth* 2G **77**
Fernbank Clo. *Wors* 3H **23**
Fernbank Dri. *Arm* 1F **35**
Fernbank Dri. *Eck* 6B **124**
Fern Clo. *D'fld* 5E **27**
Fern Clo. *Donc* 3A **34**
Fern Clo. *Eck* 6B **124**
Ferncroft Av. *Mosb* 2C **124**
Ferndale Clo. *Coal A* 6H **123**
Ferndale Dri. *Braml* 3G **81**
Ferndale Ri. *Coal A* 6H **123**
Ferndale Rd. *Coal A* 6H **123**
Ferndale Rd. *Con* 3D **58**
Ferndale Vw. *Dron* 4H **31**
Fernhall Clo. *Kirk S* 4E **21**
Fernhall Cft. *Womb* 6C **26**
Fern Hollow. *Wick* 6G **81**
Fernhurst Rd. *Donc* 3A **34**
Fernlea Clo. *Cusw* 4H **31**
Fern Lea Gro. *Bol D* 1H **41**
Fern Lea Gro. *E'fld* 1F **75**
Fernleigh Dri. *B'wth* 1B **90**
Fern Rd. *S6* 5H **85**
Fernvale Wlk. *Swint* 5B **56**
Fern Way. *Eck* 6B **124**
Fernwood Clo. *Has* 6E **139**
Ferrara Clo. *D'fld* 3C **26**
Ferrars Clo. *S9* 1H **89**
Ferrars Dri. *S9* 2H **89**
Ferrars Rd. *S9* 6G **77**
Ferrars Way. *S9* 2H **89**
Ferrers Rd. *Donc* 4F **33**
Ferriby Rd. *S6* 1H **85**
Ferry Boat La. *Roth* 1G **57**
(in two parts)
Ferry La. *Con* .2E **59**
Ferry Moor La. *Cud* 6D **10**
Ferrymoor Way. *Grim* 6E **11**
Ferrymore Ho. Donc 1C **46**
(off St James St.)
Ferry Ter. *Con* 2E **59**
Fersfield St. *S4* 5H **87**
Festival Clo. *Kiv P* 5G **117**
Festival Rd. *Wath D* 6F **41**
Fewston Way. *Donc* 3H **47**
Fiddle Neck La. *Ast* 2D **116**
Fiddler's Dri. *Arm* 5G **35**
Field Clo. *D'fld* 3E **27**
Field Clo. *Dron W* 1A **128**
Field Dri. *Cud* .2H **15**
Fielders Way. *Ed'tn* 2C **60**
Fieldfare Ho. *Old W* 1B **132**
Field Ga. *Ross* 3E **63**
Field Head Ct. *Hoy* 5A **38**
Fieldhead Rd. *S8* 6E **99**
Field Head Rd. *Hoy* 6A **38**
Fieldhead Way. *Ches* 5E **131**
Field Ho. Rd. *Spro* 3D **44**
Fieldhouse Way. *S4* 4H **87**
Fielding Dri. *Braml* 4H **81**
Fielding Gro. *Rawm* 6F **55**
Fielding Rd. *S6* 1A **86**
Field La. *B'ley* .2E **25**
Field La. *Kil* .4H **125**
Field La. *Upt* .4D **92**
Fields End. *Oxs* 6H **143**

Fields End Bus. Pk. *Thurn* 3F **29**
Fieldsend Gdns. *E'fld* 1F **75**
Fields End Rd. *Gold* 3F **29**
Fieldside. *E'thpe* 6D **20**
Field Vw. *B'wth* 2C **90**
Field Vw. *Ches* 6A **138**
Fieldview Pl. *Ches* 5E **131**
Field Way. *Roth* 1D **78**
Fife Clo. *S9* 5C **76**
Fife Gdns. *S9* 5C **76**
Fife St. *S9* 5C **76**
Fife St. *B'ley* 1F **23**
Fife Way. *S9* 5C **76**
Fifth Av. *W'land* 4D **16**
Fig Tree La. *S1* 2E **5**
Filby Rd. *Donc* 4G **31**
Filey Av. *Roy* 1F **9**
Filey La. *S3* 3C **98** (5A **4**)
Filey St. *S10* 2C **98** (4A **4**)
Finch Clo. *Thry* 5D **70**
Finch Gdns. *Braml* 2E **81**
Finch Ri. *Ast* 1C **116**
Finch Rd. *Donc* 5H **45**
Finchwell Clo. *S13* 3H **101**
Finchwell Cres. *S13* 3H **101**
Finchwell Rd. *S13* 3H **101**
Findon Cres. *S6* 3G **85**
Findon Pl. *S6* 3G **85**
Findon Rd. *S6* 3G **85**
Findon St. *S6* 3H **85**
Finkle St. *Ben* 1B **32**
Finlay Rd. *Roth* 1G **79**
Finlay St. *S3* 1C **98** (1A **4**)
Finningley Lodge. *Kiv P* 5H **117**
(off Station Rd.)
Finsbury Clo. *Dinn* 2C **106**
Firbeck Av. *Lghtn* 1E **107**
Firbeck Ho. Donc 1C **46**
(off St James St.)
Firbeck La. *Lghtn* 6G **95**
Firbeck Rd. *S8* 4C **110**
Firbeck Rd. *Donc* 1F **47**
Firbeck Way. *Ross* 3F **63**
Fir Clo. *Wath D* 6F **41**
Fircroft Av. *S5* 4H **75**
Fircroft Rd. *S5* 4A **76**
Fire & Police Mus. 1E **99** (1E **5**)
Firham Clo. *Roy* 1C **8**
Fir Pl. *S6* 6A **86**
Fir Pl. *Kil* 4A **126**
Fir Rd. *Eck* 6H **125**
Firsby La. *Con* 6A **58**
Firshill Av. *S4* .3F **87**
Firshill Clo. *S4* 3E **87**
Firshill Cres. *S4* 3E **87**
Firshill Cft. *S4* 3E **87**
Firshill Gdns. *S4* 3E **87**
Firshill Glade. *S4* 3E **87**
Firshill M. S3 .3F **87**
(off Pitsmoor Rd.)
Firshill Ri. *S4* .3F **87**
Firshill Rd. *S4* 3F **87**
Firshill Wlk. *S4* 3E **87**
Firshill Way. *S4* 3E **87**
Firs La. *H'swne* 1D **142**
First Av. *Roth* .1G **79**
First Av. *Roy* 1F **9**
First Av. *W'land* 3E **17**
Firs, The. *B'ley* 3C **24**
Firs, The. *Roy* .1C **8**
First La. *Ans* .4G **119**
First La. *Wick* 6G **81**
Fir St. *S6* 6A **86**
Fir St. *Holl* 2H **133**
Firth Av. *Cud* .2G **15**
Firth Cres. *Maltby* 5G **83**
Firth Cres. *New R* 4C **62**
Firth Dri. *S4* 5H **87**
Firth Park. **6H 75**
Firth Pk. Av. *S5* 6A **76**
Firth Pk. Cres. *S5* 6H **75**
Firth Pk. Rd. *S5* 6H **75**
Firth Rd. *Wath D* 5B **40**
Firth's Homes. *S11* 5F **97**
Firth St. *B'ley* .5H **13**
Firth St. *Donc* 2B **46**
Firth St. *Roth* .4C **68**
Firthwood Av. *Coal A* 6H **123**
Firthwood Clo. *Coal A* 6H **123**
Firthwood Rd. *Coal A* 6H **123**
Fir Tree Dri. *Wal* 5E **117**
Firtree Ri. *C'town* 3E **65**
Fir Vale. **2H 87**

Fir Va. Pl. *S5* .2G **87**
Fir Va. Rd. *S5* .2G **87**
Firvale Rd. *Walt* 5D **136**
Fir Vw. *Walt* .3H **87**
Fir Wlk. *Maltby* 4C **82**
Fisher Clo. *Ches* 5F **9**
Fisher Clo. *Ches* 6H **137**
Fisher Clo. *Roth* 3C **78**
Fisher La. *S9* 6E **89**
Fisher Rd. *Maltby* 5H **83**
Fisher St. *Ben* .5B **18**
Fisher Ter. *Donc* 4A **32**
Fish Pond La. *B'well* 1G **83**
Fishponds Rd. *S13* 5E **101**
Fishponds Rd. W. *S13* 5E **101**
Fitzalan Rd. *S13* 4H **101**
Fitzalan Sq. *S1* 2F **99** (3F **5**)
Fitzgerald Rd. *S10* 1H **97**
Fitzhubert Rd. *S2* 5D **88**
Fitzmaurice Rd. *S9* 5D **88**
Fitzroy Rd. *S2* 1F **111**
Fitzwalter Rd. *S2* 3H **99**
Fitzwilliam Av. *Con* 3B **58**
Fitzwilliam Av. *Wath D* 6E **41**
Fitzwilliam Ct. *Rawm* 3F **69**
Fitzwilliam Ct. *Wath D* 5E **41**
Fitzwilliam Dri. *H'ton* 2G **43**
Fitzwilliam Ga. *S1* 3E **99** (6C **4**)
Fitzwilliam Rd. *D'fld* 3G **27**
Fitzwilliam Rd. *S Kirk* 2E **79**
Fitzwilliam Sq. Else 1D **52**
(off Wath Rd.)
Fitzwilliam Sq. *Roth* 3B **68**
Fitzwilliam St. *S1* 2D **98** (4B **4**)
Fitzwilliam St. *B'ley* 6G **13**
Fitzwilliam St. *Else* 6C **38**
Fitzwilliam St. *H'fld* 4D **38**
Fitzwilliam St. *Hoy* 6F **37**
Fitzwilliam St. *P'gte* 4F **69**
Fitzwilliam St. *Swint* 2A **56**
(in three parts)
Fitzwilliam St. *Wath D* 6E **41**
Five Oaks. *Ark* .4E **19**
Five Trees Av. *S17* 3G **121**
Five Trees Clo. *S17* 3G **121**
Five Trees Dri. *S17* 3G **121**
Five Weirs Wlk. *S9* 5B **88**
Fixby Ho. Donc 1C **46**
(off St James St.)
Flamsted Cres. *Ches* 5A **132**
Flanders Ct. *Thpe H* 2B **66**
Flanderwell. **3F 81**
Flanderwell Av. *Braml* 4G **81**
Flanderwell Ct. *Braml* 3G **81**
Flanderwell Gdns. *Braml* 3G **81**
Flanderwell La. *Braml* 2F **81**
Flash La. *Braml* 2E **81**
Flask Vw. *S6* 4C **84**
Flat La. *L Hou* .4A **28**
Flat La. *Whis* 2H **91**
Flat St. *S1* 2F **99** (3F **5**)
Flatts Clo. *Tree* 6E **91**
Flatts La. *Tree* .6E **91**
Flatts La. *Wath D* 5D **40**
Flaxby Rd. *S9* .6D **88**
Flax Lea. *Wors* 4A **24**
Fleet Clo. *Bram B* 4B **40**
Fleet Hill Cres. *B'ley* 2A **14**
Fleet La. *Worr* .5E **73**
Fleet St. *S9* 4B **88**
Fleetwood Av. *B'ley* 2C **14**
Fleming Pl. *B'ley* 1G **23**
Fleming Sq. *Wath D* 5E **41**
Fleming Way. *Flan* 4E **81**
Fletcher Av. *Dron* 2E **129**
Fletcher Ho. Roth 2E **79**
(off Wharncliffe Hill)
Fleury Clo. *S14* 3A **112**
Fleury Cres. *S14* 3A **112**
Fleury Pl. *S14* 3A **112**
Fleury Ri. *S14* 3A **112**
Fleury Rd. *S14* 3A **112**
Flint Rd. *Donc* .3A **34**
Flintway. *Wath D* 2F **55**
Flockton Av. *S13* 5C **102**
Flockton Ct. *S1* 2D **98** (4C **4**)
Flockton Cres. *S13* 5B **102**
Flockton Dri. *S13* 5C **102**
Flockton Ho. *S1* 4C **4**
Flockton Rd. *S13* 5B **102**
Flodden St. *S10* 1H **97**
Floodgate Dri. *E'fld* 1F **75**
Flora St. *S6* 5C **86**

Florence Av. *Donc* 3A **46**
Florence Av. *Swal* 6B **104**
Florence Ri. *D'fld* 4D **26**
Florence Rd. *S8* 5C **110**
Florence Rd. *Roth* 3B **78**
Flower St. *Gold* 4H **29**
Flowitt St. *Donc* 1B **46**
Flowitt St. *Mexb* 6D **42**
Folderings La. *Bols* 6E **141**
Folder La. *Spro* 2C **44**
Foldings. **1A 72**
Folds Cres. *S8* 6A **110**
Folds Dri. *S8* .6A **110**
Folds La. *S8* .6A **110**
Fold, The. *Roth* 1B **80**
Foley Av. *Womb* 1E **39**
Foley St. *S4* 6H **87**
Foljambe Av. *Ches* 5F **137**
Foljambe Cres. *New R* 4B **62**
Foljambe Dri. *Dalt* 6G **71**
Foljambe Rd. *Brim* 3E **133**
Foljambe Rd. *Ches* 2H **137**
Foljambe Rd. *Roth* 1H **79**
Foljambe St. *P'gte* 3F **69**
Folkwood Gro. *S11* 2E **109**
Follett Rd. *S5* .4G **75**
Folly La. *Thurls* 2A **142**
Fonteyn Ho. *Donc* 3F **33**
Fontwell Dri. *Mexb* 5F **43**
Foolow Av. *Ches* 4H **137**
Foolow Ct. *Ches* 4H **137**
Footgate Clo. *O'bri* 2D **72**
Forbes Rd. *S6* .4A **86**
Ford Clo. *Dron* 2D **128**
Ford La. *S'bri* 2E **141**
Fordoles Head La. *Maltby* 1C **82**
Ford Rd. *S11* 1H **109**
Fordstead La. *Ark* 2F **17**
Fore Hill Av. *Donc* 5B **48**
Foremark Rd. *S5* 5H **75**
Fore's Rd. *Arm* .4G **35**
Forest Clo. *O'bri* 5F **73**
Forest Edge. *S11* 6G **109**
Forest Grange. *Donc* 2C **48**
Forest Ri. *Donc* 6G **45**
Forest Rd. *B'ley* 5B **8**
Forge Hill. *O'bri* 2D **72**
Forge La. *Else* .1D **52**
Forge La. *Kil* 2H **125**
Forge La. *O'bri* 2D **72**
Forge La. *O'bri & Wort* 1H **141**
Forge La. *Roth* .3D **78**
Forge Rd. *Wal* 4D **117**
Forge, The. *Dron* 2E **129**
Formby Clo. *B'ley* 1D **14**
Forncett St. *S4* 5H **87**
Fornham St. *S2* 3F **99** (6F **5**)
(in two parts)
Forres Av. *S10* 2G **97**
Forres Rd. *S10* 2G **97**
Forrester Clo. *Flan* 3F **81**
Forrester's La. *Coal A* 5G **123**
Forster Rd. *Donc* 5B **46**
Forth Av. *Dron W* 1B **128**
Fort Hill Rd. *S9* 6B **76**
Fortway Rd. *B'wth* 1C **90**
Fossard Clo. *Donc* 2G **33**
Fossard Way. *Scawt* 6H **17**
Fossdale Rd. *S7* 2B **110**
Foster Rd. *Wick* 4F **81**
Foster's Clo. *Swint* 2A **56**
Fosters, The. *High G* 6B **50**
Forster St. *B'ley* 1D **24**
Foster Way. *High G* 5B **50**
Foston Dri. *Ches* 6D **130**
Fothergill Dri. *E'thpe* 4E **21**
Foulstone Row. *Womb* 1G **39**
Foundry Climbing Cen., The. 6E **87**
Foundry Ct. *S3* 4F **87**
Foundry Rd. *Donc* 2B **46**
Foundry St. *B'ley* 1G **23**
(in two parts)
Foundry St. *Ches* 3A **132**
Foundry St. *Else* 6C **38**
Foundry St. *P'gte* 4F **69**
Foundry St. Ind. Est. Ches 3A **132**
(off Foundry St.)
Foundry, The. *Ches* 3B **138**
Fountain Clo. *Dart* 4C **6**
Fountain Ct. *B'ley* 4A **8**
Fountain Ct. *Ross* 5F **63**
Fountain Pde. *M'well* 5G **7**
Fountain Precinct. *S1* 3E **5**

Fountains Cl. *Kirk S* 3C **20**
Fountain Sq. *Dart* 4C **6**
Fountains Way. *B'ley* 4D **14**
Fountside. *S7* 1B **110**
Fourlands Clo. *Bar G* 2A **12**
Four Lane Ends. 2F 113
(Frecheville)
Fourlane Ends. 3D 110
(Norton Woodseats)
Fourth Av. *W'land* 4D **16**
Fourwells Dri. *S12* 3A **114**
Fowler Bri. Rd. *Ben* 1C **32**
Fowler Cres. *New R* 4C **62**
Fowler St. *Old W* 1H **131**
Foxbrook Clo. *Ash* 6B **130**
Foxbrook Ct. *Ches* 5D **136**
Foxbrook Dri. *Ches* 4D **136**
Fox Clo. *Roth* 5F **67**
Foxcote Lea. *Thry* 5E **71**
Foxcote Way. *Walt* 5D **136**
Fox Ct. *Swint* 4B **56**
Foxcovert Clo. *Gold* 6E **29**
Fox Cft. *Hoy* 6H **37**
Foxcroft Chase. *Kil* 3A **126**
Foxcroft Dri. *Kil* 3A **126**
Foxcroft Gro. *Kil* 3A **126**
Foxcroft Meadows. *Maltby* 5F **83**
Foxdale Av. *S12* 2D **112**
Foxen Cft. *B'ley* 3E **15**
Fox Farm Ct. *Bram* 4A **40**
Fox Fields. *Oxs* 6G **143**
Foxfield Wlk. *B'ley* 3D **24**
Fox Glen Rd. *Deep* 4F **141**
Foxglove Clo. *Cal* 2G **139**
Foxglove Rd. *S5* 5A **76**
Fox Gro. *Warm* 5E **45**
Foxhall La. *S10* 1A **108**
Fox Hill. *S3* 5F **87**
Fox Hill Av. *S6* .4A **74**
Fox Hill Clo. *S6* 4A **74**
Fox Hill Cres. *S6* 4A **74**
Fox Hill Dri. *S6* 4A **74**
Fox Hill Pl. *S6* .3A **74**
Fox Hill Rd. *S6* 5A **74**
Fox Hill Way. *S6* 3A **74**
Foxland Av. *Swint* 3G **55**
Fox La. *S12* 5E **113**
Fox La. *S17* .3B **122**
Fox La. *Barn* 1G **43**
Fox La. Ct. *S12* 3E **113**
Fox La. Vw. *S12* 3E **113**
Fox Rd. *S6* 5C **86**
Foxroyd Clo. *B'ley* 1F **25**
Foxley Oaks. *Old W* 2B **132**
Fox's Pl. *Ches* 3F **137**
Fox St. *S3* 5E **87**
Fox St. *Roth* 3G **77**
Foxtone Clo. *Stav* 3B **134**
Fox Wlk. *S6* 5B **86**
Foxwood Av. *S12* 1D **112**
Foxwood Clo. *Ches* 2G **131**
Foxwood Clo. *Has* 6D **138**
Foxwood Dri. *S12* 1D **112**
Foxwood Gro. *S12* 2D **112**
Foxwood Ind. Pk. *Ches* 2H **131**
Foxwood Rd. *S12* 1D **112**
Foxwood Rd. *Ches* 1G **131**
Foxwood Way. *Ches* 1G **131**
Foyers Way. *Ches* 2B **138**
Framlingham Pl. *S2* 6H **99**
Framlingham Rd. *S2* 6H **99**
Frances Rd. *S6* 2D **84**
Frances St. *Donc* 6D **32**
France St. *P'gte* 4F **69**
Francis Clo. *Brim* 4D **132**
Francis Cres. N. *Roth* 6B **80**
Francis Cres. S. *Roth* 6B **80**
Francis Dri. *Roth* 5B **80**
Francis Gro. *High G* 6B **50**
Francis Rd. *S6* .4E **79**
Francus Royd. *B'ley* 4E **9**
Frank Hillock Fld. *Deep* 3G **141**
Franklin Cres. *Donc* 6F **33**
Franklin Rd. *Ches* 1G **137**
Frank Pl. *S9* 4C **88**
Frank Rd. *Donc* 3B **32**
Fraser Clo. *S8* 4C **110**
Fraser Cres. *S8* 4C **110**
Fraser Dri. *S8* 4D **110**
Fraser Rd. *S8* 4C **110**
Fraser Rd. *Roth* 4F **79**
Fraser Wlk. *S8* 5D **110**
Frecheville. 3F 113

Frecheville St.—Gileswood Cres.

Frecheville St. *Stav* . . . 2B **134**
Frederick Av. *B'ley* . . . 1F **23**
Frederick Dri. *Gren* . . . 6A **64**
Frederick Rd. *S7* . . . 6D **98**
Frederick St. *S9* . . . 6D **88**
Frederick St. *Cat* . . . 6C **90**
Frederick St. *Gold* . . . 4G **29**
Frederick St. *Mexb* . . . 1D **56**
Frederick St. *Roth* . . . 2D **78**
Frederick St. *Wath D* . . . 4D **40**
Frederick St. *Womb* . . . 6A **26**
Frederic Pl. *B'ley* . . . 2H **23**
Freebirch Vw. *Ches* . . . 4D **130**
Freedom Ct. *S6* . . . 4B **86**
Freedom Rd. *S6* . . . 5A **86**
Freeman Gdns. *High G* . . . 1B **64**
Freeman Rd. *Wick* . . . 4F **81**
Freeman St. *B'ley* . . . 1H **23**
Freemans Yd. *B'ley* . . . 6H **13**
Freesia Clo. *Ans* . . . 3E **119**
Freeston Pl. *S9* . . . 4C **88**
French Ga. *Donc* . . . 5C **32**
(in two parts)
Frenchgate Shop. Cen. *Donc* . . . 6C **32**
French St. *Ben* . . . 5B **18**
Fretson Clo. *S2* . . . 5C **100**
Fretson Grn. *S2* . . . 5C **100**
Fretson Rd. *S2* . . . 5C **100**
Fretson Rd. S. *S2* . . . 6C **100**
Fretwell Clo. *Maltby* . . . 3E **83**
Fretwell Rd. *H'by* . . . 4B **82**
Fretwell Rd. *Roth* . . . 1A **80**
Freydon Way. *Cal* . . . 2G **139**
Friar Clo. *S6* . . . 5D **84**
Friars Ga. *Donc* . . . 5C **32**
Friar's Rd. *B'ley* . . . 4E **15**
Frickley Bri. La. *Brie* . . . 1E **11**
Frickley Rd. *S11* . . . 5F **97**
Friers Cft. *W'wth* . . . 4D **52**
Frinton Clo. *Ches* . . . 6H **137**
Frithbeck Clo. *Arm* . . . 3F **35**
Frith Clo. *S12* . . . 2D **112**
Frith Rd. *S12* . . . 2D **112**
Frobisher Gro. *Maltby* . . . 3E **83**
Froggatt Clo. *Ink* . . . 5A **134**
Froggatt La. *S1* . . . 3E **99** (5E **5**)
Frogmore Clo. *Braml* . . . 3H **81**
Frog Wlk. *S11* . . . 5C **98**
Front St. *Tree* . . . 1E **103**
Frostings Clo. *Gren* . . . 6A **64**
(in two parts)
Frostings, The. *Gren* . . . 6A **64**
Fulford Clo. *S9* . . . 6E **89**
Fulford Clo. *Ches* . . . 5E **137**
Fulford Clo. *Dart* . . . 4E **7**
Fulford Pl. *S9* . . . 6E **89**
Fulford Way. *Con* . . . 2G **59**
Fuller Dri. *Ches* . . . 5C **132**
Fullerton Av. *Con* . . . 3B **58**
Fullerton Cres. *Thry* . . . 4C **70**
Fullerton Dri. *B'wth* . . . 3B **90**
Fullerton Rd. *Roth* . . . 5C **78**
Fulmar Way. *Thpe H* . . . 1C **66**
Fulmer Clo. *B'ley* . . . 1B **14**
Fulmere Cres. *S5* . . . 3C **74**
Fulmere Rd. *S5* . . . 3C **74**
Fulmer Rd. *S11* . . . 6A **98**
Fulney Rd. *S11* . . . 5F **97**
Fulton Rd. *S6* . . . 6A **86**
Fulwood. . . . **5C 96**
Fulwood Chase. *S10* . . . 5E **97**
Fulwood Dri. *Donc* . . . 1H **61**
Fulwood La. *S10* . . . 3A **108**
Fulwood Rd. *S10* . . . 6D **96**
Furlong Ct. *Gold* . . . 6F **29**
Furlong Meadows. *Bram* . . . 5H **39**
Furlong Rd. *Bol D & Gold* . . . 1B **42**
Furlong Rd. *H'ton* . . . 2E **43**
Furlong Vw. *Barn* . . . 1F **43**
Furlong Vw. *H'ton* . . . 1F **43**
Furnace Hill. *S3* . . . 1E **99** (1D **4**)
Furnace Hill. *Ches* . . . 3G **137**
Furnace La. *S13* . . . 6E **103**
Furnace La. *Barl* . . . 1B **130**
Furnace La. *Brim* . . . 5F **133**
Furnace Yd. *Else* . . . 1D **52**
Furness Clo. *S6* . . . 4D **84**
Furness Clo. *Dinn* . . . 6F **107**
Furness Dene. *B'ley* . . . 2D **14**
Furness Rd. *High G* . . . 6A **50**
Furniss Av. *S17* . . . 3D **120**
Furniss M. *S17* . . . 3E **121**
Furnival Clo. *Tod* . . . 2A **118**
Furnival Ga. *S1* . . . 3E **99** (5D **4**)
Furnivall Rd. *Donc* . . . 3A **46**
Furnival Rd. *S4* . . . 1F **99** (2G **5**)
Furnival Rd. *Tod* . . . 2A **118**
Furnival Sq. *S1* . . . 3E **99** (5E **5**)
Furnival St. *S1* . . . 3E **99** (5E **5**)
Furnival Way. *Whis* . . . 2B **92**
Future Wlk. *Ches* . . . 2H **137**
Fylde Clo. *B'ley* . . . 1D **14**

G

Gainsborough Clo. *Flan* . . . 4F **81**
Gainsborough Rd. *S11* . . . 6B **98**
Gainsborough Rd. *Dron* . . . 3C **128**
Gainsborough Way. *B'ley* . . . 3B **14**
Gainsford Rd. *S9* . . . 1E **101**
Gaitskell Clo. *Gold* . . . 6F **29**
Gaitskell Clo. *Maltby* . . . 5H **83**
Gala Cres. *Maltby* . . . 3D **82**
Gallery, The. *S1* . . . 1F **99** (2G **5**)
Galley Dri. *Wat* . . . 6D **114**
Gallow Tree Rd. *Roth* . . . 5A **80**
Galpharm Way. *Dod* . . . 1A **22**
Galsworthy Av. *S5* . . . 6D **74**
Galsworthy Clo. *Donc* . . . 6H **45**
(in two parts)
Galsworthy Rd. *S5* . . . 1C **86**
Galway Clo. *Rawm* . . . 1G **69**
Galway Clo. *Roy* . . . 1E **9**
Gamston Rd. *S8* . . . 6D **98**
Gannow Clo. *Kil* . . . 2D **126**
Gannow Hill. . . . **2D 126**
Ganton Pl. *B'ley* . . . 6A **8**
Ganton Rd. *S6* . . . 1H **85**
Garbroads Cres. *Thry* . . . 5C **70**
Garbutt St. *Bol D* . . . 2B **42**
Garden Clo. *Roth* . . . 1G **91**
Garden Ct. *B'ley* . . . 6D **12**
Garden Cres. *Roth* . . . 1G **91**
Garden Dri. *Bram* . . . 3A **40**
Garden Gro. *H'fld* . . . 3E **39**
Garden Ho. Clo. *B'ley* . . . 2C **14**
Garden Ho. Dri. *Kiv P* . . . 4B **118**
Gardenia Rd. *Kirk S* . . . 4C **20**
Garden La. *Donc* . . . 2H **45**
Garden La. *Rav* . . . 4H **71**
Garden La. Roth . . . *2C 78*
(off Amen Corner)
Gardens La. *Con* . . . 3D **58**
Gardens, The. *S7* . . . 5C **98**
Gardens, The. *Donc* . . . 4B **48**
Garden St. *S1* . . . 1D **98** (2C **4**)
Garden St. *B'ley* . . . 1H **23**
Garden St. *D'fld* . . . 4E **27**
Garden St. *Gold* . . . 4H **29**
Garden St. *Mexb* . . . 6E **43**
Garden St. *Roth* . . . 2B **78**
Garden St. *Thurn* . . . 1F **29**
Garden St. *Wath D* . . . 4D **40**
Garden Ter. *Ben* . . . 1B **32**
Garden Village. . . . **3C 140**
Garden Wlk. *Beig* . . . 4G **115**
Garden Wlk. *Roth* . . . 1G **91**
Gardom Clo. *Dron W* . . . 2B **128**
Garfield Mt. *Roth* . . . 3E **79**
Garland Clo. *W'fld* . . . 1E **125**
Garland Cft. *W'fld* . . . 2E **125**
Garland Dri. *S6* . . . 2E **85**
Garland Mt. *W'fld* . . . 1E **125**
Garland Way. *W'fld* . . . 2E **125**
Garry Rd. *S6* . . . 2H **85**
Garside's Bldgs. P'stne . . . *4C 142*
(off Stottercliffe Rd.)
Garter St. *S4* . . . 4H **87**
Garth Clo. *S9* . . . 6C **88**
Garth Way. *Dron* . . . 2D **128**
Garth Way Clo. *Dron* . . . 2D **128**
Gartrice Gdns. *Half* . . . 4G **125**
Gartrice Gro. *Half* . . . 4G **125**
Gashouse La. *Mosb & Eck* . . . 4D **124**
Gate Cres. *Dod* . . . 1B **22**
Gatefield Clo. *Ches* . . . 5E **131**
Gatefield Rd. *S7* . . . 1C **110**
Gateland La. *Dron* . . . 6C **128**
Gate, The. *Dod* . . . 1B **22**
Gateway Clo. *P'gte* . . . 6E **69**
Gateway Ct. *P'gte* . . . 5E **69**
Gateway Ind. Est., The. *P'gte* . . . 5E **69**
Gateway Pl. *P'gte* . . . 6E **69**
Gateway, The. *P'gte* . . . 5E **69**
Ga. Wood La. *Cant & Bran* . . . 1G **49**
Gattison La. *New R* . . . 5D **62**
Gatty Rd. *S5* . . . 2H **75**
Gaunt Clo. *S14* . . . 4H **111**
Gaunt Clo. *Braml* . . . 3H **81**
Gaunt Clo. *Kil* . . . 3A **126**
Gaunt Dri. *S14* . . . 4H **111**
Gaunt Dri. *Braml* . . . 3H **81**
Gaunt Pl. *S14* . . . 3H **111**
Gaunt Rd. *S14* . . . 4H **111**
Gaunt Rd. *Braml* . . . 3H **81**
Gaunt Way. *S14* . . . 4H **111**
Gawber. . . . **4D 12**
Gawber Rd. *B'ley* . . . 4E **13**
Gawtress Row. *Wath D* . . . 5E **41**
Gayle Ct. *B'ley* . . . 5F **13**
Gayton Clo. *Donc* . . . 6A **46**
Gayton Ct. *Donc* . . . 6A **46**
Gayton Rd. *S4* . . . 3G **87**
Gelderd Pl. *Dron* . . . 3E **129**
Gell St. *S3* . . . 2C **98** (4A **4**)
Genn La. *B'ley & Wors* . . . 3F **23**
Genoa Clo. *D'fld* . . . 2C **26**
Genoa St. *Mexb* . . . 6F **43**
George Pl. *Mexb* . . . 6G **43**
George Pl. *Rawm* . . . 2G **69**
George Sq. *B'ley* . . . 6G **13**
George St. *S1* . . . 2F **99** (3F **5**)
George St. *Arm* . . . 2D **34**
George St. *B'ley* . . . 6G **13**
George St. *Ben* . . . 5A **18**
George St. *Brim* . . . 3E **133**
George St. *Cud* . . . 5C **10**
George St. *Gold* . . . 4E **29**
George St. *Hoy* . . . 6A **38**
George St. *L Hou* . . . 2H **27**
George St. *M'well* . . . 4F **7**
George St. *Old W* . . . 1H **131**
George St. *Roth* . . . 2D **78**
(in two parts)
George St. *Thurn* . . . 2H **29**
George St. *Womb* . . . 1F **39**
(High St.)
George St. *Womb* . . . 5D **26**
(Stonyford Rd.)
George St. *Wors* . . . 5A **24**
(Broomroyd)
George St. *Wors* . . . 5C **24**
(High St.)
George Woofindin Almshouses.
S11 . . . 5A **98**
George Yd. *B'ley* . . . 6G **13**
Georgian M. *Cat* . . . 5C **90**
Gerald Clo. *B'ley* . . . 2C **24**
Gerald Cres. *B'ley* . . . 1C **24**
Gerald Pl. *B'ley* . . . 2C **24**
Gerald Rd. *B'ley* . . . 2C **24**
Gerald St. *S9* . . . 4C **88**
Gerald Wlk. *B'ley* . . . 2C **24**
Gerard Av. *Thry* . . . 5E **71**
Gerard Clo. *S8* . . . 1F **111**
Gerard Clo. *Ches* . . . 4E **137**
Gerard Rd. *Roth* . . . 4E **79**
Gerard St. *S8* . . . 1F **111**
Gertrude St. *S6* . . . 5C **86**
Gervase Av. *S8* . . . 3C **122**
Gervase Dri. *S8* . . . 3C **122**
Gervase Pl. *S8* . . . 3C **122**
Gervase Rd. *S8* . . . 3C **122**
Gervase Wlk. *S8* . . . 3C **122**
Gibbing Greaves Rd. *Roth* . . . 5C **80**
Gibbons Dri. *S14* . . . 5A **112**
Gibbons Wlk. S14 . . . *5A 112*
(off Gibbons Dri.)
Gibbons Way. *S14* . . . 5A **112**
Gibraltar St. *S3* . . . 1E **99** (1D **4**)
Gibson La. *S'bri* . . . 2D **140**
Gibson Wlk. Swint . . . *4B 56*
(off Haythorne Way)
Gifford Dri. *Warm* . . . 5F **45**
Gifford Rd. *S8* . . . 6E **99**
Gilbert Av. *Ches* . . . 5F **137**
Gilbert Ct. *S2* . . . 5H **5**
Gilbert Gro. *B'ley* . . . 1D **24**
Gilberthorpe Ct. *Roth* . . . 3F **79**
Gilberthorpe Dri. *Roth* . . . 3G **79**
Gilberthorpe Rd. *Donc* . . . 4H **45**
Gilberthorpe St. *Roth* . . . 3F **79**
Gilbert Row. *S2* . . . 2G **99** (3H **5**)
Gilbert St. *S2* . . . 2F **99** (3G **5**)
Gilder Way. *Shaf* . . . 3C **10**
Gildhurst Ct. *Birdw* . . . 5D **36**
Giles Av. *Wath D* . . . 5C **40**
Gileswood Cres. *Bram* . . . 4A **40**

Gill Clo. *Wick* 6G **81**
Gill Cft. *S6* 5C **84**
Gilleyfield Av. *S17* 2E **121**
Gill Meadows. *S6* 5C **84**
Gillott Dell. *Wick* 6F **81**
Gillott Ind. Est. *B'ley* 5F **13**
Gillott La. *Wick* 6F **81**
(in two parts)
Gillott Rd. *S6* 5A **74**
Gill St. *Donc* 1D **46**
Gill St. *Hoy* 6B **38**
Gilpin La. *S6* 6C **86**
Gilpin St. *S6* 5C **86**
Gilroyd. **3C 22**
Gilroyd La. *Dod* 4C **22**
Ginhouse La. *Roth* 1C **78**
Gipsy Grn. La. *Wath D* 1F **55**
Gipsy La. *Old W* 2B **132**
Gisborne Ga. *S11* 1H **109**
Glade Clo. *Ches* 6G **131**
Glade Cft. *S12* 3C **112**
Glade Lea. *S12* 3C **112**
Glade, The. *S10* 4H **97**
Glade, The. *Ches* 2F **137**
Glade Vw. *Kirk S* 3D **20**
Gladstone M. *S10* 4E **97**
Gladstone Pl. *Mexb* 6C **42**
Gladstone Rd. *S10* 4F **97**
Gladstone Rd. *Ches* 1H **137**
Gladstone Rd. *Donc* 2A **46**
Gladstone Rd. *Maltby* 3E **83**
Gladwin Gdns. *Ches* 5F **137**
Gladwin Ind. Pk. *Kiln* 6C **56**
Gladys St. *Roth* 3G **79**
Glaisdale Clo. *Dinn* 2C **106**
Glaisdale Ct. *Dinn* 2C **106**
Glamis Rd. *Donc* 6G **33**
Glasshouse La. *Kiln* 6C **56**
Glasshouse Rd. *Kiln* 6C **56**
Glasshouse St. *Roth* 2C **78**
Glastonbury Ga. *Donc* 4F **31**
Gleadless. **3C 112**
Gleadless Av. *S12* 3B **112**
Gleadless Bank. *S12* 3B **112**
Gleadless Comn. *S12* 1B **112**
Gleadless Ct. *S2* 1F **111**
Gleadless Ct. *S12* 2B **112**
Gleadless Dri. *S12* 3B **112**
Gleadless Mt. *S12* 4C **112**
Gleadless Rd. *S2* 6E **99**
Gleadless Rd. *S14 & S12* 2A **112**
Gleadless Townend. **4C 112**
Gleadless Valley. **3A 112**
Gleadless Vw. *S12* 2B **112**
Glebe Clo. *Swint* 4A **56**
Glebe Ct. *Old W* 1A **132**
Glebe Ct. *Tank* 6D **36**
Glebe Cres. *Thry* 6C **70**
Glebe Farm Clo. *Arm* 2E **35**
Glebeland Clo. *Rawm* 6E **55**
Glebelands Rd. *S'bri* 4E **141**
Glebe Rd. *S10* 1A **98**
Glebe Rd. *Swint* 4A **56**
Glebe St. *Warm* 5F **45**
Glebe, The. Old W 1A **132**
(off Glebe Way, The)
Glebe Way, The. *Old W* 1A **132**
Gledhill Av. *P'stne* 6C **142**
Gledhill Clo. *Dron* 2E **129**
Glenalmond Rd. *S11* 6H **97**
Glencairn Clo. Maltby 4H **83**
(off Lumley Clo.)
Glencoe Dri. *S2* 3G **99**
Glencoe Pl. *S2* 3G **99**
Glencoe Rd. *S2* 3G **99** (5H **5**)
Glencoe Way. *Ches* 1D **136**
Glencroft. *S11* 6G **97**
Glendale Clo. *B'ley* 5D **12**
Glendale Rd. *Spro* 2D **44**
Gleneagles Clo. *Ches* 5E **137**
Gleneagles Dri. *Donc* 5F **49**
Gleneagles Ri. *Swint* 3B **56**
Gleneagles Rd. *Dinn* 5F **107**
Glen Fld. Av. *Donc* 2A **46**
Glenfield Cres. *Ches* 4H **131**
Glen Head. *S17* 6D **108**
Glenholme Dri. *S13* 6G **101**
Glenholme Pl. *S13* 6H **101**
Glenholme Rd. *S13* 5H **101**
Glenholme Way. *S13* 5G **101**
Glenmoor Av. *B'ley* 1D **22**
Glenmore Clo. *Ink* 6H **133**
Glenmore Cft. *S12* 1D **112**

Glenmore Ri. *Womb* 2G **39**
Glenorchy Rd. *S7* 2B **110**
Glen Rd. *S7* 1C **110**
Glen Rd. *Bran* 3H **49**
Glen, The. *S10* 4H **97**
Glenthorne Clo. *Ches* 3E **137**
Glentilt Rd. *S7* 2B **110**
Glen Vw. *S11* 5F **97**
Glen Vw. Rd. *S8* 1C **122**
Glenville Clo. *Hoy* 6H **37**
Glenwood Ct. *S6* 6F **73**
Glenwood Cres. *C'town* 2F **65**
Glenwood Dri. *S6* 6F **73**
Glenwood M. *S6* 6F **73**
Gliwice Way. *Donc* 2H **47**
Glossop La. *S10* 2C **98**
Glossop Rd. *S10* 3A **98** (4A **4**)
Glossop Row. *O'bri* 2D **72**
Glossop's Cft. *Old W* 1B **132**
Gloucester Av. *Ches* 5H **131**
Gloucester Cres. *S10* 3C **98**
Gloucester Rd. *Ches* 6H **131**
Gloucester Rd. *Donc* 4G **33**
Gloucester Rd. *Roth* 6H **67**
Gloucester St. *S10* 3C **98**
Glover Rd. *S8* 6E **99**
Glover Rd. *S17* 5F **121**
Glumangate. *Ches* 2A **138**
Glyn Av. *Donc* 5E **33**
Goathland Clo. *S13* 6D **102**
Goathland Dri. *S13* 6D **102**
Goathland Pl. *S13* 6D **102**
Goathland Rd. *S13* 6D **102**
Goddard Av. *S'bri* 2B **140**
Goddard Hall Rd. *S5* 2G **87**
Godley Clo. *Roy* 1F **9**
Godley St. *Roy* 1F **9**
Godric Dri. *B'wth* 2B **90**
Godric Grn. *B'wth* 2B **90**
Godric Rd. *S5* 2G **75**
Godstone Rd. *Roth* 4E **79**
Goldcrest Ho. *Old W* 1B **132**
Goldcrest Wlk. *Thpe H* 2C **66**
Gold Cft. *B'ley* 1A **24**
Golden Oak Dell. *S6* 4C **84**
Golden Smithies La.
Swint & Wath D 2H **55**
Goldsborough Rd. *Donc* 6G **33**
Goldsmith Dri. *Roth* 3H **79**
Goldsmith Rd. *Donc* 5C **46**
Goldsmith Rd. *Roth* 3H **79**
Gold St. *B'ley* 1A **24**
Goldthorpe. **4H 29**
Goldthorpe Grn. *Gold* 5F **29**
Goldthorpe Ind. Est. *Gold* 5D **28**
Goldthorpe Rd. *Gold* 5G **29**
Gomersal La. *Dron* 2E **129**
Gomersal Av. *Con* 3B **58**
Gooder Av. *Roy* 2E **9**
Goodison Boulevd. *Donc* 3C **48**
Goodison Ct. *Donc* 3C **48**
Goodison Cres. *S6* 5F **85**
Goodison Ri. *S6* 5F **85**
Goodman Ct. *Cal* 2G **139**
Goodwin Av. *Rawm* 1F **69**
Goodwin Cres. *Swint* 1A **56**
Goodwin Rd. *S8* 1E **111**
Goodwin Rd. *Roth* 3A **68**
Goodwin Way. *Roth* 3A **68**
Goodwood Gdns. *Donc* 1B **48**
Goodyear Cres. *Womb* 1F **39**
Goole Green. **6D 96**
Goore Av. *S9* 3D **100**
Goore Dri. *S9* 2D **100**
Goore Rd. *S9* 3D **100**
Gooseacre Av. *Thurn* 1E **29**
Goosebutt Ct. *P'gte* 3F **69**
Goosebutt St. *P'gte* 3F **69**
Goose Carr La. *Tod* 6H **105**
Goosecroft Av. *Thry* 5C **70**
Goosehill Ct. *Bal* 1H **61**
Goose La. *Wick* 5G **81**
Gordon Av. *S8* 5E **111**
Gordon Rd. *S11* 5B **98**
Gordon Rd. *Edl'tn* 3B **60**
Gordon St. *B'ley* 1E **25**
Gordon St. *Donc* 6C **32**
Gordon Ter. *Roth* 3F **79**
Gorehill Clo. *Wath D* 5G **41**
Gorman Clo. *Ches* 3G **131**
Gorse Clo. *Bram* 5H **39**
Gorse Dri. *Kil* 4B **126**
Gorseland Ct. *Wick* 5E **81**

Gorse La. *S10* 6A **96**
Gorse, The. *Roth* 4A **80**
Gorse, The. *Wick* 6F **81**
Gorse Valley Rd. *Has* 6E **139**
Gorse Valley Way. *Has* 6E **139**
Gorsey Brigg. *Dron W* 2B **128**
Gosber Rd. *Eck* 6E **125**
Gosber St. *Eck* 6D **124**
Gosforth Clo. *Dron* 2D **128**
Gosforth Cres. *Dron* 2D **128**
Gosforth Dri. *Dron* 2B **128**
Gosforth Grn. *Dron* 2D **128**
Gosforth La. *Dron* 2D **128**
Gosling Ga. Rd. *Gold* 4G **29**
Gotham Rd. *B'wth* 1C **90**
Gough Clo. *Roth* 5A **80**
Goulding St. *Mexb* 1D **56**
Gowdall Grn. *Ben* 4A **18**
Gower Cres. *Ches* 6E **131**
Gower St. *S4* 5G **87**
Gower St. *Womb* 1G **39**
Goyt Side Rd. *Ches* 3F **137**
Goyt Ter. *Ches* 3G **137**
Grace Rd. *Edl'tn* 2C **60**
Grace St. *B'ley* 1F **15**
Graftdyke Clo. *Ross* 4F **63**
Grafton St. *S2* 3G **99** (5H **5**)
Grafton St. *B'ley* 6F **13**
Grafton Way. *Roth* 2E **79**
Graham Av. *B'wth* 4D **90**
Graham Ct. *S10* 5F **97**
Graham Knoll. *S10* 5F **97**
Graham Ri. *S10* 4E **97**
Graham Rd. *S10* 4E **97**
Graham Rd. *Kirk S* 4D **20**
Graham's Orchard. *B'ley* 6G **13**
Grainger Clo. *Edl'tn* 4A **60**
Grainger Ct. *S10* 4E **97**
Grammar St. *S6* 4B **86**
(in two parts)
Grampian Clo. *B'ley* 5D **12**
Grampian Clo. *Donc* 4G **31**
Grampian Cres. *Ches* 1D **136**
Granary Clo. *Ches* 4C **130**
Granary Ct. *Ans* 1F **119**
(off Quarry La.)
Granby Ct. *Arm* 4G **35**
Granby Cres. *Donc* 1F **47**
Granby La. *New R* 3B **62**
Granby Rd. *S5* 1H **87**
Granby Rd. *Edl'tn* 3C **60**
Grange Av. *Aug* 4A **104**
Grange Av. *Donc* 4A **46**
Grange Av. *Dron W* 2C **128**
Grange Clo. *Bram M* 6H **93**
Grange Clo. *Brie* 2F **11**
Grange Clo. *Donc* 5D **48**
Grange Ct. *Bes* 5D **48**
Grange Ct. *Donc* 3B **32**
Grange Ct. *Wick* 6F **81**
Grange Cres. *S11* 5C **98**
Grange Cres. *B'ley* 5E **15**
Grange Cres. *Thurn* 1G **29**
Grange Cres. Rd. *S11* 5C **98**
Grange Dri. *H'by* 5B **82**
Grange Dri. *Roth* 6F **67**
Grange Farm Clo. *B'wth* 4D **90**
Grange Farm Dri. *Ast* 2C **116**
Grange Farm Dri. *Worr* 2C **84**
Grangefield Av. *New R* 4D **62**
Grangefield Cres. *New R* 4D **62**
Grangefield Ter. *New R* 4D **62**
Grange Gdns. *Tod* 6H **105**
Grange Ho. *Brie* 2F **11**
Grange Lane. **1B 76**
Grange La. *S5 & Thpe H* 1B **76**
Grange La. *S13* 5A **102**
Grange La. *A'ley* 1E **61**
(in two parts)
Grange La. *B'ley* 6E **15**
Grange La. *B'wth* 6A **78**
Grange La. *H'ton* 1H **43**
Grange La. *Maltby* 4G **83**
Grange La. *New R* 5B **62**
(in two parts)
Grange La. Ind. Est. *B'ley* 6D **14**
Grange Mill La. *S5 & S9* 1B **76**
Grangemill Pl. *Stav* 3A **134**
Grange Pk. *Kirk S* 2E **21**
Grange Pk. Av. *Brim* 1F **139**
Grange Pk. Golf Course. 5C **66**
Grange Rd. *S11* 5C **98**

Grange Rd. *Beig* 4F **115**
Grange Rd. *Brie* .2F **11**
Grange Rd. *Donc* 5D **48**
Grange Rd. *New R* 5C **62**
Grange Rd. *Rawm* 6G **55**
Grange Rd. *Roth* 1H **91**
Grange Rd. *Roy* .2C **8**
Grange Rd. *Swint* 3H **55**
Grange Rd. *Toll B* 3A **18**
Grange Rd. *Wath D* 6D **40**
Grange Rd. *W'land* 4E **17**
Grange St. *Thurn* 1G **29**

Grange, The. *Ash* 1B **136**
Grange, The. *Scho* 5E **67**
Grange Vw. *Bal* .3A **46**
Grange Vw. *Bla H* 2H **37**
Grange Vw. Cres. *Roth* 1F **77**
Grange Vw. Rd. *Roth* 1F **77**
Grange Way. *Den M* 2B **58**
Grangewood Rd. *Ches* 6H **137**
Grangewood Rd. *Lghtn* 1E **107**
Granham Acre. *Shaf* 3C **10**
Gransden Way. *Ches* 5E **137**
Grantham St. *New R* 4C **62**
Grantley Clo. *Womb* 3H **39**
Granville Clo. *Has* 5D **138**
Granville Rd. *S2* 3F **99** (6G **5**)
Granville Sq. *S2* 3F **99** (6G **5**)
Granville St. *S2* 3F **99** (6G **5**)
Granville St. *B'ley* 4F **13**
Granville Ter. *Roth* 3F **79**
Grasby Ct. *Braml* 2H **81**
Grasmere Av. *Donc* 5A **34**
Grasmere Clo. *Ans* 1H **119**
Grasmere Clo. *Bol D* 2A **42**
Grasmere Clo. *Ches* 4F **131**
Grasmere Clo. *Mexb* 5H **43**
Grasmere Clo. *P'stne* 3D **142**
Grasmere Cres. *Dart* 3E **7**
Grasmere Rd. *S8* 2C **110**
Grasmere Rd. *B'ley* 6A **14**
Grasmere Rd. *Con* 3D **58**
Grasmere Rd. *Dron W* 2B **128**
Grasscroft Clo. *Ches* 5F **131**
Grassdale Vw. *S12* 4H **113**
Grassholme Clo. *Donc* 4H **47**
Grassington Clo. *S12* 4B **114**
Grassington Dri. *S12* 4B **114**
Grassington Way. *C'town* 1D **64**
Grassmoor Clo. *S12* 2B **112**
Grassthorpe Rd. *S12* 3D **112**
Grattan St. *Roth* 3G **77**
Gratton St. *Stav* 1D **134**
Graven Clo. *Gren* 1H **73**
Graves Art Gallery. 2F **99** (4F **5**)
Graves Pk. Animal Farm. 5F **111**
Graves Tennis & Leisure Cen. 2F **123**
Graves Trust Homes. *S8* 1D **122**
(Greenhill Av.)
Graves Trust Homes. *S8* 1E **123**
(Lit. Norton La.)
Graves Trust Homes. *S12* 2C **112**
Gray Av. *Swal* .5B **104**
Gray Clo. *Roth* .1E **79**
Gray Gdns. *Donc* 5B **46**
Grays Ct. *Den M* 1C **58**
Grayshott Wlk. *Ches* 5H **137**
Grayson Clo. *Rav* 1H **81**
Grayson Clo. *S'bri* 4E **141**
Grayson Rd. *Roth* 3A **68**
Gray's Rd. *B'ley* 4E **9**
Gray St. *Else* 6C **38**
Gray St. *Mosb* .2C **124**
Greasbro Rd. *S9* 1F **89**
Greasbrough. .4C **68**
Greasbrough La. *Rawm* 3C **68**
Greasbrough Rd. *P'gte* 4D **68**
Greasbrough Rd. *Roth* 5C **68**
(in three parts)
Greasbrough St. *Roth* 2C **78**
Gt. Bank Rd. *Roth* 5A **80**
Gt. Broad Ing. *B'ley* 3D **12**
Gt. Central Av. *Donc* 3B **46**
Gt. Cliffe Rd. *Dod* 1A **22**
Great Cft. *Dron W* 1B **128**
Gt. Eastern Way. *P'gte* 5F **69**
Gt. North Rd. *Adw S & W'land* 1B **16**
Gt. North Rd. *Donc* 4B **48**
Gt. North Rd. *Ross & Baw* 2G **63**
Gt. North Rd. *W'land & Scawt* 5E **17**
Gt. Park Rd. *Roth* 1G **77**

Greaves Clo. *S6* 5C **84**
Greaves Fold. *B'ley* 5D **12**
Greaves La. *S6* .5C **84**
Greaves La. *High G* 3B **50**
Greaves Rd. *S5* .1E **75**
Greaves Rd. *Roth* 2A **78**
Greaves Sike La. *M'brng* 1B **82**
Greaves St. *S6* .4B **86**
Green Acres. *Grim* 6G **11**
Green Acres. *Hoy* 6A **38**
Green Acres. *P'stne* 4E **143**
Green Acres. *Rawm* 2G **69**
Greenacres Clo. *Dron* 4G **129**
Grn. Arbour Ct. *Thur* 6A **94**
Grn. Arbour Rd. *Thur* . . . . . . .5A **94** & 1A **106**
(in two parts)
Green Bank. *B'ley* 4B **8**
Greenbank Dri. *Ches* 1E **137**
Grn. Bank Dri. *S'side* 1G **81**
Greenbank Wlk. *Grim* 6F **11**
Green Boulevd. *Donc* 3C **48**
Green Brook Pl. *P'stne* 5D **142**
Green Chase. *Eck* 6C **124**
Green Clo. *Ink* .5A **134**
Green Comn. *Arm* 4F **35**
Green Ct. *S'side* 2G **81**
Greencroft. *Roth* 5F **79**
Green Cross. *Dron* 1F **129**
Greendale Av. *Holy* 5A **136**
Greendale Ct. *Dron* 1F **129**
Greendale Shop. Cen. *Dron* 1F **129**
Grn. Dyke La. *Donc* 2C **46**
Grn. Dyke Way. *B'ley* 3C **12**
Grn. Farm Clo. *Ches* 5E **131**
Grn. Farm Hamlet. *S'bri* 3A **140**
Greenfield. *Rawm* 2F **69**
Greenfield Clo. *S8* 2D **122**
Greenfield Clo. *Arm* 4G **35**
Greenfield Clo. *Barn D* 1E **21**
Greenfield Clo. *Roth* 1B **80**
Greenfield Cotts. *B'ley* 5E **9**
Greenfield Ct. *Adw D* 3D **42**
Greenfield Ct. *Flan* 3F **81**
Greenfield Dri. *S8* 2D **122**
Greenfield Gdns. *B'ley* 4A **8**
Greenfield Gdns. *Donc* 4E **49**
Greenfield Gdns. *Flan* 3F **81**
Greenfield La. *Donc* 2A **46**
Greenfield Rd. *S8* 2D **122**
Greenfield Rd. *Hoy* 5A **38**
Greenfield Rd. *Roth* 1B **80**
Green Fields. *Eck* 6C **124**
Greenfinch Clo. *B'wth* 3D **90**
Greenfoot Clo. *B'ley* 4F **13**
Greenfoot La. *B'ley* 3F **13**
(in two parts)
Greengate Clo. *S13* 1D **114**
Grn. Gate Clo. *Bol D* 6F **29**
Greengate Clo. *Ches* 3E **137**
Greengate La. *S13* 1C **114**
Greengate La. *High G* 1B **64**
Greengate Rd. *S13* 1D **114**
Green Glen. *Ches* 3E **137**
Greenhall Rd. *Eck* 6C **124**
Greenhead Gdns. *C'town* 2E **65**
Greenhead La. *C'town* 2E **65**
Greenhill. 2C **122**
Greenhill Av. *S8* 1C **122**
Greenhill Av. *B'ley* 4H **13**
Greenhill Av. *H'by* 5B **82**
Grn. Hill Gro. *H'swne* 1G **143**
Greenhill Main Rd. *S8* 2C **122**
Greenhill Parkway. *S8* 3B **122**
Greenhill Rd. *S8* 5D **110**
Green Ho. Rd. *Donc* 3H **33**
Greenhow St. *S6* 6A **86**
Green Ings La. *Bol D* 4G **41**
Greenland. 4E **89**
Greenland. *Bla H* 2H **37**
Greenland Av. S. *Maltby* 3G **83**
(in two parts)
Greenland Clo. *S9* 5E **89**
Greenland Clo. *Ans* 1F **119**
Greenland Ct. *S9* 5E **89**
Greenland Dri. *S9* 5E **89**
Greenland Rd. *S9* 4E **89**
Greenland Rd. Ind. & Bus. Pk. *S9* 4E **89**
Greenlands Av. *Ross* 3E **63**
Greenland Vw. *S9* 6E **89**
Greenland Vw. *Wors* 5H **23**
Greenland Wlk. *S9* 5E **89**
Greenland Way. *S9* 5E **89**
(Greenland Dri.)

Greenland Way. *S9* 4E **89**
(Greenland Rd.)
Greenland Way. *Maltby* 2G **83**
Green La. *S3* 6D **86** (1D **4**)
Green La. *Ast* 2F **119**
Green La. *Cant* .6E **105**
Green La. *Cat* 4B **90**
Green La. *Ches* 1D **138**
Green La. *Cut* 4A **130**
Green La. *Dod* 3C **22**
Green La. *D'ville* 2F **129**
Green La. *Dron* .4G **21**
Green La. *E'fld* .1G **75**
Green La. *Hoy* 6E **37**
Green La. *Kil* 5A **126**
Green La. *K'wth* .2E **77**
Green La. *Maltby* 3E **95**
Green La. *Rawm* 2F **69**
Green La. *Roth* .1G **91**
Green La. *Scawt* 5A **16**
Green La. *S'bri* .2A **140**
Green La. *Thur* .2H **93**
Green La. *Ulley* .1B **104**
Green La. *Wadw* 6G **61**
Green La. *Wath D* 2D **54**
Green La. *Wick* .4E **81**
Green La. *W'land* 3C **16**
Green La. *Wors* .4E **23**
Green Lea. *Dron W* 1A **128**
Greenleafe Av. *Donc* 2A **34**
Green Moor. 1G **141**
Grn. Moor Rd. *Wort* 1F **141**
Grn. Oak Av. *S17* 5E **121**
Grn. Oak Cres. *S17* 5E **121**
Grn. Oak Dri. *S17* 5E **121**
Grn. Oak Dri. *Wal* 5E **117**
Grn. Oak Gro. *S17* 5E **121**
Grn. Oak Rd. *S17* 6E **121**
Grn. Oak Vw. *S17* 5E **121**
Greenock St. *S6* 3H **85**
Green Ri. *Rawm* 6D **54**
Green Rd. *P'stne* 5D **142**
Greenset Vw. *B'ley* 4A **8**
Greenside. 4G **7**
Greenside. *H'swne* 1G **143**
Greenside. *M'well* 4G **7**
Greenside. *Roth* 4B **68**
Greenside Av. *Ches* 4H **131**
Greenside Av. *Kiv P* 5G **117**
Greenside Av. *M'well* 4G **7**
Greenside Est. *Shaf* 1B **10**
Greenside Gdns. *H'swne* 1G **143**
Greenside Ho. *M'well* 4G **7**
Greenside La. *Hoy* 4A **38**
Greenside M. *S12* 4B **114**
Greenside Pl. *M'well* 4G **7**
Grn. Spring Av. *Birdw* 3D **36**
Greens Rd. *Roth* 3H **79**
Green St. *Deep* .3F **141**
Green St. *Donc* .5H **45**
Green St. *Hoy* 5A **38**
Green St. *Old W* 1A **132**
Green St. *Roth* .3B **68**
Green St. *Wors* .4C **24**
Green, The. 5D **142**
Green, The. *S9* .1E **101**
(off Avenue, The)
Green, The. *S17* 5D **120**
Green, The. *S26* 4B **116**
Green, The. *Ans* 1F **119**
Green, The. *Barn* 1H **43**
Green, The. *Bol D* 6E **29**
Green, The. *Has* 6D **138**
Green, The. *H'fld* 4E **39**
Green, The. *Hood G* 6A **22**
Green, The. *Old De* 2G **57**
Green, The. *P'stne* 5C **142**
Green, The. *Roth* 6F **79**
Green, The. *Roy* .2E **9**
(in two parts)
Green, The. *Shaf* 2B **10**
Green, The. *S'side* 2G **81**
Green, The. *Swint* 3H **55**
Green, The. *Thurls* 3A **142**
Green, The. *Whis* 3H **91**
Green Vw., The. *Shaf* 1B **10**
Greenway. *Kiv P* 5H **117**
Greenways. *Ches* 5E **137**
Greenway, The. *S8* 1D **122**
Greenway, The. *Deep* 4G **141**
Greenway Vw. *H'fld* 4F **39**
Greenwood Av. *S9* 2C **100**
Greenwood Av. *Bal* 3H **45**

Greenwood Av. *Wors* 4B **24**
Greenwood Clo. *S9* 2D **100**
Greenwood Cres. *S9* 2C **100**
Greenwood Cres. *Roy* 1D **8**
Greenwood Cres. *Wick* 4G **81**
Greenwood Dri. *S9* 2C **100**
Greenwood La. *S13* 6D **102**
Greenwood Rd. *S9* 2D **100**
Greenwood Rd. *High G* 6D **50**
Greenwood Rd. *Kiln* 6C **56**
Greenwood Ter. *B'ley* 5G **13**
Greenwood Way. *S9* 2C **100**
Greeton Dri. *O'bri* 3E **73**
Gregg Ho. Cres. *S5* 4H **75**
Gregg Ho. Rd. *S5* 3H **75**
Greggs Ct. *B'ley* 2D **24**
Gregory Clo. *Brim* 3D **132**
Gregory La. *Brim* 2D **132**
Gregory Rd. *S8* 1E **111**
Grendon Vs. *Roth* 2G **79**
Grenfell Av. *Mexb* 6F **43**
Grenfolds Rd. *Gren* 1B **74**
Grenobank Rd. *Gren* 1B **74**
Greno Cres. *Gren* 1B **74**
Greno Ga. *Gren* 6A **64**
Greno Ho. *Gren* 6A **64**
Grenomoor Clo. *Gren* 1A **74**
Greno Rd. *Swint* 3B **56**
Grenoside. **6A 64**
Grenoside Crematorium. *Gren* 2H **73**
Grenoside Mt. *Gren* 2B **74**
Greno Vw. *Hood G* 6A **22**
Greno Vw. *Hoy* 6G **37**
Greno Vw. Rd. *High G* 6C **50**
Greno Wood Ct. *Gren* 6A **64**
Grenville Pl. *B'ley* 4E **13**
Grenville Rd. *Donc* 5G **45**
Gresham Av. *B'wth* 2C **90**
Gresham Rd. *S6* 5A **86**
Gresley Rd. *S8* 4C **122**
Gresley Rd. *Bal* 2B **46**
Gresley Wlk. *S8* 4C **122**
Greyfriars. *S11* 6G **97**
Greyfriars Rd. *Donc* 5C **32**
Greystock St. *S4* 5A **88**
. . . .(Corby St.)
Greystock St. *S4* 6H **87**
. . . . (Sutherland St.)
Greystones. **6G 97**
Greystones Av. *S11* 6H **97**
Greystones Av. *Wors* 5H **23**
Greystones Cliffe. **6F 97**
Greystones Clo. *S11* 6G **97**
Greystones Ct. *S11* 6G **97**
Greystones Ct. *H'hill* 3H **127**
Greystones Cres. *S11* 6G **97**
Greystones Dri. *S11* 6G **97**
Greystones Grange. *S11* 6G **97**
Greystones Grange Cres. *S11* 6G **97**
Greystones Grange Rd. *S11* 6G **97**
Greystones Hall Rd. *S11* 5G **97**
Greystones Ri. *S11* 6G **97**
Greystones Rd. *S11* 6F **97**
Greystones Rd. *Whis* 2B **92**
Grice Clo. *Donc* 1D **48**
Griffen Clo. *Stav* 3C **134**
Griffin Rd. *Swint* 2H **55**
Griffiths Clo. *P'gte* 3F **69**
Griffiths Rd. *High G* 1C **64**
Griffs. **5A 84**
Grimesthorpe. **2B 88**
Grimesthorpe Rd. *S4* 5G **87**
. . . .(in three parts)
Grimethorpe. **6G 11**
Grimesthorpe Rd. S. *S4* 5G **87**
Grimsell Clo. *S6* 2B **74**
Grimsell Cres. *S6* 2B **74**
Grimsell Dri. *S6* 2B **74**
Grimsell Wlk. *S6* 3B **74**
Grinders Hill. *S1* 5F **5**
Grinders Wlk. *S6* 2F **85**
Grindlow Av. *Ches* 4H **137**
Grindlow Clo. *S14* 1G **111**
Grindlow Dri. *S14* 1G **111**
Grindon Clo. *Ches* 6E **131**
Grinton Wlk. *Ches* 5H **137**
Grisedale Wlk. *Dron W* 2C **128**
Grizedale Av. *Soth* 5G **115**
Grizedale Clo. *Soth* 5G **115**
Grosvenor Cres. *Ark* 5D **18**
Grosvenor Cres. *Warm* 5F **45**
Grosvenor Dri. *B'ley* 6E **13**
Grosvenor Rd. *Roth* 1F **79**

Grosvenor Rd. *W'land* 2D **16**
Grosvenor Sq. *S2* 5D **98**
Grosvenor Ter. *Warm* 5F **45**
Grouse Cft. *S6* 5B **86**
Grouse St. *S6* 4A **86**
Grove Av. *S6* 1G **85**
Grove Av. *S17* 5D **120**
Grove Av. *Donc* 4A **32**
Grove Clo. *P'stne* 6D **142**
Grove Clo. *Wath D* 3C **40**
Grove Cotts. Ches 3F **137**
. . . .(off Walton Rd.)
Grove Ct. Maltby 4D **82**
. . . .(off Leslie Av.)
Gro. Farm Clo. *Brim* 4E **133**
Grove Gdns. *Brim* 1F **139**
Gro. Hall Clo. *E'thpe* 5E **21**
Gro. Hill Rd. *Donc* 2A **34**
Grove Ho. Ct. *S17* 4E **121**
Grove Pl. *Donc* 1C **46**
Grove Rd. *S7* 4A **110**
Grove Rd. *S17* 4E **121**
Grove Rd. *Brim* 6E **133**
Grove Rd. *Ches* 4A **132**
Grove Rd. *K Ind* 3B **20**
Grove Rd. *M'well* 4E **7**
Grove Rd. *Roth* 4D **78**
Grove St. *Wath D* 3C **40**
Grove Sq. *S6* 4C **86**
Grove St. *B'ley* 6A **14**
Grove St. *Deep* 4H **141**
Grove St. *Has* 5C **138**
Grove St. *Wors* 4C **24**
Grove, The. *S6* 3E **85**
Grove, The. *S17* 5D **120**
Grove, The. *Barn D* 1G **21**
Grove, The. *Cud* 4B **10**
Grove, The. *Donc* 4A **32**
. . . .(in two parts)
Grove, The. *Pool* 3E **135**
Grove, The. *Rawm* 2G **69**
Grove, The. *Roth* 2H **79**
Grove, The. *Wick* 4F **81**
Grove Va. *Donc* 2A **34**
Grove Way. *Brim* 6F **133**
Guernsey Rd. *S2* 6E **99**
Guest La. *Warm* 4F **45**
Guest Pl. *Hoy* 4A **38**
Guest Pl. *Roth* 5F **79**
Guest Rd. *S11* 5A **98**
Guest Rd. *B'ley* 4F **13**
Guest Rd. *Roth* 5F **79**
Guest St. *Hoy* 4A **38**
Guildert Av. *Thur* 6A **94**
Guildford Av. *S2* 5H **99**
Guildford Av. *Ches* 5F **137**
Guildford Clo. *S2* 5H **99**
Guildford Dri. *S2* 5H **99**
Guildford Ri. *S2* 5A **100**
Guildford Rd. *Donc* 2H **33**
Guildford Rd. *Roy* 1D **8**
Guildford Vw. *S2* 6A **100**
Guildford Wlk. *S2* 5A **100**
Guildford Way. *S2* 5H **99**
Guildhall Ind. Est. *K Ind* 4C **20**
Guild Rd. *Roth* 3H **79**
Guildway. *Tod* 2A **118**
Guilthwaite. **4A 92**
Guilthwaite Comn. La.
. . . . . *Whis* 6A **92**
Guilthwaite Cres. *Whis* 2G **91**
Guilthwaite Hill. *Whis* 5A **92**
Gullane Dri. *Warm* 5F **45**
Gulling Wood Dri. *Thry* 5E **71**
Gunhills La. *Arm* 2G **35**
Gunhills La. Ind. Est. *Arm* 2G **35**
Gun La. *S3* 1F **99** (1G **5**)
Gurney Rd. *Donc* 5B **46**
Gurth Av. *E'thpe* 5E **21**
Gurth Av. Cvn. Site. *E'thpe* 5E **21**
Gurth Dri. *Thur* 6A **94**
Gwendoline M. *Wath D* 6F **41**
Gypsy La. *Womb* 2G **39**

H

Habershon Ct. *C'town* 2E **65**
Habershon Dri. *C'town* 1D **64**
Habershon Rd. *Roth* 6H **67**
Hackenthorpe. **4B 114**
Hackings Av. *P'stne* 6C **142**
Hackness La. *B'wth* 2B **90**

Hackney La. *Barl* 1B **130**
Hackthorn Rd. *S8* 4D **110**
Haddon Clo. *Ches* 3E **137**
Haddon Clo. *Dod* 2A **22**
Haddon Clo. *Dron* 1F **129**
Haddon Pl. *Stav* 3B **134**
Haddon Ri. *Mexb* 5H **43**
Haddon Rd. *B'ley* 1B **14**
Haddon St. *S3* 5D **86**
Haddon Way. *Ast* 6D **104**
Haden St. *S6* 3A **86**
Hadfield St. *S6* 6A **86**
Hadfield St. *Womb* 2F **39**
Hadleigh Clo. *Rawm* 3F **69**
Hadrian Rd. *B'wth* 1C **90**
Hadrians Clo. *Ross* 6E **63**
Hady. **3D 138**
Hady Cres. *Ches* 3C **138**
Hady Hill. *Ches* 3B **138**
Hady La. *Ches* 3D **138**
Haggard Rd. *S6* 3B **86**
Hagg Hill. *S6* 4H **73**
. . . .(Midhurst Rd.)
Hagg Hill. *S6* 6F **85**
. . . . (Rivelin Valley Rd.)
Hagg La. *S10* 2C **96**
. . . .(in two parts)
Hagg La. Cotts. *S10* 1D **96**
Haggstones Dri. *O'bri* 3C **72**
Haggstones Rd. *O'bri & Worr* 3C **72**
Hague Av. *Rawm* 6E **55**
Hague La. *High G* 6A **50**
Hague La. *W'wth* 1D **66**
Hague Row. *S2* 2G **99** (3H **5**)
Haids Clo. *Maltby* 2F **83**
Haids La. *Maltby* 2F **83**
Haids Rd. *Maltby* 2F **83**
Haig Cres. *New R* 5C **62**
Haigh Clo. *H'swne* 1F **143**
Haigh Ct. *Bram* 5H **39**
Haigh Cft. *Roy* 1D **8**
Haigh Head Rd. *H'swne* 1F **143**
Haigh La. *Haigh* 1A **6**
Haigh La. *H'swne* 1G **143**
Haigh Memorial Homes. S8 . . . . .2E **123**
. . . .(off Meadowhead)
Haigh Moor Clo. *S13* 4H **101**
Haigh Moor Dri. *Dinn* 4C **106**
Haigh Moor Rd. *S13* 5H **101**
Haigh Moor Wlk. *S13* 5G **101**
Haigh Moor Way. *Roy* 1E **9**
Haigh Moor Way. *Swal* 6G **103**
Haigh Rd. *Donc* 4A **46**
Hail Mary Dri. *S13* 5D **102**
Haise Mt. *Dart* 4E **7**
Hakehill Clo. *Donc* 5B **48**
Halcyon Clo. *S12* 4H **113**
Haldane Clo. *Brie* 2F **11**
Haldane Rd. *Roth* 1G **79**
Haldene. *Wors* 5B **24**
Haldynby Gdns. *Arm* 3G **35**
Hale St. *S7* 1D **110**
Halesworth Clo. *Ches* 5D **136**
Halesworth Rd. *S13* 3G **101**
Halfacre La. *Uns* 3H **129**
Half Cft. *Brim* 4F **133**
Halfway. **2E 125**
Halfway Cen. *Half* 2E **125**
Halfway Dri. *Half* 2E **125**
Halfway Gdns. *Half* 2E **125**
Halifax Av. *Con* 3C **58**
Halifax Cres. *Donc* 3H **31**
Halifax Hall. *S10* 4A **98**
Halifax Rd. *S6* 5B **74**
Halifax Rd. *P'stne & H'swne* 1C **142**
Halifax St. *B'ley* 3G **13**
Hallam Chase. *S10* 4H **97**
. . . .(Endcliffe)
Hallam Chase. *S10* 3D **96**
. . . .(Sandygate)
Hallam Clo. *Aug* 4A **104**
Hallam Clo. *Donc* 4A **48**
Hallam Ct. S10 . . . . .4B **98**
. . . .(off Clarke Dri.)
Hallam Ct. *Bol D* 2H **41**
Hallam Ct. *Dron* 3E **129**
Hallam Dale Ct. *Rawm* 6G **55**
Hallamgate Rd. *S10* 3H **97**
Hallam Grange Clo. *S10* 5C **96**
Hallam Grange Cres. *S10* 4C **96**
Hallam Grange Cft. *S10* 4C **96**
Hallam Grange Ri. *S10* 4C **96**
Hallam Grange Rd. *S10* 4C **96**

Hallam Head. 3D 96
Hallam La. S1 . . . . .3E 99 (6E 5)
Hallam Pl. Rawm 2G 69
Hallam Rd. Roth 1F 91
Hallam Rock. S5 . . . . .2F 87
Hallamshire Bus. Pk. S11 . . . . .4C 98
Hallamshire Clo. S10 . . . . .5B 96
Hallamshire Ct. C'town 2E 65
Hallamshire Dri. S10 . . . . .5B 96
Hallamshire Golf Course. 3B 96
Hallamshire Rd. S10 . . . . .5B 96
Hallam Way. E'fld 1F 75
Hall Av. Jump 4C 38
Hall Av. Mexb 6F 43
Hall Balk La. B'ley 4F 13
Hall Broome Gdns. Bol D 6E 29
Hallcar St. S4 . . . . .6G 87
Hall Clo. Ans 1F 119
Hall Clo. Bram B 4B 40
Hall Clo. Cut 3A 130
Hall Clo. Dron W 1A 128
Hall Clo. Wors 1E 37
Hall Clo. Av. Whis 2A 92
Hall Cotts. Morth 3F 93
Hall Ct. Dinn 5E 107
Hall Ct. Rav 3G 71
Hall Cres. Roth 1H 91
Hall Cft. Wick 5G 81
Hall Cft. Womb 5D 26
Hallcroft Dri. Arm 5G 35
Hall Cft. Ri. Roy 2D 8
Hall Cross Av. Womb 2H 39
Hall Cross Hill. Donc 1E 47
Hall Dri. Wath D 6D 40
Hall Farm Clo. Aug 3A 104
Hall Farm Clo. Has 6D 138
Hall Farm Cft. Dinn 5F 107
Hall Farm Dri. Thurn 2F 29
Hall Farm Gro. H'swne 1G 143
Hall Farm Ri. Thurn 2F 29
Hallflash La. Cal 5G 139
Hall Flat La. Donc 4A 46
Hall Ga. Donc 6D 32
Hall Ga. Mexb 1G 57
Hall Ga. P'stne 3D 142
Hallgate. Thurn 2F 29
Hallgate Rd. S10 . . . . .2G 97
Hall Gro. M'well 4G 7
Hall Gro. Roth 4E 79
Halliwell Clo. S5 . . . . .6B 74
Halliwell Cres. S5 . . . . .6C 74
Hall La. H'swne 1G 143
Hall La. Stav 1C 134
Hall Mdw. Cft. Half 4F 125
Hall Mdw. Dri. Half 3F 125
Hall Mdw. Gro. Half 4F 125
Hall M. Rav 3G 71
Hallowes. 3G 129
Hallowes Ct. Dron 2F 129
Hallowes Dri. Dron 3F 129
Hallowes Golf Course. 4F 129
Hallowes La. Dron 2F 129
Hallowes Ri. Dron 3G 129
Hallowmoor. 2G 85
Hallowmoor Rd. S6 . . . . .2F 85
Hall Pk. Head. S6 . . . . .6D 84
Hall Pk. Hill. S6 . . . . .6E 85
Hall Pk. Mt. S6 . . . . .6E 85
Hall Pl. B'ley 3C 14
Hall Rd. S9 . . . . .2G 101
Hall Rd. S13 . . . . .3G 101
Hall Rd. Aug 4A 104
Hall Rd. Brim 4E 133
Hall Rd. Maltby 4C 82
Hall Rd. Roth 4E 79
Hallside Ct. Cant 2F 49
Hallside Clo. Mosb 3D 124
Hall's Row. Ches 3F 137
Hall St. Gold 5G 29
Hall St. Hoy 5A 38
Hall St. Roth 3C 78
Hall St. Womb 1G 39
Hallsworth Av. H'fld 4D 38
Hall Vw. C'town 1E 65
Hall Vw. Ches 5G 131
Hall Vw. Rd. Ross 6E 63
Hall Villa La. Toll B 2A 18
Hall Wood Rd. C'town 2A 64
Hallyburton Clo. S2 . . . . .1G 111
Hallyburton Dri. S2 . . . . .1G 111
Hallyburton Rd. S2 . . . . .1G 111
Halmshaw Ter. Ben 1A 32
Halsall Av. S9 . . . . .2E 101

Halsall Dri. S9 . . . . .2D 100
Halsall Rd. S9 . . . . .2E 101
Halsbury Rd. Roth 1G 79
Halstead Gro. M'well 3E 7
Halsteads. S13 . . . . .4F 101
Halton Clo. Ches 2G 131
Halton Ct. S12 . . . . .4C 114
Hamble Ct. M'well 5G 7
Hambleton Clo. Ches 6E 131
Hambleton Clo. B'ley 5D 12
Hambleton Clo. Else 5D 38
Hameline Rd. Con 3D 58
Hamer Wlk. Roth 2A 80
Hamilton Clo. Donc 2F 47
Hamilton Clo. Mexb 5G 43
Hamilton Pk. Rd. Donc 3F 31
Hamilton Rd. S5 . . . . .1H 87
Hamilton Rd. Donc 2F 47
Hamilton Rd. Gold 3H 29
Hamilton Rd. Maltby 5H 83
Hammerton Clo. S6 . . . . .4A 86
Hammerton Rd. S6 . . . . .4A 86
Hammond St. S3 . . . . . . .1C 98 (1A 4)
Hampden Rd. Mexb 6E 43
Hamper La. H'swne 1F 143
(in two parts)
Hampole Dri. Thurn 2E 29
Hampson Gdns. E'thpe 4E 21
Hampstead Grn. Roth 6G 67
Hampton Rd. S5 . . . . .2G 87
Hampton Rd. Donc 6F 33
Hampton St. Ches 6D 138
Hanbury Clo. B'ley 3D 14
Hanbury Clo. Ches 6C 130
Hanbury Clo. Donc 1G 61
Hanbury Clo. Dron 2D 128
Handby St. Has 5D 138
Handley St. S3 . . . . .6F 87
Handley Rd. S10 . . . . .1A 98
Handsworth. 4B 102
Handsworth Av. S9 . . . . .2F 101
Handsworth Cres. S9 . . . . .2F 101
Handsworth Gdns. Arm 3G 35
Handsworth Grange Clo. S13 . . . . . . .5A 102
Handsworth Grange Cres. S13 . . . . . . .4A 102
Handsworth Grange Dri. S13 . . . . . . .4B 102
Handsworth Grange Rd. S13 . . . . .4A 102
Handsworth Grange Way. S13 . . . . . . .4B 102
Handsworth Hill. 1F 101
Handsworth Rd. S9 & S13 . . . . .2F 101
Hanging Bank Ct. Ans 2G 119
Hanging Water. 5F 97
Hangingwater Clo. S11 . . . . .5F 97
Hangingwater Cotts. S11 . . . . .6F 97
(off Hangingwater Rd.)
Hangingwater Rd. S11 . . . . .6F 97
Hangman La. S11 . . . . .3B 98
Hangthwaite La. W'land 4E 17
Hanley Clo. S12 . . . . .3B 114
Hanmoor Rd. S6 . . . . .5C 84
Hannah Rd. S13 . . . . .6D 102
Hanover Royd. Dod 2C 22
Hanover Ct. S3 . . . . .3C 98 (6A 4)
Hanover Ct. Wors 4A 24
Hanover Sq. S3 . . . . .3D 98 (6B 4)
Hanover Sq. Thurn 1G 29
Hanover St. S3 . . . . .3D 98 (6A 4)
Hanover St. Thurn 1G 29
Hanover Way. S3 . . . . . . .3C 98 (5A 4)
Hanslope Vw. Kirk S 2C 20
Hanson Rd. S6 . . . . .3D 84
Hanson St. B'ley 5H 13
Hanwell Clo. E'fld 1F 75
Harbord Rd. S8 . . . . .5C 110
Harborough Av. S2 . . . . .2B 100
Harborough Clo. S2 . . . . .3C 100
Harborough Dri. S2 . . . . .3C 100
Harborough Hill Rd. B'ley 6H 13
Harborough Ri. S2 . . . . .3C 100
Harborough Rd. S2 . . . . .3C 100
Harborough Way. S2 . . . . .4C 100
Harbury St. S13 . . . . .3E 103
Harcourt Clo. Ches 6C 138
Harcourt Clo. Donc 4A 48
Harcourt Cres. S10 . . . . .1B 98
Harcourt Ri. C'town 3F 65
Harcourt Rd. S10 . . . . .2B 98
Harcourt Ter. Roth 3F 79
Hardcastle Dri. S13 . . . . .6A 102
Hardcastle Gdns. S13 . . . . .6A 102
Hardcastle Rd. S13 . . . . .1A 114
Harden Clo. B'ley 5C 12

Harden Clo. P'stne 5D 142
Hardhurst. 5H 129
Hardie Clo. Maltby 5H 83
Hardie Pl. Rawm 1F 69
Hardie Pl. Stav 3B 134
Hardie St. Eck 6D 124
Harding Av. Rawm 5D 54
Harding Clo. Rawm 6D 54
Harding Ct. Rawm 5D 54
Harding St. S9 . . . . .5D 88
Hard La. Kiv P 6A 118
Hardwick. 4G 105
Hardwick Av. New W 1D 132
Hardwick Clo. Ast 6D 104
Hardwick Clo. Dron 1F 129
Hardwick Clo. Wors 5A 24
Hardwick Ct. Stav 1C 134
(off Devonshire St.)
Hardwick Cres. S11 . . . . .5A 98
Hardwick Cres. B'ley 6C 8
Hardwicke Rd. Roth 1E 79
Hardwick Gro. Dod 3B 22
Hardwick La. Ast 6F 105
Hardwick St. Ches 1A 138
Hardwick St. Roth 1B 80
Hardwicks Yd. Ches 3G 137
Hardy Pl. S6 . . . . .5B 86
Hardy Rd. Donc 3E 33
Hardy St. Roth 2C 78
Haredon Clo. M'well 3E 7
Harefield Rd. S11 . . . . .5B 98
Harehill Rd. Ches 6H 137
Harehills Rd. Roth 4E 79
Harewood Av. B'ley 6D 12
Harewood Av. Kirk S 3D 20
Harewood Av. W'land 2B 16
Harewood Ct. Ross 5F 63
Harewood Gro. Braml 3H 81
Harewood Rd. Donc 6G 33
Harewood Way. S11 . . . . .5G 109
Hargrave Pl. Thry 5D 70
Harland Rd. S11 . . . . .4C 98
Harlech Clo. C'town 1D 64
Harlech Fold. S10 . . . . .4A 96
Harlech Grn. S10 . . . . .4A 96
Harlech Gro. S10 . . . . .4A 96
Harlech Mead. S10 . . . . .4A 96
Harleston St. S4 . . . . .5H 87
(in two parts)
Harley. 4H 51
Harley Rd. S11 . . . . .2F 109
Harley Rd. Harl 4H 51
Harlington. 1G 43
Harlington Ct. Den M 2C 58
Harlington Rd. Adw D 3D 42
Harlington Rd. Mexb 6F 43
Harmer La. S1 . . . . .2F 99 (4F 5)
Harmony Way. Cat 5C 90
Harney Clo. S9 . . . . .6E 89
Harold Av. B'ley 3E 15
Harold Av. W'land 2C 16
Harold Cft. Roth 3C 68
Harold St. S6 . . . . .5B 86
Harperhill Clo. Ches 6H 137
Harriet Clo. B'ley 2A 24
Harrington Ct. B'ley 3E 15
Harrington Rd. S2 . . . . .5E 99
Harrington St. Donc 5D 32
Harrison La. S10 . . . . .6A 96
Harrison Rd. S6 . . . . .4H 85
Harrison St. Roth 3A 78
Harry Rd. S6 . . . . .1H 85
Harry Rd. B'ley 4B 14
Hartcliff Av. P'stne 4C 142
Hartcliff Rd. P'stne 6A 142
Hartfield Clo. Has 6B 138
Hartford Clo. S8 . . . . .4E 111
Hartford Rd. S8 . . . . .4E 111
Harthill. 3H 127
Hart Hill. Rawm 5D 54
Harthill Rd. S13 . . . . .6D 100
Harthill Rd. Con 4C 58

Hartington Av. *S7* 4A **110**
Hartington Clo. *Roth* 3A **78**
Hartington Ct. *Dron* 1F **129**
Hartington Dri. *B'ley* 3H **13**
Hartington Rd. *S7* 4A **110**
Hartington Rd. *Ches* 3C **138**
Hartington Rd. *Dron* 1F **129**
Hartington Rd. *Roth* 3A **78**
Hartland Av. *Soth* 5G **115**
Hartland Ct. *Soth* 5G **115**
Hartland Cres. *E'thpe* 5D **20**
Hartland Dri. *Soth* 5G **115**
Hartland Way. *Old W* 2A **132**
Hartley Brook Av. *S5* 3G **75**
Hartley Brook Rd. *S5* 3G **75**
Hartley Clo. *Swint* 4B **56**
Hartley La. *Roth* 2C **78**
Hartley St. *S2* 6E **99**
Hartley St. *Mexb* 1D **56**
Hartopp Av. *S2* 1G **111**
Hartopp Clo. *S2* 1G **111**
Hartopp Dri. *S2* 1H **111**
Hartopp Rd. *S2* 1G **111**
Harts Head. *S1* 1F **99** (2E **5**)
Hartshead Sq. *S1* 2F **5**
Hartside Clo. *Ches* 6F **131**
Harvest Clo. *Bal* 3H **45**
Harvest Clo. *E'thpe* 4E **21**
Harvest Clo. *Maltby* 5C **82**
Harvest Clo. *Wors* 5A **24**
Harvest La. *S3* 6E **87**
Harvest Rd. *Wick* 4F **81**
Harvest Way. *Ash* 6C **130**
Harvey Clough M. *S8* 4F **111**
Harvey Clough Rd. *S8* 4E **111**
Harvey Rd. *C'town* 2E **65**
Harvey Rd. *Ches* 3E **139**
Harvey St. *B'ley* 1F **23**
Harvey St. *Deep* 3F **141**
Harwell Rd. *S8* 6D **98**
Harwich Rd. *S2* 4A **100**
Harwood Clo. *S2* 5E **99**
Harwood Dri. *Wat* 6D **114**
Harwood Gdns. *Wat* 6E **115**
Harwood St. *S2* 5E **99**
Harwood Ter. *B'ley* 5E **15**
Haslam Ct. *Ches* 1A **138**
Haslam Cres. *S8* 3B **122**
Haslam Pl. *Maltby* 3H **83**
Haslam Rd. *New R* 4D **62**
Hasland. **6D 138**
Hasland By-Pass. *Has* 4C **138**
Hasland Green. **6C 138**
Hasland La. *Cal* 5G **139**
Hasland Rd. *Ches* 4B **138**
            (in two parts)
Haslehurst Rd. *S2* 3A **100**
Haslemere Ct. *Ben* 3A **32**
Haslemere Gro. *Donc* 3A **32**
Hassocky La. *Temp N & Cal* 6H **139**
Hassop Clo. *Ches* 5E **131**
Hassop Clo. *Dron* 1G **129**
Hassop Rd. *Stav* 1D **134**
Hastilar Clo. *S2* 5D **100**
Hastilar Rd. *S2* 5D **100**
Hastilar Rd. S. *S13* 5E **101**
Hastings Clo. *Ches* 5F **131**
Hastings Mt. *S7* 3A **110**
Hastings Rd. *S7* 3A **110**
Hastings St. *Grim* 6G **11**
Hatchell Dri. *Donc* 6E **49**
Hatchell Wood Vw. *Donc* 6F **49**
Hatfield Clo. *B'ley* 6A **8**
Hatfield Cres. *Dinn* 3C **106**
Hatfield Gdns. *Roy* 1D **8**
Hatfield Ho. Donc 1C **46**
         (off St James St.)
Hatfield Ho. Ct. *S5* 4H **75**
Hatfield Ho. Cft. *S5* 4H **75**
Hatfield Ho. La. *S5* 5G **75**
Hatfield La. *Barn D* 2H **21**
            (in two parts)
Hatfield La. *E'thpe & Arm* 5F **21**
Hatherley Rd. *S9* 6G **77**
Hatherley Rd. *Roth* 1E **79**
Hatherley Rd. *Swint* 6B **42**
Hathern Clo. *Brim* 1F **139**
Hathersage Rd. *Grin & S17* 1A **120**
Hatter Dri. *Edl'tn* 5B **60**
Hatton Clo. *Dron W* 3B **128**
Hatton Dri. *Ches* 6D **130**
Hatton Rd. *S6* 4B **86**
Haugh Grn. *Rawm* 5D **54**

Haugh La. *S11* 3F **109**
Haugh Rd. *Rawm* 5C **54**
Haughton Rd. *S8* 5D **110**
Havelock Rd. *Donc* 2C **46**
Havelock St. *S10* 3C **98** (5A **4**)
Havelock St. *B'ley* 1F **23**
Havelock St. *D'fld* 4E **27**
Havenfield. *D'fld* 3E **27**
Havens, The. *Ches* 2F **137**
Haven, The. *Kiv P* 5D **118**
Havercroft Pl. *Kil* 3H **125**
Havercroft Rd. *S8* 3C **110**
Havercroft Ter. *Roth* 6A **80**
Havercroft Ter. *Kil* 2H **125**
Haverdale Ri. *B'ley* 4F **13**
Haverlands La. *Wors* 5F **23**
Haverlands Ridge. *Wors* 5H **23**
Hawes Clo. *Mexb* 5G **43**
Hawfield Clo. *Donc* 2A **46**
Hawke Clo. *Rawm* 6C **54**
Hawke Rd. *Donc* 3F **33**
Hawke St. *S9* 3C **88**
Hawk Hill La. *Thur* 1H **105**
Hawkhills. *S6* 5F **85**
Hawking Houses. *Ches* 6F **131**
Hawkins Av. *Burn* 2C **64**
Hawkshead Av. *Dron W* 2B **128**
Hawkshead Cres. *Ans* 1H **119**
Hawkshead Rd. *S4* 2B **88**
Hawksley Av. *S6* 3A **86**
Hawksley Av. *Ches* 6G **131**
Hawksley Clo. *Arm* 3F **35**
Hawksley Ct. *Arm* 2F **35**
Hawksley M. *S6* 3A **86**
Hawksley Ri. *O'bri* 3D **72**
Hawksley Rd. *S6* 3A **86**
Hawksway. *Eck* 6B **124**
Hawksworth Clo. *Roth* 2A **80**
Hawksworth Rd. *S6* 5B **86**
Hawksworth Rd. *Roth* 2A **80**
Hawkwell Bank. *Ard* 1G **25**
Hawley St. *S1* 1E **99** (2D **4**)
Hawley St. *Rawm* 2F **69**
Haworth Bank. *Roth* 2F **91**
Haworth Clo. *B'ley* 4B **14**
Haworth Cres. *Roth* 2F **91**
Hawshaw La. *Hoy* 5G **37**
Hawson St. *Womb* 1G **39**
Hawthorn Av. *Arm* 1F **35**
Hawthorn Av. *Maltby* 4D **82**
Hawthorn Av. *Wat* 6D **114**
Hawthorne Av. *Ans* 4F **119**
Hawthorne Av. *Dron* 6E **123**
Hawthorne Av. *Rawm* 2G **69**
Hawthorne Av. *S'bri* 2B **140**
Hawthorne Chase. *Swint* 2A **56**
Hawthorne Clo. *Kil* 4B **126**
Hawthorne Ct. *Dart* 5A **6**
Hawthorne Ct. *Roth* 2H **79**
Hawthorne Cres. *Dod* 1A **22**
Hawthorne Cres. *Mexb* 6C **42**
Hawthorne Cft. *Gold* 4E **29**
Hawthorne Dri. *Bol D* 1B **42**
Hawthorne Farm Ct. Bol D 1B **42**
         (off Station Rd.)
Hawthorne Flats. *Thurn* 1F **29**
Hawthorne Gro. *Ben* 5B **18**
Hawthorne Pl. *Ast* 6C **104**
Hawthorne Rd. *Wath D* 6G **41**
Hawthornes, The. *Beig* 3F **115**
Hawthorne St. *S6* 5H **85**
Hawthorne St. *B'ley* 1G **23**
Hawthorne St. *Ches* 4B **138**
Hawthorne St. *Shaf* 2C **10**
Hawthorne Way. *Shaf* 2C **10**
Hawthorn Gro. *Con* 5C **58**
Hawthorn Rd. *S6* 3H **85**
Hawthorn Rd. *Eck* 6G **125**
Hawthorn Rd. *High G* 6C **50**
Hawthorn Ter. S10 . . . . .2A **98**
         (off Parker's La.)
Hawthorn Way. *Ash* 6B **130**
Haxby Clo. *S13* 1G **113**
Haxby Pl. *S13* 1G **113**
Haxby St. *S13* 1G **113**
Haybrook Ct. *S17* 4E **121**
Haydn Rd. *Maltby* 5H **83**
Haydock Clo. *Mexb* 5F **43**
Haydon Gro. *Flan* 3F **81**
Hayes Ct. *Half* 3E **125**
Hayes Cft. *B'ley* 6H **13**
Hayes Dri. *Half* 3D **124**
Hayfield Clo. *Barn D* 1E **21**

Hayfield Clo. *Dod* 2A **22**
Hayfield Clo. *Dron W* 2B **128**
Hayfield Clo. *Stav* 1D **134**
Hayfield Cres. *S12* 4F **113**
Hayfield Dri. *S12* 4F **113**
Hayfield La. *Auc & Donc F* 2G **63**
Hayfield Pl. *S12* 4F **113**
Hayfield Vw. *Eck* 6B **124**
Hayfield Wlk. Roth 6G **67**
          (off Byrley Rd.)
Hayford Way. *Stav* 2C **134**
Hay Green. **3D 36**
Hay Grn. La. *Birdw* 4D **36**
Hayhurst Cres. *Maltby* 5G **83**
Hayland St. *S9* 1D **88**
Haylock Clo. *Hghm* 4A **12**
Haymarket. *S1* 1F **99** (2F **5**)
Haythorne Way. *Swint* 4B **56**
Haywagon Mobile Home Pk.
       Adw S 1F **17**
Haywood Av. *Deep* 3F **141**
Haywood Clo. *Roth* 2A **80**
Haywood La. *Deep* 3F **141**
Haywood Rd. *Deep* 3F **141**
Hazel Av. *Kil* 4A **126**
Hazelbadge Cres. *S12* 4G **113**
Hazel Clo. *Dron* 3G **129**
Hazel Ct. *Dron* 3F **129**
Hazel Ct. *Rav* 1H **81**
Hazel Dri. *Ches* 5F **137**
Hazel Gro. *Arm* 2G **35**
Hazel Gro. *C'town* 3E **65**
Hazel Gro. *Con* 4D **58**
Hazel Gro. *New R* 5D **62**
Hazel Gro. *Wick* 4G **81**
Hazelhurst. S8 . . . . .3F **123**
        (off Jordanthorpe Cen.)
Hazelhurst Clo. *Dalt* 6B **70**
Hazel Rd. *Eck* 6H **125**
Hazel Rd. *Edl'tn* 3B **60**
Hazel Rd. *Maltby* 4D **82**
Hazelshaw. *Dod* 3C **22**
Hazelshaw Gdns. *High G* 6B **50**
Hazelwood. *B'ley* 2A **14**
Hazelwood Clo. *Dron W* 2A **128**
Hazelwood Dri. *Swint* 5B **56**
Hazlebarrow Clo. *S8* 3F **123**
Hazlebarrow Ct. *S8* 2F **123**
Hazlebarrow Cres. *S8* 3F **123**
Hazlebarrow Dri. *S8* 2F **123**
Hazlebarrow Gro. *S8* 2G **123**
Hazlebarrow Rd. *S8* 3F **123**
Hazledene Cres. *Shaf* 4D **10**
Hazledene Rd. *Shaf* 4C **10**
Hazlehurst Av. *Ches* 6A **132**
Hazlehurst La. *Ches* 6A **132**
Headford Gdns. *S3* 3D **98** (5A **4**)
Headford Gro. *S3* 3D **98** (5B **4**)
Headford M. *S3* 3D **98** (6B **4**)
Headford Pde. *S3* 5B **4**
Headford St. *S3* 3D **98** (5B **4**)
Headingley Clo. *Kirk S* 2D **20**
Headingley Way. *Edl'tn* 2C **60**
Headland Clo. *Brim* 4E **133**
Headland Dri. *S10* 2G **97**
Headland Rd. *S10* 2G **97**
Headland Rd. *Brim* 4E **133**
Headlands Rd. *Hoy* 5H **37**
Heads La. *Bols* 6B **140**
Healaugh Way. *Ches* 5B **138**
Heath Av. *Kil* 4B **126**
Heath Bank Rd. *Donc* 2A **34**
Heathcote Dri. *Has* 5E **139**
Heathcote St. *S4* 2H **87**
Heath Ct. *Ches* 5A **138**
Heath Ct. *Warm* 4F **45**
Heatherbank Rd. *Donc* 4C **48**
Heather Clo. *Cal* 2G **139**
Heather Clo. *Roth* 5E **79**
Heather Ct. *Bol D* 6D **28**
Heather Ct. *Braml* 5H **81**
Heatherdale Rd. *Maltby* 4H **83**
Heather Gdns. *Has* 6E **139**
Heather Knowle. *Dod* 2C **22**
Heather Lea Av. *S17* 2C **120**
Heather Lea Pl. *S17* 2C **120**
Heather Rd. *S5* 6A **76**
Heather Va. Clo. *Has* 6E **139**
Heather Va. Rd. *Has* 6D **138**
Heather Wlk. *Bol D* 6D **28**
Heatherwood Clo. *Donc* 3A **34**
Heathfield Av. *Ches* 2F **137**
Heathfield Clo. *Barn D* 1E **21**

Heathfield Clo. *Dron* 3D **128**
Heathfield Rd. *S12* 3F **113**
Heath Gro. *Bol D* 2H **41**
Heath Ho. *Donc* 1C **46**
        (off St James St.)
Heath Rd. *S6* 5B **74**
Heath Rd. *Deep* 4F **141**
Heaton Clo. *Dron W* 2B **128**
Heaton Gdns. *Edl'tn* 3C **60**
Heatons Bank. *Rawm* 1G **69**
Heaton St. *Ches* 3E **137**
Heavens Wlk. *Donc* 2D **46**
Heavygate Av. *S10* 5H **85**
Heavygate Rd. *S10* 5A **86**
Hedge Hill Rd. *Thurls* 4A **142**
Hedge La. *Dart* 6B **6**
        (in three parts)
Hedgerows, The. *Adw D* 3E **43**
Hedley Dri. *Brim* 3C **132**
Heeley. **1F 111**
Heeley Bank Rd. *S2* 6F **99**
Heeley Baths. **1D 110**
Heeley City Farm. **6E 99**
Heeley Grn. *S2* 1F **111**
Heeley Retail Pk. *S8* 1D **110**
Heelis St. *B'ley* 1H **23**
Heighton Vw. *Aug* 4B **104**
Helena Clo. *B'ley* 1F **23**
Helena St. *Mexb* 6E **43**
Helensburgh Clo. *B'ley* 5E **13**
Hellaby. **4B 82**
Hellaby (Euroway) Ind. Est. *H'by* 3A **82**
Hellaby Hall Rd. *H'by* 5B **82**
Hellaby La. *H'by* 4B **82**
        (in two parts)
Hellaby Vw. *Rav* 2H **81**
Helliwell Ct. *Deep* 5G **141**
Helliwell La. *Deep* 5G **141**
Helmsley Av. *Half* 2D **124**
Helmsley Clo. *Ches* 4E **131**
Helmsley Clo. *Swal* 1A **116**
Helmton Dri. *S8* 5E **111**
Helmton Rd. *S8* 5D **110**
Helston Clo. *Has* 5B **138**
Helston Cres. *B'ley* 4B **14**
Helston Ri. *S7* 3A **110**
Hemingfield. **4E 39**
Hemmingfield Rd. *Womb* 2D **38**
Hemmingway Clo. *Tree* 1E **103**
Hemper Gro. *S8* 2B **122**
Hemper La. *S8* 3B **122**
Hemp Pits Rd. *Ark* 6D **18**
Hemsworth. **5H 111**
Hemsworth By-Pass.
     Brie & Hems 1H **11**
Hemsworth Rd. *S8* 5E **111**
Henderson Glen. *Roy* 2C **8**
Hendon St. *S13* 4H **101**
Hengist Rd. *Donc* 1H **45**
Henley Av. *S8* .1F **123**
Henley Gro. Rd. *Roth* 2B **78**
        (in two parts)
Henley La. *Roth* 1A **78**
Henley Ri. *Roth* 1A **78**
Henley Rd. *Donc* 4A **34**
Henley Way. *Roth* 1A **78**
Hennings Clo. *Donc* 4H **47**
Hennings La. *Donc* 3H **47**
Hennings Rd. *Donc* 6A **48**
Henry Clo. *Shaf* 2C **10**
Henry Ct. *P'gte* 4F **69**
Henry Ct. *Roth* 2D **78**
Henry La. *New R* 3B **62**
Henry Pl. *Mexb* 6G **43**
Henry Rd. *Wath D* 5G **41**
Henrys St. *Wors* 4A **24**
Henry St. *S3* 6D **86** (1B **4**)
Henry St. *Ches* 3B **132**
Henry St. *Eck* .6D **124**
Henry St. *High G* 6A **50**
Henry St. *Roth* 2D **78**
        (in two parts)
Henry St. *Womb* 5D **26**
Henshall St. *B'ley* 1A **24**
Henson St. *S9* .5D **88**
Heppenstall La. *S9* 5B **88**
Heptinstall St. *Wors* 4B **24**
Hepworth Dri. *Swal* 6B **104**
        (in two parts)
Hepworth Rd. *Donc* 4H **45**
Herald Rd. *E'thpe* 6C **20**
Herbert Clo. *Donc* 4A **32**
Herbert Rd. *S7* 1C **110**

Herbert Rd. *Donc* 4A **32**
Herbert St. *Mexb* 6F **43**
Herbert St. *Roth* 2G **77**
Herdings. **4A 112**
Herdings Ct. *S12* 4C **112**
Herdings Rd. *S12* 4C **112**
Herdings Vw. *S12* 4B **112**
Hereford Dri. *Brim* 3F **133**
Hereford Rd. *Donc* 2H **33**
Hereford St. *S1* 4E **99** (6D **4**)
        (in three parts)
Hereward Ct. *Con* 3G **59**
Hereward Rd. *S5* 3G **75**
Hereward's Rd. *S8* 6H **111**
Hermitage St. *S2* 4D **98**
Hermit La. *Hghm* 5A **12**
Heron Ct. *Con* .3H **59**
Heron Dri. *Bram* 4H **39**
Heron Hill. *Ast* 1C **116**
Heron Mt. *S2* .3A **100**
Herons Way. *Bal* 4D **46**
Herons Way. *Birdw* 3D **36**
Herrick Gdns. *Donc* 5C **46**
Herrick Rd. *Barn D* 1H **21**
Herries Av. *S5* .1E **87**
Herries Dri. *S5* 1E **87**
Herries Pl. *S5* .1E **87**
Herries Rd. *S6 & S5* 1A **86**
        (in two parts)
Herries Rd. S. *S6* 1A **86**
Herringthorpe. **4H 79**
Herringthorpe Av. *Roth* 5H **79**
Herringthorpe Clo. *Roth* 4H **79**
Herringthorpe Gro. *Roth* 5A **80**
Herringthorpe La. *Roth* 4A **80**
Herringthorpe Valley Rd. *Roth* 1A **80**
Herriot Dri. *Ches* 4B **138**
Herschell Rd. *S7* 6D **98**
        (in two parts)
Herten Way. *Donc* 2H **47**
Hesketh Dri. *Kirk S* 3E **21**
Hesley Bar. *Thpe H* 3A **66**
Hesley Ct. *Den M* 2B **58**
Hesley Ct. *Swint* 4A **56**
Hesley Grange. *Scho* 5D **66**
Hesley Gro. *C'town* 3G **65**
Hesley La. *Thpe H* 3A **66**
Hesley M. *Scho* 5E **67**
Hesley Rd. *S5* .2H **75**
Hesley Rd. *New R* 5D **62**
Hesley Ter. *S5* .2H **75**
Heslow Gro. *Thpe H* 2A **66**
Hessey St. *S13* 1H **113**
Hessle Rd. *S6* .1H **85**
Hethersett Way. *New R* 6C **62**
Hewitt St. *Mexb* 6G **43**
Hexthorpe. **1B 46**
Hexthorpe Bus. Pk. *Donc* 2B **46**
Hexthorpe Rd. *Donc* 2B **46**
Heyhouse Dri. *C'town* 6D **50**
Heyhouse Way. *C'town* 6D **50**
Heysham Grn. *B'ley* 1D **14**
Heywood St. *Brim* 3E **133**
Hibberd Pl. *S6* 3G **85**
Hibberd Rd. *S6* 3G **85**
        (in two parts)
Hibbert Ter. *B'ley* 2H **23**
        (off Walnut Clo.)
Hickleton Ct. *Thurn* 2E **29**
Hickleton St. *Den M* 2B **58**
Hickleton Ter. *Thurn* 2G **29**
Hickmott Rd. *S11* 5B **98**
Hickson Dri. *B'ley* 3E **15**
Hicks St. *S3* 5E **87**
Hides St. *S9* 3D **88**
High Alder Rd. *Bes* 3A **48**
Higham. **4A 12**
Higham Comn. Rd.
     Hghm & Bar G 4A **12**
Higham Ct. *Hghm* 4A **12**
Higham La. *Hghm & Dod* 5A **12**
Higham Vw. *Dart* 6B **6**
High Ash Dri. *Ans* 4F **119**
High Bank. *Thry* 5C **70**
High Bank. *Thurls* 3A **142**
High Bank La. *Thurls* 4A **142**
Highbury Av. *Donc* 3C **48**
Highbury Cres. *Donc* 3C **48**
Highbury Rd. *Ches* 6H **131**
Highbury Va. *Edl'tn* 4A **60**
Highcliffe Ct. *S11* 6G **97**
Highcliffe Ct. *Swint* 2B **56**
Highcliffe Dri. *S11* 1F **109**

Highcliffe Dri. *O'bri* 3D **72**
Highcliffe Dri. *Swint* 2B **56**
Highcliffe Pl. *S11* 1F **109**
Highcliffe Rd. *S11* 6F **97**
High Clo. *Dart* .4B **6**
High Ct. *S1* 1F **99** (2F **5**)
Highcroft. *S17* 6G **97**
High Cft. *Hoy* .6A **38**
High Cft. Dri. *B'ley* 5B **8**
Higher Albert St. *Ches* 1A **138**
Higher Stubbin. **6B 54**
Highfield. **4E 99**
Highfield. *Wath D* 5F **41**
Highfield Av. *B'ley* 1A **14**
Highfield Av. *Ches* 6G **131**
Highfield Av. *Gold* 4F **29**
Highfield Av. *Kiv P* 4A **118**
Highfield Av. *Wors* 3H **23**
Highfield Clo. *Barn D* 1E **21**
Highfield Ct. *Swint* 2A **56**
Highfield Ct. *Womb* 6A **26**
Highfield Gro. *Wath D* 4A **40**
Highfield La. *S13* 3B **102**
Highfield La. *Ches* 5G **131**
Highfield Pk. *Maltby* 3H **83**
Highfield Pl. *S2* 5E **99**
Highfield Range. *D'fld* 2E **27**
Highfield Ri. *S6* 5B **84**
Highfield Rd. *Ches* 6H **131**
Highfield Rd. *Con* 3F **59**
Highfield Rd. *D'fld* 3E **27**
Highfield Rd. *Donc* 5E **33**
Highfield Rd. *Roth* 5C **68**
Highfield Rd. *Swint* 2H **55**
Highfields. **5D 16**
Highfields. *H'swne* 1F **143**
Highfields Cres. *Dron* 3E **129**
High Fld. Spring. *S13* 1A **102**
Highfields Rd. *Dart* 5A **6**
Highfields Rd. *Dron* 3E **129**
Highfield Ter. *Ches* 6H **131**
Highfield Vw. *Cat* 5C **90**
Highfield Vw. Rd. *Ches* 6H **131**
        (in two parts)
High Fisher Ga. *Donc* 5D **32**
Highgate. **4E 29**
Highgate. *S9* 1G **89**
        (in two parts)
Highgate. *Womb* 1B **40**
Highgate Clo. *New R* 5E **63**
Highgate Ct. *Gold* 5E **29**
Highgate Dri. *Dron* 4G **129**
Highgate La. *Bol D & Gold* 6E **29**
Highgate La. *Dron* 4F **129**
High Ga. Way. *Shaf* 3C **10**
Highgreave. *S5* 2G **75**
High Greave Av. *S5* 2F **75**
High Greave Ct. *S5* 2G **75**
High Greave Rd. *Roth* 2A **80**
High Greave Rd. *Roth* 1A **80**
High Green. **3B 50**
Highgrove Clo. *Ches* 3A **132**
Highgrove Ct. *Donc* 5E **49**
High Hazel Ct. *Tree* 1E **103**
High Hazel Cres. *Cat* 5C **90**
High Hazel Rd. *Tree* 1F **103**
High Hazels Clo. *S9* 1F **101**
High Hazels Mead. *S9* 1F **101**
High Hooton Rd.
     Lghtn & Hoot L 3G **95**
High Ho. Farm Ct. *Wal* 5F **117**
High Ho. Ter. *S6* 4B **86**
Highlands Pl. *Ches* 2H **131**
Highlane. **6G 113**
High La. *S12* 6G **113**
High La. *Thur* 3F **105**
High Lee La. *H'swne* 2F **143**
Highlightly La. *Barl* 6A **128**
Highlow Clo. *Ches* 6E **131**
Highlow Vw. *B'wth* 2C **90**
High Matlock Av. *S6* 5D **84**
High Matlock Rd. *S6* 4D **84**
Highmill Av. *Swint* 2G **55**
High Moor. **4D 126**
Highmoor Av. *Kiv P* 5G **117**
Highnam Cres. Rd. *S10* 2A **98**
High Nook Rd. *Dinn* 5G **107**
High Pavement Row. *S2* 1G **99**
High Ridge. *Wors* 4H **23**
Highridge Clo. *Con* 4F **59**
High Rd. *Donc* .4A **46**
High Rd. *Edl'tn* 4B **60**
High Rd. *Warm* 5E **45**

High Royd Av. *Cud*	1H **15**
High Royd La. *Hoy*	3F **37**
High Royd La. *H'swne*	2G **143**
Highroyds. *Wors*	3H **23**
Highstone Av. *B'ley*	2G **23**
Highstone Corner. *Wors*	3H **23**
Highstone Ct. *B'ley*	2H **23**
Highstone Cres. *B'ley*	2G **23**
Highstone La. *Wors*	3H **23**
Highstone Rd. *B'ley*	2H **23**
Highstone Va. *B'ley*	2G **23**
High Storrs Clo. *S11*	1F **109**
High Storrs Cres. *S11*	6G **97**
High Storrs Dri. *S11*	1F **109**
High Storrs Ri. *S11*	6G **97**
High Storrs Rd. *S11*	1F **109**
High St. *S1*	2F **99** (3E **5**)
High St. *S9*	1E **89**
High St. *S17*	2D **120**
High St. *Ans*	3F **119**
High St. *Ark*	5D **18**
High St. *Barn D*	2G **21**
High St. *B'ley*	5G **13**
High St. *Beig*	3G **115**
High St. *Ben*	2A **32**
High St. *Bol D*	1A **42**
High St. *Brim*	3F **133**
High St. *Ches*	2A **138**
High St. *Con*	3E **59**
High St. *Dart*	3E **7**
High St. *Dod*	2B **22**
High St. *Donc*	6C **32**
High St. *Dron*	2E **129**
High St. *D'ville*	4H **21**
High St. *E'fld*	1E **75**
High St. *Eck*	6C **124**
High St. *Gold*	4G **29**
High St. *Grim*	6F **11**
High St. *Hoy*	5A **38**
High St. *Kil*	3B **126**
High St. *K'wth*	2G **77**
High St. *Lghtn*	6F **95**
High St. *L Hou*	2B **28**
High St. *Maltby*	4G **83**
High St. *Mexb*	1E **57**
High St. *Monk B*	3C **14**
High St. *Mosb*	2C **124**
High St. *Old W*	1A **132**
High St. *P'stne*	4D **142**
High St. *Rawm*	3F **69**
High St. *Roth*	3D **78**
High St. *Roy*	2C **8**
High St. *Shaf*	2C **10**
High St. *Stav*	1C **134**
High St. *Swal*	6A **104**
High St. *Thurn*	1D **28**
High St. *Wadw*	6H **61**
High St. *Wath D*	5F **41**
High St. *Whis*	2H **91**
High St. *Womb*	6B **26**
High St. *Wors*	4B **24**
High St. La. *S2*	2G **99** (3H **5**)
High St. M. *Mosb*	2C **124**
Highthorne Way. *Kiv P*	4B **118**
Highthorn Rd. *Kiln*	4B **56**
Highthorn Vs. *Kiln*	4C **56**
Highton St. *S6*	5A **86**
High Trees. *S17*	2D **120**
High Trees. *Roth*	6H **79**
High Vw. *S5*	3E **87**
High Vw. *Roy*	2D **8**
High Vw. Clo. *Ches*	3D **138**
High Vw. Clo. *D'fld*	3F **27**
High Wincobank.	**5C 76**
Highwood Clo. *Dart*	5A **6**
Highwood Pl. *Eck*	6C **124**
Highwoods.	**6C 42**
Highwoods Cres. *Mexb*	6C **42**
Highwoods Rd. *Mexb*	6C **42**
High Wray Clo. *S11*	3H **109**
Hilary Way. *Swal*	6B **104**
Hilda Ter. *Grim*	6F **11**
Hillary Ho. *Donc*	3F **33**
Hillberry Ri. *Ches*	6H **137**
Hill Clo. *S6*	5C **84**
Hill Clo. *Roth*	5C **80**
Hillcote Clo. *S10*	4D **96**
Hillcote Dri. *S10*	4D **96**
Hillcote M. *S10*	4D **96**
Hillcote Ri. *S10*	4D **96**
Hill Crest. *Hoy*	6G **37**
Hill Crest. *Thry*	4C **70**
Hillcrest. *Thurn*	2E **29**
Hillcrest Dri. *Ans*	3F **119**
Hillcrest Dri. *O'bri*	3C **72**
Hill Crest Rd. *Deep*	4H **141**
Hill Crest Rd. *C'town*	2D **64**
Hillcrest Rd. *Deep*	4G **141**
Hillcrest Rd. *Donc*	3G **33**
Hillcrest Rd. *Has*	6D **138**
Hill Crest Rd. *Roth*	2H **79**
Hill End Rd. *M'well*	6G **7**
Hill Farm Clo. *Thurn*	2D **28**
Hillfoot.	**4C 86**
	(Owlerton)
Hillfoot.	**4D 120**
	(Totley)
Hillfoot Ct. *S17*	5D **120**
Hillfoot Rd. *S3*	5C **86**
Hillfoot Rd. *S17*	4C **120**
Hillman Dri. *Ink*	5A **134**
Hillsborough.	**1H 85**
Hillsborough Arc., The. *S6*	3A **86**
Hillsborough Barracks Bus. & Shop. Cen.	
S6	3B **86**
Hillsborough Golf Course.	**6D 72**
Hillsborough Leisure Cen.	**2B 86**
Hillsborough Pl. *S6*	3A **86**
Hillsborough Rd. *S6*	3A **86**
Hillsborough Rd. *Donc*	3C **48**
Hills Clo. *Spro*	1G **45**
Hillside.	**3G 11**
Hillside. *Ans*	1F **119**
Hillside. *B'ley*	1G **25**
Hillside. *Mosb*	2C **124**
Hill Side. *Thpe H*	3B **66**
Hill Side. *Thry*	5C **70**
Hill Side. *Whis*	2H **91**
Hillside Av. *S5*	3F **75**
Hillside Clo. *H'swne*	1F **143**
Hillside Ct. *Roth*	6D **68**
Hillside Ct. *Spro*	3D **44**
Hillside Cres. *Brie*	3G **11**
Hillside Dri. *Ches*	4F **137**
Hillside Dri. *Edl'tn*	4A **60**
Hillside Dri. *Hoy*	6B **38**
Hillside Gro. *Brie*	3F **11**
Hill Side La. *Thurls*	5A **142**
Hillside Mt. *Brie*	3G **11**
Hillside Rd. *Donc*	2A **34**
Hills Rd. *Deep*	3F **141**
Hill St. *S2*	4D **98**
Hill St. *B'ley*	1E **25**
Hill St. *D'fld*	4E **27**
Hill St. *Else*	6C **38**
Hill Top.	**1H 13**
	(Barnsley)
Hill Top.	**6B 58**
	(Conisbrough)
Hill Top.	**3E 129**
	(Dronfield)
Hill Top.	**2E 109**
	(Heeley)
Hill Top.	**1B 72**
	(Oughtibridge)
Hill Top.	**3E 77**
	(Rotherham)
Hilltop. *Brie*	2F **11**
Hilltop Av. *B'ley*	4A **8**
Hill Top Clo. *B'wth*	2B **90**
Hill Top Clo. *K'wth*	3F **77**
Hill Top Clo. *Maltby*	3D **82**
Hill Top Cres. *Donc*	2A **34**
Hill Top Cres. *Edl'tn*	5B **60**
Hill Top Cres. *Wat*	6D **114**
Hilltop Dri. *O'bri*	1B **72**
Hilltop Gdns. *Den M*	3B **58**
Hilltop Grn. *S5*	6D **74**
Hill Top La. *B'ley*	4D **12**
Hill Top La. *Gren*	1G **73**
Hill Top La. *Roth* (S61)	3F **77**
Hill Top La. *Roth & Flan* (S65, S66)	
	2D **80**
Hill Top La. *Wort*	1E **141**
Hill Top Ri. *Gren*	2B **74**
Hill Top Rd. *Birdw*	3D **36**
Hill Top Rd. *Den M & Con*	2A **58**
Hilltop Rd. *Dron*	3E **129**
Hill Top Rd. *Gren*	2B **74**
Hilltop Rd. *Old W*	1A **132**
Hill Top Smithies. *B'ley*	1H **13**
Hilltop Way. *Dron*	4F **129**
Hill Turrets Clo. *S11*	3F **109**
Hill Vw. E. *Roth*	1F **77**
Hill Vw. Rd. *Brim*	3E **133**
Hill Vw. Rd. *Roth*	1F **77**
Hilton Dri. *E'fld*	1F **75**
Hilton St. *B'ley*	5F **13**
Hindburn Clo. *Donc*	4H **47**
Hinde Ho. Cres. *S4*	1A **88**
Hinde Ho. Cft. *S4*	1A **88**
Hinde Ho. La. *S4*	2H **87**
Hinde St. *S4*	2A **88**
Hindewood Clo. *S4*	1A **88**
Hindle St. *B'ley*	6F **13**
Hind Rd. *Whis*	1A **92**
Hipley Clo. *Ches*	5D **130**
Hipper St. *Ches*	3A **138**
Hipper St. S. *Ches*	3A **138**
Hipper St. W. *Ches*	3G **137**
Hirst Comn. La. *S6*	3H **73**
Hirst Dri. *Roth*	2B **80**
Hirst Ga. *Mexb*	6G **43**
Hobart St. *S11*	5D **98**
Hobner La. *Ink*	3A **134**
Hobson Av. *S6*	4C **86**
Hobson Pl. *S6*	4C **86**
Hodder Ct. *C'town*	1D **64**
Hodgkinson Av. *P'stne*	4D **142**
Hodgson St. *S3*	3D **98** (6C **4**)
Hodroyd Clo. *Shaf*	4D **10**
Hodroyd Cotts. *Brie*	3G **11**
Hodroyd La. *Shaf*	4D **10**
Hogarth Ri. *Dron*	3D **128**
Holbeach Dri. *Ches*	5G **137**
Holbeck Clo. *Ches*	1B **138**
Holbein Clo. *Dron*	3D **128**
Holberry Clo. *S10*	3C **98** (5A **4**)
Holberry Gdns. *S10*	3C **98** (5A **4**)
Holborn Av. *Dron*	1E **129**
Holbourne Gro. *High G*	4B **50**
Holbrook.	**1G 125**
Holbrook Av. *H'brk*	1F **125**
Holbrook Clo. *Ches*	5E **137**
Holbrook Dri. *S13*	1D **112**
Holbrook Grn. *H'brk*	1G **125**
Holbrook Pl. *Ink*	4A **134**
Holbrook Ri. *H'brk*	6F **115**
Holbrook Rd. *S13*	6D **100**
Holbrook Trad. Est. *H'brk*	1G **125**
Holden Ct. *B'ley*	6G **13**
Holderness Dri. *Swal*	5B **104**
Holdings Rd. *S2*	4H **99**
Holdroyds Yd. *Dod*	3B **22**
Holdworth La. *S6*	5A **72**
Hole Ho. La. *S'bri*	3D **140**
Holgate. *Womb*	4H **25**
Holgate Av. *S5*	4D **74**
Holgate Clo. *S5*	3D **74**
Holgate Cres. *S5*	3E **75**
Holgate Dri. *S5*	3E **75**
Holgate Mt. *Wors*	3H **23**
Holgate Rd. *S5*	3E **75**
Holgate Vw. *Brie*	2G **11**
Holiwell Clo. *Maltby*	3H **83**
Holkham Ri. *S11*	5F **109**
Holland Clo. *Rawm*	6F **55**
Holland Pl. *S2*	5E **99**
Holland Rd. *S2*	5E **99**
Holland Rd. *High G*	6B **50**
Holland Rd. *Old W*	1H **131**
Holland St. *S1*	2D **98** (3C **4**)
Hollens Way. *Ches*	6B **130**
Hollies Clo. *Dron*	3G **129**
Hollinberry La. *Wort*	4A **50**
Hollin Busk.	**5D 140**
Hollin Busk La. *Deep*	5E **141**
Hollin Busk Rd. *Deep*	4E **141**
Hollin Clo. *Ches*	3E **131**
Hollin Clo. *Ross*	3F **63**
Hollin Cft. *Dod*	1C **22**
Hollindale Dri. *S12*	2E **113**
Hollin Edge La. *Bols*	6H **141**
Holling Cft. *Deep*	3G **141**
Holling Hill La. *Wick*	5D **80**
Holling Moor La. *Wick*	5E **81**
Holling's La. *Thry & Rav*	5D **70**
Hollingswood Way. *S'side*	2G **81**
Hollingwood.	**2G 133**
Hollingwood Cres. *Holl*	1G **133**
Hollingwood Est. *Holl*	2G **133**
Hollingworth Clo. *Mexb*	5H **43**
Hollin Ho. La. *S6*	1A **84**
Hollin La. *Bols*	6E **141**
Hollin Rd. *O'bri*	3C **72**
Hollins Clo. *S6*	6F **85**
Hollins Ct. *S6*	5F **85**
Hollins Dri. *S6*	6G **85**

Hollins End. 2E **113**
Hollinsend Av. *S12* 2E **113**
Hollinsend Pl. *S12* 2E **113**
Hollinsend Rd. *S12* 3C **112**
Hollins La. *Ash* 5F **85**
Hollins Spring Av. *Dron* 3E **129**
Hollins Spring Rd. *Dron* 3E **129**
Hollins, The. *Dod* 3C **22**
Hollis Clo. *Rawm* 5D **54**
Hollis Cft. *S1* 1D **98** (2C **4**)
Hollis Cft. *Woodh* 1A **114**
Hollis La. *Ches* 3B **138**
(in two parts)
Hollowdene. *B'ley* 4D **12**
Hollowgate. **3C 40**
Hollowgate. *Barn* 1F **43**
Hollow Ga. *C'town* 2B **64**
Hollowgate. *Roth* 4E **79**
Hollow Ga. *Whis* 2H **91**
Hollowgate Av. *Wath D* 3C **40**
Hollow La. *Half* 3D **124**
Hollows, The. *Donc* 5C **48**
Holly Av. *Donc* 2A **32**
Hollybank Av. *S12* 1E **113**
Hollybank Clo. *S12* 1F **113**
Hollybank Cres. *S12* 1E **113**
Hollybank Dri. *S12* 1E **113**
Hollybank Rd. *S12* 1E **113**
Hollybank Way. *S12* 1F **113**
Holly Barn Fold. *Hoot R* 1G **71**
Holly Bush Dri. *Thurn* 1F **29**
Holly Bush La. *Kirk S* 4D **20**
Hollybush St. *P'gte* 4F **69**
Holly Clo. *C'town* 3D **64**
Holly Clo. *Kil* 4A **126**
Holly Ct. *S10* 4H **97**
Holly Ct. B'ley 2H **23**
(off Hornby St.)
Holly Cres. *S'side* 3G **81**
Hollycroft Av. *Roy* 2D **8**
Holly Dene. *Arm* 1E **35**
Holly Dri. *Ben* 5B **18**
Holly Farm. *Shaf* 2C **10**
Holly Gdns. *S12* 1E **113**
Holly Ga. *Wors* 4C **24**
Holly Gro. *S12* 1E **113**
Holly Gro. *Brie* 2G **11**
Holly Gro. *Gold* 4E **29**
Holly Gro. *Ross* 3E **63**
Holly Gro. *Wath D* 1F **55**
Holly Hall La. *Wort* 1H **141**
Holly La. *S1* 2E **99** (3D **4**)
Holly Mt. *Wick* 5G **81**
Holly St. *S1* 2E **99** (3D **4**)
(in two parts)
Holly St. *Donc* 2C **46**
Holly Ter. *Donc* 4H **45**
Holly Ter. *Swal* 5A **104**
Hollythorpe Clo. *Has* 5D **138**
Hollythorpe Cres. *S8* 3E **111**
Hollythorpe Ri. *S8* 3F **111**
Hollythorpe Rd. *S8* 3F **111**
Hollytree Av. *Maltby* 3D **82**
Hollywell Clo. *Rawm* 6H **55**
Holmbrook Wlk. *Ches* 6E **131**
Holm Clo. *Dron W* 1B **128**
Holmebank Clo. *Ches* 1G **137**
Holmebank E. *Ches* 1G **137**
Holmebank Vw. *Ches* 1G **137**
Holmebank W. *Ches* 1G **137**
Holme Brook Vw. *Ches* 5E **131**
Holme Clo. *S6* 3A **86**
Holme Ct. *Gold* 5E **29**
Holme Ct. *Roth* 1E **91**
Holmefield Clo. *Arm* 4G **35**
Holme Hall Cres. *Ches* 5D **130**
Holme La. *S6* 4H **85**
Holme La. *Gren* 2B **74**
Holme Oak Way. *S6* 4C **84**
Holme Pk. Av. *Ches* 4D **130**
Holme Rd. *Ches* 5A **132**
Holmeroyd Rd. *Adw S* 1G **17**
Holmes. **4A 78**
Holmes Carr Cres. *New R* 4B **62**
Holmes Carr Rd. *Donc* 5B **48**
Holmes Carr Rd. *New R* 4B **62**
Holmes Ct. *Roth* 3B **78**
Holmes Cres. *Tree* 1E **103**
Holmesdale. **1G 129**
Holmesdale Clo. *Dron* 6G **123**
Holmesdale Rd. *Dron* 6F **123**
Holmesfield. Roth 3A **78**
(off Rosebery St.)

Holmesfield Rd. *Dron W* 2A **128**
Holmesfield Rd. *O'bri* 3D **72**
Holmes La. *Hoot R* 5F **57**
Holmes La. *Roth* 3A **78**
Holmes Mkt., The. Donc 5E **33**
(off Holmes, The)
Holmes Rd. *Braml* 5H **81**
Holmes, The. *Donc* 5D **32**
Holme, The. *Dron* 6F **123**
Holme Vw. Rd. *Dart* 5A **6**
Holme Wood Ct. *E'thpe* 5E **21**
Holme Wood Gdns. *Donc* 4C **48**
Holme Wood La. *Arm* 3H **35**
(in two parts)
Holm Flatt St. *P'gte* 4E **69**
Holmhirst Clo. *S8* 5C **110**
Holmhirst Dri. *S8* 4C **110**
Holmhirst Rd. *S8* 4C **110**
Holmhirst Way. *S8* 4C **110**
Holmley Bank. *Dron* 6E **123**
Holmley Common. **6E 123**
Holmley La. *Coal A* 6E **123**
Holmoak Clo. *Swint* 4B **56**
Holmshaw Dri. *S13* 5G **101**
Holmshaw Clo. *E'thpe* 4E **21**
Holmshaw Gro. *S13* 5G **101**
Holt Ho. Gro. *S7* 3B **110**
Holtwood Rd. *S4* 4F **87**
Holwick Ct. *B'ley* 6G **13**
Holy Grn. *S1* 3E **99** (6D **4**)
Holymoor Rd. *Holy* 6A **136**
Holymoorside. **6A 136**
Holyoake Av. *S13* 4G **101**
Holyrood Ri. *Braml* 2H **81**
Holyrood Rd. *Donc* 6G **33**
Holywell Ct. *S4* 1C **88**
Holywell La. *B'well* 1G **83**
Holywell La. *Con* 4E **59**
Holywell Pl. Roth 2E **79**
(off Nottingham St.)
Holywell Rd. *S4 & S9* 2B **88**
Holywell Rd. *Kiln* 4B **56**
Holywell St. *Ches* 1A **138**
Homecroft Rd. *Gold* 4F **29**
Homefield Cres. *Donc* 1G **31**
Homeport M. *Ches* 1A **138**
Homestead Clo. *S5* 4H **75**
Homestead Dri. *B'wth* 2B **90**
Homestead Dri. *Rawm* 6F **55**
Homestead Rd. *S5* 4G **75**
Homestead, The. *Ben* 6B **18**
Honeysuckle Clo. *D'fld* 5E **27**
Honeysuckle Rd. *S5* 6B **76**
Honeywell. **4H 13**
Honeywell Clo. *B'ley* 4H **13**
Honeywell Gro. *B'ley* 3H **13**
Honeywell La. *B'ley* 4G **13**
Honeywell Pl. *B'ley* 4G **13**
Honeywell St. *B'ley* 4H **13**
Honister Clo. *Bram B* 4A **40**
Hoober. **4A 54**
Hoober Av. *S11* 2F **109**
Hoober Ct. *Rawm* 5D **54**
Hoober Fld. Rd.
Rawm & Wath D 4A **54**
Hoober Hall La.
W'wth & Wath D 2G **53**
Hoober La. *Rawm* 4A **54**
Hoober Rd. *S11* 2G **109**
Hoober St. *Wath D* 4B **40**
Hoober Vw. *Rawm* 5D **54**
Hoober Vw. *Womb* 2H **39**
Hood Green. **6A 22**
Hood Grn. Rd. *Hood G* 6A **22**
Hood Hill. **5H 51**
Hoodhill Rd. *W'wth* 5H **51**
Hoole La. *S10* 3A **98**
Hoole Rd. *S10* 3A **98**
Hoole St. *S6* 5A **86**
Hoole St. *Has* 5D **138**
Hooley Rd. *S13* 1D **114**
Hooton Clo. *Lghtn* 6G **95**
Hooton La. *Hoot L* 5E **83**
Hooton La. *Lghtn* 6G **95**
Hooton La. *Rav* 4G **71**
Hooton Levitt. **5E 83**
Hooton Rd. *Kiln* 6C **56**
Hooton Roberts. **6H 57**
Hope Av. *Gold* 4F **29**
Hope Rd. *S12* 3F **113**
Hopefield Av. *S12* 3F **113**
Hope Rd. *O'bri* 3E **73**
Hope Sq. *S9* 3B **88**

Hope St. *B'ley* 1F **15**
(Burton Rd.)
Hope St. *B'ley* 5F **13**
(Gawber Rd.)
Hope St. *Ches* 2G **137**
Hope St. *M'well* 5G **7**
Hope St. *Mexb* 1E **57**
Hope St. *Roth* 2C **78**
Hope St. *S'bri* 3E **141**
Hope St. *Womb* 1G **39**
(Gower St.)
Hope St. *Womb* 5D **26**
(Pitt St.)
Hope St. Ind. Est. *Roth* 1C **78**
Hopewell St. *B'ley* 1D **24**
Hopwood La. *S6* 1B **96**
Hopwood St. *B'ley* 5G **13**
Horace St. *Roth* 4E **79**
Horbiry End. *Tod* 2A **118**
Horbury La. *Burn* 3C **64**
Horbury Rd. *Coal* 5B **10**
Hornbeam Clo. *C'town* 3D **64**
Hornbeam Clo. *Holl* 1G **133**
Hornbeam Rd. *Flan* 3F **81**
Hornby Ct. *S11* 6G **97**
Hornby St. *B'ley* 2H **23**
(in two parts)
Horndean Rd. *S5* 2H **87**
Horner Clo. *S'bri* 3D **140**
Horner Rd. *S7* 6D **98**
Hornes La. *M'well* 4G **7**
Horninglow Clo. *S5* 6G **75**
Horninglow Clo. *Donc* 4E **49**
Horninglow Mt. *S5* 6G **75**
Horninglow Rd. *S5* 6G **75**
Hornsby Rd. *Arm* 4G **35**
Hornthorpe Rd. *Eck* 6G **125**
Hornthwaite Hill Rd. *Thurls* 5A **142**
Horse Carr Vw. *B'ley* 1G **25**
Horse Cft. La. *Whar S* 1B **72**
Horsefair Clo. *Swint* 2B **56**
Horsehills La. *Arm* 4E **35**
Horsemoor Rd. *Thurn* 1D **28**
Horseshoe Clo. *Wal* 4G **117**
Horse Shoe Ct. *Donc* 4H **45**
Horseshoe Gdns. *Wal* 4F **117**
Horsewood Clo. *B'ley* 1D **22**
Horsewood Rd. *S13* 5D **102**
Horsewood Rd. *Walt* 5D **136**
Horsley Clo. *Ches* 6C **130**
Horten Vw. *Kirk S* 2C **20**
Horton Clo. *Half* 2E **125**
Horton Dri. *Half* 2E **125**
Hough La. *Womb* 1E **39**
Houghton Rd. *N Ans* 4B **106**
Houghton Rd. *Thurn* 1C **28**
Houldsworth Dri. *Ches* 3D **138**
Hound Hill La. *Adw D* 3B **42**
Hound Hill La. *Wors* 5F **23**
Houndkirk Rd. *S11* 4A **108**
Hounsfield Cres. *Roth* 2B **80**
Hounsfield La. *S3* 2C **98** (4A **4**)
Hounsfield Rd. *S3* 2C **98** (3A **4**)
Hounsfield Rd. *Roth* 2B **80**
Housley La. *C'town* 2D **64**
Housley Pk. *C'town* 1D **64**
Houstead Rd. *S9* 2F **101**
Hoveringham Ct. *Swal* 1A **116**
Howard Dri. *Old W* 1A **132**
Howard Hill. **6A 86**
Howard La. *S1* 3F **99** (5F **5**)
Howard Rd. *S6* 6A **86**
Howard Rd. *Braml* 4H **81**
Howard Rd. *Maltby* 5H **83**
Howards Clo. *Thur* 5C **94**
Howard St. *S1* 3F **99** (5F **5**)
Howard St. *B'ley* 2H **23**
Howard St. *D'fld* 4G **27**
Howard St. *Dinn* 4G **107**
Howard St. *Roth* 2D **78**
(in two parts)
Howarth Dri. *B'wth* 4D **90**
Howarth La. *B'wth* 3E **91**
(in two parts)
Howarth Rd. *B'wth* 3D **90**
Howbeck Clo. *Edl'tn* 4A **60**
Howbeck Dri. *Edl'tn* 4A **60**
Howbrook Clo. *High G* 5A **50**
Howden Clo. *Dart* 4D **6**
Howden Clo. *Donc* 5A **48**
Howden Clo. *Stav* 1D **134**
Howden Rd. *S9* 4C **88**
Howdike La. *Hoot R* 6F **57**

Howe La. *Lghtn* 3G **95**
Howell Gdns. *Thurn* 2E **29**
Howlett Clo. *Whis* 2B **92**
Howlett Dri. *B'wth* 4C **90**
Howse St. *Else* 5D **38**
Howson Clo. *Rav* 1H **81**
Howson Rd. *Deep* 3F **141**
Hoylake Av. *Ches* 6E **137**
Hoylake Dri. *Swint* 4B **56**
Hoyland. **5A 38**
Hoyland Common. **6F 37**
Hoyland Leisure Cen. 5G **37**
Hoyland Lowe. **4G 37**
Hoyland Mkt. *Hoy* 5A **38**
Hoyland Rd. *S3* 4C **86**
Hoyland Rd. *Hoy* 6F **37**
Hoyland St. *Maltby* 5H **83**
Hoyland St. *Womb* 1F **39**
Hoyland Swaine. **1G 143**
Hoy La. *Adw D* 4C **42**
Hoyle Cft. La. *B'well* 1E **83**
Hoyle Mill. **6B 14**
Hoyle Mill La. *Thurls* 3B **142**
Hoyle Mill Rd. *B'ley* 1D **24**
Hoyle St. *S3* 1D **98** (1C **4**)
Hucklow Av. *Ches* 5H **137**
Hucklow Av. *Ink* 4A **134**
Hucklow Dri. *S5* 6H **75**
Hucklow Rd. *S5* 1H **87**
Hucknall Av. *Ches* 1E **137**
Huddersfield Rd. *B'ley* 3E **13**
Huddersfield Rd. *Dart* 1A **6**
Huddersfield Rd. *P'stne* 1A **142**
Hudson Haven. *Womb* 6H **25**
Hudson Rd. *S13* 5E **103**
Hudson Rd. *Roth* 5G **67**
Hudson's M. *Donc* 6C **32**
Humberside Way. *B'ley* 1D **14**
Humphrey Rd. *S8* 1C **122**
Humphries Av. *Rawm* 6D **54**
Hungerhill Clo. *Roth* 1F **77**
Hungerhill La. *E'thpe* 5B **20**
Hunger Hill La. *Whis* 2A **92**
Hungerhill Rd. *K'wth* 6F **67**
Hunger Hill Rd. *Whis* 1H **91**
Hunloke Av. *Ches* 4F **137**
Hunloke Cres. *Ches* 4G **137**
Hunningley Clo. *B'ley* 2D **24**
Hunningley La. *B'ley* 4D **24**
. . . . (in two parts)
Hunsdon Rd. *Eck* 6C **124**
Hunshelf La. *E'fld* 5F **65**
Hunshelf Pk. *S'bri* 2E **141**
Hunshelf Rd. *C'town* 2D **64**
Hunshelf Rd. *S'bri* 2D **140**
. . . .(Pea Royd La.)
Hunshelf Rd. *S'bri* 1B **140**
. . . .(Underbank La.)
Hunsley St. *S4* 3A **88**
Hunster Clo. *Donc* 4D **48**
Hunster Flat La. *New R* 6D **62**
Hunster Gro. *New R* 5D **62**
Hunstone Av. *S8* 2E **123**
Hunt Clo. *B'ley* 3C **14**
Hunter Ct. *S11* 6H **97**
Hunter Ho. Rd. *S11* 6H **97**
Hunter Hill Rd. *S11* 5A **98**
Hunter Rd. *S6* 3H **85**
Hunter's Av. *B'ley* 1C **22**
Hunters Bar. *S11* 5A **98**
Hunters Chase. *Dinn* 2F **107**
Hunters Clo. *Dinn* 2F **107**
Hunters Ct. *Dinn* 2F **107**
Hunters Dri. *Dinn* 2F **107**
Hunters Gdns. *S6* 2D **84**
Hunters Gdns. *Dinn* 2F **107**
Hunters Grn. *Dinn* 2F **107**
Hunters La. *S13* 1E **113**
Hunters Pk. *Dinn* 2F **107**
Hunters Ri. *B'ley* 6C **12**
Hunters Way. *Dinn* 2F **107**
Huntingdon Cres. *S11* 5C **98**
Huntingdon Rd. *Donc* 4A **34**
Huntington St. *Ben* 5A **18**
Huntington Way. *Maltby* 2E **83**
Huntingtower Rd. *S11* 6H **97**
Hunt La. *Donc* 4B **32**
Huntley Clo. *Ink* 3H **133**
Huntley Gro. *S11* 1F **109**
Huntley Rd. *S11* 1F **109**
Huntsman Rd. *S9* 1F **101**
Huntsman Rd. *Stav* 1C **134**
Huntsmans Gdns. *S9* 4E **89**

Hunt St. *Hoy* 6F **37**
Hurl Dri. *S12* 2B **112**
Hurley Cft. *Bram B* 4A **40**
. . . . (in two parts)
Hurl Field. **2A 112**
Hurlfield Av. *S12* 2B **112**
Hurlfield Ct. *S12* 1C **112**
Hurlfield Dri. *S12* 1B **112**
Hurlfield Rd. *Rav* 2H **81**
Hurlfield Rd. *S12* 2A **112**
Hurlfield Vw. *S12* 1B **112**
Hurlingham Clo. *S11* 2A **110**
Hurlstone Clo. *E'thpe* 4E **21**
Hursley Clo. *Soth* 6G **115**
Hursley Dri. *Soth* 6G **115**
Hurst Grn. *High G* 6B **50**
Hurst La. *Auc* 4H **63**
Hutchinson Ct. *Roth* 4E **79**
Hutchinson La. *S7* 4B **110**
Hutchinson Rd. *S7* 4B **110**
Hutchinson Rd. *Rawm* 1G **69**
Hutcliffe Dri. *S8* 5B **110**
Hutcliffe Wood Crematorium.
. *S8* 5B **110**
Hutcliffe Wood Rd. *S8* 5B **110**
Hut La. *Kil* .5D **126**
Hutton Cft. *S12* 4B **114**
Hutton Rd. *Roth* 6G **67**
Huxterwell Dri. *Bal* 1H **61**
Hyacinth Clo. *S5* 6B **76**
Hyacinth Rd. *S5* 6B **76**
Hyde Park. **1E 47**
Hyde Pk. Ind. Est. *Donc* 3E **47**
Hyde Pk. Ter. *S2* 2G **99** (3H **5**)
Hyde Pk. Wlk. *S2* 2G **99**
Hyland Cres. *Donc* 5G **45**
Hyman Clo. *Warm* 4F **45**
Hyperion Way. *New R* 5C **62**

I

Ians Way. *Ches* 1E **137**
Ibberson Av. *M'well* 5F **7**
Ibbotson Rd. *S6* 5A **86**
Ibsen Cres. *Barn D* 1H **21**
Ickles. **5B 78**
Ickles Roundabout. *Roth* 4C **78**
Ickles Way. *Roth* 5B **78**
Icknield Way. *B'wth* 3C **90**
Ida Gro. *Maltby* 3D **82**
Ida's Rd. *Eck* 5D **124**
Idsworth Rd. *S5* 1H **87**
Ilam Clo. *Ink* 5A **134**
Ilkley Cres. *Swal* 1A **116**
Ilkley Rd. *S5* 5H **75**
Illsley Rd. *D'fld* 3E **27**
Immingham Gro. *Stav* 2B **134**
Imperial Bldgs. *Roth* 3D **78**
Imperial Cres. *Donc* 5F **33**
Imperial St. *B'ley* 2H **23**
Imrie Pl. *Kiv P* 5H **117**
Industry Rd. *S9* 6D **88**
Industry Rd. *Car* 6E **9**
Industry St. *S6* 5A **86**
. . . . (in two parts)
Infield La. *S9* 1F **101**
Infirmary Rd. *S6* 1C **86**
Infirmary Rd. *Ches* 1B **138**
Infirmary Rd. *P'gte* 4G **69**
Ingbirchworth Rd. *Thurls* 3A **142**
Ingelow Av. *S5* 4F **75**
Ingfield Av. *S9* 1G **89**
Ingleborough Cft. *C'town* 1D **64**
Ingleborough Dri. *Donc* 1G **45**
Ingleby Clo. *Dron W* 2A **128**
Ingledene M. *Barn D* 2H **21**
Ingle Gro. *Donc* 1G **45**
Inglenook Ct. *Maltby* 5H **83**
. . . .(off Sousa St.)
Ingleton Rd. *Has* 6B **138**
Ingleton Wlk. *B'ley* 5F **13**
Inglewood. *Dart* 4E **7**
Inglewood Av. *Soth* 6G **115**
Inglewood Ct. *Soth* 6G **115**
Inglewood Dell. *Soth* 6G **115**
Ingram Clo. *S2* 3H **99**
Ingram Rd. *S2* 3H **99**
Ingsfield La. *Bol D* 1E **41**
. . . . (in two parts)
Ingshead Av. *Rawm* 2F **69**
Ings La. *Ark* 5F **19**
. . . .(Arksey Comn. La.)

Ings La. *Ark* 1G **45**
. . . .(Melton Rd.)
Ings La. *Ark* 5E **19**
. . . .(Station Rd.)
Ings La. *L Hou* 2F **27**
. . . . (in two parts)
Ings Rd. *Donc* 4B **32**
Ings Rd. *Womb* 5D **26**
. . . . (in two parts)
Ings Way. *Ark* 5D **18**
Inkerman Cotts. *Ches* 1E **137**
Inkerman Rd. *D'fld* 4E **27**
Inkersall. **5B 134**
Inkersall Dri. *W'fld* 1E **125**
Inkersall Farm Cotts. *Stav* 5C **134**
Inkersall Green. **4A 134**
Inkersall Grn. Rd. *Ink* 3H **133**
Inkersall Rd. *Stav* 4C **134**
Innovation Way. *B'ley* 3E **13**
Insley Gdns. *Donc* 4C **48**
Intake. **5H 35**
. . . .(Doncaster)
Intake. **2C 112**
. . . .(Sheffield)
Intake Cres. *Dod* 3B **22**
Intake Gdns. *B'ley* 5D **12**
. . . .(off Wade St.)
Intake La. *B'ley* 4D **12**
Intake La. *Cud* 1H **13**
Interchange Way. *B'ley* 5H **13**
Ireland Clo. *Stav* 1D **134**
Ireland Ind. Est. *Stav* 3C **134**
Ireland St. *Stav* 1D **134**
Irongate. *Ches* **2A 138**
. . . .(off High Street)
Ironside Clo. *S14* 5H **111**
Ironside Pl. *S14* 4A **112**
Ironside Rd. *S14* 5H **111**
Ironside Wlk. *S14* 5H **111**
Ironstone Cres. *C'town* 6D **50**
Ironstone Dri. *C'town* 6D **50**
. . . . .1D **52**
. . . .(off Forge La.)
Ironworks Pl. *Else* 1D **52**
. . . .(off Forge La.)
Ironworks Row. *Else* 1D **52**
. . . .(off Forge La.)
Irving St. *S9* 1E **101**
Irwell Gdns. *Donc* 1B **48**
Island Clo. *Roth* 6A **80**
Islay St. *S10* 2H **97**
Issott St. *B'ley* 4H **13**
Ivanbrook Clo. *Dron W* 2A **128**
Ivanhoe Av. *Kiv P* 4A **118**
Ivanhoe Clo. *Donc* 5H **31**
Ivanhoe M. *Swal* 5A **104**
Ivanhoe Rd. *S6* 5G **85**
Ivanhoe Rd. *Con* 3D **58**
Ivanhoe Rd. *Donc* 5G **45**
Ivanhoe Rd. *E'thpe* 6D **20**
Ivanhoe Rd. *Thur* 5A **94**
Ivanhoe Way. *Donc* 5H **31**
Ivor Gro. *Donc* 3A **46**
Ivy Clo. *Old W* 1A **132**
Ivy Clo. *Ross* 4E **63**
Ivy Cottage La. *S11* 1D **108**
Ivy Cotts. *S11* 6E **97**
Ivy Cotts. *Roy* 1F **9**
Ivy Ct. *S8* .5G **111**
Ivy Ct. *Cud* 1H **15**
Ivy Ct. *Old De* 2H **57**
Ivy Dri. *S10* 1B **98**
Ivy Farm Clo. *B'ley* 4F **9**
Ivy Farm Cft. *Dalt* 6B **70**
Ivy Gro. *S10* 1B **98**
. . . .(off Ivy Dri.)
Ivy Hall Rd. *S5* 3A **76**
Ivy La. *Beig* 3G **115**
Ivy Pk. Ct. *S10* 4E **97**
Ivy Pk. Rd. *S10* 3E **97**
Ivy Side Clo. *Kil* 3B **126**
Ivy Side Gdns. *Kil* 3B **126**
Ivy Ter. *B'ley* 1A **24**

J

Jack Clo. Orchard. *Roy* 1E **9**
Jackey La. *O'bri* 2B **72**
Jackson Cres. *Rawm* 6E **55**
Jackson St. *Cud* 1G **15**
Jackson St. *Gold* 4G **29**
Jacobs Clo. *S5* 5A **76**
Jacobs Dri. *S5* 5A **76**

Jacobs Hall Ct. *Dart* 5A **6**
Jacques Pl. *B'ley* 5D **14**
Jamaica St. *S4* 4H **87**
James Andrew Clo. *S8* 2D **122**
James Andrew Cres. *S8* 2C **122**
James Andrew Cft. *S8* 2D **122**
James Rd. *Adw S* 1F **17**
James St. *S9* 2E **101**
James St. *B'ley* 5H **13**
James St. *Ches* 5A **132**
James St. *Mexb* 6H **43**
James St. *Roth* 2C **78**
(in two parts)
James St. *Wors D* 4C **24**
James Walton Ct. *Half* 2F **125**
James Walton Dri. *Half* 2F **125**
James Walton Pl. *Half* 2F **125**
James Walton Vw. *Half* 2F **125**
Janet's Wlk. *Womb* 5G **25**
Janson St. *S9* 3C **88**
Jardine Clo. *S9* 5C **76**
Jardine St. *S9* 5D **76**
Jardine St. *Womb* 1F **39**
Jarratt St. *Donc* 1D **46**
Jarrow Rd. *S11* 5B **98**
Jasmine Av. *Beig* 4F **115**
Jasmine Clo. *Con* 4F **59**
Jaunty Av. *S12* 4D **112**
Jaunty Clo. *S12* 4D **112**
Jaunty Cres. *S12* 3D **112**
Jaunty Dri. *S12* 4D **112**
Jaunty La. *S12* 3D **112**
Jaunty Mt. *S12* 4E **113**
Jaunty Pl. *S12* 4D **112**
Jaunty Rd. *S12* 4E **113**
Jaunty Vw. *S12* 4E **113**
Jaunty Way. *S12* 3D **112**
Jaw Bones Hill. *Ches* 5A **138**
Jay La. *Ast* 1C **116**
Jebb Gdns. *Ches* 3E **137**
Jedburgh Dri. *S9* 5C **76**
Jedburgh St. *S9* 5C **76**
Jeffcock Pl. *High G* 6C **50**
Jeffcock Rd. *S9* 1E **101**
Jeffcock Rd. *High G* 6C **50**
Jefferson Av. *Donc* 6B **20**
Jeffery Cres. *Deep* 4F **141**
Jeffery Grn. *S10* 6A **96**
Jeffery St. *S2* .1F **111**
Jenkin Av. *S9* .1C **88**
Jenkin Clo. *S9* 6C **76**
Jenkin Dri. *S9* .1C **88**
Jenkin Rd. *S5* .6B **76**
Jenkin Wood Clo. *S'side* 2G **81**
Jennings Clo. *Roth* 1E **79**
Jenny La. *Cud* 1H **15**
Jepson Rd. *S5* 5B **76**
Jepson Rd. *Ches* 6C **138**
Jericho St. *S3* 1D **98** (1A **4**)
Jermyn Av. *S12* 3G **113**
Jermyn Clo. *S12* 4H **113**
Jermyn Cres. *S12* 4H **113**
Jermyn Cft. *Dod* 2B **22**
Jermyn Dri. *S12* 4H **113**
Jermyn Sq. *S12* 4H **113**
Jermyn Way. *S12* 4H **113**
Jersey Rd. *S2* 6E **99**
Jervis Pl. *Ink* 5H **133**
Jesmond Av. *Roy* 2D **8**
Jessamine Rd. *S5* 5A **76**
Jessell St. *S9* .6B **88**
Jessop Ct. *Dinn* 3F **107**
Jessop St. *S1* 3E **99** (6D **4**)
Jewitt Rd. *Roth* 5G **67**
Jew La. *S1* 3G **5**
Joan La. *Hoot L* 5E **83**
Joan Royd La. *P'stne* 6B **142**
Joan's Wlk. *Jump* 4B **38**
Jockell Dri. *Rawm* 2F **69**
Jockey Rd. *Oxs* 4H **143**
John Calvert Rd. *Woodh* 1D **114**
John Eaton's Almshouses. *S8* 5F **111**
John Hartop Pl. *Else* 1D **52**
(off Forge La.)
John Hibbard Av. *S13* 6E **103**
John Hibbard Clo. *S13* 6E **103**
John Hibbard Cres. *S13* 6E **103**
John Hibbard Ri. *S13* 6E **103**
John La. *New R* 4C **62**
Johnson Ct. *Edl'tn* 2C **60**
Johnson Ct. *Roth* 4F **79**
(off Johnson St.)
Johnson La. *S3* 1F **99** (1F **5**)

Johnson La. *E'fld* 6F **65**
Johnson St. *S3* 6F **87** (1F **5**)
Johnson St. *B'ley* 5F **13**
Johnson St. *Roth* 4F **79**
Johnson St. *S3* 3D **140**
Johnstone Clo. *Ches* 4H **137**
John St. *S2* 4D **98**
John St. *B'ley* .1H **23**
John St. *Brim* .5H **137**
(in two parts)
John St. *Ches* 2G **137**
John St. *Eck* 6D **124**
John St. *Gt Hou* 1B **28**
John St. *L Hou* 2A **28**
John St. *Mexb* 1E **57**
John St. *Roth* .3C **78**
John St. *Thur* .4A **94**
John St. *Thurn* 1F **29**
John St. *Womb* 6A **26**
John St. *Wors* .5A **24**
John Trickett Ho. *C'town* 2D **64**
(off Lansbury Av.)
John Ward St. *S13* 6D **102**
John West St. *S'bri* 4D **140**
Joiner St. *S3* 1F **99** (1F **5**)
Jones Av. *Womb* 6H **25**
Jordan. **4H 77**
Jordan Cres. *Roth* 4G **77**
Jordanthorpe. **3F 123**
Jordanthorpe Cen. *S8* 3F **123**
Jordanthorpe Grn. *S8* 3G **123**
Jordanthorpe Parkway. *S8* 4E **123**
Jordanthorpe Vw. *S8* 2G **123**
Joseph Ct. *B'ley* 1H **23**
Josephine Rd. *Roth* 3A **78**
Joseph Rd. *S6* 6A **86**
Joseph St. *B'ley* 1H **23**
Joseph St. *Eck* 6D **124**
Joseph St. *Grim* 6G **11**
Joshua Rd. *S7* 1C **110**
Josselin Ct. *C'town* 2D **64**
Jossey La. *Donc & Ben* 1F **31**
Jowitt Clo. *Maltby* 5H **83**
Jowitt Rd. *S11* 1H **109**
Jubb Clo. *Roth* 5B **80**
Jubilee Cotts. *B'wth* 2B **90**
Jubilee Cotts. *Cal* 4G **139**
Jubilee Cotts. *Hoy* 6E **37**
Jubilee Ct. *Donc* 3A **34**
Jubilee Cres. *Kil* 2C **126**
Jubilee Gdns. *Roy* 1F **9**
Jubilee Rd. *S9* 5D **88**
Jubilee Rd. *Donc* 4E **33**
Jubilee St. *Roth* 5D **78**
Jubilee Ter. *B'ley* 1B **24**
Judith Rd. *Ast* .1B **116**
Judy Row. *B'ley* 3C **14**
Julian Rd. *S9* .6D **76**
Julian Way. *S9* 6D **76**
Jumble La. *E'fld* 6H **65**
Jumble St. *S11* 6A **108**
Jump. **4C 38**
Junction Clo. *Womb* 2A **40**
Junction Rd. *S11* 5A **98**
Junction Rd. *New R* 5C **62**
Junction Rd. *Woodh* 6D **102**
Junction St. *B'ley* 1B **24**
Junction St. *Womb* 2H **39**
Junction Ter. *B'ley* 1B **24**
Junction 34 Ind. Est. *S9* 1F **89**
June Rd. *Woodh* 6D **102**
Juniper Clo. *Holl* 1G **133**
Juniper Ri. *Kil* .4A **126**

K

Kariba Clo. *Ches* 2B **138**
Kashmir Gdns. *S9* 6D **88**
Katherine Ct. *Thur* 5A **94**
Katherine Rd. *Thur* 4A **94**
Katherine St. *Thur* 5B **94**
Kathleen Gro. *Gold* 3H **29**
Kathleen St. *Gold* 3H **29**
Kay Cres. *Rawm* 5C **54**
Kaye Pl. *S10* 1B **98**
Kaye St. *B'ley* .5H **13**
Kay's Ter. *B'ley* 2E **25**
Kay St. *Hoy* 6F **37**
Kea Pk. Clo. *H'by* 4A **82**
Kearsley La. *Con* 5D **58**
Kearsley Rd. *S2* 5E **99**
Keats Dri. *Dinn* 5H **107**

Keats Gro. *P'stne* 3D **142**
Keats Rd. *S6* 3B **74**
Keats Rd. *Ches* 3H **131**
Keats Rd. *Donc* 5B **46**
Keble Martin Way. *Wath D* 5D **40**
Kedleston Clo. *Ches* 4E **131**
Kedleston Ct. *Stav* 1C **134**
(off Devonshire St.)
Keeper La. *Notton* 1H **7**
Keepers Clo. *S5* 5H **75**
Keepers Clo. *Ross* 3F **63**
Keeton Hall Rd. *Kiv P* 4B **118**
Keeton's Hill. *S2* 5D **98**
Keighley Wlk. *Con* 4B **58**
Keilder Ct. *Ches* 4F **137**
Keir Pl. *Rawm* .1H **69**
Keir St. *B'ley* 5F **13**
Keir Ter. *B'ley* .5F **13**
Kelburn Av. *Ches* 4E **137**
Kelgate. *Mosb* 3D **124**
Kelham Bank. **2C 46**
Kelham Ct. *Donc* 2C **46**
Kelham Island. **6E 87**
Kelham Island St. *S3* 6E **87**
Kelham Island Mus. **6E 87**
Kelham St. *Donc* 2C **46**
Kelly St. *Gold* 4G **29**
Kelsey Gdns. *Donc* 6C **48**
Kelsey Ter. *B'ley* 2H **23**
Kelso Dri. *Warm* 4F **45**
Kelvin Ct. *Scho* 5E **67**
Kelvin Gro. *Womb* 1G **39**
Kelvin St. *Mexb* 6E **43**
Kemp Clo. *Kil* .3A **126**
Kempton Gdns. *Mexb* 5G **43**
Kempton Pk. Rd. *Donc* 3F **31**
(in two parts)
Kempton St. *Donc* 1B **48**
Kempwell Dri. *Rawm* 5F **55**
Kenbourne Gro. *S7* 6C **98**
Kenbourne Rd. *S7* 6C **98**
Kendal Av. *Ans* 1H **119**
Kendal Clo. *Spro* 2C **44**
Kendal Cres. *Con* 3F **59**
Kendal Cres. *Wors* 5A **24**
Kendal Dri. *Bol D* 2A **42**
Kendal Dri. *Dron W* 2C **128**
Kendal Grn. *Wors* 5G **23**
Kendal Grn. Rd. *Wors* 5G **23**
Kendal Gro. *B'ley* 1G **25**
Kendal Pl. *S6* 3H **85**
Kendal Rd. *S6* .3H **85**
Kendal Rd. *Ches* 3G **131**
Kendal Rd. *Donc* 2A **32**
Kendal Va. *Wors B* 5A **24**
Kendray. **2C 24**
Kendray St. *B'ley* 6H **13**
Kenilworth Clo. *Donc* 3F **31**
Kenilworth Ct. *S11* 3F **109**
Kenilworth Pl. *S11* 5A **98**
Kenilworth Rd. *Donc* 4G **45**
Kenmare Cres. *Donc* 4G **33**
Kennedy Ct. *S10* 2H **97**
Kennedy Dri. *Gold* 6F **29**
Kennedy Rd. *S8* 5C **110**
Kenneth St. *Roth* 2E **79**
Kennet Va. *Ches* 6F **131**
Kenninghall Clo. *S2* 6H **99**
Kenninghall Dri. *S2* 6H **99**
Kenninghall Rd. *S2* 6H **99**
Kennington Av. *W'land* 2B **16**
Kennington Gro. *Edl'tn* 2C **60**
Kenrock Clo. *Ark* 6E **19**
Kensington Av. *Thurls* 3A **142**
Kensington Clo. *Dinn* 3C **106**
Kensington Dri. *S10* 5A **96**
Kensington Rd. *B'ley* 4F **13**
Kent Av. *Rawm* 6E **55**
Kent Clo. *Ches* 6H **131**
Kent Clo. *Roy* 1E **9**
Kentmere Clo. *Dron W* 2C **128**
Kentmere Dri. *Donc* 4H **47**
Kent Rd. *S8* 2F **111**
Kent Rd. *Donc* .4B **46**
Kent Rd. *Roth* .6G **67**
Kent St. *Ches* .5C **138**
Kenwell Dri. *S17* 4H **121**
Kenwood Av. *S7* 6C **98**
Kenwood Bank. *S7* 5C **98**
Kenwood Chase. *S7* 5D **98**
(off Wostenholm Rd.)
Kenwood Clo. *B'ley* 1D **24**
Kenwood Pk. Rd. *S7* 6C **98**

Kenwood Ri. Braml 3G 81
Kenwood Rd. S7 . . . . .6B 98
Kenworthy Rd. B'ley 2H 23
Kenworthy Rd. S'bri 4D 140
Kenyon All. S1 . . . . .2B 4
Kenyon Rd. Ches 4E 139
Kenyon St. S1 . . . . .1D 98 (2B 4)
Keppel Dri. Scho 5D 66
Keppel Heights. Scho 5D 66
Keppel Pl. S5 . . . . .3A 76
Keppel Rd. S5 . . . . .3B 76
Keppel Rd. Scho 5D 66
Keppel's Column. 5D 66
Keppel Vw. Rd. Roth 1F 77
Kepple Clo. New R 6D 62
Keresforth Clo. B'ley 1E 23
Keresforth Ct. B'ley 1E 23
Keresforth Hall Dri. B'ley 2E 23
Keresforth Hall Rd. B'ley 2F 23
Keresforth Hill Rd. B'ley 3D 22
                              (in two parts)
Keresforth Rd. Dod 3B 22
Kerwin Clo. S17 . . . . .1C 120
Kerwin Dri. S17 . . . . .1C 120
Kerwin Rd. S17 . . . . .1C 120
Kestrel Av. Thpe H 2C 66
Kestrel Clo. Kil 2H 125
Kestrel Dri. Adw S 1D 16
Kestrel Dri. Eck 6B 124
Kestrel Dri. Ross 4E 63
Kestrel Grn. S2 . . . . .3A 100
Kestrel Ri. Birdw 3D 36
Kestrel Ri. Swal 6G 103
Keswick Clo. S4 . . . . .3E 85
Keswick Clo. Donc 1A 32
Keswick Cres. B'wth 4B 90
Keswick Dri. Ches 4E 131
                              (in two parts)
Keswick Pl. Dron W 2B 128
Keswick Rd. S7 . . . . .3C 110
Keswick Rd. Dart 2E 7
Keswick Wlk. B'ley 1G 25
Keswick Way. Ans 1H 119
Ket Hill La. Brie 2F 11
Kettlebridge Rd. S9 . . . . .2C 100
Ketton Av. S8 . . . . .4F 111
Ketton Wlk. B'ley 4E 13
Kevin Gro. H'by 5B 82
Kew Cres. S12 . . . . .5B 112
Kexbrough. 5A 6
Kexbrough Dri. Dart 5B 6
Key Av. Hoy 5B 38
Keyworth Pl. S13 . . . . .1A 114
Keyworth Rd. S6 . . . . .2A 86
Khartoum Rd. S11 . . . . .4B 98
Kibroyd Dri. Dart 6A 6
Kibworth Clo. Ches 6C 138
Kidsley Clo. Ches 6C 130
Kieran Clo. Dinn 3C 106
Kier Hardie Av. New R 5D 62
Kilburn Rd. Dron W 2A 128
Kildale Gdns. Mosb 2D 124
Kildonan Gro. S12 . . . . .4E 113
Killamarsh. 3B 126
Killamarsh La. H'hill 4E 127
Kilner Way. S6 . . . . .6B 74
Kiln Hill. Coal A 6G 123
Kilnhurst. .6C 56
Kilnhurst Bus. Pk. Kiln 1C 70
Kilnhurst Rd. Hoot R 6D 56
Kilnhurst Rd. Rawm & Kiln 6G 55
Kiln Rd. Roth 1H 77
Kilnsea Wlk. B'ley 6G 13
                         (off Fitzwilliam St.)
Kilton Hill. S3 . . . . .5F 87
Kilton Pl. S3 .5F 87
Kilvington Av. S13 . . . . .6D 100
Kilvington Cres. S13 . . . . .1D 112
Kilvington Rd. S13 . . . . .1D 112
Kimberley St. S9 . . . . .5B 88
Kimberworth. 2G 77
Kimberworth Park. 6H 67
Kimberworth Pk. Rd. Roth 5F 67
                          (in three parts)
Kimberworth Rd. Roth 2H 77
Kinder Gdns. S5 . . . . .4F 75
Kinder Rd. Ink 5H 133
King Av. Maltby 5H 83
King Av. New R 4C 62
King Egbert Rd. S17 . . . . .4E 121
King Edward Rd. Donc 3B 46
King Edwards. S6 . . . . .1B 96
King Edwards App. S6 . . . . .2B 96

King Edwards Gdns. B'ley 1G 23
King Edward St. B'ley 1D 14
Kingfield Ct. S11 . . . . .6B 98
Kingfield Rd. S11 . . . . .6B 98
Kingfisher Clo. Donc 2H 33
Kingfisher Ct. Con 3H 59
Kingfisher Ct. Ross 4E 63
Kingfisher Gro. Swal 6G 103
Kingfisher Ho. Old W 1B 132
Kingfisher Ri. Thpe H 1C 66
Kingfisher Rd. Adw S 1D 16
King Georges Clo. New R 5B 62
King George Sq. Kirk S 3D 20
King George's Rd. New R 3B 62
King George Ter. B'ley 1B 24
King James St. S6 . . . . .5B 86
Kingsclere Wlk. Ches 6H 137
Kings Coppice. S17 . . . . .3D 120
Kings Ct. S1 .6B 4
Kings Ct. Roth 1G 91
Kings Cres. Edl'tn 2B 60
Kingscroft Clo. S17 . . . . .1E 121
Kingsforth La. Thur 3A 94
Kingsforth Rd. Thur 4A 94
Kingsgate. Donc 6D 32
Kingsgate Flats. Donc 6D 32
                          (off Kingsgate)
Kingsland Ct. Roy 1F 9
Kingsley Av. Ches 5H 137
Kingsley Av. Donc 5H 31
Kingsley Clo. B'ley 1A 14
Kingsley Cres. Arm 3G 35
Kingsley Pk. Av. S7 . . . . .3H 109
Kingsley Pk. Gro. S11 . . . . .3H 109
Kingsley Rd. Adw S 2C 16
Kingsmead Dri. Bran 3H 49
Kingsmede Av. Ches 4F 137
Kings M. Donc 6D 32
Kings M. Eck 6E 125
King's Own Yorkshire Light Infantry Mus.
                     (Mus. and Art Gallery)
                                        . . . .6D 32
King's Rd. Cud 4C 10
King's Rd. Donc 5E 33
King's Rd. Mexb 6F 43
King's Rd. Womb 1G 39
King's Stocks. L Hou 3A 28
King's St. Donc 6D 32
King's St. Grim 6G 11
Kingstone. 2F 23
Kingstone Pl. B'ley 2F 23
Kingston Rd. Donc 5H 33
Kingston St. S4 . . . . .4H 87
King St. S3 . . . . .1F 99 (2F 5)
King St. Arm .2D 34
King St. B'ley .1H 23
King St. Brim 2F 133
King St. C'town 1E 65
King St. Gold .4G 29
King St. Hoy .5A 38
King St. Swal 5A 104
King St. Swint 2B 56
King St. Thurn 2G 29
King St. N. Ches 4A 132
King St. S. Ches 6A 138
Kingsway. M'well 4E 7
Kings Way. Roth 1G 91
Kingsway. Thurn 1E 29
Kingsway. Womb 1F 39
Kingsway Clo. New R 6E 63
Kingsway Complex. Dinn 4F 107
Kingsway Gro. Thurn 1E 29
Kingsway Ho. Donc 6D 32
Kingswood. S6 . . . . .6F 73
Kingswood. S11 . . . . .1B 110
Kingswood Av. Lghtn 1E 107
Kingswood Av. Owl 5A 114
Kingswood Clo. Ches 3F 131
Kingswood Clo. Owl 5A 114
Kingswood Cres. Hoy 4A 38
Kingswood Cft. Owl 5A 114
Kingswood Gro. Owl 5A 114
Kingswood Hall. S6 . . . . .6F 73
Kingwell Cres. Wors 3H 23
Kingwell M. Wors 4A 24
Kingwell Rd. Wors 4H 23
Kinharvie Rd. S5 . . . . .6D 74
Kinnaird Av. S5 . . . . .4G 75
Kinnaird Pl. S5 . . . . .4G 75
Kinnaird Rd. S5 . . . . .4G 75
Kinsey Rd. High G 6A 50

Kipling Av. Donc 5H 45
Kipling Clo. Dron 4G 129
Kipling Rd. S6 . . . . .3A 86
Kipling Rd. Barn D 1H 21
Kipling Rd. Ches 3H 131
Kirby Clo. S9 . . . . .1E 101
Kirby Clo. Ches 6C 138
Kirby La. C'town 5H 51
Kirby Row. Thpe H 2B 66
Kirby St. Mexb 6E 43
Kirk Balk. Hoy 5H 37
Kirkby Av. S12 . . . . .3C 112
Kirkby Av. B'ley 5C 8
Kirkby Av. Donc 3A 32
Kirkby Dri. S12 . . . . .3C 112
Kirkby Rd. S12 . . . . .3C 112
Kirkby Vw. S12 . . . . .3C 112
Kirkby Way. S12 . . . . .4C 112
Kirkcroft Av. Kil 2B 126
Kirkcroft Clo. Thpe H 2C 66
Kirkcroft Dri. Kil 3B 126
Kirkcroft La. Kil 3B 126
Kirk Cft. Rd. Lghtn 1E 107
Kirk Cross Cres. Roy 3E 9
Kirkdale Clo. Ches 5B 138
Kirkdale Cres. S13 . . . . .4B 102
Kirkdale Dri. S13 . . . . .4B 102
Kirk Edge Av. Worr 5D 72
Kirk Edge Dri. Worr 5C 72
Kirk Edge Rd. O'bri & Worr 4A 72
Kirkfield Way. Roy 3E 9
Kirkhall Clo. Arm 4G 35
Kirkham Clo. B'ley 4C 14
Kirkham Pl. B'ley 6F 9
Kirkhill Bank. P'stne 6C 142
Kirk Ho. Roth 4H 79
                       (off Browning Rd.)
Kirklands Dri. Rawm 1E 69
Kirk Sandall. 3D 20
Kirk Sandall Ind. Est. K Ind 3B 20
                          (in three parts)
Kirkstall Clo. Ans 4F 119
Kirkstall Clo. B'wth 2A 90
Kirkstall Clo. Donc 4F 31
Kirkstall Rd. S11 . . . . .5A 98
Kirkstall Rd. B'ley 6A 8
Kirkstead Abbey M. Thpe H 5C 66
Kirkstead Gdns. S13 . . . . .6E 103
Kirkstead Rd. Roth 2C 76
Kirkstone Clo. Donc 2A 32
Kirkstone Rd. S6 . . . . .4A 86
Kirkstone Rd. Ches 3E 131
Kirk St. S4 . . . . .5G 87
Kirk St. Donc 1D 46
Kirk Vw. Hoy .5H 37
Kirk Way. B'ley 4D 14
Kirstead Ct. Donc 6F 49
Kirton Rd. S4 .4G 87
Kitchen Rd. Womb 6H 25
Kitchen Wood La. Dron W 3A 128
Kitson Dri. B'ley 4D 14
Kiveton Gdns. Kiv P 4B 118
Kiveton La. Tod & Kiv P 2B 118
Kiveton Park. 5H 117
Kiveton Park Station. 6D 118
Knab Clo. S7 . . . . .2A 110
Knab Cft. S7 . . . . .2A 110
Knab Rd. S7 . . . . .2A 110
Knapton Av. Rawm 1E 69
Knaresborough Clo. Swal 6A 104
Knaresborough Rd. S13 . . . . .4A 110
Knaresborough Rd. Con 4B 58
Knavesmire Gdns. Donc 1B 48
Knifesmith Ga. Ches 2A 138
Knighton Clo. Ches 6B 138
Knollbeck Av. Bram 3A 40
Knoll Beck Clo. Gold 5E 29
Knollbeck Cres. Bram 3A 40
Knollbeck La. Bram 3A 40
Knoll Clo. S'bri 3E 141
Knoll, The. Dron 3B 136
Knoll, The. Dron 6H 123
Knoll Top. 3E 141
Knowle Clo. S6 . . . . .5C 84
Knowle Ct. S11 . . . . .2H 109
Knowle Cft. S11 . . . . .2G 109
Knowle Grn. S17 . . . . .2C 120
Knowle La. S11 . . . . .2F 109
Knowle Rd. S5 . . . . .3F 75
Knowle Rd. Wors 3B 24
Knowles Av. Deep 4F 141

Knowles St. *P'stne* 5F **143**
Knowle Top. 5C **84**
Knowle Top. *Half* 2E **125**
Knowsley St. *B'ley* 6F **13**
Knutton Cres. *S5* 3C **74**
Knutton Ri. *S5* 2C **74**
Knutton Rd. *S5* 3C **74**
Kyle Clo. *S5* 5C **74**
Kyle Cres. *S5* 5C **74**
Kynance Cres. *B'wth* 4B **90**

L

Laburnum Av. *S'side* 3F **81**
Laburnum Clo. *Ans* 3F **119**
Laburnum Clo. *C'town* 3E **65**
Laburnum Ct. *Cal* 2G **139**
Laburnum Dri. *Arm* 2G **35**
Laburnum Gro. *Con* 4C **58**
Laburnum Gro. *Kil* 4A **126**
Laburnum Gro. *S'bri* 4D **140**
Laburnum Gro. *Wors* 5B **24**
Laburnum Pde. *Maltby* 4D **82**
Laburnum Pl. *Ben* 5B **18**
Laburnum Rd. *Donc* 5H **45**
Laburnum Rd. *Maltby* 4D **82**
Laburnum Rd. *Mexb* 5D **42**
Laburnum St. *Holl* 2H **133**
Laceby Clo. *Braml* 2H **81**
Laceby Ct. *B'ley* 2E **23**
Ladies Spring Ct. S17 ....2G **121**
(off Ladies Spring Gro.)
Ladies Spring Dri. *S17* 2G **121**
Ladies Spring Gro. *S17* 2G **121**
Ladock Clo. *B'ley* 4B **14**
Lady Bank Dri. *Donc* 2E **47**
Ladybank Rd. *Mosb* 3D **124**
Ladybank Vw. *Eck* 5D **124**
Ladybower Ct. *S17* 4G **121**
Ladybower La. *Stav* 3B **134**
Ladycroft. *Bol D* 1A **42**
Lady Cft. *Wath D* 5E **41**
Lady Cft. La. *H'fld* 4E **39**
Ladycroft Rd. *Arm* 5F **35**
Lady Fld. Rd. *Kiv S & Thor S* 6D **118**
Lady Ida's Dri. *Eck* 5A **124**
(in two parts)
Ladymead. *B'ley* 3B **14**
Lady Oak Rd. *Roth* 6A **70**
Ladyroyd Cft. *Cud* 1H **15**
Lady's Bri. *S3* 1F **99** (1F **5**)
Ladysmith Av. *S7* 1B **110**
Ladywood Dri. *Ches* 4E **131**
Ladywood Rd. *Grim* 6H **11**
Laird Av. *S6* 2G **85**
Laird Dri. *S6* 2G **85**
Laird Rd. *S6* 2G **85**
Lairds Way. *P'stne* 4E **143**
Laithe Cft. *Dod* 2B **22**
Laithes Clo. *B'ley* 6D **8**
Laithes Cres. *B'ley* 6B **8**
Laithes La. *B'ley* 6B **8**
Lake Clo. *Edl'tn* 4A **60**
Lake Ct. *W'land* 3E **17**
Lakeen Rd. *Donc* 5G **33**
Lakeland Clo. *Cud* 2H **15**
Lakeland Dri. *Ans* 1G **119**
Lake Rd. *W'land* 4E **17**
Lakeside. *S6* 4F **85**
Lakeside Boulevd. *Donc* 4G **47**
Lakeside Clo. *S'side* 1G **81**
Lakeside Ct. *Bram* 4H **39**
Lakeside Vw. *P'stne* 1A **142**
Lake Vw. Av. *Ches* 4E **137**
Lambcote Way. *Maltby* 3H **83**
Lambcroft La. *S13* 1C **114**
Lambcroft Vw. *Woodh* 1C **114**
Lamb Dri. *S5* 6B **74**
Lambcroft. *B'ley* 4E **9**
Lambe Flatt. *Dart* 5A **6**
Lambert Fold. *Dod* 2C **22**
Lambert Rd. *B'ley* 2C **24**
Lamberts La. *Thry* 4D **70**
Lambert St. *S3* 1E **99** (2D **4**)
Lambert Wlk. *B'ley* 1C **24**
Lambert Wlk. *Wath D* 3C **40**
Lambeth Rd. *Donc* 4B **46**
Lambeth Rd. Cvn. Pk.
  Donc 4B **46**
Lamb Hill Clo. *S13* 6F **101**
Lamb La. *B'ley* 2C **14**
Lambra Rd. *B'ley* 6H **13**

Lambrell Av. *Kiv P* 5G **117**
Lambrell Grn. *Kiv P* 5G **117**
Lamb Rd. *S5* 6B **74**
Lambs Flat La. *Dart* 6A **6**
Lanark Dri. *Mexb* 4G **43**
Lanark Gdns. *Donc* 4A **34**
Lancar Ct. *B'ley* 3B **14**
Lancaster Av. *Donc* 5A **34**
Lancaster Av. *Kirk S* 3D **20**
Lancaster Ga. *B'ley* 6G **13**
Lancaster Rd. *Ches* 3G **131**
Lancaster Rd. *S'bri* 3D **140**
Lancaster St. *S3* 6D **86**
Lancaster St. *B'ley* 6F **13**
Lancaster St. *Thurn* 1G **29**
Lancelot Clo. *Ches* 5F **137**
Lancing Rd. *S2* 5E **99**
(in two parts)
Landon Clo. *Walt* 6D **136**
Landseer Clo. *S14* 5H **111**
Landseer Clo. *Dron* 3C **128**
Landseer Ct. *Flan* 3F **81**
Landseer Dri. *S14* 5A **112**
Landseer Pl. *S14* 5A **112**
Landseer Wlk. *S14* 5A **112**
Lane Cotts. *Roy* 2E **9**
Lane End. 1E **65**
Lane End. *C'town* 6D **50**
Lane End Rd. *Roth* 6G **79**
Lane End M. *Thurn* 1D **28**
Lane End Rd. *Roth* 6G **79**
Lane End Vw. *Roth* 6G **79**
Lane Head. *Gren* 1H **73**
Lane Head Clo. *M'well* 3E **7**
Lane Head Clo. *Rawm* 1G **69**
Lane Head Ri. *M'well* 3E **7**
Lane Head Rd. *S17* 5C **120**
Laneside Clo. *Donc* 2A **46**
Lanes, The. *Roth* 2H **79**
Lane, The. *Roy* 1E **9**
Langar Clo. *Toll B* 3A **18**
Lang Av. *B'ley* 5E **15**
Langcliff Clo. *M'well* 3E **7**
Lang Cres. *B'ley* 5E **15**
Langdale Clo. *Ches* 6B **130**
Langdale Dri. *Donc* 1H **31**
Langdale Dri. *Dron* 6G **123**
Langdale Rd. *S8* 2C **110**
Langdale Rd. *B'ley* 6A **14**
Langdale Rd. *Bar G* 2A **12**
Langdale Sq. *Brim* 3D **132**
Langdale Way. *Dinn* 6F **107**
Langdon Rd. *Roth* 1G **77**
Langdon St. *S11* 5D **98**
Langdon Wlk. *B'ley* 5G **13**
Langdon Wlk. *Roth* 1G **77**
Langer Fld. Av. *Ches* 6A **138**
Langer La. *Wing & Ches* 6H **137**
Langer St. *Donc* 2A **46**
Langford Clo. *Dod* 2C **22**
Langhurst Rd. *Ches* 1F **137**
Langley Clo. *Ches* 6C **130**
Langley Clo. *Roth* 2B **80**
Langsett Av. *S6* 1G **85**
Langsett Clo. *S6* 4B **86**
Langsett Ct. *B'ley* 6A **8**
Langsett Ct. *Donc* 3H **47**
Langsett Cres. *S6* 4B **86**
Langsett Gro. *S6* 5B **86**
Langsett Ri. *S6* 4B **86**
Langsett Rd. *S6* 3A **86**
Langsett Rd. *B'ley* 6A **8**
Langsett Rd. N. *O'bri* 1C **72**
Langsett Rd. S. *O'bri* 2D **72**
Langsett Wlk. *S6* 4B **86**
Langthwaite La. *Scawt* 5F **17**
Langthwaite Rd. *Donc* 6F **17**
Langtree Av. *Old W* 2A **132**
Lansbury Av. *C'town* 2D **64**
Lansbury Av. *Maltby* 5H **83**
Lansbury Av. *New R* 4E **63**
Lansbury Pl. *Rawm* 1A **70**
Lansbury Rd. *Eck* 6D **124**
Lansdowne Av. *Ches* 4G **131**
Lansdowne Clo. *Thurn* 1E **29**
Lansdowne Cres. *Dart* 6B **6**
Lansdowne Cres. *Swint* 3B **56**
Lansdowne Rd. *S11* 4D **98**
Lansdowne Rd. *Brim* 4D **132**
Lansdowne Rd. *Donc* 4A **34**
Lanyon Way. *B'ley* 4B **14**

Lapwater Rd. *Roth* 4H **67**
Lapwater Wlk. *Roth* 4H **67**
Lapwing Va. *Thpe H* 1C **66**
Larch Av. *Kil* 4A **126**
Larch Av. *Wick* 4F **81**
Larch Clo. *D'fld* 4E **27**
Larch Dri. *Arm* 3F **35**
(in two parts)
Larches, The. *Swint* 2A **56**
Larchfield Pl. *B'ley* 2D **14**
Larchfield Rd. *Donc* 4H **45**
Larch Gro. *Ast* 5C **104**
Larch Gro. *C'town* 3E **65**
Larch Gro. *Con* 5C **58**
Larch Hill. *S9* 2G **101**
Larch M. *Roth* 1H **79**
Larch Pl. *B'ley* 3B **24**
Larch Rd. *Eck* 6G **125**
Larch Rd. *Maltby* 3D **82**
Larch Way. *Ches* 6F **131**
Lark Av. *B'wth* 3D **90**
Larkhill Clo. *P'gte* 4F **69**
Larkspur Clo. *E'thpe* 6D **20**
Larkspur Clo. *Swint* 5A **56**
Lark St. *S6* 5H **85**
Larwood Gro. *Edl'tn* 2C **60**
Latham Sq. *S11* 2E **109**
Latham Sq. *Kirk S* 2E **21**
Lathe Rd. *Roth* 1A **92**
Lathkill Av. *Ink* 5A **134**
Lathkill Clo. *S13* 6E **101**
Lathkill Rd. *S13* 6E **101**
Latimer Clo. *Kiv P* 5B **118**
Latin Gdns. *Donc* 2E **31**
Lauder Rd. *Donc* 3A **32**
Lauder St. *S4* 1H **87**
Laudsdale Clo. *Roth* 2B **80**
Laudsdale Rd. *Roth* 1A **80**
Laughton Common. 2C **106**
Laughton Comn. Rd. *Thur* 1A **106**
Laughton en le Morthen. 6G **95**
Laughton Rd. *S9* 6D **76**
Laughton Rd. *Dinn* 5F **107**
Laughton Rd. *Donc* 1B **46**
Laughton Rd. *Thur* 5B **94**
Launce Rd. *S5* 5D **74**
Laura Av. *B'ley* 2D **24**
Laurel Av. *Braml* 4H **81**
Laurel Av. *Donc* 4G **31**
Laurel Clo. *Ans* 4F **119**
Laurel Clo. *Eck* 6H **125**
Laurel Ct. *S10* 4H **97**
Laurel Cres. *Holl* 2G **133**
Laurel Dri. *Kil* 5A **126**
Laurel Gth. Clo. *Old W* 1B **132**
Laurel Rd. *Arm* 2F **35**
(in two parts)
Laurel Ter. *Donc* 4A **46**
Lavender Clo. *Con* 4F **59**
Laverack St. *S13* 4H **101**
Laverack St. *S13* 4H **101**
Laverdene Av. *S17* 5F **121**
Laverdene Clo. *S17* 5E **121**
Laverdene Dri. *S17* 5F **121**
Laverdene Rd. *S17* 5E **121**
Laverdene Way. *S17* 5F **121**
Laverock Way. *S5* 4H **75**
Lavinia Rd. *Gren* 1C **74**
Lawn Av. *Donc* 6E **33**
Lawn Av. *W'land* 1B **16**
(in two parts)
Lawndale Fold. *Dart* 4D **6**
Lawn Gth. *Donc* 2A **32**
Lawn Rd. *Donc* 6E **33**
Lawns, The. *S11* 1H **109**
Lawnswood Ct. *Bes* 3A **48**
Lawn, The. *Dron* 1F **129**
(in two parts)
Lawn Vs. *Cal* 2G **139**
Lawnwood Dri. *Gold* 4E **29**
Lawrence Clo. *Flan* 4F **81**
Lawrence Clo. *Hghm* 3A **12**
Lawrence Clo. *Old W* 1A **132**
Lawrence Ct. *Swint* 4A **56**
Lawrence Dri. *Swint* 3A **56**
Lawrence St. *S9* 5B **88**
Lawson Rd. *S10* 3H **97**
Lawton La. *Roth* 6E **79**
Lawton Ter. *S6* 3H **85**
Laxey Rd. *S6* 6E **85**
Laxfield Clo. *Ches* 5E **137**
Laxton Clo. *Maltby* 3D **82**
Laxton Rd. *B'ley* 5B **8**

Laycock Av. *Ast* 6C **104**
Layden Ct. *Maltby* 5E **83**
Layden Dri. *Donc* 1E **31**
Layton Dri. *Old W* 2B **132**
Lea Brook. 2G **53**
Lea Brook La. *W'wth* 2G **53**
Leabrook Rd. *Dron W* 2A **128**
Leach La. *Mexb* 1F **57**
Leadbeater Rd. *S12* 2B **112**
Leadbeater Rd. *S12* 3B **112**
Leader Ct. *S6* 2H **85**
Leader Rd. *S6* 2H **85**
Leadhill Clo. *Ches* 1C **136**
Leadley St. *Gold* 4G **29**
Leadmill Rd. *S2* 4F **99** (6F **5**)
Leadmill St. *S1* 3F **99** (6F **5**)
Leaf Clo. *Maltby* 3H **83**
Leake Rd. *S6* 1A **86**
Leamington Gdns. *Donc* 4H **33**
Leamington St. *S10* 1A **98**
Leander Ct. *Stav* 1D **134**
Leapings La. *Thurls* 4A **142**
(in two parts)
Lea Rd. *B'ley* 6D **8**
Lea Rd. *Dron* 2E **129**
Lease Ga. Rd. *Whis* 1H **91**
Leas, The. *Cusw* 4H **31**
Lea, The. *Swint* 3H **55**
Lea, The. *Wat* 5D **114**
Leaton Clo. *S6* 2D **84**
Leavy Greave. *S3* 2C **98** (4A **4**)
Leavygreave Rd. *S3* 2C **98** (3A **4**)
(in two parts)
Leawood Pl. *S6* 5D **84**
Ledbury Gdns. *Donc* 4F **31**
Ledbury Rd. *B'ley* 1H **13**
Ledger Clo. *Kiv P* 5G **117**
Ledsham Ct. *Else* 4D **38**
Ledsham Rd. *Roth* 5G **79**
Ledstone Rd. *S8* 3C **110**
Lee Av. *Deep* 3F **141**
Leebrook Av. *Owl* 6B **114**
Leebrook Ct. *Owl* 6B **114**
Leebrook Dri. *Owl* 6B **114**
Leebrook Pl. *Owl* 6B **114**
Lee Cft. *S1* 1E **99** (2E **5**)
Lee Cft. *Maltby* 6H **83**
Leedham Clo. *S5* 5B **76**
Leedham Rd. *S5* 5B **76**
Leedham Rd. *Roth* 5A **80**
Leeds Av. *Ans* 6E **107**
Leeds Rd. *S9* 5C **88**
Lee Ho. La. *S'bri* 4B **140**
Lee La. *Roy* 3H **7**
Lee Moor La. *S6* 4A **84**
Lee Rd. *S6* 2D **84**
Lee Rd. *Ches* 3E **139**
Lees Av. *P'stne* 4D **142**
Lees Comn. *Barl* 6B **128**
Lees Hall Av. *S8* 2F **111**
Lees Hall Golf Course. 5G **111**
Lees Hall Pl. *S8* 2F **111**
Lees Hall Rd. *S8* 2F **111**
Lees Ho. Ct. *S8* 3E **111**
Lees Nook. *S8* 2E **111**
Lees, The. *S8* 4E **111**
Lees, The. *Ard* 1H **25**
Leeswood Clo. *Ches* 3F **131**
Leewood Clo. *Bram* 5H **39**
Leger Ct. *Donc* 6E **33**
Leger Way. *Donc* 1G **47**
Legion Dri. *Ast* 6C **104**
Leicester Av. *Donc* 6G **33**
Leicester Rd. *Dinn* 4G **107**
Leicester Wlk. *S3* 1D **98** (2B **4**)
Leigh St. *S9* 4C **88**
Leighton Clo. *B'ley* 4H **13**
Leighton Dri. *S14* 4B **112**
Leighton Pl. *S14* 4B **112**
Leighton Rd. *S14* 3A **112**
Leighton Vw. *S14* 2A **112**
Leinster Av. *Donc* 4G **33**
Lemont Rd. *S17* 5E **121**
Lengdale Ct. *Rawm* 2F **69**
Lennox Rd. *S6* 2H **85**
Lennox Rd. *Donc* 4H **33**
Lenthall's Bk. Row. *Ches* 2F **137**
Lenton St. *S2* 4F **99** (6F **5**)
Leonard Clo. *S2* 6C **100**
Leopold Av. *Dinn* 5H **107**
Leopold St. *S1* 2E **99** (3D **4**)
Leopold St. *B'ley* 1F **23**
Leopold St. *Dinn* 4F **107**

Leppings La. *S6* 1A **86**
(in two parts)
Lepton Gdns. *B'ley* 3D **24**
Lescar La. *S11* 5A **98**
Lesley Rd. *Gold* 4G **29**
Leslie Av. *Con* 3C **58**
Leslie Av. *Maltby* 4D **82**
Leslie Rd. *S6* 2H **85**
Leslie Rd. *B'ley* 1D **24**
Lesmond Cres. *L Hou* 3A **28**
Lestermoor Av. *Kiv P* 5G **117**
Letard Dri. *B'wth* 2C **90**
Letsby Av. *S9* 5G **89**
Letwell Ct. *Donc* 6F **49**
Levens Way. *Ches* 3G **131**
Leverick Dri. *Rawm* 6A **56**
Leverton Dri. *S11* 4D **98**
Leverton Gdns. *S11* 4D **98**
Leverton Way. *Dalt* 6C **70**
Leveson St. *S4* 6H **87**
Levet Rd. *Donc* 2D **48**
Lewdendale. *Wors* 5A **24**
Lewden Farm La. *Wors D* 5D **24**
Lewden Gth. *Wors D* 5D **24**
Lewes Rd. *Con* 4D **58**
Lewis Rd. *S13* 6E **101**
Lewis Av. *B'ley* 3E **15**
Lewyns Dri. *Donc* 2D **48**
Leybourne Rd. *Roth* 6G **67**
Leyburn Clo. *Ches* 6G **131**
Leyburn Clo. *Donc* 4D **48**
Leyburn Dri. *Swal* 5A **104**
Leyburn Gro. *C'town* 1E **65**
Leyburn Rd. *S8* 1D **110**
(in two parts)
Ley End. *Wors* 5H **23**
Leyfield Ct. *Arm* 4G **35**
Leyfield Pl. *Womb* 5D **26**
Leyfield Rd. *S17* 2D **120**
Leylands, The. *B'ley* 3D **12**
Leyland Wlk. *B'ley* 3D **12**
Leys Clo. *Donc* 1F **61**
Leys La. *Dinn* 4H **107**
Liberty Clo. *S6* 6E **85**
Liberty Dri. *S6* 6E **85**
Liberty Hill. 6E **85**
Liberty Hill. *S6* 6E **85**
Liberty Pl. *S6* 6E **85**
Liberty Rd. *S6* 6E **85**
Library Clo. *Roth* 4A **68**
Lichen Clo. *E'thpe* 6D **20**
Lichfield Gdns. *Edl'tn* 4A **60**
Lichfield Rd. *Ches* 5E **137**
Lichfield Rd. *Donc* 3F **33**
Lichfield Way. *B'wth* 3D **90**
Lichford Rd. *S2* 1G **111**
Lidgate La. *Shaf* 2B **10**
Lidget Clo. *Donc* 4C **48**
Lidget Clo. *Swal* 1H **115**
Lidget La. *Braml* ....3H **81** & 2A **82**
(in two parts)
Lidget La. *Thurn* 1G **29**
Lidget La. Ind. Est. *Thurn* 1H **29**
Lidget La. *Dinn* 5F **107**
Lidget La. *Tank* 6B **36**
Lidgett Way. *Roy* 1E **9**
Lidster La. *Ans* 3G **119**
Lifestyle Ho. *S10* 3A **98**
Liffey Av. *Donc* 4G **33**
Lifford Pl. *Else* 6D **38**
Lifford Rd. *Donc* 4F **33**
Lifford St. *S9* 6G **77**
Lightwood. 6A **112**
Lightwood La. *S8* 6A **112**
Lilac Av. *S'bri* 3F **119**
Lilac Clo. *Ans* 4B **60**
Lilac Cres. *Edl'tn* 4A **38**
Lilac Cres. *Hoy* 5F **81**
Lilac Farm Clo. *Wick* 4G **81**
Lilac Gro. *Braml* 4G **81**
Lilac Gro. *Con* 4C **58**
Lilac Gro. *Donc* 3D **48**
Lilac Gro. *Maltby* 4D **82**
Lilac Rd. *S5* 6A **76**
Lilac Rd. *Arm* 2G **35**
Lilac Rd. *Beig* 4F **115**
Lilacs, The. *Roy* 1G **9**
Lilac St. *Holf* 2G **133**
Lilian St. *Roth* 4E **79**
Lilian St. S. *Roth* 4E **79**
Lilford Rd. *Bran* 3H **49**
Lilly Hall Clo. *Maltby* 3D **82**
Lilly Hall Rd. *Maltby* 3D **82**

Lilydene Av. *Grim* 6F **11**
Lily Ter. *Jump* 4B **38**
Limb La. *S17* 1D **120**
Limbreck Ct. *Ben* 6A **18**
Limbrick Clo. *S6* 4A **86**
Limbrick Rd. *S6* 4A **86**
Lime Av. *Stav* 2C **134**
Lime Clo. *Cal* 2G **139**
Lime Clo. *Rav* 5H **71**
Lime Ct. *Spro* 2F **45**
Limedale Vw. *Barn D* 1E **21**
Lime Gro. *B'ley* 4E **9**
Lime Gro. *C'town* 3E **65**
Lime Gro. *Maltby* 4H **83**
Lime Gro. *Roth* 5G **79**
Lime Gro. *S'bri* 4D **140**
Lime Gro. *Swint* 3B **56**
Limekilns. *Ans* 1F **119**
Limelands Rd. *Dinn* 4E **107**
Lime Rd. *Eck* 6G **125**
Limes Av. *B'ley* 4D **12**
Limes Av. *M'well* 3G **7**
Limes Clo. *M'well* 3G **7**
Limestone Cottage La. *S6* 5H **73**
Lime St. *S6* 5C **86**
Lime St. *Beig* 3F **115**
Limesway. *B'ley* 4D **12**
Limesway. *Maltby* 4F **83**
Lime Tree Av. *Arm* 2F **35**
(in two parts)
Lime Tree Av. *Donc* 1E **47**
Lime Tree Av. *Kil* 4A **126**
Limetree Av. *Kiv P* 4G **117**
Limetree Av. *Thur* 5B **94**
Limetree Clo. *Brim* 5F **133**
Lime Tree Clo. *Cud* 6B **10**
Lime Tree Ct. *Donc* 2F **47**
Lime Tree Cres. *New R* 5E **63**
Lime Tree Cres. *Rawm* 5G **79**
Lime Tree Wlk. *Den M* 1B **58**
Limpool Clo. *Donc* 4D **48**
Limpsfield Rd. *S9* 1C **88**
Linacre Reservoirs Vis. Cen. 5A **130**
Linacre Rd. *Ches* 1C **136**
Linaker Rd. *S6* 5G **85**
Linburn Clo. *Roy* 1C **8**
Linburn Rd. *S8* 5D **110**
Linby Rd. *B'ley* 5B **8**
Lincoln Clo. *Den M* 3D **58**
Lincoln Gdns. *Gold* 4F **29**
Lincoln Rd. *Donc* 3F **33**
Lincoln St. *S9* 1D **88**
Lincoln St. *Ches* 5A **138**
Lincoln St. *Maltby* 5G **83**
Lincoln St. *New R* 3C **62**
Lincoln St. *Roth* 1D **78**
Lincroft Dri. *P'gte* 4F **69**
Lindale Clo. *Ans* 2H **119**
Lindale Gdns. *Gold* 5H **29**
Lindale Rd. *Ches* 3F **131**
Lindales, The. *B'ley* 5E **13**
Linden Av. *S8* 5C **110**
Linden Av. *Ches* 4D **136**
Linden Av. *Dron* 6F **123**
Linden Av. *Wick* 3G **81**
Linden Ct. *S10* 4H **97**
Linden Ct. *E'fld* 6F **65**
Linden Cres. *S'bri* 3D **140**
Linden Dri. *Has* 6D **138**
Linden Gro. *Edl'tn* 4B **60**
Linden Gro. *Maltby* 4D **82**
Linden Pk. Gro. *Ches* 2G **137**
Linden Rd. *E'fld* 6F **65**
Linden Rd. *Wath D* 5B **40**
Linden Wlk. *Toll B* 3A **18**
Lindholme Dri. *Ross* 3F **63**
Lindholme Gdns. *Owl* 5C **114**
Lindhurst Lodge. *B'ley* 5B **8**
Lindhurst Rd. *B'ley* 5A **8**
Lindisfarne Ct. *Ches* 4E **137**
Lindisfarne Rd. *Dron* 3F **129**
Lindley Cres. *Thurn* 2F **29**
Lindley Rd. *S5* 1H **87**
Lindley's Cft. *Tod* 2B **118**
Lindley St. *Roth* 1E **79**
Lindrick Av. *Swint* 3C **56**
Lindrick Clo. *Con* 2G **59**
Lindrick Clo. *Cud* 4C **10**
Lindrick Dri. *Donc* 5A **48**
Lindrick Dri. *Arm* 4F **35**
Lindrick Gdns. *Ches* 5E **137**
Lindsay Av. *S5* 5F **75**
Lindsay Clo. *S5* 4F **75**

Lindsay Cres. *S5* 4F 75
Lindsay Dri. *S5* 4F 75
Lindsay Pl. *Swal* 6B 104
Lindsay Rd. *S5* 4F 75
Lindsey Clo. *Donc* 6B 48
Lindum Dri. *Wick* 5G 81
Lindum St. *Donc* 1B 46
Lindum Ter. *Roth* 3E 79
             (off Doncaster Rd.)
Lingamore Leys. *Thurn* 1F 29
Lingard Ct. *B'ley* 5F 13
Lingard La. *Worr* 4D 72
Lingard St. *B'ley* 4F 13
Lingfield Dri. *Donc* 4F 31
Lingfield Wlk. *Mexb* 5G 43
Lingfoot Av. *S8* 3F 123
Lingfoot Clo. *S8* 3F 123
Lingfoot Cres. *S8* 3F 123
Lingfoot Dri. *S8* 3F 123
Lingfoot Pl. *S8* 3F 123
Lingfoot Wlk. *S8* 3G 123
Lingmoor Clo. *Donc* 5G 45
Lingodell Clo. *Lghtn* 1F 107
Ling Rd. *Ches* 5F 137
Lings La. *Wick* 5G 81
Lings, The. *Arm* 4H 35
Lings, The. *Braml* 5H 81
Lingwaite. *Dod* 2C 22
Link Rd. *Roth* .5E 71
Link Row. *S2* .1G 99
             (off Bernard St.)
Links Rd. *Dron* 3F 129
Links Vw. *M'well* 3F 7
Linkswood Av. *Donc* 2A 34
Linkswood Rd. *Dalt* 6B 70
Link, The. *Dod* 3C 22
Linkway. *Donc* 3H 33
Linley La. *S12* 2F 113
Linnet Ho. *Old W* 1A 132
Linnet Mt. *Thpe H* 2B 66
Linscott Clo. *Ches* 4F 131
Linscott Rd. *S8* 5C 110
Linthwaite La.
    Else & W'wth 1E 53
Linton Clo. *B'ley* 1D 22
Linton Rd. *Ches* 5E 137
Lipp Av. *Kil* 2A 126
Liskeard Pl. *Adw S* 2C 16
Lisle Rd. *Roth* .5G 79
Lismore Rd. *S8* 2F 111
Lister Av. *S12* 3D 112
Lister Av. *Donc* 3B 46
Lister Av. *Rawm* 6E 55
Lister Clo. *S12* 4D 112
Lister Clo. *Ches* 1A 138
Lister Ct. *Donc* 4G 33
Lister Cres. *S12* 4C 112
Listerdale. 5E 81
Listerdale Shop. Cen. *Roth* 5C 80
Lister Dri. *S12* 4D 112
Lister Pl. *S12* 4D 112
Lister Rd. *S6* 4A 86
Lister St. *S9* 1E 101
Lister St. *Roth* 3F 79
Lister Way. *S12* 4D 112
Lit. Bridge Rd. *P'gte* 6E 69
Lit. Brind Rd. *Ches* 4D 130
Lit. Cockhill La. *Old E* 6B 60
Little Common. 4F 109
Lit. Common La. *S11* 4F 109
Lit. Common La. *K'wth* 2F 77
             (in two parts)
Lit. Common La. *Whis* 2C 92
Littledale Rd. *S9* 3E 101
Little Fld. La. *Womb* 6B 26
             (in two parts)
Littlefield Rd. *Dinn* 4E 107
Lit. Haynooking La. *Maltby* 4F 83
Littlehey Clo. *Maltby* 3D 82
Little Houghton. 2H 27
Lit. Houghton La. *D'fld* 3F 27
Little La. *S4* 2A 88
Little La. *S12* .1D 112
Little La. *Donc* 6A 20
Little La. *Scho* .3D 66
Little La. *Spro* .5C 30
Little La. *Thpe H* 1A 66
Little La. Ind. Est. *Donc* 6H 19
Little Leeds. *Hoy* 5A 38
Lit. London Pl. *S8* 1D 110
Lit. London Rd. *S8* 3C 110
Lit. Matlock Gdns. *S6* 5D 84
Lit. Matlock Way. *S6* 5D 84

Littlemoor. *Ches* 4F 131
Littlemoor. *Eck* 6E 125
Littlemoor Av. *Kiv P* 5G 117
Littlemoor Cen. *Ches* 4G 131
Littlemoor Cres. *Ches* 4F 131
Littlemoor La. *Donc* 2B 46
Littlemoor St. *Donc* 2B 46
Lit. New Clo. *Gawber* 4D 12
Little Norton. 1E 123
Lit. Norton Av. *S8* 2E 123
Lit. Norton Dri. *S8* 1E 123
Lit. Norton La. *S8* 1E 123
Lit. Norton M. *S8* 2E 123
Lit. Norton Way. *S8* 2E 123
Little Sheffield. 4D 98
Little Westfields. *Roy* 1C 8
Littlewood Dri. *S12* 4C 112
Littlewood Rd. *S12* 4C 112
Littlewood St. *Donc* 1B 46
Littlewood Way. *Maltby* 3H 83
Littleworth. 4F 63
Littleworth Clo. *Ross* 4F 63
Littleworth La. *B'ley* 3D 14
Littleworth La. *Ross* 3F 63
Littleworth M. *Ross* 3F 63
Litton Clo. *Shaf* 2C 10
Litton Clo. *Stav* 3A 134
Litton Wlk. *B'ley* 5F 13
Litton Wlk. *Shaf* 2C 10
Liverpool Av. *Donc* 3F 33
Liverpool Pl. *S9* 4B 88
Liverpool St. *S9* 4B 88
Livesey St. *S6* .3B 86
Livingstone Av. *Donc* 6B 20
Livingstone Cres. *B'ley* 2B 14
Livingstone Rd. *C'town* 2C 64
Livingstone Ter. *B'ley* 1G 23
Livingston Rd. *S9* 5A 88
Lloyd St. *S4* 2H 87
Lloyd St. *P'gte* .4F 69
Loakfield Dri. *S5* 2D 74
Lobelia Ct. *Ans* 3F 119
Lobelia Cres. *Kirk S* 4D 20
Lobwood. *Wors* 4A 24
Lobwood La. *Wors* 4B 24
Lockeaflash Cres. *B'ley* 2D 24
Locke Av. *B'ley* 1G 23
Locke Av. *Wors* 3H 23
Locke Rd. *Dod* .3C 22
Lockesley Av. *Con* 3C 58
Locke St. *B'ley* .2F 23
Lock Ho. Rd. *S9* 2E 89
Locking Dri. *Arm* 4G 35
Lock La. *S9* 5G 77
Lockoford La. *Ches* 5A 132
          (in four parts)
Lockoford Rd. *Ches* 5A 132
Locksley Av. *E'thpe* 5D 20
Locksley Dri. *Thur* 5A 94
Locksley Gdns. *Birdw* 5D 36
Lock St. *S6* 5C 86
Lockton Clo. *High G* 5A 50
Lockton Way. *Con* 2F 59
Lockwood Av. *Ans* 4F 119
Lockwood Clo. *Roth* 2A 80
Lockwood Gdns. *H'swne* 1G 143
Lockwood La. *B'ley* 2H 23
Lockwood La. *Thurn* 2G 29
Lockwood Rd. *Donc* 4E 33
Lockwood Rd. *Gold* 4G 29
Lockwood Rd. *Roth* 2A 80
Lodge Clo. *Brim* 1G 139
Lodge Dri. *Harl* .4H 51
Lodge Farm Clo. *Ans* 1F 119
Lodge Farm Clo. *Walt* 6D 136
Lodge Farm M. *Ans* 1F 119
Lodge La. *S6 & S10* 2A 96
Lodge La. *Ast* .1B 116
Lodge La. *Dinn* 4H 107
Lodge La. *Thpe H* 4B 66
Lodge Moor. 4A 96
Lodge Moor Rd. *S10* 5A 96
Lodge Pl. *Ink* .5A 134
Lodge, The. *S11* 2G 109
Lodge Wlk. *Ink* 5A 134
Lodge Way. *B'wth* 2C 90
Logan Rd. *S9* .1F 101
Loicher La. *E'fld* 6G 65
Lomas Clo. *S6* .4C 84
Lomas Lea. *S6* .5B 84
Lombard Clo. *B'ley* 4G 13
Lombard Cres. *D'fld* 4C 26
London Rd. *S2* 4D 98

London Way. *Thpe H* 3A 66
Long Acre. *B'ley* .4D 8
Longacre Clo. *H'brk* 6G 115
Longacre Rd. *Dron* 4E 129
Longacre Vw. *H'brk* 1G 125
Longacre Way. *H'brk* 1G 125
Long Balk. *B'ley* 2A 12
Longcar La. *B'ley* 1F 23
Long Causeway. *B'ley* 3C 14
Long Cliffe Clo. *Shaf* 3C 10
Longcliff Wlk. *Ches* 5F 131
Long Clo. *Donc* 6B 48
Long Cft. *M'well* .4F 7
Longcroft Av. *Dron W* 1A 128
Longcroft Clo. *Ches* 6H 137
Longcroft Cres. *Dron W* 1A 128
Longcroft Rd. *Dron W* 1A 128
Longdale Cft. *B'ley* 3B 14
Long Edge La. *Donc* 6G 17
Longfellow Dri. *Roth* 4H 79
Longfellow Rd. *Donc* 5C 46
Longfield Clo. *Womb* 5H 25
Longfield Dri. *Donc* 5B 48
Long Fld. Dri. *E'thpe* 5E 21
Longfield Dri. *M'well* 4F 7
Longfield Dri. *Rav* 1H 81
Longfield Grange. *Ches* 5E 131
Longfield Rd. *S10* 6H 85
Long Fld. Rd. *E'thpe* 4E 21
Longfields Cres. *Hoy* 5H 37
Long Fold. *Wath D* 5C 40
Long Henry Row. *S2* 2G 99 (3H 5)
Longlands Av. *Kiv P* 5G 117
Longlands Dri. *M'well* 5F 7
Longlands Dri. *Thry* 4E 71
Long Lands La. *Brod* 3A 16
Long La. *S6* 6D 84
Long La. *S6 & Worr* 2C 84
Long La. *S10* 1E 97
Long La. *Kil* 3C 126
Long La. *P'stne* 2B 142
             (Anna La.)
Long La. *P'stne* 6F 143
            (Castle La.)
Long La. *Spro* .5D 30
Long La. *S'bri* .4A 140
Long La. *Whis* 3F 91
Long La. *Worr* .2B 72
Longley Av. W. *S5* 1C 86
Longley Clo. *S5* 1F 87
Longley Clo. *Bar G* 3A 12
Longley Cres. *S5* 6F 75
Longley Dri. *S5* 1F 87
Longley Est. *S5* 6F 75
Longley Farm Vw. *S5* 1F 87
Longley Hall Gro. *S5* 1F 87
Longley Hall Ri. *S5* 6F 75
Longley Hall Rd. *S5* 6G 75
Longley Hall Way. *S5* 1G 87
Longley Ings. *Oxs* 5G 143
Longley La. *S5* .1F 87
Long Leys La.
    Maltby & B'well 6A 60
Longley St. *Bar G* 3A 12
Long Line. *S11* 5A 108
Longman Rd. *B'ley* 4G 13
Long Plantation. *E'thpe* 5E 21
Longridge Rd. *B'ley* 1D 14
Long Rd. *Thur* .2H 105
Long Sandall. .5B 20
Long Sandall Bri. *Donc* 4A 20
Long Shambles. Ches 2A 138
             (off High St.)
Longshaw Clo. *Stav* 3B 134
Longside Way. *B'ley* 5C 12
Longsight Rd. *M'well* 4E 7
Longspring Gro. *Tank* 6C 36
Long Steps. *S2* .2H 5
Longstone Cres. *S12* 3F 113
Longthwaite Clo. *Lghtn* 1E 107
Longton Rd. *Kirk S* 3E 21
Long Wlk. *S10* .1G 97
Lonsdale Av. *B'ley* 1H 25
Lonsdale Av. *Donc* 6H 33
Lonsdale Clo. *Ans* 1H 119
Lonsdale Ho. *Donc* 4A 34
Lonsdale Rd. *S6* 4A 86
Loosemore Dri. *S12* 2B 112

Lopham Clo. *S3* 6F **87**
Lopham St. *S3* 5F **87**
    (in two parts)
Lordens Hill. *Dinn* 4G **107**
Lord Roberts Rd. *Ches* 4A **138**
Lords Clo. *Edl'tn* 2C **60**
Lord's Head La. *Warm* 6E **45**
Lordsmill Ga. *Ches* 3B **138**
Lordsmill St. *Ches* 3B **138**
Lord St. *B'ley* 5C **14**
Lord St. *Roth* 2G **79**
Loretta Cotts. *Hoy* 5H **37**
Lorna Rd. *Mexb* 6E **43**
Lorne Clo. *Dron W* 1B **128**
Lorne Rd. *Thurn* 1D **28**
Loscoe Gro. *Gold* 4E **29**
Lothian Rd. *Donc* 4A **34**
Louden Rd. *Scho* 5D **66**
Louden Rd. *Scho* 5D **66**
Lounde Clo. *Spro* 2E **45**
Loundes Wood Av. *Ches* 3E **131**
Lound Rd. *S9* 2F **101**
Lound Side. *C'town* 1E **65**
Loundsley Ct. *Ash* 1B **136**
Loundsley Green. **6E 131**
Loundsley Grn. Rd. *Ches* 1D **136**
Lousy Busk La. *Mexb* 5C **42**
Louth Rd. *S11* 6H **97**
Lovell St. *S4* .6H **87**
Loversall Clo. *Donc* 6B **46**
Love St. *S3* 1E **99** (1E **5**)
Lovetot Av. *Ast* 5B **104**
Lovetot Av. *S9* 6A **88**
    (in two parts)
Lovetot Rd. *Roth* 5G **67**
Low Barugh. 1B **12**
Lowburn Rd. *S13* 6E **101**
Low Comn. Rd. *Dinn* 4D **106**
Low Cft. *Roy* .1F **9**
Low Cft. *Womb* 6C **26**
Low Cronkhill La. *B'ley* 3G **9**
Low Cudworth. *Cud* 2H **15**
Low Cudworth Grn. *Cud* 2H **15**
Lowedges. .3D **122**
Low Edges. *S8* 3E **123**
Lowedges Cres. *S8* 3D **122**
Lowedges Dri. *S8* 3D **122**
Lowedges Pl. *S8* 3E **123**
Lowedges Rd. *S8* 4B **122**
    (in three parts)
Lowe La. *S'bgh* 6A **22**
Lowell Av. *Donc* 5B **46**
Lower All. *Cal* 4G **139**
Lower Bradway. 3A **122**
Lwr. Castlereagh St. *B'ley* 6G **13**
Lower Crabtree. 3G **87**
Lwr. Dolcliffe Rd. *Mexb* 6D **42**
Lwr. Grove Rd. *Ches* 2H **137**
Lwr. Haigh Head. *H'swne* 1F **143**
Lwr. High Royds. *Dart* 5E **7**
Lower Lewden. 5D **24**
Lwr. Malton Rd. *Scaw* 2G **31**
Lwr. Mill Clo. *Gold* 5E **29**
Lower Pilley. 6C **36**
Lwr. Thomas St. *B'ley* 6G **13**
Lwr. Unwin St. *P'stne* 5D **142**
Lowfield. 6E **99**
Lowfield Av. *S12* 6G **113**
Lowfield Av. *Roth* 4C **68**
Lowfield Clo. *Barn D* 1F **21**
Lowfield Ct. *S2* 6E **99**
Lowfield Farm Clo. *Bol D* 1B **42**
Lowfield Gro. *Bol D* 2C **42**
Lowfield La. *Bol D* 1C **42**
Lowfield Meadows. *Bol D* 2B **42**
Lowfield Rd. *Bol D* 1B **42**
Lowfield Rd. *Donc* 2A **34**
Lowfields. *Stav* 1E **135**
Lowfield Wlk. *Den M* 1B **58**
Lowgate. *Donc* 2G **31**
Lowgates. *Stav* 1D **134**
Low Golden Smithies. *Swint* 1A **56**
Low Grange Rd. *Thurn* 1E **29**
Low Grange Sq. *Thurn* 1E **29**
Lowgreave. *Roth* 1A **80**
Lowhouse Rd. *S5* 5H **75**
Low Laithe La. *Deep* 2H **141**
Low Laithes. 3H **25**
Low Laithes Vw. *Womb* 5H **25**
Lowlands Clo. *B'ley* 2D **14**
Lowlands Clo. *Ben* 4B **18**

Low La. *Donc* 5A **48**
Low La. *Maltby* 1E **95**
Low La. *Roth* 1H **77**
Low Matlock La. *S6* 4D **84**
Low Pasture Clo. *Dod* 2C **22**
Low Pavement. *Ches* 2A **138**
Low Riddings. *S'side* 3F **81**
Low Rd. *S6* 5G **85**
Low Rd. *Con* .2E **59**
Low Rd. *Donc* 4A **46**
Low Rd. *O'bri* 2D **72**
Low Rd. E. *Warm* 5F **45**
    (in two parts)
Low Rd. W. *Warm* 6E **45**
Low Row. *Dart* 2C **6**
Lowry Dri. *Dron* 2D **128**
Low St. *Dod* .3D **22**
Lowther Rd. *S6* 2B **86**
Lowther Rd. *Donc* 4E **33**
Lowton Way. *H'by* 4A **82**
Low Vw. *Dod* 2A **22**
Low Valley. 5D **26**
Low Wood Clo. *Swint* 4A **56**
Low Wincobank. 4C **76**
Loxley. 3D **84**
Loxley Av. *Womb* 1E **39**
Loxley Bottom. 3G **85**
Loxley Clo. *Ches* 2D **136**
Loxley Ct. *S6* 4A **86**
Loxley Ct. *Roth* 1F **91**
Loxley New Rd. *S6* 4H **85**
Loxley Rd. *S6* 1A **84**
Loxley Rd. *B'ley* 4F **15**
Loxley Vw. Rd. *S10* 6H **85**
Loy Clo. *Roth* 4A **68**
Lucas Rd. *Ches* 5G **131**
Lucas St. *S4* 4G **87**
Lucknow Ct. *S7* 1C **110**
Ludgate Clo. *New R* 6E **63**
Ludham Clo. *Ches* 4H **131**
Ludham Gdns. *Ches* 4H **131**
Ludwell Hill. *Barn* 1H **43**
Lugano Gro. *D'fld* 3C **26**
Luke La. *S6* 2F **85**
Lulworth Clo. *B'ley* 1B **24**
Lumb La. *S6 & Whar S* 1A **72**
Lumley Clo. *Maltby* 4H **83**
Lumley Cres. *Maltby* 5H **83**
Lumley Dri. *Dinn* 3C **106**
Lumley Dri. *Maltby* 5H **83**
Lumley St. *S4* 1H **99**
Lumley St. *S9* 1B **100**
Lump La. *Gren* 6A **64**
Lumsdale Rd. *Stav* 5B **112**
Luna Cft. *S12* 1H **125**
Lunbreck Rd. *Warm* 6E **45**
Lund Av. *B'ley* 4F **15**
Lund Clo. *B'ley* 4F **15**
Lund Cres. *B'ley* 4F **15**
Lundhill Clo. *Womb* 2G **39**
Lundhill Farm M. *H'fld* 3F **39**
Lundhill Gro. *Womb* 2G **39**
Lund Hill La. *Roy* 1H **9**
Lundhill Rd. *Womb* 3G **39**
Lund Rd. *Worr* 4D **72**
Lundwood. .4E **15**
Lundwood Clo. *Owl* 5C **114**
Lundwood Dri. *Owl* 5C **114**
Lundwood Gro. *Owl* 5C **114**
Lundwood Ho. Donc 1C **46**
    (off Bond Clo.)
Lundy Rd. *Dron* 3F **129**
Lunn Rd. *Cud* 1H **15**
Lupin Way. *Cal* 2G **139**
Lupton Cres. *S8* 3D **122**
Lupton Dri. *S8* 3D **122**
Lupton Rd. *S8* 3D **122**
Lupton Wlk. *S8* 3E **123**
Luterel Dri. *Swal* 5B **104**
Lutterworth Dri. *Adw S* 1C **16**
Lych Ga. Clo. *Donc* 4E **49**
Lydden Clo. *Brim* 3E **133**
Lydford Av. *Old W* 2B **132**
Lydgate. 2G **97**
Lydgate Ct. *S10* 2H **97**
Lydgate Hall Cres. *S10* 2G **97**
Lydgate La. *S10* 2G **97**
Lydgate. *Bram* 5H **39**
Lyme St. *Roth* 3C **78**
Lyminster Rd. *S6* 4A **74**
Lyminton La. *Tree* 1E **103**

Lymister Av. *Roth* 1F **91**
Lyncroft Clo. *B'wth* 3D **90**
Lyndale Av. *E'thpe* 6C **20**
Lynden Av. *Adw S* 2C **16**
Lyndhurst Bank. *P'stne* 5D **142**
Lyndhurst Clo. *S11* 6A **98**
Lyndhurst Cres. *E'thpe* 4C **20**
Lyndhurst Rd. *S11* 6A **98**
Lynham Av. *Birdw* 5D **36**
Lynmouth Rd. *S7* 2C **110**
Lynn Pl. *S9* 3D **88**
Lynthwaite Clo. *Bram* 4H **39**
Lynton Av. *Roth* 6G **79**
Lynton Dri. *E'thpe* 5C **20**
Lynton Pl. *Dart* 5B **6**
Lynton Rd. *S11* 5B **98**
Lynwood Clo. *Dron W* 2B **128**
Lynwood Dri. *B'ley* 4E **9**
Lynwood Dri. *Mexb* 6E **43**
Lyons Clo. *S4* 4G **87**
Lyons Rd. *S4* 4G **87**
Lyons St. *S4* 4G **87**
Lytham Av. *B'ley* 1D **14**
Lytham Av. *Dinn* 6F **107**
Lytham Clo. *Donc* 5F **49**
Lyttleton Cres. *P'stne* 6C **142**
Lytton Av. *S5* 4C **74**
Lytton Clo. *Donc* 5B **46**
Lytton Cres. *S5* 4C **74**
Lytton Dri. *S5* 4C **74**
Lytton Rd. *S5* 4C **74**

M

M1 Commerce Pk. *Duck* 6F **135**
Mabel St. *Roth* 4F **79**
Macaulay Cres. *Arm* 3G **35**
McConnel Cres. *New R* 4B **62**
Machin Ct. *Dron* 1E **129**
Machin Dri. *Rawm* 5C **54**
Machin La. *S'bri* 2A **140**
Machon Bank. *S7* 1C **110**
Machon Bank Rd. *S7* 6B **98**
McIntyre Rd. *S'bri* 3D **140**
Mackenzie Cres. *S10* 3C **98** (6A **4**)
Mackenzie Cres. *Burn* 3B **64**
Mackenzie St. *S11* 5C **98**
McKenzie Way. *Kiv P* 5H **117**
Mackey Cres. *Brie* 2E **11**
Mackey La. *Brie* 2E **11**
Mackinnon Av. *Kiv P* 5H **117**
McLaren Cres. *Maltby* 5G **83**
McLintock Way. *B'ley* 6F **13**
McLoughlin Way. *Kiv P* 5H **117**
McMahon Av. *Ink* 5H **133**
McManus Av. *Rawm* 5F **55**
Macmillan M. *Ches* 2D **136**
Macnaughten Rd. *Tank* 6D **36**
Macro Rd. *Womb* 1G **39**
Madam La. *Barn D* 1G **21**
Madehurst Gdns. *S2* 6F **99**
Madehurst Ri. *S2* 6F **99**
Madehurst Rd. *S2* 6F **99**
Madehurst Vw. *S2* 6F **99**
Madin Dri. *Ink* 5H **133**
Madingley Clo. *Donc* 6A **46**
Madin St. *Ches* 1A **138**
Mafeking Pl. *C'town* 1E **65**
Magellan Rd. *Maltby* 3E **83**
Magna Clo. *Flan* 3F **81**
Magna Cres. *Flan* 3E **81**
Magna La. *Dalt* 6B **70**
Magna Science Adventure Cen. 5H **77**
Magnolia Clo. *Ans* 4F **119**
Magnolia Clo. *Kirk S* 4D **20**
Magnolia Clo. *Shaf* 3D **10**
Magnolia Ct. *S10* 5E **97**
Magpie Gro. *S2* 3A **100**
Mahon Av. *Rawm* 1F **69**
Maidstone Rd. *S6* 5B **74**
Maidwell Way. *Kirk S* 3C **20**
Main Av. *S17* 5E **121**
Main Av. *Edl'tn* 2B **60**
Main Rd. *S9* .6E **89**
Main Rd. *S12* 6G **113**
Main Rd. *App* 4H **129**
Main Rd. *Barl* 1A **130**
Main Rd. *Cut* 4A **130**
Main Rd. *Mar L* 6A **124**
Main Rd. *Whar S* 1C **72**
Main St. *S12* 3B **114**
Main St. *Ans* 2F **119**

Main St. Aug 4A 104
Main St. Braml 4H 81
Main St. Cant 2F 49
Main St. Cat 6D 90
Main St. Gold 4G 29
Main St. Greasb 3C 68
Main St. Gren 6A 64
Main St. Mexb 6D 42
Main St. Rav 4H 71
Main St. Rawm 1G 69
Main St. Roth 3C 78
Main St. Spro 3D 44
Main St. Swal 6A 104
Main St. Ulley 1C 104
Main St. Wadw 6H 61
Main St. W'wth 4C 52
Main St. Womb 6A 26
Main St. Shop. Cen. Braml 4H 81
Mair Ct. Roth 2G 91
Majuba St. S6 . . . . .5B 86
Makin St. Mexb 1G 57
Malcolm Clo. B'ley 1D 24
Malham Clo. Ches 6F 131
Malham Clo. Shaf 2C 10
Malham Ct. B'ley 5F 13
Malham Gdns. Half 2D 124
Malham Gro. Half 2E 125
Malham Pl. C'town 1D 64
Malham Tarn Ct. Donc 3H 47
Malia Rd. Ches 5C 132
Malinbridge. 4H 85
Malincroft. M'well 5F 7
Malinda St. S3 . . . . . . .6D 86 (1B 4)
Malin Rd. S6 . . . . .4G 85
Malin Rd. Roth 1B 80
Malkin St. Ches 2B 138
Mallard Av. Barn D 1D 20
Mallard Clo. Donc 5H 45
Mallard Clo. Thpe H 1C 66
Mallard Ct. Stav 1D 134
Mallard Dri. Kil 2H 125
Mallinder Clo. Kil 3B 126
Mallory Av. Rawm 1E 69
Mallory Dri. Mexb 5H 43
Mallory Rd. Roth 1A 80
Mallory Way. Cud 6C 10
Malson Way. Ches 5H 131
Maltas Ct. Wors 4C 24
Maltby. .4G 83
Maltby Ho. Donc 1C 46
(off Burden La.)
Maltby St. S9 . . . . .4C 88
Malthouse Cotts. Kiv S 6D 118
Malthouse Ct. Ches 1A 138
Malthouse Rd. B'ley 6H 13
Malting La. S4 . . . . .1H 5
Maltings Ct. Kirk S 2D 20
Maltings, The. P'stne 5C 142
(off Mortimer Rd.)
Maltings, The. Roth 4D 78
Maltkiln Cotts. Kirk S 2D 20
Maltkiln St. Roth 4D 78
Malton Dri. Ast 6C 104
Malton Pl. B'ley 6A 8
Malton Rd. Intake 4H 33
Malton Rd. Scaw 2F 31
Malton St. S4 . . . . .4G 87
Malton Wlk. Ches 6H 137
Maltravers Clo. S2 . . . . .3A 100
Maltravers Cres. S2 . . . . .2H 99
Maltravers Pl. S2 . . . . .2A 100
Maltravers Rd. S2 . . . . .1H 99
Maltravers Ter. S2 . . . . .3A 100
(in two parts)
Maltravers Way. S2 . . . . .2A 100
Malvern Av. Donc 4G 31
Malvern Clo. B'ley 5D 12
Malvern Dri. S'side 2F 81
Malvern Rd. S9 . . . . .6D 88
Malvern Rd. Ches 1G 137
Malvern Rd. Donc 5A 34
Malvern Way. S'side 2F 81
Malwood Way. Maltby 3H 83
Manchester Rd. S6 & S10 . . . . . . .2A 96
Manchester Rd. Mill G & Thurls . .4A 142
Manchester Rd. S'bri & Deep 1A 140
Mandale Rd. Barn D 1H 21
Mandeville St. S9 . . . . .6E 89
Mangham Rd. & P'gte 6D 68
Mangham Way. Roth 6D 68
Manifold Av. Stav 3B 134
Manknell Rd. Ches 3A 132

Mannering Rd. Donc 5G 45
Manners St. S3 . . . . .5D 86
Manor. .4D 100
Manor App. Roth 2G 77
Manor Av. Brim 4F 133
Manor Av. Gold 4G 29
Manor Bungalows. Dron 2D 128
Manor Clo. Barn D 2G 21
Manor Clo. Bram B 4B 40
Manor Clo. Maltby 4F 83
Manor Clo. Rawm 5C 54
Manor Clo. Tod 2B 118
Manor Ct. Den M 2B 58
Manor Ct. H'ton 1G 43
Manor Ct. Roth 1B 80
Manor Ct. Roy 2C 8
Manor Cres. B'wth 3B 90
Manor Cres. Ches 2F 137
Manor Cres. Dron 2D 128
Manor Cres. Grim 5G 11
Manor Dri. Brim 4F 133
Manor Dri. Ches 2E 137
(in two parts)
Manor Dri. Dinn 3E 107
Manor Dri. Donc 1F 47
Manor Dri. Roy 2D 8
Manor Dri. Tod 2B 118
Manor Dri. Whis 2A 92
Manor End. Wors 4H 23
Manor Est. Toll B 3H 17
Mnr. Farm Clo. Adw S 1D 16
Mnr. Farm Clo. Aug 3B 104
Mnr. Farm Ct. B'ley 5F 9
Mnr. Farm Ct. B'ley 1H 25
(off Doncaster Rd.)
Mnr. Farm Ct. Beig 4G 115
Mnr. Farm Ct. Cud 1H 15
Mnr. Farm Ct. Kil 4B 126
Mnr. Farm Ct. Thry 3D 70
Mnr. Farm Dri. Swint 3A 56
Mnr. Farm Est. Rawm 5C 54
Mnr. Farm Gdns. Ans 3F 119
Mnr. Farm M. Beig 4G 115
(off Broomwood Clo.)
Mnr. Fields. Roth 1G 77
Manor Gdns. B'ley 1H 25
Manor Gdns. Shaf 3C 10
Manor Gdns. Spro 2D 44
Manor Gro. Grim 5F 11
Manor Gro. Roy 2D 8
Manor Ho. S6 . . . . .5C 84
Manor Ho. Hoy 5A 38
Manor Ho. Ct. Scawt 6H 17
Mnr Ho. Rd. Roth 1G 77
Mnr. Laith Rd. S2 . . . . .3H 99
Manor La. S2 . . . . .2B 100
Manor La. Adw D 3D 42
Manor La. Dinn 2G 107
Manor La. Oxs 6H 143
Mnr. Oaks Clo. S2 . . . . .2A 100
Mnr. Oaks Ct. S2 . . . . .2H 99
Mnr. Oaks Dri. S2 . . . . .2G 99
Mnr. Oaks Gdns. S2 . . . . .2G 99
Mnr. Oaks Pl. S2 . . . . .3A 100
Mnr. Oaks Rd. S2 . . . . .2G 99
Mnr. Occupation Rd. Roy 1D 8
Manor Park. 3C 100
Mnr. Park Av. S2 . . . . .4B 100
Mnr. Park Cen. S2 . . . . .3B 100
Mnr. Park Clo. S2 . . . . .3B 100
Mnr. Park Ct. S2 . . . . .4B 100
Mnr. Park Cres. S2 . . . . .4B 100
Mnr. Park Dri. S2 . . . . .4B 100
Mnr. Park Ind. Est. S9 . . . . .1C 100
Mnr. Park Ri. S2 . . . . .3B 100
Mnr. Park Rd. S2 . . . . .3B 100
Mnr. Park Way. S2 . . . . .3B 100
Manor Pl. Hoy 5B 38
Manor Pl. Rawm 2G 69
Manor Ri. Wadw 6H 61
Manor Rd. Barn D 1G 21
Manor Rd. Bram B 4A 40
Manor Rd. Brim 4F 133
Manor Rd. B'wth 3B 90
Manor Rd. Ches 2E 137
(in two parts)
Manor Rd. Cud 1G 15
Manor Rd. Dinn 2F 107
Manor Rd. H'ton 2G 43
Manor Rd. H'hill 6B 118
Manor Rd. Kil 4C 126
Manor Rd. K'wth 3G 77

Manor Rd. Maltby 4G 83
Manor Rd. Swint 3B 56
Manor Rd. Thurn 1E 29
Manor Rd. Toll B 3A 18
Manor Rd. Wal 4F 117
Manor Sq. Thurn 1E 29
Manor St. B'ley 5F 9
Manor Vw. Half 2E 125
Manor Vw. S2 . . . . .1A 100
Manor Wlk. Wadw 6H 61
Manor Way. S2 . . . . .1A 100
Manor Way. Bol D 1B 42
Manor Way. Hoy 5A 38
Manor Way. Tod 2B 118
Manse Clo. Donc 3E 49
Mansel Av. S5 . . . . .3C 74
Mansel Ct. S5 . . . . .3C 74
Mansel Cres. S5 . . . . .3C 74
Mansel Rd. S5 . . . . .3C 74
Mansfeldt Cres. Ches 5G 131
Mansfeldt Rd. Ches 5G 131
Mansfield Cres. Arm 2C 34
Mansfield Dri. S12 . . . . .1D 112
Mansfield Rd. S12 . . . . .1C 112
Mansfield Rd. B'ley 5B 8
Mansfield Rd. Donc 2B 46
Mansfield Rd. Has & Temp N 6D 138
Mansfield Rd. Kil 2D 126
Mansfield Rd. Swal & Wal B 6A 104
(in two parts)
Mansfield Vw. S12 . . . . .1D 112
Manton Ho. Donc 1C 46
(off St James St.)
Manton St. S2 . . . . .4F 99 (6F 5)
Manvers Clo. Ans 6E 107
Manvers Clo. Swal 6B 104
Manvers Ct. Ches 1A 138
Manvers Rd. S6 . . . . .4A 86
Manvers Rd. Beig 3F 115
Manvers Rd. Cal 1G 139
Manvers Rd. Mexb 6C 42
Manvers Rd. Swal 6A 104
Manvers Way. Manv 2C 40
Maori Av. Bol D 1G 41
Maple Av. Donc 3D 48
Maple Av. Maltby 4D 82
Maplebeck Dri. S9 . . . . .1H 89
Maplebeck Rd. S9 . . . . .1H 89
Maple Clo. B'ley 2B 24
Maple Ct. Rawm 2G 69
Maple Ct. Tank 2B 50
Maple Cft. Cres. S9 . . . . .6B 76
Maple Cft. Rd. S9 . . . . .6B 76
Maple Dri. Flan 3F 81
Maple Dri. Kil 4A 126
Maple Gro. S9 . . . . .2G 101
Maple Gro. Arm 2F 35
Maple Gro. Ast 5D 104
Maple Gro. Con 5B 58
Maple Gro. S'bri 4D 140
Maple Leaf Ct. Mexb 6D 42
Maple Pl. C'town 3E 65
Maple Rd. Kiv P 4G 117
Maple Rd. M'well 4E 7
Maple Rd. Mexb 6D 42
Maple Rd. Tank 2B 50
Maple Ter. Holl 3H 133
Mapperley Rd. Dron W 2A 128
Mappin Ct. S1 . . . . .2D 98 (4B 4)
(off Mappin St.)
Mappin's Rd. Cat 6C 90
Mappin St. S1 . . . . .2D 98 (3B 4)
Mapplebeck Rd. High G 6C 50
Mapplewell. 4G 7
Mapplewell Dri. M'well 5G 7
Maran Av. D'fld 4G 27
Marbeck Clo. Dinn 4D 106
Marcham Dri. Beig 3G 115
March Bank. Thry 4E 71
March Flatts Rd. Thry 5E 71
March Ga. Con 4E 59
March St. S9 . . . . .4D 88
March St. Con 4E 59
March Va. Ri. Con 4E 59
Marchwood Av. S6 . . . . .5E 85
Marchwood Clo. Ches 1H 137
Marchwood Dri. S6 . . . . .4E 85
Marchwood Rd. S6 . . . . .5E 85
Marcliff Clo. Wick 5D 80
Marcliff Cres. Wick 5D 80
Marcliff La. Wick 5D 80
Mardale Clo. Ches 2G 131

Mardale Wlk. *Donc* 3A **34**
Marden Rd. *S7* 1C **110**
Margaret Clo. *Ast* 1B **116**
Margaret Clo. *D'fld* 4D **26**
Margaret Rd. *D'fld* 4D **26**
Margaret Rd. *Womb* 1G **39**
Margaret St. *S1* 4E **99**
Margaret St. *Maltby* 6H **83**
Margate Dri. *S4* 3H **87**
Margate St. *S4* .3A **88**
Margate St. *Grim* 6G **11**
Margerison St. *S8* 6E **99**
Margetson Cres. *S5* 3D **74**
Margetson Dri. *S5* 3D **74**
Margetson Rd. *S5* 3D **74**
Marian Rd. *E'thpe* 4C **20**
Marigold Clo. *S5* 6A **76**
Marina Ri. *D'fld* 4C **26**
Marine Dri. *Ches* 2C **138**
Marion Rd. *S6* .1H **85**
Markbrook Dri. *High G* 5A **50**
Market Clo. *B'ley* 6A **14**
Market Hall. *Ches* 2A **138**
Market Hill. *B'ley* 6G **13**
Market Pde. *B'ley* 6H **13**
Market Pl. *S1* 1F **99** (2F **5**)
Market Pl. *C'town* 2F **65**
Market Pl. *Ches* 2A **138**
Market Pl. *Cud* 6B **10**
Market Pl. *Dinn* 4F **107**
Market Pl. *Donc* 6C **32**
Market Pl. *Else* 6C **38**
Market Pl. *Gold* 4G **29**
Market Pl. Maltby 4G **83**
(off Blyth Rd.)
Market Pl. *P'stne* 4D **142**
Market Pl. *Roth* 3D **78**
Market Pl. *Stav* 1C **134**
Market Pl. *Womb* 1G **39**
Market Rd. *Donc* 5D **32**
Market Sq. *S13* 1C **114**
Market Sq. *Gold* 4G **29**
Market Sq. Roth 3D **78**
(off Market Pl.)
Market Sq. *Roth* 2E **79**
(Henry St.)
Market St. *S9* .1E **89**
Market St. *S13* 1C **114**
Market St. *B'ley* 6G **13**
Market St. *C'town* 2F **65**
Market St. *Cud* 6B **10**
Market St. *Eck* 6D **124**
Market St. *Gold* 1E **29**
(Church St.)
Market St. *Gold* 4G **29**
(Doncaster Rd.)
Market St. *High* 5D **16**
Market St. *Hoy* 4A **38**
Market St. *Mexb* 1E **57**
(Bank St., in two parts)
Market St. *Mexb* 2C **56**
(William St.)
Market St. *P'stne* 4D **142**
Market St. *Roth* 3D **78**
Market St. *Stav* 1C **134**
Markfield Dri. *Flan* 3F **81**
Mark Gro. *Flan* 4F **81**
Markham Av. *Arm* 2E **35**
Markham Av. *Con* 3C **58**
Markham Cotts. Con 3C **58**
(off Leslie Av.)
Markham Ct. *Con* 3C **58**
Markham Ct. *Duck* 6E **135**
(Duckmanton Rd.)
Markham Ct. *Duck* 6F **135**
(Markham Rd.)
Markham Cres. *Stav* 1D **134**
Markham Ho. Donc 1C **46**
(off Burden Clo.)
Markham La. *Duck* 6F **135**
Markham Quay. Ches 3B **138**
(off Carnlough Wlk.)
Markham Rd. *Ches* 3H **137**
Markham Rd. *Duck* 6E **135**
Markham Rd. *Edl'tn* 3B **60**
Markham Sq. *Edl'tn* 3C **60**
Markham Ter. *S8* 1D **110**
Markham Ter. *Edl'tn* 3B **60**
Markham Vs. Duck 6E **135**
(off Markham Rd.)
Mark La. *S10* 1A **108**
Mark St. *B'ley* .6G **13**
Marlborough Av. *Donc* 5H **31**

Marlborough Clo. *Ans* 6D **106**
Marlborough Clo. *Thurn* 1E **29**
Marlborough Ri. *Ast* 1C **116**
Marlborough Rd. *S10* 2A **98**
Marlborough Rd. *Donc* 5F **33**
Marlborough Ter. *B'ley* 1G **23**
Marlcliffe Rd. *S6* 6G **73**
Marley Rd. *S2* 4A **100**
Marifield Cft. *E'fld* 1F **75**
Marlow Clo. *Donc* 5H **81**
Marlowe Clo. *Braml* 4H **79**
Marlowe Dri. *Roth* 1H **21**
Marlowe Rd. *Barn D* 4H **79**
Marlowe Rd. *Roth* 4A **34**
Marlowe Rd. *Donc* 4A **34**
Marmion Rd. *S11* 6H **97**
(Ecclesall Rd.)
Marmion Rd. *S11* 5H **97**
(Rustlings Rd.)
Marples Clo. *S8* 6D **98**
Marples Dri. *S8* 6D **98**
Marquis Gdns. *Barn D* 2H **21**
Marr Grange La. *Marr* 2A **30**
Marrick Ct. *C'town* 2D **64**
Marriott Rd. *Rawm* 1G **69**
Marriott La. *S7* 4B **110**
Marriott Pl. *Rawm* 6D **54**
Marriott Rd. *Rawm* 4B **110**
Marriott Rd. *Swint* 1C **56**
Marrison Dri. *Kil* 3A **126**
Marr Ter. *S10* .4F **97**
Marsala Wlk. *D'fld* 3D **26**
Marsden Ind. Est. *S13* 3H **101**
Marsden La. *S3* 1D **98** (2B **4**)
Marsden Pl. *Ches* 3F **137**
(Chatsworth Rd.)
Marsden Pl. *Ches* 1A **138**
(Spencer St.)
Marsden Rd. *S'bri* 3E **141**
Marsden St. *Ches* 2A **138**
Marshall Av. *Donc* 4A **46**
Marshall Clo. *P'gte* 4F **69**
Marshall Gro. *Wath D* 6F **41**
Marshall Hall. *S10* 4B **98**
Marshall Rd. *S8* 5C **110**
Marsh Av. *Dron* 6F **123**
Marsh Clo. *Mosb* 3C **124**
Marshfield. *Birdw* 2D **36**
Marshfield Gro. *Stav* 1E **135**
Marsh Ga. *Donc* 5B **32**
Marsh Hill. *M'brng* 1C **82**
Marsh Ho. Rd. *S11* 1F **109**
Marsh La. *S10* .2F **97**
Marsh La. *Ark* .2D **18**
(in two parts)
Marsh La. *Barn D* 1A **20**
Marsh Rd. *Donc* 4C **32**
Marsh St. *Deep* 3F **141**
Marsh St. *Roth* 4C **78**
Marsh St. *Womb* 6C **26**
Marsh Vw. *Eck* 6G **125**
Marsh Wlk. S2 .1H **99**
(off St John's Rd.)
Marson Av. *W'land* 2B **16**
Marston Clo. *Dron W* 3B **128**
Marston Cres. *B'ley* 1H **13**
Marstone Cres. *S17* 4E **121**
Marston Rd. *S10* 1H **97**
Martin Clo. *S6* .6C **86**
Martin Clo. *Aug* 3A **104**
Martin Clo. *Birdw* 3D **36**
Martin Ct. *Eck* 6C **124**
Martin Cres. *S5* 3F **75**
Martindale Ter. *C'town* 2E **65**
(off Greenhead Gdns.)
Martin La. *Bla H* 2H **37**
Martin Ri. *Eck* 6C **124**
Martin Ri. *Thpe H* 1C **66**
Martin's Rd. *B'ley* 4F **15**
Martin St. *S6* 1C **98** (1A **4**)
(in three parts)
Martin Well's Rd. *Edl'tn* 4C **60**
Marton Rd. *Toll B* 2H **17**
Marvell Rd. *Donc* 3F **31**
Mary Ann Clo. *B'ley* 5D **14**
Maryhill Clo. *Tree* 1F **103**
Mary La. *D'fld* .4F **27**
Mary's Pl. *B'ley* 5E **13**
Mary St. *S1* 4E **99** (6E **5**)
Mary St. *Bar G* 3A **12**
Mary St. *Eck* .6D **124**
Mary St. *L Hou* 2A **28**
Mary St. *Roth* .2C **78**

Marys Wlk. *S2* .1H **99**
(off St John's Rd.)
Mary Tozer Ho. *S10* 2H **97**
Masbrough. 3B **78**
Masbrough Roundabout. *Roth* 3C **78**
Masbrough St. *Roth* 3B **78**
(in two parts)
Masefield Clo. *Dinn* 5G **107**
Masefield Flats. Wath D 4C **40**
(off Masefield Rd.)
Masefield Rd. *S13* 6E **101**
Masefield Rd. *Donc* 2A **34**
Masefield Rd. *Wath D* 4C **40**
Masham Rd. *Donc* 4C **48**
Mason Av. *Swal* 4B **104**
Mason Cres. *S13* 6F **101**
Mason Dri. *Swal* 4B **104**
Mason Gro. *S13* 6F **101**
Mason Lathe Rd. *S5* 4A **76**
Mason St. *Gold* 4G **29**
Masons Way. *B'ley* 3C **24**
Mason Way. *Hoy* 4H **37**
Massey Rd. *Woodh* 2D **114**
Masson Clo. *Ches* 6F **131**
Mastall La. *Ark* .5E **19**
Masters Cres. *S5* 4F **75**
Masters Rd. *S5* 4F **75**
Mather Av. *S9* 2D **100**
Mather Ct. *S9* 2D **100**
Mather Cres. *S9* 2D **100**
Mather Dri. *S9* 2D **100**
Mather Rd. *S9* 2D **100**
Mather Wlk. *S9* 2D **100**
Matilda La. *S1* 3F **99** (6F **5**)
Matilda St. *S1* 3E **99** (5D **4**)
(in three parts)
Matilda Way. *S1* 3E **99** (5D **4**)
Matlock Dri. *Ink* 6A **134**
Matlock Rd. *S6* 6A **86**
Matlock Rd. *B'ley* 1B **14**
Matlock Rd. *Walt & Ches* 6D **136**
Mattersey Clo. *Donc* 6C **48**
Matthews Av. *Wath D* 5D **40**
Matthews Clo. *Wath D* 6E **41**
Matthews Dri. *Wick* 6F **81**
Matthews Fold. *S8* 6G **111**
Matthews La. *S8* 6G **111**
Matthews La. *S8* 6D **86** (1C **4**)
Mauds Ter. *B'ley* 2C **14**
Maugerhay. *S8* 6G **111**
Maulays Ct. *Ross* 5F **63**
Mauncer Cres. *S13* 6B **102**
Mauncer Dri. *S13* 6B **102**
Mauncer La. *S13* 1B **114**
Maun Way. *S5* .6G **75**
Maurice St. *P'gte* 4F **69**
Mawfa Av. *S14* 5H **111**
(in two parts)
Mawfa Cres. *S14* 5H **111**
Mawfa Dri. *S14* 5H **111**
Mawfa La. *S14* 4H **111**
(in two parts)
Mawfa Rd. *S14* 6H **111**
Mawfa Wlk. *S14* 5H **111**
Mawfield Rd. *B'ley* 3B **12**
Maxey Pl. *S8* .1E **111**
Maxfield Av. *S10* 2A **98**
Maxwell St. *S4* 5G **87**
Maxwell Way. *S4* 5G **87**
May Av. *Donc* .1A **48**
May Av. *Old W* 1C **132**
Maycock Av. *Roth* 5F **67**
May Day Grn. *B'ley* 6H **13**
May Day Grn. Arc. B'ley 6H **13**
(off May Day Grn.)
Mayfield. *B'ley* .3B **14**
Mayfield. *Oxs* .6H **143**
Mayfield Ct. *S5* 5C **96**
Mayfield Ct. *Oxs* 6H **143**
Mayfield Cres. *New R* 5D **62**
Mayfield Cres. *Wors* 3G **23**
Mayfield Heights. *S10* 6D **96**
Mayfield Rd. *S10* 6A **96**
Mayfield Rd. *Ches* 3E **137**
Mayfield Rd. *Donc* 4A **32**
Mayfields. *Scawt* 6F **17**
Mayflower Cres. *Warm* 6E **45**
Mayflower Rd. *Warm* 5E **45**
Maynard Rd. *Ches* 4H **137**
Maynard Rd. *Roth* 6A **80**
May Rd. *S6* 3H **85**
May Ter. *B'ley* .6E **13**
Maythorne Clo. *M'well* 5G **7**

Maytree Clo. *D'fld* 5E **27**
May Tree Clo. *Wat* 6E **115**
May Tree Cft. *Wat* 6E **115**
May Tree La. *Wat* 6E **115**
Meaburn Clo. *Donc* 3D **48**
Meadow Av. *Rawm* 6D **54**
Mdw. Bank Av. *S7* 6B **98**
Meadowbank Clo. *Roth* 3A **78**
Mdw. Bank Ind. Est. *Roth* 4H **77**
Mdw. Bank Rd. *S11* 6B **98**
Meadow Bank Rd. *Roth* 5E **77**
Mdw. Bank Works. *Roth* 4F **77**
Meadowbrook Ind. Est. *Half* 1G **125**
Meadowbrook Pk. *Half* 2G **125**
Meadow Clo. *Coal* L 5G **123**
Meadow Clo. *Dalt* 6C **70**
Meadow Clo. *Kiv P* 4B **118**
Meadow Clo. *New W* 1D **132**
Meadowcourt. *S9* 1D **88**
Meadow Ct. *Adw S* 1E **17**
Meadow Ct. *New R* 5C **62**
Meadow Ct. *Roy* 2F **9**
Meadow Cres. *Grim* 6F **11**
Meadow Cres. *Mosb* 2B **124**
Meadow Cres. *Roy* 1F **9**
Meadow Cft. *E'thpe* 5E **21**
Meadow Cft. *Shaf* 2C **10**
Meadow Cft. *Spro* 3F **45**
Meadow Cft. *Swint* 5A **56**
Meadowcroft Clo. *Whis* 3H **91**
Meadowcroft Gdns. *W'fld* 1E **125**
Meadowcroft Glade. *W'fld* 1E **125**
Meadowcroft Ri. *W'fld* 1E **125**
Meadow Dri. *B'ley* 3D **14**
Meadow Dri. *C'town* 2C **64**
Meadow Dri. *D'fld* 4F **27**
Meadow Dri. *Swint* 3A **56**
Meadowfield Dri. *Hoy* 1A **52**
Meadowgate. *Bram* 5H **39**
Meadow Ga. *Womb* 2A **40**
Mdw. Gate Av. *Soth* 4H **115**
Mdw. Gate Clo. *Soth* 5H **115**
Meadowgate Lake Nature Reserve.
. . . . .1B **126**
Mdw. Gate La. *Soth* 6H **115**
Meadowgates. *Bol D* 6E **29**
Meadow Gro. *S17* 5E **121**
Mdw. Grove Rd. *S17* 5D **120**
Meadowhall. 6E **77**
Meadowhall Dri. *S9* 2D **88**
Meadowhall Retail Pk. *S9* 3E **89**
Meadowhall Rd. *S9* 1D **88**
Meadowhall Rd. *Roth* 4E **77**
Meadowhall Shop. Mall. *S9* 1E **89**
Meadowhall Way. *S9* 6E **77**
Meadow Head. 5D **110**
Meadowhead. *S8* 6D **110**
Mdw. Head Av. *S8* 2C **122**
Mdw. Head Clo. *S8* 2C **122**
Mdw. Head Dri. *S8* 1D **122**
Meadowhill Rd. *Has* 5D **138**
Meadow Ho. Dri. *S10* 4D **96**
Meadowland Ri. *Cud* 2H **15**
Meadow La. *Dart* 6C **6**
Meadow La. *Maltby* 5G **83**
Meadow La. *Old De* 2E **57**
Meadow La. *Rawm* 5D **54**
Meadowpark Cft. *Dinn* 5E **107**
Meadow Ri. *Ash* 1B **136**
Meadow Ri. *Barn D* 1E **21**
Meadow Ri. *Wadw* 6H **61**
Meadow Rd. *Roy* 2F **9**
Meadows Ct. *Ross* 5F **63**
Meadows Dri. *Stav* 2C **134**
Meadows Rd. *Manv* 4G **41**
Meadows, The. *Ash* 6B **130**
Meadows, The. *Tod* 2A **118**
Meadow St. *S3* 6D **86** (1B **4**)
Meadow St. *B'ley* 5H **13**
Meadow St. *Dinn* 3C **106**
. . . . (in two parts)
Meadow St. *Roth* 3A **78**
Meadow Ter. *S11* 5A **98**
Meadow, The. *Spro* 2E **45**
Meadow View. 5B **56**
Meadow Vw. *Ches* 5C **136**
Meadow Vw. *H'swne* 1F **143**
Meadow Vw. *Wors* 4A **24**
Mdw. View Clo. *Hoy* 6H **37**
Mdw. View Dri. *Rav* 1H **81**
Mdw. View Rd. *S8* 1D **122**
Mdw. View Rd. *Kiln* 5B **56**

Meadow Wlk. *E'thpe* 4E **21**
Meadow Way. *Swint* 2D **56**
. . . . (in two parts)
Meadstead Dri. *Roy* 2D **8**
Meads, The. *S8* 1F **123**
Mead, The. *Has* 5C **138**
Meadway Dri. *S17* 2C **120**
Meadway, The. *S17* 2D **120**
Meakin St. *Has* 5D **138**
Mears Clo. *P'stne* 4E **143**
Measborough Dike. 1B **24**
Mede, The. *W'land* 2B **16**
Medina Way. *Bar G* 2A **12**
Medley Vw. *Con* 4F **59**
Medlock Clo. *S13* 4A **102**
Medlock Clo. *Walt* 6D **136**
Medlock Ct. *Dinn* 5F **107**
Medlock Cres. *S13* 3A **102**
Medlock Cft. *S13* 3A **102**
Medlock Dri. *S13* 4A **102**
Medlock Rd. *S13* 4A **102**
Medlock Rd. *Ches* 5E **137**
Medlock Way. *S13* 3A **102**
Medway Clo. *Bar G* 2B **12**
Medway Pl. *Womb* 2H **39**
Meersbrook. 2F **111**
Meersbrook Av. *S8* 2D **110**
Meersbrook Bank. 2E **111**
Meersbrook Pk. Rd. *S8* 1E **111**
Meersbrook Rd. *S8* 2F **111**
Meetinghouse Cft. *S13* 1C **114**
Meetinghouse La. *S1* 1F **99** (2F **5**)
Meetinghouse La. *Woodh* 1C **114**
Mekyll Clo. *S'side* 3F **81**
Melbeck Ct. *C'town* 2C **64**
Melbourne Av. *S10* 3A **98**
Melbourne Av. *Ast* 5C **104**
Melbourne Av. *Bol D* 1H **41**
Melbourne Av. *Dron W* 2A **128**
Melbourne Ct. *Stav* 1C **134**
. . . . (off Devonshire St.)
Melbourne Rd. *Donc* 5G **45**
Melbourne Rd. *S'bri* 3C **140**
Melbourn Rd. *S10* 1A **98**
Melciss Rd. *Wick* 5E **81**
Meld Clo. *New R* 6D **62**
Melford Clo. *M'well* 4F **7**
Melford Dri. *Donc* 5G **45**
Melfort Glen. *S10* 2F **97**
Melia Av. *Hoy* 5A **38**
Melling Av. *Donc* 6H **31**
Melling Clo. *Ches* 5H **137**
Melling Ct. *Ches* 5H **137**
Mellington Clo. *S8* 5G **111**
Mellor La. *Barl* 2A **130**
Mellor Lea Farm Chase. *E'fld* 5F **65**
Mellor Lea Farm Clo. *E'fld* 5F **65**
. . . . (off Mellor Lea Farm Dri.)
Mellor Lea Farm Dri. *E'fld* 5F **65**
Mellor Lea Farm Gth. *E'fld* 5F **65**
. . . . (off Mellor Lea Farm Dri.)
Mellor Rd. *Womb* 1F **39**
Mellor Way. *Ches* 6A **138**
Mellow Fields Rd. *Lghtn* 1D **106**
Mellwood Gro. *H'fld* 3E **39**
Melrose Clo. *Ches* 2E **137**
Melrose Clo. *Donc* 4G **45**
Melrose Clo. *Thur* 5H **93**
Melrose Cotts. *Whis* 2A **92**
Melrose Gro. *Roth* 1G **91**
Melrose Rd. *S3* 4F **87**
Melrose Way. *B'ley* 5D **14**
Meltham La. *Ches* 5B **132**
Melton Av. *Bram* 3B **40**
Melton Av. *Gold* 4G **29**
Melton Ct. *Ast* 6E **105**
Melton Ct. *Den M* 1B **58**
Meltonfield Clo. *Arm* 4G **35**
Melton Gdns. *Spro* 2D **44**
Melton Grn. *Wath D* 5C **40**
Melton Gro. *Owl* 5A **114**
Melton High St. *Wath D* 5C **40**
Melton Rd. *Donc & Spro* 2A **44**
Melton St. *Bram* 3B **40**
Melton St. *Mexb* 1G **57**
Melton Ter. *Wors* 4C **24**
Melton Way. *Roy* 1E **9**
Melton Wood Gro. *Spro* 2D **44**
Melville Av. *Donc* 4A **46**
Melville Cres. *Brim* 1F **139**
Melville Rd. *S2* 5C **100**
Melville St. *Womb* 6B **26**
Melvinia Cres. *B'ley* 3F **13**

Melwood Ct. *Arm* 5G **35**
Memoir Gro. *New R* 6C **62**
Mendip Clo. *B'ley* 5D **12**
Mendip Clo. *Donc* 4G **31**
Mendip Cres. *Ches* 1D **136**
Mendip Ri. *B'wth* 4D **90**
Merbeck Dri. *High G* 4C **50**
Merbeck Gro. *High G* 5C **50**
Mercaston Clo. *Ches* 6C **130**
Mercel Av. *Arm* 1G **35**
Merchants Cres. *S4* 1G **99** (2G **5**)
Mercia Dri. *S17* 3E **121**
Meredith Cres. *Donc* 5B **46**
Meredith Rd. *S6* 3H **85**
Mere Gro. *Arm* 1E **35**
Mere La. *E'thpe & Arm* 6E **21**
Merlin Clo. *Adw S* 1D **16**
Merlin Clo. *Birdw* 3D **36**
Merlin Way. *S5* 6G **75**
Merlin Way. *Thpe H* 1C **66**
Merrick Clo. *Ches* 6F **131**
Merrill Rd. *Thurn* 1E **29**
Merton La. *S9* 5D **76**
Merton Ri. *S9* 5D **76**
Merton Rd. *S9* 5D **76**
Metcalfe Av. *Kil* 3A **126**
Methley Clo. *S12* 1B **112**
Methley Ho. Donc 1C **46**
. . . . (off St James St.)
Methley St. *Cud* 1H **15**
Metrodome Leisure Complex, The.
. . . . .5A **14**
Metro Trad. Cen. *B'ley* 2A **12**
Mews Ct. *Owl* 5A **114**
Mexborough. 1E **57**
Mexborough Bus. Cen. *Mexb* 6F **43**
Mexborough Pk. Homes. *Mexb* 1G **57**
Mexborough Rd. *Bol D* 2B **42**
Meynell Clo. *Ches* 3E **137**
Meynell Cres. *S5* 5B **74**
Meynell Rd. *S5* 5B **74**
Meynell Way. *Kil* 3A **126**
Meyrick Dri. *Dart* 6B **6**
Michael Cft. *Wath D* 5D **40**
Michael Rd. *B'ley* 5E **15**
Michael's Est. *Grim* 6G **11**
Mickelden Way. *B'ley* 6C **12**
Micklebring Gro. *Con* 5C **58**
Micklebring Way. *H'by* 2B **82**
Mickley. 6H **121**
Mickley La. *S17 & Dron W* 5E **121**
Middle Av. *Rawm* 2F **69**
Middle Bank. *Donc* 3E **47**
Middleburn Clo. *B'ley* 2A **24**
Middlecliff Clo. *Wat* 6E **115**
Middlecliff Cotts. *L Hou* 2A **28**
Middlecliff Ct. *Wat* 6E **115**
Middlecliffe. 2A **28**
Middlecliff La. *L Hou* 1G **27**
Middlecliff Ri. *Wat* 6E **115**
Middle Clo. *Dart* 4A **6**
Middlecroft. 3A **134**
Middlecroft Rd. *Stav* 4A **134**
Middle Dri. *Roth* 2F **91**
Middlefield Clo. *S17* 2C **120**
Middlefield Cft. *S17* 2C **120**
Middlefield Rd. *Donc* 4B **48**
Middlefield Rd. *Roth* 1G **91**
Middlefields Dri. *Whis* 2A **92**
Middlegate. *Donc* 6G **17**
. . . . (in two parts)
Middleham Rd. *Donc* 4C **48**
Middle Hay Clo. *S14* 2A **112**
Middle Hay Pl. *S14* 3A **112**
Middle Hay Ri. *S14* 3A **112**
Middle Hay Vw. *S14* 3A **112**
Middle La. *S6* 5G **85**
Middle La. *Gren* 6A **64**
Middle La. *Roth* 2F **79**
Middle L. S. *Roth* 3G **79**
Middle Ox Clo. *Half* 3F **125**
Middle Ox Gdns. *Half* 3F **125**
Middle Pavement. Ches 2A **138**
. . . . (off Low Pavement)
Middle Pl. *Roth* 2H **79**
Middlesex St. *B'ley* 2H **23**
Middle Shambles. Ches 2A **138**
. . . . (off Shambles, The)
Middle Shambles. *Ches* 2A **138**
. . . . (off High St.)
Middleton Av. *Dinn* 5E **107**
Middleton Dri. *Ink* 6H **133**
Middleton La. *Gren* 1B **74**

Middleton Rd. *Roth* 3F **79**
Middlewood. 5F **73**
Middlewood Chase. *S6* 6G **73**
Middlewood Dri. *S6* 6F **73**
Middlewood Dri. *Scho* 5E **67**
Middlewood Dri. E. *S6* 6F **73**
Middlewood Rd. *S6* 5G **73**
Middlewood Rd. N. *O'bri* 3E **73**
Middlewoods. *Dod* 2C **22**
Midfield Rd. *S10* 1G **97**
Midhill Rd. *S2* 6F **99**
Midhope Way. *B'ley* 6C **12**
Midhurst Gro. *Bar G* 2A **12**
Midhurst Rd. *S6* 3H **73**
Midland Ct. *Has* 6B **138**
Midland Ct. *Roth* 3B **78**
Midland Rd. *Roth* 3A **78**
Midland Rd. *Roy* 1E **9**
Midland Rd. *Swint* 2C **56**
Midland St. *S1* 4E **99**
Midland St. *B'ley* 6H **13**
Midland St. *P'gte* 5F **69**
Midland Ter. *Has* 6B **138**
(in two parts)
Midvale Av. *S6* 5C **86**
Midvale Clo. *S6* 5C **86**
(off Midvale Av.)
Milano Ri. *D'fld* 4D **26**
Milbanke St. *Donc* 5D **32**
Milburn Ct. *Soth* 6G **115**
Milburn Gro. *Soth* 6G **115**
Milden Pl. *B'ley* 2A **24**
Milden Rd. *S6* 1G **85**
Milefield Ct. *Grim* 6F **11**
Milefield La. *Grim* 6F **11**
Milefield Vw. *Grim* 6F **11**
Mile Oak Rd. *Roth* 2E **87**
Miles Clo. *S5* 2E **87**
Miles Rd. *S5* 2D **86**
Miles Rd. *High G* 6C **50**
Milethorn La. *Donc* 4D **32**
Milford Av. *Else* 5D **38**
Milford Rd. *Ink* 6A **134**
Milford St. *S9* 3D **88**
Milgate St. *Roy* 1F **9**
Milgrove Cres. *High G* 5B **50**
Milking La. *Bram* 4A **40**
Millais Ri. *Flan* 2F **81**
Millard La. *Maltby* 4G **83**
Millbank Clo. *High G* 1B **64**
Mill Clo. *Lghtn* 5C **78**
Mill Clo. *Roth* 3B **118**
Mill Clo. *Tod* 6F **65**
Mill Ct. *E'fld* 4A **24**
Mill Ct. *Wors* 1A **130**
Millcross La. *Barl* 6E **131**
Milldale Clo. *Ches* 4F **121**
Milldale Rd. *S17* 2B **92**
Milldyke Clo. *Whis* 4E **5**
Millennium Galleries. *Ches* 2G **131**
Millennium Way. *Ches* 1A **114**
Miller Cft. *S13* 4D **90**
Miller Dale Dri. *B'wth* 6D **98**
Miller Rd. *S7* 1E **9**
Millers Cft. *Roy* 5A **24**
Millers Dale. *Wors* 3H **141**
Miller St. *Deep* 1E **21**
Millfield Ct. *Barn D* 6C **18**
Millfield Ind. Est. *Ben* 1C **32**
Millfield Rd. *Ben* 3A **118**
Mill Fields. *Tod* 1B **32**
Mill Ga. *Ben* 1C **134**
Mill Grn. *Stav* 2F **119**
Mill Haven. *Ans* 2A **92**
Mill Hill. *Whis* 5H **25**
Mill Hill. *Womb* 5G **35**
Millhill Clo. *Arm* 6H **31**
Mill Hill Clo. *Donc* 2B **118**
Mill Hills. *Tod* 1A **108**
Mill House Animal Sanctuary. 6A **70**
Millhouse Ct. *Dalt* 1C **134**
Mill Ho. M. *Stav* 3H **27**
Millhouses. . . . .
(Darfield)
Millhouses. 4B **110**
(Heeley)
Millhouses Ct. *S11* 3H **109**
Millhouses Glen. *S11* 3H **109**
Millhouses La. *S11 & S7* 2G **109**
Millhouses St. *Hoy* 6A **38**
Millicent Sq. *Maltby* 5G **83**
Millindale. *Maltby* 5G **83**
Mill La. *S9* 4F **121**

Mill La. *Adw S* 1D **16**
Mill La. *Ans* 2F **119**
Mill La. *Bran* 3G **49**
Mill La. *Ches* 3F **137**
Mill La. *Dart* 4C **6**
Mill La. *Deep* 3H **141**
Mill La. *Dron* 2F **129**
Mill La. *H'ton* 2G **43**
Mill La. *Thurls* 4A **142**
Mill La. *Tree* 1D **102**
Mill La. *Warm* 3D **44**
Mill La. *Wath D* 6C **40**
Mill La. *W'wth* 3B **52**
Mill Mdw. Clo. *Soth* 6H **115**
Mill Mdw. Gdns. *Soth* 6H **115**
Millmoor Ct. *Womb* 5D **26**
Millmoor La. *Roth* 3B **78**
Millmoor Rd. *Donc* 3C **48**
Millmoor Rd. *Womb* 5C **26**
Millmount Rd. *S8* 2D **110**
Millmount Rd. *Hoy* 6B **38**
Millrace Dri. *Gold* 5E **29**
Mill Rd. *E'fld* 6F **65**
Mill Rd. *Eck* 5D **124**
Mill Rd. *Tree* 1D **102**
Mill Rd. Clo. *E'fld* 6F **65**
Millsands. *S3* 6F **87** (1F 5)
Millside. *Shaf* 2C **10**
Millside St. *Ben* 1B **32**
Millside Wlk. *Shaf* 2C **10**
Millstone Clo. *Dron W* 1B **128**
Millstone Dri. *Swal* 5B **104**
Millstones. *S6* 6H **143**
Mill Stream Clo. *Ches* 4E **137**
Millstream Clo. *Spro* 2F **45**
Mill St. *Arm* 3F **35**
Mill St. *B'ley* 6B **14**
Mill St. *Ches* 2B **138**
Mill St. *Roth* (S60) 4D **78**
Mill St. *Roth* (S61) 3B **68**
Millthorpe Rd. *S5* 5H **75**
Mill Vw. *Bol D* 2H **41**
Mill Wlk. *S3* 1F **99** (1F 5)
Millwood Rd. *Donc* 6H **45**
Millwood Vw. *S6* 4C **84**
Milner Av. *P'stne* 3B **142**
Milner Clo. *Braml* 3H **81**
Milner Ga. *Con* 3F **59**
(in two parts)
Milner Ga. Ct. *Con* 3G **59**
Milner Ga. La. *Con* 3F **59**
Milner Rd. *Donc* 4H **45**
Milnes St. *B'ley* 1A **24**
Milne St. *Bar G* 3A **12**
Milnrow Cres. *S5* 3D **74**
Milnrow Dri. *S5* 3D **74**
Milnrow Rd. *S5* 3D **74**
Milnrow Vw. *S5* 3D **74**
Milton. 1A **52**
Milton Av. *Donc* 5H **31**
Milton Clo. *Jump* 4B **38**
Milton Clo. *Roth* 3B **68**
Milton Clo. *Wath D* 3B **40**
Milton Ct. *Donc* 1D **46**
Milton Ct. *Swint* 2A **56**
Milton Cres. *Ches* 5A **138**
Milton Cres. *Hoy* 6A **38**
Milton Gro. *Arm* 3F **35**
Milton Gro. *E'thpe* 5D **20**
Milton Gro. *Womb* 1G **39**
Milton La. *S3* 3D **98** (6C 4)
Milton Pl. *Stav* 1D **134**
Milton Rd. *S7* 6C **98**
Milton Rd. *Burn* 2B **64**
Milton Rd. *Dinn* 5G **107**
Milton Rd. *Hoy* 6A **38**
Milton Rd. *Mexb* 6E **43**
Milton Rd. *Roth* 1F **75**
Milton St. *S3 & S1* 3D **98** (6B 4)
Milton St. *Maltby* 5F **83**
Milton St. *Roth* 1C **78**
Milton St. *Swint* 2A **56**
Milton Wlk. *Donc* 1C **46**
Minden Clo. *Wick* 5F **81**
Minden Ct. *Ben* 1B **32**
Minimum Ter. *Ches* 3G **137**
Minna Rd. *S3* 4F **87**
Minneymoor Hill. *Con* 2F **59**
Minneymoor La. *Con* 3F **59**
Minster Clo. *Ches* 4E **49**
Minster Clo. *E'fld* 1G **75**
Minster Rd. *E'fld* 1F **75**
Minster Way. *B'ley* 4D **14**

Minto Rd. *S6* 2H **85**
Miriam Av. *Ches* 5C **136**
Mission Fld. *Bram* 3A **40**
Mitchell Clo. *Wors* 4D **24**
Mitchell Rd. *S8* 5D **110**
Mitchell Rd. *Womb* 4A **26**
Mitchells Enterprise Cen. *Womb* . . .4A **26**
Mitchell St. *S3* 1C **98** (2A 4)
Mitchell St. *Swait* 4E **25**
Mitchells Way. *Womb* 5A **26**
Mitchelson Av. *Dod* 2A **22**
Moat Clo. *S'side* 2G **81**
Moat Cft. *Scawt* 6H **17**
Moat Hills Ct. *Ben* 6B **18**
Moat Ho. Way. *Con* 2E **59**
Moatlands. *Wick* 1G **93**
Moat La. *Wick* 2G **93**
Modena Ct. *D'fld* 3C **26**
Moffat Gdns. *Donc* 6B **20**
Moffatt Rd. *S2* 6F **99**
Molineaux Clo. *S5* 4H **75**
Molineaux Rd. *S5* 3G **75**
Molineux Av. *Stav* 2B **134**
Molloy Pl. *S8* 1E **111**
Molloy St. *S8* 1E **111**
Mona Av. *S10* 1A **98**
Mona Rd. *S10* 1A **98**
Mona Rd. *Donc* 3B **46**
Mona St. *B'ley* 5F **13**
Monckton Rd. *S5* 6B **76**
Moncrieffe Rd. *S7* 1C **110**
Monk Bretton. 3C **14**
Monk Bretton Priory. 5E **15**
(remains of)
Monk's Bri. Rd. *Dinn* 3C **106**
Monk's Bri. Trad. Est. *Dinn* 3C **106**
Monks Clo. *Roth* 5E **67**
Monkspring. *Wors* 4C **24**
Monks Way. *B'ley* 4D **14**
Monk Ter. *B'ley* 2E **15**
Monkton Way. *Roy* 1E **9**
Monkwood Rd. *Ches* 3F **131**
Monkwood Rd. *Rawm* 6D **54**
Monmouth Rd. *Donc* 4H **45**
Monmouth St. *S3* 3C **98** (5A 4)
Monsal Cres. *B'ley* 6C **8**
Monsal Cres. *Ink* 5H **133**
Monsal St. *Thurn* 1E **29**
Montague Av. *Con* 3C **58**
Montague St. *S6* 4B **86**
Montague St. *S11* 4C **98**
Montague St. *Cud* 5C **10**
Montague St. *Donc* 5D **32**
Montagu Rd. *Mexb* 1G **45**
Montagu Sq. *Mexb* 1F **57**
Monteney Cres. *S5* 1E **75**
Monteney Gdns. *S5* 2E **75**
Monteney Rd. *S5* 2E **75**
Montfort Dri. *S3* 5F **87**
Montgomery Av. *S7* 6C **98**
Montgomery Ct. *S11* 2G **109**
Montgomery Dri. *S7* 6C **98**
Montgomery Gdns. *Donc* 3A **34**
Montgomery Rd. *S7* 1C **110**
Montgomery Rd. *Wath D* 5F **41**
Montgomery Sq. *Wath D* 5F **41**
Montgomery Ter. Rd. *S6* 6D **86**
Montrose Av. *Dart* 4D **6**
Montrose Av. *Donc* 4H **33**
Montrose Ct. *S11* 3F **109**
Montrose Pl. *Dron W* 1B **128**
Montrose Rd. *S7* 2A **110**
Mont Wlk. *Womb* 5G **25**
Monument Dri. *Brie* 3F **11**
Monyash Clo. *Stav* 4A **134**
Moonpenny Way. *Dron* 2E **129**
Moonshine La. *S5* 6D **74**
Moonshine Way. *S5* 1D **86**
Moorbank Clo. *S10* 3D **96**
Moorbank Clo. *B'ley* 3E **13**
Moorbank Clo. *Womb* 5H **25**
Moorbank Ct. *S10* 2D **96**
Moorbank Dri. *S10* 2E **97**
Moorbank Rd. *S10* 2D **96**
Moorbank Rd. *Womb* 4H **25**
Moorbank Vw. *Womb* 4H **25**
Moorbridge Cres. *Bram* 2B **40**
Moor Cres. *Mosb* 2C **124**
Moorcrest Ri. *M'well* 3F **7**
Moorcroft Av. *S10* 6B **96**
Moorcroft Clo. *S10* 6B **96**
Moorcroft Dri. *S10* 6B **96**

Moorcroft Rd.—Myrtle Gro.

Moorcroft Rd. *S10* 6B **96**
Moordale Vw. *Rawm* 6A **56**
Moor End Rd. *S10* 1A **98**
Moore St. *S3* 4D **98** (6B **4**)
Moor Farm Av. *Mosb* 1B **124**
Moor Farm Gth. *Mosb* 1C **124**
Moor Farm Ri. *Mosb* 1B **124**
Moorfield Av. *Rav* 2H **81**
Moorfield Clo. *Rav* 2H **81**
Moorfield Dri. *Arm* 4F **35**
Moorfield Gro. *Rav* 2H **81**
Moorfields. *S3* 1E **99** (1D **4**)
Moorfields Flats. S3 6E ***87*** *(1D* ***4****)*
(off Moorfields)
Moorfoot. *S1* 6D **4**
Moor Gap. *Bran* 3H **49**
Moorgate. 1G 91
Moorgate Av. *S10* 1B **98**
Moorgate Av. *Roth* 5E **79**
Moorgate Bus. Cen. Roth 4E ***79***
(off Moorgate Rd.)
Moorgate Chase. *Roth* 4E **79**
Moorgate Ct. *Roth* 4E **79**
Moorgate Cres. *Dron* 3F **129**
Moorgate Gro. *Roth* 5F **79**
Moorgate La. *Roth* 5E **79**
Moorgate Rd. *Roth* 4E **79**
Moorgate Rd. *Roth* 4E **79**
Moorgate St. *Roth* 3D **78**
Moor Grn. Clo. *B'ley* 6C **12**
Moorhay Clo. *Ches* 4D **130**
Moorhead. *S1* 5D **4**
Moorhead Way. *Braml* 1E **81**
Moorhouse Clo. *Whis* 2B **92**
Moorhouse La. *Whis* 2A **92**
Moorland Av. *B'ley* 1D **22**
Moorland Av. *M'well* 3F **7**
Moorland Ct. *Donc* 6E **33**
Moorland Cres. *M'well* 3F **7**
Moorland Dri. *S'bri* 3C **140**
Moorland Gro. *Donc* 2A **48**
Moorland Pl. *S6* 5C **84**
Moorlands. *Wick* 5D **80**
Moorlands Ct. *Wath D* 3C **40**
Moorlands Cres. *Whis* 2A **92**
Moorland Vw. *S12* 5C **112**
Moorland Vw. *Ast* 6C **104**
Moorland Vw. *Wath D* 3C **40**
Moorland Vw. Rd. *Ches* 5E **137**
Moor La. *Birdw* 6D **36**
Moor La. *Cal* 6H **139**
Moor La. *Kirk S* 2B **20**
Moor La. *M'brng* 1B **82**
Moor La. N. *Rav* 5H **71**
Moor La. S. *Rav* 1H **81**
Moorlawn Av. *Holy* 6A **136**
Moorley. *Birdw* 2C **36**
Moor Oaks Rd. *S10* 2A **98**
Moor Pk. Av. *Ches* 5E **137**
Moor Rd. *Roth* 3H **79**
Moor Rd. *Wath D* 5F **41**
Moorside. *S10* 5A **96**
Moorside Av. *P'stne* 5D **142**
Moorside Clo. *M'well* 5F **7**
Moorside Clo. *Mosb* 1C **124**
Moorsyde Av. *S10* 6H **85**
Moorsyde Cres. *S10* 6H **85**
Moor, The. *S1* 3E **99** (6D **4**)
Moorthorpe Bank. *Owl* 5B **114**
Moorthorpe Dell. *Owl* 5B **114**
Moorthorpe Gdns. *Owl* 5H **113**
Moorthorpe Grn. *Owl* 5H **113**
Moorthorpe Ri. *Owl* 6B **114**
Moorthorpe Vw. *Owl* 6A **114**
Moorthorpe Way. *Owl* 5H **113**
(in two parts)
Moortown Av. *Dinn* 6G **107**
Moor Valley. *Mosb* 5H **113**
Moor Valley Clo. *Mosb* 6A **114**
Moor Vw. *Bran* 3H **49**
Moorview. *Roth* 3F **77**
Moorview Clo. *Brim* 4D **132**
Moorview Ct. *S17* 4H **121**
Moorview Ct. *Roth* 3F **77**
Moor Vw. Dri. *S8* 4C **110**
Moor Vw. Rd. *S8* 5C **110**
Moor Vw. Rd. *Stav* 1E **135**
Moor Vw. Ter. *S11* 2E **109**
Moorwinstow Cft. *S17* 2E **121**
Moorwoods Av. *C'town* 2E **65**
Moorwoods La. *C'town* 2E **65**
Moray Pl. *Dron W* 1B **128**
Mordaunt Rd. *S2* 1B **112**
More Hall La. *Bols* 6G **141**
Morgan Av. *S5* 1D **86**
Morgan Clo. *S5* 6D **74**
Morgan Rd. *S5* 1D **86**
Morgan Rd. *Donc* 5A **34**
Morland Clo. *S14* 4B **112**
Morland Dri. *S14* 4B **112**
Morland Pl. *S14* 4B **112**
Morland Rd. *S14* 4A **112**
Morley Av. *Ches* 1E **137**
Morley Clo. *Dron W* 2A **128**
Morley Pl. *Con* 4D **58**
Morley Rd. *Donc* 4E **33**
Morley Rd. *Roth* 6G **67**
Morley St. *S6* 4H **85**
Morley St. *P'gte* 3F **69**
Morpeth Gdns. *S3* 1B **4**
Morpeth St. *S3* 1D **98** (1B **4**)
Morpeth St. *Roth* 3E **79**
Morrall Rd. *S5* 2D **74**
Morrell St. *Maltby* 5G **83**
Morris Av. *Ches* 6G **131**
Morris Av. *Rawm* 5F **55**
Morris Dri. *Ches* 6G **131**
Morrison Av. *Maltby* 3G **83**
Morrison Dri. *New R* 5E **63**
Morrison Pl. *D'fld* 3E **27**
Morrison Rd. *D'fld* 3D **26**
Mortain Rd. *Roth* 1F **91**
Mortains. *Tod* 1B **118**
Morthen. 4F 93
Morthen Cotts. *Morth* 4E **93**
Morthen Hall La. *Morth* 4F **93**
Morthen La. *Thur* 3E **93**
Morthen La. *Whis* 5C **92**
Morthen Rd. *Wick & Thur* 5F **81**
Mortimer Dri. *P'stne* 6C **142**
Mortimer Heights. *P'stne* 6C **142**
Mortimer Rd. *Maltby* 5H **83**
Mortimer Rd. *P'stne* 6C **142**
Mortimer St. *S1* 3F **99** (6F **5**)
Mortlake Rd. *S5* 1H **87**
Mortomley. 6C 50
Mortomley Clo. *High G* 6C **50**
Mortomley Hall Gdns.
High G 6C **50**
Mortomley La. *High G* 5C **50**
Morton Clo. *B'ley* 2D **14**
Morton Gdns. *Half* 3F **125**
Morton Mt. *Half* 2F **125**
Morton Pl. *Gren* 1A **74**
Morton Rd. *Mexb* 6F **43**
Mosborough. 2D 124
Mosborough Hall Dri. *Half* 4E **125**
Mosborough Moor. *Mosb* 1B **124**
Mosborough Parkway. *S13* 4F **101**
Mosborough Rd. *S13* 6D **100**
Moscar Cotts. *S7* 3B **110**
Moscrop Clo. *S13* 6C **102**
Moss Beck Ct. *Eck* 6H **125**
Moss Clo. *Wick* 5F **81**
Mossdale Av. *Mosb* 2D **124**
Mossdale Clo. *Donc* 2G **31**
Moss Dri. *Kil* 4B **126**
Moss Gro. *S12* 4D **114**
Moss Ri. Pl. *Eck* 6C **124**
Moss Rd. *S17* 5A **120**
Moss Vw. *Mosb* 3B **124**
Moss Way. *S20* 2D **124**
Moston Wlk. *Ches* 6G **137**
Motehall Dri. *S2* 4C **100**
Motehall Pl. *S2* 4D **100**
Motehall Rd. *S2* 4C **100**
Motehall Wlk. *S2* 4D **100**
Motehall Way. *S2* 4C **100**
Motte, The. *Roth* 1H **77**
Mottram St. *B'ley* 5H **13**
Mound Rd. *Ches* 4A **138**
Mount Av. *Grim* 5G **11**
Mountbatten Dri. *Burn* 2B **64**
Mountcastle St. *Ches* 3H **131**
Mountcastle Wlk. *Ches* 3H **131**
Mount Cres. *Hoy* 4H **37**
Mountenoy Rd. *Roth* 4D **78**
Mountford Cft. *S17* 4E **121**
Mount Olive. *S'bri* 3D **140**
Mt. Osborne Ind. Pk.
B'ley 1B **24**
Mount Pleasant. *C'town* 1E **65**
Mount Pleasant. *Donc* 4A **46**
Mount Pleasant. *Grim* 5G **11**
Mount Pleasant. *Old W* 1A **132**
Mount Pleasant. *Wors* 5B **24**
Mt. Pleasant Clo. *C'town* 1E **65**
Mt. Pleasant Rd. *S7* 5D **98**
Mt. Pleasant Rd. *Roth* 2B **78**
Mt. Pleasant Rd. *Wath D* 1F **55**
Mount Rd. *S3* 4D **86**
Mount Rd. *C'town* 2C **64**
Mount Rd. *Grim* 5G **11**
Mount St. *S11* 4D **98**
Mount St. *Ard* 1F **25**
Mount St. *B'ley* 1G **23**
Mount St. *Roth* 2B **78**
Mount Ter. *Wath D* 5C **40**
Mount Ter. *Womb* 6A **26**
Mount, The. *E'thpe* 6E **21**
Mount, The. *S'side* 2F **81**
Mt. Vernon Av. *B'ley* 2H **23**
Mt. Vernon Cres. *B'ley* 3A **24**
Mt. Vernon Rd.
B'ley & Wors 2A **24**
Mount Vw. *Edl'tn* 4B **60**
Mt. View Av. *S8* 4E **111**
Mt. View Gdns. *S8* 4E **111**
Mt. View Rd. *S8* 5E **111**
Mousehole Clo. *Dalt* 6C **70**
Mousehole La. *Dalt* 6C **70**
Mouse Pk. Ga. *O'bri* 1F **73**
Mowbray Gdns. *Roth* 1A **80**
Mowbray Pl. *Roth* 1A **80**
Mowbray St. *S3* 6E **87**
Mowbray St. *Roth* 1H **79**
Mowson Cres. *Worr* 4D **72**
Mowson Dri. *Worr* 4D **72**
Mowson Hollow. *Worr* 4E **73**
Mowson La. *Worr* 4D **72**
Moxon Clo. *Deep* 4G **141**
Mucky La. *B'ley* 6G **15**
Mucky La. *S'bri* 1C **140**
(Hunshelf Rd.)
Mucky La. *S'bri* 5B **140**
(Lee Ho. La.)
Muglet La. *Maltby* 6H **83**
Muirfield Av. *Donc* 5F **49**
Muirfield Av. *Swint* 3C **56**
Muirfield Clo. *Ches* 5B **132**
Muirfield Clo. *Cud* 4C **10**
Muirfields, The. *Dart* 4E **7**
Mulberry Clo. *Cusw* 4F **31**
Mulberry Clo. *D'fld* 5E **27**
Mulberry Clo. *Gold* 4E **29**
Mulberry Clo. *P'gte* 4F **69**
Mullberry Ct. *Warm* 5F **45**
Mulberry Rd. *Ans* 1G **119**
Mulberry Rd. *Eck* 6G **125**
Mulberry St. *S1* 2F **99** (3F **5**)
Mulberry Way. *Arm* 5F **35**
Mulberry Way. *Kil* 4H **125**
Mulehouse Rd. *S10* 1G **97**
Mundella Pl. *S8* 4E **111**
Mungy La. *Thry* 5B **70**
Munro Clo. *Kil* 3B **126**
Munsbrough La. *Roth* 5B **68**
Munsbrough Ri. *Roth* 4B **68**
Munsdale. *Roth* 4B **68**
Murdoch Pl. *B'ley* 6A **8**
Murdock Rd. *S5* 5D **74**
Murrayfield Dri. *Half* 3E **125**
Murray Rd. *S11* 1H **109**
Murray Rd. *Kil* 2C **126**
Murray Rd. *Rawm* 1G **69**
Musard Pl. *Stav* 2B **134**
Musard Way. *Kil* 3A **126**
Musgrave Cres. *S5* 2E **87**
(in three parts)
Musgrave Dri. *S5* 2E **87**
Musgrave Pl. *S5* 2E **87**
Musgrave Rd. *S5* 2D **86**
Musgrove Av. *Thry* 5E **71**
Mushroom La. *S10 & S3* 2B **98** (2A **4**)
Muskoka Av. *S11* 2E **109**
Muskoka Dri. *S11* 1E **109**
Mutual St. *Donc* 1B **46**
Muxlow. *S11* 1B **110**
Myers Av. *O'bri* 1D **72**
Myers Gro. La. *S6* 4F **85**
(in two parts)
Myers La. *S6* 6A **72**
Mylnhurst Rd. *S11* 2H **109**
Mylor Ct. *B'ley* 4C **14**
Mylor Rd. *S11* 1G **109**
Myndon Wlk. *Den M* 2C **58**
Myrtle Cres. *Wick* 4G **81**
Myrtle Gro. *Holl* 2G **133**
Myrtle Gro. *Kiv P* 5G **117**

Myrtle Rd. *S2* 6E **99**
Myrtle Rd. *Womb* 6A **26**
Myrtle Springs. *S12* 2B **112**
Myrtle Springs Dri. *S12* 2B **112**
Myrtle St. *B'ley* 5E **13**
Myton Rd. *S9* 1C **100**

N

Nairn Dri. *Dron W* 2B **128**
Nairn St. *S10* 2H **97**
Nancy Rd. *Grim* 6H **11**
Nanny Hill. *S'bri* 3E **141**
Nanny Marr Rd. *D'fld* 4E **27**
Napier Mt. *Wors* 4H **23**
Napier St. *S11* 4C **98**
Narrow La. *Ans* 2G **119**
Narrow Twitchell. Roth 3E **79**
(off Hollowgate)
Narrow Wlk. *S10* 2A **98**
Nascot Gdns. *Aug* 3A **104**
Naseby Av. *Donc* 3F **31**
Naseby St. *S9* 1C **88**
Nasmyth Row. Else 1D **52**
(off Wath Rd.)
Nathan Ct. *Wat* 6F **115**
Nathan Dri. *Wat* 5F **115**
Nathan Gro. *Wat* 5E **115**
Navan Rd. *S2* 6C **100**
Navigation Way. *Bram* 2A **40**
Naylor Gro. *Dod* 2B **22**
Naylor Gro. *O'bri* 3C **72**
Naylor Rd. *O'bri* 2C **72**
Naylor St. *P'gte* 4F **69**
Neale Bank. *Brim* 4D **132**
Neale Rd. *Donc* 1H **33**
Nearcroft Rd. *Roth* 1H **77**
Nearfield Rd. *Donc* 5B **48**
Needham Way. *S7* 2A **110**
Needlewood. *Dod* 3B **22**
Neepsend. **5C 86**
Neepsend La. *S3* 5C **86**
Neill Rd. *S11* 5A **98**
Nelson Av. *B'ley* 3A **14**
Nelson Clo. *B'wth* 3D **90**
Nelson Mandela Wlk. S2 . . . . .4D **100**
(off Saxonlea Av.)
Nelson Pl. *Burn* 2B **64**
Nelson Rd. *S6* 5F **85**
Nelson Rd. *Edl'tn* 3B **60**
Nelson Rd. *Maltby* 4H **83**
Nelson Rd. *New R* 4B **62**
Nelson Rd. Flats. Edl'tn 3B **60**
(off Nelson Rd.)
Nelson St. *B'ley* 6G **13**
Nelson St. *Ches* 5A **132**
Nelson St. *Donc* 2D **46**
Nelson St. *Roth* 2E **79**
Nemesia Clo. *Ans* 3E **119**
Nesfield. **2B 130**
Nesfield Clo. *Ches* 3F **131**
Nesfield Way. *S5* 5H **75**
(in two parts)
Nether Av. *Gren* 6B **64**
Nether Av. *Kil* 3A **126**
Nether Cantley. **1F 49**
Nether Cantley La. *Cant* 1F **49**
Nether Cres. *Gren* 6B **64**
Nethercroft. *Bar G* 2A **12**
Nether Cft. Clo. *Brim* 4E **133**
Nether Cft. Rd. *Brim* 4E **133**
Netherdene Rd. *Dron* 2E **129**
(in two parts)
Nether Edge. **1C 110**
Nether Edge Rd. *S7* 1C **110**
Nether Farm Clo. *Brim* 6F **133**
Netherfield. *Hoy* 5B **38**
Netherfield Clo. *Deep* 4H **141**
Netherfield Clo. *Stav* 1E **135**
Netherfield Cft. *Roth* 1E **79**
Netherfield Cft. *Shaf* 3C **10**
Netherfield La. *P'gte* 3F **69**
Netherfield Rd. *S10* 6H **85**
Netherfield Rd. *Ches* 5C **136**
Netherfields Cres. *Dron* 3E **129**
Netherfield Vw. *Roth* 1B **80**
Nethergate. **6C 84**
Nethergate. *S6* 6B **84**
Nether Green. **5E 97**
Nethergreen Av. *Kil* 2B **126**
Nethergreen Ct. *Kil* 2B **126**

Nethergreen Gdns. *Kil* 2B **126**
Nethergreen Rd. *S11* 5F **97**
Nether Hall Rd. *Donc* 6D **32**
Nether Haugh. **1B 68**
Nether La. *E'fld* 5F **65**
Netherleigh Ct. *Ches* 2D **136**
Netherleigh Rd. *Ches* 2D **136**
Nether Ley Av. *C'town* 2E **65**
Nether Ley Cft. *C'town* 2E **65**
Nether Ley Ct. *C'town* 2E **65**
Nether Ley Gdns. *C'town* 2E **65**
Nethermoor Av. *Kil* 2B **126**
Nethermoor Clo. *Kil* 2B **126**
Nethermoor Dri. *Kil* 2B **126**
Nethermoor La. *Wick* 1G **93**
Nether Oak Clo. *Soth* 5H **115**
Nether Oak Dri. *Soth* 5H **115**
Nether Oak Vw. *Soth* 5H **115**
Nether Rd. *E'fld* 6F **65**
Nether Shire La. *S5* 2G **75**
Netherthorpe. **6E 105**
(Aston)
Netherthorpe. **2B 126**
(Killamarsh)
Netherthorpe. **1C 98**
(Sheffield)
Netherthorpe. . . . .
(Woodthorpe)
Netherthorpe. *Stav* 1E **135**
Netherthorpe Clo. *Kil* 2A **126**
Netherthorpe Clo. *Stav* 1D **134**
Netherthorpe La. *Kil* 3A **126**
Netherthorpe Pl. *S3* 6D **86** (1B **4**)
Netherthorpe Rd. *S3* 2C **98** (3A **4**)
Netherthorpe Rd. *Stav* 1D **134**
Netherthorpe St. *S3* 1D **98** (1B **4**)
Netherthorpe Wlk. *S3* 1D **98** (1B **4**)
Netherthorpe Way. *Ans* 6E **107**
Nether Wheel Row. *S13* 2H **113**
Netherwood Rd. *Womb* 4B **26**
Nettleham Rd. *S8* 4D **110**
Neville Av. *B'ley* 2D **24**
Neville Clo. *S3* 6F **87**
Neville Clo. *B'ley* 2D **24**
Neville Clo. *Womb* 5H **25**
Neville Ct. *Womb* 5H **25**
Neville Cres. *B'ley* 2D **24**
Neville Dri. *S3* 5F **87**
Neville Rd. *Roth* 6H **67**
Neville St. *Roth* 2D **78**
Nevis Clo. *Ches* 1F **137**
Newark. W'fld 1E **125**
(off Shortbrook Clo.)
Newark Clo. *M'well* 3F **7**
Newark Rd. *Mexb* 6C **42**
Newark St. *S9* 4C **88**
Newark St. *New R* 3C **62**
New Beetwell St. *Ches* 2A **138**
Newbiggin Dri. *P'gte* 3E **69**
Newbiggin Dri. *P'gte* 3E **69**
Newbold. **5F 131**
Newbold Av. *Ches* 5G **131**
Newbold Bk. La. *Ches* 5F **131**
(in two parts)
Newbold Ct. *Ches* 4F **131**
Newbold Dri. *Ches* 5G **131**
Newbold Moor. **3H 131**
Newbold Rd. *Ches* 3C **130**
Newbold Ter. *Ches* 4H **31**
Newbold Village. **5G 131**
Newbolt Rd. *Donc* 5B **46**
Newbould Cres. *Beig* 4G **115**
Newbould La. *S10* 3A **98**
Newbridge Ct. *Monk B* 4B **14**
Newbridge Ct. *Old W* 2A **132**
Newbridge Dri. *Brim* 3D **132**
New Bri. Gro. *Edl'tn* 3C **60**
Newbridge Gro. *Monk B* 4B **14**
Newbridge La. *Old W & Brim* 1A **132**
(in three parts)
Newbridge St. *Old W* 2A **132**
New Brimington. **2F 133**
Newburn Dri. *S9* 1G **89**
Newburn Dri. *S9* 1F **89**
(off Town St.)
Newbury Rd. *S10* 1H **97**
Newbury Way. *Donc* 3F **31**
Newby Cres. *Donc* 6A **46**
Newby Rd. *Ches* 3E **131**
Newcastle Clo. *Ans* 6E **107**
Newcastle St. *S1* 2D **98** (3C **4**)
New Chapel Av. *P'stne* 6C **142**

Newcomen Rd. *Donc* 4A **32**
Newcroft Clo. *Soth* 4H **115**
New Cross Dri. *S13* 1A **114**
New Cross Wlk. *S13* 1A **114**
New Cross Way. *S13* 1A **114**
Newdale Av. *Cud* 2G **15**
New Droppingwell Rd. *Roth* 3D **76**
New Edlington. **4B 60**
Newent La. *S10* 1H **97**
Newfield Av. *B'ley* 3D **14**
Newfield Clo. *Barn D* 1F **21**
Newfield Ct. *S10* 5D **96**
Newfield Cres. *S17* 2C **120**
Newfield Cres. *Wath D* 6D **40**
Newfield Cft. *S17* 1C **120**
Newfield Farm Clo. *S14* 2A **112**
Newfield Green. **2H 111**
Newfield Grn. Rd. *S2* 1H **111**
Newfield La. *S17* 2C **120**
Newfield Pl. *S17* 2C **120**
Newgate. **2A 130**
Newgate Clo. *High G* 6B **50**
Newhall. **3C 88**
Newhall Av. *Wick* 1G **93**
New Hall Cres. *S'bri* 2B **140**
New Hall La. *B'ley* 2H **25**
Newhall Grange. *Maltby* 6A **82**
New Hall La. *Maltby* 6A **82**
New Hall La. *S'bri* 3A **140**
Newhall Rd. *S9* 3A **88**
New Hall Rd. *Ches* 3F **137**
Newhall Rd. *Kirk S* 4E **21**
New Haven Clo. *Ches* 4D **136**
New Haven Gdns. *S17* 5E **121**
New Hill. *Con* 3E **59**
Newhill. *Wath D* 6C **40**
Newhill Av. *B'ley* 2A **14**
Newhill Rd. *Wath D* 6D **40**
New Houses. *Ches* 2C **138**
New Ings. *Arm* 3E **35**
Newington Av. *Cud* 5B **10**
Newington Clo. *Donc* 4D **48**
Newington Dri. *Ast* 6C **104**
Newington Rd. *S11* 5A **98**
Newland Av. *Cud* 2G **15**
Newland Av. *Maltby* 5H **83**
Newland Dale. *Ches* 1A **138**
Newland Gdns. *Ches* 6G **131**
Newland Rd. *B'ley* 6A **8**
Newlands Av. *S12* 1C **112**
Newlands Av. *Ches* 2E **137**
Newlands Clo. *Donc* 4D **48**
Newlands Dri. *S12* 1C **112**
Newlands Dri. *Donc* 4H **31**
Newlands Gro. *S12* 1D **112**
Newlands Rd. *S12* 1C **112**
Newlands Way. *Womb* 2A **40**
New La. *Bol D* 5H **27**
(in two parts)
New La. *Ross* 4E **63**
New La. *Spro* 2C **44**
New Lodge. **6A 8**
New Lodge Cres. *B'ley* 6A **8**
Newlyn Dri. *B'ley* 4B **14**
Newlyn Pl. *S8* 4D **110**
Newlyn Rd. *S8* 4D **110**
Newman Av. *B'ley* 4E **9**
Newman Clo. *S9* 5D **76**
Newman Clo. *S9* 5D **76**
Newman Ct. *Roth* 1G **91**
Newman Dri. *S9* 5C **76**
Newman Rd. *S9* 6C **76**
Newman Rd. *Roth* 1G **91**
Newmarch St. *S9* 6G **77**
Newmarket Rd. *Donc* 1B **48**
New Meadows. *Rawm* 5D **54**
New Mill Bank. *Bols* 6E **141**
New Orchard La. *Thur* 4A **94**
(in two parts)
New Orchard Rd. *Thur* 4A **94**
New Oxford Rd. *Mexb* 1F **57**
New Queen St. *Ches* 1A **138**
New Rd. *Bran* 3H **49**
New Rd. *Deep* 3F **141**
New Rd. *Dinn* 5F **107**
(Laughton Rd.)
New Rd. *Dinn* 1E **119**
(Penny Piece La.)
New Rd. *H'fld* 4F **39**
New Rd. *Holy* 6A **136**
New Rd. *M'well* 3E **7**
New Rd. *Roth* 4D **76**
New Rd. *Tank* 6B **36**

New Rd. *Wal B* 3C **116**
New Rd. *Wath D* 5F **41**
New Rossington. 4C **62**
Newsam Rd. *Kiln* 4B **56**
New School Clo. *Mosb* 2C **124**
New School Ct. *Mosb* 2C **124**
New School Rd. *Mosb* 2C **124**
Newsham Rd. *S8* 3D **110**
New Smithy Av. *Thurls* 3A **142**
New Smithy Dri. *Thurls* 3A **142**
Newsome Av. *Womb* 6H **25**
New Sq. *Ches* 2A **138**
New Sta. Rd. *Swint* 2C **56**
Newstead Av. *S12* 5G **113**
Newstead Av. *O'bri* 1D **72**
Newstead Clo. *S12* 4G **113**
Newstead Clo. *Dron W* 2A **128**
Newstead Dri. *S12* 5G **113**
Newstead Gro. *S12* 4G **113**
Newstead Pl. *S12* 5G **113**
Newstead Ri. *S12* 5H **113**
Newstead Rd. *S12* 4G **113**
Newstead Rd. *B'ley* 5A **8**
Newstead Rd. *Donc* 1H **31**
Newstead Way. *S12* 5G **113**
New St. *S1* 1E **99** (2E **5**)
New St. *B'ley* (S70) 1G **23**
(in two parts)
New St. *B'ley* (S71) 1E **25**
New St. *Ben* 1A **32**
New St. *Bol D* 2B **42**
New St. *Cat* 5D **90**
New St. *Ches* 3A **138**
New St. *D'fld* 4E **27**
New St. *Deep* 3G **141**
New St. *Dinn* 4F **107**
New St. *Dod* 3B **22**
New St. *Donc* 2C **46**
New St. *Greasb* 3B **68**
New St. *Gt Hou* 1A **28**
New St. *Grim* 6G **11**
New St. *H'fld* 4D **38**
New St. *High G* 5B **50**
New St. *H'brk* 2G **125**
New St. *Lghtn* 1E **107**
New St. *M'well* 4F **7**
New St. *Mexb* 6H **43**
New St. *Rawm* 2F **69**
New St. *Roy* 2E **9**
New St. *Thpe H* 3B **66**
New St. *Womb* 6C **26**
New St. *Wors* 5C **24**
(Edmunds Rd.)
New St. *Wors* 5A **24**
(West St.)
New St. La. *S2* 1G **99** (2H **5**)
Newton. 6H **31**
Newton Av. *S'bri* 2B **140**
Newton Chambers Rd. *C'town* 5D **50**
Newton Cft. *S13* 1B **114**
Newton Dri. *Donc* 6H **31**
Newton Dri. *Roth* 3G **79**
Newton Gdns. *C'town* 6E **51**
Newton La. *S1* 3E **99** (6E **5**)
Newton La. *Donc* 6H **31**
Newton La. *S'bri* 2B **140**
Newton Pl. *Thpe H* 4B **66**
Newton Rd. *High G* 6C **50**
Newton St. *B'ley* 5F **13**
Newton St. *Roth* 3G **79**
Newton Va. *C'town* 5D **50**
New Totley. 5E **121**
Newtown Av. *Cud* 2G **15**
Newtown Av. *Roy* 1D **8**
Newtown Grn. *Cud* 2H **15**
Newtree Dri. *Wadw* 6H **61**
Newven Ho. Roth 2F **79**
(off St Leonard's Rd.)
New Village. 5B **18**
New Winterwell. *Wath D* 4D **40**
New Wortley Rd. *Roth* 2A **78**
New York. .4C **78**
Niagara Rd. *S6* 6A **74**
Niagara Yd. *S6* 6A **74**
Nicholas La. *Gold* 4E **29**
Nicholas St. *B'ley* 6F **13**
Nicholas St. *Has* 6D **138**
Nicholson Av. *Bar G* 3A **12**
Nicholson Av. *Wath D* 6D **40**
Nicholson Pl. *S8* 1F **111**
Nicholson Rd. *S8* 1E **111**
Nicholson Rd. *Donc* 2A **46**
Nichols Rd. *S6* 6G **85**

Nickerwood Dri. *Ast* 1B **116**
Nickleby Ct. *Cat* 5B **90**
Nidderdale Pl. *S'side* 3G **81**
Nidderdale Rd. *Roth* 4H **67**
Nidd Rd. *S9* 6C **88**
Nidd Rd. E. *S9* 6D **88**
Nightingale Clo. *Ches* 2A **138**
Nightingale Clo. *Roth* 4D **78**
Nightingale Ct. *Roth* 4D **78**
Nightingale Cft. *Thpe H* 1C **66**
Nightingale Rd. *Gren* 1B **74**
Nile St. *S10* 3A **98**
Nine Trees Ind. Est. *Thur* 3H **93**
Ninian Gro. *Donc* 3C **48**
Noble St. *Hoy* 6B **38**
Nodder Rd. *S13* 5E **101**
Noehill Pl. *S2* 4D **100**
Noehill Rd. *S2* 4D **100**
Nook End. 5D **84**
Nookery Clo. *Maltby* 3H **83**
Nooking Clo. *Arm* 2G **35**
Nook La. *S6* 5C **84**
Nook La. *Cal* 2H **139**
Nook La. *P'stne* 6E **143**
Nook, The. *S8* 3D **110**
Nook, The. *H'swne* 1G **143**
Nora St. *Gold* 3H **29**
Norborough Rd. *S9* 1G **89**
Norborough Rd. *Donc* 4F **33**
Norbreck Cres. *Warm* 1C **60**
Norbreck Rd. *Warm* 6E **45**
Norbriggs. 1F **135**
Norbriggs Rd. *Mas M* 1F **135**
Norbrook Way. *Whis* 2B **92**
Norburn Dri. *Kil* 3B **126**
Norbury Clo. *Ches* 6D **130**
Norbury Clo. *Dron W* 2B **128**
Norcroft. *Wors* 3H **23**
Norcross Gdns. *D'fld* 4F **27**
Norfolk Clo. *B'ley* 3B **14**
Norfolk Clo. *Walt* 5D **136**
Norfolk Ct. *Roth* 2E **79**
(off Wharncliffe Hill)
Norfolk Dri. *Ans* 1G **119**
Norfolk Hill. *Gren* 6A **64**
Norfolk Hill Cft. *Gren* 6A **64**
Norfolk La. *S1* 5E **5**
Norfolk Pk. Av. *S2* 4H **99**
Norfolk Pk. Dri. *S2* 4G **99**
Norfolk Pk. Rd. *S2* 4F **99**
Norfolk Pk. Students Residence.
S2 . . . . .4H **99**
Norfolk Pl. *Maltby* 4G **83**
Norfolk Rd. *S2* 3G **99** (5H **5**)
Norfolk Rd. *Donc* 5B **46**
Norfolk Rd. *Gt Hou* 1A **28**
Norfolk Row. *S1* 2E **99** (3E **5**)
Norfolk St. *S1* 2E **99** (4E **5**)
(in two parts)
Norfolk St. *Roth* 2E **79**
Norfolk Way. *Roth* 1G **91**
Norgreave Way. *Half* 2E **125**
Norman Clo. *B'ley* 3C **14**
Norman Clo. *Wors* 4A **24**
Norman Cres. *Donc* 2F **31**
Norman Cres. *New R* 4C **62**
Normancroft Ct. *S2* 4D **100**
Normancroft Cres. *S2* 4E **101**
Normancroft Dri. *S2* 4D **100**
Normancroft Way. *S2* 4E **101**
Normandale. 3E **85**
Normandale Av. *S6* 3E **85**
Normandale Rd. *S6* 4B **86**
Norman St. *S9* 4B **88**
Norman St. *Thurn* 1G **29**
Normanton Gdns. *S4* 4G **87**
Normanton Gro. *S13* 1H **113**
Normanton Hill. *S13* 1E **113**
Normanton Spring. 1G **113**
Normanton Spring Ct. *S13* 1H **113**
Normanton Spring Rd. *S13* 2G **113**
Normanville Av. *B'wth* 2B **90**
Norrel's Cft. *Roth* 5F **79**
Norrels Dri. *Roth* 5F **79**
Norris Rd. *S6* 3H **85**
Norroy St. *S4* 5H **87**
Norstead Cres. *Braml* 1E **81**
Northampton Rd. *Donc* 4A **34**
North Anston. 2G **119**
N. Anston Bus. Cen. *Ans* 5C **106**
N. Anston Trad. Est. *Ans* 5B **106**
N. Bridge Rd. *Donc* 5B **32**

N. Carr La. *B'ley* 1E **27**
N. Church St. *S1* 1E **99** (2E **5**)
N. Cliff Rd. *Con* 2D **58**
North Clo. *Roy* 2E **9**
Northcote Av. *S2* 1F **111**
Northcote Ho. S8 . . . . .4D **110**
(off Chantrey Rd.)
Northcote Rd. *S2* 1F **111**
Northcote Ter. *B'ley* 5E **13**
North Cres. *Duck* 5E **135**
North Cres. *Kil* 1C **126**
North Cres. *Roth* 2G **79**
Northcroft. *Shaf* 3C **10**
North Dri. *Roth* 1D **78**
N. End Dri. *H'ton* 1F **43**
Northern Av. *S2* 6A **100**
Northern Comn.
Dron W . . . . .6H **121** & 1A **128**
N. Farm Ct. *Ast* 6D **104**
Northfield. 1D **78**
North Fld. *Dod* 1B **22**
Northfield Av. *S10* 6H **85**
Northfield Av. *Rawm* 6F **55**
Northfield Clo. *S10* 6A **86**
Northfield Clo. *S10* 6H **85**
Northfield Ct. *Wick* 4F **81**
Northfield Ind. Est. *Roth* 1D **78**
N. Field La. *Barn D* 1G **21**
Northfield La. *Wick* 4E **81**
Northfield Rd. *S10* 1H **97**
Northfield Rd. *Donc* 4A **32**
Northfield Rd. *Roth* 2D **78**
Northgate. *B'ley* 4E **13**
North Ga. *Eck* 6D **124**
North Ga. *Mexb* 6G **43**
North Gro. *Duck* 5E **135**
N. Hill Rd. *S5* 5D **74**
Northlands. *Adw S* 1C **16**
Northlands. *Roy* 1E **9**
Northlands Rd. *S5* 5D **74**
North La. *Cut* 6A **130**
North Mall. Donc 6C **32**
(off French Ga.)
N. Moor Clo. *Brim* 4F **133**
Northmoor Vw. *Brim* 4F **133**
Northorpe. *Dod* 3D **22**
N. Pitt St. *Roth* 3H **77**
North Pl. *B'ley* 4D **12**
North Pl. *Roth* 2G **79**
Northpoint Ind. Est. *S9* 6D **76**
North Quadrant. *S5* 5H **75**
N. Quay Dri. *S2* 1G **99** (1H **5**)
North Rd. *Cal* 2F **139**
North Rd. *Roth* 2G **79**
North Rd. *Roy* 1F **9**
N. Royds Wood. *B'ley* 4B **8**
Northside Rd. *Wath D* 5F **41**
North Sq. *Edl'tn* 3C **60**
North St. *D'fld* 3E **27**
North St. *Donc* 2E **47**
North St. *Edl'tn* 3C **60**
North St. *Rawm* 6G **55**
North St. *Roth* 2C **78**
North St. *Swint* 2C **56**
N. Swaithe Clo. *Ben* 5A **18**
North Ter. *Has* 6B **138**
Northumberland Av. *Donc* 4H **33**
Northumberland Av. *Hoy* 4A **38**
Northumberland La. *Den M* 2A **58**
Northumberland Rd. *S10* 2B **98**
Northumberland Way. *B'ley* 1F **25**
North Vw. *Grim* 6F **11**
Northwood. *S6* 5G **73**
Northwood Dri. *S6* 5F **73**
Northwood Pl. *S6* 6G **73**
Norton. 6G **111**
Norton Av. *S8* 6H **111**
Norton Av. *S14* & *S12* 5A **112**
Norton Av. *Ches* 5C **136**
Norton Chu. Glebe. *S8* 6F **111**
Norton Chu. Rd. *S8* 6F **111**
Norton Grn. Clo. *S8* 6G **111**
Norton Hammer. 3C **110**
Norton Hammer La. *S8* 3C **110**
Norton La. *S8* 2E **123**
Norton Lawns. S8 . . . . .6G **111**
(off School La. Clo.)
Norton Lees. 3E **111**
Norton Lees Clo. *S8* 4E **111**
Norton Lees Cres. *S8* 3E **111**
Norton Lees La. *S8* 3D **110**
Norton Lees Rd. *S8* 2D **110**
Norton Lees Sq. *S8* 3E **111**

Norton M. *S8* 6G **111**
Norton Pk. Av. *S8* 1F **123**
Norton Pk. Cres. *S8* 1E **123**
Norton Pk. Dri. *S8* 1E **123**
Norton Pk. Rd. *S8* 2E **123**
Norton Pk. Vw. *S8* 1E **123**
Norton Rd. *Donc* 4H **33**
Norton Rd. *Wath D* 4D **40**
Norton Woodseats. 4F **111**
Norville Cres. *D'fld* 3F **27**
Norwich Rd. *Donc* 2G **33**
Norwich Row. *S2* 2G **99** (3H **5**)
Norwith Rd. *Donc* 5B **48**
Norwood. 1D **126**
Norwood Av. *S5* 1F **87**
Norwood Av. *Has* 6D **138**
Norwood Av. *Maltby* 3F **83**
Norwood Clo. *S5* 2F **87**
Norwood Clo. *Has* 6E **139**
Norwood Clo. *Maltby* 3F **83**
Norwood Cres. *Kil* 2D **126**
Norwood Cres. *Kiv P* 5G **117**
Norwood Dri. *S5* 2F **87**
Norwood Dri. *Bar G* 2A **12**
Norwood Dri. *Ben* 4B **18**
Norwood Dri. *Brie* 2G **11**
Norwood Grange Dri. *S5* 1F **87**
Norwood La. *Thurls* 2A **142**
Norwood Pl. *Kil* 2D **126**
Norwood Rd. *S5* 2F **87**
Norwood Rd. *Con* 3D **58**
Norwood St. *Dalt* 6B **70**
Nostel Ho. *Donc* 1C **46**
. . . . *(off St James St.)*
Nostell Fold. *Dod* 3B **22**
Nostell Pl. *Donc* 5B **48**
Nottingham Cliff. *S3* 5F **87**
Nottingham Clo. *Ans* 3F **119**
Nottingham Clo. *B'ley* 2G **25**
Nottingham Clo. *Donc* 3F **31**
Nottingham St. *S3* 5F **87**
Nottingham St. *Roth* 2E **79**
Novello St. *Maltby* 5H **83**
Nowill Ct. *S8* 1E **111**
Nowill Pl. *S8* 1E **111**
Nunnery Cres. *Cat* 5C **90**
Nunnery Dri. *S2* 1B **100**
Nunnery Ter. *S2* 2B **100**
Nunnington Way. *Kirk S* 3C **20**
Nursery Cres. *Ans* 1F **119**
Nursery Dri. *Cat* 5C **90**
Nursery Dri. *E'fld* 1F **75**
Nursery Gdns. *B'ley* 2E **25**
Nursery Gro. *E'fld* 1G **75**
Nursery La. *S3* 6F **87** (1F **5**)
Nursery La. *Spro* 4C **44**
Nursery Rd. *Ans & Dinn* 1G **119**
. . . . *(in two parts)*
Nursery Rd. *Swal* 5A **104**
Nursery St. *S3* 6F **87** (1F **5**)
Nursery St. *B'ley* 1G **23**
Nuttack La. *Old Br* 1A **136**
. . . . *(in two parts)*
Nuttall Pl. *S2* 2H **99**
Nutwell. 4G **35**
Nutwell Clo. *Donc* 5C **48**
Nutwell La. *Arm & Cant* 3G **35**
Nutwood Trad. Est. *S6* 4H **73**

O

Oadby Dri. *Ches* 6C **138**
Oakamoor Clo. *Ches* 6D **130**
Oak Apple Wlk. *S6* 4C **84**
Oak Av. *Wath D* 6G **41**
Oak Bank Av. *Old W* 1B **132**
Oakbank Clo. *Swint* 5B **56**
Oakbank Ct. *S17* 4E **121**
Oakbrook Ct. *S10* 5F **97**
Oakbrook Rd. *S11* 5F **97**
Oakbrook Vw. *S10* 4G **97**
Oakbrook Wlk. *Roth* 1H **79**
Oakburn Ct. *S10* 4B **98**
Oak Clo. *Brim* 4D **132**
Oak Clo. *Flan* 3F **81**
Oak Clo. *Hoy* 6H **37**
Oak Clo. *Kil* 4A **126**
Oak Clo. *Mexb* 6C **42**
Oak Clo. *Wath D* 1G **55**
Oak Ct. *Spro* 2F **45**
Oakcrest. *Donc* 1F **63**

Oakdale. *Wors* 4B **24**
Oakdale Clo. *E'thpe* 6D **20**
Oakdale Clo. *Wors* 5B **24**
Oakdale Pl. *Roth* 3H **77**
Oakdale Rd. *S7* 1B **110**
Oakdale Rd. *Ans* 2H **119**
Oakdale Rd. *Roth* 3H **77**
Oak Dale Rd. *Warm* 1C **60**
Oakdell. *Dron* 6H **123**
Oakdene. *New R* 5D **62**
Oaken Wood Clo. *Thpe H* 2C **66**
Oaken Wood Rd. *Thpe H* 2B **66**
Oakes Grn. *S9* 5A **88**
Oakes Pk. Vw. *S14* 6H **111**
Oakes St. *S9* 5D **76**
Oakfern Gro. *High G* 5B **50**
Oakfield Av. *Ches* 4D **136**
Oakfield Ct. *M'well* 4E **7**
Oakfield Wlk. *B'ley* 5D **12**
Oak Gro. *Arm* 1E **35**
Oak Gro. *Con* 4C **58**
Oak Gro. *Thur* 4B **94**
Oakham Dri. *S3* 5D **86**
Oakham Pl. *B'ley* 4E **13**
Oakhill Rd. *S7* 1B **110**
Oakhill Rd. *Donc* 3H **33**
Oakhill Rd. *Dron* 1G **129**
Oakholme Rd. *S10* 4A **98**
Oakholme Rd. *S10* 3A **98**
Oakland. *Wors* 5B **24**
Oakland Ct. *S6* 3H **85**
Oakland Rd. *S6* 3H **85**
Oaklands. *Bes* 1G **63**
Oaklands. *Wick* 6G **81**
Oaklands Av. *B'ley* 3D **14**
Oaklands Dri. *Donc* 3B **48**
Oaklands Gdns. *Donc* 4B **48**
Oaklands Pl. *Wath D* 6E **41**
Oakland Ter. *Edl'tn* 3B **60**
Oak Lea. *Roth* 4B **68**
Oak Lea. *Wors* 5C **24**
Oak Lea Av. *Wath D* 4C **40**
Oaklea Clo. *M'well* 3F **7**
Oakley Av. *Ches* 1G **137**
Oakley Rd. *S13* 3G **101**
Oak Lodge Rd. *High G* 6A **50**
Oak Meadows. *Roth* 1H **79**
Oak Pk. *S10* 3H **97**
Oak Pk. Ri. *B'ley* 2A **24**
Oak Pl. *S10* 3H **97**
Oak Rd. *S12* 5C **112**
Oak Rd. *Arm* 1E **35**
Oak Rd. *Beig* 3F **115**
Oak Rd. *Maltby* 4D **82**
Oak Rd. *Mexb* 6C **42**
Oak Rd. *Shaf* 3D **10**
Oak Rd. *Thurn* 1F **29**
Oak Rd. *Wath D* 6G **41**
Oaks Av. *S'bri* 3C **140**
Oaks Bus. Pk. *B'ley* 6C **14**
Oaks Cres. *B'ley* 1C **24**
Oaks Farm Clo. *Dart* 4D **6**
Oaks Farm Dri. *Dart* 4D **6**
Oaks Farm La. *Cal* 3G **139**
Oaks Fold. *S5* 3A **76**
Oaks Fold Av. *S5* 4A **76**
Oaks Fold Rd. *S5* 4A **76**
Oaks La. *S5* 4A **76**
Oaks La. *B'ley* (S70) 1C **24**
Oaks La. *B'ley* (S71) 6C **14**
. . . . *(in two parts)*
Oaks La. *Roth* 6E **67**
Oaks, The. *S10* 3H **97**
Oak St. *S8* 6E **99**
Oak St. *B'ley* 6F **13**
Oak St. *Holl* 2G **133**
Oak St. *Mosb* 1C **124**
Oaks Wood Dri. *Dart* 5D **6**
Oak Ter. *Donc* 2C **46**
Oak Ter. *Swal* 5H **103**
Oak Tree Av. *Cud* 6B **10**
Oak Tree Clo. *Dart* 5B **6**
Oak Tree Clo. *Wick* 4G **81**
Oak Tree Cotts. *Cal* 4G **139**
Oak Tree Rd. *Bran* 2H **49**
Oakwell Bus. & Youth Enterprise Cen.
. . . *B'ley* 6B **14**
Oakwell Clo. *Maltby* 3G **83**
Oakwell La. *B'ley* 6A **14**
Oakwell Ter. *B'ley* 1A **24**
Oakwell Vw. *B'ley* 1A **24**
Oakwood Av. *S5* 2D **74**
Oakwood Av. *Roy* 1E **9**

Oakwood Clo. *Wors* 5C **24**
Oakwood Cres. *Rawm* 6E **55**
Oakwood Cres. *Roy* 1D **8**
Oakwood Cres. *Worr* 4D **72**
Oakwood Dri. *Arm* 4E **35**
Oakwood Dri. *Bran* 3H **49**
Oakwood Dri. *Roth* 5G **79**
Oakwood Flats. *S5* 2F **87**
Oakwood Gro. *Roth* 5G **79**
Oakwood Hall Dri. *Roth* 1F **91**
Oakwood Rd. *Donc* 4H **45**
Oakwood Rd. *Roy* 1D **8**
Oakwood Rd. E. *Roth* 6G **79**
Oakwood Rd. W. *Roth* 6F **79**
Oakwood Sq. *Dart* 5A **6**
Oakworth Clo. *B'ley* 4D **14**
Oakworth Clo. *Half* 3E **125**
Oakworth Dri. *Half* 3D **124**
Oakworth Gro. *Half* 3D **124**
Oakworth Vw. *Half* 3D **124**
Oasis, The. *S9* 1E **89**
Oates Av. *Rawm* 2F **69**
Oates Clo. *Roth* 2A **78**
Oates Orchard. *Mosb* 3D **124**
Oates St. *Roth* 2A **78**
Oberon Cres. *D'fld* 3D **26**
Occupation La. *S6* 2D **84**
Occupation La. *S12* 4G **113**
Occupation Rd. *Ches* 3H **131**
Occupation Rd. *Harl* 4H **51**
Occupation Rd. *P'gte* 3E **69**
Ochre Dike Clo. *Wat* 5E **115**
Ochre Dike La. *Wat* 5D **114**
Ochre Dike Wlk. *Roth* 3H **67**
Octagon Cen. *S10* 2C **98**
. . . . *(off Western Bank)*
Octavia Clo. *B'wth* 1C **90**
Odom Ct. *S2* 1F **111**
Ogden Pl. *S8* 1E **123**
Ogden Rd. *Donc* 1B **34**
Oil Mill Fold. *Roth* 3D **78**
Oldale Clo. *S13* 2C **114**
Oldale Ct. *S13* 1C **114**
Oldale Gro. *S13* 2C **114**
Old Anna La. *P'stne* 3A **142**
Old Bakery Clo. *Old W* 1A **132**
Old Brick Works La. *Ches* 5A **132**
Old Clifton La. *Roth* 3F **79**
Oldcotes Clo. *Dinn* 3F **107**
Oldcotes Rd. *Dinn* 2F **107**
Old Cottage Clo. *S13* 6D **102**
Old Cross La. *Wath D* 4F **41**
Old Cubley. 6C **142**
Old Denaby. 2G **57**
Old Denaby Wetlands Nature Reserve.
. . . . .2G **57**
Old Doncaster Rd. *Wath D* 5H **41**
Old Edlington. 6A **60**
Old Farm Ct. *Mexb* 5C **42**
Oldfield Av. *Con* 3B **58**
Oldfield Clo. *S6* 5D **84**
Oldfield Clo. *Barn D* 1F **21**
Oldfield Clo. *Hoy* 5A **38**
Oldfield Rd. *S6* 6B **84**
Oldfield Rd. *Roth* 2B **80**
Old Fld. Shutt La. *Roth* 1D **80**
Oldfield Ter. *S6* 6D **84**
Old Forge Bus. Pk. *S2* 6E **99**
. . . . *(off Guernsey Rd.)*
Old Fulwood Rd. *S10* 6D **96**
Old Garden Dri. *Roth* 2G **79**
Old Ga. La. *Thry* 6B **70**
Old Guildhall Yd. *Donc* 6C **32**
Old Hall Clo. *Braml* 4H **81**
Old Hall Clo. *Lghtn* 1D **106**
Old Hall Clo. *Spro* 2E **45**
Old Hall Clo. *Tod* 1A **118**
Old Hall Cres. *Ben* 1B **32**
Old Hall Dri. *Braml* 4H **81**
Old Hall Farm. *K'wth* 2G **77**
Old Hall La. *Braml* 4H **81**
. . . . *(off Old Hall Dri.)*
Old Hall M. *Braml* 4H **81**
Old Hall Pl. *Ben* 1B **32**
Old Hall Rd. *S9* 4C **88**
Old Hall Rd. *Ben* 1B **32**
Old Hall Rd. *Ches* 3F **137**
Old Hall Rd. *Wors* 1B **36**
Oldhay Clo. *S17* 3D **120**
Old Hay Gdns. *S17* 3C **120**
Old Hay La. *S17* 4C **120**

Old Haywoods. 3G 141
Old Hellaby La. H'by 4B 82
Old Hexthorpe. Donc 2H 45
Old Hill. Con 3E 59
Old Hill La. Roth 2D 80
Old Ho. Clo. H'fld 4E 39
Old Ho. Rd. Ches 5F 131
Old Houses. Ches 2C 138
Old Kirk Sandall. 3C 20
Old La. Half 2G 125
Old La. O'bri 3A 72
Old Mnr. Dri. Oxs 6H 143
Old Mkt. Pl. Womb 1F 39
Old Mill. .4A 14
Old Mill Dri. Ches 4C 130
Old Mill La. B'ley 5G 13
Old Mill Rd. Con 4F 59
Old Moor La. Wath D 2C 40
Old Moor Wetland Cen. (Nature Reserve)
. . . . .1D 40
Old Moor Wetland Cen. Vis. Cen.
. . . . .2C 40
Old Pk. Av. S8 . . . . .2B 122
Old Pk. Rd. S8 . . . . .2B 122
Old Peverel Rd. Duck 6E 135
Old Quarry Av. Kiv P 4F 117
Old Retford Rd. S13 . . . . .5C 102
Oldridge Clo. Ches 5D 130
Old Rd. B'ley 2A 14
Old Rd. Ches 2C 136
Old Rd. Con 5B 58
Old Row. Else 6D 38
Old School Clo. Arm 3F 35
Old School Clo. Hoy 4A 38
Old School Clo. Roth 3C 68
Old School Ct. Bar G 2A 12
Old School Dri. S5 . . . . .4F 75
Old School La. Cal 3F 139
Old School La. Cat 5D 90
Old School La. Wadw 6H 61
Old Sheffield Rd. Roth 4D 78
Old Ship La. Ches 3A 138
Old Sta. Dri. S7 . . . . .4B 110
Old Sta. Yd. Brim 3C 132
Old St. S2 . . . . .1G 99 (2H 5)
Old Town. 4E 13
Old Town Hall. Roth 2D 78
(off Howard St.)
Old Warren Va. Rawm 6F 55
Oldwell Clo. S17 . . . . .5D 120
Old Wheel. 3B 84
Old Whittington. 1A 132
Old Wortley Rd. Roth 1G 77
Old Yew Ga. Whar S 1E 73
Olive Clo. Swal 6B 104
Olive Cres. S8 . . . . .5C 112
Olive Gro. Rd. S2 . . . . .6F 99
Olive Rd. Mosb 2D 124
Olive Rd. S'bri 3D 140
Oliver Rd. S7 . . . . .3A 110
Oliver Rd. Donc 4A 46
Olivers Dri. S9 . . . . .1F 101
Olivers Mt. S9 . . . . .1F 101
Oliver St. Mexb 6D 42
Olivers Way. Cat 4B 90
Olive Ter. S6 . . . . .4D 84
Olivet Rd. S8 . . . . .4D 110
Ollerton Rd. B'ley 4B 8
Onchan Rd. S6 . . . . .6E 85
Onesacre. 2B 72
Onesacre. O'bri 2B 72
Onesmoor Bottom. S6 & O'bri 3A 72
Onslow Rd. S11 . . . . .6H 97
Orange St. S1 . . . . .2D 98 (3C 4)
Orchard Av. Ans 6E 107
Orchard Clo. S5 . . . . .2F 75
Orchard Clo. B'ley 2C 14
Orchard Clo. Cat 5D 90
Orchard Clo. Kirk S 3C 20
Orchard Clo. Lghtn 6G 95
Orchard Clo. M'well 4F 7
Orchard Clo. Mexb 6E 43
Orchard Cres. S5 . . . . .2F 75
Orchard Cft. Dart 5C 6
Orchard Cft. Dod 3C 22
Orchard Cft. Dron 2F 129
Orchard Cft. Wal 4F 117
Orchard Flatts Cres. Roth 5A 68
Orchard Gdns. Ans 3F 119
Orchard Gro. Maltby 3D 82
Orchard La. S1 . . . . .2E 99 (3D 4)
Orchard La. Beig 5F 115
Orchard La. Cusw 4F 31

Orchard La. Wal 5F 117
Orchard Lea Dri. Swal 6B 104
Orchard M. B'ley 4G 13
Orchard M. Donc 4H 31
Orchard Pl. Cud 2H 15
Orchard Pl. Kil 3B 126
Orchard Pl. Roth 3C 78
Orchard Pl. Wath D 5D 40
Orchard Rd. S6 . . . . .5A 86
Orchard Sq. S1 . . . . .2E 99 (3E 5)
Orchard Sq. Dron W 1B 128
Orchard Sq. Shop. Cen. S1 . . .2E 99 (3E 5)
Orchard St. S1 . . . . .2E 99 (3E 5)
Orchard St. Deep 4H 141
Orchard St. Donc 2B 46
Orchard St. Gold 5G 29
Orchard St. O'bri 2D 72
Orchard St. Womb 6B 26
Orchards Way. Ches 4E 137
Orchard, The. Ans 1G 119
Orchard, The. Thurn 2E 29
Orchard Vw. Rd. Ches 1E 137
Orchard Vs. Thry 5D 70
Orchard Wlk. B'ley 4H 13
Orchard Way. B'wth 4C 90
Orchard Way. Thurn 1F 29
Orchard Wells. Wick 5G 81
Orchid Clo. Cal 2G 139
Orchid Way. Ans 3E 119
Ordnance Ter. Roth 3H 77
(off Up. Clara St.)
Orgreave. 3B 102
Orgreave Clo. S13 . . . . .4C 102
Orgreave Cres. S13 . . . . .4C 102
Orgreave Dri. S13 . . . . .4C 102
Orgreave Ho. Donc 1C 46
(off Burden Clo.)
Orgreave La. S13 . . . . .4A 102
Orgreave Pl. S13 . . . . .3B 102
Orgreave Ri. S13 . . . . .5D 102
Orgreave Rd. S13 . . . . .4B 102
Orgreave Rd. Cat 6C 90
Orgreave Way. S13 . . . . .5C 102
Oriel Mt. S10 . . . . .6C 96
Oriel Rd. S10 . . . . .6D 96
Oriel Way. B'ley 4D 14
Ormesby Clo. Dron W 2A 128
Ormesby Cres. Donc 4G 31
Ormesby Way. Braml 1E 81
Ormes Mdw. Owl 5C 114
Ormond Clo. S8 . . . . .3F 123
Ormond Clo. Walt 6D 136
Ormond Dri. S8 . . . . .3F 123
Ormonde Way. New R 5C 62
Ormond Rd. S8 . . . . .3F 123
Ormond Way. S8 . . . . .2F 123
Ormsby Clo. Donc 1G 61
Ormsby Rd. Ches 4H 131
Orpen Dri. S14 . . . . .5A 112
Orpen Way. S14 . . . . .5A 112
Orphanage Rd. S3 . . . . .3F 87
Orwell Clo. Womb 2H 39
Orwins Clo. Ches 4F 131
Osbert Dri. Thur 4A 94
Osberton Pl. S11 . . . . .5B 98
Osberton St. Rawm 1H 69
Osberton St. Wadw 6H 61
Osberton Way. Dalt 6A 70
Osbert Rd. Roth 6H 79
Osborne Av. Ast 5C 104
Osborne Av. W'land 2B 16
Osborne Clo. S11 . . . . .6A 98
Osborne Ct. S11 . . . . .6A 98
Osborne Ct. B'ley 3D 14
Osborne Dri. Tod 2B 118
Osborne M. S11 . . . . .6B 98
Osborne M. B'ley 1A 24
Osborne Rd. S11 . . . . .6A 98
Osborne Rd. Donc 5F 33
Osborne Rd. Kiv P 5B 118
Osborne Rd. Tod 2B 118
Osborne St. B'ley 1A 24
Osborne Wlk. S11 . . . . .1B 110
Osgathorpe Cres. S4 . . . . .3G 87
Osgathorpe Dri. S4 . . . . .3G 87
Osgathorpe Rd. S4 . . . . .3G 87
(in two parts)
Osmaston Rd. S8 . . . . .5D 110
Osmond Dri. Wors 4A 24
Osmond Pl. Wors 4A 24
Osmond Way. Wors 4A 24
Osmund Ct. Eck 6C 124
Osmund Rd. Eck 6B 124

Osprey Av. Birdw 3D 36
Osprey Clo. Adwk S 1D 16
Osprey Gdns. S2 . . . . .3A 100
Osprey Rd. Ast 1C 116
Oswestry Rd. S5 . . . . .5G 75
Oswin Av. Bal 3H 45
Otley Clo. Con 3F 59
Otley Wlk. S6 . . . . .5B 86
Otter St. S9 . . . . .5B 88
Oughtibridge. 2D 72
Oughtibridge Bri. O'bri 2D 72
Oughtibridge La. O'bri 2E 73
Oughton Way. S4 . . . . .4H 87
Oulton Av. Braml 3H 81
Oulton Dri. Cud 6C 10
Oulton Ri. Mexb 5H 43
Our Lady Bridge Chapel. 2D 78
Ouseburn Cft. S9 . . . . .6C 88
Ouseburn Rd. S9 . . . . .1C 100
Ouseburn St. S9 . . . . .6C 88
Ouse Rd. S9 . . . . .6C 88
Ouse Ter. Con 2E 59
Ouson Gdns. B'ley 4E 9
Outgang La. Dinn 2C 106
Outgang La. Maltby 6H 83
(in two parts)
Outram Rd. S2 . . . . .3A 100
Outram Rd. Ches 5H 131
Oval Rd. Roth 2H 79
Oval, The. S5 . . . . .6G 75
Oval, The. Ans 1G 119
Oval, The. Con 2E 59
Oval, The. Donc 2A 48
Oval, The. W'land 1B 16
Overcroft Ri. S17 . . . . .5D 120
Overdale Av. Wors 3B 24
Overdale Gdns. S17 . . . . .3C 120
Overdale Ri. S17 . . . . .3C 120
Overdale Rd. Womb 2G 39
Overend Clo. S14 . . . . .3H 111
Overend Dri. S14 . . . . .3H 111
Overend Rd. S14 . . . . .3H 111
Overend Way. S14 . . . . .3H 111
Oversley Rd. Donc 3F 33
Oversley St. S9 . . . . .6G 77
Overton Clo. Stav 1D 134
Overton Rd. S6 . . . . .1H 85
Owen Clo. S6 . . . . .3B 74
Owen Clo. Roth 1E 79
Owen Falls Av. Ches 2C 138
Owen Pl. S6 . . . . .3B 74
Owen Wlk. S6 . . . . .3B 74
Owler Car La. Coal A 5H 123
Owler Ga. Whar S 1A 72
Owler La. S4 . . . . .2H 87
(in three parts)
Owlerton. 3B 86
Owlerton Grn. S6 . . . . .3B 86
Owlerton Sports Stadium. 2B 86
Owlet La. S4 . . . . .2A 88
Owlings Pl. S6 . . . . .3G 85
Owlings Rd. S6 . . . . .2G 85
Owlthorpe. 5B 114
Owlthorpe Clo. Mosb 1B 124
Owlthorpe Dri. Mosb 1B 124
Owlthorpe Greenway. Wat 6D 114
Owlthorpe Gro. Mosb 1B 124
Owlthorpe La. Mosb 1B 124
Owlthorpe Ri. Mosb 1B 124
Owram St. D'fld 4E 27
Ox Carr. Arm 3E 35
Oxclose. .3G 125
Ox Clo. Av. Roth 4G 121
Ox Clo. Av. Roth 6G 67
Oxclose Dri. Dron W 2A 128
Oxclose La. Dron W 2A 128
Oxclose Pk. Gdns. Half 3F 125
Oxclose Pk. Rd. Half 2F 125
Oxclose Pk. Rd. N. Half 2F 125
Oxclose Pk. Vw. Half 3F 125
Oxclose Pk. Way. Half 3F 125
Oxford Clo. Brim 3F 133
Oxford Clo. Roth 4C 68
Oxford Pl. Donc 1C 46
Oxford Pl. S'foot 1E 25
Oxford Rd. Brim 3F 133
Oxford St. S6 . . . . .1B 98 (1A 4)
Oxford St. B'ley 2A 24
Oxford St. Mexb 6C 42
Oxford St. New R 4C 62
Oxford St. Roth 2G 79
Oxford St. S'foot 1E 25

Oxford Vs. Roth 2G 79
(off Oxford St.)
Ox Hill. Half .4G 125
Oxley Clo. S'bri 3C 140
Oxley Ct. Roth 5F 79
Oxley Gro. Roth 5F 79
Oxspring. 6H 143
Oxspring Bank. S5 . . . . .1B 86
Oxspring La. Oxs 3G 143
Oxted Rd. S9 . . . . .1C 88
Oxton Dri. Warm 5F 45
Oxton Rd. B'ley 5B 8

P

Packhorse La. High G 5C 50
Packington Rd. Donc 4E 49
Packman La. H'hill 6D 118
Packman Rd. Wath D 4B 40
(Brampton Rd.)
Packman Rd. Wath D & Rawm 6C 40
(Rotherham Rd.)
Packmans Clo. Gren 6A 64
Packmans Way. Gren 6A 64
Packman Way. Wath D 5B 40
Packwood Clo. Maltby 3H 83
Paddington Clo. Dinn 3C 106
Paddock Clo. Donc 4G 31
Paddock Clo. M'well 4G 7
Paddock Cres. S2 . . . . .2A 112
Paddock Cft. Swint 2H 55
Paddock Dri. S'side 2G 81
Paddock Gro. Cud 6C 10
Paddock Rd. M'well 4G 7
Paddocks, The. Ast 6C 104
Paddocks, The. Donc 4F 31
Paddocks, The. Mas M 1G 135
Paddocks, The. Rav 1H 81
Paddocks, The. Thry 5E 71
Paddock, The. Adw S 1E 17
Paddock, The. Barn D 1G 21
Paddock, The. D'fld 3E 27
Paddock, The. H'fld 3E 39
Paddock, The. Scho 3D 66
Paddock Vw. Tod 2A 118
(Holmesdale Rd.)
Paddock Way. Dron 6F 123
(Stonelow Rd.)
Paddock Way. Dron 1F 129
Padley Clo. Dod 2A 22
Padley Wlk. S5 . . . . .5H 75
Padley Way. S5 . . . . .5G 75
Padua Ri. D'fld 4D 26
Page Hall Rd. S4 . . . . .2H 87
Pagenall Dri. Swal 5B 104
Paget St. S9 .4B 88
Pagnell Av. Thurn 2D 28
Paisley Clo. Stav 3A 134
Palermo Fold. D'fld 3D 26
Palgrave Cres. S5 . . . . .5C 74
Palgrave Rd. S5 . . . . .5B 74
Palington Gro. Donc 2C 48
Pall Mall. B'ley 6H 13
Palm Av. Arm 2G 35
Palmer Clo. P'stne 6C 142
Palmer Cres. Dron 2F 129
Palmer Rd. S9 . . . . .5E 89
Palmersgate. Ches 2A 138
(off Parker's Row)
Palmerston Av. Maltby 3E 83
Palmerston Rd. S10 . . . . .2B 98
Palmer St. S9 . . . . .6B 88
Palmer St. Donc 2E 47
Palmers Way. Thur 5H 93
Palm La. S6 .5A 86
Palm St. S6 .5A 86
Palm St. B'ley 4F 13
Pamela Dri. Warm 5E 45
Pangbourne Rd. Thurn 1E 29
Pantry Grn. Wors 5C 24
Pantry Hill. Wors 4C 24
Pantry Well. Wors 5C 24
Paper Mill Rd. S5 . . . . .2A 76
Parade, The. S12 . . . . .1C 112
Parade, The. Hoy 6H 37
Parade, The. Rawm 6E 55
Paradise La. S1 . . . . .2E 5
Paradise Sq. S1 . . . . .1E 99 (2E 5)
Paradise St. S1 . . . . .1E 99 (2E 5)
Parish Way. B'ley 4D 14

Park Av. S10 .5H 97
Park Av. Ans & Dinn 6E 107
Park Av. Arm .2D 34
Park Av. B'ley (S70) 6G 13
Park Av. B'ley (S71) 6B 8
Park Av. Brie .2H 11
Park Av. C'town 3E 65
Park Av. Con .4E 59
Park Av. Cud .6B 10
Park Av. Dron 1F 129
Park Av. Grim 5G 11
Park Av. Mexb 6E 43
Park Av. P'stne 4C 142
Park Av. Roy 2F 9
Park Av. Spro .2E 45
Park Av. Tree .1F 103
Park Av. Whis 1A 92
Park Clo. Arm .3F 35
Park Clo. Ches 6A 138
Park Clo. M'well 5G 7
Park Clo. Spro 2E 45
Park Clo. Swint 2A 56
Park Clo. Thry 5D 70
Park Cotts. Wors 6A 24
Park Ct. Gren 1A 74
Park Ct. Thurn 1F 29
Park Cres. S10 . . . . .3B 98
Park Cres. Bol D 1B 42
Park Cres. E'fld 1F 75
Park Cres. Roy 2F 9
Park Cres. Warm 6E 45
Park Dri. Ches 4B 138
Park Dri. Spro 2D 44
Park Dri. S'bgh 5D 22
Park Dri. S'bri 3D 140
Park Dri. Swal 6H 103
Park Dri. Way. S'bri 2D 140
Park End Rd. Gold 5F 29
Parker Av. Cal 1F 139
Parker's La. S10 . . . . .2A 98
Parkers La. S17 . . . . .1D 120
Parker's Rd. S10 . . . . .2A 98
Parkers Row. Ches 2A 138
Parker's Ter. Birdw 4C 36
Parker St. B'ley 6F 13
Parkers Yd. Ches 2B 138
Park Farm. Dron W 1A 128
Parkfield Ct. P'gte 4F 69
(off Naylor St.)
Parkfield Pl. S2 . . . . .5E 99
Parkfield Rd. Roth 3F 79
Parkgate. 4F 69
Parkgate Av. Con 3C 58
Parkgate Bus. Pk. P'gte 5F 69
Parkgate Clo. Mosb 1A 124
Parkgate Ct. P'gte 5E 69
(off Gateway, The)
Parkgate Dri. Mosb 6A 114
Parkgate Dri. Mosb 6A 114
Pk. Grange Cft. S2 . . . . .5G 99
Pk. Grange Cft. S2 . . . . .4G 99
Pk. Grange Dri. S2 . . . . .5G 99
Pk. Grange Mt. S2 . . . . .5G 99
Pk. Grange Ri. S2 . . . . .5G 99
Pk. Grange Rd. S2 . . . . .4G 99
Pk. Grange Vw. S2 . . . . .6H 99
Park Gro. B'ley 6G 13
Park Gro. Braml 4H 81
Park Gro. Rawm 6F 55
Park Gro. S'bri 2D 140
Pk. Hall Av. Walt 5C 136
Pk. Hall Clo. Walt 6D 136
Pk. Hall Gdns. Walt 5D 136
Parkhead. 3F 109
(Hemsworth)
Park Head. 6D 84
(Stannington)
Parkhead Clo. Roy 1C 8
Parkhead Ct. S11 . . . . .3F 109
Parkhead Cres. S11 . . . . .3F 109
Parkhead Rd. S11 . . . . .4E 109
Park Hill. 2H 99 (3H 5)
Park Hill. Barn D 2E 21
Park Hill. D'fld 3F 27
Park Hill. Eck 6E 125
Park Hill. Swal 6H 103
Parkhill Cres. Barn D 2H 21
Pk. Hill Gdns. Swal 6H 103
Pk. Hill Gro. Dod 1B 22
Parkhill Rd. Barn D 2H 21
Pk. Hill Rd. Womb 6C 26
Park Hollow. Womb 1G 39
Park Ho. La. S9 . . . . .2H 89

Parkinson St. Donc 4D 32
Parkland Dri. Ross 4F 63
Parklands. E'thpe 6D 20
Parklands Av. Dinn 5E 107
Parklands Clo. Ross 4E 63
Parklands Vw. Ast 2C 116
Parkland Vw. Lund 2F 15
Park La. S9 . . . . .6E 77
Park La. S10 .3B 98
Park La. C'town 4E 51
Park La. Ches 4H 131
Park La. Con & Rav . . . . .6C 58 & 1A 82
(in two parts)
Park La. Dinn 3C 106
Park La. Donc 1A 48
Park La. D'ville 4H 21
Park La. P'stne 4C 142
Park La. S'bri 2E 141
Park La. Thry .5D 70
Pk. Lane Ct. Thry 4D 70
Pk. Lane Rd. D'ville 3H 21
Park Mt. Roth .3E 79
Park Nook. Thry 5C 70
Park Pl. Roth .2H 79
Park Rd. S6 . . . . .5F 85
Park Rd. B'ley 2F 23
Park Rd. Ben .6A 18
Park Rd. Brie .2H 11
Park Rd. Ches 2A 138
(off New Beetwell St.)
Park Rd. Ches 4H 137
(Boythorpe Rd.)
Park Rd. Con .4D 58
Park Rd. Donc 6D 32
Park Rd. Grim 6G 11
Park Rd. Mexb 6E 43
Park Rd. Roth 2H 79
Park Rd. Swint 3H 55
Park Rd. Thurn 1E 29
Park Rd. Wath D 6E 41
Park Rd. Wors 6A 24
Park Side. 6D 84
Parkside. Car .4F 9
Parkside. Ches 4A 132
Parkside La. S6 . . . . .6D 84
Parkside M. Wors B 4A 24
Parkside Rd. S6 . . . . .2A 86
Parkside Rd. Hoy 1F 51
Parkside Shop. Cen. Kil 2B 126
Parkside Vw. Ches 5D 130
Parkson Rd. Roth 1H 91
Pk. Spring Dri. S2 . . . . .5G 99
Pk. Spring Rd. Grim . . . . .6F 11 & 1F 27
(in two parts)
Pk. Spring Way. S2 . . . . .5G 99
Park Sq. S2 . . . . .2F 99 (2G 5)
Parkstone Cres. H'by 5B 82
Parkstone Delph. S12 . . . . .5C 112
Parkstone Way. Donc 2A 34
Park St. B'ley 1G 23
Park St. Ches 6A 138
Park St. Rawm 1F 69
Park St. Roth .2B 78
Park St. Swal 4A 104
Park St. Womb 1G 39
Park Ter. C'town 3F 65
Park Ter. Donc 6D 32
Park Ter. Thry 5C 70
Park, The. W'land 4C 16
Pk. Vale Dri. Thry 5D 70
Park Vw. Adw S 2E 17
Park Vw. B'ley 2F 23
Park Vw. Brie .2H 11
Park Vw. Dod .2B 22
Park Vw. Has 6D 138
Park Vw. Kiv P 4A 118
Park Vw. Maltby 4H 83
(in two parts)
Park Vw. Mexb 6C 42
Park Vw. Roy 1F 9
Park Vw. Shaf 3C 10
Park Vw. Thpe H 3A 66
Park Vw. Wors 4B 24
Pk. View Av. Half 2E 125
Parkview Ct. S8 . . . . .5E 111
Pk. View Rd. S6 . . . . .2A 86
Pk. View Rd. C'town 3E 65
Pk. View Rd. M'well 4H 7
Pk. View Rd. Roth 4E 77
Park Wlk. S2 . . . . .1H 99
(off St John's Rd.)
Park Way. Adw S 1D 16
Parkway. Arm 4F 35

Parkway Av. *S9* 1B **100**
Parkway Clo. *S9* 1B **100**
Parkway Dri. *S9* 2C **100**
Parkway Mkt. *S9* 1D **100**
Parkway N. *Donc* 3F **33**
Parkway S. *Donc* 3F **33**
Parkwood Ind. Est. *S3* 5E **87**
Parkwood Ri. *Barn D* 2E **21**
Parkwood Rd. *S3* 4C **86**
Parkwood Rd. N. *S5* 1D **86**
Parkwood Springs. 4D **86**
Parliament St. *S11* 4C **98**
Parma Ri. *D'fld* 4C **26**
Parsley Hay Clo. *S13* 4H **101**
Parsley Hay Dri. *S13* 4H **101**
Parsley Hay Gdns. *S13* 4H **101**
Parsley Hay Rd. *S13* 4H **101**
Parsonage Clo. *Mosb* 3D **124**
Parsonage Ct. *S6* 5A **86**
(off Parsonage Cres.)
Parsonage Cres. *S6* 5A **86**
Parsonage St. *S6* 5A **86**
Parson Cross. 4D **74**
Parson Cross Rd. *S6* 5A **74**
Parson La. *Dod* 3A **22**
Partridge Clo. *Eck* 6B **124**
Partridge Flatt Rd. *Donc* 5D **48**
Partridge Pl. *Ast* 1C **116**
Partridge Ri. *Donc* 5D **48**
Partridge Rd. *Barn D* 2H **71**
Partridge Vw. *S2* 3A **100**
Parwich Clo. *Ches* 6C **130**
Pashley Cft. *Womb* 1D **38**
Passfield Rd. *New R* 5E **63**
Passhouses Rd. *S4* 3F **87**
Pasture Clo. *Arm* 4E **35**
(in two parts)
Pasture Ct. *Ross* 5F **63**
Pasture Cft. *Thur* 4B **94**
Pasture Gro. *Eck* 6C **124**
Pasture La. *Bol D* 5H **27**
Pastures Rd. *Mexb* 6H **43**
Pastures, The. *Tod* 2A **118**
Paternoster Row. *S1* 3F **99** (5F **5**)
Paterson Clo. *S'bri* 2C **140**
Paterson Ct. *S'bri* 2C **140**
Paterson Cft. *S'bri* 2C **140**
Paterson Gdns. *S'bri* 2C **140**
Paterson Rd. *Dinn* 4G **107**
Patmore Rd. *S5* 5H **75**
Paton Gro. *Brim* 3D **132**
Patrick Stirling Ct. *Donc* 2A **46**
Patterdale Clo. *Dron W* 2C **128**
Patterdale Way. *Ans* 1H **119**
Pavement, The. *S2* 3H **5**
Pavilion Clo. *Brie* 2G **11**
Pavilion Clo. *Ink* 4A **134**
Pavilion La. *B'wth* 1B **90**
Pavilion Way. *S5* 5H **75**
Pavillion Clo. *Edl'tn* 2C **60**
Paxton Ct. *S14* 3B **112**
Paxton Cres. *Arm* 2D **34**
Paxton La. *S10* 3B **98**
Paxton Rd. *Ches* 6C **132**
Peacehaven. *Barn D* 2H **21**
Peacock Clo. *Kil* 3A **126**
Peacock Clo. *Thpe H* 1B **66**
Peacock Heritage Cen. 2A **138**
Peak Chase. *Brie* 3G **11**
Peak Clo. *S'side* 2F **81**
Peakdale Cres. *S12* 2G **113**
Peake Av. *Con* 3C **58**
Peak La. *Hoot L* 6E **83**
Peakley Hill. 6A **128**
Peak Pl. *Ink* 4B **134**
Peak Rd. *B'ley* 6C **8**
Peaks Mt. *Cry P* 4E **115**
Peak Sq. *Cry P* 5E **115**
Peakstone Clo. *Bal* 4H **45**
Peakstone M. *Rawm* 2F **69**
Peak Vw. Rd. *Ches* 1F **137**
Pearce Rd. *S9* 2E **101**
Pearce Wlk. *S9* 1E **101**
Pearl St. *S11* 5C **98**
Pearmain Dri. *Maltby* 3D **82**
Pea Royd La. *S'bri* 2E **141**
Pearson Cres. *Womb* 4H **25**
Pearson Cft. *Ches* 5E **131**
Pearson Pl. *S8* 2D **110**
Pearson's Clo. *Roth* 5A **80**
Pearson's Fld. *Womb* 6B **26**
Pearson St. *S'bri* 2D **140**
Pear St. *S11* 4C **98**

Pear Tree Av. *Braml* 4H **81**
Peartree Av. *Thurn* 1E **29**
Pear Tree Clo. *B'wth* 3D **90**
Pear Tree Clo. *Holl* 3G **133**
Pear Tree Clo. *Kil* 4A **126**
Pear Tree Ct. *Thurn* 1E **29**
Peartree Orchard. *Roy* 1F **9**
Pear Tree Rd. *S5* 3H **75**
Pearwood Cres. *Donc* 6H **45**
Peasehill Clo. *B'ley* 1G **23**
Peashill St. *Rawm* 2F **69**
Peatfield Rd. *Kil* 2D **126**
Peckham Rd. *High G* 1D **64**
Peck Mill Vw. *Kiv S* 6D **118**
Pedley Av. *W'fld* 6E **115**
Pedley Clo. *W'fld* 6E **115**
Pedley Dri. *W'fld* 1E **125**
Pedley Gro. *W'fld* 6E **115**
Peel Clo. *Maltby* 3E **83**
Peel Gdns. *Dron* 2D **128**
Peel Pde. *B'ley* 6G **13**
Peel Pl. *B'ley* 4A **14**
Peel Sq. *B'ley* 6G **13**
Peel St. *S10* 3A **98**
Peel St. *B'ley* 2H **23**
(Highstone Rd.)
Peel St. *B'ley* 6G **13**
(Peel Sq.)
Peel St. Arc. *B'ley* 6G **13**
Peel Ter. *S10* 2C **98** (4A **4**)
Peet Wlk. *Jump* 4B **38**
Peg Folly. *S'bri* 3A **140**
Peggy La. *E'fld* 6A **66**
Peggy La. *Gren* 6B **64**
Pell's Clo. *Donc* 6C **32**
Pembrey Ct. *Soth* 5G **115**
Pembridge Ct. *Roy* 1E **9**
(off Ruston Dri.)
Pembroke Av. *Donc* 5A **46**
(in two parts)
Pembroke Clo. *Ches* 4E **137**
Pembroke Ct. *Ches* 4G **131**
Pembroke Cres. *High G* 1B **64**
Pembroke Ri. *Ans* 3F **119**
Pembroke Rd. *Donc* 3F **31**
Pembroke Rd. *Dron* 3E **129**
Pembroke St. *S11* 4C **98**
Pembroke St. *Roth* 3H **77**
Pendeen Rd. *S11* 5F **97**
Pendlebury Gro. *Roy* 6G **37**
Pendle Cft. *Soth* 6H **115**
Pendon Ho. *P'stne* 4D **142**
Pengeston Rd. *P'stne* 4B **142**
Penistone. 4D **142**
Penistone Ct. *P'stne* 4E **143**
Penistone Rd. *S6* 2A **86**
Penistone Rd. *C'town & Gren* 1A **64**
Penistone Rd. *Gren* 1B **74**
Penistone Rd. N. *S6* 6A **74**
Penistone Sports Cen. 3B **142**
Penistone St. *Donc* 5D **32**
Penley St. *S11* 5D **98**
Penmore Clo. *Has* 4C **138**
Penmore Gdns. *Has* 5C **138**
Penmore La. *Has* 5C **138**
Penmore St. *Has* 5C **138**
Pennine Cen., The. *S1* 2D **4**
Pennine Clo. *Dart* 3E **7**
Pennine Gdns. *Maltby* 3D **82**
Pennine Vw. *Dart* 3E **7**
Pennine Vw. *S'bri* 5D **140**
Pennine Way. *B'ley* 5D **12**
Pennine Way. *Ches* 6E **131**
Pen Nook Clo. *Deep* 5F **141**
Pen Nook Dri. *Deep* 5G **141**
Pen Nook Dri. *Deep* 5G **141**
Pen Nook Gdns. *Deep* 5G **141**
Pen Nook Glade. *Deep* 4G **141**
Penns Rd. *S2* 1G **111**
Penny Engine La. *Eck* 5E **125**
Penny Hill La. *Ulley & Thur* 1D **104**
Pennyholme Clo. *Kiv P* 5B **118**
Penny La. *S17* 5C **120**
Penny Piece La. *Ans* 1F **119**
Penny Piece Pl. *Ans* 1F **119**
Penrhyn Rd. *S11* 6A **98**
Penrhyn Wlk. *B'ley* 1G **25**
Penrith Clo. *S5* 1C **86**
Penrith Cres. *S5* 1C **86**
Penrith Gro. *B'ley* 1F **25**
Penrith Rd. *S5* 1C **86**
Penrith Rd. *Donc* 5A **34**
Penrose Pl. *S13* 1A **114**

Penthorpe Clo. *S12* 1D **112**
Pentland Clo. *Ches* 6E **131**
Pentland Gdns. *Wat* 5D **114**
Pentland Rd. *Dron W* 2B **128**
Penton St. *S1* 2E **99** (3D **4**)
Penyghent Clo. *C'town* 1D **64**
Pepper Clo. *Roth* 5F **67**
Pepper St. *Hoy* 3A **38**
Percy St. *S3* 6D **86**
Percy St. *Roth* 3E **79**
Peregrine Dri. *Birdw* 3D **36**
Peregrine Way. *H'hill* 4H **127**
(in two parts)
Perigree Rd. *S8* 4C **110**
Periwood Av. *S8* 4C **110**
Periwood Clo. *S8* 4C **110**
Periwood Dri. *S8* 4C **110**
Periwood Gro. *S8* 4C **110**
Periwood La. *S8* 4C **110**
Perkyn Rd. *S5* 2H **75**
Perkyn Ter. *S5* 2H **75**
Perran Gro. *Cusw* 4H **31**
Perseverance St. *B'ley* 6F **13**
Persimmon Clo. *New R* 6D **62**
Perth Clo. *Mexb* 5G **43**
Petal Clo. *Maltby* 3H **83**
Peterborough Clo. *S10* 5A **96**
Peterborough Dri. *S10* 5A **96**
Peterborough Rd. *S10* 4A **96**
Peterdale Clo. *Brim* 3E **133**
Peterdale Rd. *Brim* 3E **133**
Peterfoot Way. *B'ley* 4D **8**
Petersgate. *Donc* 1H **31**
Peter St. *Edl'tn* 4B **60**
Peter St. *Roth* 2G **77**
Peter St. *Thur* 4A **94**
Peters Yd. *Roth* 2G **77**
(off Peter St.)
Petre Dri. *S4* 4H **87**
Petre St. *S4* 4H **87**
Pettyclose La. *Ches* 6D **132**
Petunia Rd. *Kirk S* 4D **20**
Petworth Cft. *Roy* 1D **8**
Petworth Dri. *S11* 5F **109**
Pevensey Av. *Ches* 5G **131**
Peveril Clo. *Ches* 4G **131**
Peveril Clo. *Kiv P* 4A **118**
Peveril Cres. *B'ley* 6H **13**
Peveril Rd. *S11* 6H **97**
Peveril Rd. *Ches* 4H **131**
Peveril Rd. *Donc* 5G **45**
Peveril Rd. *Eck* 5E **125**
Pexton Rd. *S4* 3G **87**
Pheasant Bank. *Ross* 4E **63**
Philadelphia. 5D **86**
Philadelphia Dri. *S6* 6C **86**
Philadelphia Gdns. *S6* 6C **86**
Philadelphia Gro. *S6* 6C **86**
Philip La. *Wort* 5A **50**
Philip Rd. *B'ley* 2D **24**
Phillimore Rd. *S9* 5D **88**
Phillips Rd. *S6* 2D **84**
Phoenix Ct. *S12* 6G **113**
Phoenix Golf Course. 1B **90**
Phoenix Gro. *B'wth* 1B **90**
Phoenix La. *Thurn* 2G **29**
Phoenix Rd. *S12* 6G **113**
Piccadilly. 4A **56**
Piccadilly. *Ben* 1A **32**
Piccadilly Rd. *Ches* 3B **138**
Piccadilly Rd. *Swint* 4A **56**
Pickard Cres. *S13* 5F **101**
Pickard Dri. *S13* 5G **101**
Pickburn La. *Pick* 4A **16**
Pickering Cres. *Swal* 1H **115**
Pickering Rd. *S3* 4A **18**
Pickering Rd. *Ben* 4A **18**
Pickhill's Av. *Gold* 4H **29**
Picking La. *E'fld* 1F **75**
Pickmere Rd. *S10* 1H **97**
Pickton Clo. *Ches* 3F **137**
Pickup Cres. *Womb* 2F **39**
Pickwick Dri. *Cat* 5B **90**
Piece End. *High G* 5B **50**
(in two parts)
Piece End Clo. *High G* 5B **50**
Pieces N., The. *Whis* 3H **91**
Pieces S., The. *Whis* 3H **91**
Pigeon Bri. Way. *Ast* 2C **116**
Pighills La. *Coal A* 5F **123**
Pike Clo. *Ches* 6D **130**
Pike Lowe Gro. *M'well* 5H **7**
Pike Rd. *B'wth* 2C **90**

Pilgrim St. *S3* 4F **87**
Pilkington's Yd. *Eck* 6E **125**
(off Station Rd.)
Pilley. 5B **36**
Pilley Green. 6B **36**
Pilley Grn. *Tank* 6B **36**
Pilley Hills. 5A **36**
Pilley La. *Tank* 5B **36**
Pilley La. End. *Tank* 4A **36**
Pinchfield Ct. *Wick* 6F **81**
Pinchfield Holt. *Wick* 1F **93**
Pinchfield La. *Wick* 6F **81**
Pinchmill. 2E **93**
Pinchmill Hollow. *Wick* 1F **93**
Pinch Mill La. *Whis* 2C **92**
Pinchwell Vw. *Wick* 6F **81**
Pindale Av. *Ink* 4A **134**
Pindar Oaks Cotts. *B'ley* 1B **24**
Pindar Oaks St. *B'ley* 1A **24**
Pindar St. *B'ley* 1B **24**
Pine Av. *Ans* 4F **119**
Pine Clo. *B'ley* 3C **24**
Pine Clo. *Hoy* 6A **38**
Pine Clo. *Kil* 4A **126**
Pine Clo. *S'side* 3G **81**
Pine Cft. *C'town* 3E **65**
Pinecroft Way. *C'town* 3E **65**
Pinefield Av. *Barn D* 1E **21**
Pinefield Rd. *Barn D* 1E **21**
Pine Gro. *Con* 5C **58**
Pinehall Dri. *B'ley* 3D **14**
Pine Hall Rd. *Barn D* 1D **20**
Pinehurst Ri. *Swint* 3B **56**
Pine Rd. *Donc* 3D **48**
Pines, The. *S10* 5A **96**
Pines, The. *Wick* 6G **81**
Pine St. *Holl* 3G **133**
Pine Vw. *Ches* 2D **136**
Pine Wlk. *Swint* 5B **56**
Pinewood Av. *Arm* 1F **35**
Pinewood Av. *Donc* 6G **45**
Pinewood Clo. *Dalt* 6B **70**
Pinfold. *Wath D* 5E **41**
Pinfold Clo. *B'ley* 1E **25**
Pinfold Clo. *Holy* 5A **136**
Pinfold Clo. *Swint* 3A **56**
Pinfold Cotts. *Cud* 1H **15**
Pinfold Ct. *Barn D* 1D **20**
Pinfold Gdns. *Cud* 2H **15**
Pinfold Hill. *Wors* 3A **24**
Pinfold Lands. *Mexb* 1F **57**
Pinfold La. *S3* 4E **87**
Pinfold La. *D'fld* 4F **27**
(in two parts)
Pinfold La. *Roth* 4E **79**
Pinfold La. *Roy* 2E **9**
(in two parts)
Pinfold St. *S1* 2E **99** (3D **4**)
Pinfold St. *Eck* 6D **124**
Pingle Av. *S7* 4A **110**
Pingle Grange. *Brim* 4E **133**
Pingle La. *Rav* 5G **71**
Pingle Rd. *S7* 4H **109**
Pingle Rd. *Kil* 2C **126**
Pingles Cres. *Thry* 5C **70**
Pinner Rd. *S11* 5A **98**
Pinstone St. *S1* 3E **99** (5E **5**)
Pioneer Clo. *Wath D* 5A **42**
Pipe Ho. La. *Rawm* 6F **55**
(in two parts)
Piper Clo. *S5* 6E **75**
Piper Ct. *S5* 6E **75**
Piper Cres. *S5* 5E **75**
Pipering La. E. *Donc* 2H **31**
Pipering La. W. *Donc* 2G **31**
Piper La. *Ast* 6D **104**
Piper La. *Old Br* 2A **136**
Piper Rd. *S5* 6F **75**
Pipeyard La. *Eck* 6C **124**
Pippin Ct. *Maltby* 3D **82**
Pipworth Gro. *S2* 4E **101**
Pipworth La. *Eck* 5F **125**
Pipworth Rd. *S2* 4D **100**
Pisgah Ho. Rd. *S10* 2A **98**
Pismire Hill. 5H **75**
Pitchford La. *S10* 4D **96**
Pithouse La. *Wal* 6C **116**
Pit La. *S12* 1C **112**
Pit La. *Thpe H* 3B **66**
Pit La. *Tree* 1F **103**
Pit La. *Womb* 1C **38**
Pitman Rd. *Den M* 2A **58**
Pit Row. *H'fld* 5E **39**

Pitsmoor. 4F **87**
Pitsmoor Rd. *S3* 5E **87**
(in two parts)
Pittam Clo. *Arm* 3F **35**
Pitt Clo. *S1* 4B **4**
Pitt La. *S1* 4B **4**
Pitt La. *M'well* 4E **7**
Pitt St. *S1* 2D **98** (4B **4**)
Pitt St. *B'ley* 6G **13**
Pitt St. *Eck* 6H **125**
Pitt St. *Mexb* 6G **43**
Pitt St. *Roth* 3H **77**
Pitt St. *Womb* 4C **26**
Pitt St. W. *B'ley* 6F **13**
Plane Clo. *Donc* 3D **48**
Plane Dri. *Wick* 4G **81**
Planet Rd. *Adw S* 1E **17**
Plantation Av. *Ans* 1G **119**
Plantation Av. *Dinn* 4F **107**
Plantation Av. *Donc* 1F **63**
Plantation Av. *Roy* 2F **9**
Plantation Clo. *Ches* 6C **130**
Plantation Clo. *Maltby* 3F **83**
Plantation Ct. *Dinn* 4F **107**
Plantation Rd. *S8* 1E **111**
Plantation Rd. *Ark* 1G **19**
Plantation Rd. *Bal* 1H **61**
Plantation Wlk. *Dinn* 4F **107**
(off Plantation Av.)
Plantin Ri. *Half* 2E **125**
Plantin, The. *Half* 2E **125**
Plaster Pits La. *Spro* 5D **30**
Platts Common. 3A **38**
Platts Comn. Ind. Est. *Hoy* 4H **37**
Platts Dri. *Beig* 3G **115**
Platts La. *O'bri* 2E **73**
Platt St. *S3* 5E **87**
Playford Yd. *Hoy* 3H **37**
Pleasant Clo. *S12* 1D **112**
Pleasant Pl. *Ches* 2F **137**
Pleasant Rd. *S12* 1D **112**
Pleasant Vw. *Cud* 3H **15**
Pleasant Vw. St. *B'ley* 3G **13**
Pleasley Rd. *Whis & Aug* 2H **91**
Ploughmans Cft. *Bram* 4H **39**
Plover Ct. *S2* 3A **100**
Plover Ct. *Ross* 4E **63**
Plover Cft. *Thpe H* 1C **66**
Plover Dri. *Birdw* 3D **36**
Plover Way. *Cal* 2F **139**
Plowmans Way. *Roth* 4H **67**
Plowright Clo. *S14* 2H **111**
Plowright Dri. *S14* 2H **111**
Plowright Mt. *S14* 2H **111**
Plowright Way. *S14* 2H **111**
Plumber St. *B'ley* 6F **13**
Plumbley. 3B **124**
Plumbley Hall M. *Mosb* 3C **124**
Plumbley Hall Rd. *Mosb* 2C **124**
Plumbley La. *Mosb* 3B **124**
Plumbleywood La.
Ridg & Mosb 3A **124**
Plum La. *S3* 1E **99** (1E **5**)
Plum Leys. *Tree* 1E **103**
Plumpers Rd. *S9* 1F **89**
Plumpton Av. *Mexb* 5G **43**
Plumpton Ct. *Thurls* 4A **142**
Plumpton Gdns. *Donc* 5E **49**
Plumpton Pk. *Shaf* 3C **10**
Plumpton Pk. Rd. *Donc* 6E **49**
Plum St. *S3* 1E **99** (1E **5**)
Plunket Rd. *Donc* 5F **33**
Plymouth Rd. *S7* 2C **110**
Pocket Handkerchief La. *Tod* 5A **106**
Pocknedge La. *Holy* 4A **136**
Pogmoor. 5D **12**
Pogmoor La. *B'ley* 5D **12**
(in two parts)
Pogmoor Rd. *B'ley* 5D **12**
Pog Well La. *Hghm* 4A **12**
(in two parts)
Point, The. *Roth* 5C **78**
Polka Ct. *S3* 4E **87**
Pollard Av. *S5* 6C **74**
Pollard Cres. *S5* 6C **74**
Pollard Rd. *S5* 6C **74**
Pollard St. *Roth* 3G **77**
Pollitt St. *B'ley* 4F **13**
Pollyfox Way. *Dod* 2B **22**
Pomona St. *S11* 4C **98**
Pond Clo. *S6* 5D **84**
Pond Hill. *S1* 2F **99** (3F **5**)

Pond Rd. *S6* 5D **84**
Ponds Forge International Sports Cen.
. . . . .2F **99** (3G **5**)
Pond Sq. *S1* 3G **5**
Pond St. *S1* 2F **99** (3F **5**)
(in two parts)
Pond St. *B'ley* 1G **23**
(in two parts)
Pond St. *Ches* 3A **138**
Pondwell Dri. *Brim* 4F **133**
Pontefract La. *Bram* 4B **40**
Pontefract Rd. *B'ley* 6H **13**
Pontefract Rd. *Bram* 3B **40**
Pontefract Rd. *Cud & Shaf* 5B **10**
Pool Dri. *Donc* 6F **49**
(in two parts)
Poole Pl. *S9* 1E **101**
Poole Rd. *S9* 1E **101**
Poolsbrook. 3E **135**
Poolsbrook Av. *Pool* 3E **135**
Poolsbrook Country Pk. 4C **134**
Poolsbrook Cres. *Pool* 3E **135**
Poolsbrook Rd. *Duck* 5E **135**
Poolsbrook Sq. *Pool* 3E **135**
Poolsbrook Vw. *Pool* 3E **135**
Pools La. *Roy* 2G **9**
Pool Sq. *S1* 2E **99** (4E **5**)
Pop Av. *Con* 3B **58**
Pop La. *Con* 3E **59**
Poplar Av. *Beig* 2F **115**
Poplar Av. *Ches* 3D **136**
Poplar Av. *Gold* 4G **29**
Poplar Av. *Shaf* 3C **10**
Poplar Av. *S'bri* 4D **140**
Poplar Av. *Thry* 5C **70**
Poplar Clo. *Bran* 2H **49**
Poplar Clo. *Dron* 4G **129**
Poplar Clo. *Kil* 4A **126**
Poplar Clo. *Mexb* 5D **42**
Poplar Clo. *O'bri* 2C **72**
Poplar Dri. *B'wth* 3B **90**
Poplar Dri. *Donc* 3A **34**
Poplar Dri. *Wath D* 1F **55**
Poplar Glade. *Wick* 5F **81**
Poplar Gro. *Con* 5D **58**
Poplar Gro. *Lund* 3E **15**
Poplar Gro. *Rav* 1H **81**
Poplar Gro. *Swint* 2B **56**
Poplar Gro. *Warm* 1C **60**
Poplar Nook. *Kiv P* 4G **117**
Poplar Pl. *Arm* 3F **35**
Poplar Pl. *Ches* 3H **131**
Poplar Ri. *Maltby* 3D **82**
Poplar Rd. *Eck* 6H **125**
Poplar Rd. *O'bri* 2C **72**
Poplar Rd. *Womb* 1G **39**
Poplars Ind. Est., The. *Cat* 6B **90**
Poplars Rd. *B'ley* 2B **24**
Poplars, The. *Con* 4D **58**
Poplar Ter. *Ben* 1B **32**
Poplar Ter. *Roy* 1F **9**
Poplar Way. *Cat* 6B **90**
Popple St. *S4* 2H **87**
Poppyfields Way. *Bran* 4G **49**
Porter Av. *B'ley* 5E **13**
Porter Brook Vw. *S11* 5B **98**
(in two parts)
Porter St. *Stav* 1C **134**
Porter Ter. *S11* 5A **98**
Porter Ter. *B'ley* 5D **12**
Portland Av. *Ast* 6C **104**
Portland Bldgs. *S6* 6C **86**
(off Portland St.)
Portland Bus. Pk. *S13* 3G **101**
Portland Clo. *Ans* 5E **107**
Portland Clo. *Ches* 1A **138**
Portland Ct. *S6* 5C **86**
Portland Ct. La. *S1* 2D **98** (4B **4**)
Portland Pl. *Donc* 6C **32**
Portland Pl. *Maltby* 4G **83**
Portland Rd. *Beig* 5G **115**
Portland Rd. *New R* 6D **62**
Portland St. *S6* 6C **86**
(in two parts)
Portland St. *B'ley* 1B **24**
Portland St. *Swint* 3B **56**
Portobello La. *S1* 2D **98** (3B **4**)
Portobello St. *S1* 2D **98** (3C **4**)
Portsea Rd. *S6* 3H **85**
Pothouse La. *S'bri* 3D **140**
Potterdyke Av. *Rawm* 5F **55**
Potter Hill. 6A **50**

Potter Hill. *Roth* 4C **68**
Potter Hill La. *High G* 6A **50**
Potteric Carr Nature Reserve. 6H **47**
Potteric Carr Rd. *Donc* 2E **47**
Potters Clo. *Old W* 1B **132**
Potters Ga. *High G* 6A **50**
 (in two parts)
Pottery Clo. *Rawm* 2F **69**
Pottery La. E. *Ches* 4B **132**
Pottery La. W. *Ches* 4A **132**
Pottery Row. *Roth* 3F **77**
Poucher St. *Roth* 1D **14**
Poulton St. *B'ley* 6C **24**
Powder Mill La. *Wors* 3A **126**
Powell Dri. *Kil* . . . .
Powell St. *S3* 1C **98** (2A **4**)
Powell St. *Wors* 5B **24**
Powerhouse Sq. *Else* . . . .(off Forge La.)
Powerleague Soccer Cen. 6B **88**
Power Sta. Rd. *Donc* 5B **32**
Powley Rd. *S6* 4B **74**
Poynton Av. *Ulley* 2C **104**
Poynton Dri. *Dinn* 3F **107**
Poynton Way. *Ulley* 2C **104**
Poynton Wood Cres. *S17* 3G **121**
Poynton Wood Glade. *S17* 3G **121**
Prescott Rd. *S6* 1G **85**
President Way. *S4* 5H **87**
Preston Av. *Jump* 4C **38**
Preston St. *S8* 6E **99**
Preston Way. *B'ley* 1D **14**
Prestwich St. *S9* 5D **76**
Prestwold Way. *Ches* 6C **138**
Prestwood Gdns. *C'town* 2C **64**
Priest Cft. La. *B'ley* 1D **26**
Priestfield Gdns. *Ches* 4D **130**
Priestley Av. *Dart* 5A **6**
Priestley Av. *Rawm* 6H **55**
Priestley Clo. *Donc* 6H **45**
Priestley St. *S2* 4F **99**
Priest Royd. *Dart* 4E **7**
Primrose Av. *S5* 5A **76**
Primrose Av. *B'wth* 4D **90**
Primrose Av. *D'fld* 4D **26**
Primrose Circ. *New R* 5E **63**
Primrose Clo. *Bol D* 6D **28**
Primrose Clo. *Kil* 2C **126**
Primrose Cres. *Beig* 4F **115**
Primrose Dri. *E'fld* 1F **75**
Primrose Hill. *S6* 5B **86**
 (in two parts)
Primrose Hill. *Hoy* 6A **38**
Primrose Hill. *Roth* 1C **78**
Primrose La. *Kil* 1C **126**
Primrose Pk. *Roth* 1C **78**
Primrose Wlk. S8 . . . .*1D **110***
 (off Broadfield Rd.)
Primrose Way. *Hoy* 1A **52**
Primulas Clo. *Ans* 3E **119**
Prince Arthur St. *B'ley* 5F **13**
Princegate. *Donc* 6D **32**
Prince of Wales Rd. *S2 & S9* 6C **100**
Prince's Cres. *Edl'tn* 2B **60**
Prince's Rd. *Donc* 2H **47**
Princess Clo. *Bol D* 1H **41**
Princess Ct. *S2* 5D **100**
Princess Dri. *Deep* 4E **141**
Princess Dri. *Thurn* 2G **29**
Princess Gdns. *Womb* 1F **39**
Princess Gro. *Tank* 6A **36**
Prince's Sq. *Kirk S* 3D **20**
Princess Rd. *Dron* 1E **129**
Princess Rd. *Gold* 4G **29**
Princess Rd. *Mexb* 6F **43**
Princess St. *S4* 6H **87**
Princess St. *B'ley* 6G **13**
Princess St. *Brim* 2F **133**
Princess St. *Ches* 1H **137**
Princess St. *Cud* 4C **10**
Princess St. *Dinn* 3C **106**
Princess St. *Hoy* 6F **37**
Princess St. *M'well* 4E **7**
Princess St. *Wath D* 4D **40**
Princess St. *Womb* 6A **26**
Princess St. *W'land* 3D **16**
Prince's St. *Donc* 6D **32**
Princes St. *Roth* 3B **78**
Prince St. *Swint* 1B **56**
Pringle Rd. *B'wth* 2B **90**
Printing Office St. *Donc* 6C **32**
Prior Rd. *Con* 4D **58**
Priory Av. *S7* 5D **98**

Priory Clo. *Con* 2E **59**
Priory Clo. *E'fld* 6E **65**
Priory Clo. *Mexb* 1G **57**
Priory Clo. *Walt* 6D **136**
Priory Clo. *Wors* 1D **36**
Priory Cres. *B'ley* 4E **15**
Priory Pl. *S7* 5D **98**
Priory Pl. *B'ley* 3E **15**
Priory Pl. *Donc* 6C **32**
Priory Rd. *S7* 6C **98**
Priory Rd. *B'ley* 3E **15**
Priory Rd. *Bol D* 1A **42**
Priory Rd. *E'fld* 6E **65**
Priory Ter. *S7* 5D **98**
Priory Way. *Ast* 6C **104**
Pritchard Clo. *S12* 4B **114**
Private Dri. *Holl* 3G **133**
Probert Av. *Gold* 4F **29**
Proctor Pl. *S6* 3A **86**
Progress Dri. *Braml* 5H **81**
Prominence Way. *S'side* 2F **81**
Prospect. *Thurls* 4A **142**
Prospect Clo. *Braml* 5H **81**
Prospect Cotts. *B'ley* 2H **23**
Prospect Ct. *S17* 4G **121**
Prospect Dri. *S17* 4F **121**
Prospect Pl. *S17* 3G **121**
Prospect Pl. *Donc* 1C **46**
Prospect Rd. *S2* 6E **99**
Prospect Rd. *S17* 4G **121**
Prospect Rd. *Bol D* 6E **29**
Prospect Rd. *Cud* 1H **15**
Prospect Rd. *Dron* 6G **123**
Prospect Rd. *Old W* 1H **131**
Prospect Rd. *Toll B* 3A **18**
Prospect St. *B'ley* 6F **13**
Prospect St. *Cud* 6B **10**
Prospect Ter. *Ches* 1G **137**
Providence Ct. *B'ley* 1G **23**
Providence Rd. *S6* 5H **85**
Providence St. *Greasb* 4C **68**
Providence St. *Roth* 3C **78**
Providence St. *Womb* 5D **26**
Provincial Ho. *S1* 1D **98** (2C **4**)
Pryor Mede. *H'hill* 4H **127**
Psalter Clo. *S11* 6A **98**
Psalter Dri. *S11* 6H **97**
Psalter La. *S11* 6H **97**
Psalters Dri. *Oxs* 6H **143**
Psalters La. *Roth* 2H **77**
Pullman Clo. *Stav* 1D **134**
Pump Riding. *Edl'tn* 4D **60**
Purbeck Av. *Ches* 1F **137**
Purbeck St. *Wat* 5D **114**
Purbeck Gro. *Wat* 5D **114**
Purbeck Rd. *Wat* 5D **114**
Purcell Clo. *Maltby* 5H **83**
Purslove Clo. *Braml* 2E **81**
Pye Av. *M'well* 5E **7**
Pye Bank Clo. *S3* 5E **87**
Pye Bank Dri. *S3* 5E **87**
Pye Bank Rd. *S3* 6E **87**
Pym Rd. *Mexb* 6E **43**
Pynot Rd. *Old W* 1B **132**

Q

Quadrant, The. *S17* 4E **121**
Quail Ri. *S2* 3A **100**
Quaker Clo. *Wath D* 6D **40**
Quaker La. *B'ley* 1G **25**
 (Doncaster Rd.)
Quaker La. *B'ley* 1F **25**
 (Northumberland Way)
Quaker La. *B'ley* 3B **14**
 (Westgate)
Quaker La. *Warm* 5F **45**
Quantock Way. *Ches* 6D **130**
Quarry Bank. *Wath D* 5B **40**
Quarry Bank Clo. *Cud* 2H **15**
Quarry Bank Rd. *Ches* 3C **138**
Quarry Clo. *B'wth* 3A **90**
Quarry Clo. *Dart* 5B **6**
Quarryfield La. *Maltby* 3F **83**
Quarry Fld. La. *Wick* 6F **81**
Quarry Fields. *Wick* 6F **81**
Quarry Hill. *Mosb* 1A **124**
Quarry Hill. *Roth* 3D **78**
Quarry Hill Ct. *Wath D* 1E **55**
Quarry Hill Rd. *Wath D* 1E **55**
Quarry Hills. 4G **27**
Quarry La. *S11* 1A **110**

Quarry La. *Ans* 1F **119**
Quarry La. *Bran* 3H **49**
Quarry La. *Ches* 3E **137**
Quarry La. *D'fld* 4G **27**
Quarry La. *Mexb* 4D **42**
Quarry La. *Roth* 1C **78**
Quarry La. *W'land* 3C **16**
Quarry Rd. *S13* 2G **101**
Quarry Rd. *S17* 4E **121**
Quarry Rd. *Bla H* 2H **37**
Quarry Rd. *Kil* 2A **126**
Quarry St. *B'ley* (S70) 1H **23**
Quarry St. *B'ley* (S71) 2A **14**
Quarry St. *Cud* 6B **10**
Quarry St. *Mexb* 1F **57**
Quarry St. *Rawm* 1F **69**
Quarry Va. *Cud* 1H **15**
Quarry Va. Gro. *S12* 3E **113**
Quarry Va. Rd. *S12* 3E **113**
Queen Av. *Maltby* 5G **83**
Queen Av. *New R* 4C **62**
Queen Mary Clo. *S2* 6C **100**
Queen Mary Cres. *S2* 5C **100**
Queen Mary Cres. *Kirk S* 3D **20**
Queen Mary Gro. *S2* 6B **100**
Queen Mary M. *S2* 6C **100**
Queen Mary Rd. *S2* 5B **100**
Queen Mary's Rd. *New R* 4C **62**
Queen Mary St. *Maltby* 6G **83**
Queen's Acre. *Swint* 2B **56**
Queen's Av. *B'ley* 5F **13**
Queen's Av. *Kiv P* 5G **117**
Queen's Av. *L Hou* 2H **27**
Queen's Av. *Swint* 1B **56**
Queensberry Rd. *Donc* 4A **34**
Queen's Ct. *Donc* 3A **32**
Queen's Cres. *Edl'tn* 2B **60**
Queens Cres. *Hoy* 6E **37**
Queens Dri. *B'ley* 4E **13**
Queen's Dri. *Cud* 4C **10**
Queen's Dri. *Dod* 2B **22**
Queen's Dri. *Donc* 3A **32**
Queen's Dri. *Shaf* 2B **10**
Queens Gdns. *B'ley* 4E **13**
Queens Gdns. *Hoy* 6F **37**
Queens Gdns. *Womb* 1F **39**
Queensgate. *Donc* 6D **32**
Queensgate. *Gren* 1B **74**
Queens Retail Pk. *S2* 5E **99**
Queen's Rd. *S2* 6E **99** (6G **5**)
Queen's Rd. *B'ley* 6H **13**
Queen's Rd. *Beig* 3F **115**
Queen's Rd. *Cud* 4C **10**
Queen's Rd. *Donc* 5E **33**
Queen's Rd. *Swal* 6A **104**
Queen's Row. *S3* 1D **98** (1C **4**)
Queen's Ter. *Mexb* 6E **43**
Queen St. *S1* 1E **99** (2E **5**)
Queen St. *B'ley* 6G **13**
Queen St. *Brim* 2F **133**
Queen St. *C'town* 1D **65**
Queen St. *Ches* 1H **137**
Queen St. *D'fld* 3F **27**
Queen St. *Dinn* 3F **107**
Queen St. *Donc* 3B **46**
 (in two parts)
Queen St. *Eck* 6E **125**
Queen St. *Gold* 4G **29**
Queen St. *Hoy* 6E **37**
Queen St. *Mosb* 2C **124**
Queen St. *P'stne* 4E **143**
Queen St. *Rawm* 6G **55**
Queen St. *Roth* 2G **79**
Queen St. *Stav* 3B **134**
Queen St. *Swint* 2B **56**
Queen St. *Thurn* 2G **29**
Queen St. N. *Ches* 3A **132**
Queen St. S. *B'ley* 6H **13**
Queensway. *B'ley* 4E **13**
Queensway. *Hoy* 5B **38**
Queensway. *Roth* 1F **91**
Queensway. *Roy* 1E **9**
Queensway. *Wors* 4B **24**
Queenswood Clo. *S6* 6G **73**
Queenswood Dri. *S6* 6F **73**
Queenswood Ga. *S6* 6F **73**
Queenswood Rd. *S6* 6F **73**
Queen Victoria Rd. *S17* 5F **121**
Quern Way. *D'fld* 3E **27**
Quest Av. *H'fld* 3E **39**
Quiet La. *S10* 1B **108**
Quilter Rd. *Maltby* 5H **83**

Quintec Ct. *Roth* 6E **69**
Quoit Green. 2F **129**
Quoit Grn. *Dron* 2F **129**
Quorn Dri. *Ches* 6C **130**

R

Raby Rd. *Donc* 4F **33**
Raby St. *S9* .6G **77**
Race Comn. Av. *P'stne* 6C **142**
Racecommon La. *B'ley* 2F **23**
(in two parts)
Racecommon Rd. *B'ley* 2F **23**
Racecourse Mt. *Ches* 3H **131**
Racecourse Rd. *Ches* 3H **131**
Racecourse Rd. *Swint* 2G **55**
Race La. *Bols* 6F **141**
Race St. *B'ley* 6G **13**
Racker Way. *S6* 4H **85**
Rackford La. *Ans* 3H **119**
Rackford Rd. *Ans* 2G **119**
Radbourne Comn. *Dron W* 2B **128**
Radburn Rd. *New R* 5C **62**
Radcliffe Clo. *Scawt* 6G **17**
Radcliffe La. *Scawt* 6G **17**
Radcliffe Mt. *Ben* 5A **18**
Radcliffe Rd. *B'ley* 5B **8**
Radcliffe Rd. *Ben* 5A **18**
Radford St. *S3* 1D **98** (2B **4**)
Radiance Rd. *Donc* 4E **33**
Radley Av. *Wick* 4F **81**
Radnor Clo. *Soth* 5G **115**
Radnor Way. *Donc* 4A **34**
Raeburn Clo. *S14* 5A **112**
Raeburn Pl. *S14* 4A **112**
Raeburn Rd. *S14* 5A **112**
Raeburn Way. *S14* 5A **112**
Ragusa Dri. *New R* 6D **62**
Raikes St. *Mexb* 1D **56**
Rail Mill Way. *P'gte* 5F **69**
Rails. 1A **96**
Rails Rd. *S6* 1A **96**
(in two parts)
Railway Av. *Cat* 6C **90**
Railway Cotts. *Cat* 5C **90**
Railway Cotts. *Dod* 2A **22**
Railway Ct. *Donc* 2D **46**
Railway Ter. *Gold* 4F **29**
Railway Ter. *Has* 6B **138**
Railway Ter. *Roth* 3C **78**
Railway Vw. *Gold* 4G **29**
Rainborough Ct. *Bram* 5H **39**
Rainborough M. *Bram B* 4B **40**
Rainborough Rd. *Wath D* 5B **40**
Rainboro Vw. *H'fld* 4E **39**
Rainbow Av. *S12* 3B **114**
Rainbow Clo. *S12* 3C **114**
Rainbow Cres. *S12* 3C **114**
Rainbow Dri. *S12* 3C **114**
Rainbow Gro. *S12* 3C **114**
Rainbow Pl. *S12* 3C **114**
Rainbow Rd. *S12* 3C **114**
Rainbow Wlk. *S12* 3B **114**
(off Carter Lodge Dri.)
Rainbow Way. *S12* 3B **114**
Rainford Dri. *B'ley* 1D **14**
Rainford Sq. *Kirk S* 2D **20**
Rainstorth. 5A **66**
Rainton Gro. *B'ley* 4D **12**
Rainton Rd. *Donc* 1E **47**
Raintree Ct. *Cusw* 4H **31**
Raisen Hall Pl. *S5* 1E **87**
Raisen Hall Rd. *S5* 6D **74**
Rakes La. *Old E* 6D **60**
Raleigh Ct. *Donc* 6H **33**
Raleigh Dri. *Burn* 2B **64**
Raleigh Rd. *S2* 1F **111**
Raleigh Ter. *Donc* 5G **45**
Raley St. *B'ley* 2F **23**
(in two parts)
Ralph Ellis Dri. *S'bri* 4D **140**
Ralph Rd. *Stav* 1E **135**
Ralston Ct. *Half* 3D **124**
Ralston Cft. *Half* 3E **125**
Ralston Gro. *Half* 3D **124**
Ralston Pl. *Half* 3D **124**
Ramper La. *Barn D* 2G **21**
Ramper Rd. *Maltby* 2D **94**
Rampton Rd. *S7* 6D **98**
Ramsay Cres. *Donc* 3H **31**
Ramsden Rd. *Donc* 1A **46**
Ramsden Rd. *Roth* 4E **79**

Ramsay Av. *Ches* 4F **137**
Ramsey Rd. *S10* 1A **98**
Ramshaw Clo. *Ches* 4E **131**
Ramsker Dri. *Arm* 4F **35**
Ramsworth Clo. *Donc* 4G **31**
Ranby Rd. *S11* 6H **97**
Randall Pl. *S2* 5D **98**
Randall St. *S2* 4E **99**
Randall St. *Eck* 6G **125**
Randerson Dri. *Kiln* 4C **56**
Rands La. *Arm* 2G **35**
Rands La. Ind. Est. *Arm* 2H **35**
Ranelagh Dri. *S11* 2H **109**
Raneld Mt. *Ches* 5E **137**
Ranfield Ct. *Rav* 1H **81**
Rangeley Rd. *S6* 6G **85**
Range Rd. *S4* 2B **88**
Ranmoor. 4F **97**
Ranmoor Chase. *S10* 4H **97**
Ranmoor Cliffe Rd. *S10* 4E **97**
Ranmoor Clo. *Has* 5C **138**
Ranmoor Ct. *S10* 5G **97**
Ranmoor Cres. *S10* 4F **97**
Ranmoor Ho. *S10* 3G **97**
Ranmoor Pk. Rd. *S10* 4F **97**
Ranmoor Ri. *S10* 4F **97**
Ranmoor Rd. *S10* 4F **97**
Ranmoor Vw. *S10* 4F **97**
Ranskill Ct. *S9* 4E **89**
Ranworth Rd. *Braml* 1E **81**
Ranyard Rd. *Donc* 4H **45**
Raseby Av. *Wat* 5E **115**
Raseby Clo. *Wat* 5E **115**
Raseby Pl. *Wat* 5E **115**
Rasen Clo. *Mexb* 5G **43**
Ratcliffe Clo. *Ches* 6C **138**
Ratcliffe Rd. *S11* 5B **98**
Ratten Row. *Dod* 3A **22**
Ratten Row. *Wadw* 6H **61**
Rattigan Ho. Donc 3G **33**
(off Beckett Rd.)
Ravencar Rd. *Eck* 6B **124**
Ravencarr Pl. *S2* 4C **100**
Ravencarr Rd. *S2* 4C **100**
Raven Dri. *Thpe H* 1C **66**
Ravenfield. 4H **71**
Ravenfield Clo. *Owl* 5A **114**
Ravenfield Common. 1H **81**
Ravenfield Dri. *B'ley* 1A **14**
Ravenfield La. *Hoot R* 1G **71**
Ravenfield Pk. 2H **71**
Ravenfield Rd. *Arm* 4G **35**
Ravenfield St. *Den M* 1B **58**
Ravenholt. *Wors* 5A **24**
Raven Meadows. *Swint* 4A **56**
Raven Rd. *S7* 1B **110**
Raven Royd. *B'ley* 4B **8**
Ravenscar Clo. *Den M* 2A **58**
Ravens Clo. *M'well* 5F **7**
Ravens Ct. *Wors* 5B **24**
Ravenscroft Av. *S13* 5G **101**
Ravenscroft Clo. *S13* 5G **101**
Ravenscroft Ct. *S13* 5G **101**
Ravenscroft Cres. *S13* 5G **101**
Ravenscroft Dri. *S13* 5G **101**
Ravenscroft Oval. *S13* 5G **101**
Ravenscroft Pl. *S13* 5G **101**
Ravenscroft Rd. *S13* 5F **101**
Ravenscroft Way. *S13* 5G **101**
Ravensdale Clo. *Ink* 6A **134**
Ravensdale Rd. *Dron W* 2A **128**
Ravenshaw Clo. *B'ley* 4D **12**
Ravenside Retail Pk. *Ches* 3A **138**
Ravensmead Ct. *Bol D* 2A **42**
Ravens Wlk. *Con* 3G **59**
Ravenswood Rd. *Ches* 6C **130**
Ravensworth Rd. *Donc* 1E **47**
Ravine, The. *S5* 2A **76**
Rawlins Ct. *Coal A* 5G **123**
Rawmarsh. 2F **69**
Rawmarsh Hill. P'gte 3F **69**
Rawmarsh Ho. P'gte 3F **69**
(off Rawmarsh Hill)
Rawmarsh Rd. *Roth* 2D **78**
Rawmarsh Shop. Cen. *Rawm* 2F **69**
Rawson Clo. *Donc* 2D **48**
Rawson Rd. *Roth* 2E **79**
Rawsons Bank. *E'fld* 1F **75**
Rawson Spring Av. *S6* 1B **86**
Rawson Spring Rd. *S6* 1B **86**
Rawson Spring Way. *S6* 1B **86**
Rawson St. *S6* 4C **86**
Raybould Rd. *Roth* 6H **67**

Rayleigh Av. *Brim* 3D **132**
Rayls Ri. *Tod* 2B **118**
Rayls Rd. *Tod* 2B **118**
Raymond Rd. *B'ley* 1D **24**
Raymond Rd. *Donc* 3H **31**
Raynald Rd. *S2* 4C **100**
Raynor Sike La. *Whar S* 1A **72**
Reader Cres. *Swint* 1B **56**
Reaper Cres. *High G* 1C **64**
Reasbeck Ter. *B'ley* 2H **13**
Reasby Av. *Rav* 1H **81**
Reaton M. *B'ley* 4D **12**
Reavill Clo. *Dinn* 3F **107**
Rebecca M. *B'ley* 1H **23**
Rebecca Row. *B'ley* 1H **23**
Recreation Av. *Thur* 5B **94**
Recreation La. *New R* 4C **62**
Recreation Rd. *Brim* 6F **133**
Recreation Rd. *Wath D* 4F **41**
Recreation Rd. *W'land* 3D **16**
Rectory Clo. *Car* 4F **9**
Rectory Clo. *Eck* 5E **125**
Rectory Clo. *S'bri* 3E **141**
Rectory Clo. *Thurn* 1D **28**
Rectory Clo. *Womb* 1F **39**
Rectory Ct. *Lgtn* 6F **95**
Rectory Dri. *Whis* 3A **92**
Rectory Gdns. *Donc* 5E **33**
Rectory Gdns. *Kil* 3B **126**
Rectory Gdns. *Old E* 6A **60**
Rectory Gdns. *Thurn* 3B **118**
Rectory La. *Thurn* 1D **28**
Rectory M. *Spro* 3D **44**
Rectory Rd. *Duck* 6E **135**
Rectory Rd. *Kil* 4B **126**
Rectory Rd. *Stav* 1C **134**
Rectory St. *Rawm* 3F **69**
Rectory Way. *B'ley* 4D **14**
Redbrook. 3D **12**
Redbrook Av. *Has* 5B **138**
Redbrook Bus. Pk. *B'ley* 2D **12**
Redbrook Ct. *B'ley* 3E **13**
Redbrook Cft. *Owl* 4A **114**
Redbrook Gro. *Owl* 4A **114**
Redbrook Rd. *B'ley* 3C **12**
Redbrook Vw. *B'ley* 3E **13**
Redbrook Wlk. *B'ley* 3E **13**
Redcar Clo. *Den M* 3A **58**
Redcar Rd. *S10* 2A **98**
Redcliffe Clo. *B'ley* 3D **12**
Redfearn St. *B'ley* 5H **13**
Redfern Av. *Wat* 6D **114**
Redfern Ct. *Wat* 6D **114**
Redfern Dri. *Wat* 6D **114**
Red Fern Gro. *S'bri* 4D **140**
Redfern Gro. *Wat* 6D **114**
Redgrave Pl. *Flan* 3F **81**
Redgrove Way. *Ches* 5E **137**
Redhall Clo. *Kirk S* 3E **21**
Red Hill. *S1* 2D **98** (2C **4**)
Red Hill. *Kiv P* 5B **118**
Redhill Av. *B'ley* 2C **24**
Redhill Ct. *Wadw* 6H **61**
Redholme. *S10* 3E **97**
Redhouse Interchange 1B **16**
Red Ho. La. *Adw S* 1C **16**
Red Ho. La. *Pick* 1A **16**
(in two parts)
Red Ho. Wlk. *Ches* 6F **131**
Redland Gro. *M'well* 3F **7**
Redland La. *S7* 4B **110**
Redland Way. *Maltby* 3E **83**
Red La. *S10* 4A **98**
Red La. *Old W* 2C **132**
Red Lion Yd. *Roth* 3D **78**
(off Effingham St.)
Redmarsh Av. *Rawm* 6E **55**
Redmires Rd. *S10* 4A **96**
Red Oak La. *S6* 4C **84**
Redrock Rd. *Roth* 1G **91**
Redscope Cres. *Roth* 5F **67**
Redscope Rd. *Roth* 6F **67**
Redthorne Way. *Shaf* 2B **10**
Redthorn Rd. *S13* 5H **101**
Redthorpe Crest. *B'ley* 3C **12**
Redvers Buller Rd. *Ches* 4A **138**
Redwall Clo. *Dinn* 3C **106**
Redwood Av. *Kil* 4A **126**
Redwood Av. *Roy* 2E **9**
Redwood Clo. *Holl* 3G **133**
Redwood Clo. *Hoy* 6H **37**

Redwood Dri. *Maltby* 4C **82**
Redwood Glen. *C'town* 3D **64**
Reed Clo. *D'fld* 4E **27**
Reedham Dri. *Braml* 1E **81**
Regency Ter. *C'town* 2E **65**
    (off Greenhead Gdns.)
Regent Av. *Arm* 4G **35**
Regent Ct. *S1* 3B **4**
Regent Ct. *S6* 3B **86**
Regent Ct. *B'ley* 3E **13**
Regent Ct. *Donc* 6E **33**
Regent Ct. *Hoy* 6E **37**
Regent Cres. *B'ley* 6B **8**
Regent Gdns. *B'ley* 4G **13**
Regent Gro. *Donc* 4H **31**
Regent Gro. *New R* 5E **63**
Regent Ho. *B'ley* 6H **13**
Regent Sq. *Donc* 6E **33**
Regent St. *S1* 2D **98** (3B **4**)
Regent St. *B'ley* 5G **13**
Regent St. *Donc* 4A **46**
Regent St. *Hoy* 6E **37**
Regent St. *Roth* 3H **77**
Regent St. *S Hien* 1E **11**
Regent St. S. *B'ley* 5H **13**
Regents Way. *Ast* 6C **104**
Regent Ter. *S3* 2D **98** (3B **4**)
Regent Ter. *Donc* 6E **33**
Regina Cres. *Brie* 3E **11**
Reginald Rd. *B'ley* 2D **24**
Reginald Rd. *Womb* 1H **39**
Rembrandt Dri. *Dron* 2C **128**
Remington Av. *S5* 2D **74**
Remington Dri. *S5* 2D **74**
Remington Rd. *S5* 2D **74**
Remount Rd. *Roth* 5F **67**
Remount Way. *Roth* 5F **67**
Rempstone Dri. *Ches* 6B **138**
Renald La. *H'swne* 1E **143**
Renathorpe Rd. *S5* 3H **75**
Rencliffe Av. *Roth* 6F **79**
Reneville Clo. *Roth* 5E **79**
Reneville Ct. *S5* 1E **75**
Reneville Ct. *Roth* 5D **78**
Reneville Cres. *S5* 1E **75**
Reneville Dri. *S5* 1E **75**
Reneville Rd. *Roth* 5D **78**
Reney Av. *S8* 3B **122**
Reney Cres. *S8* 3B **122**
Reney Dri. *S8* 3B **122**
Reney Rd. *S8* 2C **122**
Reney Wlk. *S8* 3B **122**
Renishaw Av. *Roth* 1H **91**
Renshaw Clo. *High G* 5A **50**
Renshaw Rd. *S11* 1G **109**
Renville Clo. *Rawm* 6E **55**
Renway Rd. *Roth* 6G **79**
Repton Clo. *Ches* 6C **130**
Repton Pl. *Dron W* 2A **128**
Reresby Cres. *Whis* 1A **92**
Reresby Dri. *Whis* 1A **92**
Reresby Rd. *Thry* 5E **71**
Reresby Rd. *Whis* 1H **91**
Reresby Wlk. *Den M* 1B **58**
Reservoir Rd. *S10* 2A **98**
Reservoir Rd. *Ulley* 1A **104**
Reservoir Ter. *Ches* 1G **137**
Retail World. *P'gte* 5F **69**
Retford Rd. *S13* 4B **102**
Retford Wlk. *Ross* 4F **63**
Revell Clo. *Roth* 2B **80**
Revill Clo. *Maltby* 3F **83**
Revill La. *Woodh* 1C **114**
Revolution House. 1A **132**
Rex Av. *S7* 3H **109**
Reynard La. *S6* 6B **84**
Reynolds Clo. *Dron* 3C **128**
Reynolds Clo. *Flan* 3F **81**
Rhodes Av. *Ches* 6G **131**
Rhodes Av. *Roth* 5F **67**
Rhodes Dri. *Whis* 1A **92**
Rhodesia Ct. *Donc* 3B **48**
Rhodesia Rd. *Ches* 3E **137**
Rhodes St. *S2* 2G **99** (4H **5**)
Rhodes Ter. *B'ley* 1A **24**
Ribble Clo. *C'town* 1E **65**
Ribblesdale Dri. *S12* 6H **113**
Ribble Way. *S5* 6G **75**
Riber Av. *B'ley* 6C **8**
Riber Clo. *S6* 5D **84**
Riber Clo. *Ink* 6A **134**
Riber Ter. *Ches* 3G **137**
Ribston Ct. *S9* 6C **88**

Ribston M. *S9* 1D **100**
Ribston Pl. *S9* 1D **100**
Ribston Rd. *S9* 1C **100**
Ribston Wlk. *S9* 1D **100**
Richard Av. *B'ley* 1A **14**
Richard La. *New R* 4C **62**
Richard Rd. *B'ley* 1A **14**
Richard Rd. *Dart* 5B **6**
Richard Rd. *Roth* 4E **79**
Richards Ct. *S2* 1F **111**
Richardson Wlk. *Womb* 5H **25**
Richards Rd. *S2* 6E **99**
    (in two parts)
Richard St. *B'ley* 6F **13**
Richards Way. *Rawm* 1G **69**
Rich Farm Clo. *Ark* 4D **18**
Richmond. 6F **101**
Richmond Av. *S13* 5G **101**
Richmond Av. *Dart* 6B **6**
Richmond Clo. *Ches* 5G **137**
Richmond Ct. *S13* 6F **101**
Richmond Farm M. *S13* 6F **101**
Richmond Gro. *S13* 5G **101**
Richmond Hall Av. *S13* 5F **101**
Richmond Hall Cres. *S13* 6F **101**
Richmond Hall Dri. *S13* 5F **101**
Richmond Hall Rd. *S13* 5F **101**
Richmond Hall Way. *S13* 6F **101**
Richmond Hill Ho. *S13* 6F **101**
Richmond Hill Rd. *S13* 6G **101**
Richmond Hill Rd. *Donc* 1G **45**
Richmond Park. 3F **77**
Richmond Pk. Av. *S13* 3G **101**
Richmond Pk. Av. *Roth* 3F **77**
Richmond Pk. Clo. *S13* 4G **101**
Richmond Pk. Cres. *S13* 3G **101**
Richmond Pk. Cft. *S13* 3G **101**
Richmond Pk. Dri. *S13* 4G **101**
Richmond Pk. Gro. *S13* 4G **101**
Richmond Pk. Ri. *S13* 3F **101**
Richmond Pk. Rd. *S13* 4G **101**
Richmond Pk. Vw. *S13* 4G **101**
Richmond Pk. Way. *S13* 4G **101**
Richmond Pl. *S13* 6F **101**
Richmond Rd. *S13* 1E **113**
Richmond Rd. *Donc* 2F **31**
Richmond Rd. *Roth* 3G **77**
Richmond Rd. *Thurn* 1E **29**
Richmond St. *S3* 5F **87**
Richmond St. *B'ley* 6F **13**
Richworth Rd. *S13* 5H **101**
Ricknald Clo. *Aug* 4B **104**
Ridal Av. *S'bri* 2C **140**
Ridal Clo. *S'bri* 2C **140**
Ridal Cft. *S'bri* 2C **140**
Riddings Clo. *S2* 6C **100**
Riddings Clo. *Thur* 5B **94**
Riddings Cft. *Ches* 5E **131**
Ridge Bank. *S6* 3A **86**
Ridge Balk La. *W'land* 2B **16**
Ridge Ct. *S10* 3C **96**
Ridge Ct. *Roth* 2F **79**
Ridgehill Av. *S12* 1C **112**
Ridgehill Gro. *S12* 2D **112**
Ridge Rd. *High* 5D **16**
Ridge Rd. *Roth* 2E **79**
Ridge, The. *S10* 4C **96**
Ridge, The. *W'land* 3B **16**
Ridge Vw. Clo. *S9* 6C **76**
Ridge Vw. Dri. *S9* 6C **76**
Ridgewalk Way. *Wors* 3H **23**
Ridgeway. *Dron* 6H **123**
Ridgeway. *Roth* 2A **80**
Ridgeway Clo. *H'by* 4A **82**
Ridgeway Clo. *Roth* 2B **80**
Ridgeway Cres. *S12* 2C **112**
Ridgeway Cres. *B'ley* 4E **9**
Ridgeway Dri. *S12* 1C **112**
Ridgeway Rd. *S12* 1C **112**
Ridgeway Rd. *B'wth* 3C **90**
Ridgewood Av. *E'thpe* 6D **20**
Ridgway Av. *D'fld* 3E **27**
Riding Clo. *Donc* 5F **49**
Riding Clo. *Flan* 4E **81**
Ridings, The. *B'ley* 2B **14**
Ridings, The. *B'ley* 2B **14**
Rig Clo. *Roth* 6H **67**
Rig Dri. *Swint* 2G **55**
Riggotts La. *Walt* 6F **137**
Riggotts Way. *Cut* 3A **130**
Riggs High Rd. *S6* 6A **84**
Riggs Low Rd. *S6* 6A **84**
Rig La. *Rawm* 1C **68**

Riley Av. *Donc* 5H **45**
Riley Rd. *Wath D* 6F **41**
Rimington Rd. *Womb* 6B **26**
Rimini Ri. *D'fld* 4C **26**
Ringinglow. 3A **108**
Ringinglow Rd. *S11* 3A **108**
Ringstead Av. *S10* 3E **97**
Ringstead Cres. *S10* 3E **97**
Ringstone Gro. *Brie* 2G **11**
Ringway. *Bol D* 1H **41**
Ringwood Av. *Ches* 4G **131**
Ringwood Av. *Stav* 3A **134**
Ringwood Cres. *Soth* 5G **115**
Ringwood Dri. *Soth* 5G **115**
Ringwood Gro. *Soth* 5G **115**
Ringwood Rd. *Brim* 3F **133**
Ringwood Rd. *Soth* 5G **115**
Ringwood Vw. *Brim* 4F **133**
Ripley Gro. *B'ley* 3D **12**
Ripley St. *S6* 4A **86**
Ripon Av. *Donc* 3F **33**
Ripon St. *S9* 6B **88**
    (in two parts)
Ripon Way. *Swal* 6A **104**
Rippon Ct. *Rawm* 6F **55**
Rippon Cres. *S6* 3H **85**
Rippon Rd. *S6* 3H **85**
Risedale Rd. *Gold* 5H **29**
Rise, The. *Ans* 2G **119**
Rise, The. *Brie* 3G **11**
Rise, The. *Swint* 3H **55**
Rising St. *S3* 5F **87**
Rivelin Bank. *S6* 4H **85**
Rivelin Ct. *S6* 2B **96**
Rivelin Glen. *S6* 1E **97**
Rivelin Glen Cotts. *S6* 1E **97**
Rivelin Nature Trail. 1F **97**
Rivelin Pk. Ct. *S6* 5G **85**
Rivelin Pk. Cres. *S6* 5G **85**
Rivelin Pk. Dri. *S6* 5F **85**
Rivelin Pk. Rd. *S6* 6G **85**
Rivelin Rd. *S6* 5G **85**
Rivelin St. *S6* 5H **85**
Rivelin Ter. *S6* 5G **85**
Rivelin Valley Rd. *S6* 2A **96**
River Bank. *O'bri* 2E **73**
River Ct. *S17* 2G **121**
    (off Ladies Spring Gro.)
Riverdale Av. *S10* 5G **97**
Riverdale Dri. *S10* 5G **97**
Riverdale M. *S10* 5F **97**
Riverdale Pk. Cvn. Site. *Stav* 1E **135**
Riverdale Rd. *S10* 4G **97**
Riverhead. *Spro* 2D **44**
Riverside. *S6* 4G **85**
Riverside Clo. *S6* 3F **85**
Riverside Clo. *Con* 2E **59**
Riverside Clo. *D'fld* 4G **27**
Riverside Clo. *Donc* 2H **45**
Riverside Ct. *S9* 4B **88**
Riverside Ct. *Dinn* 2C **106**
Riverside Ct. *Mexb* 1G **57**
Riverside Cres. *Holy* 6A **136**
Riverside Dri. *Spro* 3E **45**
Riverside Gdns. *Bol D* 2B **42**
Riverside M. *S6* 3A **86**
    (off Langsett Rd.)
Riverside Pk. *S2* 4F **99**
Riverside Precinct. *Roth* 3D **78**
    (off Corporation St.)
Riverside Way. *Roth* 4C **78**
River Ter. *S6* 3A **86**
River Vw. Rd. *O'bri* 2D **72**
Riviera Mt. *Donc* 4B **32**
Riviera Pde. *Donc* 4B **32**
Rix Rd. *Kiln* 5B **56**
Roache Dri. *Gold* 5E **29**
Roach Rd. *S11* 6A **98**
Robert Av. *B'ley* 5D **14**
Robert Rd. *S8* 2D **122**
Roberts Av. *Con* 4F **59**
Robertshaw Cres. *Deep* 3F **141**
Robertson Dri. *S6* 5G **85**
Robertson Rd. *S6* 6G **85**
Roberts Rd. *Donc* 2B **46**
Roberts Rd. *Edl'tn* 4C **60**
Roberts St. *Cud* 6B **10**
Roberts St. *Womb* 1E **39**
Robert St. *Roth* 3B **78**
Robey St. *S4* 2H **87**
Robinbrook La. *S12* 6E **113**
Robincroft. *Ches* 6H **137**

Robinets Rd. *Roth* 4A **68**
Robin Hood Av. *Roy* 1F **9**
Robin Hood Chase. *S6* 4C **84**
Robin Hood Cres. *E'thpe* 6E **21**
Robin Hood Rd. *S9* 5C **76**
Robin Hood Rd. *E'thpe* 6E **21**
Robin La. *Beig* 2F **115**
Robin La. *Roy* 1F **9**
Robin Pl. *Ast* 1C **116**
Robins Clo. *Ast* 6C **104**
Robinson Rd. *S2* 3G **99**
Robinson's Sq. *Birdw* 4C **36**
Robinson St. *Roth* 5D **78**
Robinson Way. *Kil* 3A **126**
Rob Royd. *Dod* 3B **22**
Rob Royd. *Wors* 4E **23**
Rob Royd La. *B'ley* 4F **23**
(in two parts)
Roche. W'fld 1E **125**
(off Shortbrook Dri.)
Roche Clo. *B'ley* 4B **14**
Roche End. *Tod* 2A **118**
Rocher Av. *Gren* 2C **74**
Rocher Clo. *Gren* 2C **74**
Rocher Gro. *Gren* 2C **74**
Rochester Clo. *S10* 4A **96**
Rochester Dri. *S10* 4A **96**
Rochester Rd. *S10* 4A **96**
Rochester Rd. *Ans* 4F **119**
Rochester Rd. *B'ley* 3B **14**
Rochester Row. *Donc* 4F **31**
Rockcliffe Dri. *Wadw* 6H **61**
Rockcliffe Dri. *Wadw* 6H **61**
Rockcliffe Houses. Rawm 3F **69**
(off Rockcliffe Rd.)
Rockcliffe Rd. *Rawm* 3F **69**
Rockingham. 4H **67**
Rockingham. W'fld 1E **125**
(off Shortbrook Dri.)
Rockingham Bus. Pk. *Birdw* 5D **36**
Rockingham Clo. *S1* 6D **4**
Rockingham Clo. *Birdw* 5D **36**
Rockingham Clo. *Ches* 2E **137**
Rockingham Clo. *Dron W* 2A **128**
Rockingham Ct. *B'ley* 6A **14**
Rockingham Ct. *Swint* 2H **55**
Rockingham Ga. *S1* 3E **99** (5D **4**)
Rockingham Ho. Donc 1C **46**
(off Elsworth Clo.)
Rockingham Ho. *Rawm* 1G **69**
Rockingham La. *S1* 2E **99** (4D **4**)
Rockingham Mausoleum, The. 6A **54**
Rockingham M. *Birdw* 5C **36**
Rockingham Rd. *Dod* 3C **22**
Rockingham Rd. *Donc* 4E **33**
Rockingham Rd. *Rawm* 1G **69**
Rockingham Rd. *Swint* 3G **55**
Rockingham Row. *Birdw* 5D **36**
Rockingham St. *S1* 2D **98** (3C **4**)
Rockingham St. *B'ley* 3G **13**
Rockingham St. *Birdw* 5D **36**
Rockingham St. *Hoy* 5F **37**
Rockingham Way. *S1* 3E **99** (5D **4**)
Rockland Dri. *Thry* 4H **67**
Rockland Dri. Thry 5C **70**
(off Doncaster Rd.)
Rockland Vs. *Thry* 5C **70**
Rocklea Clo. *Swint* 3A **56**
Rockley Av. *Birdw* 3C **36**
Rockley Av. *Womb* 2D **38**
Rockley Clo. *Ches* 6G **137**
Rockley Cres. *Birdw* 4C **36**
Rockley La. *Wors* 6E **23**
Rockley Meadows. *B'ley* 2E **23**
Rockley Nook. *Donc* 2H **33**
Rockley Rd. *S6* 1H **85**
Rockleys. *Dod* 3C **22**
Rockley Vw. *Tank* 5B **36**
Rockcliffe Av. *Donc* 5B **38**
Rock Mt. *Hoy* 5B **38**
Rockmount Rd. *S9* 5D **76**
Rock Pl. *Deep* 3F **141**
Rockside Rd. *Thurls* 4A **142**
Rock St. *S3* 6E **87**
Rock St. *B'ley* 5F **13**
Rock Ter. *Con* 4D **58**
Rockwood Clo. *C'town* 2C **64**
Rockwood Clo. *Dart* 4D **6**
Roddis Clo. *Dinn* 4D **106**
Roden Way. *Rawm* 5C **54**
Rodger Rd. *S13* 6D **102**
Rodger St. *Roth* 2B **78**
Rodman Dri. *S13* 5D **102**

Rodman St. *S13* 5D **102**
Rod Moor Rd. *Dron W* 5H **121**
Rodney Hill. *S6* 3D **84**
Rodsley Clo. *Ches* 6D **130**
Rodwell Clo. *Tree* 1E **103**
Roebuck Hill. *Jump* 3B **38**
Roebuck Rd. *S6* 1B **98**
Roebuck St. *Womb* 1G **39**
Roeburn Clo. *M'well* 3E **7**
Roecar Clo. *Old W* 1B **132**
Roe Cft. Clo. *Spro* 1D **44**
Roehampton Ri. *B'ley* 1G **25**
Roehampton Ri. *B'wth* 2A **90**
Roehampton Ri. *Donc* 4F **31**
Roe La. *S3* 3F **87**
Roewood Ct. S3 . . . . .3F **87**
(off Orphanage Rd.)
Roger Rd. *B'ley* 5E **15**
Rojean Rd. *Gren* 1B **74**
Rokeby Dri. *S5* 3E **75**
Rokeby Rd. *S5* 3E **75**
Rollestone. 3H **111**
Rolleston Av. *Maltby* 5E **83**
Rolleston Rd. *S5* 5G **75**
Rollin Dri. *S6* 2H **85**
Rolling Dales Clo. *Maltby* 3E **83**
Rolls Cres. *Rawm* 5C **54**
Roman Ct. *Roth* 3G **77**
Roman Cres. *B'wth* 1C **90**
Roman Cres. *Rawm* 1H **69**
Romandale Gdns. *S2* 4E **101**
Roman Ridge. *Donc* 2G **31**
Roman Ridge Rd. *S9* 6D **76**
Roman Rd. *Dart* 6B **6**
Roman Rd. *Donc* 1G **47**
Roman St. *Thurn* 1H **29**
Roman Terrace. 6C **42**
Romney Clo. *Flan* 3F **81**
Romney Dri. *Dron* 2C **128**
Romney Gdns. *S2* 1H **97**
Romsdal Rd. *S10* 2G **55**
Romwood Av. *Swint* 1E **101**
Ronald Rd. *S9* 1A **46**
Ronald Rd. *Donc* 3A **76**
Ronksley Cres. *S5* 3H **75**
Ronksley Rd. *S5* 3D **12**
Rookdale Clo. *B'ley* 4H **141**
Rookery Bank. *Deep* 4H **141**
Rookery Chase. *Deep* 4H **141**
Rookery Clo. *Deep* 4H **141**
Rookery Clo. *Kiv P* 4G **117**
Rookery Dell. *Deep* 4H **141**
Rookery Ri. *Deep* 5H **141**
Rookery Rd. *Swint* 3H **55**
Rookery, The. *Deep* 4H **141**
Rookery Va. *Deep* 4H **141**
Rookhill. *Wors* 4C **24**
Rosamond Av. *S17* 3G **121**
Rosamond Clo. *S17* 3G **121**
Rosamond Ct. *S17* 3G **121**
Rosamond Dri. *S17* 3G **121**
Rosamond Glade. *S17* 3G **121**
Rosamond Pl. *S17* 3G **121**
Rosamond Rd. *S10* 1A **98**
Roscoe Bank. *S6* 1D **96**
Roscoe Ct. *S6* 5F **85**
Roscoe Dri. *S6* 6F **85**
Roscoe Mt. *S6* 6F **85**
Roscoe Rd. *S3* 6D **86**
Roscoe Vw. *S6* 1D **96**
Rose Av. *Beig* 4F **115**
Rose Av. *Cal* 2G **139**
Rose Av. *D'fld* 2D **26**
Rose Av. *S17* 3B **46**
Roseberry Clo. *Hoy* 1A **52**
Roseberry St. *B'ley* 1D **24**
Rosebery St. *Roth* 3A **78**
Rosebery Ter. *B'ley* 1H **23**
Rose Clo. *B'wth* 4D **90**
Rose Cottage. *Barn D* 1H **21**
Rose Cotts. *Ches* 3C **138**
Rose Cotts. *Bal* 3A **46**
Rose Ct. *Wick* 5E **81**
Rose Cres. *Donc* 2G **31**
Rose Cres. *Rawm* 1H **69**
Rosedale Av. *Ches* 5B **138**
Rosedale Av. *Rawm* 1F **69**
Rosedale Clo. *Ast* 5C **104**
Rosedale Gdns. *S11* 5B **98**
Rosedale Gdns. *B'ley* 6E **13**
Rosedale Rd. *S11* 5B **98**
Rosedale Rd. *Ast* 5B **104**
Rosedale Rd. *Ben* 5A **18**

Rosedale Rd. *Donc* 2F **31**
Rosedale Vw. *Walt* 6D **136**
Rosedale Way. *S'side* 3G **81**
Rose Gth. Av. *Ast* 4G **81**
Rose Gth. Av. *Ast* 5B **104**
Rosegarth Clo. *Ches* 4C **138**
Rosegarth Clo. *Donc* 2H **31**
Rosegreave. *Gold* 4F **29**
Rose Gro. *Arm* 3E **35**
Rose Gro. *Womb* 5H **25**
Rose Hill. *Ches* 2H **137**
Rose Hill. *Donc* 2A **48**
Rose Hill. *Mosb* 1B **124**
Rosehill. *Rawm* 6F **55**
Rose Hill Av. *Mosb* 6G **55**
Rose Hill Cemetery & Crematorium.
 Donc 2C **48**
Rose Hill Clo. *Mosb* 1B **124**
Rose Hill Clo. *P'stne* 5D **142**
Rosehill Cotts. *Harl* 4A **52**
Rosehill Ct. *B'ley* 5G **13**
Rose Hill Ct. *Donc* 1A **48**
Rose Hill Dri. *Dod* 2B **22**
Rose Hill Dri. *Mosb* 1B **124**
Rose Hill E. *Ches* 2A **138**
Rose Hill M. *Mosb* 1B **124**
Rose Hill Ri. *Donc* 2A **48**
Rosehill Rd. *Rawm* 1F **69**
Rose Hill Vw. *Mosb* 1B **124**
Rose Hill W. *Ches* 2H **137**
Rose Ho. *Arm* 3E **35**
Rose La. *Lghtn* 5D **94**
Roselle St. *S6* 3A **86**
Rosemary Ct. S10 . . . . .6A **86**
(off Bank Rd.)
Rosemary Ct. S10 . . . . .5A **86**
(off Heavygate Rd.)
Rosemary Rd. *Beig* 3F **115**
Rosemary Rd. *Wick* 4E **81**
Rosene Cotts. *Cut* 4A **130**
Rose Pl. *Womb* 5A **26**
Rose Tree Av. *Cud* 6B **10**
Rose Tree Ct. *Cud* 6B **10**
Rose Way. *Kil* 4B **126**
Rosewell Ct. *Roth* 1H **79**
Rose Wood Clo. *Ches* 3F **131**
Rosewood Dri. *Barn D* 2G **21**
Roslin Rd. *S10* 2A **98**
Rossendale Clo. *Ches* 5G **137**
Rosser Av. *S12* 5B **112**
Rossetti Mt. *Flan* 3F **81**
Rossington. 4E **63**
Rossington Ho. Donc 2C **46**
(off Elsworth Clo.)
Rossington Rd. *S11* 5A **98**
Rossington St. *Den M* 1B **58**
Rossiter Rd. *Roth* 4C **68**
Rosslyn Av. *Ast* 5C **104**
Rosslyn Cres. *Ben* 5B **18**
Ross St. *S9* 1F **101**
Rosston Rd. *Maltby* 4H **83**
Rostholme. 5A **18**
Rostholme Sq. *Ben* 5B **18**
Roston Clo. *Dron W* 2B **128**
Rothay Clo. *Dron W* 3C **128**
Rothay Rd. *S4* 2B **88**
Rothbury Clo. *Soth* 5G **115**
Rothbury Ct. *Soth* 5G **115**
Rothbury Way. *B'wth* 2C **90**
Rother Av. *Brim* 3D **132**
Rother Clo. *Ches* 5G **137**
Rother Ct. *P'gte* 5E **69**
Rother Cres. *Tree* 1E **103**
Rother Cft. *Hoy* 5A **38**
Rotherham. 3D **78**
Rotherham Cemetery & Crematorium.
 Roth 3B **80**
Rotherham Central Library & Arts Cen.
 . . . . .2E **79**
Rotherham Clo. *Kil* 1D **126**
Rotherham Gateway. *Cat* 5B **90**
Rotherham Golf Course. 2D **70**
Rotherham La. *Lghtn* 6E **95**
Rotherham Rd. *S13* 3B **102**
Rotherham Rd. *B'ley* 1A **14**
Rotherham Rd. *Beig* 3G **115**
Rotherham Rd. *Cat* 5D **90**
Rotherham Rd. *Dinn* 3C **106**
Rotherham Rd. *Eck* 5E **125**
Rotherham Rd. *Half* 2F **125**
Rotherham Rd. *Kil & Blbgh* 5E **127**
(High Moor)

Rotherham Rd. Kil 2D **126**
(Norwood)
Rotherham Rd. L Hou & Gt Hou . . .3A **28**
Rotherham Rd. Maltby 4C **82**
Rotherham Rd. Roth & P'gte 6E **69**
Rotherham Rd. Swal 6A **104**
Rotherham Rd. Wath D 5B **40**
Rotherham Rd. N. Half 2F **125**
Rotherham St. S9 . . . . .4C **88**
Rotherham United F.C. 3B **78**
Rotherhill Clo. Roth 2G **79**
Rothermoor Av. Kiv P 5G **117**
Rother Rd. Roth 6D **78**
Rotherside Rd. Eck 5F **125**
Rotherstoke Clo. Roth 5E **79**
Rother St. Bram 3A **40**
Rother Ter. Roth 6D **78**
Rothervale Clo. Beig 3G **115**
Rothervale Rd. Ches 5A **138**
(Derby Rd.)
Rothervale Rd. Ches 6A **138**
(Storforth La.)
. . . . .5A **116**
Rother Valley Way. H'brk 1H **125**
Rother Vw. Clo. Swal 6G **103**
Rother Vw. Gdns. Swal 6G **103**
Rother Vw. Rd. Roth 6D **78**
Rother Way. Ches 5B **132**
Rother Way. H'by 3A **82**
Rotherway. Roth 3E **91**
Rotherwood Av. S13 . . . . .5D **102**
Rotherwood Clo. Donc 3F **31**
Rotherwood Cres. Thur 5A **94**
Rotherwood Rd. Kil 2C **126**
Rothesay Clo. Cusw 4H **31**
Rothey Gro. Ches 6B **130**
Rotunda Bus. Cen. C'town 6E **51**
Roughbirchworth 6G **143**
Roughbirchworth La. Oxs 6H **143**
Rough La. Gren . . . . .6A **64** & 1H **73**
Roughwood Grn. Rawm 4A **68**
Roughwood Rd. Roth 5G **67**
Roughwood Way. Roth 5G **67**
Roundel St. S9 . . . . .6B **88**
Round Grn. La. S'bgh & Wors 5D **22**
Round Hill. Dart 4E **7**
Round Hill Ct. Donc 3H **47**
Roundwood Ct. Wors 5A **24**
Roundwood Golf Course. 3H **69**
Roundwood Gro. Rawm 2G **69**
Roundwood Way. D'fld 3D **26**
Rowan Clo. B'ley 2H **23**
Rowan Clo. C'town 3E **65**
Rowan Clo. Gold 4E **29**
Rowan Ct. Donc 3A **34**
Rowan Dri. B'ley 4D **13**
Rowan Dri. Braml 4G **81**
Rowan Gth. Donc 3A **32**
Rowan Mt. Donc 3H **33**
Rowan Ri. Maltby 4D **82**
Rowan Rd. Eck 6H **125**
Rowan Tree Clo. Kil 4A **126**
Rowan Tree Dell. S17 . . . . .6E **121**
Rowan Tree Rd. Kil 3H **125**
Rowborn Dri. O'bri 5F **73**
Rowdale Cres. S12 . . . . .2F **113**
Rowell La. S6 . . . . .3B **84**
Rowena Av. E'thpe 6D **20**
Rowena Dri. Donc 3F **31**
Rowena Dri. Thur 4A **94**
Rowena Rd. Con 3D **58**
Rowernfields. Dinn 6H **107**
Rowland Pl. Donc 1C **46**
Rowland Rd. S2 . . . . .5E **99**
Rowland Rd. B'ley 4E **13**
Rowland St. S3 . . . . .6E **87**
Rowland St. Roy 1F **9**
Rowms La. Swint 2C **56**
Rowsley Cres. Stav 3A **134**
Rowsley St. S2 . . . . .4F **99**
Row, The. Cant 2F **49**
Roxby Clo. Donc 5B **48**
Roxton Av. S8 . . . . .1D **122**
Roxton Rd. S8 . . . . .6C **110**
Royal Av. Donc 5E **33**
Royal Ct. Bar G 1A **12**
Royal Ct. Ches 1A **138**
Royal Ct. Hoy 5B **38**
Royale Clo. Eck 6E **125**
Royal St. B'ley 6G **13**
Royalty La. Ark 1H **19**
Royd. 5G **141**

Royd Av. Cud 1H **15**
Royd Av. M'well 4F **7**
Royd Clo. Wors 5H **23**
Roydfield Clo. Wat 5D **114**
Roydfield Dri. Wat 5D **114**
Roydfield Gro. Wat 5D **114**
Royd Fld. La. P'stne 6D **142**
Royd La. Deep 5F **141**
Royd La. Hghm 4A **12**
(in two parts)
Royd Moor Ct. Thurls 3A **142**
Royd Moor Rd. Thurls 3A **142**
Royds Av. Whis 1A **92**
Royds Clo. Cres. Thry 5C **70**
Royds La. S4 . . . . .5A **88**
Royds La. Else 6E **39**
Royds Moor. 2C **92**
Royds Moor Hill. Whis 2D **92**
Royd, The. Deep 5F **141**
Roy Vw. Brie 4A **12**
Roy Kilner Rd. Womb 5H **25**
(in two parts)
Royston. .2E **9**
Royston Av. Donc 2A **32**
Royston Av. Owl 5A **114**
Royston Clo. Owl 5A **114**
Royston Clo. Walt 6D **136**
Royston Cotts. Hoy 5H **37**
Royston Cft. Owl 5A **114**
Royston Gro. Owl 5A **114**
(off Royston Clo.)
Royston Hill. Hoy 5H **37**
Royston La. Roy & B'ley 3E **9**
Royston Leisure Cen. 1E **9**
Royston Rd. Cud 4A **10**
Rubens Clo. Dron 2D **128**
Rubens Row. S2 . . . . .1G **99**
(off Bernard St.)
Rud Broom Clo. P'stne 5B **142**
Rud Broom La. P'stne 5B **142**
Ruddle La. M'brng 6A **60**
Rudyard M. S6 . . . . .3A **86**
Rudyard Rd. S6 . . . . .3A **86**
Rufford Av. B'ley 5C **8**
Rufford Clo. Ches 4G **137**
Rufford Ct. Soth 5G **115**
Rufford Ri. Gold 5E **29**
Rufford Ri. Soth 5G **115**
Rufford Rd. Donc 2F **47**
Rufus La. New R 4B **62**
Rugby St. S3 . . . . .5E **87**
Rundle Dri. S7 . . . . .6C **98**
Rundle Rd. S7 . . . . .6C **98**
Rundle Rd. S'bri 3D **140**
Runnymede Rd. Donc 5H **33**
Rupert Rd. S7 . . . . .2C **110**
Rural Cres. Bran 3H **49**
Rural La. S6 . . . . .1F **85**
Ruscombe Pl. B'ley 4E **9**
Rushby St. S4 . . . . .2H **87**
Rushdale Av. S8 . . . . .2E **111**
Rushdale Mt. S8 . . . . .2E **111**
Rushdale Rd. S8 . . . . .2E **111**
Rushdale Ter. S8 . . . . .2E **111**
Rushen Mt. Ches 6H **137**
Rushey Clo. Rawm 5E **55**
Rushleigh Ct. S17 . . . . .2D **120**
Rushley Av. S17 . . . . .1D **120**
Rushley Clo. S17 . . . . .1D **120**
Rushley Dri. S17 . . . . .1D **120**
Rushley Rd. S17 . . . . .1D **120**
Rushworth Clo. Dart 5A **6**
Ruskin Av. Mexb 5F **43**
Ruskin Clo. Wath D 4C **40**
Ruskin Dri. Arm 3G **35**
Ruskin Rd. Donc 5A **46**
Ruskin Sq. S8 . . . . .1E **111**
Russell Clo. B'ley 2B **14**
Russell Clo. Swal 6H **103**
Russell Ct. S11 . . . . .5G **109**
Russell Pl. Maltby 3G **83**
Russell Rd. Kiln 6C **56**
Russell St. S3 . . . . .6E **87** (1D **4**)
Russell St. Roth 1E **79**
Russett Ct. Maltby 3D **82**
Rustlings Ct. S10 . . . . .5F **97**
Rustlings Rd. S11 . . . . .5G **97**
Ruston Clo. Ches 5D **130**
Ruston Dri. Roy 1E **9**
Ruthin St. S4 . . . . .3A **88**
Ruth Sq. S10 . . . . .3C **98**
Ruthven Dri. Warm 4F **45**
Rutland Av. Ans 6D **106**

Rutland La. New R 4B **62**
Rutland Pk. S10 . . . . .3A **98**
Rutland Pl. Womb 1D **38**
Rutland Rd. S3 . . . . .6D **86**
Rutland Rd. Ches 2H **137**
Rutland St. S3 . . . . .5E **87**
Rutland St. Donc 5E **33**
Rutland St. Old W 1A **132**
Rutland Ter. Barl 1A **130**
Rutland Way. S3 . . . . .5D **86**
Rutland Way. B'ley 4E **13**
Ryan Dri. S13 . . . . .6E **103**
Ryan Pl. P'gte 3F **69**
Rydal Clo. Bol D 2A **42**
Rydal Clo. Dinn 6F **107**
Rydal Clo. Dron W 2B **128**
Rydal Clo. P'stne 3D **142**
Rydal Ct. Donc 1G **61**
Rydal Cres. Ches 3G **131**
Rydalhurst Av. S6 . . . . .1G **85**
Rydall Pl. Donc 1H **31**
Rydal Rd. S8 . . . . .2C **110**
Rydal Rd. Dinn 6F **107**
Rydal Ter. B'ley 6A **14**
Rydal Way. Mexb 5G **43**
Rye Bank. Whis 2B **92**
Rye Ct. Roth 1E **91**
Ryecroft. 1H **69**
Rye Cft. B'ley 1A **14**
Rye Cft. Con 3G **59**
Ryecroft Glen Rd. S17 . . . . .1G **121**
Ryecroft Rd. Rawm 1A **70**
Ryecroft Vw. S17 . . . . .1D **120**
Ryedale Wlk. Donc 6F **31**
Ryegate Cres. S10 . . . . .2H **97**
Ryegate Rd. S10 . . . . .3H **97**
Ryehill Av. Ches 3C **136**
Ryeview Gdns. Roth 5B **68**
Ryhill Dri. Owl 5A **114**
Rykneld Sq. Ches 2A **138**
(off Church Way)
Ryle Rd. S7 . . . . .6C **98**
Rylstone Ct. S12 . . . . .4B **114**
Rylstone Gro. S12 . . . . .4B **114**
Rylstone Wlk. B'ley 3D **24**
Ryton Av. Womb 2H **39**
Ryton Clo. Maltby 4G **83**
Ryton Rd. Ans 3F **119**
Ryton Way. Donc 5E **49**

S

Sackerville Ter. Kil 3H **125**
Sackup La. Dart 4D **6**
Sackville Clo. Walt 5D **136**
Sackville Rd. S10 . . . . .1H **97**
Sackville St. B'ley 5F **13**
Saddler Av. Wat 6D **114**
Saddler Clo. Wat 6D **114**
Saddler Grn. Wat 6D **114**
Saddler Gro. Wat 6D **114**
Sadler Ga. B'ley 5G **13**
Sadler's Ga. Womb 5A **26**
St Agnes' Rd. Donc 1G **47**
St Aidan's Av. S2 . . . . .5H **99**
St Aidan's Clo. S2 . . . . .4A **100**
St Aidan's Dri. S2 . . . . .5A **100**
St Aidan's Mt. S2 . . . . .5A **100**
St Aidan's Pl. S2 . . . . .5A **100**
St Aidan's Rd. S2 . . . . .5A **100**
St Aidan's Way. S2 . . . . .5A **100**
St Albans Clo. S10 . . . . .4C **96**
St Alban's Ct. Wick 5F **81**
St Albans Dri. S10 . . . . .4B **96**
St Albans Rd. S10 . . . . .4B **96**
St Alban's Way. Wick 5E **81**
St Andrew Rd. Deep 4G **141**
St Andrew's Clo. S11 . . . . .6B **98**
St Andrew's Clo. Braml 2G **81**
St Andrews Clo. Dinn 5F **107**
St Andrews Clo. Donc 5F **49**
St Andrews Clo. Swint 4B **56**
St Andrews Cres. Hoy 5A **38**
St Andrews Dri. Dart 4E **7**
St Andrews Ri. Ches 5E **137**
St Andrew's Rd. S11 . . . . .6B **98**
St Andrew's Rd. Con 4D **58**
St Andrews Rd. Hoy 5A **38**
St Andrew's Sq. Bol D 1A **42**
St Andrew's Ter. Donc 2D **46**

St Andrew's Wlk.—Sale St.

St Andrew's Wlk. *B'wth* 2A **90**
St Andrew's Way. *Barn D* 1E **21**
St Andrews Way. *B'ley* 2G **25**
St Anne's Clo. *Stav* 3B **134**
St Anne's Dri. *B'ley* 6F **9**
St Anne's Rd. *Donc* 1G **47**
St Ann's. 2E **79**
St Ann's Rd. *Deep* 3F **141**
St Ann's Rd. *Roth* 1E **79**
St Ann's Roundabout. *Roth* 2E **79**
St Anthony Rd. *S10* 1G **97**
St Augustines. 5A **138**
St Augustines Av. *Ches* 5A **138**
St Augustines Cres. *Ches* 5A **138**
St Augustines Dri. *Ches* 4A **138**
St Augustines Mt. *Ches* 5A **138**
St Augustines Ri. *Ches* 5A **138**
St Augustines Rd. *Ches* 5H **137**
St Augustine's Rd. *Donc* 2A **48**
St Austell Dri. *Bar G* 3A **12**
St Barbara's Clo. *Maltby* 5E **83**
St Barbara's Rd. *D'fld* 4D **26**
St Barnabas La. *S2* 5E **99**
St Barnabas Rd. *S2* 5E **99**
St Bartholomew's Clo. *Maltby* 5E **83**
St Bartholomews Ri. *Donc* 3B **48**
St Bart's Ter. *B'ley* 1H **23**
St Bede's Rd. *Roth* 3C **78**
St Benedicts Ct. *S2* 5H **99**
St Catherine's Av. *Donc* 3B **46**
St Catherine's Way. *B'ley* 6D **12**
St Cecilia's Rd. *Donc* 2G **47**
St Chad's Sq. *Den M* 1B **58**
St Chad's Way. *Ches* 3A **132**
St Chad's Way. *Spro* 2E **45**
St Charles St. *S9* 5A **88**
*St Christopher's. Donc 4A **46***
(off Hall Flat La.)
St Christophers Clo. *B'ley* 2G **25**
St Christopher's Cres. *Donc* 3G **31**
St Clements Clo. *B'ley* 2G **25**
St Clement's Clo. *Donc* 3F **31**
St David Rd. *Deep* 4G **141**
St David's Dri. *Ans* 4F **119**
St David's Dri. *B'ley* 1F **25**
St David's Dri. *B'wth* 2A **90**
St David's Dri. *Donc* 3F **31**
St David's Ri. *Ches* 5F **137**
St David's Rd. *Con* 3D **58**
St Dominic's Clo. *Spro* 3D **44**
St Edmund's Av. *Thur* 6A **94**
St Edward's Av. *B'ley* 1F **23**
St Elizabeth Clo. *S2* 5F **99**
St Eric's Rd. *Donc* 3B **48**
St Francis Boulevd. *B'ley* 6F **9**
St Francis Clo. *S10* 3E **97**
St Francis Clo. *Braml* 2G **81**
St George Ga. *Donc* 6C **32**
St George Rd. *Deep* 4G **141**
St George's Av. *Swint* 2H **55**
St George's Clo. *S3* 1C **98** (2A **4**)
St George's Ct. *S3* 3B **4**
St George's Dri. *B'wth* 2A **90**
St George's Rd. *B'ley* 6G **13**
St George's Rd. *Donc* 2H **47**
St George's Ter. *S1* 2D **98** (3B **4**)
*St Georges Ter. S11 5D **98***
(off Sharrow La.)
St Giles Clo. *Ches* 5B **138**
St Giles Ga. *Donc* 4F **31**
St Giles Sq. *C'town* 2D **64**
St Helen Rd. *Deep* 5G **141**
St Helen's. 2D **14**
St Helen's Av. *B'ley* 2B **14**
St Helen's Boulevd. *B'ley* 1B **14**
St Helen's Clo. *Ches* 1A **138**
St Helens Clo. *Thurn* 1D **28**
St Helen's Clo. *Tree* 2F **103**
St Helens Ct. *Else* 5B **38**
St Helen's La. *Barn* 1H **43**
(in two parts)
St Helen's Rd. *Donc* 1G **47**
St Helen's Sq. *Kirk S* 3D **20**
St Helen's St. *Ches* 1A **138**
St Helen's St. *Else* 5C **38**
St Helen's Way. *B'ley* 2D **14**
St Helier Dri. *B'ley* 5D **12**
St Hilda Av. *B'ley* 6E **13**
St Hilda Clo. *Deep* 5G **141**
St Hilda's Rd. *Donc* 1G **47**
St James Av. *Ans* 3F **119**
St James Clo. *Ches* 4C **138**
St James Clo. *Kirk S* 3D **20**
St James Clo. *Wath D* 5G **41**
St James' Clo. *Wors* 5A **24**
St James Ct. *Donc* 1D **46**
St James' Dri. *Rav* 4H **71**
St James' Gdns. *Donc* 2B **46**
St James' Row. *S1* 1E **99** (2E **5**)
St James's Bri. *Donc* 1C **46**
*St James Sq. Ches 2A **138***
(off Vicar La.)
St James' St. *S1* 2E **99** (3E **5**)
St James St. *Donc* 1C **46**
St James' Vw. *Rav* 4H **71**
St James Wlk. *S13* 5D **102**
St Joan Av. *Deep* 5G **141**
St John's. *H'swne* 1F **143**
St John's Av. *Bar G* 3A **12**
St John's Av. *Roth* 3B **78**
St John's Av. *S'side* 3G **81**
St John's Clo. *S2* 1G **99**
St John's Clo. *Dod* 2A **22**
St John's Clo. *P'stne* 5C **142**
St John's Clo. *Roth* 1G **79**
St Johns Clo. *Walt* 6D **136**
St John's Ct. *Lghtn* 1E **107**
St Johns Ct. *Roth* 3B **78**
St John's Ct. *S'side* 3G **81**
St John's Cft. *Wadw* 6H **61**
St Johns Grn. *Roth* 6G **67**
St John's Mt. *Ches* 3H **131**
St Johns Pl. *Stav* 2B **134**
St John's Rd. *S2* 1H **99**
St John's Rd. *B'ley* 1G **23**
St John's Rd. *Ches* 4G **131**
(in two parts)
St John's Rd. *Cud* 1H **15**
St John's Rd. *Deep* 4H **141**
St John's Rd. *Donc* 3A **46**
St John's Rd. *Edl'tn* 3B **60**
St John's Rd. *Lghtn* 1E **107**
St John's Rd. *Roth* 1G **79**
St Johns Rd. *Stav* 2A **134**
St John's Rd. *Swint* 2A **56**
St John's Wlk. *Adw D* 3E **43**
St John's Wlk. *Roy* 2F **9**
St Joseph's Ct. *Dinn* 4F **107**
St Joseph's Gdns. *B'ley* 1B **24**
St Joseph's Rd. *S13* 3H **101**
St Laurence Ct. *Adw S* 1C **16**
St Lawrence Glebe. *S9* 1G **89**
St Lawrence Rd. *S9* 6G **77**
St Lawrence's Ter. *Adw S* 1E **17**
St Leger Av. *Dinn* 3C **106**
St Leger Way. *Dinn* 3F **107**
St Leonard's Av. *Thry* 5D **70**
St Leonard's Clo. *Dinn* 5E **107**
St Leonards Ct. *S5* 6F **75**
St Leonard's Cft. *Thry* 4D **70**
St Leonards Dri. *Ches* 4C **138**
St Leonard's La. *Roth* 2F **79**
St Leonard's Lea. *Donc* 3G **31**
St Leonard's Pl. *Roth* 2F **79**
St Leonard's Rd. *Roth* 2E **79**
St Leonards Way. *B'ley* 2G **25**
St Luke's Clo. *D'ville* 3H **21**
St Lukes Ct. *Ches* 3H **131**
St Lukes Way. *B'ley* 4C **14**
St Margaret Av. *Deep* 4G **141**
St Margaret's Av. *Barn* 1G **43**
St Margaret's Dri. *Ches* 2H **137**
St Margaret's Dri. *Swint* 2H **55**
St Margaret's Rd. *Donc* 1G **47**
St Margarets Rd. *E'fld* 2F **75**
St Mark Rd. *Deep* 4G **141**
St Mark's Cres. *S10* 3B **98**
St Mark's Rd. *Ches* 2G **137**
St Martin Clo. *Deep* 4G **141**
St Martin's Av. *Donc* 3G **31**
St Martin's Clo. *B'ley* 6D **12**
St Martin's Clo. *Ches* 5F **131**
St Mary Cres. *Deep* 5G **141**
St Mary's & All Saints' Church (Crooked Spire) 2B 138
St Mary's Clo. *Cud* 6B **10**
St Marys Clo. *E'fld* 6E **65**
St Mary's Cres. *Donc* 5E **33**
St Mary's Cres. *Swint* 1A **56**
St Mary's Dri. *Arm* 3G **35**
St Mary's Dri. *Cat* 5C **90**
St Marys Gdns. *Wors* 1E **37**
St Mary's Ga. *S2* 4D **98** (6C **4**)
St Mary's Ga. *B'ley* 5G **13**
St Mary's Ga. *Ches* 2B **138**
St Marys La. *E'fld* 6E **65**
St Mary's Pl. *B'ley* 5G **13**
*St Mary's Pl. Ches 2B **138***
(off St Mary's Ga.)
St Mary's Rd. *S1 & S2* 4E **99** (6E **5**)
St Mary's Rd. *D'fld* 4F **27**
St Mary's Rd. *Donc* 4E **33**
St Mary's Rd. *Edl'tn* 4C **60**
St Mary's Rd. *Gold* 3H **29**
St Mary's Rd. *Rawm* 2G **69**
St Mary's Rd. *Womb* 1E **39**
St Mary's Sq. *S1* 4D **98** (6C **4**)
St Mary's St. *P'stne* 4D **142**
*St Mary's Ter. Bols 6E **141***
(off Walders La.)
St Mary's Vw. *Roth* 4B **68**
St Mary's Wlk. *Spro* 3D **44**
St Matthews Way. *B'ley* 4C **14**
St Matthias Rd. *Deep* 5G **141**
St Michael's Av. *B'ley* 1D **14**
St Michaels Av. *Ross* 3E **63**
St Michael's Av. *Swint* 1B **56**
St Michaels Clo. *E'fld* 1F **75**
St Michaels Clo. *Gold* 4F **29**
St Michaels Cres. *S35* 1F **75**
St Michael's Rd. *Bes & Donc* 2H **47**
St Michaels Rd. *E'fld* 1F **75**
St Nicholas Clo. *E'thpe* 5C **20**
St Nicolas Rd. *Rawm* 1G **69**
St Nicolas Wlk. *Rawm* 1H **69**
St Oswald's Dri. *E'thpe* 5D **20**
St Owens Dri. *B'ley* 5D **12**
St Pancras Clo. *Dinn* 3B **106**
St Patrick Rd. *Deep* 4G **141**
St Patrick's Rd. *Donc* 4G **33**
St Patrick's Way. *Donc* 3F **31**
St Paul Clo. *Deep* 4G **141**
St Paul Clo. *Tod* 2A **118**
St Paul Rd. *B'ley* 4E **13**
St Pauls Av. *Has* 6D **138**
St Pauls Clo. *Dinn* 2C **106**
St Paul's Pde. *S1* 4E **5**
St Paul's Pde. *B'ley* 1F **25**
St Paul's Pde. *Donc* 4F **31**
St Peter Av. *Deep* 4H **141**
St Peter's Clo. *S1* 1E **99** (2E **5**)
St Peter's Clo. *Barn D* 1G **21**
St Peter's Clo. *B'wth* 3A **90**
St Peter's Dri. *Con* 4D **58**
St Peter's Rd. *Con* 4D **58**
St Peter's Rd. *Donc* 4G **45**
St Peter's Ter. *B'ley* 1A **24**
St Philip's Clo. *Maltby* 5E **83**
St Philip's Dri. *Has* 5B **138**
St Philip's La. *S3* 6D **86**
St Philip's Rd. *S3* 1C **98** (2A **4**)
(in three parts)
St Quentin Clo. *S17* 4H **121**
St Quentin Dri. *S17* 4H **121**
St Quentin Mt. *S17* 4H **121**
St Quentin Ri. *S17* 4H **121**
St Quentin Vw. *S17* 4H **121**
St Ronan's Rd. *S7* 6D **98**
St Sepulchre Ga. *Donc* 6C **32**
St Sepulchre Ga. W. *Donc* 1C **46**
St Stephens Dri. *Ast* 5B **104**
St Stephen's Rd. *S3* 1C **98** (1A **4**)
St Stephen's Rd. *Roth* 2E **79**
St Stephen's Wlk. *S3* 1C **98** (2A **4**)
St Stephens Wlk. *Donc* 4G **31**
St Thomas' Ct. *Donc* 5B **48**
St Thomas Rd. *S10* 2H **97**
St Thomas's Clo. *Donc* 5G **45**
St Thomas's Rd. *B'ley* 3C **12**
St Thomas St. *S1* 2D **98** (3C **4**)
St Thomas St. *Ches* 3E **137**
St Ursula's Rd. *Donc* 1G **47**
St Veronica Rd. *Deep* 4H **141**
St Vincent Av. *Donc* 5E **33**
St Vincent Av. *W'land* 1B **16**
St Vincent Rd. *Donc* 5E **33**
St Vincent's Av. *Bran* 4G **49**
St Wandrilles Clo. *E'fld* 6F **65**
*St Wilfrids Ct. Donc 3C **48***
(off Masham Rd.)
St Wilfrid's Rd. *S2* 5E **99**
St Wilfrid's Rd. *Donc* 2A **48**
St Withold Av. *Thur* 5A **94**
Salcey Sq. *Ches* 4F **137**
Salcombe Clo. *M'well* 5G **7**
Sale Hill. *S10* 3H **97**
Salerno Way. *D'fld* 3C **26**
Sale St. *Hoy* 6E **37**

Salisbury Av. *Ches* 4G **131**
Salisbury Av. *Dron* 3E **129**
Salisbury Cres. *Ches* 4H **131**
Salisbury Rd. *S10* 1H **97**
Salisbury Rd. *Donc* 2A **46**
Salisbury Rd. *Dron* 4F **129**
Salisbury St. *Maltby* 3F **83**
Salisbury St. *B'ley* 4F **13**
Salmon St. *S11* 5D **98**
Salt Box Gro. *Gren* 1A **74**
Salt Box La. *Gren* 2A **74**
Saltergate. *Ches* 2H **137**
Salter Oak Cft. *B'ley* 4E **9**
Saltersbrook. *Gold* 4F **29**
Saltersbrook Flats. *Gold* 4F **29**
Saltersbrook Rd. *D'fld* 2D **26**
Salters Way. *P'stne* 5D **142**
Samson St. *S2* 3G **99**
Samuel Clo. *S2* 6H **99**
Samuel Dri. *S2* 6H **99**
Samuel Pl. *S2* 5H **99**
Samuel Rd. *S2* 6H **99**
Samuel Rd. *B'ley* 4D **12**
Samuel Sq. *B'ley* 4D **12**
Samuel St. *Donc* 5H **45**
Sanctuary Fields. *Ans* 6D **106**
Sandal Ct. *Roth* 2B **78**
Sandall Beat La. *Donc* 3B **34**
Sandall Beat (Nature Reserve) 5C **34**
Sandall Beat Rd. *Donc* 6H **33**
Sandall Carr Rd. *K Ind* 4C **20**
Sandall La. *K Ind* 2B **20**
(in two parts)
Sandall Pk. Dri. *Donc* 2A **34**
Sandall Ri. *Donc* 3H **33**
Sandall Stones Rd. *K Ind* 4B **20**
(in two parts)
Sandall Vw. *Dinn* 2C **106**
Sandal Rd. *Con* 4C **58**
Sandalwood Clo. *Donc* 1A **34**
Sandalwood Ri. *Swint* 5B **56**
Sandbeck Clo. *B'ley* 4H **13**
Sandbeck Ct. *Den M* 2B **58**
Sandbeck Ct. *Ross* 5E **63**
Sandbeck Ho. *Donc* 1C **46**
(off Grove Pl.)
Sandbeck Pl. *S11* 5B **98**
Sandbeck Rd. *Donc* 1F **47**
Sandbeck Way. *H'by* 4A **82**
Sandbed Rd. *S3* 4C **86**
Sandbergh Rd. *Roth* 5G **67**
Sandby Ct. *S14* 5A **112**
Sandby Cft. *S14* 5A **112**
Sandby Dri. *S14* 5A **112**
Sandcliffe Rd. *Donc* 3H **33**
Sandcroft Clo. *Hoy* 6G **37**
Sandeby Dri. *Rav* 2H **81**
Sanderson St. *S9* 4B **88**
Sandford Ct. *B'ley* 6F **13**
Sandford Ct. *Donc* 4A **46**
Sandford Gro. Rd. *S7* 2C **110**
Sandford Rd. *Donc* 5A **46**
Sandhill. .6H **55**
(Rawmarsh)
Sandhill. .1B **28**
(Thurnscoe)
Sandhill Clo. *Rawm* 6H **55**
Sandhill Ct. *Gt Hou* 1B **28**
Sandhill Golf Course. 1H **27**
Sandhill Gro. *Grim* 4G **11**
Sandhill Rd. *Rawm* 6H **55**
Sandhurst Pl. *S10* 1A **98**
Sandhurst Rd. *Cant* 4E **49**
Sandiron Ho. *S7* 6H **109**
Sandiway. *Ches* 5E **137**
Sandon Vw. *S10* 6A **4**
Sandown Clo. *Eck* 6B **124**
Sandown Gdns. *Donc* 1B **48**
Sandown Rd. *Mexb* 5F **43**
Sandpiper Rd. *Thpe H* 1B **66**
Sandpit Hill. *Bran* 3G **49**
Sandringham Av. *Whis* 2H **91**
Sandringham Clo. *Cal* 1G **139**
Sandringham Clo. *Ches* 3A **132**
Sandringham Clo. *Thurls* 3A **142**
Sandringham Pl. *Rav* 1H **81**
Sandringham Rd. *Cal* 1G **139**
Sandringham Rd. *Donc* 6G **33**
Sandrock Dri. *Donc* 4C **48**
Sands Clo. *S14* 3A **112**
Sandstone Av. *S9* 1B **88**
Sandstone Av. *Walt* 5D **136**

Sandstone Clo. *S9* 6C **76**
Sandstone Dri. *S9* 1B **88**
Sandstone Rd. *S9* 1B **88**
Sandwith Rd. *Tod* 2A **118**
Sandy Acres Clo. *Wat* 6F **115**
Sandy Acres Dri. *Wat* 6F **115**
Sandybridge La. Ind. Est.
Shaf .1B **10**
Sandycroft Cres. *Donc* 4G **45**
Sandy Flat La. *Wick* 2E **93**
Sandygate. 3D **96**
Sandygate. *Wath D* 5F **41**
(in two parts)
Sandygate Ct. *S10* 3D **96**
Sandygate Cres. *Wath D* 1F **55**
Sandygate Grange Dri. *S10* 3E **97**
Sandygate Gro. *S10* 3D **96**
Sandygate La. *S10* 3E **97**
Sandygate La. *B'ley* 1E **25**
Sandygate Pk. *S10* 3C **96**
Sandygate Pk. Cres. *S10* 3D **96**
Sandygate Pk. Rd. *S10* 3D **96**
Sandygate Rd. *S10* 3D **96**
Sandy La. *Braml* . . . . .6H **81** & 6A **82**
(in two parts)
Sandy La. *Burn* 3A **64**
Sandy La. *Donc* 2G **47**
Sandy La. *Thur* 4B **94**
Sandy La. *Womb* 1A **38**
Sandymount Rd. *Wath D* 6G **41**
Sanforth St. *Ches* 5A **132**
Sankey Sq. *Gold* 4F **29**
Sarah Ct. *Arm* 2H **35**
Sarah St. *Mexb* 1E **57**
Sarah St. *Roth* 3B **78**
Sark Rd. *S2* 6E **99**
Sarrius Ct. *Cant* 3C **48**
Saundby Clo. *Donc* 4A **48**
Saunderson Rd. *P'stne* 3B **142**
Saunders Pl. *S2* 2A **100**
Saunders Rd. *S2* 2A **100**
Saunders' Row. *Womb* 1E **39**
Savage La. *S17* 2D **120**
Savile St. *S4* 6G **87**
Savile St. E. *S4* 6H **87**
Savile Wlk. *Brie* 2H **11**
Saville Ct. *Hoy* 6F **37**
Saville Hall La. *Dod* 3B **22**
Saville La. *Thurls* 4A **142**
Saville Rd. *Dod* 3B **22**
Saville Rd. *Wath D* 5E **41**
Saville St. *Whis* 2H **91**
Saville St. *Cud* 6B **10**
Saville St. *Dalt* 6A **70**
Saville Ter. *B'ley* 1G **31**
Sawdon Rd. *S11* 4C **98**
Sawn Moor Av. *Thur* 5B **94**
Sawn Moor Rd. *Thur* 6B **94**
Sawston Clo. *Donc* 1G **61**
Saxon Cres. *Wors* 4A **24**
Saxonlea Av. *S2* 4E **101**
Saxonlea Ct. *S2* 4E **101**
Saxonlea Cres. *S2* 4E **101**
Saxonlea Dri. *S2* 4D **100**
Saxon Rd. *S8* 1E **111**
Saxon Rd. *Kiv P* 5B **118**
Saxon Rd. *Roth* 3F **77**
Saxon Row. *Con* 4G **59**
Saxon St. *Cud* 1H **15**
Saxon St. *Thurn* 1G **29**
Saxton Av. *Donc* 3A **48**
Saxton Clo. *Else* 5D **38**
Saxton Dri. *Roth* 2F **91**
Sayers Clo. *H'ton* 1G **43**
Scafell Pl. *Ans* 1H **119**
Scaftworth Clo. *Donc* 4A **48**
Scammadine Clo. *B'wth* 3D **90**
Scamming La. *Lghtn* 6H **95**
Scampton Lodge. *S5* 1F **87**
Scarborough Clo. *Ans* 6E **107**
Scarborough La. *New R* 4B **62**
Scarborough Rd. *S9* 6E **89**
Scarborough Rd. *Wick* 4F **81**
Scarbrough Cres. *Maltby* 5G **83**
Scarbrough Farm Ct. *Maltby* 4F **83**
Scarfield Clo. *B'ley* 1F **25**
Scargill Cft. *S3* 1E **99** (2E **5**)
Scar La. *Ard* 1F **25**
Scarlett Oak Mdw. *S6* 5C **84**
Scarll Rd. *Donc* 2A **46**
Scarsdale Clo. *Dron* 3F **129**
Scarsdale Cres. *Brim* 4D **132**
Scarsdale Cross. *Dron* 2F **129**

Scarsdale Rd. *S8* 4D **110**
Scarsdale Rd. *Ches* 3A **132**
Scarsdale Rd. *Dron* 2E **129**
Scarsdale St. *Dinn* 4G **107**
Scarth Av. *Donc* 3B **46**
Scawsby. .3F **31**
Scawsby La. *Scaw* 1D **30**
Scawthorpe. 1G **31**
Scawthorpe Av. *Donc* 1F **31**
Scawthorpe Cotts. *Scawt* 1E **31**
Sceptone Gro. *Shaf* 2C **10**
Sceptre Gro. *New R* 6C **62**
Schofield Dri. *D'fld* 3E **27**
Schofield Pl. *D'fld* 3E **27**
Schofield Rd. *D'fld* 3E **27**
Schofield Rd. *Deep* 3F **141**
Schofield St. *Mexb* 6D **42**
Schole Av. *P'stne* 4C **142**
Schole Hill La. *P'stne* 5B **142**
(in two parts)
Scholes. .4D **66**
Scholes Fld. Clo. *Scho* 5E **67**
Scholes Grn. *Scho* 3E **67**
Scholes La. *Scho* 4C **66**
Scholes Ri. *E'fld* 1F **75**
Scholes Vw. *E'fld* 6F **65**
Scholes Vw. *Hoy* 6A **38**
Scholes Vw. *Jump* 4B **38**
Scholey Rd. *Wick* 4F **81**
Scholey St. *S3* 6F **87** (1G **5**)
Scholfield Cres. *Maltby* 5H **83**
School Av. *Half* 2E **125**
School Board La. *Ches* 3G **137**
School Clo. *Half* 2F **125**
School Clo. *Wal* 4F **117**
School Ct. *Donc* 5D **32**
(off Dockin Hill Rd.)
Schoolfield Dri. *Rawm* 6F **55**
School Grn. La. *S10* 6B **96**
School Gro. *Ast* 6C **104**
School Hill. *Cud* 6B **10**
School Hill. *Cut* 4A **130**
School Hill. *Whis* 2A **92**
School La. *S2* 2G **99** (4H **5**)
School La. *S6* 6C **84**
School La. *S8* 2D **122**
(Greenhill Main Rd.)
School La. *S8* 6G **111**
(Norton La.)
School La. *Cant* 3F **49**
School La. *Dron* 2E **129**
School La. *Gren* 6A **64**
School La. *P'gte* 4E **69**
School La. *Thry* 4D **70**
School La. Clo. *S8* 6G **111**
School Rd. *S10* 2H **97**
School Rd. *Beig* 4G **115**
School Rd. *Ches* 4A **132**
School Rd. *High G* 6C **50**
School Rd. *Lghtn* 1D **106**
School Rd. *Thur* 5B **94**
School Rd. *Wal* 5E **117**
School St. *B'ley* 4F **13**
School St. *Bol D* 1A **42**
School St. *Cud* 5B **10**
School St. *D'fld* 3F **27**
School St. *Dart* 4C **6**
School St. *Dinn* 4F **107**
School St. *Eck* 6D **124**
School St. *H'fld* 4E **39**
School St. *M'well* 4G **7**
School St. *Mosb* 2D **124**
School St. *S'foot* 1D **24**
School St. *Swal* 6A **104**
School St. *Thry* 5C **70**
School St. *Thurn* 1F **29**
School St. *Womb* 6B **26**
School Ter. *Con* 3D **58**
School Wlk. *Den M* 1B **58**
School Wlk. *Maltby* 4F **83**
School Wlk. *Old E* 6A **60**
Scorah's La. *Swint* 2G **55**
Scotia Clo. *S2* 5B **100**
Scotia Dri. *S2* 5B **100**
Scotland St. *S3* 1D **98** (1C **4**)
Scot La. *Donc* 6D **32**
Scott Av. *Barn* 1G **43**
Scott Av. *Con* 3C **58**
Scott Clo. *Thur* 5A **94**
Scott Cres. *E'thpe* 4C **20**
Scott Hill. *Spro* 3D **44**
Scott Rd. *S4* 3F **87**
Scott St. *S4* 3A **88**

Scott Wlk. *Maltby* 3D **82**
Scott Way. *C'town* 3D **64**
Scout Dike. **1B 142**
Scovell Av. *Rawm* 6D **54**
Scovell Ho. *Rawm* 6D **54**
Scowerdons Clo. *S12* 2H **113**
Scowerdons Dri. *S12* 2H **113**
Scraith Wood Dri. *S5* 1B **86**
Scrooby Dri. *Roth* 4C **68**
Scrooby La. *P'gte* 4D **68**
Scrooby Pl. *Roth* 4C **68**
Scrooby St. *Roth* 4C **68**
Sea Breeze Ter. *S13* 5F **101**
Seabrook Rd. *S2* 3H **99**
Seagrave Av. *S12* 3D **112**
Seagrave Cres. *S12* 4C **112**
Seagrave Dri. *S12* 3D **112**
Seagrave Dri. *Ches* 6C **138**
Seagrave Rd. *S12* 3C **112**
Searby Rd. *Braml* 2H **81**
Seaton Clo. *S2* 3B **100**
Seaton Cres. *S2* 3B **100**
Seaton Gdns. *New R* 6D **62**
Seaton Pl. *S2* 3B **100**
Seaton Way. *S2* 3B **100**
Sebastian Vw. *B'wth* 1C **90**
Second Av. *W'land* 3E **17**
Second La. *Ans* 4G **119**
Second La. *Wick* 1G **93**
Sedan St. *S4* 4G **87**
Sedbergh Cres. *Ches* 4F **131**
Sedge Clo. *Braml* 2E **81**
Sedgefield Way. *Mexb* 5F **43**
Sedgemoor Clo. *Ches* 1D **136**
Sedgley Rd. *S6* 3B **86**
Sefton Ct. *S10* 6E **97**
Sefton Rd. *S10* 6D **96**
Selborne Rd. *S10* 3G **97**
Selborne St. *Roth* 1E **79**
Selbourne Clo. *Bar G* 2A **12**
Selby Clo. *Ches* 5E **137**
Selby Clo. *Swal* 6A **104**
Selby Rd. *S4* 2H **87**
Selby Rd. *B'ley* 6B **8**
Selby Rd. *Donc* 4G **33**
Selhurst Cres. *Donc* 4C **48**
Selhurst Rd. *Ches* 6H **131**
Selig Pde. *S12* 5E *113*
(off White La.)
Selkirk Av. *Warm* 5F **45**
Selkirk Rd. *Donc* 3A **34**
Sellars Rd. *Roth* 6G **67**
Sellars Row. *High G* 5B **50**
Sellers St. *S8* 6D **98**
Selly Oak Gro. *S8* 3G **123**
Selly Oak Rd. *S8* 3G **123**
Selmer Ct. *Brim* 3D **132**
Selwood Flats. *Roth* 2F **79**
Selwyn St. *Roth* 1E **79**
Senior St. *S9* 1F **101**
Senior Rd. *Donc* 1A **46**
Seniors Pl. *C'town* 1E **65**
Sennen Cft. *B'ley* 4B **14**
Serlby Ho. *Donc* 1C *46*
(off St James St.)
Serpentine Wlk. *S8* 1E **123**
Setcup La. *Eck* 6H **125**
Seth Ter. *B'ley* 1A **24**
Sevenairs Fold. *Beig* 4E **115**
Sevenairs Rd. *Beig* 4E **115**
Sevenairs Vw. *Beig* 4E **115**
Sevenfields Ct. *S6* 2G **85**
Sevenfields La. *S6* 2G **85**
Seven Yards Rd. *Bran* 1H **49**
Severn Ct. *S10* 2B **98**
Severn Rd. *S10* 2B **98**
Severnside Dri. *S13* 6A **102**
Severnside Gdns. *S13* 6A **102**
Severnside Pl. *S13* 6A **102**
Severnside Wlk. *S13* 6A **102**
Sewage Cotts. *Roth* 6G **69**
Sewell Rd. *Half* 3F **125**
Sexton Dri. *Braml* 5H **81**
Seymore Rd. *Ast* 1B **116**
Seymour La. *Mas M* 2G **135**
(in two parts)
Seymour Rd. *Maltby* 4H **83**
Shackleton Rd. *Donc* 6B **20**
Shackleton Vw. *P'stne* 5D **142**
Shady Side. *Donc* 2A **46**
(in three parts)
Shaftesbury Av. *Ches* 2F **137**
Shaftesbury Av. *Donc* 6H **33**

Shaftesbury Dri. *Hoy* 6H **37**
Shaftesbury Ho. *Donc* 4A **34**
Shaftesbury Sq. *Roth* 2E **79**
Shaftesbury St. *B'ley* 1E **25**
Shaftholme. **2D 18**
Shaftholme La. *Ark* 1B **18**
Shaftholme Rd. *Ark* 4D **18**
(in two parts)
Shafton. **2C 10**
Shafton Hall Dri. *Shaf* 2B **10**
Shafton Rd. *Roth* 1H **91**
Shafton Two Gates. **3D 10**
Shakespeare Av. *W'land* 1B **16**
Shakespeare Cres. *Dron* 3G **129**
Shakespeare Dri. *Dinn* 5G **107**
Shakespeare Rd. *Ben* 6B **18**
Shakespeare Rd. *Roth* 1F **79**
Shakespeare Rd. *Wath D* 4D **40**
Shaldon Gro. *Ast* 6B **104**
Shalesmoor. *S3* 6D **86** (1C **4**)
Shambles St. *B'ley* 6G **13**
Shambles, The. Ches 2A *138*
(off High St.)
Shap Clo. *Ches* 6E **131**
Shardlow Gdns. *Donc* 5D **48**
Sharlston Gdns. *Ross* 4F **63**
Sharpe Av. *S8* 1C **122**
Sharpfield Av. *Rawm* 5E **55**
Sharrard Clo. *S12* 2D **112**
Sharrard Dri. *S12* 2D **112**
Sharrard Gro. *S12* 1D **112**
Sharrard Rd. *S12* 2D **112**
Sharrow. **6B 98**
Sharrow General Cemetery. *S11* 5C **98**
Sharrow Head. **5C 98**
Sharrow La. *S11* 5C **98**
Sharrow Mt. *S11* 6B **98**
Sharrow St. *S11* 5D **98**
Sharrow Vale. **5B 98**
Sharrow Va. Rd. *S11* 5A **98**
Sharrow Vw. *S7* 5C **98**
Shaw Ct. *Arm* 4G **35**
Shaw Lands. **6F 13**
Shaw La. *B'ley* 6E **13**
Shaw La. *Car* 4F **9**
Shaw La. *Donc* 1B **34**
Shaw La. *M'well* 3G **7**
Shaw La. Ind. Est. *Donc* 1C **34**
Shaw Rd. *E'wd T* 1G **79**
Shaw Rd. *Edl'tn* 2C **60**
Shawsfield Rd. *Roth* 6F **79**
Shaws Row. *Ches* 3F **137**
Shaw St. *B'ley* 6F **13**
Shaw St. *Ches* 3A **132**
Shaw St. *Coal A* 5G **123**
Shaw Wood Way. *Donc* 2B **34**
Shay House. **3D 140**
Shay Ho. La. *S'bri* 4D **140**
Shay Rd. *S'bri* 3D **140**
Shay, The. *Donc* 4C **48**
Sheaf Bank. *S2* 6E **99**
Sheaf Clo. *Con* 4F **59**
Sheaf Ct. *B'ley* 2D **24**
Sheaf Cres. *Bol D* 2B **42**
Sheaf Gdns. *S2* 4F **99**
Sheaf Gdns. Ter. *S2* 4F **99**
Sheaf Sq. *S1* 3F **99** (5F **5**)
Sheaf St. *S1* 2F **99** (5G **5**)
Sheardown St. *Donc* 1B **46**
Sheards Clo. *Dron W* 1D **128**
Sheards Dri. *Dron W* 2C **128**
Sheards Way. *Dron W* 2D **128**
Shearman Av. *Roth* 5F **67**
Shearwood Rd. *S10* 2B **98**
Shed La. *S'bgh* 6B **22**
Sheepbridge. **1G 131**
Sheepbridge La. *Ches* 1G **131**
Sheep Bri. La. *Ross* 4E **63**
Sheepbridge Works. *Ches* 1G **131**
Sheepcote Rd. *Kil* 3A **126**
Sheep Cote Rd. *Roth* 6B **80**
Sheep Dike La. *Morth* 3G **93**
Sheephill Rd. *S11* 4A **108**
Sheep La. *Donc* 5A **30**
Sheerien Clo. *B'ley* 6A **14**
Sheffield. **2E 99** (4E **5**)
Sheffield Airport Bus. Pk. *S9* 4F **89**
(Europa Link)
Sheffield Airport Bus. Pk. *S9* 5G **89**
(Letsby Av.)

Sheffield Arena. 4D **88**
Sheffield Bus Mus. 2E **89**
Sheffield City Mus. & Mappin Art Gallery.
. . . . .2B **98**
Sheffield Hallam University 4B **98**
Sheffield Ice Sports Cen. 4F **99**
Sheffield La. *Cat* 6C **90**
Sheffield Lane Top. **5G 75**
Sheffield Park. **4A 100**
Sheffield Parkway.
S2 & S9 . . . . .1G **99** (2H **5**)
Sheffield Rd. *S9 & Roth* 2E **89**
Sheffield Rd. *S12* 5H **113**
Sheffield Rd. *S13 & Swal* 5E **103**
Sheffield Rd. *Ans* 2F **119**
Sheffield Rd. *B'ley* 1H **23**
Sheffield Rd. *Birdw* 2C **36**
Sheffield Rd. *Ches & Uns* 1G **131**
Sheffield Rd. *Con* 5B **58**
Sheffield Rd. *Dron* 6D **122**
(in two parts)
Sheffield Rd. *Hoy* 6E **37**
Sheffield Rd. *Kil* 2H **125**
Sheffield Rd. *P'stne & Oxs* 4E **143**
Sheffield Rd. *Tod* . . . . .6G **105** & 1B **118**
(in two parts)
Sheffield Rd. *Warm* 1B **60**
Sheffield Rd. *Whit M* 3A **132**
(in three parts)
Sheffield Rd. *Woodh* 1A **114**
Sheffield St Marie's R.C. Cathedral.
. . . . .2E **99** (3E **5**)
Sheffield St Peter & St Paul's Cathedral.
. . . . .1E **99** (2E **5**)
Sheffield Ski Village. 4D **86**
Sheffield Technology Pk. *S9* 5C **88**
Sheffield Transport Dept. Golf Course.
. . . . .2D **122**
Sheffield United F.C. 4E **99**
Sheffield Wednesday F.C. 1A **86**
Sheldon Av. *Con* 4F **59**
Sheldon La. *S6* 5C **84**
Sheldon Rd. *S7* 1C **110**
Sheldon Rd. *Ches* 6D **130**
Sheldon Rd. *S'bri* 3E **141**
Sheldon Row. *S3* 1F **99** (1G **5**)
Sheldon St. *S2* 4E **99**
Sheldrake Clo. *Thpe H* 1B **66**
Shelley Av. *Donc* 5B **46**
Shelley Clo. *P'stne* 3D **142**
Shelley Dri. *Arm* 3G **35**
Shelley Dri. *B'ley* 4A **14**
Shelley Dri. *Dinn* 5H **107**
Shelley Dri. *Dron* 4G **129**
Shelley Dri. *Roth* 4H **79**
Shelley Gro. *Donc* 6H **31**
Shelley Ri. *Adw S* 2C **16**
Shelley Rd. *Roth* 3H **79**
Shelley Way. *Wath D* 4C **40**
Shenstone Dri. *Roth* 5H **79**
Shenstone Rd. *S6* 1A **86**
Shenstone Rd. *Roth* 5H **79**
Shepcote La. *S9 & Tins I* 4E **89**
Shepcote Way. *S9* 4E **89**
Shephard's Clo. *Den M* 2B **58**
Shepherd Dri. *High G* 1C **64**
Shepherd La. *Thurn* 2F **29**
Shepherd St. *S3* 1D **98** (1C **4**)
Shepherd Wheel. 5F **97**
(Water Wheel)
Shepley Cft. *High G* 1C **64**
Shepley St. *Ches* 3F **137**
Shepleys Yd. *Ches* 2A **138**
Sheppard Rd. *Donc* 4A **46**
Shepperson Rd. *S6* 2H **85**
Sherbourne Av. *Ches* 3G **131**
Sherburn Ga. *C'town* 1D **64**
Sherburn Rd. *B'ley* 6A **8**
Sherde Rd. *S6* 6C **86**
Sheridan Av. *Donc* 5C **46**
Sheridan Ct. *B'ley* 6D **14**
Sheridan Dri. *Roth* 3A **80**
Sheridan Rd. *Barn D* 1H **21**
Sheringham Clo. *High G* 6B **50**
Sheringham Gdns. High G 6B *50*
(off Sheringham Clo.)
Sherwood Av. *Con* 4C **58**
Sherwood Av. *Donc* 3F **31**
Sherwood Av. *E'thpe* 5D **20**
Sherwood Chase. *S17* 4E **121**
Sherwood Cres. *Roth* 3E **79**
Sherwood Dri. *Donc* 6G **45**
Sherwood Glen. *S7* 6H **109**

Sherwood Pl. *Dron W* 2B **128**
Sherwood Rd. *Dron W* 2B **128**
Sherwood Rd. *Harw* 5E **63**
Sherwood Rd. *Kil* 2C **126**
Sherwood St. *B'ley* 6H **13**
Sherwood St. *Ches* 4B **138**
Sherwood Way. *Cud* 4A **10**
Shetland Gdns. *Donc* 4H **33**
Shetland Rd. *Dron* 3F **129**
Shield Av. *Wors* 4A **24**
Shinwell Av. *Ink* 4H **133**
Shipcroft Clo. *Womb* 1G **39**
Ship Hill. *Roth* 3D **78**
Shipman Ct. *Mosb* 2D **124**
Shipton St. *S6* 6C **86**
Shirburn Gdns. *Donc* 2D **48**
Shirebrook Rd. *S8* 1E **111**
Shirecliffe. 1C **86**
Shirecliffe Clo. *S3* 3F **87**
Shirecliffe La. *S3* 4E **87**
Shirecliffe Rd. *S5* 1E **87**
Shiregreen. 3A **76**
Shiregreen La. *S5* 5A **76**
Shiregreen Ter. *S5* 4H **75**
Shirehall Cres. *S5* 2H **75**
Shirehall Rd. *S5* 3H **75**
Shire Oak Dri. *Else* 6D **38**
Shireoaks Rd. *Dron* 1G **129**
Shires Clo. *Spro* 2D **44**
Shirewood Clo. *Bram* 5A **40**
Shirland Av. *B'ley* 1A **14**
Shirland Clo. *S9* 5B **88**
Shirland Ct. *S9* 6D **88**
Shirland La. *S9* 5B **88**
Shirland M. *S9* 6C **88**
Shirland Pl. *S9* 6D **88**
Shirland St. *Ches* 1A **138**
Shirley Clo. *Ches* 6D **130**
Shirley Rd. *S3* 4F **87**
Shirley Rd. *Donc* 2A **46**
Shooters Hill Dri. *Ross* 5F **63**
Shop. Mall. *S'bri* 3E **141**
Shore Ct. *S10* 3G **97**
Shoreham Av. *Roth* 2G **91**
Shoreham Dri. *Roth* 2F **91**
Shoreham Rd. *Roth* 2F **91**
Shoreham St. *S1 & S2* 5E **99** (6E **5**)
. . . . (in two parts)
Shore La. *S10* 3G **97**
Shorland Dri. *Tree* 1F **103**
Shortbrook Bank. *W'fld* 1E **125**
Shortbrook Clo. *W'fld* 1E **125**
Shortbrook Cft. *W'fld* 1E **125**
Shortbrook Dri. *W'fld* 1E **125**
Shortbrook Rd. *W'fld* 1E **125**
Shortbrook Wlk. *W'fld* 1F **125**
. . . . (off Eastcroft Way)
Shortbrook Way. *W'fld* 1E **125**
Shortfield Ct. *B'ley* 5A **8**
Short Ga. *Wadw* 6F **61**
Short La. *Donc* 4H **47**
Shortridge St. *S9* 5B **88**
Short Rd. *Donc* 5A **34**
Short Row. *B'ley* 2H **13**
Shorts La. *S17* 3B **120**
Short St. *Hoy* 6F **37**
Short Wood Clo. *Birdw* 2D **36**
Shortwood Vs. *Hoy* 4E **37**
Shotton Wlk. *Donc* 1C **46**
Shrewsbury Almshouses.
S2 . . . . .3G **99** (5H **5**)
Shrewsbury Clo. *Mexb* 6D **42**
Shrewsbury Clo. *P'stne* 4D **142**
Shrewsbury Rd. *S2* 3F **99** (6G **5**)
Shrewsbury Rd. *P'stne* 4D **142**
Shrewsbury Ter. *S17* 5D **120**
Shrewsbury Ter. *Roth* 3H **77**
Shroggs Head Clo. *D'fld* 3F **27**
Shrogs Wood Rd. *Roth* 6B **80**
Shubert Clo. *S13* 5B **102**
Shude Hill. *S1* 1F **99** (2G **5**)
Shuttle Clo. *Ross* 5F **63**
Shuttleworth Clo. *Ross* 5E **63**
Sibbering Row. *Deep* 4H **141**
Sicey Av. *S5* 5H **75**
Sicey La. *S5* 5H **75**
Sidcop Rd. *Cud* 4A **10**
. . . . (in two parts)
Siddall St. *S1* 2D **98** (3B **4**)
Sidings Ct. *Donc* 3E **47**
Sidlaw Clo. *Ches* 6E **131**
Sidney Rd. *Donc* 5H **33**
Sidney St. *S1* 3E **99** (6E **5**)

Sidney St. *Swint* 2B **56**
Sidons Clo. *Roth* 5G **67**
Siemens Clo. *S9* 1G **89**
Siena Clo. *D'fld* 3C **26**
Sike Clo. *Dart* 4A **6**
Sike La. *P'stne* 6A **142**
Sikes Rd. *Ans* 2F **119**
Silkstone Clo. *S12* 3G **113**
Silkstone Clo. *Tank* 6B **36**
Silkstone Cres. *S12* 3G **113**
Silkstone Dri. *S12* 3F **113**
Silkstone Pl. *S12* 3G **113**
Silkstone Rd. *S12* 3G **113**
Silkstone Vw. *Hoy* 3A **38**
Silver Birch Av. *S10* 6C **96**
Silverdale Clo. *S11* 3G **109**
Silverdale Clo. *Bran* 3H **49**
Silverdale Clo. *Ches* 2G **131**
Silverdale Ct. *S11* 2H **109**
. . . . (off Silverdale Rd.)
Silverdale Cres. *S11* 2G **109**
Silverdale Cft. *S11* 2G **109**
Silverdale Dri. *B'ley* 2D **14**
Silverdale Gdns. *S11* 3H **109**
Silverdale Glade. *S11* 3H **109**
Silverdale Rd. *S11* 3G **109**
Silverdales. *Dinn* 4G **107**
Silver Hill Rd. *S11* 2H **109**
Silver Jubilee Clo. *Donc* 3A **34**
Silver Mill Rd. *S2* 5E **99**
Silvermoor Dri. *Rav* 1H **81**
Silverstone Av. *Cud* 6C **10**
Silver St. *S1* 1E **99** (2E **5**)
Silver St. *B'ley* 1G **23**
. . . . (in two parts)
Silver St. *Dod* 3B **22**
Silver St. *Donc* 6D **32**
Silver St. *Thry* 5C **70**
Silver St. Head. *S1* 1E **99** (2D **4**)
Silver Well Dri. *Stav* 3B **134**
Silverwood Ho. *Donc* 2C **46**
. . . . (off Elsworth Clo.)
Silverwood Vw. *Con* 3D **58**
Silverwood Wlk. *Flan* 3F **81**
Simcrest Av. *Kil* 4B **126**
Simmonite Rd. *Roth* 5G **67**
Simon Ct. *S10* 5F **97**
Simons Way. *Womb* 4H **25**
Simpson Pl. *Mexb* 2D **42**
Sims St. *S1* 1E **99** (2D **4**)
Sincil Way. *Whis* 4C **48**
Singleton Cres. *S6* 4A **86**
Singleton Gro. *S6* 4A **86**
Singleton Rd. *S6* 4A **86**
Site Gallery. 3F **99** (5F **5**)
Sitka Clo. *Roy* 3D **8**
Sitwell. *W'fld* 1F **125**
. . . . (off Shortbrook Way)
Sitwell Av. *Ches* 4H **137**
Sitwell Av. *S'bri* 3C **140**
Sitwell Dri. *Roth* 6G **79**
Sitwell Gro. *Roth* 1G **91**
Sitwell Gro. *Swint* 3B **56**
Sitwell La. *Wick* 6F **81**
Sitwell Pk. Golf Course. 1C **92**
Sitwell Pk. Rd. *Roth* 6B **80**
Sitwell Pl. *S7* 5D **98**
Sitwell Rd. *S7* 5D **98**
. . . . (in two parts)
Sitwell St. *Eck* 6G **125**
Sitwell Ter. *Wick* 6F **81**
. . . . (off Sitwell La.)
Sitwell Vw. *Roth* 6F **79**
Sitwell Vw. *Whis* 2B **92**
Sivilla Rd. *Kiln* 5B **56**
Skeldale Dri. *Ches* 5B **138**
Skelton Av. *M'well* 4F **7**
Skelton Clo. *S13* 2B **114**
Skelton Dri. *S13* 1B **114**
Skelton Gro. *S13* 1B **114**
Skelton La. *Beig* 4F **115**
Skelton La. *Woodh* 1B **114**
Skelton Ri. *O'bri* 3D **72**
Skelton Rd. *S8* 2E **111**
Skelton Wlk. *S13* 1C **114**
Skelton Way. *S13* 1B **114**
Skelwith Clo. *S4* 2B **88**
Skelwith Clo. *Ches* 3F **131**
Skelwith Dri. *S4* 1B **88**
Skelwith Rd. *S4* 2B **88**
Skew Hill La. *Gren* 1H **73**
Skiddaw Clo. *Ches* 5F **131**
Skiers Vw. Rd. *Hoy* 6G **37**

Skiers Way. *Hoy* 6G **37**
Skinnerthorpe Rd. *S4* 2H **87**
Skinpit La. *H'swne* 1G **143**
Skipton Clo. *Den M* 2A **58**
Skipton Rd. *S4* 3G **87**
Skipton Rd. *Swal* 6A **104**
Skipwith Gdns. *New R* 5C **62**
Skye Cft. *Roy* 1E **9**
Skye Edge Av. *S2* 3H **99**
Skye Edge Rd. *S2* 3H **99**
Slack Fields La. *Whar S* 1B **72**
Slack La. *Ches* 2D **136**
Slacks La. *Braml* . . . . . .6H **81** & 1A **94**
. . . . (in two parts)
Slade Hooton. 4G **95**
Slade Rd. *Swint* 3A **56**
Slaidburn Av. *C'town* 1D **64**
Slate St. *S2* 6F **99**
Slayleigh Av. *S10* 5C **96**
Slayleigh Delph. *S10* 5D **96**
Slayleigh Dri. *S10* 5D **96**
Slayleigh La. *S10* 5C **96**
Sleaford St. *S9* 5B **88**
Sledgate Dri. *Wick* 6D **80**
Sledgate La. *Wick* 6D **80**
. . . . (in two parts)
Sledmere Rd. *Donc* 3G **31**
Slinn St. *S10* 1A **98**
Slitting Mill La. *S9* 5B **88**
Smallage La. *S13* 4F **103**
Small Bridge. 2A **48**
Smalldale Rd. *S12* 3F **113**
Smeaton Clo. *Rav* 1H **81**
Smeaton St. *S7* 5D **98**
Smelter Wood Av. *S13* 6G **101**
Smelter Wood Clo. *S13* 6G **101**
Smelter Wood Ct. *S13* 6G **101**
. . . . (off Smelter Wood Way)
Smelter Wood Cres. *S13* 6H **101**
Smelter Wood Dri. *S13* 6G **101**
Smelter Wood La. *S13* 6G **101**
Smelter Wood Pl. *S13* 6H **101**
Smelter Wood Ri. *S13* 6H **101**
Smelter Wood Rd. *S13* 6G **101**
Smelter Wood Way. *S13* 6G **101**
Smeltinghouse La. *Barl* 1A **130**
Smillie Rd. *New R* 5E **63**
Smith Av. *Ink* 4H **133**
Smith Cres. *Ches* 4D **138**
Smithey Clo. *High G* 1B **64**
Smithfield. *S3* 1E **99** (1D **4**)
Smithfield Av. *Ches* 6C **138**
Smithfield Rd. *S12* 5C **112**
Smithies. .3A **14**
Smithies La. *S13* 3G **13**
Smithies Rd. *Swint* 1B **56**
Smithies St. *B'ley* 3G **13**
Smithley. .6F **25**
Smithley La. *Womb* 6F **25**
Smith Rd. *S'bri* 3D **140**
Smith Sq. *Donc* 4H **45**
Smith St. *C'town* 2E **65**
Smith St. *Donc* 4H **45**
Smith St. *Womb* 6C **26**
Smithy Bri. La. *H'fld* 4F **39**
. . . . (in two parts)
Smithy Carr Av. *C'town* 2D **64**
Smithy Carr Clo. *C'town* 2D **64**
Smithy Clo. *Roth* 6H **67**
Smithy Cft. *Dron W* 1A **128**
Smithy Green. 2H **13**
Smithy Moor. 2B **140**
Smithy Moor Av. *S'bri* 1A **140**
Smithy Moor La. *S'bri* 2A **140**
Smithy Wood Cres. *S8* 3C **110**
. . . . (in two parts)
Smithy Wood La. *Dod* 3B **22**
Smithy Wood Rd. *S8* 3C **110**
Smithywood Rd. *Thpe H* 3H **65**
Snail Hill. *Roth* 3D **78**
Snailsden Way. *M'well* 5H **7**
Snaithing La. *S10* 4E **97**
Snaithing Pk. Clo. *S10* 4E **97**
Snaithing Pk. Rd. *S10* 4E **97**
Snake La. *Con* 4F **59**
Snape Hill. 4E **27**
. . . . (Darfield)
Snape Hill. 1E **129**
. . . . (Dronfield)
Snape Hill. *Dron* 1E **129**
Snapehill Clo. *Dron* 6E **123**
Snapehill Cres. *Dron* 6E **123**

Snapehill Dri. *Dron* 6E **123**
Snape Hill La. *Dron* 1E **129**
Snape Hill Rd. *D'fld* 4F **27**
Snape Hill Rd. *Womb* 4D **26**
Snelston Clo. *Dron W* 2A **128**
Snetterton Clo. *Cud* 6C **10**
Snig Hill. *S3* 1F **99** (2F **5**)
Snowberry Clo. *Swint* 5A **56**
Snowden Ter. *Womb* 6B **26**
Snowdon Way. *B'wth* 4D **90**
Snow Hill. *Dod* 3B **22**
Snow Hill Row. *S2* 1G **99** (2H **5**)
. . . .(off Bernard St.)
Snow La. *S3* 1E **99** (1D **4**)
Snydale Rd. *Cud* 6B **10**
Soaper La. *Dron* 1E **129**
Soap Ho. La. *S13* 6E **103**
. . . .(in two parts)
Society St. *Donc* 6D **32**
Sokell Av. *Womb* 1E **39**
Solario Way. *New R* 6C **62**
Solferino St. *S11* 4D **98**
Solly St. *S1* 1D **98** (3B **4**)
Solway Ri. *Dron W* 1B **128**
Somercotes Rd. *S12* 2F **113**
Somersall Clo. *Ches* 4C **136**
Somersall Hall Dri. *Ches* 5C **136**
Somersall La. *Ches* 5C **136**
Somersall Pk. Rd. *Ches* 4C **136**
Somersall Willows. *Ches* 4C **136**
Somersby Av. *Donc* 5H **31**
Somersby Av. *Walt* 6D **136**
Somerset Ct. *Cud* 1H **15**
Somerset Dri. *Brim* 2F **133**
Somerset Rd. *S3* 5F **87**
Somerset Rd. *Donc* 1D **46**
Somerset St. *S3* 5F **87**
Somerset St. *B'ley* 5F **13**
Somerset St. *Cud* 1H **15**
Somerset St. *Maltby* 5H **83**
Somerton Dri. *Donc* 4C **48**
Somerville Ter. *S6* 5B **86**
Somin Ct. *Bal* 6C **46**
Sopewell Rd. *Roth* 3F **77**
Sorby Hall. *S10* 4H **97**
Sorby Rd. *Swal* 6H **103**
Sorby St. *S4* 6G **87**
Sorby Way. *Wick* 6E **81**
Soresby St. *Ches* 2A **138**
Sorrel Rd. *S'side* 3G **81**
Sorrelsykes Clo. *Whis* 3H **91**
Sorrento Way. *D'fld* 2D **26**
Sothall. .5G **115**
Sothall Clo. *Beig* 4F **115**
Sothall Ct. *Beig* 4F **115**
Sothall Grn. *Beig* 4F **115**
Sothall M. *Beig* 4F **115**
Sough Hall Av. *Thpe H* 2B **66**
Sough Hall Clo. *Thpe H* 2B **66**
Sough Hall Cres. *Thpe H* 2B **66**
Sough Hall Rd. *Thpe H* 3B **66**
Sousa St. *Maltby* 5H **83**
Southall St. *S8* 1E **111**
South Anston. 3F **119**
South Av. *New W* 3H **55**
Southbourne Ct. *S17* 3D **120**
Southbourne Hall. *S10* 3B **98**
Southbourne M. *S10* 4A **98**
Southbourne Rd. *S10* 3A **98**
South Clo. *Roy* 3E **9**
Southcote Dri. *Dron W* 2B **128**
South Ct. *S17* 2E **121**
South Cres. *Dod* 2B **22**
South Cres. *Duck* 6E **135**
South Cres. *Kil* 2C **126**
South Cres. *Roth* 2H **79**
South Cft. *Shaf* 2C **10**
Southcroft Gdns. *S7* 1D **110**
Southcroft Wlk. S7 . . . . .1D **110**
. . . .(off Southcroft Gdns.)
Southdown Av. *Ches* 1E **137**
South Dri. *Bol D* 2H **41**
South Dri. *Roy* 3E **9**
Southend Pl. *S2* 3A **100**
Southend Rd. *S2* 3A **100**
Southey Av. *S5* 6E **75**
Southey Clo. *S5* 6D **74**
. . . .(in two parts)
Southey Cres. *S5* 6D **74**
Southey Cres. *Maltby* 4G **83**
Southey Dri. *S5* 6E **75**
Southey Green. 5C **74**
Southey Grn. Clo. *S5* 6D **74**

Southey Grn. Rd. *S5* 5B **74**
Southey Hall Dri. *S5* 6E **75**
Southey Hall Rd. *S5* 6D **74**
Southey Hill. *S5* 5C **74**
Southey Pl. *S5* 6D **74**
Southey Ri. *S5* 6D **74**
Southey Rd. *Maltby* 4G **83**
Southey Wlk. *S5* 6D **74**
Southfield Av. *Has* 6D **138**
Southfield Cotts. *B'ley* 4E **9**
Southfield Cres. *Thurn* 2D **28**
Southfield Dri. *Dron* 3G **129**
Southfield La. *Thurn* 3D **28**
. . . .(in two parts)
Southfield Mt. *Dron* 3G **129**
S. Field Rd. *Arm* 3E **35**
Southgate. *B'ley* 4E **13**
Southgate. *Eck* 6E **125**
Southgate. *Hoy* 5A **38**
Southgate. *P'stne* 5E **143**
Southgate. *Shaf* 3D **10**
Southgate Ct. *Eck* 6E **125**
S. Grove Dri. *Hoy* 6H **37**
Southgrove Rd. *S10* 4B **98**
Southlands Way. *Ast* 6C **104**
South La. *S1* 4D **98** (6C **4**)
Southlea Av. *Hoy* 6B **38**
Southlea Clo. *Hoy* 6B **38**
Southlea Dri. *Hoy* 6B **38**
Southlea Rd. *Hoy* 6B **38**
S. Lodge Ct. *Ches* 2D **136**
South Mall. Donc 6C **32**
. . . .(off French Ga.)
Southmoor Av. *Arm* 3E **35**
Southmoor Clo. *Brim* 1F **139**
Southmoor La. *Arm* 4E **35**
South Pde. *S3* 6E **87** (1D **4**)
South Pde. *Donc* 6D **32**
South Pl. *B'ley* 4D **12**
South Pl. *Ches* 3F **137**
. . . .(Barker La.)
South Pl. *Ches* 3A **138**
. . . .(Beetwell St.)
South Pl. *Womb* 6H **25**
S. Quay Dri. *S2* 1G **99** (1H **5**)
South Rd. *S6* 5A **86**
South Rd. *Dod* 2B **22**
South Rd. *High G* 6B **50**
South Rd. *Roth* 2G **77**
Southsea Rd. *S13* 1A **114**
South St. *S2* 2G **99** (3H **5**)
South St. *B'ley* 6F **13**
South St. *Ches* 3A **138**
South St. *D'fld* 4E **27**
South St. *Dinn* 4F **107**
South St. *Dod* 3B **22**
South St. *Donc* 2D **46**
South St. *Greasb* 4C **68**
South St. *High* 5D **16**
South St. *Mosb* 3D **124**
South St. *Rawm* 1G **69**
South St. *Roth & K'wth* 4G **77**
. . . .(in three parts)
South St. N. *New W* 1D **132**
South Ter. *Kiv P* 4D **116**
South Ter. Roth 3D **78**
. . . .(off Moorgate St.)
S. Vale Dri. *Thry* 5D **70**
South Vw. *D'fld* 4E **27**
South Vw. *Edl'tn* 4A **60**
South Vw. *Grim* 6F **11**
South Vw. *H'brk* 2G **125**
South Vw. *Kiv P* 5H **117**
S. View Clo. *S6* 2E **85**
S. View Cres. *S7* 6D **98**
S. View Ri. *S6* 2E **85**
S. View Rd. *S7* 5D **98**
S. View Rd. *Roy* 3E **9**
S. View Ter. *Cat* 6C **90**
Southwell Gdns. *Swal* 6G **103**
Southwell Ri. *Mexb* 5F **43**
Southwell Rd. *S4* 2B **88**
Southwell Rd. *Donc* 3F **33**
Southwell Rd. *Rawm* 1H **69**
Southwell St. *B'ley* 5F **13**
Southwood Av. *Dron* 4E **129**
Southwood Gro. *S6* 6G **73**
South Yorkshire Mus. of Life. 5F **31**
. . . .(Cusworth Hall)
South Yorkshire Railway. 5D **76**
S. Yorkshire (Redbrook) Ind. Est.
B'ley .2C **12**

Sowters Row. *Ches* 2A **138**
. . . .(off High St.)
Spa Brook Clo. *S12* 3H **113**
Spa Brook Dri. *S12* 2H **113**
. . . .(in two parts)
Spa Houses. 6G **91**
Spa La. *S13* 2C **114**
Spa La. *Ches* 2B **138**
. . . .(in two parts)
Spa La. Cft. *S13* 1C **114**
Spalton Rd. *P'gte* 3F **69**
Spansyke St. *Donc* 1B **46**
Sparkfields. *M'well* 5F **7**
Spark La. *Bar G & M'well* 6E **7**
Spartan Vw. *Maltby* 2D **82**
Spa Vw. Av. *S12* 4H **113**
Spa Vw. Dri. *S12* 4H **113**
Spa Vw. Pl. *S12* 4H **113**
Spa Vw. Rd. *S12* 4H **113**
Spa Vw. Ter. *S12* 4H **113**
Spa Vw. Way. *S12* 4H **113**
Spa Well Cres. *Tree* 6E **91**
Spa Well Gro. *Brie* 2G **11**
Spa Well Ter. *B'ley* 5H **13**
Speedwell Ind. Est. *Stav* 2C **134**
Speeton Rd. *S6* 4A **86**
Spencer Av. *Donc* 5E **33**
Spencer Av. *Mas M* 1F **135**
Spencer Ct. *Whis* 2B **92**
Spencer Dri. *Rav* 2H **81**
Spencer Grn. *Whis* 2B **92**
Spencer Pk. *Roth* 1C **78**
Spencer Rd. *S2* 6E **99**
Spencer St. *B'ley* 1G **23**
Spencer St. *Ches* 1A **138**
Spencer St. *Mexb* 1C **56**
Spencer Rd. *Roth* 4H **79**
Spey Clo. *M'well* 6G **7**
Spilsby Clo. *Donc* 5E **49**
Spink Hall. 4D **140**
Spink Hall Clo. *S'bri* 4E **141**
Spink Hall La. *S'bri* 4D **140**
Spinkhill Av. *S13* 5E **101**
Spinkhill Dri. *S13* 5F **101**
Spinkhill Rd. *S13* 5E **101**
Spinkhill Rd. *Kil* 6B **126**
Spinners Wlk. Roth 4E **79**
. . . .(off Warwick St.)
Spinney Clo. *Roth* 6G **79**
Spinneyfield. *Roth* 1G **91**
Spinney Hill. *Spro* 3D **44**
Spinney, The. *Barn D* 1E **21**
Spinney, The. *Brim* 3D **132**
Spinney, The. *Donc* 6H **45**
Spire Lodge. *Ches* 6A **132**
Spital. 3C **138**
Spital Brook Clo. *Ches* 4C **138**
Spitalfields. *S3* 6F **87**
Spital Gdns. *Ches* 4C **138**
Spital Gro. *Ross* 6E **63**
Spital Hill. *S4* 6G **87**
Spital La. *S3* 6G **87**
Spital La. *Ches* 3B **138**
Spital St. *S3 & S4* 6F **87**
Spofforth Rd. *S9* 6C **88**
Spooner Dri. *Kil* 3A **126**
Spooner Rd. *S10* 3A **98**
Spoon Glade. *S6* 5C **84**
Spoonhill Rd. *S6* 5F **85**
Spoon La. *S6* 5A **84**
Spoon M. *S6* 5C **84**
Spoon Oak Lea. *S6* 5C **84**
Spoon Way. *S6* 5C **84**
Spotswood Dri. *S14* 3A **112**
Spotswood Dri. *S14* 3A **112**
Spotswood Mt. *S14* 3H **111**
Spotswood Pl. *S14* 3H **111**
Spotswood Rd. *S14* 3H **111**
Spout Copse. *S6* 5B **84**
Spout La. *S6* 4B **84**
Spout Spinney. *S6* 5B **84**
Spreadeagle Yd. *Ches* 3A **138**
. . . .(off Beetwell St.)
Springbank. *D'fld* 4F **27**
Springbank. *Uns* 3H **129**
Springbank Clo. *B'ley* 5E **9**
Spring Bank Rd. *Ches* 2H **137**
Spring Bank Rd. *Con* 5D **58**
Spring Clo. *Whis* 2A **92**
Spring Clo. Dell. *S14* 3B **112**
Spring Clo. Dri. *S14* 3B **112**
Spring Clo. Mt. *S14* 3B **112**
Spring Clo. Vw. *S14* 3A **112**

Spring Cres. *Spro* 2D **44**
Spring Cft. *Roth* 6H **67**
Springcroft Dri. *Donc* 1G **31**
Spring Dri. *Bram* 3A **40**
Springfield. *Bol D* 1G **41**
Springfield Av. *S7* 2A **110**
Springfield Av. *Ches* 2F **137**
Springfield Clo. *S7* 3A **110**
Springfield Clo. *Arm* 4G **35**
Springfield Clo. *D'fld* 4F **27**
Springfield Clo. *Eck* 6C **124**
Springfield Clo. *Roth* 6D **68**
Springfield Ct. *Donc* 4G **31**
Springfield Cres. *D'fld* 4F **27**
Springfield Cres. *Hoy* 6G **37**
Springfield Dri. *Thry* 5E **71**
Springfield Glen. *S7* 3H **109**
Springfield Path. *Mexb* 1E **57**
Springfield Pl. *B'ley* 6F **13**
Springfield Rd. *S7* 3H **109**
Springfield Rd. *Edl'tn* 3C **60**
Springfield Rd. *Grim* 6F **11**
Springfield Rd. *Hoy* 6F **37**
Springfield Rd. *Kiln* 6C **56**
Springfield Rd. *Wick* 4E **81**
Springfields. *B'ley* 3C **12**
Springfield St. *B'ley* 6E **13**
Springfield Ter. *Ans* 6C **106**
Springfield Ter. *B'ley* 6F **13**
Springfield Way. *Burn* 2B **64**
Spring Gdns. *B'ley* 3C **14**
Spring Gdns. *Cant* 2G **49**
Spring Gdns. *Donc* 6C **32**
Spring Gdns. *Hoy* 5A **38**
Spring Gro. *B'ley* 4F **9**
Spring Hill. *S10* 1A **98**
Springhill Av. *Bram* 3A **40**
Spring Hill Clo. *Spro* 2D **44**
Spring Hill Rd. *S10* 1A **98**
Spring Ho. Clo. *Ash* 6B **130**
Spring Ho. Rd. *S10* 1A **98**
Spring La. *S2* 5A **100**
Spring La. *B'ley* 5F **9**
Spring La. *New C* 1G **7**
Spring La. *Spro* 5D **30**
Spring Pl. *Ches* 2A **138**
Spring Ram Bus. Pk. *Dart* 3A **6**
Springs Leisure Cen., The. 1B **112**
Spring St. *S3* 1E **99** (1E **5**)
Spring St. *B'ley* 1G **23**
Spring St. *Roth* 2E **79**
Spring Vale. 4E **143**
Spring Va. Av. *Wors* 5H **23**
Springvale Clo. *Maltby* 3F **83**
Springvale Clo. *Wick* 1G **93**
Springvale Gro. *P'stne* 4E **143**
Springvale Rd. *S6 & S10* 1H **97**
Spring Va. Rd. *Brim* 3D **132**
Springvale Wlk. *S6* 6B **86**
Spring Vw. Rd. *S10* 1A **98**
Spring Wlk. Roth 2E **79**
(off Wharncliffe Hill)
Spring Wlk. *Womb* 5H **25**
Spring Water Av. *S12* 4A **114**
Spring Water Clo. *S12* 4H **113**
Spring Water Dri. *S12* 4A **114**
Spring Well. *Beig* 3E **115**
Springwell Av. *Beig* 3E **115**
Springwell Clo. *Maltby* 3H **83**
Springwell Cres. *Beig* 3E **115**
Springwell Dri. *Beig* 3E **115**
Springwell Gdns. *Bal* 5H **45**
Springwell Gro. *Beig* 3E **115**
Springwell La. *Donc* 5H **45**
(in two parts)
Springwell Pk. Dri. *Ink* 4A **134**
Springwood. *S5* 1C **86**
Springwood Av. *Aug* 4A **104**
Springwood Clo. *Bran* 4G **49**
Spring Wood Clo. *Ches* 3E **131**
Springwood Ct. *Aug* 4B **104**
Springwood Gro. *Thurn* 2E **29**
Springwood Ho. Thurn 1C **46**
(off Elsworth Clo.)
Springwood La. *High G* 6A **50**
Springwood Rd. *S8* 1E **111**
Springwood Rd. *Donc* 1G **31**
Springwood Rd. *Hoy* 6G **37**
Springwood Vw. *P'stne* 4F **143**
Sprotborough Flash Nature Reserve.
. . . . .5C **44**
Sprotbrough. 2D **44**
Sprotbrough La. *Marr* 3A **30**

Sprotbrough Park. 2E **45**
Sprotbrough Rd. *Donc* 6H **31**
Spruce Av. *Roy* 2D **8**
Spruce Av. *Wick* 4G **81**
Spruce Ri. *Kil* 4A **126**
Spurley Hey Gro. *S'bri* 4E **141**
Spurr La. *S2* 1G **111**
Spurr St. *S2* 5F **99**
Square E., The. *S'side* 2G **81**
Square, The. *B'ley* 1F **23**
Square, The. *Cut* 4B **130**
Square, The. *Harl* 4H **51**
Square, The. *Wal* 5F **117**
Square W., The. *S'side* 2F **81**
Squirrel Cft. *Roth* 3H **67**
Stable Gdns. *Spro* 3E **44**
Stables, The. *Swint* 2H **55**
Stacey Bank. *S6* 1A **84**
Stacey Cres. *Grim* 6F **11**
Stacey Dri. *Thry* 4D **70**
Stackyard, The. *B'ley* 1H **25**
Stacye Av. *Woodh* 1D **114**
Stacye Ri. *Woodh* 1D **114**
Stadium Ct. *P'gte* 5E **69**
Stadium Way. *S9* 6B **88**
Stadium Way. *P'gte* 6F **69**
Stafford Clo. *Dron W* 1A **128**
Stafford Cres. *S2* 2F **91**
Stafford Dri. *Roth* 2F **91**
Stafford La. *S2* 3H **99**
Stafford M. S2 . . . . .3H **99**
(off Stafford La.)
Stafford Pl. *Den M* 2B **58**
Stafford Rd. *S2* 3H **99**
Stafford Rd. *W'land* 3E **17**
Staffordshire Clo. *Maltby* 4H **83**
Stafford St. *S2* 3G **99** (4H **5**)
Stafford Way. *Burn* 2D **64**
Stag Clo. *Roth* 6A **80**
Stag Cres. *Roth* 6A **80**
Stag La. *Roth* 6H **79**
Stainborough. 5B **22**
Stainborough Castle 6B **22**
Stainborough Clo. *Dod* 3B **22**
Stainborough La. *Hood G* 6A **22**
Stainborough Rd. *Dod* 3B **22**
Stainborough Vw. *Tank* 5B **36**
Stainborough Vw. *Wors* 4H **23**
Staincross. .3E **7**
Staincross Comn. *M'well* 3F **7**
Staindrop Clo. *C'town* 1D **64**
Staindrop Vw. *C'town* 1E **65**
Stainforth Rd. *Barn D* 2H **21**
Stainley Clo. *B'ley* 3D **12**
Stainmore Av. *Soth* 5G **115**
Stainton Clo. *B'ley* 1G **13**
Stainton La. *S'ton* 2H **83**
Stainton Rd. *S11* 5H **97**
Stainton St. *Den M* 2B **58**
Stairfoot. 1E **25**
Stairfoot Bus. Pk. *B'ley* 2E **25**
Stair Rd. *S4* 3G **87**
Staithes Wlk. *Den M* 1C **58**
Stalker Lees Rd. *S11* 5B **98**
Stalker Wlk. *S11* 4C **98**
Stamford St. *S9* 4B **88**
Stamford Way. *M'well* 3F **7**
Stanage Ri. *S12* 2G **113**
Stanage Way. *Ches* 6B **130**
Stanbury Clo. *B'ley* 3D **12**
Standhill Cres. *B'ley* 6A **8**
Standish Av. *S5* 3E **87**
Standish Bank. *S5* 3E **87**
Standish Clo. *S5* 2E **87**
Standish Dri. *S5* 2E **87**
Standish Gdns. *S5* 3E **87**
Standish Rd. *S5* 2E **87**
Standish Way. *S5* 3E **87**
Standon Cres. *S9* 4C **76**
Standon Dri. *S9* 4C **76**
Standon Rd. *S9* 4C **76**
Stand Pk. Ind. Est. *Ches* 4A **132**
Stand Rd. *Ches* 3H **131**
Staneford Ct. *Wat* 6D **114**
Stanford Clo. *Maltby* 5H **83**
Stanford Rd. *Dron W* 2A **128**
Stanford Way. *Walt* 5D **136**
Stanhope Gdns. *B'ley* 4E **13**
Stanhope Rd. *S12* 2E **113**
Stanhope Rd. *Donc* 4E **33**
Stanhope St. *B'ley* 6F **13**
Staniforth Av. *Eck* 6B **124**
Staniforth Cres. *Tod* 2A **118**

Staniforth Rd. *S9* 6B **88**
Stanley Av. *Ink* 5H **133**
Stanley Ct. Maltby 4D **82**
(off Stanley Ter.)
Stanley Gdns. *Donc* 2B **46**
Stanley Gro. *Ast* 5C **104**
(in two parts)
Stanley La. *S3* 6F **87** (1G **5**)
Stanley Rd. *S8* 2F **111**
Stanley Rd. *B'ley* 1E **25**
Stanley Rd. *C'town* 1B **64**
Stanley Rd. *Donc* 2F **31**
Stanley Rd. *S'bri* 4E **141**
Stanley Sq. *Kirk S* 3D **20**
Stanley St. *S3* 6F **87** (1F **5**)
Stanley St. *B'ley* 6F **13**
Stanley St. *Ches* 3C **138**
Stanley St. *Kil* 2B **126**
Stanley St. *Roth* 3D **78**
Stanley Ter. *Maltby* 4D **82**
Stannington. 5C **84**
Stannington Glen. *S6* 5E **85**
Stannington Ri. *S6* 4G **85**
Stannington Rd. *S6 & Stann* 5B **84**
Stannington Vw. Rd. *S10* 1G **97**
Stanton Cres. *S12* 3F **113**
Stanwell Av. *S9* 5C **76**
Stanwell Clo. *S9* 5C **76**
Stanwell St. *S9* 5C **76**
Stanwell Wlk. *S9* 5C **76**
Stanwood Av. *S6* 5F **85**
Stanwood Cres. *S6* 5F **85**
Stanwood Dri. *S6* 5F **85**
Stanwood Dri. *Walt* 5D **136**
Stanwood M. *S6* 5F **85**
Stanwood Rd. *S6* 5F **85**
Staple Grn. *Thry* 5E **71**
Stapleton Rd. *Warm* 6F **45**
(in two parts)
Star La. *B'ley* 6G **13**
Star La. *Con* 3E **59**
Starling Mead. *S2* 3H **99**
Starnhill Clo. *E'fld* 6G **65**
Station App. Donc 6C **32**
(off Factory La.)
Sta. Back La. *Ches* 2B **138**
Station Cotts. *Dart* 4C **6**
Station Ct. *Ans* 2F **119**
Station Ct. *Donc* 6C **32**
Station La. *S9* 1C **88**
Station La. *Old W & New W* 1B **132**
Station La. *O'bri* 2D **72**
Station La. Ind. Est. *Old W* 1B **132**
Station Rd. *S9* 1E **101**
Station Rd. *Ark* 6D **18**
Station Rd. *Barn D* 1D **20**
Station Rd. *B'ley* 5F **13**
Station Rd. *Bol D* 1A **42**
Station Rd. *Brim* 3C **132**
Station Rd. *Cat* 5C **90**
Station Rd. *C'town* 2F **65**
Station Rd. *Ches* 2B **138**
Station Rd. *Con* 2E **59**
Station Rd. *Dart* 4C **6**
Station Rd. *Deep* 3H **141**
Station Rd. *Dinn* 2C **106**
Station Rd. *Dod* 2A **22**
Station Rd. *E'fld* 6G **65**
Station Rd. *Eck* 6E **125**
Station Rd. *Holl* 2F **133**
Station Rd. *Kil* 3H **125**
Station Rd. *Kiv P* 5H **117**
Station Rd. *Lund* 2F **15**
Station Rd. *Mexb* 1E **57**
(in two parts)
Station Rd. *Mosb & Half* 2D **124**
Station Rd. *Ross* 4E **63**
Station Rd. *Roth* 3B **78**
Station Rd. *Roy* 1D **8**
Station Rd. *Spin* 6B **126**
Station Rd. *Thurn* 1F **29**
Station Rd. *Tree* 1E **103**
Station Rd. *Wath D* 4F **41**
Station Rd. *Whit M* 2A **132**
Station Rd. *Womb* 6C **26**
(in two parts)
Station Rd. *Woodh* 1C **114**
Station Rd. *Wors* 5C **24**
Station Rd. Ind. Est. *Womb* 5C **26**
Station St. *Swint* 2B **56**
Station Ter. *Brim* 3C **132**
Station Ter. *Roy* 1G **9**
Station Way. *Dinn* 2C **106**

Staton Av. *Beig* 3G 115
Statutes, The. *Roth* 3D 78
Staunton Clo. *Ches* 6A 138
Staunton Rd. *Donc* 4E 49
Staveley. 1C 134
Staveley La. *Eck & Stav* 6E 125
Staveley Rd. *S8* 6E 99
Staveley Rd. *Ark T* 6C 134
Staveley Rd. *New W* 1E 133
Staveley Rd. *Pool* 3D 134
Staveley St. *Edl'tn* 2B 60
Steade Rd. *S7* 6D 98
Steadfield Rd. *Hoy* 1F 51
Steadfolds Clo. *Thur* 5C 94
Steadfolds Gdns. *Thur* 5C 94
Steadfolds La. *Thur* 4B 94
Steadfolds Ri. *Thur* 5C 94
Steadlands, The. *Rawm* 6D 54
Stead La. *Hoy* 6F 37
Stead M. *Eck* 6D 124
Stead St. *Eck* 6D 124
Steel Bank. 6A 86
Steel City Plaza. *S1* 3D 4
Steele Av. *Ink* 5H 133
Steele St. *Hoy* 6E 37
Steel Hill. *Gren* 2A 74
Steelhouse La. *S3* 1E 99 (1E 5)
Steel Rd. *S11* 5A 98
Steel St. *Roth* 4A 78
Steeping Clo. *Brim* 3E 133
Steep La. *H'swne* 3F 143
Steeplegate. *Ches* 2A 138
Steeton Ct. *B'ley* 5C 38
Stemp St. *S11* 5D 98
Stenson Ct. *Donc* 3A 46
Stenton Rd. *S8* 2D 122
Stentons Ter. *Mexb* 1F 57
Stephen Dri. *S10* 2F 97
Stephen Dri. *Gren* 1H 73
Stephen Hill. 2F 97
Stephen Hill. *S10* 2F 97
Stephen Hill Rd. *S10* 2F 97
Stephen La. *Gren* 1H 73
Stephenson Ct. *Ches* 3D 136
Stephenson Hall. *S10* 4A 98
Stephenson Pl. *Ches* 2A 138
Stephenson Pl. *Swint* 1B 56
Stephenson Rd. *Stav* 2C 134
Stepney Row. *S2* 2H 5
Stepney St. *S2* 1C 99 (2H 5)
Stepping La. *Gren* 6A 64
Sterland St. *Ches* 2G 137
Sterndale Rd. *S7* 4A 110
Steven Clo. *C'town* 3D 64
Steven Cres. *C'town* 2D 64
Steven Pl. *C'town* 3D 64
Stevenson Dri. *Hghm* 3A 12
Stevenson Dri. *Roth* 4H 79
Stevenson Rd. *S9* 5A 88
Stevenson Rd. *Donc* 5B 46
Stevenson Way. *S9* 5B 88
Stevens Rd. *Donc* 2B 46
Steventon Rd. *Thry* 5E 71
Stewart Rd. *S11* 5B 98
Stewarts Rd. *Rawm* 1H 69
Stewart St. *Donc* 1C 46
Sticking Hill. 4D 42
Sticking La. *Adw D* 4B 42
Stillman Clo. *Has* 5C 138
Stirling Clo. *Else* 5C 38
Stirling Ct. *Ches* 1A 138
Stirling St. *Donc* 1C 46
Stirling Way. *S2* 5C 100
Stockarth La. *O'bri* 4E 73
Stockarth Pl. *O'bri* 5F 73
Stockbridge. 5C 18
Stockbridge Av. *Donc* 2A 32
Stockbridge Cvn. Site. *Ben* 6C 18
Stockbridge La. *Ben* 6C 18
Stockil Rd. *Donc* 1E 47
Stock Rd. *S2* 4A 100
Stocksbridge. 3E 141
Stocksbridge & District Golf Course.
. . . . .5F 141
Stocks Grn. Ct. *S17* 5D 120
Stocks Grn. Dri. *S17* 5D 120
Stocks Hill. *E'fld* 6E 65
Stocks Hill Clo. *B'ley* 4E 9
Stock's La. *B'ley* 5E 13
Stock's La. *Rawm* 2F 69
Stockton Clo. *S3* 6F 87
Stockwell Av. *Kiv P* 6G 117
Stockwell La. *Wal* 6F 117

Stoddart Way. *P'gte* 5F 69
Stoke St. *S9* 6A 88
Stoket La. *Ulley* 6D 92
Stokewell Rd. *Wath D* 4C 40
Stoneacre Av. *S12* 4B 114
Stoneacre Clo. *S12* 4B 114
Stoneacre Dri. *S12* 5B 114
Stoneacre Ri. *S12* 4B 114
Stonecliffe Clo. *S2* 4C 100
Stonecliffe Dri. *S'bri* 5D 140
Stonecliffe Pl. *S2* 4C 100
Stonecliffe Rd. *S2* 4C 100
Stonecliffe Wlk. *S2* 4D 100
Stonecliff Wlk. *Den M* 1C 58
Stone Clo. *Coal A* 6G 123
Stone Clo. *Kiv P* 5A 118
Stone Clo. *Rav* 2H 81
Stone Cotts. *Toll B* 2H 17
Stone Cres. *Wick* 4F 81
Stonecroft Rd. *S17* 4F 121
Stone Cross Dri. *Spro* 1D 44
Stonecross Gdns. *Donc* 3E 49
Stone Delf. *S10* 4C 96
Stone Font Gro. *Donc* 4D 48
Stonegarth Clo. *Cud* 1H 15
Stonegravels. 5A 132
Stonegravels Cft. *Half* 3E 125
Stonegravels La. *Ches* 6A 132
Stonegravels Way. *Half* 3F 125
Stone Gro. *S10* 2B 98
Stonehill Clo. *Hoy* 4G 37
Stone Hill Dri. *Swal* 6B 104
Stonehill Ri. *Cud* 1H 15
Stonehill Ri. *Donc* 1G 31
Stonehill Ri. *P'stne* 6C 142
Stone La. *S13* 2A 114
Stone Leigh. *Tank* 6B 36
Stoneleigh Clo. *Dinn* 6H 107
Stoneleigh Cft. *B'ley* 2H 23
Stoneley Clo. *S12* 6D 112
Stoneley Cres. *S12* 6D 112
Stoneley Dell. *S12* 6D 112
Stoneley Dri. *S12* 6D 112
Stonelow Ct. Dron 1F 129
(off Stonelow Rd.)
Stonelow Cres. *Dron* 1G 129
Stonelow Grn. *Dron* 1F 129
Stonelow Rd. *Dron* 1F 129
Stonely Brook. *Rav* 3H 81
Stone Moor Rd. *S'bri & Bols* 4C 140
Stone Pk. Clo. *Maltby* 4H 83
Stone Riding. *Edl'tn* 6D 60
Stone Ridings. *Edl'tn* 4A 60
Stone Rd. *Coal A* 5G 123
Stone Row. *Ches* 3G 137
Stone Row Ct. *Tank* 1B 50
Stonerow Way. *P'gte* 6E 69
Stonesdale Clo. *Mosb* 2D 124
Stones Inge. *High G* 6B 50
Stone St. *B'ley* 3G 13
Stone St. *Mosb* 2D 124
Stonewood Ct. *S10* 3D 96
Stonewood Gro. *S10* 3D 96
Stoney Bank Dri. *Kiv P* 5A 118
Stoney Cft. *Hoy* 6F 37
Stoney Ga. *High G* 5B 50
Stoney Rd. *B'ley* 4B 8
Stoney Wlk. *S6* 4A 86
Stonyford Rd. *Womb* 5D 26
Stony La. *O'bri* 2B 72
Stoops Clo. *Ches* 5F 131
Stoops La. *Donc* 4H 47
(in two parts)
Stoops Rd. *Donc* 6B 48
Stopes Rd. *S6* 5A 84
Stoppard Row. *Ches* 3E 137
Store St. *S2* 4F 99
Storey's Ga. *Womb* 6H 25
Storey St. *Swint* 2A 56
Storforth La. *Ches & Has* 6A 138
Storforth La. Ter. *Has* 5B 138
Storforth La. Trad. Est. *Has* 4A 134
Stormont Gro. *Ink* 4A 84
Storrs. 2A 84
Storrs Bri. La. *S6* 2A 84
Storrs Grn. *S6* 3A 84
Storrs Hall Rd. *S6* 5H 85
Storrs La. *Mosb* 4A 84
Storrs La. *Wort* 3A 50
Storrs Rd. *Ches* 3D 136
Storth Av. *S10* 5E 97

Storth La. *S10* 4E 97
Storth La. *Kiv P* 4F 117
Stortholme M. *S10* 4E 97
Storth Pk. *S10* 6D 96
Storthwood Ct. *S10* 4E 97
Stotfold Dri. *Thurn* 1E 29
Stothard Ct. *S10* 1H 97
Stothard Rd. *S10* 1H 97
Stottercliffe Rd.
Thurls & P'stne 4B 142
(in three parts)
Stour Clo. *Brim* 3E 133
Stour La. *S6* 1F 85
Stovin Dri. *S9* 5D 88
Stovin Gdns. *S9* 5D 88
(in two parts)
Stow Bri. La. *Whis* 5C 92
Stowe Av. *S7* 3A 110
Stradbroke Av. *S13* 6F 101
Stradbroke Clo. *S13* 6G 101
Stradbroke Cres. *S13* 6G 101
Stradbroke Dri. *S13* 6G 101
Stradbroke Pl. *S13* 6G 101
Stradbroke Ri. *Ches* 5E 137
Stradbroke Rd. *S13* 6F 101
Stradbroke Wlk. *S13* 6G 101
Stradbroke Way. *S13* 6G 101
Strafford Av. *Else* 5C 38
Strafford Av. *Wors* 3H 23
Strafford Gro. *Birdw* 5D 36
Strafford Ind. Est. *Dod* 4C 22
Strafford Pl. *Thpe H* 2A 66
Strafford Rd. *Donc* 4E 33
Strafford Rd. *Roth* 5G 67
Strafford St. *Dart* 5A 6
Strafford Wlk. *Dod* 3B 22
Straforth Ho. *Den M* 2A 58
(off Ravenscar Clo.)
Straight La. *Gold* 4G 29
Straight Riding. *Edl'tn* 5C 60
Strait La. *Wath D* 5E 41
Stratford Rd. *S10* 4D 96
Stratford Way. *Braml* 2E 81
Strathmore Gro. *Wath D* 5F 41
Strathmore Rd. *Donc* 6G 33
Strathtay Rd. *S11* 6H 97
Strauss Cres. *Maltby* 5H 83
Strawberry Av. *S5* 3F 75
Strawberry Gdns. *Roy* 1E 9
Strawberry Lee La. *S17* 4B 120
Straw La. *S6* 6C 86
Streatfield Cres. *New R* 5C 62
Street. 3G 53
Streetfield Cres. *Mosb* 3D 124
Streetfield La. *Half* 3E 125
Streetfields. *Half* 3E 125
Street La. *W'wth* 3F 53
Strelley Av. *S8* 6C 110
Strelley Rd. *S8* 6C 110
Strelley Rd. *B'ley* 5A 8
Stretton Clo. *Donc* 3E 49
Stretton Rd. *S11* 6A 98
Stretton Rd. *B'ley* 2A 14
Stride, The. *Ches* 6H 137
Stringers Cft. *Whis* 2B 92
Stripe Rd. *Ross & New R* 4E 63
Struan Rd. *S7* 2A 110
Strutt Rd. *S3* 4E 87
Stuart Clo. *Ches* 5C 132
Stuart Gro. *C'town* 3F 65
Stuart Rd. *C'town* 3F 65
Stuart St. *Thurn* 1G 29
Stubbin. 3G 141
Stubbin Clo. *Rawm* 6D 54
Stubbing. 6C 72
Stubbing Ho. La. *S6* 2G 73
Stubbing La. *Worr* 3B 72
Stubbing Rd. *Ches* 6H 137
Stubbin La. *S5* 5G 75
Stubbin La. *Rawm* 5C 54
(in two parts)
Stubbin Rd. *Rawm* 6B 54
Stubbins Hill. *Edl'tn* 3B 60
Stubbins Riding. *Edl'tn* 4C 60
Stubbs Cres. *Roth* 6H 67
Stubbs Rd. *Womb* 1E 39
Stubbs Wlk. *Roth* 6H 67
Stubley Clo. *Dron W* 6C 122
Stubley Cft. *Dron W* 1B 128
Stubley Dri. *Dron W* 1C 128
Stubley Hollow. *Dron* 6C 122
Stubley La. *Dron* 1B 128

Stubley Pl. *Dron* 1C **128**
Studfield Cres. *S6* 3F **85**
Studfield Dri. *S6* 2F **85**
Studfield Gro. *S6* 3F **85**
Studfield Hill. **3F 85**
Studfield Hill. *S6* 3E **85**
Studfield Ri. *S6* 2F **85**
Studfield Rd. *S6* 2F **85**
Studios, The. **2G 137**
(off School Board La.)
Studley Ct. *S9* 1E **101**
Studmoor Rd. *Roth* 5F **67**
Studmoor Wlk. *Roth* 5F **67**
Stump Cross. **3F 53**
Stump Cross Gdns. *Bol D* 1H **41**
Stump Cross Rd. *Wath D* 6E **41**
Stumperlowe. **5D 96**
Stumperlowe Av. *S10* 5E **97**
Stumperlowe Clo. *S10* 5E **97**
Stumperlowe Cres. Rd. *S10* 5D **96**
Stumperlowe Cft. *S10* 4D **96**
Stumperlowe Hall Chase. *S10* . . .4D **96**
Stumperlowe Hall Rd. *S10* 5D **96**
Stumperlowe La. *S10* 5D **96**
Stumperlowe Mans. *S10* 5D **96**
Stumperlowe Pk. Rd. *S10* 5D **96**
Stumperlowe Vw. *S10* 4D **96**
Stupton Rd. *S9* 1C **88**
Sturge Cft. *S2* 1F **111**
Sturton Clo. *Donc* 5A **48**
Sturton Cft. *Dalt* 6C **70**
Sturton Rd. *S4* 3G **87**
Sub-Station La. *Ches* 3A **132**
(off Queen St. N.)
Sudbury Clo. *Ches* 6D **130**
Sudbury Dri. *Ast* 6C **104**
Sudbury St. *S3* 6D **86** (1B **4**)
Sudhall Clo. *Ches* 3F **131**
Sudhall Cl. *Ches* 3F **131**
Suffolk Clo. *Ans* 1G **119**
Suffolk La. *S2* 3F **99** (6G **5**)
Suffolk Rd. *S2* 3F **99** (5F **5**)
Suffolk Rd. *Donc* 5B **46**
Suffolk Vw. *Den M* 3B **58**
Sulby Gro. *B'ley* 3D **24**
Summerdale Rd. *Cud* 1G **15**
Summerfield. **3A 98**
Summerfield. *S10* 3A **98**
Summerfield. *Roth* 3E **79**
Summerfield Cres. *Brim* 3D **132**
Summerfield Rd. *Ches* 4H **137**
Summerfield Rd. *Dron* 6F **123**
Summerfield St. *S11* 4C **98**
Summer La. *S17* 5D **120**
Summer La. *B'ley* 5G **13**
Summer La. *Roy* 1D **8**
Summer La. *Womb* 6H **25**
Summerley Wlk. *Ches* 6F **131**
Summer Rd. *Roy* 1D **8**
Summerskill Grn. *Ink* 4A **134**
Summer St. *S3* 1C **98** (2A **4**)
Summer St. *B'ley* 5F **13**
(in two parts)
Summerwood La. *Dron* 6D **122**
Summerwood Pl. *Dron* 1D **128**
Sumner Rd. *Roth* 1F **79**
Sunbury Ct. *S10* 3A **98**
Sunderland St. *S11* 4C **98**
Sunderland Ter. *B'ley* 1A **24**
Sundew Cft. *High G* 5B **50**
Sundew Gdns. *High G* 5B **50**
Sundown Pl. *S13* 5H **101**
Sundown Rd. *S13* 5H **101**
Sunlea Flats. *Roth* 2F **79**
(off St Leonard's Rd.)
Sunningdale Av. *Dart* 4E **7**
Sunningdale Clo. *Ches* 5G **137**
Sunningdale Clo. *Donc* 5F **49**
Sunningdale Clo. *Swint* 4B **56**
Sunningdale Dri. *Cud* 5C **10**
Sunningdale Mt. *S11* 2H **109**
Sunningdale Ri. *Ches* 5E **137**
Sunningdale Rd. *Dinn* 5F **107**
Sunningdale Rd. *Donc* 4G **33**
Sunny Bank. *S10* 4C **98** (6A **4**)
Sunny Bank. *E'thpe* 6E **21**
Sunny Bank. *High G* 6B **50**
Sunny Bank. *Jump* 4B **38**
Sunnybank Cres. *B'wth* 3C **90**
Sunny Bank Dri. *Cud* 2H **15**
Sunny Bank Ri. *Else* 5C **38**
Sunny Bank Rd. *Bols* 6E **141**
Sunny Bar. *Donc* 6D **32**

Sunnybrook Clo. *Hoy* 1A **52**
Sunnyfields. **2F 31**
Sunnyside. **5C 20**
(Kirk Sandall)
Sunnyside. **4C 20**
(Rotherham)
Sunnyside. *E'thpe* 4C **20**
Sunnyside Clo. *Ans* 1G **119**
Sunny Springs. *Ches* 1A **138**
Sunnyvale Av. *S17* 5D **120**
Sunnyvale Rd. *S17* 5D **120**
Sunny Vw. Cvn. Pk. *A'ley* 1F **61**
Sunrise Mnr. *Hoy* 4A **38**
Surbiton St. *S9* 3D **88**
Surrey Clo. *B'ley* 5H **23**
Surrey La. *S1* 3F **99** (4F **5**)
(in two parts)
Surrey Pl. *S1* 2F **99** (4F **5**)
Surrey St. *S1* 2E **99** (4E **5**)
Surrey St. *Donc* 4B **46**
Surtees Clo. *Maltby* 2E **83**
Sussex Gdns. *Den M* 2B **58**
Sussex Rd. *S4* 6G **87**
Sussex Rd. *C'town* 2E **65**
Sussex St. *S4* 6G **87** (1H **5**)
Sussex St. *Donc* 4B **46**
Suthard Cross Rd. *S10* 1H **97**
Sutherland Ho. *Donc* 3G **33**
Sutherland Rd. *S4* 5G **87**
Sutherland St. *S4* 5H **87**
Sutton Av. *B'ley* 5B **8**
Sutton Cres. *Ink* 4A **134**
Sutton Rd. *Kirk S* 2E **21**
Sutton St. *S3* 2C **98** (3A **4**)
Sutton St. *Donc* 2A **46**
Swaddale Av. *Ches* 5B **132**
Swaddale Clo. *Ches* 5B **132**
Swaith Av. *Donc* 2H **31**
Swaithe. **4E 25**
Swaithedale. *Wors* 4C **24**
Swaithe Vw. *Wors* 4D **24**
Swalebank Clo. *Ches* 5B **138**
Swale Clo. *Bol D* 1B **42**
Swale Ct. *Roth* 1F **91**
Swaledale Dri. *Womb* 6C **26**
Swaledale Rd. *S7* 2B **110**
Swale Dri. *C'town* 2C **64**
Swale Gdns. *S9* 1E **101**
Swale Rd. *Roth* 4A **68**
Swallow Clo. *Birdw* 3D **36**
Swallow Clo. *Dart* 5B **6**
Swallow Ct. *Ross* 4E **63**
Swallow Hill. **6E 7**
Swallow Hill Rd. *Bar G* 6E **7**
Swallow La. *Ast* 1C **116**
Swallownest. **6A 104**
Swallownest Ct. *Swal* 5A **104**
Swallowood Ct. *Bram* 5H **39**
Swallow's La. *Mosb* 1C **124**
Swallow Wood Clo. *Tree* 1E **103**
Swallow Wood Ct. *S13* 1A **114**
Swallow Wood Rd. *Swal* 6G **103**
Swamp Wlk. *S6* 4B **86**
Swanbourne Clo. *Has* 5C **138**
Swanbourne Pl. *S5* 5G **75**
Swanbourne Rd. *S5* 4G **75**
Swanee Rd. *B'ley* 2B **24**
Swangate. *Bram* 4H **39**
Swannington Clo. *Donc* 4F **49**
Swan Rd. *Ast* 1C **116**
Swan St. *Ben* 6B **18**
Swan St. *Roth* 4D **78**
Swanwick St. *Old W* 1A **132**
Swarcliffe Rd. *S9* 6C **88**
Sweeney Ho. *S'bri* 3C **140**
Sweet La. *Wadw* 6H **61**
Sweyn Cft. *Wors* 4A **24**
Swifte Rd. *Roth* 6G **79**
Swift Ri. *Thpe H* 1C **66**
Swift Rd. *Gren* 1B **74**
Swift St. *B'ley* 4F **13**
Swift Way. *S2* 4A **100**
Swinburne Av. *Adw S* 2C **16**
Swinburne Av. *Donc* 5B **46**
(in two parts)
Swinburne Clo. *Barn D* 1H **21**
Swinburne Pl. *Roth* 4H **79**
Swinburne Rd. *Roth* 4H **79**
Swinscoe Way. *Ches* 6C **130**
Swinston Hill Gdns. *Dinn* 5G **107**
Swinston Hill Rd. *Dinn* 5F **107**
Swinton. **2B 56**
Swinton Bridge. **2D 56**

Swinton Meadows Bus. Pk.
  Swint 2D **56**
Swinton Meadows Ind. Est.
  Swint 2D **56**
Swinton Rd. *Mexb* 1D **56**
(in two parts)
Swinton St. *S3* 6E **87**
Swithland Clo. *Ches* 6C **138**
Sycamore Av. *Arm* 2G **35**
Sycamore Av. *Ches* 4G **137**
Sycamore Av. *Cud & Grim* 6B **10**
Sycamore Av. *Dron* 6E **123**
Sycamore Av. *Kiv P* 5F **117**
Sycamore Av. *Wick* 4G **81**
Sycamore Cen. *E'wd T* 6H **69**
Sycamore Ct. *Mexb* 6C **42**
Sycamore Cres. *Wath D* 6G **41**
Sycamore Dri. *Cal* 2E **139**
Sycamore Dri. *Kil* 4A **126**
Sycamore Dri. *Roy* 2C **8**
Sycamore Dri. *Thur* 4B **94**
Sycamore Farm Clo. *Wick* 6F **81**
Sycamore Flats. *Wath D* 6F **41**
(off Burman Rd.)
Sycamore Gro. *Con* 4C **58**
Sycamore Gro. *Donc* 3D **48**
Sycamore Ho. Rd. *S5* 3A **76**
Sycamore La. *Holl* 2G **133**
Sycamore La. *H'swne* 1G **143**
Sycamore Rd. *Barn D* 2H **21**
Sycamore Rd. *E'wd T* 6H **69**
Sycamore Rd. *E'fld* 1F **75**
Sycamore Rd. *Holl* 2F **133**
Sycamore Rd. *Mexb* 6C **42**
Sycamore Rd. *S'bri* 4C **140**
Sycamore St. *B'ley* 5E **13**
Sycamore St. *Beig* 3F **115**
Sycamore St. *Mosb* 1C **124**
Sycamore Vw. *Spro* 2F **45**
Sycamore Wlk. *P'stne* 4D **142**
Sycamore Wlk. *Thurn* 1F **29**
Sydney Rd. *S6* 1B **98**
Sydney St. *Ches* 2G **137**
Sydney Ter. *B'ley* 1H **23**
Sykes Av. *B'ley* 5F **13**
Sykes Ct. *Swint* 4B **56**
Sykes St. *King* 2F **23**
Sylvan Clo. *Ches* 4B **138**
Sylvan Clo. *Maltby* 3H **83**
Sylvester Av. *Donc* 2C **46**
Sylvester Gdns. *S1* 3E **99** (6E **5**)
Sylvester St. *S1* 3E **99** (6D **4**)
Sylvestria Ct. *Ross* 4E **63**
Sylvia Clo. *S13* 6D **102**
Sylvia Rd. *Uns* 5H **129**
Symes Gdns. *Donc* 2D **48**
Symonds Av. *Rawm* 5C **54**
Symons Cres. *S5* 5D **74**

T

Tadcaster Clo. *Den M* 3A **58**
Tadcaster Cres. *S8* 3D **110**
Tadcaster Rd. *S8* 3D **110**
Tadcaster Way. *S8* 3D **110**
Taddington Rd. *Ches* 6D **130**
Tait Av. *Edl'tn* 5B **60**
Talbot Av. *Barn D* 2H **21**
Talbot Circ. *Barn D* 2H **21**
Talbot Cres. *S2* 3G **99** (5H **5**)
Talbot Cres. *Has* 6D **138**
Talbot Gdns. *S2* 3G **99** (5H **5**)
Talbot Pl. *S2* 3G **99** (5H **5**)
Talbot Rd. *S2* 3G **99** (4H **5**)
Talbot Rd. *P'stne* 3C **142**
Talbot Rd. *Swint* 2D **56**
Talbot St. *S2* 3G **99** (5H **5**)
Talbot St. *Has* 6D **138**
Talmont Rd. *S11* 1H **109**
Tamar Clo. *Hghm* 4A **12**
Tanfield Clo. *Roy* 1C **8**
Tanfield Rd. *S6* 2B **86**
Tanfield Way. *Wick* 5F **81**
Tankersley. **1D 50**
Tankersley La. *Hoy* 1D **50**
Tankersley Pk. Golf Course. **3C 50**
Tank Row. *B'ley* 6D **14**
Tannery Clo. *S13* 1B **114**
Tannery St. *S13* 1B **114**
Tan Pit La. *Gold* 6F **29**
Tansley Dri. *S9* 5D **76**

Tansley Dri. *Ches* 6C **130**
Tansley St. *S9* 5D **76**
Tansley Way. *Ink* 5A **134**
Tanyard. *Dod* 3A **22**
Tanyard Cft. *Brie* 2G **11**
Tap La. *Ches* 2G **137**
Taplin Rd. *S6* 3H **85**
Tapton. **5C 132**
Tapton. *S10* 2A **98**
Tapton Bank. *S10* 3G **97**
Tapton Ct. *S10* 3H **97**
Tapton Cres. Rd. *S10* 3G **97**
Tapton Grange. *Brim* 6E **133**
Tapton Gro. *Brim* 6E **133**
Tapton Hill. **3G 97**
Tapton Hill Rd. *S10* 2G **97**
Tapton Ho. Rd. *S10* 3H **97**
Tapton La. *Ches* 2B **138**
Tapton Lock Hill. *Ches* 5B **132**
Tapton Lock Vis. Cen. **5B 132**
Tapton M. *S10* 2H **97**
Tapton Mt. Clo. *S10* 3H **97**
Tapton Pk. Gdns. *S10* 4G **97**
Tapton Pk. Mt. *S10* 4G **97**
Tapton Pk. Municipal Golf Course.
. . . . .1C **98**
Tapton Pk. Rd. *S10* 4F **97**
Tapton Ter. *Ches* 1B **138**
Tapton Va. *Ches* 6C **132**
Tapton Vw. Rd. *Ches* 6H **131**
Taptonville Cres. *S10* 3A **98**
Taptonville Rd. *S10* 2A **98**
Tapton Wlk. *S10* 3H **97**
Tapton Way. *Cal* 2F **139**
Tarleton Clo. *Kirk S* 3E **21**
Tasker Rd. *S10* 1H **97**
Tasman Gro. *Maltby* 3E **83**
Tatenhill Gdns. *Donc* 4E **49**
Taunton Av. *S9* 6D **76**
Taunton Gdns. *Mexb* 5G **43**
Taunton Gro. *S9* 5D **76**
Taverner Clo. *High G* 4B **50**
Taverner Cft. *High G* 5C **50**
Taverner Way. *High G* 5B **50**
Tavistock Rd. *S7* 1D **110**
Tavy Clo. *Bar G* 2A **12**
Tay Clo. *Dron W* 1B **128**
Tay Clo. *M'well* 6G **7**
Taylor Cres. *Ches* 4D **138**
Taylor Row. *B'ley* 1H **23**
Taylor Row. *Wath D* 1D **54**
Taylor's Clo. *P'gte* 5E **69**
Taylor's Ct. *P'gte* 5F **69**
Taylor's La. *P'gte* 5E **69**
Taylor St. *Con* 3F **59**
Tay St. *S6* 1B **98**
Teesdale Rd. *S12* 6H **113**
Teesdale Rd. *Roth* 4H **67**
Teeside Clo. *Donc* 4F **31**
Telford Cres. *Stav* 1D **134**
Telford Rd. *Donc* 4A **32**
Telson Clo. *Swint* 2G **55**
Temperance St. *Swint* 2B **56**
Tempest Av. *D'fld* 2E **27**
Templar Clo. *Thur* 5H **93**
Templeborough. **6H 77**
Templeborough Enterprise Pk.
Roth 5C **78**
Temple Cres. *Braml* 5H **81**
Temple Gdns. *Donc* 4E **49**
Templestowe Ga. *Con* 3G **59**
Temple Way. *B'ley* 4D **14**
Ten Acre Rd. *Roth* 1H **77**
Tenby Gdns. *Donc* 4A **46**
Tennyson Av. *Arm* 3F **35**
Tennyson Av. *Ches* 2H **137**
Tennyson Av. *Donc* 5H **31**
Tennyson Av. *Mexb* 5F **43**
Tennyson Clo. *Dinn* 5G **107**
Tennyson Clo. *P'stne* 3D **142**
Tennyson Ri. *Wath D* 3C **40**
Tennyson Rd. *S6* 5B **86**
Tennyson Rd. *B'ley* 3B **14**
Tennyson Rd. *Ben* 6B **18**
Tennyson Rd. *Maltby* 5G **83**
Tennyson Rd. *Roth* 4G **79**
Ten Pound Wlk. *Donc* 3C **46**
Tenter Balk La. *Adw S* 2C **16**
Tenterden Rd. *S5* 5B **76**
Tenter Hill. *Thurls* 3A **142**
Tenter La. *Warm* 5E **45**
Tenter Rd. *Warm* 5E **45**
Tenters Grn. *Wors* 5H **23**

Tenter St. *S1* 1E **99** (2D **4**)
Tenter St. *Roth* 2C **78**
Terminus Rd. *S7* 4A **110**
Terrace Rd. *P'gte* 3F **69**
Terrace, The. *S5* 6A **76**
Terrace Wlk. *S11* 5A **98**
Terrey Rd. *S17* 4E **121**
Terry St. *S9* 3D **88**
Tetney Rd. *S10* 3F **97**
Tewitt Rd. *Toll B* 3A **18**
Teynham Dri. *S5* 1D **86**
Teynham Rd. *S5* 1C **86**
Thackeray Av. *Rawm* 6H **55**
Thames St. *Roth* 2C **78**
Thatch Pl. *Roth* 4A **68**
Thealby Gdns. *Donc* 4A **48**
(in three parts)
Theatre La. *Ches* 2B **138**
Theatre Yd. *Ches* 2A **138**
(off Low Pavement)
Thellusson Av. *Donc* 3E **31**
Theobald Av. *Donc* 2F **47**
Theobald Clo. *Donc* 2E **47**
Thicket Dri. *Maltby* 3H **83**
Thicket La. *P'stne* 6E **143**
Thicket La. *Wors* 5C **24**
Third Av. *W'land* 3E **17**
Thirlmere Ct. *Mexb* 5H **43**
Thirlmere Dri. *Ans* 1H **119**
Thirlmere Dri. *Dron* 1E **129**
Thirlmere Gdns. *Kirk S* 4D **20**
Thirlmere Rd. *S8* 2C **110**
Thirlmere Rd. *B'ley* 6A **14**
Thirlmere Rd. *Ches* 4E **131**
Thirlwall Av. *Con* 3C **58**
Thirlwell Rd. *S8* 1E **111**
Thirsk Clo. *Den M* 3A **58**
Thomas St. *S1* 3D **98** (5C **4**)
(in two parts)
Thomas St. *D'fld* 1H **23**
Thomas St. *D'fld* 4F **27**
Thomas St. *Edl'tn* 4B **60**
Thomas St. *Kiln* 6D **56**
Thomas St. *Kiv P* 5H **117**
Thomas St. *Swint* 1B **56**
Thomas St. *Wors* 4A **24**
Thompson Av. *Edl'tn* 3B **60**
Thompson Clo. *Ches* 3A **132**
Thompson Clo. *Maltby* 2E **83**
Thompson Clo. *Rawm* 5C **54**
Thompson Clo. *Wath D* 5F **41**
Thompson Dri. *Swint* 4A **56**
Thompson Gdns. *High G* 5A **50**
Thompson Hill. *High G* 6A **50**
Thompson Rd. *S11* 4B **98**
Thompson Rd. *Womb* 1F **39**
Thompson St. *Ches* 3A **132**
(Brimington Rd.)
Thompson St. *Ches* 4A **132**
(King St. N.)
Thomson Av. *Donc* 4H **45**
Thoresby Av. *B'ley* 4C **14**
Thoresby Av. *Donc* 2F **47**
Thoresby Clo. *Ast* 6D **104**
Thoresby Pl. *Ink* 5A **134**
Thoresby Rd. *S6* 4A **86**
Thornborough Clo. *S2* 6G **99**
Thornborough Pl. *S2* 6G **99**
Thornborough Rd. *S2* 6F **99**
Thornbridge Av. *S12* 4F **113**
Thornbridge Clo. *S12* 4F **113**
Thornbridge Cres. *S12* 4G **113**
Thornbridge Cres. *Ches* 6H **137**
Thornbridge Dri. *S12* 4F **113**
Thornbridge Gro. *S12* 4F **113**
Thornbridge La. *S12* 4G **113**
Thornbridge Pl. *S12* 4F **113**
Thornbridge Ri. *S12* 4G **113**
Thornbridge Rd. *S12* 5F **113**
Thornbridge Way. *S12* 4G **113**
Thornbrook Clo. *C'town* 1F **65**
Thornbrook Gdns. *C'town* 1F **65**
Thornbrook M. *C'town* 1E **65**
Thorncliffe Clo. *Swal* 1H **115**
Thorncliffe Ind. Est. *C'town* 5D **50**
Thorncliffe La. *C'town* 6D **50**
Thorncliffe Pk. Est. *C'town* 6E **51**
Thorncliffe Rd. *C'town* 5E **51**
Thorncliffe Vw. *C'town* 6D **50**
Thorncliffe Vs. *C'town* 6D **50**
Thorncliffe Way. *Tank* 6C **36**
Thorndale Ri. *B'wth* 3D **90**
Thorndene Clo. *Ches* 5A **132**

Thorndon Way. *Ches* 5E **137**
Thorne Clo. *Ash* 1B **136**
Thorne Clo. *B'ley* 6A **8**
Thorne End Rd. *M'well* 3F **7**
Thornely Av. *Dod* 1B **22**
Thorne Rd. *S7* 2C **110**
Thorne Rd. *Donc* 6D **32**
Thorne Rd. *E'thpe* 6C **20**
Thornfield Av. *Ches* 4D **136**
Thornfield Ct. *Ches* 6A **132**
Thorn Gth. *Donc* 3A **32**
Thornham Clo. *Arm* 4F **35**
Thorn Hill. **2C 78**
Thornhill Av. *B'wth* 4B **90**
Thornhill Av. *Donc* 3H **33**
Thornhill Edge. *Roth* 2C **78**
Thornhill Pl. *Wath D* 5E **41**
Thorn La. *Donc* 5B **20**
Thornlea Ct. *Edl'tn* 4A **60**
Thornley Cotts. *Dod* 2B **22**
Thornley Sq. *Dod* 2B **22**
Thornley Sq. *Thurn* 1D **28**
Thornley Vs. *Birdw* 4C **36**
Thorn Rd. *Kiln* 4B **56**
Thornsett Ct. *S11* 5C **98**
Thornsett Gdns. *S17* 2F **121**
Thornsett Rd. *S7* 5C **98**
Thorntondale Rd. *Donc* 2F **31**
Thornton Pl. *Dron W* 2A **128**
Thornton Rd. *B'ley* 2C **24**
Thornton St. *Roth* 4G **77**
Thornton Ter. *B'ley* 2C **24**
Thornton Ter. *Roth* 4G **77**
Thorntree Clo. *Thpe H* 3B **66**
Thorntree Ct. *Ches* 6H **137**
Thorntree La. *B'ley* 4F **13**
Thorntree Rd. *Thpe H* 4B **66**
Thornwell Gro. *Cud* 1G **15**
Thornwell La. *Thpe H* 1B **66**
Thorogate. *Rawm* 6E **55**
Thorold Pl. *Kirk S* 2D **20**
Thorp Clo. *S2* 5E **99**
Thorpe Av. *Coal A* 5G **123**
Thorpe Bridle Rd. *Kiv S* 6F **119**
Thorpe Clo. *Ches* 3H **131**
Thorpe Common. **4B 66**
Thorpe Dri. *Wat* 6E **115**
Thorpefield Clo. *Thpe H* 2B **66**
Thorpefield Dri. *Thpe H* 2B **66**
Thorpe Grn. *Wat* 6D **114**
Thorpehall Rd.
Kirk S & E'thpe 4E **21**
(in two parts)
Thorpe Hesley. **2B 66**
Thorpe Ho. Av. *S8* 3E **111**
Thorpe Ho. Ri. *S8* 3E **111**
Thorpe Ho. Rd. *S8* 3E **111**
Thorpe La. *Spro* 2D **44**
Thorpe St. *Thpe H* 2A **66**
Thorpleigh Rd. *Mas M* 1F **135**
Three Hills Clo. *Thry* 4D **70**
Three Nooks La. *Cud* 4B **16**
Threshfield Way. *S12* 4B **114**
Throapham. **2F 107**
Thrush Av. *B'wth* 3D **90**
Thrush St. *S6* 5H **85**
Thruxton Clo. *Cud* 6C **10**
Thrybergh. **4D 70**
Thrybergh Country Pk. & Reservoir.
. . . . .2F **71**
Thrybergh Country Pk. Vis. Cen. . .2E **71**
Thrybergh Ct. *Den M* 2D **58**
Thrybergh Hall Rd. *Rawm* 1H **69**
Thrybergh La. *Thry* 4E **71**
Thundercliffe Rd. *Roth* 2D **76**
Thurbrook Gdns. *Thur* 4C **94**
Thurcroft. **4A 94**
Thurcroft Ho. *Donc* 1C **46**
(off St James St.)
Thurcroft Ind. Est. *Thur* 3A **94**
Thurlstone. **3A 142**
Thurlstone Rd. *P'stne* 4B **142**
Thurnscoe. **1E 29**
Thurnscoe Bri. La. *Thurn* 3F **29**
Thurnscoe East. **1G 29**
Thurnscoe La. *Gt Hou* 1B **28**
Thurnscoe La. Bus. Pk.
Thurn 2G **29**
Thurnscoe Rd. *Bol D* 1A **42**
Thurstan Av. *S8* 1C **122**
Tiber Vw. *B'wth* 2C **90**
Tickhill Rd. *Donc* 4A **46**
(in two parts)

Tickhill Rd. *Maltby* 4H **83**
Tickhill Sq. *Den M* 2B **58**
Tickhill St. *Den M* 1B **58**
Tickhill Way. *Ross* 5F **63**
Tideswell Clo. *Stav* 3H **133**
Tideswell Ct. *S5* 6G **75**
Tideswell Rd. *S5* 6G **75**
Tiercel M. *Dinn* 4E **107**
Tilford Rd. *S13* 1C **114**
Tillotson Clo. *S8* 1E **111**
Tillotson Ri. *S8* 1E **111**
Tillotson Rd. *S8* 1E **111**
Tiltshills. **1B 18**
Tiltshills La. *Ben* 1A **18**
Tilts La. *Ben* 1D **18**
Timothy Wood Av. *Birdw* 3D **36**
Tingle Bri. Av. *H'fld* 4E **39**
Tingle Bri. Cres. *H'fld* 4E **39**
Tingle Bri. La. *H'fld* 4E **39**
Tingle Clo. *H'fld* 4E **39**
Tinker La. *S6 & S10* 6H **85**
Tinker La. *Hoy* 5E **37**
Tinker Rd. *Rawm* 1G **69**
Tinsley. **1G 89**
Tinsley Ind. Est. *S9* 5E **89**
Tinsley Pk. Clo. *S9* 4E **89**
Tinsley Pk. Golf Course. 6H **89**
Tinsley Pk. Rd. *S9* 5D **88**
                                   (in two parts)
Tinsley Rd. *Hoy* 4H **37**
Tippit La. *Cud* 2H **15**
Tipsey Ct. *M'well* 4H **7**
Tipsey Hill. *M'well* 4H **7**
Tipton St. *S9* 6C **76**
Tissington Clo. *Ches* 6D **130**
Tithe Barn Av. *S13* 6B **102**
Tithe Barn Clo. *S13* 6C **102**
Tithe Barn Ct. *Adw D* 3D **42**
Tithe Barn La. *S13* 1B **114**
Tithe Barn Way. *S13* 6B **102**
Tithe Laithe. *Hoy* 5A **38**
Titterton Clo. *S9* 5C **88**
Titterton St. *S9* 5C **88**
Tiverton Clo. *Swint* 3B **56**
Tivydale Dri. *Dart* 6C **6**
Toad Holes La. *Ross* 2D **62**
Toad La. *Bram M* 6H **93**
Tockwith Rd. *S9* 6D **88**
Todmorden Clo. *Den M* 2A **58**
Todwick. **2A 118**
Todwick Grange. *Tod* 6H **105**
Todwick Ho. Gdns. *Tod* 1A **118**
Todwick Rd. *S8* 4C **110**
Todwick Rd. *Ast* 5A **106**
Todwick Rd. Ind. Est. *Dinn* 4B **106**
Todwick Vs. *Tod* 2A **118**
Toecroft La. *Spro* 2B **44**
Tofield Rd. *Wadw* 5G **61**
Tofts. **1C 96**
Tofts La. *S6* 1C **96**
Toftstead. *Arm* 4F **35**
Toftwood Av. *S10* 1G **97**
Toftwood Rd. *S10* 1H **97**
Togo Bldgs. *Thurn* 2E **29**
Togo St. *Thurn* 2E **29**
Toll Bar. **3A 18**
Toll Bar Av. *S12* 2A **112**
Toll Bar Clo. *S12* 2A **112**
Tollbar Clo. *Oxs* 6H **143**
Toll Bar Dri. *S12* 2B **112**
Toll Bar Rd. *S12* 2A **112**
Toll Bar Rd. *Roth* 4C **80**
Toll Bar Rd. *Swint* 3H **55**
Tollbridge Rd. *Mas M* 1F **135**
Tollgate Clo. *Shaf* 4D **10**
Tollgate Ct. *S3* 4F **87**
Toll Ho. Mead. *Mosb* 2D **124**
Tom La. *S10* 4D **96**
Tom La. *Duck* 6C **134**
Tomlinson Rd. *Else* 5B **38**
Tontine Rd. *Ches* 3A **138**
Tooker Rd. *Roth* 4E **79**
Topcliffe Rd. *B'ley* 2A **14**
Top Fld. La. *Roth* 1B **80**
Top Fold. *Ard* 1G **25**
Top Fold Cotts. *Old De* 3G **57**
Top Hall Rd. *Donc* 5D **48**
Top La. *Donc* 4H **47**
Top La. *S'ton* 1H **83**
Toppham Dri. *S8* 3D **122**
Toppham Rd. *S8* 3D **122**
Toppham Way. *S8* 3D **122**
Top Pingle Clo. *Brim* 4E **133**

Top Rd. *Barn D* 2H **21**
Top Rd. *Cal* 3F **139**
Top Rd. *Worr* 4D **72**
Top Row. *Dart* 2C **6**
Top Side. *Gren* 6A **64**
Tops, The. *Rawm & P'gte* 1C **68**
                                   (in two parts)
Top Ter. S10 . . . . .2A **98**
                                   (off Parker's La.)
Top Tree Way. *Thry* 4D **70**
Top Vw. Cres. *Edl'tn* 5B **60**
Top Warren. *C'town* 5F **51**
Torbay Rd. *S4* 4H **87**
Tor Clo. *B'ley* 2B **14**
Torksey Clo. *Donc* 6C **48**
Torksey Rd. *S5* 5H **75**
Torksey Rd. W. *S5* 5H **75**
Torne Clo. *Donc* 5E **49**
Torrington Clo. *Adw S* 1C **16**
Torry Ct. *S13* 1C **114**
Tortmayns. *Tod* 2A **118**
Torver Dri. *Bol D* 2A **42**
Tor Way. *B'wth* 3D **90**
Tor Wood Dri. *S8* 2C **122**
Totley. **5D 120**
Totley Brook. **4E 121**
Totley Brook Clo. *S17* 4D **120**
Totley Brook Cft. *S17* 4D **120**
Totley Brook Glen. *S17* 3D **120**
Totley Brook Gro. *S17* 4D **120**
Totley Brook Rd. *S17* 4D **120**
Totley Brook Way. *S17* 4D **120**
Totley Clo. *B'ley* 6D **8**
Totley Grange Clo. *S17* 5D **120**
Totley Grange Dri. *S17* 5D **120**
Totley Grange Rd. *S17* 5D **120**
Totley Hall Cft. *S17* 6D **120**
Totley Hall Dri. *S17* 5D **120**
Totley Hall La. *S17* 5D **120**
Totley Hall Mead. *S17* 6D **120**
Totley La. *S17* 5G **121**
                                   (Longford Rd.)
Totley La. *S17* 5F **121**
                        (Mickley La., in two parts)
Totley Mt. *Brim* 3D **132**
Totley Rise. **4F 121**
Tourist Info. Cen. 6H **13**
                                   (Barnsley)
Tourist Info. Cen. 2A **138**
                                   (Chesterfield)
Tourist Info. Cen. 6D **32**
                                   (Doncaster)
Tourist Info. Cen. 2E **79**
                                   (Rotherham)
Tourist Info. Cen. 2E **99** (4E **5**)
                                   (Sheffield)
Towcester Way. *Mexb* 5G **43**
Tower Clo. *S2* 5G **99**
Tower Clo. *Scawt* 6F **17**
Tower Dri. *S2* 5G **99**
Tower St. *B'ley* 2G **23**
Town End. **4H 141**
                                   (Stannington)
Town End. **6E 85**
                                   (Stocksbridge)
Town End. *Donc* 5B **32**
Town End Av. *Ast* 5C **104**
Townend Av. *Dalt* 6C **70**
Townend Clo. *Tree* 1E **103**
Town End Ind. Est. *Donc* 5A **32**
Townend La. *Deep* 5G **141**
Town End Rd. *E'fld* 1D **74**
Townend St. *S10* 6A **86**
Town Fields Av. *E'fld* 1G **75**
Town Fld. Vs. *Donc* 6E **33**
Towngate. *M'well* 4F **7**
Towngate. *Thurls* 3A **142**
Towngate Gro. *Worr* 4D **72**
Towngate Rd. *Worr* 4C **72**
Townhead. **2C 120**
                                   (Dore)
Town Head. . . . .
                                   (Worrall)
Townhead Rd. *S17* 2C **120**
Townhead St. *S1* 2E **99** (3D **4**)
Town Moor Av. *Donc* 5F **33**
Town St. *S9* 6F **77**
Town St. *Roth* 5D **78**
Town Vw. Av. *Scaw* 1D **30**
Town Wells Ct. *Ans* 2F **119**
Toyne St. *S10* 1H **97**
Traditional Heritage Mus. 5A **98**

Trafalgar Ct. *S1* 3D **98** (5C **4**)
Trafalgar Rd. *S6* 5A **74**
Trafalgar St. *S1* 2D **98** (4C **4**)
Traffic Ter. *Has* 6B **138**
Trafford Ct. *Donc* 6C **32**
Trafford Way. *Donc* 6C **32**
Tranmoor Av. *Donc* 4C **48**
Tranmoor Ct. *Hoy* 5A **38**
Tranmoor La. *Arm* 4F **35**
                                   (in two parts)
Tranquil Wlk. *New R* 5B **62**
Trap La. *S11* 1E **109**
Travey Rd. *S2* 6C **100**
Travis Gdns. *Donc* 2H **45**
                                   (in three parts)
Travis Pl. *S10* 3C **98** (6A **4**)
Tredis Clo. *B'ley* 3G **13**
Treecrest Ri. *B'ley* 3G **13**
Treefield Clo. *Roth* 4A **68**
Treelands. *B'ley* 4D **12**
Tree Neuk Clo. *Ches* 2D **136**
Tree Root Wlk. *S10* 2B **98**
Treeton. **1E 103**
Treeton Enterprise Cen.
                   Tree 2F **103**
Treeton Ho. *Donc* 1C **46**
                                   (off St James St.)
Treeton La. *Aug* 2A **104**
Treeton La. *Cat* 6D **79**
Treetown Cres. *Tree* 6E **91**
Treherne Rd. *Roth* 4F **79**
Trelawney Way. *Wors* 4H **23**
Trent Clo. *Edl'tn* 2C **60**
Trent Gdns. *Kirk S* 2D **20**
Trent Gro. *Dron* 6F **123**
Trentham Clo. *B'wth* 3D **90**
Trenton Clo. *Woodh* 1D **114**
Trenton Ri. *Woodh* 1D **114**
Trent St. *S9* 5A **88**
Trent Ter. *Con* 2E **59**
Trent Vs. *Kiv P* 5H **117**
Treswell Cres. *S6* 3A **86**
Trevose Clo. *Ches* 6E **137**
Trewan Ct. *B'ley* 4B **14**
Trickett Rd. *S6* 4A **86**
Trickett Rd. *High G* 5A **50**
Trinity Clo. *S3* 1H **137**
Trinity Rd. *Kiv P* 5B **118**
Trinity St. *S3* 1E **99** (1D **4**)
Trippet Ct. *S10* 5F **97**
Trippet La. *S1* 2D **98** (3C **4**)
Tristford Clo. *Cat* 5D **90**
Troon Clo. *Ches* 5E **137**
Troon Wlk. *Dinn* 5F **107**
Troughbrook Hill. *Stav* 3A **134**
Troughbrook Rd. *Holl* 2H **133**
Trough Dri. *Thry* 5E **71**
Troutbeck Clo. *Thurn* 2E **29**
Troutbeck Rd. *S7* 3C **110**
Troutbeck Way. *New R* 6C **62**
Trowell Way. *B'ley* 5B **8**
Trueman Grn. *Maltby* 3E **83**
Trueman Ter. *B'ley* 5E **15**
Truman Gro. *Deep* 3H **141**
Truman St. *Ben* 6A **18**
Truro Av. *Donc* 1H **33**
Truro Ct. *B'ley* 4B **14**
Truswell Av. *S10* 1G **97**
Truswell Rd. *S10* 2G **97**
Tudor Dri. *Barn D* 1D **20**
Tudor Rd. *Donc* 5G **33**
Tudor Rd. *W'land* 1F **95**
Tudor Sq. *S1* 2F **99** (4F **5**)
Tudor St. *New R* 5D **62**
Tudor St. *Stav* 1D **134**
Tudor St. *Thurn* 1G **29**
Tudor Way. *Wors* 4A **24**
Tuffolds Clo. *S2* 6C **100**
Tulip Tree Clo. *Beig* 2G **115**
Tullibardine Rd. *S11* 1H **109**
Tulyar Clo. *New R* 6D **62**
Tumbling La. *B'ley* 1F **15**
Tummon Rd. *S2* 3A **100**
Tummon St. *Roth* 3B **78**
Tune St. *B'ley* 1A **24**
Tune St. *Womb* 1E **39**
Tunstall Grn. *Ches* 4F **137**
Tunstall Way. *Ches* 4F **137**
Tunwell Av. *S5* 2F **75**
Tunwell Dri. *S5* 2F **75**
Tunwell Greave. *S5* 2F **75**
Tunwell Rd. *Maltby* 3E **83**
Turham Ct. *Ross* 5F **63**

Turie Av. *S5* 3E **75**
Turie Cres. *S5* 3E **75**
Turnberry Clo. *Ches* 5E **137**
Turnberry Ct. *Ben* 1A **32**
Turnberry Gro. *Cud* 5C **10**
Turnberry Way. *Dinn* 6F **107**
Turnbull Clo. *Ches* 4H **137**
Turner Av. *Womb* 6H **25**
Turner Bus. Pk. *S13* 3G **101**
Turner Clo. *Dron* 2D **128**
Turner Clo. *P'gte* 3G **69**
Turner Dri. *Ink* 3H **133**
Turner La. *Whis* 2H **91**
Turner Mus. of Glass. 2D **98** (3B **4**)
Turner's Clo. *Jump* 4B **38**
Turners La. *S10* 3A **98**
Turner St. *S2* 3F **99** (5F **5**)
Turner St. *Gt Hou* 1A **28**
Turnesc Gro. *Thurn* 2F **29**
Turnoaks Bus. Pk. *Ches* 6B **138**
Turnoaks La. *Ches* 6A **138**
(in three parts)
Turnpike Cft. *Gren* 6A **64**
Turnshaw Av. *Aug* 4A **104**
Turnshaw Rd. *Ulley* 4C **104**
Tutbury Gdns. *Donc* 4E **49**
Tuxford Cres. *B'ley* 5D **14**
Tween Woods La. *Wadw* 4F **61**
Twelve Lands Clo. *Tank* 6C **36**
Twelve O'Clock Ct. *S4* 6G **87**
Twenty Lands, The. *Tree* 2E **103**
Twentywell La. S17 . . . . .2G **121**
(off Ladies Spring Ct.)
Twentywell Dri. *S17* 3H **121**
Twentywell La. *S17* 2G **121**
Twentywell Ri. *S17* 3H **121**
Twentywell Rd. *S17* 4H **121**
Twentywell Vw. *S17* 4H **121**
Twibell St. *B'ley* 4A **14**
Twickenham Clo. *Half* 3E **125**
Twickenham Ct. *Half* 3E **125**
Twickenham Cres. *Half* 3E **125**
Twickenham Glade. *Half* 3E **125**
Twickenham Glen. *Half* 4F **125**
Twickenham Gro. *Half* 3E **125**
Twigg Ct. *Swint* 4C **56**
Twitchill Dri. *S13* 1B **114**
Two Gates Way. *Shaf* 3C **10**
Twyford Clo. *Swint* 2G **55**
Tyas Pl. *Mexb* 6G **43**
Tyas Rd. *S5* 2E **75**
Tye Rd. *Beig* 4G **115**
Tyers Hill. 1B **26**
Tyler St. *S9* 1D **88**
Tyler Way. *S9* 6D **76**
Tylney Rd. *S2* 3H **99**
Tylney Rd. *Ches* 5D **136**
Tynedale Ct. *Kirk S* 3E **21**
Tynker Av. *Beig* 4G **115**
Tyzack Rd. *S8* 5C **110**

U

Ulley. 1C **104**
Ulley Beeches. *Thur* 2F **105**
Ulley Country Pk. 2A **104**
Ulley Cres. *S13* 6D **100**
Ulley La. *Ast* 4C **104**
Ulley La. *Aug* 3B **104**
Ulley Rd. *S13* 6D **100**
Ulley Vw. *Aug* 3B **104**
Ulley Water Activities Cen. 1A **104**
Ullswater Av. *Half* 3E **125**
Ullswater Clo. *Ans* 6E **107**
Ullswater Clo. *Bol D* 2A **42**
Ullswater Clo. *Dron W* 1C **128**
Ullswater Clo. *Half* 3E **125**
Ullswater Dri. *Dron W* 2C **128**
Ullswater Pl. *Dron W* 1C **128**
Ullswater Pl. *Dron W* 1C **128**
Ullswater Rd. *B'ley* 1H **25**
Ullswater Rd. *Mexb* 5H **43**
Ullswater Wlk. *Donc* 2E **31**
Ulrica Dri. *Thur* 5A **94**
Ulverston Rd. *S8* 3C **110**
Ulverston Rd. *Ches* 4F **131**
Underbank. 5B **84**
Underbank La. *S'bri* 1A **140**
Undercliffe Rd. *S6* 6F **85**
Undergate Rd. *Dinn* 3E **107**
Underhill. *Wors* 5B **24**
Underhill La. *S6* 4H **73**

Under Tofts. 1D **96**
Underwood Av. *Wors* 3B **24**
Underwood Rd. *S8* 3D **110**
Union Ct. *B'ley* 1H **23**
Union Dri. *S11* 1B **110**
Union La. *S1* 3E **99** (6D **4**)
(in two parts)
Union Rd. *S11* 1B **110**
Union St. *S1* 3E **99** (5E **5**)
Union St. *B'ley* 1H **23**
Union St. *Donc* 1C **46**
Union St. *Roth* 3B **78**
Union Wlk. *Ches* 2A **138**
Unity Pl. *Roth* 3D **78**
Universal Clo. *N Ans* 5B **106**
Universal Cres. *N Ans* 5B **106**
University of Sheffield 2C **98** (3B **4**)
Unsliven Rd. *S'bri* 1A **140**
Unstone. 4H **129**
Unstone Dronfield By-Pass.
Dron 2D **128**
Unstone Hill. *Uns* 3H **129**
Unstone St. *S2* 4E **99**
Unwin Cres. *P'stne* 5D **142**
Unwin St. *P'stne* 5D **142**
Upland Ri. *Ches* 4F **137**
Uplands Av. *Dart* 5A **6**
Uplands Rd. *Arm* 3G **35**
Uplands Way. *Rawm* 1E **69**
Up. Albert Rd. *S8* 3E **111**
Up. Allen St. *S3* 1D **98** (2B **4**)
Upper Bradway. 4H **121**
Up. Castle Folds. *S1* 2G **5**
Up. Clara St. *Roth* 3H **77**
Up. Cliffe Rd. *Dod* 1A **22**
Upper Crabtree. 2G **87**
Up. Croft Clo. *Brim* 4E **133**
Upper Cudworth. 4C **10**
Upperfield Clo. *Maltby* 3F **83**
Up. Field La. *H Hoy* 5A **6**
Upperfield Rd. *Maltby* 3E **83**
Upper Folderings. *Dod* 2B **22**
Up. Forest Rd. *B'ley* 5B **8**
Upper Gate. 6B **84**
Uppergate Rd. *S6* 6B **84**
Up. Hanover St. *S3* 3C **98** (5A **4**)
(in two parts)
Upper Haugh. 6D **54**
Up. High Royds. *Dart* 5E **7**
Upper Hoyland. 4G **37**
Up. Hoyland Rd. *Hoy* 3F **37**
Up. King St. *Brim* 2F **133**
Up. Ley Ct. *C'town* 3E **65**
Up. Ley Dell. *C'town* 2E **65**
Up. Lum Clo. *Ches* 3D **138**
Up. Lunns Clo. *Roy* 2G **9**
Upper Millgate. *Roth* 3D **78**
Up. Moor St. *Ches* 3D **136**
Upper Newbold. 3C **130**
Up. Newbold Clo. *Ches* 4D **130**
Up. New St. *B'ley* 1H **23**
Up. Rye Clo. *Whis* 2B **92**
Up. School La. *Dron* 3F **129**
Up. Sheffield Rd. *B'ley* 2A **24**
Upper Swithen. 2A **6**
Upper Tankersley. 2C **50**
Upperthorpe. 4B **126**
(Killamarsh)
Upperthorpe. 6C **86**
(Sheffield)
Upperthorpe. *S6* 6B **86**
(in two parts)
Upperthorpe Glen. *S6* 6B **86**
Upperthorpe Rd. *S6* 6C **86** (1B **4**)
Upperthorpe Rd. *Kil* 4B **126**
Upperthorpe Vs. *Kil* 4B **126**
Up. Valley Rd. *S8* 2E **111**
Upper Whiston. 5B **92**
Up. Whiston La. *Whis* 4A **92**
Upperwood Rd. *D'fld* 3C **26**
Up. Wortley Rd.
Thpe H & Scho 3A **66**
Upton Clo. *Maltby* 2E **83**
Upton Clo. *Womb* 5H **25**
Upwell Hill. *S4* 2A **88**
Upwell La. *S4* 2A **88**
Upwell St. *S4* 2A **88**
Upwood Clo. *Ches* 6C **130**
Upwood Rd. *S6* 2H **85**
Urban Rd. *Donc* 2A **46**
Urch Clo. *Con* 4E **59**
Utah Ter. *S12* 4C **114**
Uttley Clo. *S9* 5D **88**

Uttley Cft. *S9* 5D **88**
Uttley Dri. *S9* 5D **88**
Uttoxeter Av. *Mexb* 5G **43**

V

Vaal St. *B'ley* 1B **24**
Vainor Rd. *S6* 1G **85**
Vale Av. *Thry* 5D **70**
Vale Clo. *Dron* 2F **129**
Vale Ct. *Thry* 5D **70**
Vale Cres. *Thry* 5D **70**
Vale Gro. *S6* 3E **85**
Valentine Clo. *S5* 4G **75**
Valentine Cres. *S5* 4G **75**
(in two parts)
Valentine Rd. *S5* 4G **75**
Vale Rd. *S3* 4D **86**
Vale Rd. *Thry* 5D **70**
Valetta Ho. P'gte 3F **69**
(off Netherfield La.)
Vale Vw. *Oxs* 6H **143**
Valiant Gdns. *Spro* 6G **31**
Valley Cres. *Ches* 3C **138**
Valley Dri. *Bran* 3H **49**
Valley Dri. *Kil* 2B **126**
Valley Dri. *Wath D* 5E **41**
Valley Gro. *Lund* 2F **15**
Valley Pk. Ind. Est. *Womb* 2A **40**
Valley Rd. *S8* 1E **111**
Valley Rd. *S12* 4C **114**
Valley Rd. *Ches* 3C **138**
Valley Rd. *High G* 1C **64**
Valley Rd. *Kil* 2B **126**
Valley Rd. *M'well* 4E **7**
Valley Rd. *Swint* 3H **55**
Valley Rd. *Womb* 5C **26**
Valley Vw. Clo. *Eck* 6H **125**
Valley Vw. Clo. *Has* 6E **139**
Valley Way. *Hoy* 5A **38**
Valley Way. *Womb* 1G **39**
Vancouver Dri. *Bol D* 1H **41**
Vanguard Trad. Est. *Ches* 6B **138**
Varley Gdns. *Flan* 3F **81**
Varney Rd. *Wath D* 6E **41**
Vaughan Av. *Donc* 5D **32**
Vaughan Rd. *B'ley* 4D **12**
Vaughton Hill. *Deep* 4H **141**
Vauxhall Clo. *S9* 5D **76**
Vauxhall Rd. *S9* 5D **76**
Velvet Wood Clo. *B'ley* 4C **12**
Venetian Cres. *D'fld* 4D **26**
Ventnor Clo. *Donc* 4H **45**
Ventnor Ct. *S7* 5D **98**
Ventnor Pl. *S7* 5D **98**
Venture Way. *Ches* 2H **131**
Venus Ct. *B'wth* 1C **90**
Verdant Way. *S5* 4H **75**
Verdon St. *S3* 5F **87**
Verelst Av. *Ast* 4B **104**
Vere Rd. *S6* 1A **86**
Verger Clo. *Ross* 4E **63**
Vernon Clo. *B'ley* 2H **23**
Vernon Cres. *Wors* 4H **23**
Vernon Delph. *S10* 2F **97**
Vernon Rd. *S17* 3E **121**
Vernon Rd. *Ches* 2F **137**
Vernon Rd. *Roth* 6H **79**
Vernon Rd. *Wors* 4H **23**
Vernon St. *B'ley* 5H **13**
Vernon St. *Birdw* 5D **36**
Vernon St. *Hoy* 6G **37**
Vernon St. N. *B'ley* 5H **13**
Vernon Ter. *S10* 3G **97**
Vernon Way. *B'ley* 4D **12**
Vernon Way. *Maltby* 3E **83**
Verona Ri. *D'fld* 4E **27**
Vesey St. *Rawm* 3F **69**
Vicarage Clo. *Donc* 4E **49**
Vicarage Clo. *Gren* 1A **74**
Vicarage Clo. *Hoy* 5A **38**
Vicarage Clo. *Mexb* 1G **57**
Vicarage Clo. *Roth* 1B **80**
Vicarage Ct. *B'wth* 4D **90**
Vicarage Cres. *Gren* 1A **74**
Vicarage Dri. *Wadw* 6H **61**
Vicarage La. *S17* 2D **120**
Vicarage La. *Roth* 3D **78**
Vicarage La. *Roy* 2E **9**
Vicarage Rd. *S9* 4B **88**
Vicarage Rd. *Gren* 1A **74**

Vicarage Wlk. *P'stne* 4D **142**
Vicarage Way. *Ark* 5E **19**
Vicar Cres. *D'fld* 4F **27**
Vicar La. *S1* 2E **99** (3E 5)
Vicar La. *Ches* 2A **138**
Vicar La. *Woodh* 6B **102**
Vicar Rd. *D'fld* 4F **27**
Vicar Rd. *Wath D* 4E **41**
Vickers Dri. *S5* 6H **75**
Vickers Rd. *S5* 1H **87**
Vickers Rd. *High G* 6B **50**
Victoria Av. *B'ley* 5G **13**
Victoria Av. *Roth* 3F **79**
Victoria Av. *Stav* 1D **134**
Victoria Clo. *Kiv P* 5A **118**
Victoria Clo. *S'bri* 3D **140**
Victoria Ct. *S11* 1B **110**
Victoria Ct. *Ben* 4B **18**
Victoria Ct. *Kiv P* 5A **118**
Victoria Cres. *B'ley* 5F **13**
Victoria Cres. *Birdw* 4C **36**
Victoria Cres. W. *B'ley* 5F **13**
Victoria Gro. *Brim* 6F **133**
Victoria Hall. *S1* 2D **98** (4C 4)
Victoria Ho. *S3* 4B 4
Victoria La. *New R* 4C **62**
Victoria M. *Kiln* 6C **56**
Victorian Cres. *Donc* 5F **33**
Victoria Pk. Rd. *Brim* 6F **133**
Victoria Quays. *S2* 1G **99** (2H 5)
Victoria Rd. *S10* 4C **98**
Victoria Rd. *Adw S* 1F **17**
Victoria Rd. *B'ley* 5G **13**
Victoria Rd. *Beig* 3F **115**
Victoria Rd. *Ben* 5B **18**
Victoria Rd. *Donc* 3B **46**
Victoria Rd. *Edl'tn* 2B **60**
Victoria Rd. *Mexb* 6E **43**
Victoria Rd. *P'gte* 3F **69**
(in two parts)
Victoria Rd. *Roy* 1F 9
Victoria Rd. *S'bri* 3D **140**
Victoria Rd. *Womb* 6B **26**
Victoria Rd. E. *Wath D* 8K **59**
Victoria Rd. W. *Wath D* 8K **59**
Victoria Sta. Rd. *S4* 1F **99** (2G 5)
Victoria St. *S3* 2D **98** (4B 4)
Victoria St. *B'ley* 5G **13**
Victoria St. *Brim* 2F **133**
Victoria St. *Cat* 5D **90**
Victoria St. *Ches* 1A **138**
Victoria St. *Cud* 6B **10**
Victoria St. *D'fld* 3F **27**
Victoria St. *Dinn* 4G **107**
Victoria St. *Dron* 1D **128**
Victoria St. *Gold* 4G **29**
Victoria St. *Hoy* 5B **38**
Victoria St. *Kiln* 6C **56**
Victoria St. *Maltby* 6G **83**
Victoria St. *Mexb* 6C **42**
Victoria St. *P'stne* 4D **142**
Victoria St. *Roth* 3B **78**
(in two parts)
Victoria St. *S'foot* 1D **24**
Victoria St. *S'bri* 3D **140**
Victoria St. N. *Old W* 1H **131**
Victoria St. W. *Ches* 3E **137**
Victoria Ter. *B'ley* 1A **24**
Victoria Vs. S6 . . . . .6C **86**
(off Blake Gro. Rd.)
Victoria Way. *Maltby* 3D **82**
Victor Rd. *S17* 2F **121**
Victor St. *S6* .4B **86**
Victor Ter. *B'ley* 1A **24**
Viewland Clo. *Cud* 2H **15**
Viewlands Clo. *Braml* 2E **81**
Viewlands Clo. *P'stne* 2D **142**
View Rd. *S2* 6E **99**
View Rd. *Roth* .1G **79**
View Rd. *Thurls* 3A **142**
Viewtree Clo. *Harl* 4H **51**
Vikinglea Clo. *S2* 5D **100**
Vikinglea Dri. *S2* 5D **100**
(in two parts)
Vikinglea Glade. *S2* 4D **100**
Vikinglea Rd. *S2* 4D **100**
Viking Way. *Kiv P* 4B **118**
Villa Gdns. *Toll B* 2A **18**
Village St. *Adw S* 1D **16**
Village St. *Donc* 4F **31**
Villa Pk. Rd. *Donc* 3C **48**
Villa Rd. *W'land* 2D **16**
Villiers Clo. *S2* 1A **112**

Villiers Dri. *S2* 1A **112**
Vincent Cres. *Ches* 3D **136**
Vincent Ho. *S1* 1D **98** (2C **4**)
Vincent La. *Ches* 3D **136**
Vincent Rd. *S7* 5D **98**
Vincent Rd. *B'ley* 4F **15**
Vincent Rd. *Rav* 2H **81**
Vincent Ter. *Thurn* 2H **29**
Vine Clo. *B'ley* 3C **14**
Vine Clo. *Roth* .3C **78**
Viola Bank. *S'bri* 3D **140**
Violet Av. *Beig* 4E **115**
Violet Av. *Edl'tn* 4B **60**
Violet Bank Rd. *S7* 1C **110**
Violet Farm Ct. *Brie* 3G **11**
Vivian Rd. *S5* .1H **87**
Vizard Rd. *Hoy* 5C **38**
Vulcan Ho. *Roth* 2G **79**
Vulcan Rd. *S9* 1D **88**
(Meadowhall Dri.)
Vulcan Rd. *S9* 1E **89**
(Meadowhall Way)

W

Wadbrough Rd. *S11* 4B **98**
Waddington Rd. *B'ley* 5D **12**
Waddington Ter. *Mexb* 1F **57**
Waddington Way. *Roth* 6G **69**
Wade Clo. *Roth* 5F **79**
Wade Mdw. *S6* 2G **85**
Wade St. *S4* 2A **88**
Wade St. *B'ley* 5D **12**
Wadsley. .1F 85
Wadsley La. *S6* 1G **85**
Wadsley Pk. Cres. *S6* 2G **85**
Wadsworth Av. *S12* 2E **113**
Wadsworth Clo. *S12* 1F **113**
Wadsworth Dri. *S12* 2F **113**
(in two parts)
Wadsworth Dri. *Rawm* 5C **54**
Wadsworth Rd. *S12* 2E **113**
Wadsworth Rd. *Braml* 5H **81**
Wadworth. 6H 61
Wadworth Av. *Ross* 4F **63**
Wadworth Hall. *Wadw* 6H **61**
Wadworth Hall La. *Wadw* 6G **61**
Wadworth Hill. *Wadw* 6H **61**
Wadworth Riding. *Edl'tn* 3D **60**
Wadworth Ri. *Dalt* 6C **70**
Wadworth St. *Den M* 2C **58**
Wager La. *Brie* 2G **11**
Wagon Rd. *Roth* 5B **68**
Wain Av. *Ches* 2B **138**
Waingate. *S3* 1F **99** (2F 5)
Wainscott Clo. *B'ley* 2C **14**
Wainwright Av. *S13* 5F **101**
Wainwright Av. *Womb* 6H **25**
Wainwright Cres. *S13* 5E **101**
Wainwright Pl. *Womb* 6H **25**
Wainwright Rd. *Donc* 1E **47**
Wainwright Rd. *Roth* 6H **67**
Wakefield Rd. *M'well* 2G 7
Wake Rd. *S7* .6C **98**
Walbank Rd. *Arm* 3G **35**
Walbert Av. *Thurn* 2E **29**
Walbrook. *Wors* 5B **24**
Walden Av. *Donc* 6G **17**
Walden Rd. *S2* 6F **99**
Walders Av. *S6* 1G **85**
Walders La. *Bols* 6E **141**
Wales. 5F 117
Wales Bar. 4D 116
Wales Ct. *Wal* .3F **117**
Walesmoor Av. *Kiv P* 5F **117**
Wales Pl. *S6* 5B **86**
Wales Rd. *Kiv P* 5F **117**
Waleswood. 4B 116
Waleswood Ind. Est. *Wal B* 3D **116**
Waleswood Rd. *Swal* 2A **116**
Waleswood Rd. *Wal B* 3D **116**
Waleswood Vw. *Ast* 1B **116**
Waleswood Vs. *Kiv P* 4D **116**
Walford Rd. *Kil* 3A **126**
Walgrove Av. *Ches* 4G **137**
Walgrove Rd. *Ches* 4F **137**
Walker Clo. *Gren* 1A **74**
Walker La. *Roth* 2E **79**
Walker Pl. Roth 2E **79**
(off Drummond St.)
Walker Rd. *Roth* 6H **67**
Walker Rd. *Tank* 6D **36**

Walker's La. *Kil* 3B **126**
Walkers Ter. *B'ley* 2C **14**
Walker St. *S3* 6F **87** (1G 5)
Walker St. *Rawm* 1H **69**
Walker St. *Swint* 2C **56**
Walker Vw. *Rawm* 1H **69**
Walkley. 5A 86
Walkley Bank. 6H 85
Walkley Bank Clo. *S6* 4A **86**
Walkley Bank Rd. *S6* 5G **85**
Walkley Cres. Rd. *S6* 5H **85**
Walkley La. *S6* 3A **86**
Walkley Rd. *S6* 5A **86**
Walkley St. *S6* 5A **86**
Walkley Ter. *S6* 5G **85**
Walk, The. *Birdw* 5C **36**
Walk, The. *Roth* 2H **79**
Wallace Rd. *S3* 4D **86**
Wallace Rd. *Donc* 5G **45**
Waller Rd. *S6* .5G **85**
Walling Clo. *S9* 1D **88**
Walling Rd. *S9* 1D **88**
Wallis Way. *Cat* 6B **90**
Wallsend Cotts. *Ches* 6G **131**
Wall St. *B'ley* .1G **23**
Walney Fold. *B'ley* 1D **14**
Walnut Clo. *B'ley* 2H **23**
Walnut Dri. *Dinn* 5F **107**
Walnut Dri. *Kil* .4A **126**
Walnut Gro. *Mexb* 5D **42**
Walnut Pl. *C'town* 3D **64**
(in two parts)
Walnut Tree Hill. *Wadw* 6H **61**
Walpole Clo. *Donc* 6H **45**
Walpole Gro. *Swal* 4B **104**
Walseker La. *H'hill* 1G **127**
Walsham Dri. *Donc* 4G **31**
Walshaw Gro. *Worr* 4C **72**
Walshaw Rd. *Worr* 4D **72**
Walters Rd. *Maltby* 4H **83**
Walter St. *S6* .4B **86**
Walter St. *Roth* 2C **78**
Waltham Cft. *Ches* 6C **138**
Waltham Gdns. *Soth* 5G **115**
Waltham St. *B'ley* 1H **23**
Waltheof Rd. *S2* 5C **100**
Walton. 5D 136
Walton Bk. La. *Walt* 6A **136**
Walton Clo. *Ches* 5D **136**
Walton Clo. *Dron W* 1A **128**
Walton Clo. *High G* 5A **50**
Walton Ct. *S8* .1C **122**
Walton Cres. *Ches* 4G **137**
Walton Dri. *Ches* 4G **137**
Walton Dri. Ct. *Ches* 4G **137**
Waltonfields Rd. *Ches* 3F **137**
Walton Ho. Donc 1C **46**
(off St James St.)
Walton Rd. *S11* 4B **98**
Walton Rd. *Ches* 3F **137**
Walton St. *B'ley* 4E **13**
Walton St. N. *B'ley* 4E **13**
Walton Wlk. *Ches* 3G **137**
Walton Works. *Ches* 3F **137**
Wannop St. *P'gte* 4F **69**
Wansfell Rd. *S4* 2B **88**
Wansfell Ter. *B'ley* 6A **14**
Wapping, The. *Hoot R* 6H **57**
Warburton Clo. *S2* 2G **99**
Warburton Gdns. *S2* 2G **99**
Warburton Rd. *S2* 2G **99**
Ward Clo. *P'stne* 5D **142**
Warde Aldam Cres. *Wick* 4E **81**
Warde Av. *Donc* 5H **45**
Warden Clo. *Donc* 3E **49**
Warden St. *Roth* 6D **78**
Wardgate Way. *Ches* 6C **130**
Ward Green. 4H 23
Wardlow Clo. *Ches* 5H **137**
Wardlow Rd. *S12* 2F **113**
Ward Pl. *S7* 5D **98**
Wardsend Rd. *S6* 1B **86**
Wardsend Rd. N. *S6* 6A **74**
Ward St. *S3* 6E **87** (1D 4)
Ward St. *P'stne* 5D **142**
Ward's Yd. Ches 3A **138**
(off Beetwell St.)
Wards Yd. *Dron* 2E **129**
Wareham Ct. *Soth* 5G **115**
Wareham Gro. *Dod* 1C **22**
Warehouse La. *Wath D* 5E **41**
Warminster Clo. *S8* 3E **111**
Warminster Cres. *S8* 3F **111**

Warminster Dri. *S8* 4F **111**
Warminster Gdns. *S8* 4E **111**
Warminster Pl. *S8* 5F **111**
Warminster Rd. *S8* 3E **111**
Warmsworth. 6E **45**
Warmsworth Ct. *Warm* 5F **45**
Warmsworth Halt. *Warm* 1B **60**
Warmsworth Halt Ind. Est.
  Warm 1C **60**
Warmsworth Rd. *Donc* 5G **45**
Warner Av. *B'ley* 5D **12**
Warner Pl. *B'ley* 5E **13**
Warner Rd. *S6* 2H **85**
Warner Rd. *B'ley* 5D **12**
Warner St. *Ches* 4B **138**
Warnington Dri. *Donc* 6E **49**
Warning Tongue La. *Donc* 3F **49**
Warren. 5F **51**
Warren Av. *Rawm* 6E **55**
Warren Clo. *Donc* 5G **33**
Warren Clo. *Roy* 1F **9**
Warren Clo. *Warm* 5E **45**
Warren Cres. *B'ley* 2H **23**
Warren Dri. *Roth* 1H **77**
Warreners Dri. *Thry* 5D **70**
Warren Gdns. *C'town* 5F **51**
Warren Hill. *Roth* 1H **77**
Warren Ho. Clo. *Braml* 4H **81**
Warren La. *C'town* 5E **51**
Warren La. *Dart* 2F **7**
Warren La. *Donc* 6D **48**
                (in two parts)
Warren La. *High G* 4D **50**
              (in three parts)
Warren Mt. *Roth* 1H **77**
Warren Pl. *B'ley* 2H **23**
Warren Quarry La. *B'ley* 2H **23**
Warren Ri. *Dron* 6G **123**
Warren Rd. *Con* 4D **58**
Warren Rd. *Wick* 4F **81**
Warren St. *S4* 6H **87**
                (in two parts)
Warren, The. *Ast* 6D **104**
Warren, The. *Ross* 3E **63**
Warren Vale. 5G **55**
Warren Va. *Rawm* 6G **55**
Warren Va. *Swint* 4G **55**
Warren Va. Rd. *Swint* 2G **55**
Warren Vw. *B'ley* 1H **23**
Warren Vw. *Roy* 1G **51**
Warren Wlk. *Roy* 1E **9**
               (Queensway)
Warren Wlk. *Roy* 1F **9**
             (Warren Clo.)
Warrington Rd. *S10* 1B **98**
Warris Clo. *Roth* 6G **67**
Warris Pl. *S2* .2H **99**
Warsop Rd. *B'ley* 4A **8**
Warwick Rd. *B'ley* 4B **14**
Warwick Rd. *Donc* 4H **33**
Warwick Rd. *Maltby* 4B **82**
Warwick St. *S10* 1A **98**
Warwick St. *Ches* 6B **138**
Warwick St. *Roth* 4E **79**
Warwick St. Ind. Est. *Ches* 6B **138**
Warwick St. S. *Roth* 4E **79**
Warwick Ter. *S10* 1A **98**
Warwick Way. *Ans* 1G **119**
Wasdale Av. *Half* 3E **125**
Wasdale Clo. *Half* 3E **125**
Washfield Cres. *Tree* 1E **103**
Washfield La. *Tree* 1E **103**
Washford Rd. *S9* 5A **88**
Wash Ho. La. *Ches* 3E **137**
Washington Av. *Con* 3B **58**
Washington Av. *Womb* 1D **38**
Washington Clo. *Dinn* 5D **106**
Washington Gro. *Donc* 2A **32**
Washington Rd. *S11* 5D **98**
Washington Rd. *E'fld* 6F **65**
Washington Rd. *Gold* 5F **29**
Washington Rd. *W'land* 2D **16**
Washington St. *Mexb* 6F **43**
Wasteneys Rd. *Tod* 2B **118**
Watch Ho. La. *Donc* 3H **31**
Watchley Gdns. *Gold* 4E **29**
Watch St. *S13* 5E **103**
Waterdale. 1D **46**
Waterdale Clo. *Spro* 3F **45**
Waterdale Rd. *Wors* 5H **23**
Waterdale Shop. Cen. Donc 6D **32**
             (off Waterdale)
Waterfield M. *W'fld* 6E **115**

Waterfield Pl. *B'ley* 1E **25**
Water Hall La. *P'stne* 3D **142**
                (in two parts)
Waterhall Vw. *P'stne* 3D **142**
Waterhouse Clo. *Dalt* 6C **70**
Wateringbury Gro. *Stav* 1D **134**
Watering La. *Ard* 1A **26**
Watering Pl. Rd. *Thurls* 4A **142**
Water La. *S17* 2F **121**
Water La. *Hoot R* 1G **71**
Water La. *Roth* 4D **78**
Water La. *W'wth* 2C **52**
Waterloo Ct. *Dinn* 2C **106**
Waterloo Rd. *S6* 4C **86**
Waterloo Rd. *B'ley* 6F **13**
Waterloo Wlk. *S6* 6D **86**
Watermead. *Eck* 6G **125**
Watermead. *Bol D* 2B **42**
Water Mdw. La. *Ches* 4D **130**
Water Royd Dri. *Dod* 2B **22**
Waterside Dri. *S'side* 1G **81**
Waterside Enterprise Pk.
  Dinn 3C **106**
Waterside Gdns. *O'bri* 2D **72**
Waterside Pk. *Womb* 1H **39**
Waterside Vw. *Con* 2E **59**
Water Slacks Clo. *S13* 1B **114**
Water Slacks Dri. *S13* 1B **114**
Water Slacks La. *S13* 1A **114**
Water Slacks Rd. *S13* 1B **114**
Water Slacks Wlk. *S13* 1B **114**
Water Slacks Way. *S13* 1B **114**
Watersmeet Rd. *S6* 4H **85**
Water St. *S3* 1E **99** (1E **5**)
Waterthorpe. 6E **115**
Waterthorpe Clo. *W'fld* 1F **125**
Waterthorpe Cres. *W'fld* 1F **125**
Waterthorpe Gdns. *W'fld* 1F **125**
Waterthorpe Glade. *W'fld* 1F **125**
Waterthorpe Glen. *W'fld* 1F **125**
Waterthorpe Greenway.
  W'fld 4D **114**
Waterthorpe Ri. *W'fld* 6F **115**
Watery St. *S3* 6D **86** (1B **4**)
Wath Golf Course. 2D **54**
Wath Rd. *S7* 1C **110**
Wath Rd. *Bol D* 2H **41**
Wath Rd. *Else* 1D **52**
Wath Rd. *Wath D & Mexb* 5B **42**
Wath Rd. *Womb & Bram* 1H **39**
Wath Roundabout. *Wath D* 5F **41**
Wath-upon-Dearne. 5F **41**
Wath W. Ind. Est. *Wath D* 3C **40**
Wath Wood. .1F **55**
Wath Wood Bottom.
  Wath D 2E **55**
Wath Wood Dri. *Swint* 2F **55**
Wath Wood Rd. *Wath D* 1F **55**
Watkinson Gdns. *Wat* 6E **115**
Watnall Rd. *B'ley* 5B **8**
Watson Clo. *Roth* 1H **77**
Watson Glen. *Roth* 1E **77**
Watson Rd. *S10* 3A **98**
Watson Rd. *Roth* 1H **77**
Watson St. *Hoy* 6F **37**
Watson Wlk. *S1* 2F **5**
Watt La. *S10* 3F **97**
Waveney Dri. *Hghm* 4A **12**
Waverley Av. *Con* 3E **59**
Waverley Av. *Donc* 4G **45**
Waverley La. *Kiv P* 4A **118**
Waverley La. *Thur* 5B **94**
Waverley La. *S13* 2H **101**
Waverley Ct. *Toll B* 3A **18**
Waverley La. *S13* 2H **101**
Waverley Rd. *S9* 1E **101**
Waverley Vw. *Cat* 6C **90**
Waycliffe. *B'ley* 4C **14**
Wayford Av. *Braml* 3H **81**
Wayford Av. *Has* 4B **138**
Wayland Av. *Wors* 4H **23**
Wayland Rd. *S11* 5B **98**
Wayside. *Brim* 3D **132**
Wayside Ct. *Brim* 3D **132**
Way, The. *Ches* 5D **136**
Weakland Clo. *S12* 5H **113**
Weakland Cres. *S12* 4H **113**
Weakland Dri. *S12* 4H **113**
Weakland Way. *S12* 4H **113**
Weavers Clo. *B'ley* 4A **12**
Weavers Clo. *Gren* 6A **64**
Webb Av. *Deep* 4G **141**
Webbs Av. *S6* 5E **85**

Webster Clo. *Roth* 1E **77**
Webster Ct. *Ches* 6G **131**
        (off Newbold Bk. La.)
Webster Cres. *Roth* 1F **77**
Webster Cft. *Old W* 1B **132**
Webster St. *S9* 2D **88**
Wedgewood Clo. *Rawm* 2F **69**
Weedon St. *S9* 2D **88**
Weetshaw Clo. *Shaf* 4C **10**
Weetshaw La. *Cud & Shaf* 4A **10**
Weetwood Dri. *S11* 1G **109**
Weetwood Rd. *Roth* 1G **91**
Weigh La. *S2* 2G **99** (4H **5**)
Weir Clo. *Hoy* 1A **52**
Weir Head. *S9* 2D **88**
Welbeck Clo. *Dron W* 1A **128**
Welbeck Clo. *Ink* 5B **134**
Welbeck Dri. *Ast* 6D **104**
Welbeck M. *Wick* 6F **81**
Welbeck Rd. *S6* 5H **85**
Welbeck Rd. *Donc* 1F **47**
Welbeck St. *B'ley* 5F **13**
                (in two parts)
Welbury Gdns. *Half* 3E **125**
Welby Pl. *S8* .2D **110**
Welfare Av. *Ches* 2F **137**
Welfare Av. *Con* 3C **58**
Welfare Rd. *Thurn* 1F **29**
Welfare Rd. *W'land* 4D **16**
Welfare Vw. *Dod* 1B **22**
Welfare Vw. *Gold* 5F **29**
Welham Dri. *Roth* 5E **79**
Welland Clo. *S3* 5D **86**
Welland Ct. *Hghm* 4A **12**
Welland Cres. *Else* 5C **38**
Wellbeck St. Stav 1C **134**
        (off Devonshire St.)
Wellbourne Clo. *C'town* 3G **65**
Wellcarr Rd. *S8* 5E **111**
Wellcliffe Clo. *Braml* 3G **81**
Well Ct. *S12* 4B **114**
Well Cft. *High G* 6B **50**
Wellcroft Clo. *Donc* 3A **34**
Wellcroft Gdns. *Braml* 2E **81**
Wellcroft Ho. Roy 2E **9**
          (off Church St.)
Well Dri. *Thry* .5E **71**
Wellesley Rd. *S10* 2B **98**
Wellfield Clo. *S6* 1B **98**
Wellfield Clo. *S12* 6G **113**
Wellfield Gdns. *Roy* 1F **9**
Wellfield Gro. *P'stne* 2D **142**
Wellfield Lodge. *Roth* 6G **67**
Wellfield Rd. *S6* 6B **86**
Wellfield Rd. *B'ley* 4F **13**
Wellfield Rd. *Roth* 5G **67**
Wellgate. *Con* 3E **59**
Wellgate. *M'well* 4F **7**
Wellgate. *Roth* 3E **79**
Wellgate Mt. *Roth* 3E **79**
Wellgate Ter. *Roth* 3E **79**
Well Grn. Rd. *S6* 6B **84**
Wellhead Rd. *S8* 1E **111**
Well Hill Gro. *Roy* 1E **9**
Well Ho. La. *P'stne* 3D **142**
             (Barnsley Rd.)
Well Ho. La. *P'stne* 1B **142**
          (Huddersfield Rd.)
Wellhouse Way. *P'stne* 2D **142**
Wellingley Rd. *Bal* 6C **46**
Wellington Av. *Ans* 6D **106**
Wellington Clo. *B'ley* 3B **14**
Wellington Cres. *Wors* 3C **24**
Wellington Gro. *Donc* 2A **32**
Wellington Pl. *S9* 1E **101**
Wellington Pl. *B'ley* 6F **13**
Wellington Rd. *S6* 5E **85**
Wellington Rd. *Edl'tn* 3B **60**
Wellington St. *S1* 3D **98** (5C **4**)
                (in two parts)
Wellington St. *B'ley* 6G **13**
Wellington St. *Gold* 4G **29**
Wellington St. *Mexb* 6E **43**
Welling Way. *Roth* 2G **77**
Well La. *S6* 1F **85**
Well La. *S12* 3B **114**
Well La. *Aug* .3A **104**
Well La. *B'ley* 2C **14**
Well La. *Gren* .6A **64**
Well La. *Tree* .1E **103**
Well La. *Wadw* 6H **61**
                (in two parts)

Well La. *Whis* 2H **91**
(Turner La.)
Well La. *Whis* 4B **92**
(Up. Whiston La.)
Well La. Ct. *L Hou* 3B **28**
Well Mdw. Dri. *S3* 1D **98** (2B **4**)
Well Mdw. St. *S3* 1D **98** (1B **4**)
Well Rd. *S8* 1E **111**
Wells Ct. *M'well* 5G **7**
Well Spring Clo. *Blbgh* 4E **133**
Wells Rd. *Donc* 3F **33**
Wells St. *Cud* 1H **15**
Well's St. *Dart* 5C **6**
Wells, The. *Ans* 2F **119**
(in two parts)
Well Vw. Rd. *Roth* 1F **77**
Wellway, The. *S'side* 2F **81**
Wellwyn Ct. *S12* 3D **112**
Welney Pl. *S6* 5A **74**
Welshpool Pl. *Ches* 2F **137**
Welshpool Yd. *Ches* 3F **137**
Welton Clo. *Donc* 5A **48**
Welwyn Clo. *S12* 3D **112**
Welwyn Clo. *Ches* 2F **137**
Welwyn Rd. *S12* 3D **112**
Wembley Av. *Con* 3C **58**
Wembley Clo. *Donc* 4A **34**
Wendel Gro. *Else* 5D **38**
Wenlock Clo. *Ches* 1F **137**
Wenlock Cres. *Ches* 1E **137**
Wenlock St. *S13* 4H **101**
Wensley Clo. *S4* 2A **88**
Wensley Ct. *S4* 1A **88**
Wensley Ct. *B'ley* 6A **8**
Wensley Ct. *Roth* 1F **91**
Wensley Cres. *Donc* 4D **48**
Wensley Cft. *S4* 1A **88**
Wensleydale Dri. *B'wth* 4D **90**
Wensleydale Rd. *Donc* 2F **31**
Wensleydale Rd. *Roth* 4H **67**
Wensley Dri. *S4* 1A **88**
Wensley Gdns. *S4* 1A **88**
Wensley Grn. *S4* 1A **88**
Wensley Rd. *B'ley* 6A **8**
Wensley St. *S4* 1A **88**
Wensley St. *Thurn* 1D **28**
Wensley Way. *Stav* 3A **134**
Wentworth 4C **52**
Wentworth Av. *S11* 5F **109**
Wentworth Av. *Ast* 1D **116**
Wentworth Av. *Ches* 5G **137**
Wentworth Castle. 6B **22**
Wentworth Castle Gardens 6B **22**
Wentworth Clo. *Thpe H* 2A **66**
Wentworth Ct. *Roth* 3B **68**
Wentworth Cres. *M'well* 5H **7**
Wentworth Cres. *P'stne* 4D **142**
Wentworth Dri. *M'well* 5G **7**
Wentworth Dri. *Rawm* 3F **69**
Wentworth Gdns. *Swint* 4A **56**
(off St James St.)
Wentworth Ind. Pk. *Tank* 1B **50**
Wentworth Meadows. *P'stne* ...3D **142**
Wentworth M. *P'stne* 4D **142**
Wentworth Pl. *Scho* 5E **67**
Wentworth Rd. *Bla H* 2H **37**
Wentworth Rd. *Dart* 5B **6**
Wentworth Rd. *Donc* 4E **33**
Wentworth Rd. *Dron W* 2A **128**
Wentworth Rd. *Else* 1C **52**
Wentworth Rd. *Jump* 4C **38**
Wentworth Rd. *M'well* 5G **7**
Wentworth Rd. *P'stne* 3C **142**
(in two parts)
Wentworth Rd. *Rawm & Swint* ...4C **54**
Wentworth Rd. *Thpe H* 2B **66**
Wentworth St. *B'ley* 4G **13**
Wentworth St. *Birdw* 4C **36**
Wentworth Vw. *Hoy* 6A **38**
(Millhouses St.)
Wentworth Vw. *Hoy* 6G **37**
(Willow Clo.)
Wentworth Vw. *Womb* 2F **39**
Wentworth Way. *Dinn* 6F **107**
Wentworth Way. *Dod* 3B **22**
Wentworth Way. *Tank* 1B **50**
Wentworth Woodhouse. 5E **53**
Wescoe Av. *Gt Hou* 1A **28**
Wesley Av. *Swal* 5B **104**
Wesley Ct. *Thpe H* 2B **66**
Wesley La. *S10* 2H **97**

Wesley Pl. *Ans* 3F **119**
Wesley Rd. *High G* 6A **50**
(in two parts)
Wesley Rd. *Kiv P* 4H **117**
Wesley St. *B'ley* 6H **13**
Wessenden Clo. *B'ley* 6C **12**
Wessex Gdns. *S17* 4D **120**
Wessington Dri. *Stav* 3A **134**
Westacre. *P'stne* 4E **143**
West Av. *Bal* 4A **46**
West Av. *Bol D* 2H **41**
West Av. *Rawm* 1F **69**
West Av. *Roy* 1F **9**
West Av. *Womb* 6H **25**
West Av. *W'land* 2B **16**
Westbank Clo. *Coal A* 5F **123**
Westbank Ct. *Coal A* 5G **123**
Westbank Dri. *Ans* 3E **119**
West Bank La. *S1* 2E **99** (3D **4**)
W. Bank Ri. *Ans* 3E **119**
West Bar. *S3* 1E **99** (1E **5**)
Westbar Grn. *S1* 1E **99** (2E **5**)
West Bars. *Ches* 2H **137**
W. Bawtry Rd. *B'wth & Roth* 2D **90**
Westbourne Gdns. *Donc* 6H **45**
Westbourne Gro. *B'ley* 4F **13**
Westbourne Gro. *Ches* 2D **136**
Westbourne Rd. *S10* 4A **98**
Westbourne Ter. *B'ley* 6E **13**
Westbrook Bank. *S11* 5B **98**
Westbrook Clo. *Ches* 3B **136**
Westbrook Dri. *Ches* 3B **136**
Westbrook Rd. *C'town* 2E **65**
Westbury Av. *C'town* 3F **65**
Westbury Clo. *B'ley* 3D **12**
Westbury St. *S9* 6B **88**
Westby Cres. *Whis* 2H **91**
Westby Wlk. *Braml* 1E **81**
W. Carr Rd. *Dinn* 4D **106**
West Clo. *Roth* 1G **77**
West Cres. *Duck* 6E **135**
West Cres. *Oxs* 5G **143**
West Cres. *S'bri* 3C **140**
W. Croft Ct. *Ink* 6H **133**
Westcroft Cres. *W'fld* 1E **125**
W. Croft Dri. *Ink* 6H **133**
Westcroft Dri. *W'fld* 2E **125**
Westcroft Gdns. *W'fld* 1E **125**
Westcroft Glen. *W'fld* 2E **125**
W. Don St. *S6* 5C **86**
W. End Av. *Donc* 2A **32**
W. End Av. *Roy* 2C **8**
W. End Ct. *Ross* 5F **63**
W. End Cres. *Roy* 2C **8**
W. End La. *New R* 4A **62**
W. End Rd. *Wath D* 4B **40**
W. End Vw. *Eck* 6H **125**
Westerdale Rd. *Donc* 2F **31**
Western Av. *Dinn* 5F **107**
Western Clo. *Dinn* 5F **107**
Western Bank. *S10* 2B **98** (3A **4**)
Western Rd. *S10* 1H **97**
Western Rd. *Roth* 2G **79**
Western St. *B'ley* 5F **13**
Western Ter. *Womb* 6A **26**
Westfield. 5A **40**
(Brampton)
Westfield. 1E **125**
(Mosborough)
Westfield Av. *S12* 4C **114**
Westfield Av. *Aug* 4A **104**
Westfield Av. *Ches* 4D **136**
Westfield Av. *Thurls* 3A **142**
Westfield Cen. *W'fld* 1E **125**
Westfield Clo. *Ches* 3D **136**
Westfield Craft Pk. *P'gte* 3E **69**
Westfield Cres. *Mosb* 1C **124**
Westfield Cres. *Thurn* 1D **28**
Westfield Ct. *Bram* 4A **40**
Westfield Gdns. *Ches* 3D **136**
Westfield Gro. *S12* 4B **114**
Westfield Ho. *S1* 4C **4**
Westfield La. *Barn* 1F **43**
Westfield La. *B'ley* 2A **12**
Westfield Northway. *W'fld* 1E **125**
(in two parts)
Westfield Rd. *Arm* 3E **35**
Westfield Rd. *Braml* 4H **81**
Westfield Rd. *Bram & Bram B* ...5A **40**
Westfield Rd. *Donc* 3B **46**
Westfield Rd. *Dron* 3G **129**
Westfield Rd. *Kil* 4A **126**

Westfield Rd. *P'gte* 4E **69**
Westfields. *Roy* 1C **8**
Westfields. *Wors* 5A **24**
Westfield Southway. *W'fld* 1E **125**
Westfield St. *B'ley* 6F **13**
Westgarth Clo. *Dinn* 4F **107**
Westgate. *B'ley* 6G **13**
Westgate. *Bram* 5A **40**
West Ga. *Mexb* 6G **43**
Westgate. *Monk B* 3B **14**
Westgate. *P'stne* 5D **142**
Westgate. *Roth* 3D **78**
West Green. 1F **15**
W. Green Dri. *Kirk S* 3C **20**
West Gro. *Donc* 4G **33**
West Gro. *Roy* 1C **8**
W. Hall Fold. *W'wth* 4C **52**
West Haven. *Cud* 2H **15**
West Hill. *Roth* 3E **77**
Westhill La. *S3* 2D **98** (4B **4**)
West Ho. *S8* 3E **111**
Westholme Rd. *Donc* 2B **46**
W. Kirk La. *L Hou* 2A **28**
W. Laith Ga. *Donc* 6C **32**
Westland Clo. *W'fld* 6E **115**
Westland Gdns. *W'fld* 6D **114**
Westland Gro. *W'fld* 1E **125**
Westland Rd. *W'fld* 1E **125**
West La. *S6* 1A **84**
West La. *Aug* 4H **103**
West La. *Maltby* 2D **94**
West Lea. *Ches* 3D **136**
Westleigh Ct. *Ches* 6G **131**
West Mall. *Cry P* 5E **115**
West Mall. Donc 6C **32**
(off French Ga.)
West Melton. 4D **40**
Westminster Av. *S10* 4B **96**
Westminster Clo. *S10* 4B **96**
Westminster Clo. *Braml* 2E **81**
Westminster Cres. *S10* 4B **96**
Westminster Cres. *Donc* 4H **33**
Westminster Dri. *D'ville* 3H **21**
Westminster Ho. *Donc* 4A **34**
Westmoor Clo. *Gold* 4E **29**
W. Moor Cres. *B'ley* 6C **12**
W. Moor La. *Arm* 2H **35**
(in two parts)
W. Moor La. *Bol D & H'ton* 1D **42**
W. Moor Link. *E'thpe* 6C **20**
W. Moor Pk. *Arm* 2H **35**
Westmoor Rd. *Brim* 1F **139**
Westmoreland St. *S6* 6C **86**
Westmorland La. *Den M* 2B **58**
Westmorland St. *Donc* 5H **45**
Westmorland Way. *Spro* 2C **44**
W. Mount Av. *Wath D* 3C **40**
Westnall Ho. *O'bri* 2D **72**
(off Glossop Row)
Westnall Rd. *S5* 2H **75**
Westnall Ter. *S5* 2H **75**
Weston Clo. *Ches* 5C **130**
Westongales Way. *Ben* 1A **32**
Weston Rd. *Donc* 5A **46**
Weston St. *S3* 1C **98** (2A **4**)
Westover Rd. *S10* 3E **97**
W. Park Dri. *Swal* 6H **103**
West Pinfold. *Roy* 2E **9**
Westpit Hill. *Bram B* 4A **40**
West Pl. *Ben* 6B **18**
West Quadrant. *S5* 5H **75**
West Rd. *B'ley* 5D **12**
West Rd. *Mexb* 6D **42**
Westside Grange. *Bal* 4A **46**
West St. *S1* 2D **98** (4B **4**)
West St. *Ans* 3F **119**
West St. *Beig* 4F **115**
West St. *Ches* 1H **137**
West St. *Con* 3E **59**
West St. *D'fld* 4E **27**
West St. *Donc* 6C **32**
West St. *Dron* 1D **128**
West St. *Eck* 6H **125**
West St. *Gold* 3G **29**
West St. *Hoy* 5G **37**
West St. *Mexb* 1E **57**
West St. *Roy* 1F **9**
West St. *Thur* 4B **94**
West St. *Wath D* 5E **41**
(in two parts)
West St. *Womb* 6A **26**
West St. *Wors* 5A **24**

West St. La. *S1* 2E **99** (3D **4**)
Westthorpe. 4B **126**
Westthorpe Fields Rd. *Kil* 5A **126**
Westthorpe Grn. *Kil* 5B **126**
Westthorpe Rd. *Kil* 4B **126**
W. Vale Gro. *Thry* 5D **70**
West Vw. *B'ley* 2G **23**
West Vw. *Stav* 2B **134**
West Vw. *Wors* 5B **24**
W. View Clo. *S17* 3F **121**
W. View Cres. *Gold* 5E **29**
W. View La. *S17* 3F **121**
W. View Rd. *Ches* 5G **131**
W. View Rd. *Mexb* 1E **57**
W. View Rd. *N'well* 3E **77**
W. View Ter. *Wors* 5B **24**
. . . . (off Ashwood Clo.)
Westville Rd. *B'ley* 4F **13**
West Way. *B'ley* 6G **13**
Westwell Pl. *Mosb* 3D **124**
Westwick Cres. *S8* 2B **122**
Westwick Gro. *S8* 2C **122**
Westwick La. *Holy* 3A **136**
Westwick Rd. *S8* 3B **122**
Westwood. 5B **50**
Westwood. *High G* 4B **50**
Westwood Av. *S6* 6F **73**
Westwood Av. *Stav* 3A **134**
Westwood Clo. *S6* 6F **73**
Westwood Clo. *Ink* 6A **134**
Westwood Country Pk. 4B **50**
Westwood Ct. *B'ley* 5G **13**
Westwood Ct. *High G* 5B **50**
Westwood Dri. *Ink* 6A **134**
Westwood Dri. Gdns. *Ink* 6H **133**
Westwood Ind. Est. *Arm* 4G **35**
Westwood La. *Brim* 1F **139**
Westwood La. *Wort* 1A **50**
Westwood New Rd.
. . . .*High G & Tank* 6A **50**
Westwood Rd. *S11* 5F **97**
Westwood Rd. *Cal* 1G **139**
Westwood Rd. *High G* 5B **50**
Wetherby Clo. *Donc* 4F **31**
Wetherby Ct. *S9* 1E **101**
Wetherby Dri. *Mexb* 5F **43**
Wetherby Dri. *Swal* 6A **104**
Wetlands La. *Ches* 1E **139**
Wet Moor La. *Wath D* 4D **40**
. . . . (in two parts)
Whaley Rd. *B'ley* 2B **12**
Wharf Clo. *Swint* 2C **56**
Wharfedale Dri. *C'town* 2C **64**
Wharfedale Rd. *B'ley* 5D **12**
Wharf La. *Ches* 1A **138**
Wharf La. *Stav* 1D **134**
Wharf Rd. *S9* 6F **77**
Wharf Rd. *Donc* 4D **32**
Wharf Rd. *Kiln* 6C **56**
Wharf St. *S2* 1G **99** (2G **5**)
Wharf St. *B'ley* 4A **14**
Wharf St. *Swint* 2C **56**
Wharncliffe. *Dod* 3C **22**
Wharncliffe Av. *Ast* 5C **104**
Wharncliffe Av. *Wath D* 5F **41**
Wharncliffe Clo. *Hoy* 1H **51**
Wharncliffe Clo. *Rawm* 5D **54**
Wharncliffe Ct. *Tank* 6A **36**
Wharncliffe Hill. *Roth* 2E **79**
Wharncliffe Ind. Complex.
. . . .*Deep* 3H **141**
Wharncliffe Rd. *S10* 3C **98** (6A **4**)
Wharncliffe Rd. *High G* 6B **50**
Wharncliffe Rd. *B'ley* 6F **13**
Wharncliffe St. *Car* 5F **9**
Wharncliffe St. *Donc* 1A **46**
Wharncliffe St. *Roth* 2E **79**
Wharton Av. *Swal* 4B **104**
Wharton Dri. *Ches* 2B **138**
Wheatacre Rd. *S'bri* 3E **141**
Wheata Dri. *S5* 2F **75**
Wheata Pl. *S5* 2E **75**
Wheata Rd. *S5* 3E **75**
Wheatbridge Retail Pk. *Ches* . . .3H **137**
Wheatbridge Rd. *Ches* 2G **137**
Wheat Cft. *Con* 3G **59**
Wheatcroft Rd. *Rawm* 1H **69**
. . . . (in two parts)
Wheatfield Clo. *Barn D* 1E **21**
Wheatfield Cres. *S5* 3H **75**
Wheatfield Dri. *Thurn* 2F **29**
Wheatfield Way. *Ash* 6B **130**
Wheathill Clo. *Ash* 1B **136**

Wheathill Clo. *Brim* 1F **139**
Wheathill La. *Ches* 1D **138**
Wheathill St. *Roth* 4D **78**
Wheatley. 3F **33**
Wheatley Clo. *B'ley* 3H **13**
Wheatley Golf Course. 3B **34**
Wheatley Gro. *S13* 4G **101**
Wheatley Hall Retail Cen. *Donc* . .2H **33**
Wheatley Hall Rd. *Donc* 3E **33**
Wheatley Hills. 3B **34**
Wheatley La. *Donc* 5E **33**
Wheatley Park. 2H **33**
Wheatley Pk. Rd. *Ben* 5A **18**
Wheatley Ri. *Den M* 2B **58**
Wheatley Ri. *M'well* 3F **7**
Wheatley Rd. *B'ley* 2E **25**
Wheatley Rd. *Kiln* 6C **56**
Wheatley Rd. *Roth* 6G **67**
Wheatley St. *Den M* 2B **58**
Wheats La. *S1* 2E **5**
Wheeldon Cres. *Brim* 3B **132**
Wheeldon St. *S1* 2D **98** (3B **4**)
Wheel La. *Gren* 1B **74**
Wheel La. *O'bri* 2B **72**
Wheel, The. *E'fld* 1C **74**
Wheldrake Rd. *S5* 1H **87**
Whernside Av. *C'town* 1D **64**
Whinacre Clo. *S8* 3F **123**
Whinacre Pl. *S8* 3E **123**
Whinacre Wlk. *S8* 3E **123**
Whinby Cft. *Dod* 2B **22**
Whinby Rd. *Dod* 1A **22**
Whinfell Clo. *Adw S* 1D **16**
Whinfell Ct. *S11* 5E **109**
. . . . (in three parts)
Whin Hill Rd. *Donc* 3B **48**
Whinmoor Rd. *S5* 6B **76**
Whinmoor Rd. *High G* 6A **50**
Whirlow Hill. 5C **70**
Whins, The. *Rawm* 1C **68**
Whiphill Clo. *Donc* 4C **48**
Whiphill La. *Arm* 4G **35**
. . . . (in two parts)
Whiphill Top La. *Bran* 2H **49**
Whirlow. .5E **109**
Whirlow Ct. Rd. *S11* 5F **109**
Whirlowdale Clo. *S11* 5E **109**
Whirlowdale Cres. *S7* 4H **109**
Whirlowdale Ri. *S11* 5F **109**
Whirlowdale Rd. *S11 & S7* 5E **109**
Whirlow Farm M. *S11* 4E **109**
Whirlow Grange Av. *S11* 5E **109**
Whirlow Grange Dri. *S11* 5E **109**
Whirlow Grn. *S11* 5E **109**
Whirlow Gro. *S11* 5F **109**
Whirlow La. *S11* 4E **109**
Whirlow M. *S11* 4F **109**
Whirlow Pk. Rd. *S11* 5F **109**
Whisperwood Clo. *Duck* 6E **135**
Whisperwood Dri. *Bal* 1H **61**
Whiston. .2H **91**
Whiston Brook Vw. *Whis* 2A **92**
Whiston Grange. *Roth* 2G **91**
Whiston Grn. *Whis* 3H **91**
Whiston Gro. *Roth* 5F **79**
Whiston Va. *Whis* 3H **91**
Whitaker Clo. *Roth* 6D **62**
Whitaker Sq. *New R* 5C **62**
Whitbeck Clo. *Wadw* 6H **61**
Whitbourne Clo. *B'ley* 2H **13**
Whitburn Rd. *Donc* 1E **47**
Whitby Rd. *S9* 6E **89**
Whitby Rd. *New R* 5C **62**
Whitcomb Dri. *New R* 6D **62**
Whitebank Clo. *Ches* 4B **138**
Whitecotes Clo. *Ches* 5G **137**
Whitecotes La. *Ches* 5G **137**
Whitecotes Pk. *Ches* 5H **137**
White Cft. *S1* 1E **99** (2C **4**)
Whitecroft Cres. *B'wth* 3C **90**
White Cross Av. *Cud* 2H **15**
White Cross Ct. *Cud* 2H **15**
White Cross La. *Wadw* 4G **61**
. . . . (in two parts)
White Cross La. *Wors* 4D **24**
White Cross Mt. *Cud* 2H **15**
White Cross Ri. *Wors* 4D **24**
White Cross Rd. *Cud* 2H **15**
White Edge Clo. *Ches* 6F **131**
White Ga. *Ans* 1H **119**
Whitegate Wlk. *Roth* 4G **67**
Whitehall Rd. *Roth* 3H **67**
Whitehall Way. *Roth* 4A **68**

White Hart Corner. *Eck* 5E **125**
Whitehead Av. *Deep* 3F **141**
Whitehead Clo. *Dinn* 4E **107**
Whitehead St. *Stav* 1D **134**
White Hill Av. *B'ley* 6C **12**
Whitehill Av. *B'wth* 3C **90**
White Hill Gro. *B'ley* 4C **90**
Whitehill Gro. *B'ley* 6D **12**
Whitehill La. *B'wth* 2C **90**
Whitehill Rd. *B'wth* 3B **90**
White Hill Ter. *B'ley* 6C **12**
Whitehouse La. *S6* 5C **86**
Whitehouse Rd. *S6* 5B **86**
Whitehouses. *Ches* 4B **138**
White Ho. Vw. *Barn D* 1G **21**
White La. *S12* 4C **112**
White La. *C'town* 6F **51**
Whitelea Gro. *Mexb* 1D **56**
Whitelea Gro. Trad. Est. *Mexb* . . .1D **56**
White Leas. *Ches* 1D **136**
Whitelee Rd. *Swint & Mexb* 2C **56**
Whiteley La. *S10* 6C **96**
Whiteleys Av. *Rawm* 6E **55**
Whiteley Wood Clo. *S11* 6F **97**
Whiteley Wood Green. 1B **108**
Whiteley Wood Rd. *S11* 1D **108**
Whiteley Woods. 6F **97**
Whitelow La. *S17* 1A **120**
White Rd. *Stav* 1E **135**
White Rose Ct. *Ben* 6C **18**
White Rose Ho. *Roth* 4D **78**
White Rose Way. *Donc* 2D **46**
White's La. *S2* 2H **99**
White Thorns Clo. *S8* 3F **123**
White Thorns Dri. *S8* 4F **123**
White Thorns Vw. *S8* 3F **123**
White Towers Cvn. Site. *Donc* . . .3C **34**
Whiteways Clo. *S4* 3H **87**
Whiteways Dri. *S4* 3H **87**
Whiteways Gro. *S4* 3H **87**
Whiteways Rd. *S4* 3H **87**
Whitewood Clo. *Roy* 3D **8**
Whitfield Rd. *S10* 6C **96**
Whitfield Rd. *Rawm* 6D **54**
Whitham Rd. *S10* 3A **98**
Whiting St. *S8* 1E **111**
Whitley. 5D **64**
Whitley Carr. *Gren* 5C **64**
Whitley Cft. *E'fld* 6F **65**
Whitley La. *Gren & E'fld* 6B **64**
Whitley Vw. *E'fld* 5F **65**
Whitley Vw. Rd. *Roth* 4D **78**
Whitney Clo. *Donc* 6G **45**
Whittier Rd. *Donc* 5A **46**
Whittington Hill. *Old W* 2A **132**
Whittington Moor. 3A **132**
Whittington St. *Donc* 4D **32**
Whittington Way. *Whit M* 2A **132**
Whitting Valley Rd. *Old W* 1A **132**
Whitton Clo. *Donc* 5A **48**
. . . . (in three parts)
Whitton Pl. *Duck* 5E **135**
Whitwell Cres. *S'bri* 3D **140**
Whitwell La. *S'bri* 4C **140**
Whitwell St. *S9* 1F **101**
Whitwell Vw. *Ross* 4F **63**
Whitworth Cft. *S10* 3F **97**
Whitworth La. *S9* 4C **88**
Whitworth Rd. *S10* 4E **97**
Whitworth Rd. *Ches* 5H **131**
Whitworth's Ter. *Thurn* 1G **29**
. . . . (off Clarke St.)
Whitworth St. *Gold* 4G **29**
Whitworth Way. *Wath D* 4E **41**
Whybourne Gro. *Roth* 4E **79**
Whybourne Ter. *Roth* 3E **79**
Whyn Vw. *Thurn* 1E **29**
Wicker. *S3* 1F **99** (1G **5**)
Wicker La. *S3* 1F **99** (1F **5**)
Wickersley. 5F **81**
Wickersley Rd. *Roth* 5G **79**
Wickett Hern Rd. *Arm* 3G **35**
. . . . (in two parts)
Wicket Way. *Edl'tn* 2C **66**
Wickfield Clo. *S12* 2H **113**
Wickfield Dri. *S12* 2H **113**
Wickfield Gro. *S12* 3G **113**
Wickfield Pl. *S12* 2G **113**
Wickfield Rd. *S12* 3H **113**
Wicklow La. *Donc* 4G **33**
Widdop Clo. *S13* 5F **101**
Widdop Cft. *S13* 5F **101**
Wigfield Dri. *Wors* 4H **23**

Wigfield Farm. 5G 23
Wigfull Rd. S11 . . . . .4A 98
Wigley Rd. Ink 5A 134
Wignall Av. Wick 5D 80
Wikeley Way. Brim 3D 132
Wike Rd. B'ley 5E 15
Wilberforce Rd. Ans 2F 119
Wilberforce Rd. Donc 6B 20
Wilbrook Ri. B'ley 3C 12
Wilby Carr Gdns. Donc 2C 48
Wilby La. B'ley 1A 24
Wilcox Clo. S6 . . . . .4B 74
Wilcox Grn. Roth 3A 68
Wilcox Rd. S6 . . . . .4A 74
Wild Av. Rawm 6C 54
Wildene Dri. Mexb 5E 43
Wilder M. Roth 2H 77
Wildflower Clo. New R 6C 62
Wilding Clo. Roth 1G 77
Wilding Way. Roth 1G 77
Wilford Rd. B'ley 4A 8
Wilfred Clo. S9 . . . . .6C 88
Wilfred Dri. S9 . . . . .6C 88
Wilfred St. Roth 3D 78
Wilfred Ter. B'ley 1G 23
Wilfrid Rd. S9 . . . . .6C 88
Wilkin Hill. Barl 2A 130
Wilkinson Av. New R 5E 63
Wilkinson Clo. Ches 6A 138
                                    (in two parts)
Wilkinson Dri. Ink 4H 133
Wilkinson La. S10 . . . . . .2C 98 (4A 4)
                                    (in two parts)
Wilkinson Rd. Else 6C 38
Wilkinson St. S10 . . . . . .2C 98 (4A 4)
                                    (in two parts)
Wilkinson St. B'ley 1H 23
Willan Dri. Cat 6C 90
Willbury Dri. S12 . . . . .1C 112
Willersley Ct. Ches 4F 131
                                  (off Bowness Rd.)
Willey St. S3 . . . . .1F 99 (1G 5)
William Clo. Mosb 3D 124
William Cres. Mosb 2D 124
William La. New R 3B 62
William Nuttall Cottage Homes. Donc
                                     . . . . .1F 47
Williamson Rd. S11 . . . . .6B 98
Williams Rd. Donc 3H 31
Williams St. P'gte 3G 69
William St. S10 . . . . .3C 98 (6A 4)
William St. Ches 5A 132
William St. Eck 6D 124
William St. Gold 4E 29
William St. Roth 3E 79
William St. Swint 2C 56
William St. Wath D 5F 41
William St. Womb 6A 26
William St. Wors 4A 24
William St. N. Old W 1H 131
Willingham Clo. Soth 6G 115
Willingham Gdns. Soth 6G 115
Willington Rd. S5 . . . . .5G 75
Willis Rd. S6 . . . . .2H 85
Willman Rd. B'ley 4F 15
Willoughby St. S4 . . . . .1A 88
Willow Av. Donc 3D 48
Willow Av. Rawm 2G 69
Willow Bank. B'ley 2F 13
                                    (in two parts)
Willow Beck. Roth 1H 79
Willow Bri. Cvn. Site. Donc 4B 32
Willow Brook Clo. M'well 5E 7
Willow Clo. Ans 4F 119
Willow Clo. B'wth 4D 90
Willow Clo. Cud 6B 10
Willow Clo. Flan 3G 81
Willow Clo. Hoy 6G 37
Willow Ct. Cal 2G 139
Willow Ct. D'fld 4E 27
Willow Ct. Rawm 1G 69
Willow Ct. Wath D 6E 41
Willow Ct. Wick 5F 81
Willow Cres. C'town 3E 65
Willowcroft. Bol D 2H 41
Willowdale Clo. Spro 3E 45
Willow Dene Rd. Grim 6G 11
Willow Dri. S9 . . . . .2G 101
Willow Dri. Edl'tn 2C 60
Willow Dri. Flan 3G 81
Willow Dri. Mexb 6D 42
Willow Gth. Rawm 1G 69
Willowgarth Av. B'wth 3C 90

Willow Gth. Rd. Ches 3E 131
Willow Glen. Bran 3H 49
Willow Gro. Ast 5D 104
Willow La. Bol D 2B 42
Willow La. Oxs 5H 143
Willow La. Ross 4E 63
Willowlees Ct. Donc 4C 48
Willow Rd. Arm 2G 35
Willow Rd. Kil 4A 126
Willow Rd. Maltby 4D 82
Willow Rd. S'bri 5D 140
Willow Rd. Thurn 1F 29
Willow Rd. Wath D 1G 55
Willows, The. D'fld 4E 27
Willows, The. Oxs 6H 143
Willows, The. Roth 4F 79
                                    (off Badsley St.)
Willows, The. Roth 5F 67
                                    (Becket Cres.)
Willow St. B'ley 1F 23
Willow St. Con 3F 59
Willow Wlk. Ben 4A 18
Wilmington Dri. Donc 4F 47
Wilsden Gro. B'ley 4D 12
Wilsic Ho. Donc 1C 46
                                    (off St James St.)
Wilson Av. P'stne 5D 142
Wilson Av. Rawm 1E 69
Wilson Dri. Dalt 6C 70
Wilson Gro. B'ley 3E 15
Wilson Pl. S8 . . . . .1E 111
Wilson Rd. S11 . . . . .5A 98
Wilson Rd. Coal A 5G 123
Wilson Rd. Deep 4H 141
Wilson St. S3 . . . . .5E 87
Wilson St. Dron 3F 129
Wilson St. Womb 6H 25
Wilson Wlk. Dod 3C 22
Wilstrop Rd. S9 . . . . .6D 88
Wilthorpe. 3E 13
Wilthorpe Av. B'ley 3E 13
Wilthorpe Cres. B'ley 3E 13
Wilthorpe Farm Rd. B'ley 3E 13
Wilthorpe Gdns. Owl 4A 114
Wilthorpe Grn. B'ley 3E 13
Wilthorpe La. B'ley 3D 12
                                    (in two parts)
Wilthorpe Rd. B'ley 3C 12
Wilton Clo. Rawm 2F 69
Wilton Ct. Roth 2A 78
Wilton Gdns. Roth 2A 78
Wilton La. Roth 3A 78
Wilton Pl. S10 . . . . .3C 98 (6A 4)
Wiltshire Av. Den M 2B 58
Wiltshire Rd. Donc 5A 34
Wimborne Cres. Ches 4G 131
Wimpenny Av. Ans 2G 119
Wincanton Clo. Mexb 5F 43
Winchester Av. S10 . . . . .5B 96
Winchester Av. Donc 3G 33
Winchester Ct. Roth 2E 79
                                  (off Nottingham St.)
Winchester Cres. S10 . . . . .5B 96
Winchester Dri. S10 . . . . .5B 96
Winchester Ho. Donc 3F 31
Winchester Rd. S10 . . . . .5B 96
Winchester Rd. Ches 4G 131
Winchester Way. B'ley 2G 25
Winchester Way. B'wth 2A 90
Winchester Way. Scaw 3G 31
Wincobank. 6B 76
Wincobank Av. S5 . . . . .6A 76
Wincobank Clo. S5 . . . . .6B 76
Wincobank La. S4 . . . . .2B 88
Wincobank Rd. S5 . . . . .6B 76
Winco Rd. S4 . . . . .2B 88
Winco Wood La. S5 . . . . .6B 76
Windam Dri. Barn D 1H 21
Windermere Av. Donc 4A 34
Windermere Av. Dron W 2C 128
Windermere Av. Gold 5G 29
Windermere Clo. Mexb 5H 43
Windermere Ct. Ans 1G 119
Windermere Cres. Kirk S 3D 20
Windermere Grange. Edl'tn 4B 60
Windermere Rd. S8 . . . . .2C 110
Windermere Rd. B'ley 4E 15
Windermere Rd. Ches 4E 131
Windermere Rd. P'stne 3D 142
Winders Pl. Womb 1F 39
Windgate Hill. Con 2F 59
Windham Clo. B'ley 4H 13
Windhill. .5G 43

Windhill Av. Dart 2E 7
Windhill Av. Mexb 6G 43
Windhill Cres. Dart 2E 7
Windhill Cres. Mexb 5G 43
Windhill Dri. Dart 2E 7
Windhill La. Dart 2E 7
Windhill Mt. Dart 2E 7
Windhill Ter. Mexb 5G 43
Windings, The. Thurn 2H 29
Windle Ct. Tree 1F 103
Windle Rd. Donc 2A 46
Windle Sq. Kirk S 3D 20
Windmill Av. Con 4F 59
Windmill Av. Grim 5F 11
Windmill Balk La.
          W'land & Adw S 3C 16
Windmill Ct. Thpe H 4C 66
Windmill Ct. Womb 1D 38
Windmill Dri. Wadw 6H 61
Windmill Est. Con 4F 59
Windmill Greenway. Half 4E 125
Windmill Hill La. C'town 3C 64
Windmill La. S5 . . . . .5A 76
Windmill La. Thurls 4A 142
Windmill Rd. Ans 1G 119
Windmill Rd. Womb 1D 38
Windmill Ter. Roy 1D 8
Windsor Av. Dart 5A 6
Windsor Av. Thurls 3A 142
Windsor Clo. Braml 3H 81
Windsor Clo. Ches 4E 137
Windsor Clo. H'ton 1G 43
Windsor Ct. S11 . . . . .3F 109
Windsor Ct. D'ville 3H 21
Windsor Cres. B'ley 4B 14
Windsor Cres. L Hou 2H 27
Windsor Dri. Dod 2B 22
Windsor Dri. Dron W 2A 128
Windsor Dri. Mexb 5G 43
Windsor Sq. Thurn 1G 29
Windsor St. S4 . . . . .6A 88
                                    (Attercliffe Rd.)
Windsor St. S4 . . . . .5H 87
                          (Savile St. E., in two parts)
Windsor St. Hoy 4H 37
Windsor St. Thurn 1G 29
Windsor Wlk. Ans 4E 119
Windsor Wlk. Donc 3G 31
Windsor Wlk. Has 4C 138
Windy Fields Rd. Holy 6A 136
Windy Ho. La. S2 . . . . .6B 100
                                    (in two parts)
Windy Ridge. Aug 4A 104
Winfield Rd. Wath D 6F 41
Wingerworth Av. S8 . . . . .1B 122
Wingerworth Way. Ches 6H 137
Wingfield. 5H 67
Wingfield Clo. Dron W 2A 128
Wingfield Clo. Roth 4A 68
Wingfield Ct. Roth 5H 67
Wingfield Cres. S12 . . . . .2E 113
Wingfield Rd. B'ley 1A 14
Wingfield Rd. Roth 4H 67
Winholme. Arm 3F 35
Winifred St. Roth 3C 78
Winkley Ter. S5 . . . . .4A 76
Winlea Av. Roth 5C 80
Winmarith Ct. Roy 2D 8
Winnat Pl. Ink 4A 134
Winnats Clo. Ches 6E 131
Winn Clo. S6 . . . . .6H 73
Winn Dri. S6 . . . . .6H 73
Winn Gdns. S6 . . . . .6H 73
Winn Gro. S6 . . . . .5G 73
Winnipeg Rd. Ben 6B 18
Winsford Rd. S6 . . . . .4A 74
Winsick. .6E 139
Winster Clo. Birdw 3D 36
Winster Cres. Dart 1A 138
Winster Rd. S6 . . . . .2A 86
Winster Rd. Stav 3A 134
Winston Av. S'bri 2B 140
Winter Av. B'ley 5E 13
Winter Av. Roy 1E 9
Winter Garden. 4E 5
Winter Hill La. Roth 2G 77
Winterhill Rd. Roth 3F 77

Winter Rd. *B'ley* 5E **13**
Wintersett Dri. *Donc* 3H **47**
Winter St. *S3* 1C **98**
Winter Ter. *B'ley* 5E **13**
Winterton Clo. *Donc* 5B **48**
Winterton Gdns. *S12* 4C **114**
Winterwell Rd. *Wath D* 4C **40**
(in two parts)
Winton Clo. *B'ley* 2A **24**
Winton Rd. *Donc* 5H **33**
Wisbech Clo. *Ches* 5G **137**
Wisconsin Dri. *Donc* 4G **47**
Wiseton Rd. *S11* 5A **98**
Wisewood. .2F **85**
Wisewood Av. *S6* 3G **85**
Wisewood La. *S6* 3G **85**
Wisewood Pl. *S6* 3G **85**
Wisewood Rd. *S6* 3G **85**
Wishing Well Grn. *Swal* 6H **103**
Wiston Way. *Ches* 6C **138**
Witham Clo. *Ches* 5C **132**
Witham Ct. *Ches* 2E **137**
Witham Ct. *Hghm* 4A **12**
Withens Av. *S6* 1H **85**
Withens Ct. *M'well* 4E **7**
Witney St. *S8* 5E **99**
Wittsend Pk. Cvn. Site. *Ark* 4E **19**
Wivelsfield Rd. *Donc* 4G **45**
Woburn Clo. *Donc* 6G **45**
Woburn Pl. *S11* 5F **109**
Woburn Pl. *Dod* 3B **22**
Wolfe Clo. *Ches* 4F **137**
Wolfe Dri. *S6* 4B **74**
Wolfe Rd. *S6* 4B **74**
Wollaton Av. *S17* 4G **121**
Wollaton Clo. *B'ley* 5A **8**
Wollaton Dri. *S17* 4G **121**
Wollaton Rd. *S17* 5F **121**
Wolseley Rd. *S8* 6E **99**
Wolsey Av. *Donc* 6G **33**
Wolverley Rd. *S13* 1A **114**
Wombwell. 6B **26**
Wombwell Av. *Wath D* 6E **41**
Wombwell (Hillies) Golf Course.
. . . . .2F **39**
Wombwell La. *B'ley* 2E **25**
Wombwell La. *Hoy* 1H **37**
Wombwell La. *Hoy* 4A **38**
Wood Acres. *B'ley* 3C **12**
Woodall. .3G **127**
Woodall La. *H'hill* 3G **127**
Woodall Rd. *Kil* 4D **126**
Woodall Rd. *Roth* 4A **80**
Woodall Rd. S. *Roth* 5A **80**
Woodbank Ct. *S17* 2G **121**
(off Ladies Spring Gro.)
Woodbank Cres. *S17* 2D **110**
Woodbank Rd. *S6* 1A **96**
Woodbine Rd. *S9* 4B **88**
Woodbourne Gdns. *Tank* 6C **36**
Woodbourn Hill. *S9* 6B **88**
Woodbourn Rd. *S9* 1B **100**
Woodbridge Ri. *Ches* 5D **136**
Woodburn Ct. *Roth* 2B **78**
(off Park St.)
Woodburn Dri. *C'town* 2F **65**
Woodbury Clo. *S9* 4C **76**
Woodbury Rd. *S9* 4C **76**
Wood Cliffe. *S10* 1B **108**
Wood Clo. *C'town* 3G **65**
Wood Clo. *Rav* 1G **81**
Wood Clo. *Rawm* 6E **55**
Woodcock Clo. *Roth* 5H **67**
Woodcock Pl. *S2* 2H **99**
Woodcock Rd. *Hoy* 6A **38**
Woodcock Way. *Adw S* 1D **16**
Wood Cft. *Roth* 6H **67**
Woodcross Av. *Donc* 4E **49**
Wood End. *Gren* 5C **64**
Wood End Av. *P'stne* 6C **142**
Woodend Clo. *S6* 4G **85**
Wood End Ct. *Dod* 3C **22**
Woodend Dri. *S6* 4G **85**
Woodfarm Av. *S6* 5F **85**
Woodfarm Clo. *S6* 5E **85**
Woodfarm Dri. *S6* 5E **85**
Woodfarm Pl. *S6* 5E **85**
Woodfield Av. *Mexb* 6F **43**
Woodfield Clo. *D'fld* 3E **27**
Woodfield Rd. *S10* 6H **85**
Woodfield Rd. *Arm* 4G **35**
Woodfield Rd. *Donc* 4A **46**
(in two parts)

Woodfield Rd. *Wath D* 5B **40**
Wood Fields. *Braml* 2E **81**
Woodfield Vs. *Roth* 5E **79**
Woodfield Way. *Bal* 1H **61**
Wood Fold. *S3* 4E **87**
Woodfoot Rd. *Roth* 2F **91**
Woodford Rd. *Barn D* 1H **21**
Woodgrove Rd. *S9* 5D **76**
Woodhall Rd. *Roth* 2A **80**
Woodhall Clo. *D'fld* 3E **27**
Woodhall Flats. *D'fld* 3E **27**
Woodhall Ri. *Swint* 3B **56**
Woodhall Rd. *D'fld* 3E **27**
Woodhead Dri. *Bla H* 2H **37**
Woodhead La. *Hoy* 1A **38**
Woodhead Rd. *S2* 5E **99**
Woodhead Rd. *Gren* 5A **64**
Wood Hill. .3H **87**
Woodholm Pl. *S11* 2H **109**
Woodholm Rd. *S11* 2H **109**
Woodhouse. 1B **114**
Woodhouse Av. *Beig* 3F **115**
Woodhouse Clo. *Rawm* 5D **54**
Woodhouse Ct. *Beig* 3E **115**
Woodhouse Cres. *Beig* 3F **115**
Woodhouse Gdns. *S13* 1C **114**
Woodhouse Grn. *Thur* 4A **94**
(in two parts)
Woodhouse La. *Beig* 2E **115**
Woodhouse La. *Bsvr* 6H **135**
Wood Ho. La. *Wadw* 6F **61**
Woodhouse La. *Wool* 1F **7**
Woodhouse Mill. 5D **102**
Woodhouse Rd. *S12* 1D **112**
Woodhouse Rd. *Donc* 3E **33**
Woodhouse Rd. *Hoy* 6H **37**
Woodlaithes. 2F **81**
Woodlaithes Rd. *S'side* 1G **81**
Woodland Av. *Ans* 2G **119**
Woodland Clo. *Cat* 6C **90**
Woodland Clo. *Wick* 6G **81**
Woodland Dri. *S12* 5D **112**
Woodland Dri. *Ans* 2G **119**
Woodland Dri. *B'ley* 1D **22**
Woodland Gdns. *Maltby* 4H **83**
Woodland Gro. *Wath D* 1F **55**
Woodland Pl. *S17* 4F **121**
Woodland Rd. *S8* 4F **111**
Woodland Rd. *Wath D* 1F **55**
Woodlands. 3C **16**
Woodlands. *Brim* 4D **132**
Woodlands Av. *Beig* 2F **115**
Woodlands Clo. *Swal* 4B **104**
Woodlands Cres. *Swint* 3G **55**
Woodlands East. 3E **17**
Woodlands Rd. *Hoy* 3A **38**
Woodlands Rd. *W'land* 3D **16**
Woodlands Ter. *Edl'tn* 4B **60**
Woodlands, The. *S10* 3G **97**
Woodlands, The. *Arm* 2G **35**
Woodlands Vw. *Hoy* 4A **38**
Woodlands Vw. *Womb* 3C **38**
Woodlands Vw. *W'land* 3C **16**
Woodlands Way. *Den M* 2B **58**
Woodland View. 5F **85**
Woodland Vw. *S12* 5D **112**
Woodland Vw. *S17* 2G **121**
Woodland Vw. *Cud* 2H **15**
Woodland Vw. *Mexb* 1G **57**
Woodland Vw. Rd. *S6* 5G **85**
Woodland Vs. *Tank* 6C **36**
Woodland Wlk. *Ches* 6B **130**
Woodland Way. *Roth* 4A **80**
Wood La. *S6* 5E **85**
Wood La. *S12* 4B **112**
Wood La. *B'ley* 3C **8**
Wood La. *Bram M* 6G **93**
Wood La. *Car* 4E **9**
Wood La. *Cat* 4A **90**
Wood La. *Old E* 6B **60**
Wood La. *Roth* 6D **78**
(in two parts)
Wood La. *Roy* 3A **8**
Wood La. *Tree* 1F **103**
Wood La. *Wadw* 3E **61**
Wood La. *Wick* 6G **81**
(in three parts)
Wood La. Clo. *S6* 5E **85**
Woodlea Gdns. *Donc* 4D **48**
Woodlea Gro. *Arm* 3F **35**
Woodlea Way. *Donc* 2A **34**
Wood Lee. .6G **83**
Woodleigh Clo. *Ches* 6B **130**

Woodleys Av. *Rawm* 5E **55**
Woodman Dri. *Swint* 3G **55**
Woodmoor St. *B'ley* 5F **9**
Woodnook. 6B **130**
Wood Nook. *Gren* 6A **64**
Woodnook Clo. *Ash* 1B **136**
Woodnook La. *Cut* 6B **130**
Woodnook Way. *Ash* 1B **136**
Wood Pk. Vw. *B'ley* 4B **8**
Woodpecker Clo. *Ast* 1C **116**
Wood Rd. *S6* 3H **85**
Wood Rd. *Roth* 6H **67**
Woodrove Av. *S13* 5D **100**
Woodrove Clo. *S13* 6D **100**
Wood Royd. 4G **141**
Woodroyd Av. *B'ley* 4E **9**
Woodroyd Clo. *B'ley* 4E **9**
Wood Royd Rd. *Deep* 3G **141**
Wood Seats. 4B **64**
(Burncross)
Woodseats. 4D **110**
(Norton Woodseats)
Woodseats. *Gren* 4B **64**
Woodseats Clo. *S8* 3C **110**
Woodseats Ho. Rd. *S8* 5D **110**
Woodseats Rd. *S8* 3C **110**
Woodsetts Rd. *Ans* 1G **119**
Woodsetts Wlk. *Con* 3G **59**
Woodside. .5E **87**
Woodside Av. *Kil* 2D **126**
Woodside Av. *Wath D* 5F **41**
Woodside Clo. *Ches* 1D **136**
Woodside Clo. *Maltby* 4H **83**
Woodside Cotts. *W'land* 4C **16**
Woodside Ct. *Maltby* 5H **83**
(off Ley Dri.)
Woodside Ct. *Wick* 6G **81**
Woodside Ct. *W'land* 3C **16**
Woodside La. *S3* 5E **87**
(in two parts)
Woodside La. *Gren* 6A **64**
Woodside Rd. *Donc* 1G **31**
Woodside Rd. *W'land* 3C **16**
Woodside Vw. *Bol D* 1B **42**
Woodside Wlk. *Roth* 4B **68**
(in two parts)
Woodspring Ct. *S4* 3A **88**
Woodstock Dri. *Has* 5C **138**
Woodstock Gdns. *B'ley* 3F **13**
Woodstock Ri. *Has* 5C **138**
Woodstock Rd. *S6* 3E **85**
Woodstock Rd. *S7* 1C **110**
Woodstock Rd. *B'ley* 3F **13**
Woodstock Rd. *Donc* 4G **45**
Wood St. *S6* 5C **86**
Wood St. *B'ley* 1G **23**
Wood St. *Donc* 6D **32**
Wood St. *Mexb* 6D **42**
Wood St. *Swint* 2C **56**
Wood St. *Thry* 5C **70**
Wood St. *Womb* 1E **39**
Wood Syke. *Dod* 2C **22**
Wood Ter. *Roth* 6D **78**
Woodthorpe. 1G **135**
Woodthorpe Cres. *S13* 5E **101**
Woodthorpe Est. *S13* 6E **101**
Woodthorpe Rd. *S13* 5E **101**
(in two parts)
Woodthorpe Rd. *Mas M* 1G **135**
Woodthorpe Rd. *Shut* 2H **135**
Woodvale Clo. *Ches* 5C **136**
Woodvale Flats. *S10* 3H **97**
Woodvale Rd. *S10* 4H **97**
Wood Vw. *Birdw* 5D **36**
Wood View. *Bran* 2H **49**
Wood Vw. *Con* 4G **59**
Wood Vw. *Edl'tn* 2C **60**
Wood Vw. *Else* 6C **38**
(in two parts)
Wood Vw. *Maltby* 4H **83**
Woodview. *Spro* 2D **44**
Wood Vw. Ho. Ct. *Eck* 6C **124**
(off Billam St.)
Wood Vw. La. *B'ley* 6D **78**
Wood Vw. Pl. *Roth* 4A **86**
Woodview Rd. *S6* 5E **97**
Woodview Ter. *S11* 4C **98**
Woodville Hall. *S10* 3A **38**
Wood Wlk. *Hoy* 3A **38**
Wood Wlk. *Mexb* 5D **42**
Wood Wlk. *Roy* 1E **9**
Woodway, The. *S'side* 2F **81**
Wood Willows. 3F **141**

Woofindin Av. *S11* 6E **97**
Woofindin Rd. *S10* 6D **96**
Wooldale Clo. *Owl* 5A **114**
Wooldale Cft. *Owl* 5A **114**
Wooldale Dri. *Owl* 5A **114**
Wooldale Gdns. *Owl* 5A **114**
Wooley Av. *Womb* 1E **39**
Woollen La. *S6* 6C **86**
Woolley Colliery Rd. *Dart* 4C **6**
Woolley Edge La. *Wool* 1D **6**
Woolley Ho. *Donc* 2C **46**
(off Elsworth Clo.)
Woolley Rd. *S'bri* 3C **140**
Woolley Wood Rd. *S5* 2A **76**
Wootton Ct. *Thry* 5C **70**
Worcester Av. *Donc* 2F **33**
Worcester Clo. *S10* 4B **96**
Worcester Dri. *S10* 4B **96**
Worcester Rd. *S10* 4A **96**
Wordsworth Av. *S5* 6C **74**
Wordsworth Av. *Dinn* 5G **107**
Wordsworth Av. *Donc* 5A **46**
Wordsworth Av. *P'stne* 5C **142**
Wordsworth Clo. *S5* 3C **74**
Wordsworth Ct. *P'stne* 3D **142**
Wordsworth Cres. *S5* 5C **74**
Wordsworth Dri. *S5* 5C **74**
Wordsworth Dri. *Donc* 5H **31**
Wordsworth Dri. *Roth* 3G **79**
Wordsworth Pl. *Dron* 4G **129**
Wordsworth Rd. *B'ley* 3B **14**
Wordsworth Rd. *Ches* 3H **131**
Wordsworth Rd. *Wath D* 4C **40**
Work Bank La. *Thurls* 3A **142**
Workhouse Green. 1A **108**
Workhouse La. *S3* 1E **99** (1E **5**)
Works La. *Cal* 3H **139**
Worksop Rd. *S9* 5C **88**
Worksop Rd. *Ans* 3F **119**
Worksop Rd. *Ast & Tod* 6E **105**
(in two parts)
Worksop Rd. *Blbgh* 1E **135**
Worksop Rd. *Swal & Ast* 6B **104**
Works Rd. *Holl* 1H **133**
Worral Av. *Tree* 6E **91**
Worral Clo. *Wors* 3H **23**
Worral Ct. *E'thpe* 5E **21**
Worrall. 4D **72**
Worrall Dri. *Worr* 4D **72**
Worrall Rd. *High G & C'town* 1C **64**
Worrall Rd. *Worr & S6* 5D **72**
Worrygoose La. *Whis* 1A **92**
Worsborough Vw. *Tank* 5B **36**
Worsbrough. 5A **24**
Worsbrough Bridge. 5B **24**
Worsbrough Common. 2H **23**
Worsbrough Dale. 5C **24**
Worsbrough Mill Country Pk. 6G **23**
Worsbrough Mill Mus. 6H **23**
Worsbrough Rd. *Birdw* 3D **36**
Worsbrough Rd. *Bla H* 2H **37**
Worsbrough Village. 1D **36**
Worsley Clo. *B'ley* 3B **24**
Worthing Cres. *Con* 3F **59**

Worthing Rd. *S9* 1A **100**
Wortley Av. *Con* 3C **58**
Wortley Av. *Swint* 2B **56**
Wortley Av. *Womb* 4H **25**
Wortley Dri. *O'bri* 2E **73**
Wortley M. *Thpe H* 3A **66**
Wortley Rd. *Deep* 3H **141**
Wortley Rd. *High G* 5A **50**
Wortley Rd. *Roth* 1G **77**
(in two parts)
Wortley St. *B'ley* 6G **13**
Wortley Vw. *Bla H* 2H **37**
Wostenholm Rd. *S7* 6D **98**
Wragby Rd. *S11* 5G **97**
Wragg La. *Ast* 2H **115**
Wragg Rd. *S2* 3A **100**
Wreakes La. *Dron* 6D **122**
Wrelton Clo. *Roy* 2D **8**
Wren Bank. *S2* 3A **100**
Wren Pk. Clo. *Ches* 6H **137**
Wrens Way. *Birdw* 3D **36**
Wren Vw. *B'ley* 2H **23**
Wright Cres. *Womb* 1F **39**
Wright's Hill. *S2* 5D **98**
Wrightson Av. *Warm* 6E **45**
Wrightson Ter. *Donc* 3B **32**
Wright St. *Ans* 1G **119**
Wroxham Clo. *Braml* 1E **81**
Wroxham Dri. *Braml* 1E **81**
Wroxham Way. *Braml* 1E **81**
Wroxham Way. *Donc* 4G **31**
Wulfric Clo. *S2* 5B **100**
Wulfric Pl. *S2* 5B **100**
Wulfric Rd. *S2* 6B **100**
(in two parts)
Wulfric Rd. *Eck* 6C **124**
Wyatt Av. *S11* 1A **110**
Wybourn. 2A **100**
Wybourn Cres. *S2* 2A **100**
Wybourn Ho. Rd. *S2* 2A **100**
Wybourn Ter. *S2* 2A **100**
Wychwood Clo. *Donc* 1F **61**
Wychwood Cft. *Soth* 5G **115**
Wychwood Glen. *Soth* 5G **115**
Wychwood Gro. *Soth* 5G **115**
Wycombe St. *B'ley* 5E **15**
Wyedale Ct. *Ches* 4G **131**
Wyedale Cft. *Beig* 3F **115**
Wyndthorpe Av. *Donc* 4C **48**
Wyn Gro. *Bram* 3A **40**
Wynmoor Cres. *Bram* 4A **40**
Wynyard Rd. *S6* 2H **85**
Wythburn Rd. *Ches* 4E **131**
Wyvern Gdns. *S17* 3E **121**

Y

Yarborough Ter. *Donc* 4B **32**
Yardley Sq. *S3* 1C **98** (2A **4**)
Yarmouth St. *S9* 2D **88**
Yarncliff Clo. *Ches* 6F **131**
Yarwell Dri. *Maltby* 3E **83**
Yates Clo. *Wick* 6F **81**

Yealand Clo. *Adw S* 1D **16**
Yearling Chase. *Swint* 2H **55**
Yeldersley Clo. *Ches* 6D **130**
Yeomans Rd. *S6* 6C **86**
Yeomans Way. *Ans* 3F **119**
Yewdale. *Wors* 4B **24**
Yew Greave Cres. *S5* 2D **74**
Yew La. *S5* 2C **74**
Yews Av. *Wors* 4B **24**
Yews Clo. *Worr* 5D **72**
Yews La. *Wors* 4B **24**
Yews Pl. *B'ley* 2B **24**
Yews, The. *Roth* 2F **79**
Yew Tree Av. *Ans* 2H **119**
Yew Tree Clo. *Thur* 4B **94**
Yew Tree Cres. *Ross* 3E **63**
Yew Tree Dri. *S9* 2H **89**
Yew Tree Dri. *Ches* 5B **136**
Yew Tree Dri. *Kil* 4A **126**
Yew Tree Rd. *Maltby* 3C **82**
Yewtrees La. *Bols* 6D **140**
Yoredale Av. *C'town* 1D **64**
York and Lancaster Regiment Mus.
. . . . .2E **79**
York Bldgs. *Edl'tn* 2B **60**
(off Eglington La.)
York Gdns. *Donc* 2B **48**
York Gdns. *Wath D* 4D **40**
York La. *Morth* 4F **93**
York Ri. *Swal* 6A **104**
York Rd. *S9* .6E **89**
York Rd. *Donc & Scawt* 1F **31**
York Rd. *Roth* 2E **79**
York Rd. *S'bri* 3D **140**
Yorkshire Outlet, The.
Donc 3F **47**
Yorkshire Way. *Arm* 2H **35**
York Sq. *Mexb* 1E **57**
York St. *S1* 1E **99** (2E **5**)
York St. *B'ley* 6G **13**
York St. *Ches* 6C **138**
York St. *Cud* .1G **15**
York St. *Hoy* .4A **38**
York St. *Mexb* 6D **42**
York St. *New R* 3C **62**
York St. *Thurn* 1G **29**
York St. *Womb* 6B **26**
York Way. *Con* 2G **59**
Youlgreave Dri. *S12* 2F **113**
Young St. *S1* 3D **98** (6C **4**)
Young St. *Donc* 6D **32**
Yvonne Gro. *Womb* 6H **25**

Z

Zamor Cres. *Thur* 6A **94**
Zenith Pk. *B'ley* 3C **12**
Zetland Pk. *Thur* 4F **33**
Zetland Rd. *Else* 6D **38**
Zion Dri. *M'well* 4F **7**
Zion La. *S9* 5B **88**
Zion Pl. *S9* 5B **88**
Zion Ter. *B'ley* 2E **25**

HOSPITALS and HOSPICES
covered by this atlas
with their map square reference

N.B. Where Hospitals and Hospices are not named on the map, the reference
given is for the road in which they are situated.

ASHGATE HOSPICE 1B **136**
Ashgate Rd.
CHESTERFIELD
Derbyshire
S42 7JD
Tel: 01246 568801

ASH GREEN 2B **136**
Ashgate Rd.
Ashgate
CHESTERFIELD
Derbyshire
S42 7JE
Tel: 01246 565000

BARNSLEY DISTRICT GENERAL HOSPITAL 4E **13**
Pogmoor Rd.
BARNSLEY
South Yorkshire
S75 2EP
Tel: 01226 730000

BARNSLEY HOSPICE 4C **12**
104 Church St.
Gawber
BARNSLEY
South Yorkshire
S75 2RL
Tel: 01226 244244

BEIGHTON HOSPITAL 4E **115**
Seveairs Rd.
Beighton
SHEFFIELD
S20 1NZ
Tel: 0114 2716500

BIRKDALE CLINIC 3F **79**
Clifton La.
ROTHERHAM
South Yorkshire
S65 2AJ
Tel: 01709 828928

CHARLES CLIFFORD DENTAL HOSPITAL 2B **98**
76 Wellesley Rd.
SHEFFIELD
S10 2SZ
Tel: 0114 2717800

CHATSWORTH SUITE (BMI) HOSPITAL 2E **139**
Chesterfield & North Derbyshire Royal Hospital
Chesterfield Rd., Calow
CHESTERFIELD
Derbyshire
S44 5BL
Tel: 01246 544400

CHESTERFIELD & NORTH DERBYSHIRE ROYAL HOSPITAL
..................................2E **139**
Chesterfield Rd., Calow
CHESTERFIELD
Derbyshire
S44 5BL
Tel: 01246 277271

CLAREMONT HOSPITAL 3D **96**
401 Sandygate Rd.
SHEFFIELD
S10 5UB
Tel: 0114 2630330

DONCASTER GATE HOSPITAL 3E **79**
Doncaster Ga.
ROTHERHAM
South Yorkshire
S65 1DW
Tel: 01709 820000

DONCASTER ROYAL INFIRMARY 4F **33**
Thorne Rd.
DONCASTER
South Yorkshire
DN2 5LT
Tel: 01302 366666

KENDRAY HOSPITAL 1C **24**
Doncaster Rd.
BARNSLEY
South Yorkshire
S70 3RD
Tel: 01226 777811

KERESFORTH CENTRE 1E **23**
Keresforth Clo.
BARNSLEY
South Yorkshire
S70 6RS
Tel: 01226 777865

LOVERSALL HOSPITAL 6C **46**
Weston Rd.
DONCASTER
South Yorkshire
DN4 8NX
Tel: 01302 796000

MALTBY HOSTEL 3F **83**
130 Braithwell Rd.
Maltby
ROTHERHAM
South Yorkshire
S65 4LP
Tel: 01709 790097

MICHAEL CARLISLE CENTRE 6B **98**
Osborne Rd., SHEFFIELD
S11 9BF
Tel: 0114 2716310

MONTAGU HOSPITAL 5E **43**
Adwick Rd., MEXBOROUGH
South Yorkshire
S64 0AZ
Tel: 01709 585171

MOUNT VERNON HOSPITAL 3H **23**
Mt. Vernon Rd., BARNSLEY
South Yorkshire
S70 4DP
Tel: 01226 777835

NORTHERN GENERAL HOSPITAL 2G **87**
Herries Rd.
SHEFFIELD
S5 7AU
Tel: 0114 2434343

ROTHERHAM DISTRICT GENERAL HOSPITAL 1F **91**
Moorgate Rd.
ROTHERHAM
South Yorkshire
S60 2UD
Tel: 01709 820000

ROTHERHAM HOSPICE, THE 4G **79**
Broom Rd.
ROTHERHAM
South Yorkshire
S60 2SW
Tel: 01709 829900

ROYAL HALLAMSHIRE HOSPITAL 3B **98**
Glossop Rd.
SHEFFIELD
S10 2JF
Tel: 0114 2711900

ST CATHERINE'S HOSPITAL 6B **46**
Tickhill Rd.
DONCASTER
South Yorkshire
DN4 8QN
Tel: 01302 796000

ST JOHN'S HOSPICE 5A **46**
Weston Rd.
DONCASTER
South Yorkshire
DN4 8JS
Tel: 01302 311611

ST LUKE'S DAY HOSPICE 4E **115**
Beighton Hospital, Sevenairs Rd.
Beighton, SHEFFIELD
S20 1NZ
Tel: 0114 2716524

ST LUKE'S HOSPICE 4F **109**
Lit. Common La.
SHEFFIELD
S11 9NE
Tel: 0114 2369911

SHEFFIELD CHILDREN'S HOSPITAL 2B **98**
Western Bank
SHEFFIELD
S10 2TH
Tel: 014 2717000

SHIRLE HILL HOSPITAL 6B **98**
6A Cherry Tree Rd.
SHEFFIELD
S11 9AA
Tel: 0114 2716860

THORNBURY BMI HOSPITAL 4G **97**
312 Fulwood Rd.
SHEFFIELD
S10 3BR
Tel: 0114 2661133

TICKHILL ROAD HOSPITAL 6B **46**
Tickhill Rd.
DONCASTER
South Yorkshire
DN4 8QL
Tel: 01302 796000

WALTON HOSPITAL 6G **137**
Whitecotes La.
CHESTERFIELD
Derbyshire
S40 3HW
Tel: 01246 277271

WATHWOOD HOSPITAL 2F **55**
Gipsy Grn. La.
Wath-Upon-Dearne
ROTHERHAM
South Yorkshire
S63 7TQ
Tel: 01709 873106

WESTON PARK HOSPITAL 2B **98**
Whitham Rd.
SHEFFIELD
S10 2SJ
Tel: 0114 2265000

WHEATA DAY HOSPICE 2E **75**
Wheata Pl.
SHEFFIELD
S5 9DZ
Tel: 0114 2571744

RAIL, ELSECAR STEAM RAILWAY AND SUPERTRAM

with their map square reference

Adwick Station. Rail 1E **17**
Arbourthorne Road Stop. ST 6H **99**
Arena Stop. ST 4D **88**
Attercliffe Stop. ST 5B **88**

Bamforth Street Stop. ST 4B **86**
Barnsley Station. Rail 5H **13**
Beighton Stop. ST 5F **115**
Bentley Station. Rail 1A **32**
Birley Lane Stop. ST 5G **113**
Birley Moor Road Stop. ST 5H **113**
Bolton-on-Dearne Station. Rail 1B **42**

Carbrook Stop. ST 2E **89**
Castle Square Stop. ST . . .2F **99** (3F **5**)
Cathedral Stop. ST 2E **99** (3E **5**)
Chapeltown Station. Rail 2E **65**
Chesterfield Station. Rail 2B **138**
City Hall Stop. ST 2E **99** (3D **4**)
Conisbrough Station. Rail 2D **58**
Cortonwood Halt Station. ESR 3G **39**
Cricket Inn Road Stop. ST 1H **99**
Crystal Peaks Stop. ST 5D **114**

Darnall Station. Rail 1E **101**
Darton Station. Rail 4C **6**
Dodworth Station. Rail 2A **22**
Doncaster Station. Rail 6C **32**
Donetsk Way Stop. ST 5C **114**
Don Valley Stop. ST 4D **88**
Dore Station. Rail 2G **121**
Drake House Lane Stop. ST 5F **115**
Dronfield Station. Rail 2E **129**

Elm Tree Stop. ST 1C **112**
Elsecar Station. Rail 6C **38**

Fitzalan Square Stop. ST
. . . . .2F **99** (3G **5**)

Gleadless Townend Stop. ST . . .4C **112**
Goldthorpe Station. Rail 4F **29**
Granville Road Stop. ST 3F **99** (6G **5**)

Hackenthorpe Stop. ST 4A **114**
Halfway Stop. ST 2F **125**
Hemingfield Halt Station. ESR 5E **39**
Herdings Park Stop. ST 5A **112**
Herdings Stop. ST 4B **112**
Hillsborough Park Stop. ST 3A **86**
Hillsborough Stop. ST 3A **86**
Hollinsend Stop. ST 2C **112**
Hyde Park Stop. ST 1H **99**

Infirmary Road Stop. ST 6D **86**

Kirk Sandall Station. Rail 3C **20**
Kiveton Bridge Station. Rail 5H **117**
Kiveton Park Station. Rail 6D **118**

Langsett Stop. ST 5C **86**
Leighton Road Stop. ST 4B **112**
Leppings Lane Stop. ST 2A **86**

Malin Bridge Stop. ST 4H **85**
Manor Top Stop. ST 1C **112**
Meadowhall South Stop. ST 1F **89**
Meadowhall Station. Rail 6D **76**
Mexborough Station. Rail 1E **57**
Middlewood Stop. ST 6H **73**
Moss Way Stop. ST 4D **114**

Netherthorpe Road Stop. ST
. . . . .2D **98** (2B **4**)
Nunnery Square Stop. ST 1A **100**

Park Grange Stop. ST 5G **99**

Penistone Station. Rail 4E **143**
Ponds Forge Stop. ST 2F **99** (3G **5**)
Primrose View Stop. ST 5C **86**

Rockingham Station. ESR 1D **52**
Rotherham Central Station. Rail . . .3D **78**

Shalesmoor Stop. ST 6D **86**
Sheffield College, The Stop. ST
. . . . .3F **99** (6G **5**)
Sheffield Hallam University Stop. ST
. . . . .2F **99** (4G **5**)
Sheffield Station. Rail 3F **99** (5G **5**)
Sheffield Station Stop. ST
. . . . .2F **99** (4G **5**)
Spring Lane Stop. ST 5A **100**
Swallownest Station. Rail 1H **115**
Swinton Station. Rail 2C **56**

Thurnscoe Station. Rail 1F **29**
Tinsley Stop. ST 1F **89**

University of Sheffield Stop. ST
. . . . .2C **98** (4A **4**)

Valley Centretainment Stop. ST
. . . . .3E **89**

Waterthorpe Stop. ST 6F **115**
Westfield Stop. ST 1F **125**
West Street Stop. ST 2D **98** (4C **4**)
White Lane Stop. ST 4D **112**
Wombwell Station. Rail 1D **38**
Woodbourn Road Stop. ST 6B **88**
Woodhouse Station. Rail 6D **102**